Portable Australian Authors
Catherine Helen Spence

PORTABLE AUSTRALIAN AUTHORS

General Editor: L.T. Hergenhan

Also in this series:

Marcus Clarke edited by Michael Wilding
Henry Lawson edited by Brian Kiernan
Five Plays for Stage, Radio and Television edited by Alrene Sykes
The 1890s: Stories, Verse and Essays edited by Leon Cantrell
Rolf Boldrewood edited by Alan Brissenden
The Jindyworobaks edited by Brian Elliott
Hal Porter edited by Mary Lord
Barbara Baynton edited by Sally Krimmer and Alan Lawson
Henry Kingsley edited by J.S.D. Mellick
Joseph Furphy edited by John Barnes
New Guinea Images in Australian Literature edited by Nigel Krauth
Australian Science Fiction edited by Van Ikin
Christopher Brennan edited by Terry Sturm
The Australian Short Story: An Anthology from the 1890s to the 1980s edited by Laurie Hergenhan
Robert D. FitzGerald edited by Julian Croft

In preparation:

James McAuley edited by Leonie Kramer
Nettie Palmer edited by Vivian Smith
John Shaw Neilson edited by Clifford Hanna

*Portable
Australian Authors*

Catherine Helen Spence

Edited with an Introduction by

Helen Thomson

180016

University of Queensland Press
ST LUCIA • LONDON • NEW YORK

First published 1987 by University of Queensland Press
Box 42, St Lucia, Queensland, Australia

Compilation, introduction and notes © Helen Thomson 1987

This book is copyright. Apart from any fair dealing for the
purposes of private study, research, criticism or review, as
permitted under the Copyright Act, no part may be reproduced
by any process without written permission. Enquiries should
be made to the publisher.

Typeset by University of Queensland Press
Printed in Australia by Australian Print Group, Maryborough

Distributed in the UK and Europe by University of Queensland Press
Dunhams Lane, Letchworth, Herts. SG6 1LF England

Distributed in the USA and Canada by University of Queensland Press
250 Commercial Street, Manchester, NH 03101 USA

Cataloguing in Publication Data

National Library of Australia

Spence, Catherine Helen, 1825–1910.
  Catherine Helen Spence.

  Bibliography.

  I. Thomson, Helen, 1943–   . II. Title.
  (Series: Portable Australian authors).

A828'.108

British Library (data available)

Library of Congress

Spence, Catherine Helen, 1825–1910.
  Catherine Helen Spence.

  (Portable Australian authors).
  Bibliography: p.

  1. Spence, Catherine Helen, 1825–1910. 2. Women social
reformers — Australia — South Australia — Biography. 3. South Australia — Social
conditions. I. Thomson, Helen. II. Title. III. Series.

HQ1822.S642   1987   303.4'84   86-16063

ISBN 0 7022 2004 3

Contents

Acknowledgments *vii*
Introduction *ix*

1 CLARA MORISON
EDITOR'S NOTE *xxviii*
  Clara Morison: A Tale of South Australia during the Gold Fever, a novel, 1854 *xxix*

2 AUTOBIOGRAPHY
EDITOR'S NOTE *411*
  Excerpts from *Catherine Helen Spence: An Autobiography*, 1910 *413*

3 LITERARY COMMENT
EDITOR'S NOTE *483*
  The Literary Calling 1880 *485*
  The Australian in Literature 1902 *492*

4 SOCIAL AND LEGAL REFORM
Women and Children *497*
EDITOR'S NOTE *497*
  Marriage Rights and Wrongs 1878 *499*
  The Boarding-Out System of South Australia 1878 *504*
Crime *509*
EDITOR'S NOTE *509*
  Heredity and Environment 1897 *510*
Progress *525*
EDITOR'S NOTE *525*
  Some Social Aspects of South Australian Life 1878 *526*

Contents

5 POLITICS
EDITOR'S NOTE   *555*
  Effective Voting 1896   *557*
  The Dangerous Classes 1878   *562*

6 RELIGION
EDITOR'S NOTE   *569*
  Sermon Excerpt   *571*

Select Bibliography   *576*

Acknowledgments

Acknowledgment is due to Rigby Ltd, Adelaide, for permission to reproduce *Clara Morison*, first published by J. W. Parker and Son, London, in 1854, and in Seal Books in 1971.

Acknowledgments are also due to the staff of the State Library of South Australia Archives for their assistance with the journalism and manuscript material of Catherine Spence; to Dr L. T. Hergenhan for his suggestions about the selection of material; to Dr D. C. Muecke for his encouragement and South Australian knowledgeability; to Dr Susan Magarey for her helpful discussions about some of the problems of Spence scholarship; to Lorraine Bullock for her patient research assistance; to Doreen Dougherty and Sheila Wilson for their early typing work, and to Gail Ward for her skilful help in the preparation of the final manuscript.

Introduction

Catherine Helen Spence's life was an extraordinary one. It began unpromisingly in the narrow world of rural Scotland in 1825, but it ended with her having earned the title of "the grand old woman of Australia" in 1910, one of Australia's best known and most admired public figures. Her subsequent neglect may have something to do with later generations forgetting the formidable obstacles facing any woman whose life spanned that of Queen Victoria's reign, and Spence was further disadvantaged by being poor, a spinster, and a colonial. In becoming a public figure in the fullest sense of the word — writer, lecturer, preacher, government adviser, political candidate, lobbyist, propagandist — Catherine Spence became a representative figure of female liberation, proving her social worth beyond the traditional private sphere of Victorian womanhood.

Spence's *Autobiography* was written in 1910 in the last year of her life. Extracts comprising more than half of the *Autobiography* can be found in part 2 of this volume. It is an essential source of information about her life and work, and also provides a history of Adelaide, for Spence had arrived as an intelligent, observant fourteen-year-old in 1839, just three years after the colony was founded, and thereafter loyally identified South Australia's interests with her own. As the *Autobiography* makes clear, she was no mere observer of the colony's growth. She documents the process by which she gradually became more and more fully drawn into public activity.

Three things emerge from a reading of the *Autobiography*. First, from her earliest adult years Spence had an interest in law, economics, politics and social reform, as well as literature. At the time, law, economics and politics were exclusively masculine

Introduction

preserves which she broached through her writing activities — initially by writing letters to the press, later through her journalism and public-speaking. Second, her participation in these "masculine" areas of knowledgeability and power was a deliberate and self-conscious attempt to prove an equality of ability — fuelled by the need to generate an income for herself and her mother — which directed much of her work towards the reform of legal disadvantages suffered by women and children. Thus while personally she was, from a feminist point of view, steadily and deliberately appropriating patriarchal territory, she was simultaneously directing her public efforts towards feminist causes. And third, as her involvement with the cause of proportional representation grew, she came to see it as the most important reform she had ever taken up, because she thought it the only political system which was truly democratic, which gave a genuine choice to every member of a society. Thus all other reformist activities were subsumed under this one, including the feminist issue of female suffrage.

Spence's *Autobiography* gives us more than an account of a remarkable life, of a woman who was a pioneer in many senses of that word; it also gives us the flavour of a thoroughly attractive personality: optimistic, generous, energetic, with a well-developed sense of humour and an intellectual adventurousness that grew with age. Catherine Spence epitomizes that central nineteenth-century concept of progress; she was consciously and deliberately utopian. History, particularly that part of it she had actually lived through, provided her with all the evidence she needed for her belief in human improvement, in a development towards a better world for all. No one reading her *Autobiography* would contest her right to such optimism, for she had devoted a long, active life to the betterment of her society with notable success.

Such a full, interesting and useful life would be worth recording in any age, and Spence's *Autobiography* is invaluable. But as a younger woman she had thought herself destined to be a novelist: at the time it seemed the line of least resistance for a talented and ambitious female, one of the very few occupational options available to a middle-class woman with a living to earn. She also taught for a few years in her youth. *Clara Morison: A Tale of South Australia during the Gold Fever*, published in 1854, one of the first novels about Australia by a woman, was Spence's first novel and remains her best. It is reproduced in full in part 1 of this volume. It has always been valued for its historical significance; the details of the ways people actually lived in 1851 and 1852,

both in Adelaide and under canvas at the Victorian diggings, are of great interest. The novel's domestic orientation and social realism give us a perspective missing from more formal historical records and most other novels of the day. In fact *Clara Morison* offers more than historical interest. It provides the best depiction of domestic life of any novel about Australian life until the late nineteenth century when the works of "Tasma", Mrs Campbell Praed and Ada Cambridge began to appear; and *Clara Morison* compares favourably with their best work.

While Sir Walter Scott was an early and abiding influence on the Scottish-born Spence, this novel's closest literary model is Jane Austen. Like Austen's novels *Clara Morison* concerns itself with questions of moral discrimination, particularly in relation to class, confines itself largely to the domestic world, employs irony, wit and satire to make its moral points, and models its plot according to romance conventions. What makes the novel distinctively Australian is its geographical and historical placement, the unambiguous defence of colonial society, particularly its egalitarianism, and the theme of vocation, not only for men, but in particular the examination of the limited options available to women who must work to support themselves. The novel ranges widely over a number of social issues, from the tragedy of the seduced and deserted woman to the problem of wresting land for smallholders from the Victorian squattocracy. For a "domestic" novel it has a surprisingly broad canvas, and already there are many indications of its author's involvement in public issues.

The novel begins with recognizably Austenian prose, employing the kind of ironic constructions which reveal the selfish reality beneath bourgeois assumptions of benevolence. The authorial stance makes moral judgment inescapable from the very first sentence:

> Mr. Morison had been sitting in his study for half an hour one morning, neither reading nor writing, but apparently settling the pros and cons of some new resolution which he had just formed, or perhaps trying to make it appear as graceful as it was convenient.

We can hardly miss the condemnation of Morison's abuse of patriarchal authority in making use of Susan's accomplishments without remuneration, and heartlessly consigning the nineteen-year-old Clara to solitary emigration. Much later in the novel the forthright Margaret Elliot delivers judgment on this act when she says to Clara, on hearing the sisters' story: "So it was convenient to keep her, but not you, poor child! There is very little generosity among those respectable people."

Introduction

In effect "respectability" is what *Clara Morison* is all about, its colonial context making possible a much broader discussion than was possible for Austen. Clara's sensibility, intelligence and moral courage mean she never really loses caste in crossing class lines to go into service, whereas the vulgarity of Miss Waterstone's blatant husband-hunting and the false gentility of Mrs Denfield and Miss Withering earn them contempt. However it is to the credit of an egalitarian colonial society that such social dislocations as Clara's can be accommodated without condemnation. As early as 1851, and despite evidence that Spence was personally unhappy and certainly poor, she is strongly partisan in defending her colonial society. Furthermore, the letters from the goldfields show the South Australian diggers' pride in their colony's superiority compared to Victoria, with Melbourne's squalid living conditions, a squatter government that was withholding land from smallholders, and the neglect of agriculture in favour of pastoralism. That key word "respectable" occurs again in Gilbert Elliot's letter to Margaret: "We [Adelaide people] consider ourselves as by far the most respectable part of the digging community . . .".

In fact taking part in a gold-rush is barely respectable at all. The ideal colonist makes his or her way through hard work, frugality and firm moral principles. The lottery of the diggings only leads to Mrs Tubbins, in whose portrait can be seen the moral damage done to the working class by unearned wealth. However seriously Spence regarded such cases, her sense of humour rewards us with a richly comic episode where Mrs Tubbins's complacent conviction that the possession of a piano in her dirt-floored cottage marks a rise in the world is contrasted with the total neglect of her children's education. Such things, Margaret points out, can only weaken the colony. In fact, a rise in the world for the working class can only be achieved when middle-class values have been absorbed by them. Spence consistently idealizes and identifies with her own middle class here as elsewhere.

The heroine Clara displays those qualities which Spence admired but did not herself possess, while Margaret Elliot is much closer to a self-portrait. Like Margaret, Catherine Spence had refused two offers of marriage, had written letters to the press under a brother's name, was attracted to the study of law, and was honest, intelligent and lacking in imagination and aesthetic sensibilities. It is Clara who has the strong imagination, the poetic sensibility, the vocation in marriage, although she also shares with Spence a taste for writing fiction and sermons. In isolating Clara from home, friends and even a position in middle-class society,

Introduction

Spence sympathetically dramatizes the real problems facing many single women of the time, herself included, but it is the revelation of the inner drama these circumstances give rise to that reminds us not only of Austen, but of Charlotte Brontë and her heroines Jane Eyre and Lucy Snowe. This is the problem of possessing a female sensibility, but needing to keep it in check, to rein in the feelings. The solitary woman has no outlet for her emotions; she must painfully learn that self-mastery is necessary for tranquillity and happiness. The alternative can mean disastrous self-destruction, as Miss Ker's story demonstrates. The pattern had already been laid down in *Jane Eyre*, with Bertha Mason the self-destructive figure of passion. And like Jane Eyre, Clara discovers, at the very limit of her psychological endurance, cousins who offer her a haven, and subsequently gains a husband originally proscribed by a legal and moral obligation to another woman. Furthermore, Spence launches her heroine into the world just as Charlotte Brontë had done with her Jane: both are orphans heartlessly cast out into the world by an unsympathetic relation.

The similarities are striking, but do not extend to the romantic hero. Charles Reginald is no Edward Rochester. On the contrary his originality lies in his possession of an essentially feminine sensibility; his literary tastes are precisely those of Clara, and they define him as a gentleman just as Clara's knowledge of Tennyson indicates to Minnie Hodges that Mrs Bantam's servant girl is quite out of the ordinary. The fact the Reginald's character was based on that of Spence's friend John Taylor, who took the manuscript of *Clara Morison* to England in 1853 to find a publisher, does not vitiate the interesting contrast he makes not only with other colonial males, but also with the "manly" Margaret Elliot. William Bell, like Reginald, possesses "feminine" characteristics, a fine and discriminating sensibility, revealed most tellingly perhaps in his generous sympathy for Miss Ker's plight. Reginald and Clara also share what modern critics have seen as a distinguishing feature of the nineteenth-century's literary symbolism: they are both in the characteristically "female" situation of enclosure, representing the constraints of the female social position. Reginald is as much imprisoned in his lonely, comfortless farmhouse as is Clara in her kitchen, territorially forbidden the comforts of the Bantams' sitting-room.

This line of analysis will not take us far, however, with *Clara Morison*. It is, after all, written by a self-confessed "Margaret Elliot", more interested in social action than reflection, identifying herself with colonial progress rather than literary symbolism. It is not that Spence's characters lack inner lives, but that she

Introduction

herself perhaps undervalues them. There are hints in the early parts of the *Autobiography* that the young Spence suffered much as Clara did; hers is certainly a feeling portrait of what emigrant experience meant for a woman. This makes Spence's championing of the South Australian colony all the more interesting — Spence's "vocation" may have been unclear to her in 1851, but it was already identified with Adelaide and its development.

As early in *Clara Morison* as Chapter I, the contempt felt for Mr Morison's selfish treatment of his nieces is extended to his opinion of Australia as a place where the second-rate can be passed off as valuable and where a shortage of females will surely solve the unmarried woman problem. Mrs Morison's patronizing view of Australians as "simple and unsophisticated" is challenged by a character like Reginald, but corroborated in a non-pejorative sense by a character like Minnie Hodges, open, unaffected, friendly and sympathetic. Mrs Hardy's kindness redeems her simplicity, as does Mrs Bantam's.

In the relentlessly satiric, and often very funny, portrait of Miss Withering, Spence hits back at those who patronize all things colonial under a quite mistaken apprehension of their cultural, material and moral superiority. The debate between Minnie and Miss Withering concerning the merits of Adelaide leaves the governess quite without credibility. The exchange makes clear the inappropriateness of an outsider's criticisms, and Spence's dislike of false gentility and snobbish narrow-mindedness.

Clara learns, as do we, the value of colonial experience. Domestic skills are painfully learned, but their usefulness extends beyond mundane practicalities, for Clara reflects that she will never see or treat servants again in the same light after her own experience of service. And "respectability" is broadened to include the Elliot girls, who must black their own grates and fetch their own water. This is a "domestic" novel with a vengeance, but it insists in true colonial fashion on the dignity of labour. That these standards are progressive and liberating (however paradoxical that may seem for women) is indicated in the contempt earned by Mr Dent, not only for his return to the petty snobbery of England, but for the wilfully unflattering description of colonial life he provides for Julia Marston. He is despised because he exploits colonial opportunities to acquire wealth only in order to finance re-entry into England's class system.

In fact while "respectability" might be the general basis for the novel's moral discriminations — and they are quite as fine and as plentiful as Austen's — they are also directed towards the end of defining Spence's ideal colonists, of whom the Elliots are the

Introduction

prime examples. Loyalty to the colony is of primary importance, and this includes an awareness of just how South Australia can be seen as superior to what has been left behind. This in turn entails the kind of faith in the future which is articulated by Margaret Elliot, and a willingness to look further than the muddy streets and humble dwellings of the colony, something the Miss Witherings and Mr Dents are incapable of doing.

A feminist reading of *Clara Morison* suggests that like so many nineteenth-century novels written by women, it is more searchingly subversive and critical of the patriarchal status quo than a casual reading might suggest. Even the initial pages, which suggest the sheer brutality of Morison's treatment of his nieces, also subtextually announce the necessarily helpless subjection of women to morally inferior men. An aunt's intervention would be fruitless, since she is also powerless. The remainder of the novel continually reiterates this dilemma caused by women's powerlessness. Morally and intellectually inferior men are repeatedly contrasted with female superiority: the weak Mr Haussen, the frivolous Mr Harris, the ungrateful Mr Dent, the stupid Mr Humberstone, the unprincipled Mr Beaufort, the bigamous "Mr Ker". No wonder Margaret Elliot is content with spinsterhood. Not that examples of female weaknesses are lacking: Mrs Haussen, Mrs Denfield, Miss Withering, even Miss Waterstone, attract their share of authorial criticism, but their faults are somewhat neutralized by their relative powerlessness. Clara's poem — solid proof that Spence's literary strengths were not poetic — is a feminist lament on the theme of a female powerlessness.

In the light of this, Spence's "feminization" of the ideal hero Reginald is an interesting and at least potentially subversive reversal. With his bookish tastes, fastidious withdrawal from boisterous male socializing, and enjoyment of domesticity, he is as far from the ethic of mateship as it is possible to be. He may live in the bush, but it has not claimed him as one of its own in the way depicted by other writers of fiction.

An early critic of *Clara Morison*, Frederick Sinnett, commented:

> This novel is no more Australian than results from the fact that the author, having been resident in Australia, having a gift for novel writing, and writing about what she knew best, unavoidably wrote an Australian novel . . . She has merely illustrated Australian life insensibly in the process of illustrating human life.

While this is praise of Spence's avoidance of Australian stereotypes and exaggerations, it does underestimate the degree to

Introduction

which the novel champions colonial life. What is interesting in so early a novel is its urban focus. Like all domestic novels its action is confined to interior scenes, cleverly expanded through the use of letters to give us something of the larger context of Melbourne and the diggings, but even when Clara herself goes to the bush to nurse Mrs Beaufort, we are told remarkably little about her physical surroundings. Certainly there are no romantic consolations in nature for Australians. Nowhere is Spence's truthful realism more evident than in her recognition that town life was to be the lot of most colonials, and their life's work, if they were idealists like herself, would lie in civic reform.

Spence "liberated" her heroine through the convention of a happy marriage. Her own liberation took a different form, and at the end of a long life she was able to look back without a shade of regret. Characteristically though, she looked forward to yet better things. The penultimate chapter of *Clara Morison* contains its "real", as opposed to fictional, conclusion, in Margaret Elliot's vision of Australia's future:

> I think that the discovery of these gold-fields will throw us at once into a more advanced state; I do not mean of morals, but it will bring us improvements in arts and sciences: we shall have steam and railways; towns will grow suddenly into cities; population will increase at an unexampled rate; and not only diggers and speculators will come to our shores, but men of intellect and enterprise. The English government will find out that the surest way to keep her colonies, is to leave them very much to act for themselves. It was the want of patronage, more than the Stamp Act, that lost her America. And, Gilbert, we shall soon be an important nation; you must get into council by-and-bye, and help to clear away the cumbrous and expensive trappings of justice. It is likely that transportation to these colonies will soon be abolished; but the effect of so many criminals having been poured into them wholesale for so many years must be long felt in every part of Australia. If you can make any improvements in our criminal law — if you can make our prison discipline reformatory — if you can do something towards raising our moral standard of education, so that we may not sink in the scale of nations through having been deluged with thieves and pickpockets — you will have lived to a great and useful purpose. Yes, Gilbert, you must get into council, and I must live to see it.

Spence's real brother, John Spence, did indeed become a member of South Australia's Legislative Council, but it turned out to be Spence herself, not a male surrogate, who was able to contribute so energetically and usefully to her country's progress through philanthropy and reform. The antagonism towards transportation expressed in this passage is also a measure of the colony's

Introduction

maturity, its sense of nationhood, and in itself it provides an important gloss on *Clara Morison*'s emphasis on respectability.

The excerpts from the *Autobiography* chart the progress of Spence's growth in public activities, and also tell us a little of her domestic life which must always have been demanding, for not only did she care for her mother until her death at ninety-seven, but she also brought up three families of orphaned children. Her generosity was far from being merely theoretical. But the *Autobiography* was written right at the end of her long life, and is coloured by the justifiably triumphant realization that she had indeed achieved more in her life than she could have dreamed of as a girl. As the *Autobiography* proceeds it records her increasing absorption into public life; what is missing, merely hinted at in the early chapters, is the personal struggle, the suffering she underwent in those unhappy early years, dogged by poverty, lack of a clear vocation, and religious pessimism. A little of this unhappiness is recorded in Clara's story in *Clara Morison*. However it was optimism which was more characteristic of Spence, and that note is sounded everywhere in her work.

Spence's *Autobiography* is an important historical document, charting as it does the growth from isolated colony to a federation of states, almost exactly coinciding with Queen Victoria's reign. But the personality of its writer, tolerant, good-humoured, broad-minded and forward-looking, is a reminder that this antipodean Victorian was one of the progressives of her time. There are regrettably few Australian autobiographies from the nineteenth century, even fewer with the interest attached to that rare Victorian individual, a woman fully involved in public life. Spence is absolutely right when she attributes her opportunities for work and reform to her geographical and historical placement. The interest in economics, law and politics, the knowledgeability which enabled her to publish many articles on these subjects, was obviously acquired, as the *Autobiography* points out, from her close proximity to the actual creation of South Australia's public institutions. This is another kind of pioneering, very different from battling with the bush, less romantic but perhaps more important, and all too often neglected.

The early chapters of the *Autobiography* also provide a useful account of the origins and background of one of the most important of ethnic immigrant groups, the Scots. That they did see themselves as historically and culturally distinct from English settlers is important, for in a new land they had an extra pride in their achievements, a pride which had its origin in an awareness of

Introduction

economic vassalage in their own country, all the more unfair in view of their educational superiority. Spence's return to Scotland in 1865, however, was a useful corrective to any romantic nostalgia, and helped define her own lifelong allegiance to South Australia. Her combination of Scots pride and Australian radicalism is nowhere better expressed than in the first paragraph of the *Autobiography* with its challenging assessment of an advantaged birth which had nothing to do with social position:

> . . . I must go back to Scotland for the roots of my character and ideals. I account myself well-born, for my father and mother loved each other. I consider myself well descended, going back for many generations on both sides of intelligent and respectable people. I think I was well brought up, for my father and mother were of one mind regarding the care of the family. I count myself well educated, for the admirable woman at the head of the school which I attended from the age of four and a half, till I was thirteen and a half, was a born teacher in advance of her times.

Summed up here are the values which informed a lifetime of work helping to create a fairer society. It is unsurprising to find Spence concluding — much later in the *Autobiography*, after travelling through America and revisiting England — that while England seemed to be developing more sophisticated political methods, America was socially superior, having discovered for herself "Intelligence and not wealth . . . to be the passport to social life among the Americans I met". If Spence's judgments about the advantages of being an Australian were partisan, they were never parochial. In assessing Spence's work we should never forget that she achieved an authentic sense of nationalism without the limitations of provincialism.

Spence wrote five more novels and two polemical works, but they brought her very little money — with *Clara Morison* she made £30. She had given up teaching at twenty-five, and increasingly turned to journalism to help support herself and her mother. A visit to Scotland and England in 1865, financed by friends, enlarged her acquaintance with notable English Unitarians, reformers and writers such as John Stuart Mill, and broadened her social and intellectual interests. When she returned to Adelaide she was glad to throw herself into work for wards of state and support for the boarding-out system, which removed children from orphan institutions and placed them in ordinary homes. But the real turning-point of her life was when she became regular outside contributor to the Adelaide newspaper *The Register* and its weekly counterpart *The Observer*. "What a glorious opening for my

Introduction

ambition and for my literary proclivities came to me in July, 1878, when I was in my fifty-third year!" she joyfully records. She certainly did not waste the opportunity. For the next six years in particular appeared scores of articles, reviews, leaders, on every subject which interested her through her wide reading and her reformist interests, and indeed she continued writing for newspapers not only in Adelaide, but also in Sydney, Melbourne and Brisbane, as well as periodicals in Australia and overseas, for most of the remainder of her life. The small sample printed in this volume cannot possibly indicate the full breadth of her interests.

"The Literary Calling" (part 3) was written by Spence when in fact she had decided to give up novel-writing herself: her two last novels, *Gathered In*[1] (which she considered to be her best work), and *Handfasted*[2] were both still unpublished in 1880. The former was serialized in *The Observer* in 1881–82, the latter, rejected in a competition run by the *Sydney Daily Mail*, had to wait more than a century for publication (1984). It is hardly surprising to find Spence's advice to the would-be author full of cautious commonsense, and rather discouraging. The interesting passage, in relation to her own work, is where she maintains that the really personal aspects of experience are necessarily suppressed — it is this which differentiates her most strongly from Charlotte Brontë, despite their shared feminist interests.

"The Australian in Literature" essay (part 3) was written almost two decades later, shortly after the federation of Australian states which made an estimate of literary national traits timely. Here the note sounded is characteristically optimistic, good humour and commonsense being appealed to as more accurate representations of the Australian character than the romantic pessimism which had marked the writing of the 1890s in particular. That this had also been a largely masculine ethos might also be remarked. In longer pieces of work, published for the most part in the *Melbourne Review*, and in public lectures, Spence undertook serious literary criticism of contemporary, non-Australian writers — Robert Browning, Elizabeth Barrett, Balzac, and George Eliot.[3] This work was of a high order, attracting praise even from George Eliot herself.[4]

More characteristic of her regular journalism were the articles broadly concerned with social justice where she could air her favourite preoccupations. A selection of these can be found in part 4. It was the legal plight of women and children which most disturbed her, and this remained a concern all through her life. She took an active interest in discussions of the Married Women's

Introduction

Property Act, the Contagious Diseases Act, the need for higher education for girls, the need for improved divorce and child maintenance laws, the plight of orphans, the need for Children's Courts, the formation of a women's cooperative and free kindergartens. In all these matters she was consistent in her rational arguments for greater legal protection, less legal victimization, of the virtually powerless members of her society. While it is true she never really identified with working-class struggles, speaking always in the voice of middle-class liberalism, it should be remembered that her interest in improving the lives of women and children cut right across class lines, since the law disadvantaged them all.

Despite the fact that in her novel *Handfasted* Spence had devised a radically ordered society based on the notion of trial marriages, thus effectively abolishing the double standard of sexual morality, in "Marriage Rights and Wrongs", written at about the same time, she maintains: "There can be no question that adultery is a greater offence in a wife than a husband . . .". Modern feminists would not agree. Nevertheless the changes she advocates in this article place her in the forefront of reformist thinkers of the day. Her reference to the *Contemporary Review* and the maintenance bill to be put to the English Parliament demonstrate that distance did not prevent her keeping absolutely up-to-date with current English ideas and movements. She is never merely parochial. Her job with *The Register* meant these ideas were widely and rapidly disseminated in the colonial context where there was often an eagerness to equal or improve on overseas legislative reform. Three weeks later, on 2 August, Spence records the successful passing of what became the Matrimonial Causes Amendment Bill, incorporating the provisions she describes.

South Australians' pride in their progressiveness is reflected in the *Sydney Morning Herald* article on the boarding-out system of South Australia, for it had introduced this humane way of dealing with the social problem of destitute children ten years earlier, largely due to the efforts of Emily Clark and Catherine Spence. This reform was very close to Spence's heart, for it translated into practical action a conviction she had held almost all her adult life — that the crucial factor in human development was environment. In part, this was a consequence of her repudiation of the Calvinist Presbyterianism of her childhood, with its emphasis on predestination and original sin.

This same conviction underlies the paper "Heredity and Environment", written nearly twenty years later, in 1897. Although Spence begins with an appeal to Christianity as the source of all

true charity, typically the remainder of the article stresses the need for human beings to shape their present and future societies with full recognition of their own responsibility to their weaker members. Here Spence is one of the many nineteenth-century thinkers and theorists trying to understand the causes of poverty and crime, largely without the benefit of sociological documents, based on statistics, which provided Spence with hard evidence for opinions she held for so long. Nothing could be more charitable than this essay's avoidance of blame for the victims of poverty, in contrast to prevailing attitudes earlier in the century. Her concern for social justice for society's outcasts, even its criminals, is characteristic of the generosity of spirit which was continually searching for pragmatic means to idealistic ends.

The influence of her visit to America in 1893 is also to be seen in this article's use of the United States as a basis for comparison and discussion of criminological problems. Her own work with outcast children, particularly the boarding-out system briefly referred to here, had provided her with evidence which was corroborated by Dugdale's book,[5] and her lifetime interest in children's education was fuelled by the same belief in the crucial importance of environment in moral development. She is ahead of her time in seeing that the importance of heredity was more social than genetic; that inherited pauperism was the real problem to be tackled. And she is never more typically colonial than when she points out the sheer pointlessness and irrationality of transportation as an answer to England's criminal problem. Her conviction of South Australia's superiority to the other Australian states was based on the fact that convicts had never been sent there.

Spence's concern with and belief in progress is evident in the articles on the social aspects of South Australian life, signed, as were so many of her newspaper writings, by "A Colonist of 1839". Even in 1878 when these articles were written, this *nom de plume* earned Spence the right to record something of South Australia's history, and the colony's achievements were justifiably a source of pride to one who had played so large a part in bringing them about. Her recollections of the colony's early days are coloured by nostalgia perhaps, but the utopian aspects of this society are just as evident in her projection of future improvements. There is consistent stress on the roles women have played in establishing their new society, and the steady expansion of opportunities for them. Typically the emphasis falls on the middle classes, in this colonial context no longer caught between the fear of dropping, irretrievably, below the rigid class line of gentility, nor oppressed by an

Introduction

equally rigid exclusion from the upper class by the necessity to earn a living.

The description of Adelaide's early days in "Some Social Aspects of South Australian Life" gives us some of the real background to *Clara Morison*, particularly its emphasis on the dignity of labour in regard to domestic work, an important aspect of Spence's utopian vision of society. As well, this series of articles reads remarkably like a feminist document, for most of it in fact is concerned with women's work and education. Spence argues strongly against the orthodoxy of "separate spheres", looks forward to women's suffrage, and generally sees the main social changes, both past and future, as being spearheaded by women whose usefulness to society will improve in direct relation to their improved status through higher education and properly remunerated work.

No reformer could fail to become involved in questions of politics, and Spence's devotion to the cause of proportional representation became total, the consuming interest of the last three decades of her life. She was convinced that all other means of achieving social justice and equity, including female suffrage, were subservient to and dependent on the achievement of a system which most accurately achieved democracy's aim, where every individual participant in the democratic process of voting could be fairly represented. The pamphlet *Effective Voting*, reproduced in part 5, is evidently one that Spence had printed to accompany her public lectures on the subject, and is a succinct account of what she hoped to achieve. It contains the essentials of a longer and earlier pamphlet, *A Plea for Pure Democracy*, written as far back as 1859, an adaptation of Thomas Hare's system of proportional representation. This pamphlet greatly impressed John Stuart Mill, and initiated a correspondence crowned by their meeting in England in 1865,[6] where they were mutually appreciative of each other's social reformist ideals and efforts.

Spence devoted more of her considerable energy to the idea of proportional representation than she did to any other issue. She considered the effectiveness of the democratic process itself was more important than any other reform activity. While she gathered much support, mainly through the many public meetings at which she spoke on the subject, such a drastic alteration in the political process was resisted by all the political parties who had their own stake in the status quo. Spence carefully kept outside party allegiances (although she initially had high hopes for the

xxii

Introduction

new Labour Party), but in fact proportional representation could only have been introduced as part of a party platform.

What makes this pamphlet interesting, in comparison to Spence's earlier writing on the subject, is its addressing itself to the newly enfranchised women voters of South Australia, about to vote in 1896 for the first time. Spence confessed herself, in the *Autobiography*, a latecomer to the female suffrage movement, always considering reform of the electoral process pre-eminently important: "I had failed to see the advantage of having a vote that might leave me after an election a disenfranchised voter, instead of an unenfranchised woman". Alas, the rousing call to gender and colonial pride in the pamphlet's last line, "Let South Australia and South Australian women lead the way!" — South Australia was the first of the Australian states to introduce female suffrage — was not answered as effectively as Spence would have wished. The *Autobiography* records her subsequent disappointment:

> the first election in this State found many women voters fairly well equipped to accept their responsibilities as citizens of the State. But in the full realization by the majority of women of their whole duties of citizenship I have been distinctly disappointed. Not that they have been on the whole less patriotic and less zealous than men voters; but, like their brothers, they have allowed their interest in public affairs to stop short at the act of voting, as if the right to vote were the beginning and end of political life. There has been too great a tendency on the part of women to allow reform work — particularly women's branches of it — to be done by a few disinterested and public-spirited women. Not only is the home the centre of woman's sphere, as it should be, but in too many cases it is permitted to be its limitation. The larger social life has been ignored, and women have consequently failed to have the effect on public life of which their political privilege is capable.

Perhaps her disappointment had also been coloured by her unsuccessful candidacy for the Federal Convention, in the previous year, when she stood on a platform of proportional representation.

The article "The Dangerous Classes" (part 5) makes Spence's own class allegiance clear, the "intelligent middle class" she sees as "the very hope and strength of our English nation and colonies". Nevertheless, her open-minded relativism strengthens her argument. Her methodology reminds us strongly of Matthew Arnold's "Culture and Anarchy"; both writers scrutinize each component of society without overt identification with any one. The thorough grasp of French history exhibited here indicates Spence's familiarity with French language and culture; she review-

Introduction

ed many French publications for *The Register*. Her political stance defines itself as typically liberal in seeing the British Parliament and constitution as an ideally workable set of checks and balances where no one party can claim all the power. Nevertheless she is critical of the colonies' Upper Houses being merely rich men's clubs, and concludes with a strong defence of the freedom to dissent.

The sermon excerpt included in part 6 represents a milestone in Spence's life, as well as in the Unitarian Church she had joined in 1855. She was not Australia's first woman preacher, but she was South Australia's. She preached more than one hundred sermons over the next thirty years, and their subjects indicate both the Unitarian tendency to "secularize" religion through emphasis on social reform, and Spence's own taste for that form of moral action. Sometimes the subjects of her newspaper articles and her sermons are almost identical. This sermon is of particular interest because Spence sets out to define Unitarianism itself, and clearly its attraction for her lay in the broadness of its parameters, in the hope it offered even to the heathen, if he were a lover of mankind.

It is fitting that Spence made the subject of her first sermon the undogmatic faith of Unitarianism, for she was thankful all her life for the avenue it gave to her religious impulses without doing violence to her rationality, nor narrowing the path to redemption with the pessimistic strictures of the Calvinism she had so happily abandoned at the age of thirty. She does not indicate precisely her own spiritual position among the alternatives she describes, but she does stress the importance of the brotherhood of man and the duty of charity. Such a religion dovetailed perfectly with her life devoted to social reform, with her characteristic optimism, belief in evolution and progress, her tolerence and generosity of spirit. This final excerpt from her writing should remind us that Catherine Spence was not simply the practical and commonsense activist, but that all her work was imbued with the sense of a spiritual reality behind the material world, and that her idealism was activated by a religious impulse which derived its moral imperatives from a conviction of sisterhood with her fellow men and women.

Notes

1. *Gathered In* serialized in *The Adelaide Observer*, 1881–82; ed. B.L. Waters and G.A. Wilkes (Sydney: Sydney University Press, 1977).

Introduction

2. Helen Thomson, ed., *Handfasted* (Ringwood: Penguin Books, 1984).
3. "George Eliot", *Melbourne Review* 1 (1876): 146-63; "Honoré de Balzac: a psychological study", *Melbourne Review* 4 (1879): 348-57; "George Eliot's life and works", *Melbourne Review* 10 (1885): 217-44. Lectures on Love Letters of Robert Browning and Elizabeth Barrett Barret (*sic*), on Robert Browning, and on the Writing of George Eliot, mss. 202/1, Mitchell Library.
4. See letter from George Eliot reproduced in Spence's *Autobiography*, chapter IX (part 2 of this volume).
5. Robert Dugdale, *The Jukes: A Study in Crime, Pauperism, Disease and Heredity* (New York: L.P. Putnam's Sons, and London: The Knickerbocker Press, 1877).
6. *Autobiography*, chapter IX.

1
Clara Morison

EDITOR'S NOTE

The account of how Catherine Spence's first novel came to be published is contained in chapter 5 of her *Autobiography*, reproduced in part 2 of this volume. We know from this account that the original manuscript was abridged by the publisher and published without Spence's final revision. Since the manuscript has disappeared, we cannot now discover the kind or extent of the cuts made. Spence herself does not record any comment, critical or otherwise, on the novel's abridgment.

The first edition of *Clara Morison* was published in 1854 in two volumes by J. W. Parker and Son of London. A one-volume 1862 edition is listed in the South Australian Libraries Bibliography, but a search has failed to locate any surviving copies. In view of this, and since Spence states in the *Autobiography* that *Tender and True* "is the only one of my books that went through more than one edition", this 1862 edition may be apocryphal.

This edition is a facsimile of the Seal Australian Fiction volume edited by Susan Eade (Magarey) and published by Rigby in 1971, which is in turn taken from the first edition.

Clara Morison

A Tale of South Australia during the Gold Fever

Catherine Helen Spence

Contents

VOLUME 1

Preface   xxxv

CHAPTER I
LIKE ALL FIRST CHAPTERS — INTRODUCTORY 1

CHAPTER II
WILL PROBABLY BE MISSED, FOR IT ONLY DESCRIBES A LONG VOYAGE .. 8

CHAPTER III
FIRST IMPRESSIONS OF ADELAIDE 17

CHAPTER IV
THE BOARDING-HOUSE 24

CHAPTER V
A SUNDAY AT MRS. HANDY'S 41

CHAPTER VI
A GLIMPSE OF A SITUATION 48

CHAPTER VII
ANOTHER GLIMPSE, AND A RESOLUTION 60

CHAPTER VIII
AT SERVICE 70

CHAPTER IX
A VISITOR 75

Contents

CHAPTER X
HOW MISS WITHERING MAKES HERSELF AGREEABLE TO MRS. BANTAM AND HER GUESTS 80

CHAPTER XI
MINNIE STANDS UP FOR HER COUNTRY 91

CHAPTER XII
THE FAMILY NEXT DOOR 100

CHAPTER XIII
CLARA HAS AN INVITATION, AND GETS A 'SUNDAY OUT' 111

CHAPTER XIV
MRS. BANTAM AND MINNIE LAY A PLOT TO GET QUIT OF MISS WITHERING 120

CHAPTER XV
CLARA HAS AN OPPORTUNITY OF SEEING HER FELLOW-PASSENGERS .. 132

CHAPTER XVI
DARKNESS AND SORROW 139

CHAPTER XVII
MR. REGINALD'S LETTER TO ENGLAND IS RECEIVED AND ANSWERED .. 146

CHAPTER XVIII
MR. REGINALD MAKES THE ACQUAINTANCE OF THE ELLIOTS 156

CHAPTER XIX
MR. AND MRS. BANTAM RETREAT BEFORE THE ENEMY 164

CHAPTER XX
SOUTH AUSTRALIA UNDER AN ECLIPSE 169

CHAPTER XXI
CLARA IS OFFERED A HOME 176

CHAPTER XXII
SWEET AND BITTER 187

Contents

VOLUME 2

CHAPTER I
CLARA LOOKS AT ADELAIDE MORE PLEASANTLY THAN BEFORE   201

CHAPTER II
A NEW NEIGHBOUR COMES NEXT DOOR 210

CHAPTER III
MR. HARRIS'S PROSPECTS OF GETTING TO THE DIGGINGS LOOK BRIGHTER 222

CHAPTER IV
LETTERS FROM THE DIGGINGS 230

CHAPTER V
MR. HUMBERSTONE'S THEORY AND PRACTICE WITH LONG ENGAGEMENTS 242

CHAPTER VI
DEPARTURES 255

CHAPTER VII
MISS WITHERING'S MATRIMONIAL SCHEME IS CROWNED WITH SUCCESS ... 261

CHAPTER VIII
MORE LETTERS FROM THE DIGGINGS 266

CHAPTER IX
SIGNS OF COLONIAL PROSPERITY! 276

CHAPTER X
A SITUATION TURNS UP FOR CLARA 287

CHAPTER XI
THE RETURN OF THE DIGGERS 294

CHAPTER XII
THE DIGGERS SETTLE DOWN 304

CHAPTER XIII
A VISITOR INQUIRES FOR MR. HAUSSEN 310

CHAPTER XIV
A RIDE TO THE BUSH 320

Contents

CHAPTER XV
LIFE AT THE BARN 326

CHAPTER XVI
THE MASTER'S RETURN 336

CHAPTER XVII
CLARA TAKES COUNSEL WITH HER FRIENDS 351

CHAPTER XVIII
GRIEF UPON GRIEF 362

CHAPTER XIX
ESCAPE 369

CHAPTER XX
THE ECHUNGA DIGGINGS 377

CHAPTER XXI
MR. REGINALD DELIVERS SOPHIE'S LETTER 383

CHAPTER XXII
A RELEASE 388

CHAPTER XXIII
BROTHER AND SISTER 394

CHAPTER XXIV
CONCLUSION 401

Preface

The following tale has for its author a young lady who, for some years, has resided in one of the provinces of that distant country in which the scene of the novel is laid. This preface is written by the friend to whose care she entrusted the manuscript; and the work has been printed without the advantage of the author's final revision.

Of the merits of the story it would be altogether unbecoming here to speak. The fair writer's aim seems to have been to present some picture of the state of society in the Australian colonies, especially as it existed in South Australia, in the year 1851, when the discovery of gold in the neighbouring province of Victoria took place. At this time the population of South Australia numbered between seventy and eighty thousand souls, the greater part of whom were remarkable for their intelligence, their industry, and their enterprise—characteristics which had doubtless been fostered by the energy shown in developing the mineral resources of the country, and which, in the instance of the Burra Burra and other copper mines, had met with such signal success. When it became known that gold in illimitable quantities, at a locality not more than three hundred miles distant from their own territory, was to be had, it can scarcely be supposed that a people, so keenly alive to their own interests, would remain unmoved. Resolute attempts were made to discover a gold field near Adelaide. Finding the gold would not come to them, the people determined to go to the gold. Accordingly, the entire male population, with comparatively few exceptions, removed in the course of a few short weeks, to the vicinity of Mount Alexander and Forest Creek. Most of them left in vessels which were gladly sent from Melbourne to convey them. Others ascended the course of the River Murray, depending partially for subsistence on the game which

abounds on that noble stream. Others, again, pursued the shorter but more adventurous route, across the inhospitable region which separates the two colonies, startling the wild tribes of the interior by their apparition, and leaving occasionally behind them small mounds of earth to mark the place where the strong man had bit the dust.

The exodus was almost complete, and entirely without parallel in the history of any country. The absence of the 'braw foresters,' so pathetically bewailed in the old ballad, was not more keenly felt by the Scottish maidens, than was that of many a husband and lover from the hearths of South Australia. None but women and children were to be seen, anywhere, and the skill manifested by them in the management of affairs was the subject of much admiration. The entire vintage of that year was gathered, and the wine made by them; and never was there better made. 'In those days,' it may be emphatically said, 'there was no king in Israel, and every woman did that which was right in her own eyes.' No sight or sound of manual labour met the ear or eye. An unwonted silence prevailed. A state of society unsung by poets, and such as was never seen before, existed, in which gentleness, and courtesy, and loving kindness reigned, and which will never be forgotten by those whom a supposed hard fortune compelled to remain behind. Had Mr Tennyson been there at the time, another book might have been added to his 'Princess.'

Marvellous successes attended those who were first on the gold-fields. The South Australian settlers were remarkable for their good fortune—it may be added for their sobriety, and for the good example they set to the rest of the diggers. A few months, in many cases a few weeks, sufficed to gratify their desires. None of them took kindly to Victoria, or thought of making a permanent abode there. They remembered, too, that warm hearts were beating for them in their own loved and beautiful province, and that bright eyes were waiting to beam brighter at their return.

And the return came; and many a green valley, and vine-clad cottage, bore witness to the welcoming back, it may almost be said 'with timbrels and dancings,' of the wanderers laden with their golden spoil.

It is the above epoch in the history of South Australia which the writer has seized on for her story. How far she has been successful in so doing, it is for the gentle reader to determine.

[William Bakewell]

Volume 1

CHAPTER I

LIKE ALL FIRST CHAPTERS—INTRODUCTORY

Mr. Morison had been sitting in his study for half an hour one morning, neither reading nor writing, but apparently settling the pros and cons of some new resolution which he had just formed, or perhaps trying to make it appear as graceful as it was convenient. At the end of his half hour's deliberation he rung the bell, and desired the servant to let Miss Susan and Miss Clara Morison know that he particularly requested their presence in his study immediately. They soon appeared, obedient to their uncle's summons; and while he is clearing his throat and making a few preliminary observations not much to the point, we will take a glance at the parties, and briefly explain their relative positions.

Mr. Morison was a grave, respectable looking man, between forty and fifty, who had a handsome house, and saw a good deal of company, in a fashionable street in Edinburgh. He had a delicate and rather *exigeante* wife and seven children, to whom he was as much attached as he could be to anything; but living up to his income, he felt that the recent death of his brother, leaving him two penniless girls to provide for, was a dreadful calamity; and it was in order, as he thought, to do the best for them with the least possible inconvenience to himself, that he sent for his nieces on this memorable morning. He did not like to be opposed in anything, and both of the young ladies knew it.

Susan was about one-and-twenty, with a plain face, and a figure barely tolerable; but her voice was exquisitely musical, her manners graceful and refined, and every accomplishment which she had cultivated was thoroughly acquired; she was a skilful musician, she drew admirably, and she understood more than one foreign language. Mr. Morison felt that she would be an excellent governess for his family, and rejoiced in the idea that he was able to do all his duty by her. But with

1

poor Clara, what was to be done? There she stood, with her soft grey eyes, sunny brown hair, radiant smile, and graceful figure, formed to delight her father's eyes and to gladden his heart, but without one accomplishment that had any marketable value. She neither played, nor sung, nor drew, but she read aloud with exquisite taste; her memory was stored with old ballads and new poems; she understood French, and was familiar with its literature, but could not speak the language; she could write short-hand, and construe Caesar's Commentaries; she played whist and backgammon remarkably well, but she hated crochet and despised worsted-work. In her father's lifetime, Clara had been the general referee at home on all miscellaneous subjects. She knew what book such a thing was in, what part of the book, and almost at what page. But alas! no one cared now for such accomplishments, and she hung her head before her matter-of-fact uncle.

'My dear girls,' said he, 'you are aware that I am not rich, and I hope that neither of you have any objections to doing something for yourselves. I think, Susan, that you could make yourself useful in instructing my three girls, for your education has been a long and expensive one, and must now be turned to account. You will be treated by me and by your aunt exactly as a daughter of our own, and visit and receive visitors with us. And, my dear Susan, as you know your poor aunt's delicate state of health, I hope you will relieve her as much as you can from the fatigue and worry of looking after servants and ordering dinner. You have, since your mother's death, three years ago, had the whole management of your father's establishment, and I am sure you take sufficient interest in us to do your utmost in mine. Now I hope, Susan, that you have no objection to make to this arrangement.'

Susan murmured, 'None whatever; but what shall Clara do?'

'Clara, unfortunately, has not made the same use of the advantages she had,' replied Mr. Morison. 'I do not see how I could get a situation for her, except perhaps as a nursery governess, with some eight or ten pounds a-year, which I am afraid Clara might think too small, and her employer too large, a remuneration for her services. My idea for Clara is, that she should emigrate to Australia.'

'Australia! sixteen thousand miles off!' cried both sisters, bursting into tears.

'What matter for distance?' said Mr. Morison. 'If Clara were to take a situation at all, you must be separated; and if you would look on the thing rationally, you would see that the greater the distance the better for her. In Australia they cannot want accomplished governesses; Clara might get fifty or sixty pounds a-year, and take a good position in society besides. And Clara, you are a pretty and a good girl; you will

Introductory

be sure to marry well in a country where young ladies are so scarce, and where nobody looks for a fortune with his wife; and then you can write for Susan, if you like, to join you.'

'But am I to go alone?' said Clara. 'I am only nineteen, and it is a dreadful thing to go through that long voyage without a friend.'

'I have spoken to Captain Whitby, of the *Magnificent*,' said her uncle, 'and he says that his wife will be a mother to you during the voyage. You will probably make friends among your fellow-passengers in a four months' voyage; and I will give you a strong letter of recommendation to my old friend Campbell, who is a rising merchant in Adelaide, and whose wife will give you a home till you get a situation. And I hope, my dear girl, that you will hold fast by your religious principles even in such a distant land, for that is my only anxiety about you; and write to us by every opportunity that offers. I am confident that you will make a capital colonist. I have spoken to Captain Whitby about an intermediate berth for you; the accommodation between decks is of a very superior description—very superior, indeed. But, my dear child, if you do not like to go, say the word.'

Clara gasped, and felt nearly choked; but managed to say—

'What does my aunt say about my going so far?'

'She thinks it highly advisable, particularly as the climate is so fine, and she does not think the long, cold Scotch winters agree with you.'

'If I am to go, when does the vessel——'

Clara could say no more.

'Oh, no hurry—not for six weeks yet. You will have to get your things in order, and I will see that your outfit is complete; but you will tell me to-morrow morning if you have any reasonable objection to make. You had better sleep upon it, Clara, and tell me to-morrow.'

The sisters withdrew into their own room—not to consult, but to weep. They had never been separated in their lives. The loss of both their parents had made them all in all to each other; and though a vague and alarming idea had crossed each of their minds that their poverty might prevent them from living together in future, it had never been expressed in words, and it was only intimated by the frequency and tenderness of their caresses, and by long silent gazes into each other's eyes, that they felt a time might come when they could neither caress nor look at one another.

Susan's tears were of unmingled sadness; but there was some indignant bitterness in Clara's. Susan felt that her uncle was kind to her, and that for Clara he was doing the best he could. But Clara, more clear-sighted, saw that her uncle wished to be spared the mortification of seeing so near a

relative reduced to be a nursery governess in his neighbourhood. But this feeling she did not communicate to Susan, when she saw that her sister did not herself perceive it; but said, she dared to say it was all for the best, but it was very sad.

They did not think of making any objection or of pleading for any delay, but prepared for the worst by fresh bursts of tears; and when they did at last speak on the subject, it was about the long letters they would write, and the prayers they would offer up to God for each other.

'I shall be comfortable,' said Susan; 'but what troubles you may have to go through, and I not near to help or comfort you! But yet, my darling, you are not appreciated here. You have finer abilities than I have; but because I make a noise on a piano, and scratch figures on Bristol board, I am extolled, and you are disparaged. They will judge better in Adelaide, I hope; and you will be marrying some rich man, and keeping your carriage; for you are very lovely, at least in my eyes. And when you are rich, and I would be no burden to you, send for me; for though my uncle and aunt are very kind, I am yours and you are mine, till death.'

'Till death,' said Clara. 'But I can form no hopes of anything brilliant in the prospect before me. I feel so helpless, so useless, as if I might perish, and no man regard it. Only in your heart would I leave a void.'

Thus all that day did the sisters grieve together; and, after a sleepless night, rose at their usual hour, and went in to breakfast. Mrs. Morison was up, and dispensing coffee, which they scarcely expected, for she had been confined to her bedroom all the preceding dreadful day.

'Well, Susan,' said she, 'this is the last day I mean to get breakfast for the family. You will, as my eldest daughter would do if she were old enough, preside at the breakfast-table in future, I hope. The effort is really too much for me. I feel now quite exhausted, and I think I caught a chill this morning. Clara, will you ring the bell for me, my dear? What a treasure you will be in any Australian family; you are so obliging and so fond of children. Your domestic virtues are quite undervalued in this country: every one looks to show and flourish here; but I believe that a truer taste pervades the communities of our colonies. I expect to hear of your being domiciled in some nice Scotch family in Adelaide, or near it. I would not like you to go far in the bush. The natives and bushrangers make it unsafe; and I have heard, too, that snakes are numerous and dangerous in the thinly-settled districts; so, for our sakes, as well as your own, do not venture far out. But every one says that the climate is delightful, and that is a grand consideration; and people are

so simple and unsophisticated: the state of society is very charming. Governesses of every kind are so much wanted, that I have heard of people going in quest of them on board every newly-arrived ship, and engaging them before they put foot on shore. But, Clara, you must follow Mr. Campbell's advice, and not take the first situation that offers. You should prefer forty pounds a-year, with a comfortable home, to sixty, where everything is not *comme il faut*. We hear of servants and distressed needle-women making brilliant marriages in Australia. So, Clara, who knows how long you may continue teaching? But let your choice fall on a man of sound principles and religious feelings, if you mean to be happy.'

Mrs. Morison had gone on, without looking at Clara's red eyes, or Susan's woe-begone face; but, in presenting to them both the idea that Clara would be appreciated in the far land they destined for her home, she had done something to comfort and encourage her. So that when, after breakfast, her uncle asked her how she felt on the subject of emigration, she replied, in a firmer voice than she could have thought possible the day before—

'I have no objection to make. I will go to Australia.'

Her uncle and aunt encouraged and indulged Clara during the short time she had still to remain with them. Every one was busied with her outfit, which was a very good one, though principally adapted for summer wearing; for English and Scotch people never reckon on Australia having a winter at all. All Mr. Morison's children gave Clara a little present to keep for their sakes. A great proportion of her friends gave her books, chiefly religious ones, with good wishes for her temporal, and especially her spiritual, prosperity, written in a bold hand on the fly-leaf.

Susan wished Clara to take all her books, as she herself did not care so much about reading as Clara did, and, besides, she would always have access to her uncle's library, and the circulating libraries in town, whereas Clara might not be able to meet with books in that distant land.

Clara accepted her sister's generous offer, leaving her only a few keep-sakes. Everything that Susan had she would have given to her sister; but, except in the matter of the books, Clara would not consent to such robbery.

Captain and Mrs. Whitby were invited several times to Mr. Morison's, that Clara might become acquainted with them.

The host and hostess thought them most excellent and delightful people; but Clara could not admire them. They took too much notice of her, and made her feel uncomfortable. They talked of the colony of South Australia with raptures, which encouraged her at first; but when she dis-

covered that this was their first voyage thither, she felt that their praises were no recommendation. Clara read every book that she could procure about the colony she was bound for; but the accounts were so contradictory, that she came to no satisfactory conclusion.

She felt nervous when she heard that a young lady, named Miss Waterstone, was to share her cabin, and must, necessarily, be her intimate companion during the long dreary voyage. Mrs. Whitby was to be a mother to Miss Waterstone likewise. Clara begged her uncle to invite this young lady to spend a few days with her before undertaking the voyage together. And Miss Waterstone accepted the invitation for the last week but one of her remaining in Edinburgh.

Miss Waterstone was apparently about twenty-five. Her charms were fully developed, her complexion florid, her voice loud, and her manner imposing. She took so much notice of Mrs. Morison's children, that this lady was fully convinced of Miss Waterstone's amiability; and, as she behaved with great deference to both her host and hostess—never allowing herself to contradict them in the slightest point—they thought her a young woman of good judgment, with very correct principles. Mr. Morison earnestly recommended his young niece to her care, and presented her with a handsome workbox, which raised her opinion of his virtues to an extravagant pitch. Miss Waterstone's final destination was Melbourne; so that, as she sometimes regretfully said, she could do nothing for Clara at the end of the voyage; though, every now and then, she forgot it, and, with singular irrationality, proposed entering into partnership and commencing a school, in which she would take all the higher branches, while Clara would look after the house, and teach the junior members of the establishment. Mrs. Morison could not see that there was much to choose between Melbourne and Adelaide, and thought it would be as well for Clara to change her destination, to secure so valuable a friend; but her husband, not knowing anybody in the colony of Victoria, but an unmarried sheep-farmer, who lived a hundred-and-fifty miles up the country, was obliged to give up the idea of the partnership, which would have been, indeed, an excellent arrangement for Clara. A few friends gave her letters of introduction to their Australian acquaintances; of which more hereafter.

Miss Waterstone had no doubt of her success: she was thoroughly competent to undertake anything in the way of education, though, as yet, she had had no experience; and she trusted to her letters of introduction bringing her at once into the best society in Melbourne. Clara tried hard to get up her confidence as well, but could not. She saw a thousand difficulties from within and from without, which no one else

Introductory

seemed to see for her. And when her friends wished her a safe and pleasant voyage, as if all would go smoothly if she were once landed in Australia, she felt that worse might follow, and that dangers by sea were the least of the risks she ran.

CHAPTER II

WILL PROBABLY BE MISSED, FOR IT ONLY DESCRIBES A LONG VOYAGE

It was late in the autumn of 1850, when Clara Morison set sail from Leith in the good ship *Magnificent*. The bitter parting from Susan was over. Miss Waterstone was drowned in tears on taking leave of all her friends; and they both felt ill and miserable as they lay in their respective berths, Clara above and Miss Waterstone below, sobbing and crying. Miss Waterstone left neither father nor mother, nor brother nor sister, behind her; and Clara thought her situation comparatively enviable, particularly as she was so hopeful of success in Victoria, till Miss Waterstone suddenly burst out with—

'Oh, how I envy you, Miss Morison, if you do not leave your heart behind you. I have tried to keep up my spirits, but really I can stand it no longer. Oh, dear Robert! I may never see you again; and I never knew how dear you were to me till now!'

'Oh!' thought Clara, 'everybody has her romance: this commonplace-looking woman may be as sensitive as I am, and have more to grieve for.'

'I fear, if you are heart-whole, Miss Morison, that you will scarcely be able to sympathize with me; for love seems a delusion to all who have not felt it; but to those who have—'

Miss Waterstone could say no more.

'I can give you my sympathy, though I have had no personal experience of the feeling,' said Clara. 'My idea of the subject is, that love is a very uncomfortable thing.'

'Ah! my dear child, that is not the term to apply to it. It is anguish or ecstasy.'

Here Miss Waterstone groaned and blew her nose.

'Do feel for me, my dear; it would do me so much good to talk about him.'

'Are you engaged, and have your friends objected to your

marriage?' said Clara. 'I suppose you expect him to follow you to Australia?'

'I certainly do,' said Miss Waterstone, 'for I know he loves me; in fact, it is just possible that he is on board this vessel; but we have seen none of our fellow-passengers yet. He intends to go to Melbourne, and that is the reason I wished to go there, and indeed, I wish you were to go there too. I am sure you will like Robert, he is so handsome and agreeable, and genteel in his manners; I never saw any one so much the gentleman, and such a lady's man he is too; reads all the new novels; he used to get them for me; and goodness! how angry my old aunts used to be when they found them in my room. They forbade him to enter the house again; but I heard from a sure hand that he was going to Melbourne, so I made up my mind to go before him, that my cross aunts might suspect nothing. And even if I do not meet him—but that thought is not to be borne;—I must not dream of it. Still one can die in Australia as well as in Scotland, and it will not take much to kill me. But oh! Miss Morison, I feel very unwell indeed. How are you feeling now?'

Clara felt too ill to make any further inquiries as to Miss Waterstone's love, though she thought she was behaving very imprudently, and was still more imprudent to confess all this to such a stranger. But the real miseries of sea-sickness, aggravated by the want of attendance and comforts which cabin passengers could command, but which are utterly unattainable in the intermediate, banished every unkind thought from her mind, and made her only pity her companion, who was suffering more from sickness than herself.

Mrs. Whitby came down to see them once, and brought something that the girls could eat and drink; but her words of encouragement were more valuable than all, and she could not stay to give them many.

Miss Waterstone eagerly asked the names of the cabin passengers, but though they were all given with precision, she seemed dissatisfied with the answer. She next falteringly inquired if there were any intermediate passengers on board besides themselves.

'Only two young men, Mr. Renton and Mr. Macnab,' said Mrs. Whitby. 'I suppose you will mess with them, for there are too few to make two messes?'

'Oh!' said Clara, 'could not Miss Waterstone and I have a table to ourselves?'

'I don't see how it could be done,' said Mrs. Whitby; 'besides, there is no steward for the intermediate, and as I fancy you will not like to go on deck to roast your coffee or get your meals, you will find these young gentlemen very useful.'

'I would like to join them by all means,' said Miss Waterstone. 'It would be so dull to be always by ourselves; don't you think so, Clara?'

Clara thought that Miss Waterstone's willingness proceeded from her knowledge of one at least of the parties spoken of, and was surprised when, on Mrs. Whitby's leaving their cabin, Elizabeth Waterstone burst into tears afresh, on account of Robert's not being on board.

'Do you think it right to mess along with two young men who are utter strangers to us?' asked Clara.

'If it had been wrong, would Mrs. Whitby have talked of it as a matter of course?' said Miss Waterstone; 'besides, they will be company for us. It would indeed be dull work this four months' voyage without a beau or two. We can get up a flirtation; I will take the tallest, and you will flirt with the shortest, and I dare say we shall have famous fun.'

'That would surely be wrong, Miss Waterstone; we cannot be too cautious in our manners to young men, thrown as we are into such close contact with them. And you an engaged woman too! It is not right to trifle with other people's feelings.'

'Tut! tut!' said Miss Waterstone, 'you know nothing of the world, or you would never put the words feelings and flirtations together. Flirtation only means lively talk, and if you would condemn me to silence or to dull prosy conversation, I shall never get through this dreary voyage at all, with such a weight on my mind as I have, too. But do you know I feel much better now. I would like to peep out and reconnoitre. Come with me, Clara; do, there's a dear.'

So Clara, forgetting that her hair was in disorder and her dress crushed and tumbled out of all shape, good-naturedly accompanied Miss Waterstone into what was to be their dining-room and common sitting-room. Clara was pleased to see that they were divided from the young gentlemen by a long, narrow deal table, with ridges like those on the desks of church pews, to prevent plates from slipping off. The young gentlemen were on deck, so that the girls could look about them. Ships were not so crowded with passengers then as they are now, and the other four cabins of the intermediate were untenanted by any living occupant, but were full of goods, chiefly stores for the cabin; for the steward and the steward's boy were continually scrambling up and down the hatchway in search of something in them. At the further end of the apartment was a small room, that seemed to run into the mainmast, which was the dormitory of the first and second mate. The sound of children crying, and people groaning and squabbling, was easily heard through the thin partition which separated the intermediate from that part of the steer-

A Long Voyage

age allotted to the married folks and their families. They heard eight bells strike, and presently saw their two fellow-passengers descend the ladder, one bearing a small pitcher of pease-soup, and the other a piece of salt pork on a tin plate. They started on seeing the two girls, but recovering themselves, begged that they would share their repast, as their allotments were put together.

Miss Waterstone begged to be introduced, and having ascertained that Mr. Renton was decidedly the tallest and best-looking, while Mr. Macnab was short and surly, with a dreadful squint, turned to Clara with a meaning smile, and said—

'Miss Morison and I, who I beg to inform you am Miss Waterstone, of Duke-street, Edinburgh, are scarcely in dinner costume, but you must excuse us for to-day, gentlemen. We will sit down with you for society, though I think neither of us can eat anything; and it does not look very tempting either.'

Tin plates, and knives and forks, were with some difficulty procured, and the two young ladies got a portion of the mess, but Clara could eat nothing. Miss Waterstone ate a little from complaisance, and endeavoured to make herself agreeable by the suavity of her manners. After dinner, Clara asked how the dishes were to be washed. Mr. Renton offered to do it, and Miss Waterstone was about to accept the offer, when Clara interfered, by saying—

'If we are spared the trouble and annoyance of going on deck to get our provisions by these gentlemen, it is the least we can do for them to keep things clean and tidy down stairs. If they would be so kind as to bring us some hot water, we will wash the dishes, and the table too, for it needs it sadly.'

Miss Waterstone would have demurred, but Clara for once insisted on having her own way, and carried the point. Hot salt water was brought, after which the gentlemen went again on deck.

'Going out on speculation, I suppose,' said Renton. 'Can't hook any one at home, and trying it on in the colonies. What an extensive affair the eldest one is, but the little one knows what she is about too. Ha! ha! What fun we'll get out of them both, Macnab! I wish I had not been in such dishabille, but on board ship one can't be always spruce, particularly through that confounded sea-sickness. And I flatter myself that I have the air of a gentleman, even in the shabbiest clothes.'

'Who cares about a body's air?' said Macnab, with a supercilious sneer; 'it is what a body has that takes the women's fancy. I dare say that they would like to be saved all trouble

in catching a husband on land, by fishing a little at sea; but they are no bait for me, I'm thinking.'

In the meantime the young ladies had retired to their cabin, and Miss Waterstone was very anxious to know Clara's first impressions of the beaux they had got. She herself saw some resemblance between Renton and Robert; there was the same look about their eyes, and their manners were very similar.

'You see that I have got the best of the two,' said she, smiling. 'Macnab is a perfect fright, and of all things in the world I abhor a squint. Oh, how I pity you, Clara! you cannot possibly flirt with such a creature. His west-country drawl is really detestable, and yet he seems to grudge his words as if they were music.'

'If I were to pass an opinion at all on the subject,' said Clara, 'on such slight grounds as I have for judging, I would say that I would rather go through this voyage with Mr. Macnab than with the other. He may be rude and surly, but Mr. Renton strikes me as being familiar, and inclined to be impudent.'

'Only kind and friendly,' said Miss Waterstone, eagerly; 'you cannot expect the stiffness and ceremony which you find in Edinburgh on board ship. There is an absence of all restraint here.'

'Ah! Miss Waterstone, I have read and heard that where there is no artificial constraint, young ladies should put a great deal of restraint upon themselves. For instance, when no one sees what you do, you should be the more careful to do nothing imprudent. I have often felt myself frozen up in a *tête-à-tête* with a gentleman whom I treated with cordiality when I met him in company.'

'Well, Miss Morison, I don't know what to make of you at all. A *tête-à-tête* is the most delightful thing in the world, but those aunts of mine would never give me any opportunity for one, and I used to lay my plans beforehand, in order to manage an interview.'

Clara now said that she would like to read a little, and took up a book into her berth with her. Miss Waterstone got out some letters from her dressing-case, and began to read them, sighing and groaning at intervals. Suddenly they were in total darkness, and Miss Waterstone rose in real alarm.

'Clara, we are going to have a dreadful storm,' said she; 'I never saw anything so sudden in my life. Oh dear! we shall all be drowned! I must see what it is.'

And throwing down her letters with precipitation, she rushed out at the cabin-door, but all was as light in the dining-room as before; and after consulting with Clara, they came

A Long Voyage

to the conclusion that something must have been put on the bull's-eye that served them for a window.

'Probably the plates for the cabin dinner,' said Clara, 'for I believe the pantry is just above us, from the noises I hear.'

Miss Waterstone was very indignant, and wanted to go on deck to remonstrate, but Clara intreated her to remain below, and not show herself in such dishabille.

'The plates cannot remain there long,' said she, 'and we can surely stay contentedly in darkness for half an hour. I cannot think of thrusting ourselves forward, during the bustle of the cabin dinner, to make complaints.'

'Whenever the gentlemen come down I'll tell them of it,' said Miss Waterstone, 'and send them up to rectify it. I don't see what right the cabin dinner has to deprive us of the light of day; it is unjustifiable. In the meantime let us open the door and let in the borrowed light from the saloon, as they call it, into our state-room.'

Clara consented to the door's being left slightly ajar, getting up herself, and smoothing her hair and arranging her dress as well as the bad light permitted her; but Miss Waterstone still remained straining her eyes over her letters, till aroused by the footsteps of Renton and Macnab descending the hatchway.

'Do go and speak to them, Clara; I am not fit to be seen. Bid them remonstrate with the steward, and get the plates taken away—my eyes ache dreadfully for want of light. Quick, Clara, before they go into their cabin.'

Timidly, Clara went out, and explained their annoyance. Mr. Renton said he was enchanted to have an opportunity to oblige the ladies—there was nothing he would not do to please the fair; and hurried off. Mr. Macnab gave a sardonic smile, and retreated into his cabin. The steward was hurried and cross, and made great objections to lifting the plates; the bull's-eye was just at his pantry-door, and it was very inconvenient to put them anywhere else; but Mr. Renton talked so much and so loudly about the deprivation and annoyance to the young ladies, that he attracted several of the cabin-passengers round the disputants. They gave decision in favour of the ladies, but could not help laughing at the vulgar importance of their champion. The steward was offended at his manner, and determined to set the plates on the bull's-eye every day, to give Renton the trouble of coming up and battling for daylight for the ladies.

Hot and triumphant, he came down stairs; Clara went out to thank him, while Miss Waterstone murmured her gratitude from the further end of her cabin.

We need not go into detail with the monotonous life on board a passenger ship during so long a voyage. To fancy

that a captain's lady can take a motherly charge of any intermediate passenger is a splendid absurdity, which nobody that had been on board a week could believe for a moment. Mrs. Whitby did more than could be expected from her; she came to see the girls once a-week, and asked after their health. She found Miss Waterstone on very good terms with her messmates, ordering Mr. Renton about in the most unscrupulous manner, but always joining the reluctant Clara in every request she made. When they went on deck, they had no proper place allotted to them, and not being permitted to go aft with the cabin passengers, sat on a bench together, amongst the steerage passengers. If Miss Waterstone's voice had not been so loud, and her flirtations with Mr. Renton so undisguised; if she had put as much restraint upon herself as she had done in her visit to Clara's uncle, Mrs. Whitby, who was not ill-natured, would have pressed Mrs. Surford and Mrs. Hastie, the principal ladies in the cuddy, to have invited the girls to the poop; and really felt for Clara, who looked uncomfortable and unhappy. But to invite Clara without Miss Waterstone was impossible; Renton and Macnab would have followed them, and the exclusive society of the after-cabin would never tolerate such a wholesale invasion of their privileges.

How Clara longed for the voyage to be over!—how she wished that she had been rather sent out alone, than with a companion who compromised her so fatally, yet so good-humouredly! Her heart sank within her when she remembered her uncle's assurances that Mrs. Whitby would be a mother to her, and that she was sure to make valuable friends on board; and a dread came over her that his golden dreams about South Australia might prove as groundless.

Miss Waterstone was continually taking notice of the children, and talking to the servants of the ladies in the cuddy, which was considered presumptuous and impertinent by those ladies; and Clara's backwardness and timidity were also misconstrued. Even what Mrs. Whitby told in the cabin about Miss Morison's good connexions—her excellent uncle, his handsome house, elegant furniture, and numerous servants —went against his niece. If she really was a good, amiable girl, why did a man of Mr. Morison's means and standing send her out alone to such a distance?

Mr. Macnab got more endurable towards the end of the voyage. Miss Waterstone thought he was becoming melted. And as for Mr. Renton, he was delightful. Clara would often have remained alone in her cabin, and allowed Miss Waterstone to go on deck without her; but she felt that her companion needed protection, though she did not wish it. How often Clara wished for solitude. How weary she was of

A Long Voyage

Miss Waterstone's long digressive descriptions of Robert and his charms; and of all the other delightful young men who either had admired her, or ought to have done so. How sick of all her companion's cross-questionings as to the state of her own heart, and whether she had ever had an offer, and if there were many beaux visiting at her father's house; or if her sister was never jealous of her superior charms. In vain Clara again and again answered in the negative to all these questions. The undaunted Miss Waterstone returned to the charge, and only felt hurt at Clara's closeness; it seemed such a bad return for all her confidence.

Then Miss Waterstone was always dreaming that Mr. Macnab had stolen her hundred sovereigns out of her dressing-case, and getting up at any hour in the night in great alarm, striking a light, and counting them all over for security. She once insisted on Clara's getting up too, and seeing that her money was safe. Poor Clara's ten sovereigns were not so hard to count. Miss Waterstone was of opinion that her uncle should have given her, at least, fifty.

'You should always have enough to take you home again, if you do not succeed, or do not keep your health in a strange country,' said she; 'and it is no wonder that I am so anxious about mine. If Robert does not come to Melbourne, I may feel too broken-spirited to take a situation, and will need all I have got. But it really is the most singular thing that I should dream this so often, and always of Mr. Macnab. I never dream of Mr. Renton taking it, or of Mr. Melvin or Mr. Macfie, the mates, doing such a thing, and I am sure they all need it more than Mr. Macnab, who is very well off indeed. It is really wonderful that I should always fix on him as the thief. He looks very avaricious certainly, and has a greedy look about the eyes. We had better both beware of him, for the thing is quite outside of the common.'

But in the morning her suspicions vanished, and she was as gracious to Macnab as ever, and that was as gracious as he would let her be. Miss Waterstone was very affable and polite to the mates, who lived in the mainmast-cabin, and got them to procure her some comforts and luxuries, which, they said, they stole for her; so, as she said, it would have been more to be expected that she should dream of their being the thieves.

But the voyage was got through at last, and, after seeing a very unpromising-looking island, about which Miss Waterstone fell into raptures, and misquoted some sentimental poetry about yon green isle, and which, they were informed, was called Kangaroo Island, they took a pilot on board, and slowly went up the creek till they got into Port Adelaide. Miss Waterstone wanted to go on shore at once; Mr. Renton

took the opportunity of the first boat that came to leave the ship; but Mr. Macnab had a considerable quantity of goods on board, and would not land till he saw them safe.

Clara cogitated within herself how she should appear before Mr. Campbell. She wished to prevail upon Mrs. Whitby to accompany her; but she was surprised to see that lady go on shore along with Mrs. Hastie and her family, merely remarking to her, that she had better go to town on the morrow, and see Mr. Campbell at his place of business in Hindley-street. Mrs. Whitby bade Clara good-by for the present, saying that she was going with Mrs. Hastie to a friend's house, some miles out of town, and left Clara in great perplexity. Miss Waterstone volunteered to go to Adelaide with her; and Clara, hoping that she would be as prudent and quiet on shore as she had seemed to be at her uncle's before she sailed, accepted of her offer, and thanked her for her kindness. Clara's boxes were got out, and she packed up all her loose property, with the exception of a book, and a few nick-nacks, which Miss Waterstone had admired, and which she now begged her to keep for her sake.

Good-humoured Miss Waterstone was much obliged. She regretted parting with her dear Clara, hoped they might meet again, and put the presents in her box. Miss Waterstone did not dream this night about the loss of her money; but though undisturbed, Clara was too much excited to sleep. The next day she was to be thrown upon the world in a strange land. All her deficiencies stared her in the face. She saw Mr. Campbell looking sternly at her, and asking what right she had to any countenance or protection from him. She saw Mrs. Campbell eyeing her from head to foot, and expressing by looks, if not by words, her annoyance at being burdened with such a helpless creature. She saw Renton shaking hands with her in an offensively familiar way before Mr. Campbell's face. She heard Miss Waterstone's loud vulgar remarks. She fancied that Mr. Campbell must have seen the cabin passengers of the *Magnificent* and heard from them what sort of people the intermediates were. And tossing to and fro in her narrow berth, she sobbed aloud at the humiliation of her position.

CHAPTER III

FIRST IMPRESSIONS OF ADELAIDE

It was a hot day, rather towards the end of an Australian summer, when Clara and Miss Waterstone went on shore, and after a little difficulty about Clara's luggage, which, after some hesitation, she directed the draymen to take to Mr. Campbell's warehouse, they got into a port cart, and drove up the miserably dusty road which leads from the port to the town. Everything looked as disconsolate as Clara's own thoughts. The grass was scanty, and so burnt up, that one wondered if it ever could have been green; there was not a flower to be seen; the sun was scorchingly hot; the wind, direct from the north, blew as if out of a furnace; the cart jolted, as if it would shake her to pieces, while the passengers abused the weather, and prayed for a railroad. Miss Waterstone's round face was streaming with perspiration; Clara's pocket-handkerchief became nearly black in her vain endeavours to keep hers clean; and the pale muslin dress and white chemisette and sleeves, which she had put on as suitable for the weather, were sadly crushed and soiled. The sight of green gardens in North Adelaide refreshed her eyes; and as the cart drove into town, her curiosity and interest in what she saw for a few minutes drove away her painful sensations. The streets, though straight, were most irregularly built upon; houses of brick, wood, earth, and stone, seemed to be thrown together without any plan whatever, and looked too incongruous even to be picturesque. The river was unworthy of the name; she had never seen a burn in Scotland so small. And when one of the gentlemen in the cart told her that on this river Torrens, the inhabitants of Adelaide were almost wholly dependent for water, she feared that there must be dreadful scarcity at times. She wondered at the complacent tone in which this gentleman talked of the colony, though he confessed that it was often as hot and as dusty

as now; and that in winter the streets and roads were dreadfully bad—almost impassable.

Miss Waterstone groaned audibly, from the effects of heat and exhaustion; and pitied Clara, who had been condemned to live in such a fiery furnace as Adelaide seemed to be. But the cart stopped, and with it her lamentations; and the driver directed them to a large building, a few doors off, which he said was Campbell's store.

Clara would fain have made a more creditable appearance than she now could, and was half inclined to ask the gentleman who had spoken to her before, if he knew of any respectable boarding house where she might rest for half an hour, but did not like to take the liberty. Miss Waterstone eagerly forced her on, being so anxious to get into the shade, that she quite overlooked the appearance they must both make—dusty, and burnt quite red with the sun.

The warehouse door was open, and the girls looked in.

'Is Mr. Campbell in?' said Miss Waterstone, taking the lead from her anxious companion; 'we have particular business with him.'

'A consignment,' muttered the clerk; 'rather a heavy article;' but he said aloud, 'Mr. Campbell has just gone out, but you will take a seat in his private room till he returns. He cannot be ten minutes.'

'Oh! most gladly will we take a seat out of the sun,' said Miss Waterstone. 'The heat is really beyond everything. Is it always like this in Adelaide? Oh, me! I feel melting away altogether.'

And Miss Waterstone sat down in Mr. Campbell's own particular chair, loosened her bonnet, wiped her face, unclasped her shawl, and spread out her clothes as much as she could, that they might come down to in-doors temperature.

'Oh! Clara,' said she, 'this is refreshing. I feel as if I were down a well, and yet the thermometer says 89 degrees. What it can be outside I cannot fancy; something very near the boiling-point, I dare say.'

Here Miss Waterstone laughed, and turned over the leaves of some newspapers that lay on the table,

'Everything seems in order here; it does not look so unlike Edinburgh in-doors as out. Maps pasted up and letters filed with the greatest propriety,' continued Miss Waterstone. 'I am sure Mr. Campbell must be an excellent man of business. I see our names are in this paper as having come by the 'Magnificent,' and I dare say Mr. Campbell is expecting us, or at least you, for I fancy he knows nothing of the Waterstones. Well, I hope you will get on well with him. You heard how much he was respected from those gentlemen in the

cart—quite at the top of the tree in the colony. I don't see why he should not engage you himself, even if he has no family, which you are not sure of; I dare say his wife would be the better of such a companion as you would make; and you would see such lots of folk in a house like his. I must say you are in luck, Clara;' forgetting how much she had pitied her ten minutes before.

In vain Clara tried to collect herself for the important meeting,—in vain she tried to frame an initiatory speech; tears started to her eyes, her heart beat wildly, and her tongue clove to the roof of her mouth. Miss Waterstone found out that she, too, was very thirsty, and was just going to rise to request a glass of water, when the door opened, and Mr. Campbell entered.

He seemed to be about the same age as Mr. Morison. He was dressed in white from head to foot, and though rather stout, had a good presence, Miss Waterstone thought. His complexion was fair, but on this hot day his face was red all over; he looked good-natured, but not very firm; and from his voice twelve years' residence in South Australia had not taken the accent so dear to Clara's heart.

Miss Waterstone snatched from Clara's passive hand the letter of her uncle, and presented it with an air of some importance to Mr. Campbell. Clara trembled as he opened it, and read to himself as follows:—

'DEAR CAMPBELL,—

'After so long a silence on my part, I fear that you will consider me as trespassing on your well-known good-nature in the request I am about to make to you.

'My poor brother William, after a tedious illness, died a few months ago, leaving his affairs in a sad state. He would speculate beyond his means, and the result has been ruinous. He left his two girls to be provided for by me, and of course I have done all in my power for them. The eldest and plainest girl I have given a home to, but I cannot afford to injure my own family so much as the additional burden of the younger would do; and as she is a thoroughly amiable, good, and pretty girl, I think she may by your good offices make her way well in a colony like yours.

'My brother made a great pet of Clara, and did not force her on so much with her education as he might have done; he selfishly trained her to minister to his own private comfort, instead of looking forward to her ultimate prospects in life. She used to read aloud to him, copy letters and accounts, play whist and backgammon, and I am aware that she has very good abilities. She has had a thorough English education, is a very fair French scholar, and a first-rate arithmetician;

but I regret to say that she is quite ignorant of music and drawing. I have found it impossible to get a situation for her in this country, but I feel convinced that she would be a treasure in any family who preferred solid acquirements to superficial accomplishments.

'I hope, dear Campbell, that for auld lang syne you will look to her a little, and that your kind-hearted wife will give her a home till she gets a situation.

'If it is impossible to get anything suitable for her, you may draw on me for as much money as will take her back to Scotland, though that is an extremity I can scarcely imagine Clara to be reduced to in your flourishing community.

'We hear great things of your mines in South Australia, and all your friends in Edinburgh expect you to come home as rich as a nabob some day soon. It is nearly twelve years now since we parted, and I cannot say that I have ever met any man that I respected or liked so much as you all that time. Mrs. Morison and I often talk of the pleasant evenings we used to spend with you in the Crescent. My family now amounts to seven—three girls and four boys, and of course they are the finest children that ever existed. They are all in great grief about parting with their cousin Clara, and all their mamma can say to them about its being for Clara's own good does not quite dry their tears.

'I hope Mrs. Campbell's motherly heart will warm to the orphan thrown upon her tender charity in a strange land. Mrs. Morison would have written to her, but all this excitement has been too much for her nerves, and she feels quite inadequate to the task. She joins me in kindest regards to Mrs. Campbell and yourself, and in the hope that you will soon revisit Auld Reekie,

'Believe me yours sincerely,
JAMES MORISON.'

After reading the letter, Mr. Campbell looked dreadfully puzzled. Which was the lady, and what was he to do with her? Miss Waterstone certainly had given him the letter, but she did not look at all like the family, and he hoped that she was not the one he was to take care of; besides, she seemed confident and comfortable, and though in some instances new comers had presented letters of introduction to him with considerable coolness, Miss Waterstone's self-possession was beyond anything he had yet seen; and when she began to speak, and complained of the dust and the heat with loud volubility, while Clara stood trembling in the background, his alarm as to his consignment found vent in words, and he exclaimed, 'Which lady is Miss Morison?'

First Impressions of Adelaide

'Oh! not me,' said Miss Waterstone, with a hearty laugh; 'only to think of me being supposed to be the principal party here! I am Miss Waterstone, a fellow-passenger of Clara's, and I accompanied her because she did not like to come by herself; and if it had not been for this dreadful heat and abominable dust, I would have liked it very much; but it is delightful here, just like a well. Can your thermometer be right, Mr. Campbell? Is it really so hot here as 89 degrees? We never suffered so much from heat, even when crossing the Line, as we have done to-day; but the sea breeze is preferable to the land breeze. I should fancy that the soil here could grow nothing, for it seems to spend 'most of its time in the air,' as the old song says. Eh, Mr. Campbell?'

Perhaps Miss Waterstone thought that she was giving Clara time to come to herself while she was speaking, but it had quite the contrary effect.

'I hope, Mr. Campbell—that is, I wish,—I am sorry. I will do anything. Will Mrs. Campbell——'

Here she came to a full stop, and felt that she had said nothing, and yet too much.

'I should have thought,' said Mr. Campbell, gravely, 'that my old friend Morison might have heard of my sad bereavement before you set sail; but I regret to be obliged to tell you that I cannot offer you Mrs. Campbell's protection, which I know she would have gladly given you. She is no more!'

Clara grieved for the bereaved husband; she grieved, too, for herself, and burst into tears. Mr. Campbell was rather pleased with her sensibility, for he overlooked the selfish part of her sorrow.

'Ah, Miss Morison, it makes a fearful blank—but I can offer you the protection of my house, if you choose to accept of it; that is, if you have no other friend,' said Mr. Campbell, hesitatingly.

Miss Waterstone signed to Clara to take advantage of this offer, but Clara mournfully shook her head, and took from her bag three other letters of introduction, which her friends had given her on her departure.

'Oh, my poor child,' said Mr. Campbell, kindly, 'these are quite valueless. One of the parties addressed, to my certain knowledge, lives at Hobarton, another in Sydney; so much for Edinburgh folks' knowledge of Australian geography.'

'But the third?' said Clara, eagerly, 'surely I may try what it can do?'

'I do not know who wrote this letter,' said Mr. Campbell, 'but if any one had given a letter of introduction to any girl I took any interest in, with such an address, I should

look on it as an insult. He bears a bad character, and you must not know him.'

'The letter is from his aunt,' said Clara; 'I understood that he was married, and that his wife would be kind to me; but take it, destroy it, or let me tear it in pieces.' So saying, she tore the letter into shreds, and exhausted and heartsick, sat down to hear what advice Mr. Campbell had to give her.

'If,' said he, 'you really have no friends here, I can give you a home. I have room enough in my place out of town.'

Visions of the whist and backgammon, and of all the little attentions Clara might pay him, floated through his mind; and burnt, and dusty, and tearful as Clara was, there was no disguising that she was a bonnie lassie; and he felt inclined to press her to become an inmate of his very dull, lonely house, but he resisted the temptation.

He felt relieved when Clara gratefully but decidedly declined his offered hospitality, and begged him to recommend her to a respectable house where she might stay till she found employment. He delicately inquired into the state of her finances, and hoped she might be able to make her money hold out till then. Clara assured him that she would do her best with her ten pounds, or rather, what was left of it, for she had been obliged to break in upon it for the day's expenses; and, turning anxiously to Mr. Campbell, said she would go to the cheapest respectable house he could point out; she did not mind about discomfort, but the place must be respectable.

Mr. Campbell good-naturedly put on his hat, and offered to accompany Miss Morison in her search for lodgings. He told Clara that Mrs. Handy's house was thought very well conducted; that Mr. Handy had gone to California on a gold-hunting expedition, and though he had been gone more than a year, did not speak of coming back soon; but that, in his absence, the boarding-house was very creditably managed by Mrs. Handy. It would not cost Clara more than eighteen shillings a-week to live at Handy's. There were often no ladies there; but she ought to keep by her hostess as much as possible.

'I will make inquiries amongst all my lady acquaintances,' said Mr. Campbell, 'and do all in my power to get a situation for you; but, Miss Morison, you must form no extravagant idea of the remuneration of governesses here. They can get no more than they do at home, and often not so much. They are frequently called upon to assist in household work, and generally are made to act as nursemaids. The only point in which their situation is better than in Scotland is, that their term of service is not generally so long. There is more

chance of promotion; but girls should be cautious in that matter, too; for I have seen some governesses make wretched marriages, from not knowing the man's character, and having no one to find out what he was for them.'

Clara thanked Mr. Campbell for all his advice and kind intentions; agreed that she would try to be useful, and would not object to a small salary. He laughed when she told him that she knew a little Latin, and could write shorthand, and thought her education had been singularly misdirected; but by this time they had reached Mrs. Handy's door; and Miss Waterstone, who was faint with heat and fatigue, declared that she would stop there a week, while the vessel was in harbour, and keep Clara company till she had got over the novelty of such a strange life. Mr. Campbell had taken as great a dislike to Miss Waterstone as it was in his nature to feel; for she was not overawed by his manner, and did not seem to know her position. He did not like this woman to stick so close to his *protégée*, but he said nothing. He recommended Miss Morison to Mrs. Handy's particular care, and left her, with a comfortable consciousness on his part, that he had done all he could, and more than could have been expected from him.

'I wonder,' thought he, as he retraced his steps to his place of business, 'if James Morison had heard of my wife's death, and sent out this pretty niece to be Mrs. Campbell number two. It looks very queer, for I sent him the paper, and there has been time in twelve months to fit out the young lady and despatch her. I think she knows nothing of the matter, however; but, upon my word, it is the boldest stroke ever James made. If not to be my wife, what should make him send the poor thing here? Everybody that can do nothing at home is sent out as quite good enough for the colonies, and generally with such a flaming high character, that we require to be cautious. I have had two clerks recommended to me by friends at home, as trustworthy and honest, who have robbed me right and left; and three others, who habitually got drunk, and neglected and mismanaged my business, who, I was informed, would prove treasures. I like to see a man earn a colonial character before I trust him far, and a woman too. And this girl may turn out like the rest of them, though she has a sweet voice, and a modest, timid manner.'

CHAPTER IV

THE BOARDING-HOUSE

Mrs. Handy regretted that she had not two rooms vacant, but she hoped that the two ladies would not object to occupying the same room. Miss Waterstone said she would prefer this arrangement, and Clara, though longing to be alone, if but for half an hour, could make no objection. The bed-room they were shown into was somewhat larger than their cabin on shipboard; and though it was scantily furnished, it looked clean and tidy. Mrs. Handy having procured them a tolerable supply of cold water, which, she said, would make them half forget how hot it was, left Miss Waterstone and Clara to arrange their toilet.

'Oh, Clara! what shall we do?' said Miss Waterstone. 'My portmanteau is in Mr. Campbell's store, and so are all your things. I hope some one will think of sending them, for we can't go in to dinner as we are.'

But there was no help for it, as neither Clara's boxes nor Miss Waterstone's portmanteau made their appearance till the following day. Mrs. Handy obligingly brought their dinner into their bed-room; but hoped that they would come into tea.

'I told the gentlemen,' said she, 'that I had two young ladies in the house, and they were like to pull me to pieces because I did not bring you in to dinner. We have tea a little after seven, and as it will then be candlelight, you need not mind about your dresses.'

So at a quarter past seven, the young ladies emerged from their apartment, and were introduced by Mrs. Handy to so many new names, that they forgot them all immediately. They sat down on each side of Mrs. Handy, and felt that they were gazed on with considerable curiosity by some eight or ten pairs of eyes. There were two clerks in situations, two on the look-out for a clerkship, a middle-aged man who did

The Boarding-House

something in the commission way, a German gentleman with a large moustache, two assistants in shops, who seemed to be looked down on by the others; the overseer of a sheep-farmer in the north, who had come into town to sell sheep and get stores for the stations; and a new comer, who, without being a clerk or accountant, or, in fact, brought up to any business at all, had come out to South Australia, in the hope that something would turn up for him there. He was very simple, and seemed to be the general butt.

Miss Waterstone felt quite happy when she saw so many people who seemed disposed to be agreeable; she saw with half an eye the great joke of the establishment was to make Mr. Blinker (the butt) show off, and she felt sure that she should not want for attention where the gentlemen formed so overwhelming a majority. Close beside her was the country overseer, Mr. Humberstone, not ill-looking, rather well-dressed, disposed to be complimentary, and labouring under the strange delusion that he was very bashful, and wanted a great deal of encouragement.

Miss Waterstone had received a piece of bread and butter from his hands with a gracious smile and had laughed at an attempted witticism on the similarity of their names, which had been received with general applause. Mrs. Handy had just asked her if her tea was sweet enough, when the door opened, and a gentleman with spurs and large straw hat on, and looking hot, dusty, and tired, entered the well-filled parlour.

'Well, Mr. Reginald,' said Mrs. Handy, with the accent of surprise.

The new comer quietly ascertained that he could be accommodated with the sofa for a bed; and having vanished for a few minutes to brush away the marks of his journey, soon reappeared, brought forward a chair, and sat down next to Clara, displacing the surprised Mr. Haussen, the German, who speaking English very imperfectly, and only by his gestures expressing politeness, had struck Clara as being by far the most gentlemanly of the party.

'Ah!' said Mrs. Handy, 'Mr. Reginald knows what he is about when he gets near the ladies. Let me introduce you. Miss Waterstone, Miss Morison, just landed to-day from the *Magnificent*; Mr. Reginald, from the North. I think you know Mr. Campbell, Mr. Reginald, a friend of Miss Morison's,—a relation, I believe?'

'No relation,' murmured Clara.

'I felt quite pleased,' said Mrs. Handy, 'at the high terms Mr. Campbell used to-day about this establishment. He said I was the only person in town he could trust ladies with.'

'Do give me a cup of tea, Mrs. Handy,' interposed Mr.

Reginald, 'for I am dying of thirst. I come near you to be well supplied; all selfishness on my part.'

Mr. Reginald saw that his newly-introduced companion was pretty and ladylike, and evidently ill at ease in the motley assembly she was thrown amongst. Her face was so intelligent and expressive, and her manner so timid, that he wondered what strange chance had sent her alone, or with such a companion as Miss Waterstone, to South Australia.

Clara, in the two half glances she had given him, saw a gentleman tall and dark, with fine eyes and a singularly pleasant smile. His age seemed to be about thirty, and his accent was English.

'Does this put you in mind of Todgers', Miss Morison?' said he, while the hostess was warmly recommending Miss Waterstone to change her mind about going to Melbourne, and remain in Adelaide, which she confidently asserted was far the better, and appealed to the gentlemen for confirmation.

How refreshing to poor Clara was this little allusion to a book! Of course Miss Waterstone had read all the current literature of the day that Robert had procured her, and considered herself, in her own phrase, a *well-read woman*; but whatever she read she made a point of forgetting, so that for those four months Clara had been debarred from her favourite topic of conversation. She smiled her assent, and Mr. Reginald continued,—

'We have a greater medley here than Mrs. Todgers had; English, Scotch, and Irish, and the German gentleman at your other hand. It is a pity he knows so little English, and has so little confidence in what knowledge he has, for he is highly accomplished, and you would find him agreeable when you got to understand him. I think I see Jenkins at the other end of the table, and perhaps that poor, ill-used individual, Blinker, might pass for Augustus Moddle. We certainly want Miss Cherry Pecksniff, though your companion makes no bad Miss Merry.'

Clara felt flattered at Miss Waterstone's being considered her companion merely, not her friend. She felt more at ease with this strange gentleman than she had done since she left home, and with a look such as her father had loved to see, said,—

'Then you do get a sight of Dickens' works here?'

'It would be too bad if we did not,' said Mr. Reginald. 'I get tired sometimes of the mighty dead, and like to hold communion with the delightful living. I get out the newest works of Dickens, Bulwer, and Thackeray. Have you seen the end of 'Pendennis,' Miss Morison?'

'It had not all come out when I left home,' said Clara, 'and I was very anxious to know how it was to wind up.'

The Boarding-House

'So am I,' said Reginald. 'It would be too trite and commonplace to kill off Blue Beard's wife, and get Laura to marry him,—but yet I do not feel that Pen deserves her. I am afraid, however, that George Warrington is too rough and gruff to suit a lady's taste.'

'O, no, indeed,' said Clara, 'I do not like Pen; he wants courage. If men knew how much women admire courage—moral courage in particular—they would not be so fond of making themselves appear small and petty in their presence, as they are.'

'What has struck me most in 'Pendennis' is that chapter about Sadducees,' said Reginald; 'it seems to be written for this colony; how many Sadducees we meet here every day! men who have no genuine faith in anything, who see things going wrong, but will not give themselves any trouble to set them right, men whose belief is only opinion, and whose love degenerates into convenience!'

'Miss Waterstone is going to sing,' said Mr. Oscar. 'Why, Mr. Reginald, you completely monopolize Miss Morison.'

Miss Morison blushed. She had forgotten the whole company; she had heard voices and laughter, but knew not what had been said, or who had been amused. She had even forgotten that Miss Waterstone was present; she had only felt happy, and was unconscious of anything else.

Miss Waterstone sung. Never had she sung so well. The hot wind clears the voice, if it has no other good effect; and a naturally fine voice, some musical talent, and a slight infusion of taste, rendered her song a very pleasing performance. Miss Morison was next entreated to sing. She said she never sung, and appealed to Miss Waterstone for confirmation.

'Indeed,' said Miss Waterstone, 'Clara has never favoured me with anything like a song the whole voyage; except, indeed, the words. I think she knows the words of every song that ever was written. And for poetry, too, I never saw such a memory.'

'Miss Morison would not sing to-night, even if she could,' said Mr. Reginald, in a low tone, to Clara.

Clara smiled. 'But, indeed, I cannot sing at all, nor play either,' said she.

'If Miss Morison knows the words of songs,' said a black-eyed puppy, with an imperial, from the other end of the room, 'she will be invaluable to Blinker. He is acquainted with all the tunes, but fails in the words. It is Miss Waterstone's privilege to call: I merely hint that Blinker sings.'

'Indeed he does, charmingly,' said half-a-dozen voices. 'You see the ladies are dying to hear you, Blinker.'

'Ask him, Miss Waterstone,' whispered the country overseer. 'It is such fun! You have no notion how soft he is.'

And Miss Waterstone, entering into the joke, pressed Mr. Blinker to sing. And Mr. Blinker would do anything to please the ladies; but he did not sing well. He knew what good singing was; he understood music; but his voice was not what it used to be. He would do his best, however, if they would not be too severe upon him. Would Mrs. Handy let him have her 'Little Warbler?'

'Oh!' said the puppy before mentioned, whose name was Brown, 'Miss Morison will enable us to dispense with the 'Little Warbler' for to-night. We must get a song of some kind from Miss Morison.'

Clara looked indignant, and with a glance made Brown lower his eyes, which saved Mr. Reginald the trouble of telling him to hold his tongue.

'Well,' said Oscar, 'here is the 'Little Warbler,' and go it, Blinker!'

So Blinker began at the beginning of the book, and sung 'The Last Rose of Summer,' in a feeble, croaky voice; but was greeted with a round of applause at the termination, and an earnest request for another. He sang the next in order, and was again applauded. He liked to sing, and whenever he seemed inclined to shut the book and give up, the other gentlemen whispered that the ladies were enchanted with his performance, and would be quite grieved if he did not continue it. The German, who had a fine taste in music, had put on his hat at the beginning of the second song and gone out; and nothing but his desire to see how his fair companion would get through what must be to her a very uncomfortable scene, prevented Reginald from following his example. Fourteen songs had been sung by the indefatigable Blinker—four comic, and ten sentimental—before he laid down the book. Then Miss Waterstone sung again. Not so well as at first, for her lungs were quite exhausted by laughter, suppressed and otherwise. Clara had not much more uninterrupted conversation with Mr. Reginald; but she felt that he understood her; and she wondered if South Australian sheep-farmers were all as agreeable. In the midst of these thoughts, she heard the clock strike. She did not know exactly what hour; but she telegraphed to her companion, who understood the signal.

Miss Waterstone wished to shake hands with Mr. Humberstone at least; but she saw that Clara's dignified reverence looked well, and ventured on an imitation. Mrs. Handy accompanied them to their bed-room; hoped they had enjoyed themselves; said that she herself had never passed a more delightful evening, and bid them good night.

'Ah, Clara!' said Elizabeth Waterstone, 'I thought that you never flirted, and could not conduct a *tête-à-tête*. Well, if you

never did in Scotland, you came off amazingly well for a beginner. You monopolized the handsomest, the richest, and the most agreeable gentleman in the room. Mr. Humberstone tells me he is a large sheep-holder, and of a good family, too; but I see you did not care to flirt till you found someone worth your while!'

'Do you call that flirting?' said Clara. 'Mr. Reginald only talked to me as my father used to do—my own dear papa! Oh, if he was with me, I should be able to bear anything! Welcome poverty and labour, if shared with him! I must try to do nothing unbecoming his memory, and, by God's help, I will do what is right in the thorny path I have to tread.'

'Dear me, Clara, you are on your high horse, to-night; but do not be so much uplifted. I think Mr. Reginald is a dreadful flirt. Mr. Brown told me as much, when he saw you so much taken up with him.'

Clara paid no attention to these words; but knelt down, and prayed long and fervently that her steps might be ordered aright. She would enter into no conversation, though Elizabeth was disposed to talk; but, contrary to her own expectation, after this exciting day, fell immediately into a sweet, sound, refreshing sleep. Next morning, Mrs. Handy told the ladies, after breakfast was over, and the gentlemen dispersed, that she considered Mr. Reginald as a king compared to the rest.

'The others may have more fun, but Mr. Reginald is always polite and gentlemanly; I never saw anybody with finer manners in or out of the colony. And they all grumble at the food I give them but Mr. Reginald. If I gave him bread and water, I believe he would make no complaint. If you only knew Mr. Oscar and the trouble he gives me, you would wonder that we have hung together so long. At first I used to fret myself sadly when he said, 'No pudding to-day, Mrs. Handy! I shall be obliged to try another house.' Or sometimes with a sneer and a toss of his head, 'The grand secret of making good coffee, is to put in *plenty* of coffee. Perhaps you do not know that, Mrs. Handy. You will be the better for the information.' Or sometimes, 'Do you think us Abyssinians to live on raw meat, Mrs. Handy?' Or, what was worse than all, when I had made a nice light pudding, and taken such pains with it, he would call it a delusion, and teach the other gentlemen to do the same. But Mr. Reginald is not like that.'

Clara's boxes and Miss Waterstone's much wished-for portmanteau arrived in the forenoon. Mrs. Handy recommended a washerwoman to Clara, telling her that the washing of her ship's-clothes was likely to cost her about thirty shillings. This would make a great hole in her finances; but Clara was

determined not to be discouraged by trifles, and sat down to write the commencement of a letter to Susan, which was tolerably cheerful.

Miss Waterstone went in to dinner this day, which was Saturday, in all the glory of a well-fitting black silk dress, a gold chain, pretty bracelets, and several handsome rings. Clara's dress was quiet and simple; her hand and arm, without ornament of any kind, were perfectly beautiful, and her throat white and slender. Mr. Reginald thought he had never seen anything so unique as this solitary girl, who seemed pleased to sit beside him and ask him questions about the colony, without either forwardness or *mauvaise honte*. It was not to every lady that Mr. Reginald could be agreeable. He had no *petits soins*, paid no compliments, and had no frivolous remarks to make. Miss Waterstone would have found him a much duller companion than the sprightly Humberstone; but Clara had a very different taste.

'I do not understand what makes people get fond of South Australia, while at the same time they own to so many disagreeables in it,' said Clara to Reginald.

'I shall find it difficult to make the feeling understood,' replied he; 'in time I hope that you will share it. When our weather is fine, it is very fine indeed; there is something in the air so clear, so bracing, that it seems to be enough of happiness to breathe it. Then, when our society is good, it is so cordial and unceremonious. There is not that universal desire to keep up appearances here which poisons English society, and renders hospitality a toil to the giver and a bore to the receiver of it. In fact, six years' residence in this colony has made me quite unfit for England, and I feel very much indisposed to submit to either its climate, its restraint, or its etiquette. But I suppose, Miss Morison, that you are disappointed with South Australia, or at least with Adelaide; you have come out at a bad season of the year, and I fear that your beautiful imaginary pictures of the Arcadian scenery and pastoral tranquillity of Australia have been too like fairyland to be ever realized.'

'Indeed, I cannot say that I expected to like the colony,' said Clara. 'Some have greatness thrust upon them, and I think I may say that emigration was thrust upon me. My uncle thought it advisable that I should come out, and endeavour to get a situation as governess here, for it is no easy matter at home; and as Mr. Campbell was an old friend, he recommended me to his and Mrs. Campbell's care; but, unhappily, Mrs. Campbell's death has deprived me of a protector and adviser; so here I am.'

Mr. Reginald saw many difficulties before this young girl,

but he talked encouragingly, and was pleased to see that she was determined to do her utmost for independence.

After tea, Mr. Brown, who liked to do rude things when he could, began a violent philippic against Scotland, concluding with his stock quotation from Byron about 'The land of meanness, sophistry, and mist,' winking with one eye to Oscar, and keeping the other fixed on the two Scotch girls. Clara's lip slightly curled, but she took no further notice of the impertinence; not so Miss Waterstone; she fired up, and defended her country.

'I am sure, sir,' said she, 'there is no country superior to Scotland, or any people better than the Scotch. Mist, indeed! mist is a far cleaner thing than that abominable dust that covers Adelaide all over like a cloak. I suppose you think we can't grow anything in Scotland, but if you just saw how green the grass is there, and what apples, and pears, and gooseberries we have, you would change your mind. And for a city, what city can beat Edinburgh, the modern Athens?'

But here Mr. Brown sought to escape from the lady's rhetoric, by calling out another accomplishment of his unfortunate butt.

'Ah, Blinker,' said he, 'it is a pity that your scruples about the gentility of the thing prevents you from starting a dancing-school. You would have all the beauty and fashion of Adelaide eager for initiation into the matchless grace of your Terpsichorean feats, or feet,—it's all the same.'

'Do you really think so, Brown?' said the hapless Blinker. 'If you will move the table aside, and whistle 'the Original,' I will give you the polka.'

'But you must have a partner,' whispered Ivory; 'can't you ask one of these ladies to dance?'

'Miss Morison is dying to dance with you,' said Brown; 'go and ask her.'

Blinker did as he was bid, but met with a chilling negative. He was next instigated to ask Miss Waterstone, but she said that she could not dance to whistling, and professed herself very anxious to see him dance, which she could not do so well if she joined him.

Thus encouraged, Blinker went through all his steps with more precision than grace. Mr. Haussen again retreated, and Clara asked Mr. Reginald if he was not inclined to leave the house with his German friend.

'This is not very pleasant,' said he, 'but for two or three days it forms a variety to me. My bush life is very solitary, and after eight or ten weeks of it, I feel wondrously charitable, even to such absurdities as these. But I hope, Miss Morison, that your stay here will not be a long one, for a week of such vulgar jokes is more than enough.'

'I do not know how long I may remain here. I do not think my uncle contemplated my going to a boarding-house; but when Miss Waterstone has left for Melbourne, I shall keep to my own room more than I can now. I feel more timid about getting a situation than I did; for it would have been better, much better, if I could have gone from Mrs. Campbell's house, than from such an establishment as this. I never met with gentlemen so familiar and presuming, except, indeed, one on board the *Magnificent*; but he was a 'single spy,' here 'they are in battalions,' and support each other.'

'We must not think too much about them,' said Reginald, gaily; 'it is too great a compliment. I want to ask you if you are an admirer of Byron's; for if you are not, you had better disguise your sentiments, if you wish for peace at Handy's. These half-gentlemen are all rabid for Byron.'

'I have read very little of his writings, and what I have read has puzzled me much,' said Clara. 'One moment I admire, next pity, then hate, then despise. I do not feel comfortable in reading Byron; my mind aches with his jerks more than my body did yesterday in the port cart. And can you tell me what he wrote for, Mr. Reginald? It seems to me that he could not help writing, but that he wrote without a purpose. He throws no light upon the path of life.'

'Only the light—the beacon of his own sad experience,' said Reginald. 'How wasted were all his powers! How contented we should be with mediocrity, when we see that such a brilliant destiny was so miserable! But you are too young, or not young enough, to admire Byron. I have, of late years, seen more earnestness in his sorrow, and I detach it as much as I can from the sneers and frivolity, which, I think, were mere excrescences on the reality of his style. But what annoys me most with these Browns and Oscars, and such like, is, that the very jerks which you feel so painful, and which to me are affectations, form his great recommendation to them. It encourages them in their frivolity and unbelief to see a man of such genius as Byron placing pathos and satire side by side in unnatural juxtaposition. One of them is out of place. I would deny the sincerity of the sneer; they would ignore the pathos.'

'How much more healthy is your Walter Scott,' continued Reginald, 'though I do not consider his genius so great; but his sympathies were wider, and his observation genial. When he paints a villain, he is generally a villain—not Byron's melodramatic half-scoundrel, half-hero, with some infusion of the fool. Still, neither Sir Walter's villains nor heroes are so much to my taste as his middling characters. His back-grounds are well filled in, all the accessories are perfect, and his minor characters never out of place. But I suppose you, like every

Scotchwoman I have met, worship Sir Walter, and think I am giving very faint praise indeed.'

'I like Sir Walter much,' said Clara; 'but my father used to be disappointed in my admiration of his novels. He considered them perfect, and incapable of improvement. I could find no fault with them; but I missed something.'

'Yes,' said Reginald, 'it is the outer life he portrays; the inner he rarely touches upon. In reading them, I feel a thousand thoughts come into my mind, deeper and higher than what are expressed in the book for me. I think that even *mediocre* people like ourselves have still depths of thought within them which they like to have stirred up sometimes.'

Clara was pleased to hear her sentiments so naturally expressed, and was still more pleased that she was called *mediocre*. Her father had taught her that a fine taste for poetry and a well cultivated mind did not make her a genius; but her aunt and uncle, and, latterly, Miss Waterstone, had been accustomed to annoy her by supposing she thought herself very clever. She had talked about books to this stranger, because he had started the subject, and because she had nothing else to talk about; but she had sometimes feared that he would think her a blue-stocking, who wished to make a parade. That very evening she had heard Miss Waterstone telling the two gentlemen nearest her, that Clara, though not accomplished, was quite a learned lady—quite intellectual, indeed.

'Intellectual!' thought Clara. 'What a vague idea Miss Waterstone has got of the meaning of words! The utmost that can be said of me is that I am intelligent. I hope Mr. Reginald thinks me so.'

The evening wore away; and, after the ladies had gone out of the room, cards were brought out: and, with the exception of Blinker, who could not play, and Reginald, who would not, the whole party sat down to loo. Reginald took up a book, and seemed all impatience till the game should be over. He went out to smoke, and came in to find the party more engrossed in their game than before. He took up the book again, and smoked another cigar; but there was no stopping them till twelve o'clock, when he dismissed them with some thankfulness that it was Saturday night, and that next night they were likely to go to bed soon.

When they were all gone, and the doors shut, Reginald took from his pocket two letters, which he had got at the post-office that day. One of them was opened, the other had the seal unbroken. He had merely glanced at the first, but had had no opportunity of reading the second, and even now he seemed to want courage to begin.

'Had Julia married me,' said he, half aloud, 'when she should have done so, and that is six years ago, what a companion this gentle girl would have made for her. Let me see, we might have had three children now, and Miss Morison would have taught them, and kept Julia from feeling dull in my absence. And Julia would have grown to be a domestic, affectionate wife—she was as wax in my hands then; but six years have been spent by me in solitude and labour, by her in dissipation and gaiety, and we are both changed. I fear that the song is not right about 'absence making the heart grow fonder.' That ship-board song, six years ago, seemed to speak to the heart; but I doubt it now.

'But I must read these letters, and perhaps answer them too, as there is a mail making up for England on Tuesday. It would be foolish to delay writing till I am in the bush, for my letter will be gloomier from Taringa than from Adelaide.'

So he got paper, pen, and ink together, preparing to answer before he began to read.

'I had better read my mother's over again first,' said he. It was as follows:—

'MY DEAR CHARLES,

'I have just got your letter of May the twelfth, and am delighted to hear that you are so well, and making your way in the world, as I always knew you would. Your letters are all most interesting to me, and I feel so glad that you do not cut them short, but give me full weight of foreign post well filled.

'Your sisters have been spending a month with me lately; Jane brought her three children for change of air; and though they were quite sickly when they left Everton, they soon were able to make noise enough for half-a-dozen, which of course delighted me; and when James came for them he was quite struck with the change in their appearance.

'He is getting on very well now in his profession, and has got all Lord L——'s agency, which is a very handsome thing; and they have got a most beautiful house in Everton now. It is in the High-street, and is twice as large as the one they used to live in. They see a great deal of company, for both Jane and Mr. Marston like society; but yet I fancy that it is greatly on Julia's account that they give so many parties. You would be proud of Julia, Charles, if you could see her now. I am very proud of her myself, though her engagement to you is not generally known. I think that she grows handsomer every year; her figure was slight and girlish when you left home, but it has developed into what everybody calls perfect. She has been taking lessons in singing from Signor

Farinelli, and her voice is considered the finest in all Everton. The Hon. Mr. Ashleigh, Lord L——'s eldest son, paid Julia great attention at the county ball, and was heard to remark that Miss Marston's air was as good as that of any lady he had ever seen.

'I am sorry to say that your sister Alice has not recovered her strength after her late severe illness. She must be nursed all winter, and when spring comes on, Edward means to take her for a tour on the Continent. She has asked Julia to accompany her, and though Julia wished to go, she asked my permission before she would consent. Of course it was just what I could have wished, for she will be a cheerful companion for Alice, and, by your quiet fireside some day, she will be able to tell you all about her wanderings, and the sights she has seen, which will be the more delightful to you, as you have never been abroad.

'I dare say Julia's fidelity has been much more tried than yours, for you can never see any one so beautiful in Australia, while here some of the handsomest and finest young men in the country have been most assiduous in their attentions. People wonder that she does not make her choice, but I never breathe a word about her reason. I say there is no hurry; but she is now twenty-five, and I hope that you will come and claim her soon, for I should like to see my only son happy before I die, and I may not be long for this world.

'Everything goes on much as usual with me at Ashfield. The garden has lost almost all its glory, but Richard promises that it will surpass all former years next summer, and be quite a great exhibition of itself. He is always asking me when you are coming back to England to see the trees you planted, which are thriving very well; he wishes to surprise you by a great many *lusus naturae*, as he calls them, but I don't exactly know what he means by the phrase. He requests you to send some more Australian seeds. Very few of those we received have come up, and even those that grow do not seem to thrive; but Richard wants to try again.

'I feel my rheumatism coming on again, and expect to be able to go out very little all this winter, but my friends are very kind in visiting me. Julia promises me a two months' visit after Christmas, which will be delightful, for she fills the house with amusing company, and saves me from the trouble of entertaining them. After she returns from the Continent, she promises me another visit, and we propose going to see the Great Exhibition together.

'I have been thinking, and Julia too, that in a short time you might be able to return to England for good and all, and settle down in the old house, or in a new one if you prefer it. It seems a burying alive of Julia to take her to

your lonely sheep station, so far from town. If you could afford a house in Adelaide for her, though it would be equally hard for me to bear, it would be different for Julia, for she is formed for society. So do, my dearest Charles, make money as fast as possible, and come back with a fortune to justify Julia's choice in the eyes of the world, and you will make the evening of my days as happy as it can be.

'When I get on this subject, I forget everything else that I ought to tell you, so I may as well conclude by subscribing myself your attached mother,

'E. REGINALD.'

Mr. Reginald next looked at the other letter. It had a very pretty seal, was inclosed in a tasteful envelope, and was addressed in a very pretty hand; but Charles Reginald felt afraid of it. The proposition that his mother had made would probably be repeated in it, and he knew that he could not accede to it. But he must read it, and did accordingly. It ran thus,—

'MY DEAREST CHARLES,

'I wish you would not write me such dull letters as your last two have been, giving me advice, and so forth. Nobody ever thinks of advising me here. From your dear, kind mother, down to our little niece Fanny, all with one accord allow me to do just as I please, and you must be as complaisant, or you and I will quarrel.

'When Jane asked me what was in your last letter, it quite took me by surprise. I could give her no answer. There was no news in it; only the names of some books you wanted me to read, and some songs you would like me to learn. I appealed to Jane if I had any time to read, or if it was possible for me to learn such antiquated songs, and your sister quite took my view of the matter.

'We have had delightful pic-nic parties this last autumn, and now we are beginning to be gay in Everton. I expect to be out two or three nights a week, and we have most pleasant parties at home. The plan of Jane's new house is so much to my taste, that I send you a copy of it, that you may get up something like it, or at least imitate the air of it, if you cannot have so large a house. The double drawing-room holds twenty couples comfortably, and the loftiness of the ceiling makes it delightful to sing in. I have got up as high as B flat in it, and you know that I used to have difficulty with G sharp not long ago.

'I am going to visit your mother about the New Year, and when Spring sets in, I go with Alice and Mr. Bisset on the Continent. Will not the tour be delightful? and I know it will do Alice much good.

The Boarding-House

'My brother James and Jane say they will never be able to do without me so long, but I dare say they will enjoy a little quiet, for I am as restless as ever, and like nothing so well as variety. Your mother and I are of opinion that as we have waited so many years already, we had better wait a few years longer, till you have made your fortune, and then you could come back, and settle near Everton in some sort of style. Your mother proposed your living at Ashfield, and getting some additions made to the old house, but it would never do. It is old-fashioned, and suits an old lady like your mother, but I never could submit to the narrow passages and low ceilings. You give me no brilliant description of your present dwelling; I assure you that I do not find it at all tempting. I know I could not live in the bush; I should mope to death. Much as I love you, Charles, I cannot consent to live so many miles from civilization, among savages and snakes. I have given up a great deal for your sake; do make an effort, or even a sacrifice, to please me. I always thought you rather contradictory; but how a man of your talents and accomplishments can profess to like a life which by your own description is monotonous and unexciting, I *cannot* understand.

'My dress at the county ball was considered the most tasteful in the room. It was a suggestion of my own that Madame Estcourt worked out, and it was quite a success. It was of white satin, trimmed *en bouillon*,—but of what use is it giving you any account of it? I suppose you would rather see me in a brown stuff dress, with a blue apron, or some such horror, than in the most elegant attire. I hope you dress like a gentleman, for I cannot bear to fancy you untidy. The sleeves of coats are worn very wide, and the collars very low. I hope you will have yours made thus.

'In all your letters you have never mentioned whether you wore a moustache or not, or if your black hair curled better in your hot climate than it used to do in England. Your mother gave me such a pretty present on *your* birthday, of a bracelet. Only one is worn now; at least, if you wear two, they must not match, but be as dissimilar as you and I. Such disparity is fashionable, you see.

'By the bye, how old are you? Either thirty or thirty-one, I know, but I am not certain which. I am twenty-five, but do not feel at all old yet. I seem to get younger every day; at least, Jane and your mother say so.

'People have forgotten, if they ever knew, that I am engaged to you; and it is so pleasant and so comfortable to be able to flirt without any danger of being caught myself; while no one knows how secure I am. I hope you dance

sometimes, and have not forgotten how to sing. I never can get such a good second as yours to join me.

'The three children send love and kisses to Uncle Charles, for though they have never seen you, grand-mamma has been talking so much about you lately, that they are quite fond of you.

'Do you know, James and Jane are so glad that I held out against being married to you when we were first engaged, and going with you to Australia. They were just saying last night, that, instead of enjoying myself for six years in my own element, and, consequently, looking well and happy, I should have been old and careworn by this time, with the dreadful long voyage, and all the hardships you described; and you would, perhaps, have ceased to admire, if not to love me. And I must have admiration as well as love; I cannot live without some incense.

'So, dear Charles, write me a very delightful letter. Put as many compliments in it as you can—conscientious, if possible; and believe me, yours ever,

JULIA MARSTON.'

Reginald sat for ten minutes in silent thought; and then took up his pen to answer Julia's letter. To his mother he could write from the country; but he felt that he must let Julia know the plain truth as soon as possible.

He wrote as follows:

'MY DEAREST JULIA,

'I am very much grieved that my letters are too dull for you. I cannot write you news, when you know nobody here. I can only write my own thoughts and feelings, which, as I have not you near me to enliven them, must necessarily be stupid, and sometimes sad. I fear, my dear girl, that the life you lead, and which you seem to enjoy so much, is no good preparation for ultimately settling down as my wife, for I am not a lively man, though I will love you truly, and devote myself to making you happy. But I cannot give parties, or go with you on tours, nor am I witty enough to keep you always amused. My mother and you seemed to have formed a very erroneous idea of my circumstances. It would be many years before I could be justified in selling off my sheep, and living like a gentleman in idleness. Even a house in town is beyond my present means; and even if I had it, I should be obliged to leave it for half the year to look after my stations; and after waiting so long, it is a cruel thing to think that I cannot have you always with me. And, dear Julia, look at the matter, not from the false point of view you at present see it from, but reasonably and generously. I have worked

hard for six years, and am now able to give you all the comforts, and even some of the elegancies of life. But you wish me to wait till all my youth is over, and I have pined and hardened in solitude, that we may be able to begin life in style, and make a respectable figure in that circle which is to you 'the world!' I do not mean to reproach you; but you have enjoyed everything that your heart could wish for these six years, and yet you object to sharing my moderate fortunes, and making a paradise of my cottage. You would rather wait till I was old, and worn, and rich. Oh, Julia, how happy you would have made me if you had married me *that* May!

'If you will promise to come out with me, I will go home after the New Year; and if you really wish it, and my circumstances will afford the expense (which they may if wool brings a good price next clip), I promise you a house in Adelaide, not so handsome as your brother James's, but as good as is expected here by people in our position.

'For my dear mother's sake, I would fain have settled down in her neighbourhood; but, perhaps, we can prevail upon her to come out with us. The climate will suit her admirably, and as for the voyage, it is not disagreeable, if you have a tolerable captain and a good protector. And my mother may make a new Ashfield of my poor station of Taringa; she shall change its name into something more English, if she pleases, and you two will make me the happiest of men. And I will not bore you with books either: you shall play and sing, and I, though rather rusty, will cultivate the second you like. And we will ask friends to see us; and I can certify, that Mrs. Charles Reginald, of Taringa, will be more admired in South Australia than Miss Marston was at any county ball, or town of Everton either.

'I wear no moustache, but, if you like it, I can easily get one up. I saw a white hair among my raven locks this morning, which set me moralizing on the departure of youth; but I am only thirty-one, after all. I shall certainly get a coat with wide sleeves and fashionable collar, though I fear that before this reaches you they will have gone out of fashion, and you will be shocked at the idea of my wearing complacently what has been exploded for months. Still, Julia, this may prove to you that I wish much to please you, and would do anything in my power to gratify your every wish, even every whim. I did wish to hear how you were dressed at the ball, and was quite disappointed when you stopped short in your description; so write me a full account of your last dress in the answer to this, which I shall weary for sadly.

'Do not think me too exacting, my dearest love, and believe me yours devotedly,

CHARLES REGINALD.'

Clara Morison

Charles sighed when this letter was finished, and lay down on the sofa to try to sleep; but the hard pillow under his head, and the anxious thoughts in his heart, kept him awake the greater part of the night.

CHAPTER V

A SUNDAY AT MRS. HANDY'S

Mrs. Handy's table was not half filled next morning at breakfast, for several of the young gentlemen preferred cold tea, or even none at all, to getting up in time for it on Sunday morning: so that the breakfast-things lay on the table till it was time to lay the cloth for dinner. Mrs. Handy complained of their laziness to the young ladies, and Miss Waterstone wondered at her submitting to it, and declared that, after a certain hour, they should have no breakfast.

'The Adelaide people are all very tender in the mornings,' said Mr. Humberstone. 'I can't sleep a wink myself after five o'clock, and it puzzles me to get through the hours before an Adelaide breakfast. I get up as usual, and get out, but there is nobody up; I have to walk about the streets for an hour and a half before I meet even a milk-man, and I should be glad to talk to him, but he cannot stop—he must serve his customers. I next see servant-girls, very untidy, with nightcaps on, coming out to get wood to light the fire, and to fill the kettle; but in fact these things should be brought in overnight. In another hour or so, I see Adelaide trying to get up and look awake, and by that time I think breakfast will be ready, and come in here to find Mrs. Handy's gentlemen snug in bed yet. It is really scandalous. They would be the better for living in the country for a year or two. And what makes all the Adelaide ladies look so pale, but their not getting up early enough? We have not many country lasses, but what rosy cheeks *they* have! Ah! Miss Waterstone, there's no flowers in the garden like those flowers; I know you are an early riser; you need say nothing about it, for in fact I am quite convinced of it.'

The ladies went to Little St. Andrew's, the church of the Scotch establishment, where the service was so delightfully familiar to Clara, that she almost forgot she was in a strange

land; and she came home soothed and tolerably cheerful; but the confusion and noise of dinner distracted her again. Mr. Reginald had been out all day, and she missed him.

In the afternoon, Miss Waterstone complained of a headache, and saying that an hour's rest would put her to rights, lay down in her own room; while Clara sat with her kindhearted hostess, and heard her talk of many things—of cookery, of servants, of washerwomen, of the difficulty of getting servants that could do anything, and of the comfortable position of servants in this colony, compared with that of their employers.

'They get good wages,' continued she, 'and have no cares; they have only their dress to find; and really my Jane, with her seven shillings a-week, dresses better than myself. To see her go out now in her flounced muslin gown, satin visite, and drawn bonnet, you would take her for the mistress, and not the servant. She is out walking with her lover, for it is her Sunday out to-day, and a good match she is making—a master carpenter, who employs three or four men, and as sober and respectable a young man as is in the colony. Ah, well! Miss Morison, I hope you will like the colony; it is hard to get a good situation here, but I am sure that you will get on well when you are once in a respectable family. Your friend, Miss Waterstone, has a nice frank manner, that will take people at first, but you need have no fear but in the long run you will succeed as well. What do you think of Mr. Reginald, Miss Morison? He is not quite so handsome as he used to be on board ship, nor perhaps so lively, but I suppose it is the dull life he leads. It was always a kind word or a smile to me when he saw me so poorly on the *Dauntless*; and my husband said that he was as considerate and polite to the poorest woman on board as to any of the young ladies in the cuddy. He is an old acquaintance of mine, you see; and I have had good reason to like him, for he has encouraged this house as much as he could, and recommended it to his friends. And really it is a good thing that I can make my own living, for Handy has sent me nothing as yet. It is a hard life: up early, and down late; but I can pay my way, and look everybody in the face. You can't think how sleepy I get Sunday afternoons. I fancy it must be the early dinner. I must lay my head on the sofa for half an hour; I see you have a book.'

Clara had a book—one of the good books she had got as parting presents from her friends; but her mind was too anxious to take in what her eyes mechanically wandered over, when Mr. Reginald came in. A heavy shower, which had fallen during the night, had refreshed everything; the wind was from the south-west, and was fresh and bracing,

A Sunday at Mrs. Handy's

and you could almost fancy that you saw something green springing up.

'Now, Miss Morison,' said Reginald, 'is not our fine weather very fine, as I said last night?'

'It is indeed,' answered Clara; 'the short walk to and from church was so delightful, that it made me quite like the country.'

'You cannot quite call this the country,' said Reginald; 'but I know that you will like the real country when you see more of it. Adelaide was never much to my taste, though I often weary to come into it, particularly in winter, when the evenings are long and the roads bad, but I am always glad to get out of it again. This weather promises me a pleasant day for my ride home to-morrow.'

Clara was sorry that he was going away so soon, for what could she say to the other gentlemen, or how escape their impertinence? She hoped that Mr. Haussen would sit beside her sometimes. She sat some minutes in silence, and so did Reginald; then he suddenly said,—

'Have you read Borrow's 'Lavengro'?'

'No; I have heard of it, and seen reviews; critics call it stupid; but I liked the 'Bible in Spain,' and I think I should like it.'

'What struck me most was, that in this book, which is either an autobiography or an imitation of one, he meets with characters, describes them, and makes you interested in them, and then they disappear, and you see them no more, and the book leaves off without ending anything, as unfinished as the lives of its readers. This is life-like, but not book-like; everything in books is jointed in and polished off—neatly, but not naturally. Have you ever observed this? I suppose it is highly probable, Miss Morison,' continued Reginald, 'that we may never meet again; yet I should not write a life of myself without describing our short acquaintance, and many like it,— pleasant passages which lead to nothing.'

'You must see many different characters in a house like this,' observed Clara.

'Of course,' said Reginald, still thinking of Lavengro, the last book he had read, and which he was glad to talk over to an intelligent listener. 'I think the most prominent characteristic of Borrow must be what phrenologists call secretiveness. He seems to delight in concealing his thoughts, his attainments, his past life and future intentions, from every one he meets, or at least Lavengro does.'

'Perhaps it is merely the invention of an imaginary character?' said Clara.

'It seems to come out of the very nature of the man,' said Reginald; 'and it has set me wondering what the man really

is, since all he tells of himself seems intended to obscure the subject.'

'I like to see the portrait of the author prefixed to a book, provided he is dead,' said Clara; 'but I am not fond of seeing living writers trying to look sublime at the commencement of their own works, and yet by some perversity that I cannot account for, I long to see the portrait anywhere else.'

'Do you draw at all, Miss Morison?' said Reginald.

'Oh, no! not at all,' said Clara. 'I am singularly destitute of accomplishments for an Edinburgh girl of the nineteenth century; but I admire drawing very much, and my sister used to make little sketches for me, and smile at the criticisms I made.'

'I have made several sketches of Australian scenery to send home to my mother and other friends,' said Reginald; 'but whether I have not done them justice, or that the scenery is not really fine, I know not, but they have not been much admired. What a splendid display of all works of art there will be in the Great Exhibition in a few months from this time. I suppose that you must regret losing the opportunity of seeing it, by coming to this wild country? Several of my friends have gone home expressly to see it, and if I could have combined business with pleasure, I should have set sail by this time.'

'I really regretted leaving my native country when it was on the eve of so wonderful a display,' said Clara. 'My sister Susan is going up to London with my uncle and aunt, but I was to go to South Australia, and everybody seemed to think, the sooner the better.'

'Your sister would fain have kept you longer, I dare say,' said Reginald.

'Indeed she would, or have gone instead of me, had that been permitted; but what my uncle thought right, she was convinced must be for the best, so she gave up her own wishes with wonderfully good grace.'

'But your inclination was not consulted any more than your sister's.'

'Ah! but I am not so good as she is. Papa used to say that girls were generally taught to place generosity before justice, and he determined to reverse the matter with us; Susan did not relish the justice-lessons much, but when she came to the generosity, she revelled in it. She seems quite to enjoy every sacrifice she makes, and has no conscience whatever on her own side; but as for poor me, I have been so engrossed with the justice, that I have never got so far as the generosity.'

'You do not mean me to believe that you would not make a sacrifice for those you love?' said Reginald.

'I could make a sacrifice,' said Clara, 'but I should know

A Sunday at Mrs. Handy's

that it was a sacrifice, and be fully aware of its extent, which Susan and all amiable girls never are.'

'Then you deserve the more credit if you do your duty because you feel it is right, and not to gratify a selfish desire to make others happy, and so promote your own enjoyment,' said Reginald.

'Do not say so,' said Clara. 'How much more beautiful is spontaneous benevolence than such calculating virtue as mine is!'

'Miss Morison,' said Reginald, kindly and gravely, 'I see you have a passion for depreciating yourself, and that you have a pleasure in telling that you want this or that good quality; but you will find that an indulgence in it will do you no good in South Australia. You must say what you can do, and look confident, or ninety-nine in a hundred will not think you capable of anything. I am a good deal older than you, so I hope you will not take my little piece of advice in bad part.'

'No, indeed,' said Clara, 'it is very kind of you; you are quite right to tell me of my faults.'

'I did not call it a fault,' said Reginald.

'Well, my imprudence,' said Clara.

'But here comes Miss Waterstone, looking well again. We have been talking of the Great Exhibition, and Mr. Reginald has been expressing his surprise that we did not delay emigrating till we had seen it. I have given my reason, that I had no choice. Will you give us yours?'

'Why,' said Miss Waterstone, looking a little confused, 'I was hurried in my departure in many ways; and even if I had stayed, it is very likely that my aunts would not have gone, or if they had, they were sure to leave me to keep the house; and perhaps it may turn out a failure after all; and a ship sailing from Leith with a married captain, was a great inducement at the time, I remember. And after all, I suppose we will see all about it in the papers; though I do hate newspapers, and never read them when I can help it; and there's nobody now to make me read them against my will, which is a great comfort, isn't it, Clara? Aunt Penny used to make me read the *Courant* and the *Witness* till I was hoarse. When the General Assembly of the Free Church was sitting, and Aunt Penny was not well enough to go to hear the speeches, she used to make me read them all; and once they took me three hours and a half, and I could not speak above my breath for a fortnight afterwards. So I just hate the papers.'

One after another the gentlemen dropped in; tea relieved Miss Waterstone's headache, and she listened to Mr. Humberstone's account of bush living—tea without milk, drunk out of pannikins three times a day, with an unvarying routine of

mutton and damper for solids, with sympathizing wonder. There was talk of a very desultory nature going on. Mr. Reginald seemed reserved, and Clara felt dull. It certainly was not proper Sunday conversation, and perhaps he would have preferred going to church. She wished to go herself, but Miss Waterstone did not feel well enough to accompany her, and she felt she could not go alone. So she sat beside Mr. Reginald, looking sad and anxious, but very pretty, while all the wit of the company was lost upon her.

Mr. Reginald liked to see her silent, for it is a rare virtue in one that can converse well; and he felt too anxious himself to talk. The letters he carried in his pocket were uncomfortable ones, and he sat contrasting in his mind's eye the quiet girl beside him with his own brilliant betrothed, as he remembered her, and as his mother's letter described her. Julia was certainly handsomer, and more striking. Her hair and eyes were darker, and her figure taller and more commanding. There was no comparison in beauty, but yet Clara looked charming. And she was going to be a governess to some half-dozen children, with domestic drudgery enough besides, and would be glad to marry any one, to put an end to it. Governnesses generally make bad wives, and their manners are often not agreeable; but Miss Morison had evidently never taught yet. But yet a lovely, accomplished English wife was preferable to a girl like this, thrown into the colony with no connexions that any one knew of, and with merely a letter-of-introduction passport into society.

When they had got into their room at night, Miss Waterstone confided to Clara her opinion that Reginald was a *stick*.

'Mr. Humberstone says that he is going out of town tomorrow, too, and will ride in Mr. Reginald's company a good bit beyond Gawler Town, though where that is I know no more than the man in the moon; so we shall both be minus our beaux. By the bye, when do you mean to see Mr. Campbell again?'

'I do not like to give him much trouble,' said Clara; 'if he sends me no message, I shall call at the end of a week to see if he has heard of anything for me.'

'Did your uncle say nothing about taking you back in case you did not succeed?'

'He did not seem to contemplate any such contingency,' said Clara, mournfully; 'but Mr. Campbell mentioned it as a pis-aller. I do not wish to return if I am unwelcome, to embitter dear Susan's happy home. So I will take any situation in South Australia rather than be sent back as returned goods, unsuited to the market.'

And Clara looked slightly scornful.

A Sunday at Mrs. Handy's

'Well,' said Miss Waterstone, 'I shall be quite sorry to leave Adelaide, for I shall be all alone in Melbourne, whereas you are as good as a sister to me here. But do you know, Clara, that my sleep in the afternoon has not made me feel wakeful now. I am dreadfully sleepy, though it is quite early. There is only ten o'clock striking.'

CHAPTER VI

A GLIMPSE OF A SITUATION

Next morning, Mr. Reginald read the newspaper till all the gentlemen had gone out but Humberstone, who was flirting with Miss Waterstone in a despairing manner, regretting that he should never see her again, entreating her not to leave Adelaide for Melbourne, and vowing that he would wear the willow for at least a year and a day; all which Miss Waterstone took as it was meant, and treated as an excellent joke. Clara was rising to leave the room, when Reginald started up, and said,—

'Come, Humberstone, we must be going; I have an English letter to post, or I should have been on the way before breakfast. Don't leave the room without bidding me goodbye, Miss Morison. We have not known each other long, but let us shake hands at parting.'

Clara looked him in the face, stretched out her little hand, which he grasped with a friendly warmth, a half-muttered good wish, and a look that said, 'If I could serve you, I would.'

The example of shaking hands once set, Miss Waterstone and Mr. Humberstone went through with it, and made many fine parting speeches. Miss Waterstone followed with her eye from the window her country friends, while Clara retreated to her room, and sat for a full half hour endeavouring to analyze her emotion. Was it right in her to be so sorry at this gentleman's departure? Why did she think so much of him? Why did her thoughts follow him to his lonely home in the distant bush? And why had she talked so much to him, and to no one else? She came to the conclusion that it was foolish, but natural, and not at all wrong. She busied herself in getting all her things arranged, in mending everything that needed mending, and in adding a few lines to her letter to Susan. Thus the day passed away, and the evening was to be spent among strangers. Her friend was gone.

A Glimpse of a Situation

'Ah, young ladies,' said Mr. Brown at dinner, 'your gallant knights are gone. They love and ride away. Blinker, you must give us that song to-night; your voice is in excellent trim, and the ladies will show their appreciation by tears if not by applause, if you sing it with feeling.'

'I am going to sail away this week,' said Miss Waterstone; 'so all the Adelaide gentlemen may ride away when they please, and where they please, for me.'

'But Miss Morison has not that consolation,' said Oscar. 'What a fellow that Reginald is to talk; but I would put no trust in him if I were you, Miss Morison.'

And so on for all the evening Clara was annoyed by the impertinence of the young men, which she could not laugh off, as Miss Waterstone did. Blinker sang appropriate songs, and was made to declaim very incorrectly several hackneyed pieces of poetry; and Clara had no refuge. She tried to get Mrs. Handy to talk to her, but that lady liked the amusement going on, and could not bear to lose any of it; so that Clara sat silent and uncomfortable, which was attributed to her not having a beau. Thus passed day after day till the Friday on which Miss Waterstone was to return to the *Magnificent*, and Clara to call at Mr. Campbell's; and they went together to his store.

Mr. Campbell had a very numerous acquaintance, but on inquiry he found that very few of them wanted governesses. Most of them sent their children to school; it was cheaper, and more convenient; some would like a governess, but had not accommodation, for the children had too little room already. Some wanted an elderly person, who had had experience in tuition; but could not think of entrusting their children to a girl of nineteen. But the want of music was the great drawback, for though most of these music-requiring ladies had no piano, they could never think of getting a governess merely to teach reading and writing; they could teach these things quite as well themselves. There was only one lady who would like to see Miss Morison, though even she was afraid she would not suit, and she wished Mr. Campbell would desire her to call. It was a nice walk, only four miles and a half out of Adelaide. Mr. Campbell gave Clara directions as to her road, which she could not easily mistake, for all the roads go straight north or south, east or west, from Adelaide; and telling her that Mrs. Denfield was a high-spirited woman, who did not like contradiction, and though she was very clever she spoilt her children a little, but that she was very amiable notwithstanding, he recommended her to go that very day, that no time might be lost. So Clara took a hurried but kind leave of Miss Waterstone, who promised to write to her whenever there was anything worth writing

about, and set off on her nice walk. The sun was overpoweringly hot, and when Clara got out of town, and had to walk between sections fenced with posts and rails, she longed for the green sheltering hedges of her own country. Here and there the corn was left on the field, though it had been reaped weeks ago, and she wondered to see how small and far apart the shocks were. Where the wheat had been reaped by the machine, and the heads merely had been taken off, the long stubble, which is reckoned of no value in Australia, had been either burned or was left standing till favourable weather came. She saw one large field which had accidentally taken fire, and watched the active exertions of all the people about to extinguish it by beating it out with boughs. It had been a very dry winter, and the crops in the plains near Adelaide had been very poor; so that she had no flattering view of the capabilities of South Australian soil. But with all this, there was an appearance of civilization and comfort in the numerous cottages on the way, each having a small garden, and generally a patch of vines, which were loaded with fruit; and what interested Clara still more, she saw many wells near the cottages, which encouraged her often to ask for a drink of water. She was unused to walking far for so many months, and the road was often so deep in sand, into which her feet sank every step, that she was very thankful when a decent-looking woman asked her to sit down out of the sun and rest a bit. She wiped a chair for the lady to sit on, and went on with her washing. Several children were about her, eating bread and butter with their grapes. They had all dirty faces, but looked healthy enough; their clothes were neither fine nor altogether whole; the furniture was scanty, and altogether Clara did not see that over-powering contrast between the exterior of this dwelling and those of people in the same rank in Scotland which she had been led to expect. But the bread and butter, and the smell of meat baking in the camp oven, and the teapot, which the eldest girl was brightening a little for father's dinner cup of tea, were all very different, and looked as if, whatever crops might be, the labourer ran no risk of being starved.

A little curly-haired boy crept up to her, and asked her her name, where she came from, and where she was going; and Clara, having no motive for concealment, gave him ready answers.

'You're going to Mrs. Denfield's; that's where my sister Louisa Jane stops,' said he. 'Mother, this lady is going to Louisa Jane's missis's.'

The mother looked rather curiously at Clara, and said, 'My Louisa Jane is coming home next week, for she can't stand the work nor the rowing she gets there no longer; and

them children are enough to tire out the patience of Job himself. I hope, miss, that you aint a going to be governess there, for the last one had a pretty time of it. The boys and the girls, too, gave her such sauce; and then if she scolded them, their mamma's tongue came cataracting down upon the poor thing; and if Mr. Denfield said a word to help Miss Dobson out, I expect he catched it too. Maybe I am too free of my tongue, miss, for Mrs. Denfield might be a friend of yours; but I can't forgive her for not letting Louisa Jane come to see me, and forbidding her to take the children out a-walking this way; for she says it is only to have a gossip at her mother's, that will spoil her for a week afterwards. I wonder what mississes think servants are made of, if they are not flesh and blood the same as them. Suppose her children had to go to service, I fancy she would like to see them odd times, particular if they lived within a mile. My Louisa Jane did not like Miss Dobson, for she held her head high, and would not speak free-like to the servants in the kitchen; for my maid has a good spirit of her own, and she thinks that as they were all working for wages, there should be an equality. But, as I says to Louisa Jane, mind Miss Dobson wears better clothes than you, and sits at table with your missis, and does no dirty work, so there should be a difference.'

'I had better go now,' said Clara; 'I feel quite rested now. I have not much further to go, I hope?'

'Only a mile and half a section,' said Mrs. Watts. 'You'll find it easy; a white house in the middle of a section, with the haystack on the left hand, and the hedge of kangaroo thorn round the garden.'

Clara met the master of the house in the doorway, who was wiping his forehead and calling on Betsy to look sharp with the dinner. He gave a slight bow as he passed the young lady, and hoped she did not feel the weather too hot. But she felt it all the hotter after her temporary shelter, and plodded on more wearily and despondingly than before.

In front of the white house was a very pretty garden, full of a variety of fruit trees and vines; and she saw there two girls and a boy, who were busy picking grapes and devouring them, seeds and stones included. They had no hats or bonnets on, and were very much freckled; they stared for a few seconds at the new comer, who found some difficulty in untying the rope that fastened up the gate, and supplied the place of the lock, which was broken; but they did not offer to assist her, and resumed their pleasant occupation. A sharp-looking girl, whom Clara conjectured to be Louisa Jane, came out.

'My word! Master Henry and Miss Lucy and Eliza,' said

she, 'won't your ma be angry to see you out without hats this broiling hot day, and eating them Muscats too. You'll all be ill as sure as I'm here. I'll just run and tell your ma. Come in, there's dears, and get on your hats; you know you'll be sunstruck.'

The two young ladies said that they never wore hats, and that their sun-bonnets were dirty—much too dirty to wear; and scolded Louisa for her laziness in not washing them, and her ill-nature in not giving them their best bonnets when the others were not fit to put on.

Clara had by this time reached the door, at which she knocked. Louisa Jane whispered to the children that most likely this was the new governess coming, at which news they hurried in at the back door, to get into the parlour as soon as she did, and have a good look at her before their mamma made her appearance. So by the time Clara was ushered into the sitting-room the whole of the juvenile Denfields were there ready to inspect her. There was the eldest, Caroline, who seemed to be about fifteen; then James; then the three whom Clara had seen in the garden, and Robert and Emily, first merely looking at her, and then asking her questions.

'What a pretty frock you have on,' said Caroline, 'though you have got it rather dusty with the walk; and your bonnet is very nicely trimmed. Have you been long in the colony, or have you just come out?'

'I only landed last week,' said Clara.

'Then why do you wear your hair in ringlets? they are quite out of fashion. All new comers wear their hair crimped and stuck out in wavy bands, and it looks so stylish. If you stay here you must wear your hair like that, for ma does not like curls at all. What is your name?'

'Clara Morison,' was the reply.

'It is a nice name, I like it. Our last governess was called Bridget Dobson; wasn't it a horrid ugly vulgar name? but she was a vulgar creature altogether.'

'I do not think it such a vulgar name,' said Clara. 'There was a Mrs. Dobson who translated Petrarch beautifully.'

Miss Denfield stared, and continued, 'If you are to be our governess you must give us nice short lessons, and let us play a great deal. I am not too old for play yet, though I am so tall, and I don't mean to give it up till I come out, and I hope that will not be long. There is Miss Robertson came out at fifteen, and I wish you would help me to persuade ma to let me accept the next invitation I get. It would be delightful to dance till daylight. It is never too hot to dance you know, and I would never miss a dancing lesson for the world, but I do hate learning spelling and grammar, and doing horrid sums when it is as hot as this. Ma says she is fit for

nothing to-day, and what can you expect of me? Master James, don't break the chairs, swinging upon them like that; and do, Miss Eliza, keep Emily from ma's work-box. She has got everything out of it; and there now, if she has not run the scissors into her hand. Oh Emily, don't cry, it is not very bad. What will ma say?'

But Emily was of opinion that it was very bad indeed, and screamed so that Caroline was forced to take her out of the room to her mamma. Clara saw the other children do a good deal of mischief, and when she mildly hinted that they had better not, they merely stared at her, and went on. Three quarters of an hour elapsed before Mrs. Denfield entered, and with considerable dignity requested Clara to resume her seat when she rose to accost her. Mrs. Denfield prided herself on two things in particular; first, that she was lady-like, and secondly that she was decided. Her manner was cold, her eye critical, her mouth hard in its expression, and her gait stiff; but still she was, in the opinion of those twenty people who formed her world, such a lady-like superior woman. She was anxious that her children should be as lady-like and firm as she was, but neither precept nor example had hitherto succeeded in producing that result. She had at last adopted the opinion that mothers were not the best instructors of their darlings, but that they needed a subordinate educating machine, such as a governess, to act under their orders, and to cram the minds of children with useful knowledge, without either inspiring any of the respect, or winning any of the affection which was due to the mother, and the mother alone.

Her cold grey eyes looked Clara over; the result was not satisfactory. As Clara's colour rose at the inspection, she supposed that she had not been accustomed to good society; and as her flexible mouth did not close like a vice, she was of opinion that she wanted firmness. Besides, she was too young, and what some people would think too pretty for a governess, though there was no mind whatever to be found in her face.

'You are, I presume,' said Mrs. Denfield, 'the young person in whose favour Mr. Campbell spoke to me on Wednesday evening? Miss Morison, I believe, is your name?'

'Yes, ma'am,' said Clara.

'Pray, have you been accustomed to tuition? for I consider that a great point.'

Clara's distressed eyes glanced at the children, who were all eagerly listening, but whether Mrs. Denfield thought that they would profit by the colloquy, or whether she thought it a good trial of the governess's patience to conduct her cross-

examination before her future pupils, she did not take the hint, but looked impatient for an answer.

'I have never been in a situation yet, but I used to teach the little ones at school,' said Clara.

'An apprentice, I suppose,' said Mrs. Denfield.

'It was only because I liked it,' said Clara; 'I think there are no such things as school apprentices in Scotland.'

'Then you are Scotch; yes, I hear you have the accent very strong. Were you at a boarding-school or a day-school, Miss Morison?'

'I have been at both,' said Clara, 'and had instruction at home besides.'

'Are you acquainted with the routine of tuition? Could you give me any idea of how you would go through one day with these young folks of mine?'

'I cannot tell until I know what progress they have made. Probably your boys go to school, and as for the young ladies I must take each separately, as there is such a difference in their ages, and they cannot learn exactly the same lessons,' said Clara.

'I understood from Mr. Campbell that you know a little Latin, Miss Morison; and if you could carry on James and Henry for a few months, to prepare them for a good school, I think it would be a good arrangement for all parties. What is the matter, Caroline?'

'Oh, ma,' said Caroline, who just now burst into the room. 'I wish you would come and speak to Louisa, she is so cross with Emily, and was just going to give her a slap, when I said I would run and tell you. And what do you think Sarah is doing, ma? She is scrubbing out your room with the same water she took to wash the passage; all her laziness to save her drawing more water from the well.'

'Servants are the plague of my life,' said Mrs. Denfield. 'You will excuse me five minutes, Miss Morison. Put on your bonnets, my dears, and pick some grapes. I dare say Miss Morison would take a few this hot day if you dip them in cold water for a few minutes to cool them.'

When Mrs. Denfield returned it was without her children, to Clara's great delight; she resumed her conversation without delay.

'Caroline, as you may see, is very sharp and observant; nothing escapes her, and as she tells me all that she sees, she prevents these girls from imposing upon me. I feel that under a mother's eye alone can daughters in particular be rightly brought up; and if we should happen to come to terms, Miss Morison, let it be on the distinct understanding that my authority is in no way delegated to you. You teach them such and such lessons, and report to me how well or ill they

A Glimpse of a Situation

have been learned, and what their behaviour has been; for my children are of such an affectionate temper that they cannot bear anybody to find fault with them but me. And in the next place, Miss Morison, I wish you to tell me exactly what you can and cannot do. I beg that you will resort to no subterfuges, for children are acute observers, and if you lay claim to any knowledge or skill which you do not possess, you will completely lose their esteem whenever they find it out.'

'I can teach all the branches of an English education,' said Clara, 'and I understand French grammatically. I could give lessons in Latin for the first year or two, and I could instruct the young ladies in plain needlework.'

'No fancy work, knitting, or crochet?' asked Mrs. Denfield.

'No, ma'am.'

'No music?'

'No, ma'am; I know only the notes.'

'Don't you draw at all?'

'No, ma'am.'

'Cannot you teach dancing?'

'Oh yes, at least I can dance well; my master always said I was his best pupil.'

'Was he a Frenchman?'

'Yes, ma'am.'

Mrs. Denfield hesitated a little, and then said, 'May I ask your age?'

'Nineteen, ma'am.'

'In what vessel did you come out?'

'In the *Magnificent*—in the intermediate.'

'I have met a Mrs. Hastie, just come from Scotland; I suppose a fellow-passenger of yours. May I inquire from her as to how you conducted yourself on board? Excuse my doing so, for in a colony like this one cannot be too careful.'

'Mrs. Hastie knows nothing whatever about me, ma'am,' said Clara. 'We never spoke to the cabin passengers all the voyage. I have no reference except to Mr. Campbell; my uncle did not even procure me certificates from the schools and masters I attended, for he thought that Mr. and Mrs. Campbell's interest would be sufficient to procure me the situation I wanted. Will you try me for a month, and see if I will not suit you?'

'Well,' said Mrs. Denfield, 'with so few accomplishments, and no recommendations, I suppose you will be glad of a home. I cannot afford to give you a high salary.'

'I would come for twenty pounds a-year,' said Clara, anxious to bring the matter to some conclusion.

'Twenty pounds a-year! what an absurdly high salary for a nursery governess! If you had known anything of music

I might have stretched a point, but I do not consider myself justified in offering you any more than fifteen.'

'That is very little,' said Clara; 'I do not see how a young lady can provide her dress and contingencies on such a small income.'

'I do not care for the young person who occupies the place of governess in my family dressing at all expensively. The plainer the better, provided she is clean and neat. Every governess I have had has assisted me with the family needlework; and Miss Dobson, to whom I gave fifteen pounds a-year, used to dress two of the younger children every morning. She was no musician, certainly, but she drew nicely; I shall be grieved if Caroline's drawing is to be at an end: and she was very skilful in all kinds of fancy work. I cannot possibly offer you any higher salary, Miss Morison; it is for you to accept or decline it.'

Clara's colour went and came several times during this speech; she knew it would be a most uncomfortable situation, but yet she thought it right to take it; for, according to Mr. Campbell's account, this was a fair specimen of colonial ladies, and no other employer might appear before her money was spent, and she was destitute. So she consented to take the salary of fifteen pounds a-year, board and washing (this last in moderation), for instructing Mrs. Denfield's seven children.

Mrs. Denfield now became tolerably gracious to Clara. She had asked her a great many questions, she had engaged her at a low salary, she had a prospect of her boys learning Latin at no expense; in fact, she had been decided, and made the governess come into her terms without binding herself in any way. So she was talking rather pleasantly about the colony and the weather, the vineyard and the dairy, and Clara was beginning to think that she would like her a little, when Mr. Denfield entered, with the children.

'Ha!' said he, 'a young lady here, and a fair one. Introduce me, Mrs. Denfield.'

'This is Miss Morison, about whom Mr. Campbell spoke to me.'

'Just so,' said Mr. Denfield; 'I am glad to see that it is Miss Morison. I hope you will like Langley, Miss Morison. I am sure, Caroline, and Lucy, and Eliza, you will like this nice lady to teach you your lessons. She does not look at all like Miss Dobson, my dears. Why do you not ask Miss Morison to take off her bonnet and what-do-you-call-it, Priscilla? she must be smothered in them.'

Mrs. Denfield was displeased at her husband for admiring the new governess, and at his taking it for granted that she was engaged without its being announced from head-quarters;

and still more at his rebuking her for a failure in courtesy. So she changed her mind, and determined that Miss Morison should have another situation to seek for.

'You are always too precipitate, Mr. Denfield,' said she. 'I have not settled matters with Miss Morison yet; there are some inquiries to make before a final engagement can be entered into.'

'A final engagement! That sounds very like a marriage,' said Mr. Denfield, laughing heartily. 'Never mind, Miss Morison, there are lots of young fellows about here who will be very desirous of entering into a final engagement with you; but in the meantime, we must allow Mrs. Denfield to have her way in the first place, and to make your prior engagement as firm and decided as she is herself. Ha! ha!'

"I am sure I shall like you,' said Miss Denfield; 'you look so good-natured.'

'I don't like a woman to teach me,' said Master James; 'I want to go to school like other boys.'

'So you shall, my boy, and Harry too,' said Mr. Denfield. 'This young lady cannot take charge of such great unruly fellows as you are; can you, Miss Morison?'

'Miss Morison has promised to do so,' said Mrs. Denfield; 'she knows Latin, and says that she can lay the foundation for that language. I hope she can do it well, for it occurs to me that there is some difference between English Latin and Scotch Latin. Is there not, William, my love?'

'Oh! to be sure there is; Scotchmen make all the vowels broad,' rejoined Mr. Denfield. I remember a chap, of the name of Macbarnet, coming to our grammar-school from the north, and how terribly he got laughed at among the boys for his way of pronouncing the words.'

'After which fashion do you pronounce the language?' said Mrs. Denfield, with such cold severity, that hot as the day was, Clara felt a shiver come over her.

'After the Scotch fashion, ma'am,' said she, flushing under the supercilious sneer of the boy James, who, knowing nothing whatever of the matter, thought it a fine thing to despise ladies' Latin.

'It is of very little consequence, Priscilla,' said Mr. Denfield, apologetically; 'Macbarnet was really the best scholar among us, and was never once out in his quantities.'

'I beg your pardon, Mr. Denfield,' said the lady, 'but I am disposed to consider it of great consequence; and I am glad I am aware of this point, Miss Morison, for I should have been sorry indeed if you had succeeded in holding it back from me. I will let you know on Monday whether I can engage you, and in case I do, you ought to hold yourself in readiness to accompany the messenger.'

Clara assented, and feeling uncomfortable under Mrs. Denfield's eye, she moved to take her leave; having merely tasted the glass of colonial wine that Mrs. Denfield had offered her, and leaving both fruit and bread much as she had got them. Mr. Denfield went out to open the gate for her, and Caroline followed with a bunch of grapes, which she insisted on her eating by the way; while Mrs. Denfield, more displeased than ever, sullenly determined that, whatever might be said on the subject, that girl should never enter her house again, to make mischief, as she was sure to do.

As Clara went home, her heart felt unaccountably lightened. She had observed Mrs. Denfield's manner, and was convinced that her answer would be unfavourable; but she was conscious that she had conceded every point, and that she was not to blame for her bad success in her first attempt to get a situation.

So she picked her grapes, and slowly returned to Adelaide, happy in the thought that on this evening, for the first time for months, she could have a little solitude, and even looking forward to a return to Mrs. Handy's cordial face with a sort of home feeling. Mrs. Denfield's coldness had made her long to return to the boarding-house. The sun was low when she got into town, and in passing Mr. Campbell's store, she found it was shut, so that she could not on this evening give him any account of her conversation with his amiable friend.

On reaching home, Clara went straight to her room to obtain a little rest, but was not long left to herself, for in half an hour Mrs. Handy tapped at the door, bringing in a cup of tea, with bread and butter; and Clara begged she would sit down to hear about her application to Mrs. Denfield, while she took the welcome tea. Mrs. Handy was convinced that Mrs. Denfield would send for Miss Morison on Monday. She knew very well that Mrs. Denfield could afford to give a better salary than fifteen pounds a-year, and concluded by advising Clara to make a stand at first both for more authority and more pay.

Clara said quietly that she did not expect to get this situation, but that even if she did, she was not in circumstances to make any stand. She must come into her employer's terms, or not be engaged at all.

'Well, Miss Morison,' said Mrs. Handy, 'I suppose it is all for the best, but things do go contrary with us all sometimes. I am losing all my pleasantest people. There's Mr. Haussen has given me notice to-day, and I believe it is just the singing and dancing they make Mr. Blinker do in the evenings that sends him off; but I cannot say a word about it, for Mr. Oscar and Mr. Brown, and some of the others, would leave if I dared to find fault. I don't think you like

the noise they make either, and I must say that it would be a great deal more gentlemanly if they would exert themselves to amuse you in a quiet way, than by making game of that poor harmless creature. We have got a new gentleman to-day, who takes half a room till Mr. Haussen goes. He is a Jew, a Mr. Samuels; but he does not mind about eating pork. He took bacon at dinner to-day, and I was rather sorry to see it, for you know that it is the most expensive article on the table; and I have had Jews who were more particular, and I liked them for boarders very well.'

CHAPTER VII

ANOTHER GLIMPSE, AND A RESOLUTION

Clara did not admire Mr. Samuels at all; on the contrary, she took a great dislike to him at first sight. He insisted on sitting beside her, and talking to her about dress, fashions, and personal ornaments; he turned his rings and brooches in every different light, in order to dazzle her by their brilliancy, and in spite of her short answers and averted head, he seemed determined to force himself upon her attention. Clara made her escape as soon as possible, not feeling quite so sure that she was glad Mrs. Denfield would not have her.

Monday brought a stiff note from that lady, saying that, after making further inquiries, she had found that Miss Morison would not suit. When Clara next saw Mr. Campbell, he seemed to think that it must have been her own fault that she had failed; and though she repeated her conversation with Mrs. Denfield nearly verbatim, he was not convinced.

Mr. Campbell was not so rich as he was supposed to be; his own affairs were puzzling him, and he felt the burden of Clara's very oppressive, though not very important. So he told her that she had better advertise. She sat down directly at his table, and promptly wrote the following:—

'Wants a situation as governess, a young lady capable of teaching thoroughly all the branches of an English education, French, dancing, and the elements of Latin. Only a moderate salary is required. Address to C. M., Post-office, Adelaide.'

'Will that do, Mr. Campbell?' said she, 'or had I better leave out the Latin, as I don't pronounce it after the orthodox fashion in South Australia. But you know the Scotch way is really the best; I asked Mr. Haussen, a German gentleman, whom I met at Mrs. Handy's, how he read Latin, and he told me it was nearly the same as ours, whereas English Latin is utterly unintelligible all over the Continent.'

'Don't leave out the Latin,' said Mr. Campbell; 'it will do

A Resolution

very well for people in the country. Scotch folks will prefer it as you pronounce it, and nine-tenths of the English don't know Latin from Greek; even English gentlemen are generally ignorant of all classical literature; Scotland is the place to be inducted into the humanities. If Mrs. Denfield had not been such a very superior woman, she would never have found out anything wrong in the broad vowels; but it cannot be helped now. I like your promptitude, Miss Morison; no sooner do I say you should do such a thing, than instead of asking how it is to be done, you set about it and accomplish it. And you wipe your pen when you have done, which looks methodical, and is good for my favourite pen. I expect that something will come of this advertisement. You must send it to one or two of the papers, for how many insertions?—let me see— I think three insertions in two newspapers will do, Miss Morison. I shall feel great pleasure in being of use to you, and of course all applicants can be referred to me. My name is good for something in Adelaide. Yes, Miss Morison, I feel convinced that this advertisement will do you good.'

Clara having still further reduced her stock of money by paying for advertising, waited with some impatience for the result. Mrs. Handy spoke to her kindly and cheerfully, and if there had been no one else in the house, Clara would have been comparatively happy; but the vulgar jokes she was subjected to from the young men in the boarding-house were intolerable.

At last came an application for her services; it was couched in these words:

'Mrs. Caumray presents her complements to C. M., and would be glad to see her on Tewsday next, at the ——— Hotel, where I am stopping for the preasant time, at three o'clock P.M.'

Clara shrugged her shoulders slightly at this elegant note, but with only thirty shillings in the world, she must not be too particular; so she showed it to Mrs. Handy, who read it twice over.

'Well, Mrs. Caumray's compliments are something new; and the paper is beautiful, though I can't say the same of the writing and spelling. I fancy she would not speak to me now, though many a good day's work she has had from me when she wanted it; for Caumray used to drink awful the first year they were here, and if it had not been that she took in washing, both her and her little girl might have starved. When he took the pledge, and they went out to the country, they never took any more notice of me. I hear they are doing very well down south, and Mr. Oscar told me that Caumray had bought three more sections of land yesterday at the land-sale. They live about thirty miles out of town, with a sort of rough

plenty about their housekeeping; but I can see by this that Mrs. Caumray wants to start in a more genteel line now, and get a governess for Janey, and make a lady of her. Set them up to get a born gentlewoman to teach a girl that I remember going about in perfect rags; but it is all of a piece, for the last time I saw Mrs. Caumray and Jane, they were riding through Adelaide on beautiful horses, and had on handsome green cloth habits. I dare say you would be kindly treated there, Miss Morison; but it seems a casting of pearls before swine—excuse the quotation—for you to go to my old washerwoman's.'

'How old is the little girl?' asked Clara.

'Let me see; she was eight years old when we landed, and that is fully six years ago; she must be going on for fifteen now. All the children she had after her died in the colony, so it must be only for Janey that she wants a governess.'

'Then they came out in the same ship with you and Mr. ——.' Here Clara stopped short.

'Yes, with me and Mr. Reginald. I knew what you were going to say. Only she was in the steerage, I was in the intermediate, and Mr. Reginald in the cabin, of course. What a good laugh he will have when I tell him that Mrs. Caumray wanted you to go to learn Janey the accomplishments, as she calls them. Really, Miss Morison, you must not go there; you are sure not to like it, and you will find it difficult to get a genteel situation afterwards. And what would Mr. Reginald think?'

'I have no choice left,' said Clara, 'for I have scarcely any money left. I will, if possible, agree with this lady. I dare say I shall be happier with her than I could have been with Mrs. Denfield; and even if I am not, we were not sent into the world to be happy.'

'What were we sent for, then?' said Mrs. Handy.

'To be useful, to be strong, to conquer our faults, to uproot our pride'—and Clara dashed a salt drop from her eye, and looked so determined that Mrs. Handy was of opinion that, though she was a gentle-looking creature, there was a great deal of spirit in Miss Morison.

'After all,' said Mrs. Handy, 'I dare say that is very true. I expected to be happy when I was as young as you, and yet my life has been only one of very hard work, with a good deal of anxiety, and very little pleasure or happiness in it at all. So I hope that as you don't seem to expect happiness, but only mean to do your best and be useful, you may find happiness by the way.'

Mrs. Caumray was a stout, good-humoured looking woman, very proud of her nice farm and beautiful dairy, but above all things proud of her only daughter, whose rosy cheeks, and

A Resolution

tall though awkward figure, gave promise that she would one day turn out a fine woman. Janey was an admirable horsewoman, and understood all about cows, and pigs, and poultry; but she had had no education but what had been picked up from young gentlemen who had been at her father's in the capacity of servants, no uncommon thing in South Australia. Generally speaking, they were what Scotch people call *'ne'er-do-weels'*; but it was a convenience in the evenings, when the day's farm-work was over, that they could hear Janey read, set her a copy, and make her work a few sums.

But, as Mrs. Caumray wisely observed, Janey was getting too old to have a young man for a teacher now; she must either go to a boarding-school or have a governess. She would be likely to pick up the finest manners at school, if she went to a first-rate one, and an inferior one was not to be thought of. So Mrs. Caumray applied to two or three of the most esteemed boarding-schools in Adelaide; but as her accent and manners were unmistakeably vulgar, she was told that they had no vacancy at present.

When Clara entered the room which Mrs. Caumray for the present occupied, she found that both her husband and daughter were with her. She hoped that they were a more united couple than Mr. and Mrs. Denfield, and they appeared to be so, so far as she could judge at sight. Miss Caumray was standing at the window, looking out at the numerous passengers, which are so irresistibly fascinating to a country girl. She looked at the young lady whom she expected to be her governess with a sort of wondering awe, as she thought of the French and Latin; but the idea of dancing crossed her mind, and made a smile pass over her face.

The awkwardness of introduction by people who did not well know how to set about it fairly over, Mrs. Caumray said,

'Jane, my dear, will you go to Miss Nicoll's, and get your dress tried on, and tell her as both yours and mine must be sent here by Saturday morning, for your father says he can't stop in town no longer.'

Jane took a parting stare at Miss Morison, and went her way.

'It is better, Miss Morison, that she should not be here while you talk over matters with Mr. Caumray and me.' In this sentiment Clara heartily joined. 'I like your appearance, and think you are sure to suit me; but would you tell me who I can refer to about your character and all that sort of thing?'

'I can refer you to Mr. Campbell, of Hindley-street, an old friend of my uncle's.'

'A most respectable gentleman, indeed,' said Mr. Caumray; 'that is quite satisfactory.'

'So it is,' concurred Mrs. Caumray. 'I don't know anybody whose recommendation is worth more; but I wish you could teach music and singing, for Miss Caumray has a wonderful ear, and is wild to learn the piano; but perhaps you know enough to begin her, and her father has promised her a piano, and I know he will have no peace till he gets it, so I wish you could give her music.'

'I know the notes of music, but I can teach nothing further.'

'Well, Jane shall get a musical question and answer book and you can teach her out of that, surely; for she is a great girl now, and has no time to lose. You will wonder that I don't send Jane to school, having only one daughter to educate.'

'I suppose you do not like to part with her,' suggested Clara.

'Indeed and I don't,' said Mrs Caumray; 'but yet I did make some inquiries about a school for her, and went to some ladies the other day; but they looked so proud and haughty, that I was afraid they would make my girl as proud as themselves. She will have a good bit of money by and by, and that makes me want her taught to be humble. She is naturally of a very meek disposition, Miss Morison; and if anybody takes exceptions to her, and finds fault, she cries dreadful, and won't speak for an hour or two; but for all that, she must be found fault with sometimes. You will have it all your own way, for I never interfere, and neither does Mr. Caumray. It's her manners that I am most particular about, for in the bush people gets so rough, and the neighbours about has no notion of gentility; so I like to keep Jane at home, at least I do my utmost. Now, Miss Morison, what salary would you be seeking?'

Clara had been instructed by Mrs. Handy to ask a tolerably high salary, and to do it coolly too; so she said, 'Forty pounds a-year.'

'That is quite a large sum for teaching one girl,' said Mrs. Caumray. 'I never heard of such a salary being given in town or country; and there is that very genteel lady, Mrs. Forbes, only gives thirty, and her governess knows music too.'

'That may be true,' said Clara, 'but does she understand English?'

'I'm sure I never thought of asking, but you know that it is a great matter to be able to play.'

'What I say I can do you will find that I will perform,' said Clara, remembering Mr. Reginald's advice. 'When my uncle sent me out to Australia, he expected that I should get at least sixty, and had poor Mrs. Campbell been alive I should

A Resolution

have been staying with her, and should have felt in no hurry to take a situation. As it is, I am anxious to have a comfortable home, and will take forty.'

The confidence and decision with which this was said produced its effect. To get a young lady, a friend of Mr. and Mrs. Campbell's, at forty pounds a-year, would, in spite of the want of music, be a grander thing than even Mrs. Forbes' thundering polka-player, who knew nobody in the colony and whom nobody knew. 'And as for the money,' thought Mrs. Caumray, 'we can afford it a mighty sight better than Mrs. Forbes can, with all her genteel airs.'

But she could not resist the temptation of satisfying her curiosity as to where Clara lived, if it was not with the Campbell's; probably it was at Mrs. Barnard's, who was a great friend of theirs, and the most elegant woman in Adelaide.

'You say that you want a comfortable home, Miss Morison; where are you stopping now?'

'I am in a boarding-house at present, and I do not like it.'

'Whose boarding-house is it? Miss Renshaw's, I suppose; that is the best in town.'

'I do not live there; I am staying at Mrs. Handy's.'

Mr. and Mrs. Caumray both flushed when Mrs. Handy's name was mentioned, but the lady's colour was the highest, and lasted longest. Clara commanded her countenance as well as she could, but her heart sank when Mrs. Caumray began to speak.

'I don't think we can come to terms, Miss Morison; you know you don't teach music, and you ask too much salary, and I don't see no use in girls learning Latin; do you, Mr. Caumray?'

'Neither do I,' said he; but he whispered something to his wife.

She shook her head. Clara tried to look unconscious, but blushed, in spite of herself.

'Will you not think of it again, Mrs. Caumray?' said she. 'If you really think the salary too high, give me what you consider reasonable.'

'She does not know yet,' said Mrs. Caumray, in an under tone to her husband. 'It will never do. We cannot have her.'

'I will call again to-morrow,' said Clara; 'perhaps you will have settled then how much you think me worth.'

'No,' said Mrs. Caumray, shaking her head, 'you will not do; how old are you?'

'Nineteen last September.'

'Oh, you are much too young for Jane; Jane is going on for fifteen. Have you ever been in a place before? I beg pardon; I mean a situation?'

'Not a regular situation,' said Clara; 'but I have taught

a good deal at school, and understand giving instruction quite as well as those who have had more experience.'

'But experience is the great thing, Miss Morison; I am sure you will not do;—I wish you a good afternoon.'

'I do the same,' said Mr. Caumray.

And presently Clara found herself in the street, without having succeeded in getting a situation. She went straight to Mr. Campbell's, and told him the result of her advertisement. He looked annoyed, but he was too honest a man to reproach her for telling the truth.

'Well, Miss Morison, I really do not know what is to be done with you. How does your money hold out?'

'I have still thirty shillings, but I must not wait till it is all spent,' said Clara; 'I am very slow at needlework, but I sew neatly; do you think I could get anything to do in that way?'

'I do not know,' said Mr. Campbell; 'I will inquire. I believe that it is a business which does not pay, all over the world. You could not, even if you were a skilful sempstress, earn so much as would pay Mrs. Handy her eighteen shillings a week.'

Mr. Campbell took two or three turns about the little room, and then took out Mr. Morison's letter, desiring her to read it.

When Clara had done so, he asked her if she would like him to draw upon her uncle for as much money as would take her home.

'No,' said Clara, 'I would rather work my fingers to the bone than be dependent on his unwilling charity.'

'I am not rich, Miss Morison,' said Mr. Campbell, 'but I daresay I could lend you a trifle till you get employment.'

'It was cruel, cruel, to send me here,' said Clara. 'In all this wide country can I get nothing to do at all? I have made no objection to any sort of drudgery.'

'Ah! Miss Morison, if you had been a strong servant girl, instead of an educated lady, there would have been no difficulty in getting you a place, and good wages, too.'

'I never thought of that before,' said Clara; 'I can go to service. I don't know anything about work yet, but I shall soon learn, and you don't know how strong I am. Do you think anybody would take me? Will you ask for a place as housemaid in a respectable family for me, and I know that I shall soon learn to work hard and well. Do let me have a trial, Mr. Campbell.'

Mr. Campbell admired the girl's independent spirit, and smiled approvingly; but when he looked at the little white hands and taper fingers, the slight figure and elegant bearing

A Resolution

of the young lady, he was rather doubtful whether anybody would take her as a servant.

'I will inquire, Miss Morison,' said he. 'By the way, Mrs. Bantam mentioned to me the day before yesterday that her last girl—one of that batch of Irish orphans who turned out so ill—had got drunk and been so furious, that Mr. Bantam was obliged to turn her out of doors; and that after she had gone, Mrs. Bantam had missed a great many things, which the girl had stolen. She told me that she would not engage another till she found one with a good character; perhaps she would take you. She is a very amiable, kind woman, and I dare say she would take pains with you, if you were willing to learn.'

'Do not tell her who I am,' said Clara; 'only say that I have never been at service before.'

'And that not having succeeded in getting employment as nursery governess or needlewoman, you wish to get a servant's place. Mrs. Bantam is an English lady, and has an idea that Scotch young ladies are ignorant of all household work; so I will not tell that you are a lady. Come in here to-morrow about this time, and I will let you know what Mrs. Bantam says.'

Mr. Campbell felt comfortable in the thought that the girl's good sense and high spirit would carry her through the world, and save him any further trouble; but Mrs. Handy was horror-struck when Clara made her acquainted with the result of her interview with Mr. and Mrs. Caumray.

'To think, Miss Morison, that your being staying in this house could do you any harm; I am so sorry about it. To be sure it must be wormwood to her that I know how poor she used to be; and as she knows me to be free-spoken enough, of course she supposes that I should tell you all about it before she saw you again. But after all, it would be hard for you to be comfortable with such a vulgar woman; and I am sure you will soon get a better opening.'

'I have made up my mind,' said Clara, 'as to what I am to do. Mr. Campbell says that if I had been a hard-working girl, I should have had no difficulty in getting employment, so I have resolved to go to service.'

'Go to service? Don't think of such a thing! You are not fit for the work, and will lay yourself up in a week; and besides, you will quite spoil your chance of getting well married; and that would be a pity.'

'No matter,' said Clara; 'I will keep out of debt and out of danger; and there is no necessity for being married.'

'Perhaps not, Miss Morison; but you would not like to be a servant, at everybody's beck and call, for your whole life. By the time you have tried it for a year, you will long

to get free; and I fancy you would not like to marry the butcher or the baker, or any of that sort of people.'

'Do gentlemen never marry so much beneath them?' asked Clara.

'Why, shopmen and clerks sometimes do marry servant-girls, and I have heard of two or three gentlemen who did the same; but then their wives are not visited by genteel people,—at least, by the lady part of them. You must not go to service, Miss Morison; I am in no hurry about the board, as my house is full; and if you could make yourself handy and useful about the house, I could easily make a deduction. Jane is so thoughtless; she forgets more than half she is told; and you could do a deal to save my poor feet. Perhaps something suitable may turn up in a week or two. Mr. Reginald will be in town again soon; wouldn't you like to see him again?'

'I feel very grateful for your very great kindness, Mrs. Handy, but Mr. Campbell says he knows of a lady who is in want of a maid-of-all-work, and has promised to speak in my favour to-day; and I am bound to him to accept of the place, if Mrs. Bantam will take such a poor, stupid thing as I am.'

'It would be quite colonial in you to change your mind to-morrow,' said Mrs. Handy.

But Clara felt that she could not trifle with Mr. Campbell, or lose the chance of what appeared to be an unexceptionable situation. Grateful as she felt to Mrs. Handy for her kind offer, she was conscious that the position of hanger-on at a boarding-house was neither very safe nor very respectable.

'If Mrs. Bantam will engage me,' said she, 'I will go there; if not, I shall really be very glad to do all in my power to assist you. In the meantime, will you let me go to the kitchen to see how you manage things there; and if you can give me any hints or advice, I shall be very much obliged to you. I see the parlour looks dusty; let me try to sweep and arrange it; I think I could manage to have it done before Jane comes to lay the cloth for dinner; and be good enough to criticise my performance when I have finished.'

Mrs. Handy was pleased with Clara's first attempt at work, and gave her a fair meed of praise. She then proceeded to give her directions about a variety of things, told her how long a joint of meat took to bake in a camp-oven, how long in a brick-oven, and how long it took to roast before the fire; how clothes should be washed, and how starch should be made; how knives and forks should be cleaned, and how German-silver could be kept from turning yellow; how floors were to be scrubbed, and hearths blackened or whitewashed; how furniture was to be oiled, and crystal polished.

A Resolution

Clara got quite confused by hearing that so much knowledge was indispensable to a good servant. Things which she had thought were done merely by instinct, she now saw required thought and management; but some of Mrs. Handy's directions remained in her mind; and she went to Mr. Campbell's next day, with the determination that if he got her a place, she would do her utmost to keep it.

Mr. Campbell had not found much difficulty in persuading Mrs. Bantam to try his *protégée* for the idea of getting a girl who was sober and honest, and who spoke the truth, was a welcome one to her after her experience of the last two or three who had so grievously imposed upon her good nature. Clara had dressed herself very plainly, in case Mrs. Bantam might wish to see her; so there was nothing to distinguish her from others except the propriety of her language; but that her Scotch accent prevented Mrs. Bantam from observing. As she was to be taught everything, Clara offered to go for the first month without wages; at the end of that time, there was to be a new agreement. Mrs. Bantam hoped that they might get on comfortably, for she said she did not like changing her servant often.

Next morning Clara had to bid Mrs. Handy good-bye; that worthy lady was not satisfied with shaking hands; she threw her arms about Clara, and kissed her affectionately.

'I will not tell any of the gentlemen where you have gone, though they may teaze me ever so much. I will not even tell Mr. Reginald when he comes into town again. He is sure to ask me about you, for he seemed to take more interest in you than I ever saw him take in anybody.'

'Do not tell anybody anything about me, my dear Mrs. Handy. I must not even come to see you again though I do like you so much; for I must only associate with my equals. I hope your Jane will not think herself very much above me.' And here Clara laughed a little sad laugh.

'My Jane shall think nothing about the matter, either good or bad, for she shall know nothing; but do come to see me sometimes, Miss Morison; Mrs. Bantam will surely let you out now and then.'

'If I can I will; and again good-bye my dear kind friend.' And Clara set out to try the world for herself, with a singular mixture of pride in what she was doing, and of contempt for all who would despise her for it. But yet she feared to meet any one she knew, and a figure slightly resembling Mr. Reginald's sent her two streets out of her way.

CHAPTER VIII

AT SERVICE

When young ladies in novels are set to any work to which they are unaccustomed, it is surprising how instanteously they always get over all the difficulties before them. They row boats without feeling fatigued, they scale walls, they rein in restive horses, they can lift the most ponderous articles, though they are of the most delicate and fragile constitutions, and have never had such things to do in their lives.

It was not so with Clara, however. She found the work dreadfully hard, and by no means fascinating; and though she was willing and anxious even to painfulness, the memory that had tenaciously kept hold of hard names and dates, which her father had trusted to as to an encyclopaedia, seemed utterly to fail her in recollecting when saucepans were to be put on and taken off, and every day brought the same puzzling uncertainty as to how plates and dishes were to be arranged at the breakfast and dinner-table, which Mrs. Bantam had more than once shown her, with a particular desire that she should do it exactly in the same way.

Then she was very awkward at lighting a fire, and would often let it go out black just when it was most wanted. The camp-oven was a perfect heart-break to her, for she could never hit upon any medium between scorching heat and lukewarmness. Mrs. Bantam said that every new comer from England was awkward with the wood-fires and the camp-oven at first, so she excused her; but Clara knew that she should have been no better if the fires had been of coal, and the oven the newest invented patent cooking apparatus, but this opinion she prudently kept to herself.

She made a considerable smashing of crockery the first week; next week she scalded her arm pretty severely, and felt almost unable to move it for two days; the third week she was becoming more fit to be trusted, but yet she was con-

scious that if Mrs. Bantam had not been a paragon of good nature she would not have patience with her even for the month that she got no wages. And as for her work ever being done, she never could see over the top of it. Mrs. Bantam came into the kitchen every day to bring up arrears, and Clara with hopeless admiration saw her quietly put one thing after another out of her hands finished.

'I am afraid I shall never learn,' said Clara to her mistress one day. 'I am sorry I am so dreadfully stupid.'

'I dare say you will learn in time, though you seem determined to take your time to it, Clara; but where in all the world can you have been brought up to be so helpless. I do not know a young *lady* in the colony so ignorant of all household matters. The people next door, whom you see sometimes in the back yard, keep no servant, and do all their own work, but yet everybody knows the Miss Elliots are ladies, though I do not visit them myself.'

'I am heartily ashamed of my ignorance,' said Clara, 'but I was a spoilt child at home, and am suffering for it now. I fear you do not think me anxious to do right from the many failures I make.'

'You are too anxious, I think, and get nervous. Keep yourself cooler in future, and you will do better.'

Clara endeavoured to keep herself cooler during the last week of her month's probation, for she was very anxious to remain with Mrs. Bantam. It seemed to be a quiet place, and neither her master nor mistress was unreasonable. She was too busy to feel her solitary kitchen dull, and though she ached all over every morning from the exertions of the preceding day, that was preferable to the headache which Mrs. Handy's young gentlemen had inflicted upon her every evening. She was subjected to no impertinence; the butcher and baker called her 'Miss' when they came with their commodities; Mrs. Bantam did not send her out on many errands, and though waiting at table was a humiliating piece of work, there had been no strangers as yet to make her feel it deeply.

The month having expired, Mrs. Bantam was of opinion that though a very great deal was yet to be learned, some progress had been made; and offered Clara four shillings a week to stay. 'You are nothing of a servant,' said she, 'but you are civil and honest, so I will try you a little longer. If you would only learn to be methodical you would suit me.'

Clara was grateful and happy, and sat down forthwith to write to her uncle, in order to give him a clear statement of the new position in which she was placed. She had not considered it advisable to write on the subject till the month of trial had expired. To Susan she would have written on the same day, but could not find time, and was forced to delay

it till the next Sunday evening, when she entered into detail, describing her mode of life at Mrs. Handy's, her two unsuccessful attempts at getting a situation as governess, and her final settlement as maid of all work, with a very kind lady.

'Do not fancy that it is so very dreadful, my dear sister, or that I am completely miserable. I am determined to be happy if it is possible, and though now I feel the toil fatiguing, because I am new to bodily labour, in time I shall feel it nothing, and have leisure in the long winter evenings which are coming on to read and to write to you.

'The house I am living in is situated in a little garden; it is a real cottage of one story, which almost all the houses in Adelaide are, with only a trap ladder leading up to the little attic where I sleep. I have a fine view of the hills from my bed-room window, and now that the great heat has moderated I think the climate delightful. I still sleep with my window open that I may have enough of fresh air, and it is no uncommon thing in summer for people to leave all their doors and windows open through the night. I think that shows that the colony must be an honest place; but you must always bear in mind that this never has been a penal settlement.

'I do not think you would fancy the trees here, at least taken separately. They are evergreens, and looked fresh when everything else was burnt up, but now the newly sprung grass makes them look rather lugubrious. They are somewhat scraggy, and the bark is white on the greater proportion of the trees around the town, which gives them quite a ghostly appearance by moonlight. There are a few near the river Torrens which look really pretty, and I have been told that in the bush there are much finer trees than in the neighbourhood of town. They say that South Australian wood, being of slow growth, and consequently very hard, makes the best fuel possible, but I find it no easy matter to kindle it, and am always getting splinters of it in my hands; but of course I shall learn to do better soon.

'I suppose that when you receive this you will be in London with my uncle and aunt to see the world, and to wonder at the Great Exhibition. But, Susan, I am seeing life, and learning lessons which I hope I shall never forget; it is not merely the things I am learning to do, useful as they undoubtedly are, but the new thoughts and feelings which my present employments awaken, which will benefit me much. I have hitherto lived too much in books, and thought them all-important; now I see what things fill the minds of nine-tenths of my sex—daily duties, daily cares, daily sacrifices. I see now the line of demarcation which separates the employers from the employed; and if I ever, by any chance,

should again have a servant under me, I shall surely understand her feelings, and be considerate and kind. How I reproach myself now for the unnecessary trouble I used to give our good faithful Peggy and Helen, and all through want of thought.

'So again I say, do not pity me much; feel for me a little, but rest assured that these little trials I meet with will do a great deal of good to

'Your most affectionate sister,
'CLARA.'

Mrs. Bantam at last found Clara useful. If she learned slowly it was surely; and at the end of three months she was really a tolerable servant—not a strong one, but industrious and tidy. She often speculated upon the girls next door. There were three of them. They must be Scotch, for they were always singing Scotch ballads, and they went to the Scotch Church.

They were all very comely, if not positively pretty, and in spite of the work they had to do Clara would have known them to be ladies even if Mrs. Bantam had not told her so. Their two brothers went to business in the morning, and returned in the evening, and Clara would sometimes see one or two of the sisters meeting them at the gate, and bringing them into the house through the little garden. They had a piano, and used to play and sing in the evenings; sometimes Clara would go into the corner of Mrs. Bantam's yard to listen, or if she happened to be passing that way she would linger near the windows to catch the words of some familiar ditty. The young men used to dig in the garden, or sometimes chop wood in the yard in the mornings.

Clara had been once sent by Mrs. Bantam to borrow a log of wood, for they happened to be out of it; and she saw the eldest Miss Elliot busy washing out her kitchen. Clara was delighted to see it, but Miss Elliot did not like quite so much to be caught by the girl next door doing the most disagreeable piece of work in the house. However, she pulled down her sleeves, and showed Clara where to get the wood, saying that Mrs. Bantam was welcome to it.

As Clara got more *au fait* in the routine of her daily duties, she found the evenings long and wearisome. She thought that she ought to employ them in sewing for herself, for her wages were not high, and the clothes she had were not suitable to her employments; so she began her first attempt at dressmaking on a dark-brown print, with unhappy looking white spots on it, which was to be a morning wrapper. She did not know how to cut it rightly, and it turned out to be a deplorable misfit; and what between the gloomy colour of the thing

itself, and the cheerless solitude in which she made it, the tears dropped often and fast over it. Stitch after stitch she put in, and thought of her old happy home—her father, her mother, her sister; of the want of some one to exchange an idea with; of the constraint of this continual reticence, till her heart felt ready to break. When the gown was really done, she brought down a blank book that she had got for a journal on board ship, but which she had written nothing upon there, and relieved her mind by expressing her thoughts.

'It is right that I have made this dress, but to make another in the same way would kill me, I think. I had better go in rags than have my heartstrings torn up like this. I must read, though I have no face to look up to when I lift my eyes from the book; I must write, though nobody but myself shall read it.

'I hope I may never meet Mr. Reginald again; I feel that once we were equals, but that now, without any fault of mine, I am hopelessly his inferior.'

Such were a very few of the thoughts which Clara committed to paper. She felt relieved by doing so, and then began to read something not very wise, or very deep, but amusing; for she did not want to over-think.

CHAPTER IX

A VISITOR

Mrs. Bantam did not much approve of her servant's studies, and after Clara had gone on with them for a week, she told her that it would be much better if she would sew, and pronounced a decided negative on either reading or writing upstairs when she had gone to bed; for, said she—

'A girl I had two years ago used to read novels in bed half the night, and was never fit for her work through the day. She was always pale, and had a startled look about her; but one night she startled us all in earnest, for she set fire to her bed, and we had difficulty in putting it out. So, since that, I have made a rule that no servant of mine shall read in bed; and I hope, Clara, that you will not break it.'

'Then do not be angry if I read or write in the kitchen, ma'am,' said Clara; 'for I feel too sad and lonely to sew much.'

'I am as fond of a book myself as anybody can be, but I never let reading interfere with my duties,' said Mrs. Bantam; 'and I hope, Clara, that you will not let a passion for novels lead you into idleness and all mischief, as it did poor Eleanore. She has turned out very ill; gone quite wrong indeed.'

Clara coloured at this comparison, but she said nothing.

'Well, Clara, we are going to have a visitor to spend a few weeks with us, so you must see that the spare bedroom next mine is very clean and comfortable, for this lady is just out from England, and seems to be very precise and particular. I do not know her myself, but she has brought letters to Mr. Bantam from a cousin of his in Staffordshire. She wants a situation as governess in a respectable family, or as teacher in a good school; and Mr. Bantam has asked her to stay with us till she meets with something to suit her.'

'Was it the lady who called yesterday?' asked Clara.

'Yes; and she comes this afternoon with her luggage. Now

see and don't make any mistake at table, Clara; for this lady is very observant, and of course will blame me as well as you, if anything is wrong.'

'I will try to get everything done *comme il faut.*'

'No slipslop French, at any rate, Clara; Miss Withering would consider that dreadfully out of place. Mr. Bantam is to be on an election committee this afternoon, and he dines in town; so you had better have dinner ready by three, when I expect Miss Withering here.'

Clara thought a great deal about Miss Withering. She had only had one glance at her face; it was neither pretty nor young, but there was a confidence about its expression which looked as if its possessor could make her way in the world.

Three o'clock came, and with it Miss Withering and her boxes in a spring cart. She had a quarrel with the driver as to the amount of his charge for bringing them, but was ultimately obliged to pay the full sum, as he would not go away without. So Miss Withering entered Mrs. Bantam's house highly malcontent, and took off her bonnet and shawl in the room her hostess showed her into, in a state, for her, of considerable excitement. She was dissatisfied with the colony generally, and as this was a very wet day, and she had got splashed in the cart, she felt justified in complaining of a climate which she had been led to believe, from books published, and general conversation in England, was the finest under the sun.

'I cannot think how you can submit to such streets, Mrs. Bantam,' said she, as she sat down to dinner. 'I feel that I have been deceived with regard to South Australia. I was told that it was Italy without its sirocco, and that the air was so mild that throughout the whole year sleeping in the open air was agreeable and innoxious. Now my experience hitherto has been very contrary to these accounts; the bracing frosts of England are luxuries compared with this plashing, continual rain.'

'I cannot say I like the rain much,' said Mrs. Bantam; 'but unless we have a great deal of rain in winter, we have short crops in summer. Last season was dry and very pleasant while it lasted, but we are suffering for it now, in high prices and scarcity both of corn and hay. We are but young people here, and Rome was not built in a day.'

'Pray, Mrs. Bantam, have you been long in South Australia?' asked Miss Withering.

'Only ten years; I cannot call myself one of the original colonists, but I have been here long enough to see great improvements, and to have ceased to think about returning to England.'

'Do you mean to say that you have lived ten whole years

A Visitor

in such a place as this? really you must have made many sacrifices, and submitted to many discomforts. No lady thinks of staying ten years in India, Mrs. Bantam.'

'You would not compare South Australia to India,' said Mrs. Bantam, warmly.

'Indeed I should prefer India of the two. I like warm weather, and a lady never needs to do anything whatever there; while here, I understand, that servants are so scarce and bad, that a lady's life is one of unmitigated slavery. You should really get Mr. Bantam to take you home again; Mr. Dillon expects that you will not be long in returning to Staffordshire.'

'There are a great many things to be considered, Miss Withering, before I could make up my mind to leave this colony. I rather think I like it too well to leave it, even if it were advisable otherwise.'

Miss Withering elevated her eyebrows at this speech, and gave her attention to her dinner and Clara, whom she watched with her pale cold blue eyes till she succeeded in making her nervous and uncomfortable. Miss Withering wanted a great deal of waiting on. She could not help herself to water from the jug, though it stood at her hand; nor hand anything past, as Mr. and Mrs. Bantam usually did.

After dinner, she asked Mrs. Bantam if she would send one of her girls to Rundle-street for the key of her work-box, which she had left at the house where she had been living for the last two days. Mrs. Bantam supposed Clara would make no objection, and Clara did not. It was not raining just then, but the streets were very wet and muddy; she was picking her steps very carefully in coming home, but just in turning an awkward corner, she met Mr. Renton full in the face. He was carrying a large parcel and a bandbox, and looked as much caught as she did.

'Ah! Miss Morison, this is an unexpected pleasure, for I have never got sight of you since we landed. Where have you hidden yourself, and how have you been this age?'

A heavy shower came on, and Clara was obliged to stand beside Mr. Renton under a broad verandah, subjected to the inspection of half-a-dozen children, who were watching the rain from the windows of the cottage.

'Got a good situation, I hope, Miss Morison. Have you heard from our extensive friend, the fair Elizabeth, yet?'

'Not yet, Mr. Renton. I suppose she has forgotten me.'

'I'll be bound she has not forgotten me,' said Mr. Renton. 'I flatter myself that I did make an impression in that quarter; but where are you living, Miss Morison?'

'I have got a very comfortable situation; I hope you have succeeded in getting into a line of business that suits you?'

'Why, not quite! I have tried several places, but the fact is, they were not suited to me; they wanted a man of less talent and less ambition than I am. I have been thinking of going to the Turon, the New South Wales gold fields, you know; but I have gone as assistant to Macnab in the meantime, and am really invaluable to him with the ladies. With servant-girls, in particular, I am irresistible. This parcel, Miss Morison, contains five pounds seventeen and sixpence worth of drapery that I induced a red-handed, coarse-looking girl, who is going to be married next week, to buy at Macnab's; and I capped the matter by offering to take the young lady's parcel home myself, so she bought a guinea bonnet out of very joy. And she came into the shop to buy a pair of shoes, an article we were out of. Really, Macnab ought to consider these things, and remunerate me accordingly.'

By this time the shower had moderated, and Clara and Renton parted. She made the best of her way home, and Mr. Renton proceeded up another street to deliver his precious parcel.

Miss Withering received her key with dignity, opened her work-box, and took out a narrow strip of muslin, which she began to hem slowly and painfully, while she talked in an oracular manner to her good-natured hostess, who grew uncomfortable under the battery of her words. The new-comer boasted herself to be a person of great discernment, and told Mrs. Bantam that she could read people's characters at a glance.

'I have astonished many persons by my singularly quick perception, and many of my friends have regretted not attending to my warnings in time. I hope you will excuse me for mentioning that I think the girl who waited at table to-day only wants an opportunity to be impertinent; and you will allow me to find fault with her in case she treats me with disrespect. I suppose you do not find your girls improve after you have had them for six months?'

'They are very seldom good for anything after that time,' said Mrs. Bantam, 'and yet I dislike changing so much that I would submit to almost anything. I have had great trouble with Clara, not from any want of respect, but from her total ignorance of every kind of work. I cannot bear to find fault, and she really is a good, well-meaning girl, though fonder of reading than I quite approve of.'

'There is nothing spoils a servant so much as a taste for reading,' said Miss Withering; 'it makes them dislike working, and besides, they fancy when they have read a few books, that they know as much as their mistresses, and then there is an end of all right subordination. The old plan was the best, to have servants in their proper places; let them learn

A Visitor

to wash and scour, bake and brew, and leave reading and writing to their betters. 'A little learning is a dangerous thing'.'

'One girl I had was quite ruined by reading,' said Mrs. Bantam; 'I told Clara about it, but she seems to think that, as she does all the work of the house, she may have the evenings to herself.'

'Ah! Mrs. Bantam, I see how you are imposed upon. I am pretty sure that a great deal of the work Clara professes to do falls upon you; and in order to let her amuse herself in the evenings, you are forced to slave half the day.'

'Well, there is some truth in that,' said Mrs. Bantam.

'It was for the girl's own good I spoke,' said Miss Withering; 'for it would be much better for herself if she would bring up her arrears, and keep the furniture brighter than she does, than to be filling her head with nonsense.'

When Mr. Bantam returned home to a late tea Miss Withering began a discussion on politics with him. Mr. Bantam was a Radical, a Dissenter, and a Voluntary; Miss Withering was very High Church indeed; so that Mrs. Bantam, whose opinions were not very decided either way, but who rather inclined to her husband's views, had great difficulty in keeping the expressions of the disputants within 'parliamentary language,' and was not sorry when bed-time put an end to the altercation.

'What a talented man Mr. Bantam is!' said Miss Withering to his wife, when she came to see that her guest was comfortable for the night. 'Very decided in his views, and prejudiced on some points, but really a masculine mind. I admire firmness in others as much as I cultivate it in myself; so do not be annoyed at our war of words, my dear Mrs. Bantam; we are only trying the stuff we are made of. I have enjoyed this little conversation more than I have done anything since I left England.'

'Well, Elinor,' said Mr. Bantam to his wife, in confidence, 'I am sure I was foolish to ask this Miss Withering to stay here, for I don't think we shall find her a comfortable guest. Do you?'

'She seems a clever, sensible woman,' replied the lady; 'she admires you very much, and thinks you very talented indeed.'

Mr. Bantam was greatly mollified.

CHAPTER X

HOW MISS WITHERING MAKES HERSELF AGREEABLE TO MRS. BANTAM AND HER GUESTS

Ere a week had passed, Mrs. Bantam found that Miss Withering was not at all a desirable guest; but still she had a great opinion of her judgment, and thought that it must be from some fault of her own that she was always uncomfortable with her. Miss Withering ordered Clara about in the most unreasonable manner, and it was only by the greatest effort that Clara could submit patiently. She despised the meanness which could lead Miss Withering to accept of hospitality from people whose existence she was embittering; for day after day she succeeded in detaching the members of the family from each other, and rendering herself the centre round which the household must revolve.

She pitied Mrs. Bantam for having so much to do; wondered why Mr. Bantam did not get her a carriage to drive about in—it would benefit her health so greatly; thought that as Mrs. Bantam did not keep two servants, she should have one strong enough and clever enough to spare her every fatigue; talked her victim into a wretched headache, and then was afraid Mr. Bantam did not feel enough for his angelic wife.

To Mr. Bantam, when she could attack him singly, she regretted his wife's weak nerves and easy temper; asked if he did not think it advisable to have a competent person in the house to look after Clara, and get her to do her duty; admired the force of his mind and the vigour of his fancy; sighed over the difficulty gentlemen find in getting ladies to enter into their projects or pursuits, or to comprehend business matters; and concluded by saying that Mrs. Bantam was the most amiable of women.

To Clara she seldom spoke, except to find fault; but after Miss Withering had been with her mistress a week, something occurred which almost made her continual watching and

reproving nothing to Clara. It was towards the close of a fine mild winter day in the end of May, when a knock called Clara to the door, where, to her great surprise, she saw and recognised Mr. Reginald; but owing to the shadow in which she was thrown, he did not know her again.

'Is Mrs. Bantam at home?' said he. Clara could not trust herself to speak, but made a gesture of assent, and opened the parlour-door to admit him, retreating to the kitchen with all possible despatch, saying to herself, 'He will not stay long. I hope he will not stay to tea. How wretchedly ill he is looking!'

'How long it is since you have been in town, or, at least since you have come to see us, Reginald,' said Mr. Bantam. 'What has kept you in the bush for so many months?'

It appeared that Mr. Reginald had suffered a long illness, and had come to Adelaide for change of air; but that, finding his usual abode at Mrs. Handy's occupied, he thought of returning the next day but one.

'Do stay with us, Reginald,' said Mr. Bantam. 'You can give your vote in Adelaide for whatever county you have qualified for; and though you and I differ on politics, we won't quarrel. You will find a powerful ally here; Miss Withering is a strong church and state lady, but I am not afraid to contend with both of you.'

Mr. Reginald hoped that it would put Mrs. Bantam to no inconvenience, and being assured that it would not, confessed that he should only be too happy to spend a month in such pleasant quarters. Mrs. Bantam's conscience pricked her a good deal that night, for having entrapped an invalid within ear-shot of Miss Withering's tongue, but as that lady had been milder and more agreeable that evening, she was inclined to think it was all for the best after all. But Clara's part was the hardest to go through. She delayed bringing in tea till Miss Withering declared that 'that girl' meant to starve them all, and rung the hand-bell with such violence as nearly to dislocate the handle.

When she did bring in candles and tea, her cheeks were painfully flushed, and her hand trembled so that she could scarcely put the cups and plates in their places. Miss Withering's eye was upon her, but that she heeded not; she saw at a glance that she was recognised. She cast one imploring look at her friend of the boarding-house, to let him know that he must take no notice of her; it was understood, and Reginald only gave one or two stolen glances to see how the young lady got on at service. She did not do Mrs. Bantam credit this evening, and made so many blunders, that Miss Withering looked from her to her mistress as if to say, 'Do you not see what an affected, stupid thing she is?'

After tea, Clara heard with despair of the arrangement that had been made, and she and Mrs. Bantam went in together to put the prophet's chamber, as they called it, into a habitable state.

'And I must wait on him here for a month,' she wrote down in her short-hand journal, 'and never speak to him, and nobody must know that we have ever met. He said that our meeting formed a page of his life; truly it fills a page in mine, too. Miss Withering is not handsome, neither is she agreeable; I am sure he will not like her. . . . How I wish she had never come here! I always was afraid of visitors, and the first has been so bad, that I never thought I could feel the second a worse infliction; but I do.'

When Clara had written this, she remembered that she had got that day through Mr. Campbell (who sometimes looked in, and was pleased to see how bravely she got on) a letter from Miss Waterstone, which she had twice opened, but only to be interrupted. Anybody's thoughts were better than her own just then, so she opened it again, and read as follows:

'MY DEAREST CLARA,

'I have been very long in writing to you, but my plans have been so unsettled, that I did not like to write till I had fixed upon something.

'You know what was my great inducement for going to Australia, and when I heard from Aunt Rachel that Robert had got a good situation in Glasgow, and had no intention of leaving the country at all, I saw that I had no chance of seeing him in Melbourne, so I had *half a mind* to go home again. But you know it would have looked a foolish-like thing in me, and I don't think Robert behaved well about it at all.

'However, I made up my mind to forget him, and to take a situation in Melbourne; and I daresay I should have succeeded if I had not foolishly (you will say) fallen in love. I could not refuse such a handsome offer as I had made to me just three weeks ago to-day, and I think you will be glad to hear that I am going to be comfortably established. Mr. Patrick Fleming is, *in my opinion* at least, very agreeable. He is in business in Melbourne; I liked him from the first day I saw him; he is tall and fair with fine blue eyes (you prefer *black*); and though he has been a great many years in Port Phillip (or Victoria I should call it now) he is as fond of Scotch music and Scotch *people* as ever.

'Melbourne is a much finer town than Adelaide; the streets are regularly built, and are kept in better repair; but the environs are not so pretty, and there are not many villages near the town. However, I prefer Melbourne on the whole, and the river is much finer than that miserable little burn

they call the Torrens; but I have *good* reason to prefer this place for it is to be my home, and my *intended* has a nice shop in one of the best streets, with a dwelling-house upstairs.

'Do write to me soon, my dear Clara; and let me know what you are doing. You must address to *Mrs. P. Fleming,* Collins-street, Melbourne. It seems queer to write the name before it is really my own, but Patrick is continually asking me if it does not sound very well?—he is *so* amusing.

'I want to know how Mr. Macnab and Mr. Renton are getting on, for I still take a great interest in all my fellow-passengers. Remember me kindly to Mrs. Handy when you see her, and believe me to be,

'Yours very affectionately,
'(for a short time only) ELIZABETH WATERSTONE.'

'A kind husband and a happy home,' sighed Clara, after reading this letter. 'Ah, Miss Waterstone! you are indeed to be envied.'

On the following morning when Clara was getting the breakfast-table arranged in the parlour, Mr. Reginald came in. Neither Mr. nor Mrs. Bantam, nor even Miss Withering, were early risers, so he was the first to make his appearance. Both of them coloured a little, but Reginald recovered first, and said, rather confusedly:—

'I hope you are well, Miss Morison. I did not know that you were living here. If I had known, I would not have accepted Mrs. Bantam's kind invitation, for I see you would rather have my absence than my company. I will go to-day if I make you uncomfortable.'

'Do not go on my account. Mrs. Bantam has a right to ask what guests she pleases. I shall get used to this; I know I looked very foolish last night, but you are the first person I had met who had known any thing of me before I went to ——.'

'Could you not have done better, Miss Morison? Could not Mr. Campbell have got you any situation as a governess? This is a sphere for which you were not formed, and it must be painful to you to submit to the position you hold here.'

'I am not heroic enough to deny that it is painful, but I had no alternative. I am not accomplished enough for Adelaide people; I had no money, so I determined that if my head was valueless I would try my hands, and I have succeeded better than you could have expected.'

'But, Miss Morison, would you not prefer to go home. I think you told me that your uncle was in good circumstances, and it would be better and happier for you to live with your sister in his house than to go through such drudgery here'

'If my uncle writes me a kind invitation to return to Scotland I will gladly go, but I will not for a cold one. It would make Susan unhappy if I were to be a burden on my uncle. So I am better here.'

'But you are pale and thin, Miss Morison; your eyes look as if you did not sleep well, and I fear you are suffering a great deal in silence. Shall I speak to Mrs. Bantam, and represent your former position to her that she may show you more consideration?'

'Do not speak, I beseech you, Mr. Reginald. She is very kind, very patient with me; she has taught me everything, for I was dreadfully stupid. I beg of you to take no notice of me at all, but just let me go on in my old way, and not try to make me discontented with the station in life in which God has seen fit to place me. I must order myself lowly and reverently to you as well to all my other betters, so good-bye, we are strangers now.'

So saying Clara returned to the kitchen, and waited till the bell summoned her before she would again encounter Reginald's eyes.

Miss Withering soon found out that colonial gentlemen were not attentive, and that Mr. Reginald was neglectful beyond all forbearance. He was at all times rather spasmodic in his efforts to please ladies, and Miss Withering trod so ruthlessly on his pet prejudices and old established opinions, that he could barely be civil to her. Mrs. Bantam required very little from her guests beyond an appearance of satisfaction with what she did for their comfort, and she did not mind though Mr. Reginald forgot to inquire after her last night's headache on the following morning, or that he required to be reminded to pass anything across the table, even though she wanted it herself. But to Miss Withering these were serious things, and she very soon began to talk at Mr. Reginald to Mrs. Bantam, and made her regret having invited Reginald to the house. But she could not send Miss Withering away; it would be cruel, for she was very poor; she was certainly clever and managing, and though she was not an agreeable or accommodating guest, she might be an admirable governess for unruly children.

Mrs. Bantam was glad when one of Miss Withering's morning tirades was stopped by the arrival of a gig at the door containing Mr. Hodges and his daughter Minnie. She had but a slight acquaintance with them, but what she had seen of them she liked very much. Mr. Bantam had sold some property for Mr. Hodges lately, and had got a good price for it; the two gentlemen were both busy electioneering on the same side at the present time; and when Mr. Bantam had taken his wife on a tour down to the south they had been

most kindly entertained at Mr. Hodges' for a week. Mrs. Hodges had been everything that was hospitable, and Minnie had walked with her guest to all the prettiest spots within walking distance, and had laid herself out to please her with the frankness and earnestness of a country girl, anxious to convince her town acquaintance that the bush is the most delightful place in the world.

Mrs. Bantam introduced the new comers to Miss Withering, who thinking that there might be a situation in this quarter, drew herself up to her full height, and looked like the concentrated essence of all the virtues and accomplishments extant. Mr. Hodges thought her ladylike, Minnie thought she was a bad specimen of a class which she generally disliked;—a newcomer, who did not take kindly to Minnie's own dear colony.

'You have not come all the way into town to-day,' said Mrs. Bantam; 'early risers as I know you to be, thirty-five miles of indifferent roads cannot be gone over by eleven o'clock.'

'No, no, Mrs. Bantam; a merciful man is merciful to his beast,' said Mr. Hodges; 'my poor grey could not do it so soon. We came in as far as the foot of the hills yesterday, and stayed all night with our friends the Summerses; and the late breakfast there, and one thing or another, has kept me out of town till now; and I have business to do, and little time to do it in. Mr. Bantam is at his office, I suppose?'

'He went nearly two hours ago,' said Mrs. Bantam. 'But though you are hurried, Miss Hodges is not. I hope she will be induced to pay me a visit of a month now, after my trespassing on her good nature last summer.'

'Don't trespass on it now, by calling me Miss Hodges; I hate the name so thoroughly. Will the new Council not be able to change our names as well as the English Parliament? I really wish, papa, you would inquire, for it would be so delightful to have a pretty name.'

'I am quite contented with my name myself,' said Mr. Hodges, 'and if you dislike it, you have it always in your power to change it for a prettier; don't you think she has no reason to complain, Mrs. Bantam?'

'I like to be called Minnie best, and you called me so in the country,' said the young lady.

'Very well, Minnie; I am sure that your father is in no hurry for you back again just now, and I should be so pleased if you would spend a few weeks with me, till business again brings Mr. Hodges into town.'

'The children will lose their lessons, and I fear mamma will have too much to do if I leave her so long. And besides,

papa, I ought to go to stay with the Elliots, if I have any time to spend in Adelaide.'

'But I am very anxious for your company just now, Minnie.'

And Mr. Hodges seemed well-disposed towards his daughter's accepting the invitation.

'We see,' he said, 'so little good society in the bush; and really Minnie grows quite wild.'

But Mr. Hodges looked very proud of his daughter, notwithstanding.

'But, papa,' said Minnie, 'I cannot do it. What *would* Annie Elliot say to see me next door, after all my promises to come to her the very next time mamma could spare me? Do you know the Elliots, Mrs. Bantam?'

'I am sorry to say that I don't; but perhaps you could take me to see them.'

'Minnie has a school-girl friendship for Annie Elliot,' said Mr. Hodges, 'and is always keeping up a correspondence with her. I can't fancy what they write about, but they fill sheet after sheet of paper.'

'Now, papa, it is a shame to say you don't know what we write about, when I read you my last letter from beginning to end, not forgetting the postscript. I was rather proud of it, do you know, Mrs. Bantam. I had made quite a hit in giving a description of papa's accident, which turned out quite harmless; and I wrote about mamma's fears that Ellen's second teeth were coming in cross; and I described Mrs. Caumray's new governess, whom I saw at church; and Miss Caumray's fashionable bonnet; and John's insane desire to learn the native language; and all about Charles losing himself in the Murray scrub, and asking for a night's lodging from a German, who looked upon him as a beggar, and would hardly let him in; (was it not disgraceful inhospitality for the bush?) and after I had read every word of it to papa, he said it was only a rigmarole about nothing.'

'Young ladies are very fond of letter-writing,' said Miss Withering, 'but I think that some restrictions should be put upon this taste. In the school which I conducted in England, I made a point of seeing every letter written by the young ladies, and sealing and addressing it myself. Also I kept a very strict watch that no letters should be interchanged by the girls or sent by the servants. I prevented a great deal of mischief by that means.'

'That is a very good old-fashioned system,' said Mr. Hodges.

'But unrestrained letter-writing gives a person a fluent style,' said Minnie.

'Yes; but not a correct or concise style,' said Miss Withering. 'How few ladies can write a business letter! they cannot

keep to the point; they enlarge and digress on every hand; and it is a common subject of complaint that after you have got through perhaps six pages, you find the only important part of a girl's letter in the postscript.'

'Very true! very true!' said Mr. Hodges. 'I must say, Miss Withering, that your views are very judicious. Now, Minnie, I hope you will not make a convenience of your kind friend here, and be constantly running out to see Annie Elliot. I have an engagement this morning, so you must excuse me for the present, ladies—I must wish you good morning.'

So saying, Mr. Hodges left the room, and presently drove off.

'By the bye, I ought to have asked Miss Withering if she has any objection to sharing her room with you, Minnie, before I induced you to stay; for Mr. Reginald occupies the only other spare room I have,' said Mrs. Bantam.

'I should be most happy,' said Miss Withering, 'if Miss Hodges would give me her company in my dormitory; I shall be only too glad to have some one to talk to while I dress and undress, for it seems such a waste of time otherwise.'

'I hope you have a tolerable servant just now,' said Minnie to Mrs. Bantam; 'for I cannot bear to think that I shall give you trouble. I can do anything for myself, but I dislike making my hostess feel uncomfortable by making her girls have more to do than usual.'

'Clara is a very fair servant,' said Mrs. Bantam, 'though she is not very strong.'

'You are too good-natured,' said Miss Withering. 'I never saw any one so easily pleased in my life.'

'I know that for one I have had better, I have had two worse than Clara, and I regard her accordingly.'

'That speaks ill for South Australian servants,' said Miss Withering; 'but Miss Hodges will judge for herself.'

'South Australian servants are not so bad as they are called,' said Minnie. 'Perhaps they are not such working machines as English servants, but we have met with so many instances of genuine good feeling in ours lately, that I am determined to find some better topic of conversation than the faults of domestics, which I have long been sick of hearing from our neighbours. I walk or ride across for a little change to see a friend, and hope to get into some agreeable conversation, when, behold! they will talk of nothing in the world but Sarah's blunders and Mary's depravity; dwelling upon trifles with severe displeasure, till I am inclined to think that if our characters were as much taken to pieces by them in the kitchen, as theirs are by us in the parlour, we should cut a very poor figure indeed.'

Miss Withering and Minnie were water and fire, and never

could agree. The water at first made the fire burn dim, and Minnie felt uncomfortable while Miss Withering dilated on the elegance and etiquette of English life, and the many blunders which novices made on the threshold of the world.

Miss Withering was of opinion that a sister was a very unfit teacher for her brothers and sisters. There could not, under her management, be the strictness or the regularity which, like the hem at the end of the garment, prevented the fraying and wasting of the loose edges of time. Punishments were rarely enforced by a sister with sufficient rigour to prevent the recurrence of the fault, and often an appeal to mamma would thwart the firmest and best-laid schemes of the amateur governess. Minnie was conscious that she was not very strict or regular with her dear pupils, and that there was a great deal of truth in what Miss Withering now insinuated gently, and then declared boldly; but she had both sense and feeling, and she was convinced that such a teacher as her disinterested adviser would be a great change for the worse.

The first opportunity Mrs. Bantam had to speak to Minnie alone, she apologized for inviting her to meet a person who, though clever, was so disagreeable; but said, that she herself was so tired of her, and had been so worried with her advice and opinions, that she hoped Minnie would excuse her, and talk to Miss Withering a little to relieve her, and contradict her as much as she pleased; 'for, my dear child, I cannot contradict any one, and I cannot make up my mind to offend her, and get quit of her at once.'

'Then I have free leave to say what I like to this lady?'—and Minnie clapped her hands. 'I will not let her talk against the colony, or despise the Elliots because they do their own work. Greek shall meet Greek, and a fine tug we shall have!'

'Remember, I don't want you to quarrel with Mr. Reginald,' said Mrs. Bantam; 'I will not forgive you if you do.'

Clara was alarmed at the announcement of a third visitor, but a sight of Minnie dispelled her apprehensions. Minnie was tall and straight, with an easy, though not fully developed figure. Her hair was dark-brown, and in great profusion; her eyes were very blue, and clear, though not sparkling; her nose was rather too large, but the effect of it was carried off by a tolerably wide mouth, with beautiful teeth, and a bewitching smile. Her hands were rather red, and she was a good deal freckled; but yet nobody could say there was anything vulgar in Minnie's appearance.

She volunteered to save Clara all further trouble with the bed-room she and Miss Withering occupied; and as, previous to her arrival, it had been left every morning deplorably untidy, this was a great relief to Clara.

'And, Clara,' said Minnie, 'as there is only you to do the

work of the house, and now it is full of visitors, you must sometimes have more than you can manage; so ask me to help you when you have a push. I can do anything in the way of making puddings and pies; indeed I am quite fond of it, and will not let our girl do them at home.'

To Mr. Reginald, Minnie was frank and agreeable; she had a piece of knitting in her hand, from which she looked up every now and then to listen and reply to what was said. Miss Withering proposed a game at whist after tea, saying that it was the only game of cards that she liked, for it was the only one which was rational and solid. Mrs. Bantam could not play, but Minnie could; so the two gentlemen sat down to play with the two young ladies — Minnie and Reginald against Miss Withering and Mr. Bantam. Mrs. Bantam was in a state of great delight when she saw Miss Withering fixed to the card-table, and felt herself free to do as she pleased. She went into the kitchen, and found Clara endeavouring to read, and silently wiping away the tears that rolled from her eyes.

"What is the matter, Clara? Are you ill?'

'No, ma'am; but I have wanted to speak to you for some time.'

'Do you want to leave me, Clara? I shall be quite sorry to part with you.'

'Shall you, indeed?' said Clara, her face brightening at the thought that some one cared a little for her. 'I am so glad to hear you say so. I did not wish to leave, but I wanted to know how I have displeased you; for you do not seem to put the same confidence in me you used to do.'

'You have not displeased me at all, Clara. It is only that Miss Withering's nonsense. I wish she had never entered the house. Never mind what she says, or what she makes me say, for I like you as well as ever, and should be grieved if you went away; and I am sure you would never get such a comfortable place as you have here. So dry your eyes, you silly child, and tell me if you don't think Miss Minnie a very much pleasanter guest.'

Clara agreed that Miss Minnie was a paragon of a visitor, and received directions from Mrs. Bantam with regard to supper with restored equanimity.

Miss Withering understood whist better than the other players, but she had decidedly the worst partner; for Mr. Bantam made many and serious blunders. She laid down the laws of the game with great precision, explained how her partner might have taken such and such tricks; and when he would have passed it off, saying, that as they were only playing for love, it was of no consequence, she would not have such a palliation.

'Excuse me, Mr. Bantam; if a thing is worth doing at all, it is worth doing well. If you mean to play whist, you must attend to the rules of the game; it is a game of skill as well as chance.'

'Really,' said Minnie, 'I do not see any pleasure in playing at anything that requires much thought. I quite hate chess for that reason. I see no use in making a labour of an amusement, any more than in turning conversation into a pitched battle.'

'Thank you, Minnie,' said Mr. Bantam; 'I see I may trust to you as an ally. Suppose we are partners tomorrow evening, you will not take my blunders much to heart, eh?'

'If you will be merciful to mine, I will overlook yours,' said Minnie.

CHAPTER XI

MINNIE STANDS UP FOR HER COUNTRY

Next day being very fine, Mrs. Bantam asked Miss Withering and Minnie to accompany her when she made some calls. Miss Withering was surprised and shocked at everything she saw; the houses were small, the furniture scanty and shabby; the children seemed like wild things, and the number of babies who were brought out to be admired was really quite intolerable. Mrs. Bantam was going round her acquaintances with families on this day, in the faint hope that some one of them might think Miss Withering a desirable governess. She could not conscientiously recommend her, but she would let her be seen and heard; thinking that her air of confidence and universal knowledge might induce an engagement. Miss Withering, though not admiring Australian society, prudently kept her thoughts for the amusement and edification of her more immediate companions; and looked more like a being from another sphere condescending to enlighten and astonish inferior creatures, than like the ill-tempered, domineering woman she really was; and when in the house of a quiet and easy, but not particularly clever or tidy lady, who had four young children, she met Mrs. Denfield, the congeniality of their natures drew them together.

Mrs. Bantam had scarcely a bowing acquaintance with Mrs. Denfield, and was not inclined to cultivate it; but she was pleased to see that she seemed to be struck with Miss Withering's appearance and manners. She ventured to ask if Mrs. Denfield was in want of a governess, for her friend Miss Withering had been highly recommended, and had had much experience in tuition. Mrs. Denfield said that she was at present but indifferently pleased with the young person she had; but as the engagement had been entered into for three months, and only six weeks had elapsed since it was made, she supposed she must keep her till the full term had expired.

But she looked at Miss Withering keenly, and asked several fishing questions as to her qualifications. Miss Withering, of course, could do everything under the sun, and had the best possible manner of imparting knowledge; she talked like a book on the subject of education, and flattered Mrs. Denfield so delicately that a certain impression was made.

'If nothing else turns up,' thought Mrs. Bantam, 'here is an opening for Miss Withering. I can, perhaps, submit to her for six weeks, but no longer.'

Minnie had meant to go to see the Elliots this afternoon, but Mrs. Bantam had a bad headache, and besought her to stay with Miss Withering, while she retired to her bedroom for a little peace and quietness. So Minnie good-naturedly gave up her pleasant visit, and endeavoured with all her powers to amuse her unwilling subject. Miss Withering would not be led into any topic of conversation; she must start it herself, and turn it, if possible, her own way. The sad state of manners in the colony was her present theme, and she dilated upon it, almost with feeling.

'It would have been a great thing for you, Miss Hodges, if you had been two or three years in a good boarding-school in England. It would have made you see things in the same light in which they appear to an Englishwoman like me.'

'And I think that a very unpleasant light,' said Minnie. 'We have gone with Mrs. Bantam to see five ladies to-day; I have been quite happy in these visits; would it really have been better if I had been as dissatisfied as you have been?'

'You would find yourself much at a loss in English society, Miss Hodges. It is not customary for young ladies there to talk about babies cutting teeth, or the wearing out of children's shoes; or to discuss the best method of ironing and clear-starching, or what shape of pinafore sits best on the shoulder, and is most easily made.'

'What is the great end of conversation, Miss Withering? Is it not to suit what you have got to say to the tastes and capacity of the person you address? I like to please those I am with, and though you may think my subjects low and common-place, I both gave pleasure and felt it.'

'That is a sort of truckling I could not submit to,' said Miss Withering. 'I was born to rule, and cannot stoop to my inferiors. A master-mind like mine was not made "to chronicle small beer".'

'I can assure you,' said Minnie, 'that Margaret Elliot, who is the very cleverest girl I know, can both make small beer and chronicle it. I am sure her mind is cultivated as highly as any English lady's, and yet she never complains of me, though I am so inferior to her on all points.'

'She cannot have a lofty mind, or she would revolt from

such drudgery as she has to do. These girls actually wash and scour; I can see them from my window.'

'She has a comprehensive mind; it can take in small things as well as great,' said Minnie, thinking she had settled the matter.

'How did you become acquainted with these Elliots, Miss Hodges? Your papa does not seem to feel cordially to them; I do not like girls having friends whom their parents do not approve of.'

'Papa cannot but approve of them,' said Minnie. 'Though he talks sometimes of foolish schoolgirl friendships, it is only in jest, for I owe more to the Elliots than we can ever repay in gratitude. We were shipmates in the *Alexander* eleven years ago, and Dr. Elliot was very attentive to mamma and me, when we had the fever on board, though he was not the surgeon of the vessel. We took a house between us when we landed here, and lived three months as one family. Of course, when we went to the bush, and they settled in Adelaide, we could not see each other so often; but when it was thought advisable that I should be sent to school, Mrs. Elliot offered to take me into her house, that I might go to school with Annie, who is of my own age.'

'Annie—that is the least of the three, is it not?'

'Yes, she is not so tall as either of her sisters, but she is a dear girl; and we became great friends in the four years that I lived at Dr. Elliot's. It was a second home to me; Margaret and George used to help us with our lessons in the evenings, and I know I learned more from them than I did at school. I am sure I was ten times happier there than I could have been at a boarding school.'

'I suppose it was quite as expensive.'

'Perhaps it was; but then I had all the advantage of a home while I was learning, and as every one of the Elliots was clever, and knew more than I, their society must have done me good besides.'

'My opinions are very different from yours upon this point,' said Miss Withering. 'Girls never learn anything thoroughly unless they are kept under strict discipline; but tell me more about your friends; their father and mother are dead now, I believe?'

'When Dr. Elliot died, after a long and severe illness, he left the two brothers to maintain the family; for he had very little notion of economy, and the trifle which he had laid aside was left to his wife; but she did not long survive him— only about twelve months, and now the girls are obliged to be very economical, in order to live on their brothers' salaries and their own little money, for George and Gilbert settled

that all their father and mother left should belong to their sisters.'

'I wonder that the young ladies do not take situations, as you say they are clever and tolerably accomplished.'

'George and Gilbert would not hear of such a thing, and the girls are too fond of being at home to wish to leave it. They are so united a family, that they cannot part with one of their number.'

'They are not all young,' said Miss Withering. 'Have they never thought of relieving their brothers by marrying, or have they had a chance? They certainly cannot be called handsome, and they want style.'

'Now, I call them all good-looking,' said Minnie. 'Grace has been engaged nearly two years, but as Mr. Henry Martin does not get a high salary, they are waiting till he has a rise. He is at the Burra mine, in the Company's employment; so they see each other very seldom, though their engagement is no secret. Grace talks about it to her friends as a matter of course. They take the thing quite coolly and comfortably, are confident that on some future day they will be made happy, and are not particularly miserable in the meantime.'

'And the second sister,' said Miss Withering, 'is there any prospect of her settling in life soon?'

'No, I do not think there is at present. Papa was quite angry with Margaret for refusing a friend of his, who was in very good circumstances. He was rather handsome too, and not stupid; but Margaret did not like him. Papa said it would have been such an advantageous connexion for the whole family.'

'Don't you think she was wrong and selfish in refusing such a connexion, Miss Hodges?'

'What would it have been worth to the family if Margaret had not been happy? George and Gilbert were quite satisfied with her conduct, and I am sure she must have been right. Do not fancy that the Elliots told me this. It was from papa I heard it. As for Annie, I hope she is not going to be married for a long time to come, for I want to keep my friend.'

'But these three girls all at home must be a great burden on their brothers; the poor young men cannot think of marrying themselves, and they seem very nice lads,' said Miss Withering, looking searchingly into Minnie's face.

'Oh! time enough for that; they are both quite young yet; indeed, Gilbert is scarcely one and twenty; and really they are so comfortable with their sisters, that they have no inducement to think of marrying. Such a man as Mr. Reginald, now, would be the better for a wife; for he is alone in the colony, and has no one to talk to at home, neither mother nor sister. Don't you like Mr. Reginald, Miss

Withering? Would you not take compassion on his solitude, and condescend to marry a bushman?'

A faint smile for a moment played on Miss Withering's thin lips, but it disappeared when she recollected that Reginald was anything but attentive to her, and that to Minnie he had been more agreeable.

'Don't you think his manners are very gentlemanly, Miss Withering?' asked Minnie.

'Anything but that. He is a bear. I have never seen such a thing as a gentleman in the colony. I suppose there are none.'

'Don't you consider Mr. Bantam a gentleman?' said Minnie.

'He is rather clever, though opinionative; but he cannot be called a gentleman.'

'And what do you call Mrs. Bantam, then?' said Minnie, in increasing wonder at the new comer's impertinence.

'A most amiable useful woman, but not a lady,' said Miss Withering, authoritatively.

Minnie would not deign any answer to this, feeling too indignant to trust herself to speak. She expressed a great wish to read that day's newspaper, and hoped Miss Withering would find a book to amuse her, for of course she did not suppose that a new comer could take any interest in colonial matters or colonial politics, or Miss Withering might have the newspaper.

'I like to get information from what I read,' said Miss Withering, taking up a book containing the driest chips of history, which Mr. Bantam had bought years ago, but which had never been cut. She asked Minnie to get her a paper knife, which after a quarter of an hour's diligent searching was found and given to her.

'There is a great deal of valuable information contained in this work,' said Miss Withering, after she had cut several leaves and read three pages. 'I have really found one fact which was new to me already.'

'Yes,' said Minnie. 'Don't we feel every book we read convince us of how little we know?' Miss Withering stared. That was not generally the result of her reading.

'I am not a very great reader myself,' said Minnie, 'and am not so fond of solid reading as I ought to be. I like a lively novel better than anything else.'

'I think time is too valuable to be frittered away over novels,' said Miss Withering, 'and even newspapers are a dissipating kind of reading. History, philosophy, biography, and science, particularly medical science, are what suit the requirements of my mind.' And so saying she again settled herself to pick up her chips for a blaze on some future occasion.

Whist this evening was pleasanter to Mr. Bantam than on

the previous night, but Miss Withering was not at all satisfied with her partner. He was absent and forgetful, and not all her remonstrances could induce him to take an interest in the game.

'There is to be a concert at the Exchange to-morrow evening,' said Mr. Bantam, who had won the rubber, and thought he had done great deeds. 'Shall we make a party and go to it, ladies? I can assure you, Miss Withering, that we have very good concerts in Adelaide considering what a young colony this is, and that it is not very populous. The many Germans who have settled amongst us have infused a taste in our audiences for what is called solid music, though I myself scarcely understand it.'

Minnie was delighted at the idea of the concert; she had not been at one since she was grown up, and knew it would be delightful. But when she remembered that she had a great deal of shopping to do next day to be in time to go to her father's by the dray, her spirits fell at the thought that she would not get her visit paid to her friends next door till she had been three whole days in town.

'I want a new carpet, Minnie,' said Mrs. Bantam, when they went out the next day, 'for Miss Withering is always fixing her eyes on the old one as if she were counting the holes and darns in it, and I feel it quite unpleasant. Will you help me to choose one?'

'I will give you my taste on the subject,' said Minnie, 'and what is more, I will help you to cut and make it, for I made all our last one at home, with very little assistance from mamma. We shall improve the appearance of the parlour greatly, I have no doubt.'

Minnie had a most miscellaneous list of articles to purchase, and had to go from one end of the town to the other in order to get what she wanted. There were commissions from both the servants at home, besides what was wanted for her mother and the children. She hesitated a long time about the cook's Sunday dress; but Mrs. Bantam was much longer in making up her mind about the carpet. It was nothing to please herself and Minnie, but she wanted to get something that Miss Withering could not greatly object to. This stripe would suit the room nicely, but Miss Withering would think it stiff; that diamond-shaped pattern looked rich, and would be serviceable, but Miss Withering would certainly think it gaudy. So they chose something not sufficiently *prononcé* to please themselves, but which the shopman called quiet and genteel, hoping that its unobtrusiveness would disarm criticism. But, alas! they might as well have got something to please themselves, for Miss Withering looked very contemptuously on the new carpet when it came home, and could not

have supposed that Mrs. Bantam meant to put it in the parlour. Kidderminster carpets, she said, were never used at home except in nurseries; Brussels and Wilton had completely exploded the homelier manufacture.

Mrs. Bantam was both tired and mortified, but a cup of tea gave her new strength and spirits, and she was quite able to go with the others to the concert. Minnie was enchanted with the music and the numbers of people she saw; she sat next to Mr. Reginald, who talked agreeably to her whenever there was a silence; her face was radiant with pleasure, and she almost forgot her disappointment at not seeing the Elliots, in the enjoyment of the moment. Of course Miss Withering had heard really good music before, and could see nothing delightful in the performance; the airs were old and hackneyed, and she smiled at the simplicity of the novices around her. She remarked many things on which she meant to comment afterwards, and particularly the words and looks of poor Minnie, who, she thought, was certainly much too free in her conduct in a public place.

While they were absent Clara thought she would try to write to her sister, but when she had begun, 'My dearest Susan,' she could proceed no further. A full tide of bitter thoughts broke in upon her. Every day lately had been so miserable, that even Mrs. Bantam's half apology for her coldness had scarcely relieved her oppressed spirit. She began to feel now that Reginald was dear to her from the pangs which his attentions to Minnie inflicted. It was in vain that she said to herself that it would have been the same had he been an old married man; her keen self-scrutinizing eye saw that her heart was implicated; and her judgment decided that if she ever hoped for peace or happiness, a love so hopeless must be crushed before it grew too strong to master her.

She did not feel that she had done wrong; it was natural that her mind should turn to the only person who seemed to understand her feelings, or to compassionate her position. Even Mr. Campbell had fancied her nature 'like the dyer's hand, subdued to what it wrought in'; Mr. Reginald alone could see that she suffered in secret, and that this life, though she had entered on it of her own free will, and was convinced that she was right in doing so, was one of much painful humiliation. But no further should this feeling on her part go. She had only answered Mr. Reginald in monosyllables, and with distant respect, even when they were by chance thrown in each other's company without witnesses. This had been but rarely since Minnie had come, for she was an early riser, and used to chat gaily with Reginald before breakfast, until the other members of the household made their appearance.

Clara did not dislike Minnie in spite of this, nor did she think that as yet there was any love between them; but it cost her great pain to see conversation going on that she was shut out from, and to observe that Reginald watched the expression of Minnie's eye while Miss Withering was speaking, enjoying its decided antagonism to the insufferable new comer. And Minnie's position was so good, her face so pleasing, and her manners so frank and prepossessing, that Clara was convinced that love would soon ensue on Reginald's part, which Minnie surely could not fail to return.

Clara stole into the empty parlour, and sat down where Reginald had been sitting at tea. She fancied Minnie sitting opposite her, and recalled her bright look and merry laugh. Then she took up the book Mr. Reginald had been reading, and looked into it. It was a novel from the circulating library, and a very silly one.

'I cannot read such trash as this,' said she; 'if he admires it, he has not such a fine taste as I had expected from him. I dare say that I have imagined many wonderful things of him, because I have seen and talked to no one else yet. After all, he may be but an ordinary mortal.'

But Clara did not feel any the better for this supposition. Her nature was one that loved to admire and look up to whatever was true and noble; and though much suffering was connected with her admiration of Mr. Reginald, it made her still more miserable to think that he was not admirable. However, she thought she had found an idea that would do her good; and she began to write down in her journal all that might lower her friend in her estimation; she enlarged upon his reserve, his bad taste in novel-reading, and his somewhat hot discussions on politics; and feeling that she had done a great deal to uproot her strong prepossession in his favour, she shut and locked up her journal with some little triumph. Two hours were yet to elapse before the pleasure-seekers were expected home; and Clara began to repeat what she called her 'household treasures,'—those pieces of poetry which she had learned in happier times, and which her father used to call for in the twilight, when he sat in his easy chair by the fire, and she was on a low stool at his feet.

Different as were her circumstances now, and different as the scene was on which her eyes rested, it was surprising how much better she felt in thus making her thoughts and memories audible to herself; poem after poem was gone through in a low, distinct voice, while her fingers mechanically endeavoured to twine the hair, which she had properly braided on going to service, into the long ringlets she had worn at home. Her kitchen brightened as she stirred the fire and snuffed the candle at intervals; her spirits rose, and life

seemed again endurable. Even the sound of Minnie's joyous voice, when she returned, and Mr. Reginald's anxious hope that she had not caught cold in the slight shower they had encountered in the walk from the Exchange, though they sent a pang through her heart, did not make her relapse into such hopeless and deep misery as she had felt when they set out.

CHAPTER XII

THE FAMILY NEXT DOOR

When Minnie promised to help Mrs. Bantam to make the carpet, she did not expect that it was to be done in such a hurry; but Mrs. Bantam had a fidgetty desire to have it put down, for she knew it would look much better on the floor than in the hand. Carpets were not things to stand being criticised without the general effect being seen; so the poor slandered Kidderminster was cut immediately after breakfast, and Minnie and Mrs. Bantam set to work, and did not stop till it was finished. Then it was laid down and admired by the makers; but Miss Withering thought it looked cold, and that the colours did not harmonize with the window curtains. Minnie was too anxious to go to see the Elliots, and make an apology to her dear friend Annie for not coming sooner, to be roused by anything Miss Withering could say. She put on her bonnet, and hurried away. Just as she got to the Elliot's gate, she saw George and Gilbert coming home to dinner, accompanied by another young gentleman who was a stranger to her. She had scarcely time to knock at the door and receive admittance, when they all came in.

'Ah, Minnie,' said George, 'you have been more than three days in town, and have never come to see us, though you were only next door.'

'I have very good excuses to make, George, if you only knew them,' said Minnie.

'That you have been so happy at Mrs. Bantam's, that you have forgotten us,' said George.

'I will make my excuses to your sisters,' said Minnie, who felt offended at George supposing such a thing as that she felt coldly to her old friends.

Minnie did excuse herself, though rather awkwardly, to the Misses Elliot. She did not like to tell them that she had wished Mrs. Bantam to call with her the first time, but that

she had refused, saying that Miss Withering would certainly wish to go with them, and that she would not bring such a torment on the Elliots for the world. Nor did she like to reveal just at first how disagreeable Miss Withering was; and that Mrs. Bantam wanted her to save her from the annoyance of her interminable harangues and uncomfortable innuendoes; so that having made the most of the shopping, and drawn out the round of calls and the making of the carpet into the utmost possible tediousness, she felt that, after all, she had made a very poor apology.

'I am glad you have come to-night, Minnie,' said her particular friend, Annie Elliot, 'for after being so gay, you would have found it very dull if we had only been in our old way; but George has brought his friend, Mr. Everard Harris (from the Burra), to spend the evening with us, and he will enliven us, if any one can. He came down from the mine yesterday, and only stays till the day after to-morrow. I liked him very much both times I have seen him, and I hope you will like him too.'

'I should much rather have come when you were alone,' said Minnie.

'But you can come some other day; you can come often before you go out of town. What do you say to giving Mrs. Bantam your mornings, and spending your evenings with us, when our brothers are at home? You used to think it pleasant.'

'So I do yet,' said Minnie, 'nor did I ever weary of mornings in your house. How often I think of your mamma's good-nature in letting us iron on Saturdays; I am sure we spoiled many of our dolls' things by ironing with too hot irons; but it was so nice.'

'Well, come in to dinner now, and we will talk of old times by and bye.'

Mr. Everard Harris was a young gentleman whom every one thought very good-looking, though he had not a good feature in his face; but there was a brilliancy in his oddly-shaped eyes, and an expression of humour in his irregular but most mobile mouth, that conveyed a feeling of pleasure which beauty itself can scarcely give. He was tall, his movements were easy and graceful, and no one disputed the symmetry of his figure. He had not been more than a year in the colony, but he was popular from the first, and was always the chief man in company. George Elliot had hitherto admiringly acquiesced in his superiority, but on this particular evening he did not like it quite so well. Mr. Harris sat between Minnie and Annie at dinner, keeping up a rattle of lively small-talk, and dividing his attentions so fairly between the two ladies, that not even George could see any difference.

Grace was always quiet, and Margaret and Gilbert had

their heads so full of politics at this particular time, that they could talk of nothing else; Annie was delightedly listening to what Mr. Harris was saying, and George, without the assistance of some one of his family, found it impossible to start a subject that would amuse Minnie, and bring himself forward.

When dinner was over, the young people sat round the fire, and George succeeded in getting beside the young lady he wished to please.

'There is to be a conversazione at the Mechanics' Institute in a fortnight, Minnie,' said George. 'Will you go with us? I think you will like it. We have a lecture, with music and singing afterwards.'

'I shall be delighted to go if I am in town, but papa has only given me a fortnight to stay in Adelaide, and three days have expired already.'

'I saw you last night at the concert with Reginald,' said Mr. Harris. 'I bowed to him, but he seemed to be too pleasantly engaged talking to you to pay any attention to me. What a queer kind of duenna that was sitting beside you; I think she is the approved mixture of whalebone and vinegar. Oh! George, you should have seen her, sitting upright, tall, thin, and bony, with a precise black silk dress, and virtuous bonnet, endeavouring to keep this young lady and Reginald quiet in their flirtation, but not succeeding.'

George looked cold, Minnie looked hot, and could not resist a hit at Miss Withering, as the most tiresome of new comers, concluding by saying,—

'If I have leave to stay in town till the day of the conversazione, you must be good enough to take me; and I shall like it quite as well as the concert; for, as Miss Withering says, it is a great thing to be able to get information; and I hope your lectures are not too abstruse for my comprehension.'

'Oh! not at all,' said George; 'they are generally too popular for me; I hear nothing but what I have known before. The music is the most pleasing part of the performance to my taste; but of course you will not think it equal to what you heard last night.'

'It was very fair,' said Harris, 'very creditable to such a place as Adelaide; but you should have heard Jenny Lind in 'La Figlia del Regimento', Miss Hodges.'

And here Mr. Harris burst forth into an opera reminiscence. From that he went to the ballet and Cerito, then to the theatre and Macready; next to the Fine Arts and Landseer, describing all the things which his auditors had never seen, and had no chance of seeing, with an animation and enthusiasm which made Annie almost wish to return to

England, and produced a greater effect upon Minnie than all Miss Withering had said upon the advantages of the mother country.

George, completely silenced by this great Tom o' Lincoln, sat wondering when Minnie would turn her face towards him; Grace was pleased and quiet as usual; but Margaret, who thought it mattered very little what people had seen, unless it was followed by reflection and action, got into a train of thought of her own about the education question, which then was agitated between the voluntary party and their opponents. The voluntary side was sure to triumph in the matter of religion, and Margaret saw with sorrow that the State grant was doomed as regarded the clergy; but she hoped that the liberal party, as they were called, would not commit so suicidal an act as to withdraw support from education unless it were divorced from religion. Gilbert was writing to the newspaper on the subject, and a few ideas that might enlighten it were crossing Margaret's mind, when Mr. Harris, leaving the ornamental, touched upon the useful, and mentioned steam and railways. He was astonished that none of his auditors had seen a railway, and that only Grace and George remembered being in a steamer. Margaret would fain have recalled her thoughts from her own subject, and fixed them on railways, but she could not manage it. Perhaps Gilbert had been thinking about his letter, too, for when he did speak, it was on quite a different subject from what was under discussion.

'Are the Burra proprietors ever going to pay dividends again?' said he; 'it is a great pity that they should have been stopped just now, when there is such a stagnation in the colony; money being scarce, and labourers coming out when there is no employment for them. The great bulk of emigrants from England are despatched in spring, and reach us in the dead of winter, which is always a slack time. If they were to land in September, in time for the sheep-shearing, or in December, for the harvest, they would soon be dispersed through the country, instead of remaining, poorly fed and ill-lodged, in town.'

'Oh! the dividends will soon be resumed,' said Mr. Harris; 'there is no fear of the company, for they have an immense quantity of ore raised, and the Patent Copper Company have ship-loads of copper smelted and ready to be taken to the port; but you know what abominable roads we have just now. It would be so expensive to get it carted down at present, that the proprietors do wisely to wait till the roads are fit to travel on. Besides, some creditors are pressing them, and they are spending their present receipts in clearing off old scores. And this monster engine for keeping the mine clear

of water has cost no trifle of money either; but what a property that copper mine is, after all. Those lucky fellows that invested in it at first are getting eight hundred per cent. on their outlay.'

'I think bad times are coming on the colony,' said Gilbert, 'and really we deserve it. These elections have made me ashamed of my fellow-colonists; such an amount of clap-trap and mock wisdom, such truckling to the masses, such abuse of the term liberty, put me too much in mind of Yankee-land.'

'I thought you were a Whig, Gilbert?' said Harris.

'So I used to consider myself, but I find that though I have changed none of my principles, I am looked upon in this land of enlightenment as a red hot Tory.'

'I must say that I feel slightly conservative myself when I am told to look up to the working-classes, as a respectable man in a fustian jacket once required me to do at a public meeting lately; but it is not *selon les règles* to talk politics to ladies; is it, Elliot?'

'Indeed!' said Annie, 'if you are to exclude politics you condemn Gilbert to silence, and Margaret too, for she is quite as enthusiastic as he is. If ever I am inclined to be merry since this excitement came on, they seem to think me childish and frivolous.'

'And what does Miss Hodges think on the subject?' said Mr. Harris, with an air of *empressement* which made Minnie blush.

'I have not quite made up my mind,' said Minnie; 'I think both parties go too far, papa on the one side, and our good friends here on the other.'

'Then you think ladies have nothing to do with politics?' said Harris.

'If ladies can understand them I think they are entitled to take as much interest in them as gentlemen,' answered Minnie.

'Do not say *gentlemen*, that is not the term,' said Harris. 'It is working-men who are the parties most capable of judging upon all political subjects, and for whose especial behoof every law must be enacted. They may form a combination against the use of machinery where it is much needed; they may petition Government to impose an export duty on corn; but yet the friends of improvement and free-trade will still consider them infallible dictators of what is right and wise in colonial policy. 'Let us protect the working man,' is the cry that wins the day in South Australia. But, for my own part, I take as little interest in politics as any lady in the land. I, like them, had no vote, and I was glad of it, for it saved me a world of trouble—

'How small, of all that human hearts endure,
That part which kings or laws can cause or cure'.'

'That couplet of Goldsmith's is a fallacy, though it sounds very well,' said Margaret. 'A great deal of our happiness depends on the good government of the country we live in. I do not like to see you so indifferent to the welfare of South Australia, Mr. Harris.'

'My father sent me here in the hope that I should learn to be more avaricious,' said Harris. 'He had heard that colonial life made people sharp and keen, and as I always made ducks and drakes of my cash at home, he thought I could not but improve here. I think I have got a little better, for no one will trust me, so I keep out of debt—but I never have a surplus. My whole energies are devoted to the task of making my month's pay satisfy my month's wants; so what stake have I in the colony? And now, when I am disposed to pass a delightful evening in such agreeable company, do not fancy that I can be stirred up to honourable action. The non-political young ladies will sing, I hope.'

The piano was opened, and Annie played an accompaniment, while Minnie and Harris joined her in singing. George had a cold, and could not sing; Gilbert read the newspaper, whose arguments he meant to demolish, and the two elder girls went into the kitchen to look after tea. Harris had a remarkably fine voice, and knew how to aid without drowning those of his companions; their voices had never sounded so well, and they were delighted with the effect. Tea was only a short interruption; for Annie insisted on Minnie's going over all their old songs together, and Mr. Harris could always extemporise a second or a third, as it was wanted.

Then Mr. Harris, after deploring the want of ladies' society at the Burra, entreated somebody to play a waltz or a polka, for he had not had a dance for six months. Minnie expected George to ask her to dance with him, but Mr. Harris engaged her beforehand, leaving the Elliots to dance with their sisters. When Minnie was tired, her partner danced with Annie, and, to her surprise, George did not ask her hand after she had rested. He spoke very little, and seemed out of spirits; he handed her a book of engravings to look at, but did not himself point out what he liked, and what he hoped she liked. When Mr. Harris was quite tired, he sat down and talked, expressing his intense enjoyment of this evening, which he said he should mark as a white day in his almanack, if he had happened to have one.

'You had rather a black day at Kooringa lately, when the floods came,' said Gilbert.

'And washed the people out of their Burra burrows,' said

Harris. 'I saw a rich scene there and then, Miss Annie. Some honest fellows, miners, who had comfortable houses in the township, went to lend their assistance to the poor half-drowned inhabitants of the holes in the side of the creek. You know, Miss Hodges, that a number of the miners make a hole, rat fashion, to put their heads in, and bring up their families in a subterranean sort of way. This was cheap, but neither healthy nor comfortable, and when the floods came it appeared to be rather an unsafe proceeding. No lives were lost, but a good deal of curious property was floated away. These good fellows I spoke of worked hard to fish out the people from one of these holes. The husband was in the mine at the time, but they had to take out the woman and her children, and she sent them back for a box of clothes, some stools, a chair, and some bedding. The water was rising very fast, and when they had brought out all these articles, and stood gasping to recover their breath, she whined out, 'Oh! please do go in again; there are two nice logs of wood on the fire, and it is a pity they should be lost.' The fellows looked quite disgusted, and walked off, leaving the woman bewailing the loss of her fuel, and wondering how people could be so disobliging. Of course I sympathised with her, though I did not offer to dive for the wood.'

'I suppose you have a considerable population both above and below ground?' said Minnie.

'Upwards of four thousand now, and I am sure they made noise enough for eight thousand at the election. It is quite a rising place, and plenty of business doing. The town will look larger when the burrows are abandoned and substantial cottages erected. The company have warned the miners that they must not live in holes for the future, and have given them six months' notice to quit; but the working men are quite offended at this; they think if they take the risk at their own valuation, the Mining Association should not interfere.'

'You don't mean to say that they have any desire to return to their holes after being so summarily ejected?' said George.

'I saw them baling out the mud the day I left Kooringa for Adelaide,' answered Harris, 'with a view to taking possession again. They are sure to live in them till they are again washed out, or till the six months are up; but they mean to petition for a longer lease. Well, I suppose they are as comfortable as the poor gold diggers on the Turon; that *is* wet work.'

'Gold may be bought too dear,' said George, sententiously. 'I should be sorry to run the risk of losing health and happiness for ever so large nuggets.'

'That monster one of a hundredweight might tempt even the philosophic George,' said Harris. 'Is not it a thousand pities it could not have been sent in time for the Exhibition?

The articles near it would have been overlooked, for such a mass of gold would be the greatest wonder in the Exhibition.'

'I do not think so,' said Margaret. 'It would not tempt me much. I would much rather see something on which skill and labour had been employed, or genius had struck out a world-wide interest from homely materials, than an ugly mass of gold, worth, when dug out of the ground, £3, 17s. 10d. per ounce.'

'I am sure it could not be ugly,' said Annie; 'and if they had carved and brightened it up, it would have looked beautiful.'

'I believe it is as pretty a sight down the Burra mine as anywhere,' said Gilbert. 'I thought when I went down with Henry that it was magnificent; the malachite and variously-coloured ores, with pieces of quartz and crystal sparkling all round, must make it more brilliant than any gold or silver mine in the world.'

It was getting late, and Minnie went to put on her bonnet. She felt that George was stiff and cold, and that she had talked more to Mr. Harris than she ought to have done in the presence of such old friends. She wanted to tell Annie again how really sorry she was not to have come before, when they were alone; but the words stuck in her throat, and when her friend asked her how she liked Mr. Harris, and was so glad that she had had an opportunity of seeing him, she could only say that he was very agreeable, and that she liked him very much. When Grace asked her to come again soon, and hoped she was happy at Mrs. Bantam's, Minnie could contain herself no longer, but told her friends, in confidence, how disagreeable Miss Withering was, and how she worried Mrs. Bantam out of health and spirits.

'So don't fancy that I am forgetting you, or that I am happier there than I should be here, if I do not come so often to see you as we could wish; but pity me for having to entertain or to quarrel with a person whom I so exceedingly dislike.'

'But,' said Margaret quietly, 'you will be happier in the evenings, for both Mr. Bantam and Mr. Reginald are said to be clever, agreeable men.'

'Oh, yes!' said Minnie, blushing, 'you would like Mr. Reginald, Margaret; he is quiet, and not at all funny; he would just suit you, besides that you would agree on politics. And Mr. Bantam plays whist so delightfully ill, and makes Miss Withering so cross; it is fun to see her bristling up with Hoyle at her finger's end when he makes a mistake.'

Mr. Harris had his hat in his hand when Minnie returned to the parlour, and would see her safe to the end of her long and perilous journey next door. George did not offer to

accompany them, nor did Gilbert, but hoped Harris would take good care of her. Minnie did not hear what her companion said, and answered yes and no at random, and was glad when Clara opened the door and she parted from him.

The family at Mr. Bantam's were just breaking up to go to bed, when Minnie entered; but Miss Withering detained her, saying that she wished to have a talk with her by the fire.

'I hope you have spent a pleasant evening, Miss Hodges,' said she; 'I saw three gentlemen going in at the gate immediately after you left us. Are there three Mr. Elliots, or was one a stranger?'

'It was a Mr. Harris, from the Burra, a friend of Grace's intended; I never saw him before.'

'He is taller than either of your friend's brothers, is he not; and a finer figure?'

'Yes, I think he is,' said Minnie.

'Well, what have you been doing all this evening, Miss Hodges? you have been in no hurry home; so I conclude that you have enjoyed yourself very much among your old friends. There is so much cordiality and freedom from restraint in such visiting as yours, and the single strange gentleman would prevent it from being too domestic. I suppose you were singing with the Elliots?'

'Annie and I were singing with Mr. Harris; he sings very well indeed.'

'Better than Mr. George Elliot?'

'Yes, I think he does,—more correctly and scientifically. Annie says she finds him easier to sing with.'

'Well, you must have been very happy. It has been a miserable evening here, for I could not prevail upon Mrs. Bantam to try whist; and though I said I had no objection to dummy, neither of the gentlemen would consent to play under such circumstances; and then, instead of talking, they sat down to read. I do not think Mr. Reginald addressed twelve words to me in the course of the evening.'

'Was he so much interested in the novel I recommended to him?' said Minnie.

'Oh, no! he threw it down, saying he wondered Miss Hodges could like such rubbish; and began to read some work of Carlyle's,—*Heroes and Hero-worship*, I think it was, which I believe he had read before. Such a puerile mind his must be, to require to read anything over again. You understand me better, Miss Hodges; and I really have some pleasure in talking to you. Your mind is a rich though an uncultivated garden, and I feel much disposed to endeavour to do something with it. What shall we talk about to-night? I think that if we were to take the life of Hannibal or Alexander the

Great, and go over the incidents in their order, we should find it a most interesting and improving study.'

'It is late,' said Minnie, 'and my head aches; I could not talk history to-night, even if I were up to the facts, which I am not.'

'How do you teach your sisters history, Miss Hodges, if you are unacquainted with its facts?'

'Oh! they are at the History of England,' said Minnie, with great simplicity; 'and I know that well enough, particularly the first part of it; and then I have the book before me. I do not like to trust to my memory; I might make some mistake.'

'Oral tuition is very much in fashion now,' observed Miss Withering; 'I know some families where they do not allow the governess to use books at all, but insist on her knowing everything independent of them, and require her to be constantly communicating information to her pupils, while they are walking and dressing and even at meal-times.'

'Oh! how I pity the poor governess's head,' exclaimed Minnie.

'Your sandal has got untied, Miss Hodges; you will be sure to break it, if you do not fasten it up.'

'Oh! so it has,' said Minnie; 'I suppose it slipped the knot when I was dancing. How untidy it must have looked!'

'You should always tie it in a double knot; I will show you how it is done. There is a right and a wrong way of doing everything.'

'Oh, Miss Withering,' cried Minnie, 'I must and shall go to bed; you did not help to make the carpet, and of course you are not tired.'

'I never did such a thing in my life,' said Miss Withering, 'and could not think of attempting it. I see you have pricked your fingers sadly; and as for poor Mrs. Bantam, she could not sew at all this evening. In England, some one is sent from the furnishing warehouse to measure the room and fit and make the carpet, which is a much better arrangement. I was forced to try to amuse Mrs. Bantam to-night; I got her to hold several skeins of silk while I wound it. Mr. Reginald never offered to do it when I brought them out.'

But Miss Withering was speaking to the fire or the table, for her auditor had escaped. What a relief it would have been to Minnie to take a good cry, but she dared not do it, for fear that this dreadful woman would observe her. Her only plan was to pretend to be asleep; so though Miss Withering addressed her several times when she came in, she gave no answer. Minnie could not sleep for a long time; she reproached herself for not apologizing to George for her somewhat snappish speech to him at first; for not denying

that she flirted with Reginald; and, above all, for receiving so much attention from Mr. Harris. He ought to have known better than to take so much notice of a stranger when there were three Miss Elliots to talk to; and if she had only had five minutes' quiet conversation with George, all would have been well. But the evening had been spent, and could not be recalled; and George thought she had found new friends whom she preferred.

'And I am sure,' thought Minnie, 'that neither of these gentlemen are half so delightful as George can be. Reginald is too grave, and Harris too flippant; George is so true and honest, and sprightly, too, when he pleases. If Gilbert had been offended with me, I could have gone straight up to him, and explained matters; but I feel more shy with George. I suppose it is because he is older, that I am more afraid of offending him. And to think that Annie really fancied I should like to see a stranger among that dear circle. I hope she does not like that Mr. Harris too well. It was very wrong in me to tell her that I thought him agreeable.'

At last Minnie fell asleep, and dreamed most disagreeable dreams, starting up in bed sometimes and occasionally receiving a sharp poke from Miss Withering's elbow, to admonish her to keep quiet.

CHAPTER XIII

CLARA HAS AN INVITATION, AND GETS A 'SUNDAY OUT'

Minnie felt too ill to get up after her miserable night; she was hot and feverish, and even Miss Withering advised her to take breakfast in bed; so Clara again met Reginald alone in the parlour.

'Miss Morison,' said he, 'I have a message to deliver to you; do not leave the room till you hear it.'

'A message for me! from whom, sir?' said Clara.

'It is from your friend, Mrs. Handy; she is quite grieved that you have never been to see her, and when she heard that I was staying at Mrs. Bantam's, she asked me how you got on. I said that you seemed to work well, but that you looked as if you were ill; and she wishes you to ask Mrs. Bantam to let you take tea with her to-morrow. You will only see her husband, who has just returned from California. Mrs. Handy says she will not believe you are comfortable at all if you do not come, for if Mrs. Bantam refuses you permission, she must be a very unfeeling mistress.'

Clara's face had brightened at the first mention of Mrs. Handy's invitation, but when she thought that all the work and Miss Withering stood in the way of her accepting it, she sighed, and said—

'I fear I cannot be spared, for with so many strangers in the house, there is a great deal to do.'

'I am going out to-morrow,' said Reginald, 'to spend Sunday with a friend in North Adelaide; so I am off the list for that day; and surely Mrs. Bantam will not object to your going out for once, for you really want a change. You will be ill, and I fear I shall have helped to make you so, from the additional work I have inconsiderately brought upon you.'

'I do not mind work, I am strong enough; but do not talk of my being ill,' said Clara nervously. 'What would become of me if I was really ill? Miss Withering would have me sent

to the hospital, and I suppose that my mistress, kind and good as she is, could not bear to be burdened with me, and would take her advice. I must not think of it.'

'If you were in distress, Miss Morison, and a friend offered you assistance, would you be too proud to take it? Will you trust me as a man and a brother, and write to me if you are in want or sickness? Here is my address. I have sisters whom I should be sorry to see friendless in a strange land, as you are. You are as well born and as well educated as they are, and knowing what they would feel, I can understand what you must suffer in your present position.'

Clara took the address in her hand. 'God only knows what is before me, sir,' said she. 'In case of sickness, I might draw on my uncle, through Mr. Campbell, but you know I should be unwilling to do so. I will keep your address, and I will not forget your kindness. It does me good to hear that I have a friend in the world. If circumstances should justify me in applying to you for temporary assistance, I am not too proud to do it—though I have no claim on anybody here, and least of all on you.'

'Only the claim that you may need help, and that I should be glad to give it. It is simple enough, and if our cases were reversed, you would see how natural and proper it is. When I see Mrs. Handy to-day, shall I tell her that you are coming at three to-morrow?'

'I will ask my mistress, and should really like to go above all things. I long to see her kind face again,' said Clara, as she left the room.

Reginald strolled out to look at the weather, and to see if any vessel was signalled. There was an English vessel coming in, if the ball at the flagstaff told the truth, and Reginald determined to go to the post-office as soon as the mail came into town, to inquire for letters. He expected a letter from Julia, not in answer to that which we saw him write at Mrs. Handy's, for the eight months, which has been our course of post, had not expired; but he had only had two short letters from his mother since, telling him that Julia had started for the continent with his sister Alice and Mr. Bisset, and hoping that she was writing to him frequently and fully, describing all she had seen; but till now he had not had a word from Julia. When he got a letter, addressed by her, at the post-office, with a foreign post-mark, and looking very thick and closely written, his spirits rose; but on opening it he found the greater part was written by his sister Alice, and a short, cold letter from Julia was all he received after months of silence. She described what she saw and whom she saw, but said very little about either herself or him. He would have preferred her lively raillery, or even her scolding,

to this chilling indifference; and when he saw that she took it for granted that he had agreed to her proposal to wait till he could return to England, and only mentioned their marriage casually as a very distant event, which she had given up thinking of, he felt doubly anxious to know how she would receive his refusal of her request.

'She loved me once,' thought he, 'and perhaps the earnestness of my appeal may awaken that affection, which all this gaiety and the foolish indulgence she meets with, have so sadly deadened. But she will never be able to accommodate herself to me, so I must try to humour and study her. If I can only make her happy, I shall be happy myself, whatever sacrifice I may have to make. How different is this poor Clara; differently placed and differently minded; but I do not think Julia would feel much for her. If I were not engaged, I should feel tempted to break through all my rules about unequal matches, and appear the most inconsistent of men, by offering a heart and a home to Mrs. Bantam's servant-girl.'

Minnie got up after breakfast, and as her knitting and cotton were done, she begged a piece of work from Mrs. Bantam, for she could not sit idle, and did not feel inclined to read. Mrs. Bantam had nothing at hand, but Miss Withering volunteered to give her employment. It was to knit her trimming for sleeves. She had seen that Minnie knitted fast and well, and as she herself despised such a mechanical kind of work, and yet wanted the thing done, it was a very good arrangement for Miss Withering. So Minnie knitted while Miss Withering talked, for though the narrow strip of muslin was always in the new comer's hands, she got on very slowly with it, for her eloquence was very exacting, and could only have full effect when her eyes were fixed upon her listener. Miss Withering's bearing with regard to Clara had now assumed a new phase; she pitied her, and hinted that she feared she was going into a consumption.

'I heard her coughing last night after you were asleep, Miss Hodges; and really she is so pale and thin, that she looks fitter for an hospital than for service. It is a pity that Mrs. Bantam does not keep two servants, for it is quite painful to look at that poor overworked creature.'

Minnie rose and left the parlour, and found Clara making her bed.

'Clara, you are not well,' said Minnie; 'I meant to do the room to-day, when I had had a rest, for I slept badly last night, and feel a little queer this morning. Let me finish it now, and go to your regular work.'

Clara would not allow this, but Minnie insisted on helping, at any rate, and in a short time all was tidy.

'Thank you, Miss Minnie; the sight of your face does me good,' said Clara.

'I suppose Miss Withering's countenance is not a cordial to you, Clara, any more than it is to me. I think she has talked me ill, and I am quite afraid to go back to sit with her. Will you fetch me my knitting, and I will stay here. Tell Mrs. Bantam where I am, if she inquires.'

Miss Withering was sitting wondering what had taken Miss Hodges away, and what she could find to say to Clara, when the latter entered, and was taking away Minnie's work.

'What a ghost you look, Clara! I think you are falling into a decline, from the cough you have; you should really take care of yourself, and not take too much fatigue. Will you bring me my pocket-handkerchief from the bed-room, and tell Miss Hodges that she has left me quite alone; and that I want the knitting to be made broader as it gets to the middle; I will show her how it is to be managed.'

Minnie reluctantly returned, and received instructions from head-quarters as to the trimming. All day she submitted to Miss Withering's persecution with an aching heart but uncomplaining tongue; but in the evening, when Mr. Bantam had gone out on business, and Mr. Reginald looked too dull to amuse her, she could hold her head up no more. She entreated Mrs. Bantam to let her go to bed.

'Certainly, my dear. I hope you may have a sleep, for that will do you more good than anything.'

'I scarcely expect to sleep, but I shall rest,' said Minnie.

'Shall I come with you to amuse you?' said Miss Withering.

'Oh no!' said Minnie, trying to disguise her horror at the proposal. 'Do not give yourself any trouble about me. I shall be well to-morrow, I dare say.'

She had lain down about ten minutes when she heard a gentle tap at the door.

'Who is there?' said she.

'It is Clara. I want to know if you would like anything— if I can do anything for you.'

'Yes, you can. Bring me a glass of water and a candle, if you please; I put mine out, and I should like to read now.'

The candle was brought, but Minnie's eyes ached, and she could not see.

'Shall I read to you?' said Clara; 'perhaps it might set you to sleep.'

'Perhaps it may,' said Minnie, recollecting the drawling way in which the servants at home read.

Clara opened the book, even the silly novel, and read so sweetly, so musically, that Minnie felt relieved by the sound of her voice. She finished the novel, for Minnie had got near the end of it; and as she declared she was not tired, her

listener began to ponder what she should like to hear next.

'Can you read poetry as well as prose?' said she. 'I like nothing so well as hearing poetry read to me, if it is well read. Get me Tennyson's Poems from the parlour, there's a good girl, and let me hear you read some of them.'

Clara returned with the news that Mr. Reginald was reading the book that was wanted. Would Miss Minnie like her to ask for it?

'Oh, no, it is of no consequence,' said Minnie.

'But, Miss Minnie, I know many of Tennyson's poems by heart. I will repeat them if you would like it.'

'I should like it exceedingly.'

So Clara repeated the 'Talking Oak' with spirit and fanciful feeling. She asked if Minnie was tired, but she was in a state of tranquil enjoyment, and begged Clara to go on. She then began 'Locksley Hall,' and gave it with all the indignant bitterness which the poet throws into it, but which, perhaps, poor Amy did not deserve. Mr. Reginald passed the door once or twice during this recitation, and stopped to listen to the sound of what he had been reading, as if life and reality had been given to it through the utterance of this poor servant-girl. When he heard her scornful way of treating a love which was not 'love for ever-more,' he thought that when Clara loved it would be for once and for ever, and he shrank from the mockery which Julia offered him as an exchange for a true heart. He determined to go home to his station on Monday morning, to relieve Clara from the trouble and humiliation of his presence—he had gratified a selfish desire to see into her character at the expense of her comfort, but he was determined to do so no more.

Clara wound up with 'The Lotos-eaters,' which she rehearsed so dreamily that it sent Minnie into a sound sleep; and then, as it was late, and Mrs. Bantam had told her she need not sit up, she went to her attic to go to bed.

What a bright day this had been to her—Mr. Reginald's interest in her, the invitation from Mrs. Handy, her mistress's consent that she should go out for the whole afternoon, the pleasure of reading aloud and repeating her favourite verses to that kind-hearted girl, whom Miss Withering had tormented as well as herself, for she was sure that Minnie's illness had been either occasioned or aggravated by that evil-disposed person—all these things filled her mind with a joy and thankfulness which could only find a vent in tears. She looked at the address again; she was glad to know Mr. Reginald's Christian name; she felt that he respected her, and that his offer of assistance was no insult. She sat half-dreaming on her box, with her face buried in her hands. 'He may love Minnie, but still he esteems me; and Minnie does not care

for him—her heart is elsewhere; I am convinced of that.'

Clara's heart was lifted up to heaven that night in devout thankfulness that life was again a blessing. One is not apt to feel religious influences when simply uncomfortably unhappy, but the depth of misery, or the lighting up of the heart after it draws the soul to the Giver of all good. In her desolation, in the sharp pangs of jealousy, in the anguish that for the last fortnight she had endured, Clara had turned for help to God, and now in her comparative happiness she acknowledged his hand.

'I shall not be at church to-morrow,' said she; 'how dreadful my uncle would think my neglect of the public ordinances of religion! but I want the sunshine of human sympathy and human friendship, and I trust that I have enough of religion within me to purify me from the worldliness of the week.'

Miss Withering was of opinion that Clara was likely to catch a severe cold if she exposed herself to the night air, and, for the girl's own sake, urged Mrs. Bantam to insist on her coming home before dark, in time to get tea for the family; but when Minnie heard that she was going to see the only friend she had in the colony, and that this was the first time she had asked for permission to pay a visit, she offered to get tea, and hoped Clara would enjoy herself. Minnie had been very much struck with Clara's accomplishments, from which she had derived benefit the previous evening; and expressed such a warm interest in her, that Mrs. Bantam resolved she would never let Miss Withering shake her confidence in her servant again.

Clara walked now through green plots and then through dirty streets, for there was nearly a mile between Mrs. Bantam's and Mrs. Handy's, and Adelaide is not half built upon. Wherever grass could grow, it came up green even in corners of streets. Wherever Clara could find it, she would even go out of her way to tread on it,—sometimes half creeping through a dilapidated fence to go over a whole acre of green turf, full of yellow flowers. She picked a few little blossoms, and found that they were fragrant enough, though the sweetest were too small to look beautiful until they were closely inspected.

She went round by the back way, in case of meeting Brown, Oscar, and Co. going out for their Sunday stroll, and found Mrs. Handy watching for her at the door. She kissed her, and brought her into her own little room.

'Handy is out for a walk, but he will be in soon,' said she; 'so tell me all the news before he comes. Of course you would not like to tell me how you like your place before him, as he is a stranger. Mr. Reginald told me that you were the most elegant hand-maid he ever saw, and that you did every-

thing so nicely. I knew you would try, but it is a wonder that you have strength to do so much. And your mistress is kind, and your master quiet; and if your visitors are all like Mr. Reginald, they will not give you much trouble.'

Mrs. Handy then took off Clara's bonnet and shawl, and drew off her gloves, saying that really her hands looked wonderful, considering; 'and I must say, Miss Morison, though you are thinner, and have lost your colour, you are quite as lady-like as ever. I did not let my husband know you were at service; he fancies you are a governess, so give yourself a few airs, and he will believe it. And tell me when you heard from Miss Waterstone, and how she is getting on.'

Clara told all she knew of her friend, and also that she had met a fellow-passenger in the street the other day, who told her he could do anything he liked with servant girls, but who had not succeeded in finding out where she lived, though he seemed very anxious to know. Then she told what difficulty she found in learning to work, and how patient Mrs. Bantam had been with her. She asked if Mr. Reginald had mentioned Miss Minnie Hodges' name, or told Mrs. Handy what a pleasant girl she was.

'He only said there were two ladies visiting at the Bantams', but mentioned no names. The Hodges are neighbours of the Caumrays, and Mrs. Caumray feels quite bitter because Mrs. Hodges will take no notice of her or her family. Now that she has got a genteel accomplished governess for Janey, she thinks she is as good, if not better, than Mrs. Hodges, whose eldest girl has to teach the little ones.'

Clara next mentioned Miss Withering, and said that she did not like her at all. She knew that it was not considered quite correct to criticise her master's guests to a stranger; but if Mrs. Handy had kept her secret from her own husband, it was not likely that any of her other revelations would be repeated; and she felt great relief in telling her troubles to ears that heard, instead of to senseless paper. She next asked how the house got on,—if the gentlemen made as much fun of poor Mr. Blinker as ever, and if Miss Waterstone's friend, the overseer, had ever been in town again; not that she cared very much to know, but she knew it would please Mrs. Handy if she expressed curiosity. She learned that poor Blinker, after having endured persecution till all his money was spent, came to the conclusion that he did not know what to do, and was much obliged to Humberstone for seizing upon him, and taking him to the country where he said he would make a man of him. He was to be a hut-keeper at first, and if he was worthy of promotion, he was to be advanced to take a flock of sheep. Oscar and Brown had

talked to him of Arcadia and corrosive sublimate; of pastoral pipes, of damper and shifting hurdles, till he was in a state bordering on distraction. He had come into the kitchen, and asked Mrs. Handy if they put corrosive sublimate into the dampers, or how did they make them damp—was it by pouring water on them after they were baked, or by boiling them for awhile? She had told him that damper was a wrong name, for it was the driest description of bread that could be made, except biscuits; but that he would be shown how it was to be made when he got to the station—he would have nothing to do but to follow directions; this had relieved him, and he went off next day with Humberstone, quite happy.

When Mr. Handy came in, Miss Morison was introduced to him, and the new girl, Leonora, got tea. It was new and delightful to Clara to take tea in company with any one—to be asked to take another cup—to be pressed to try another piece of seed-cake. Mr. Handy was cumbrously polite and paid her several slow compliments, but Clara was in elysium, and not at all critical; she thought the attention and the compliments could not be improved, they were so pleasant. Mr. and Mrs. Handy talked a good deal about Reginald, and all in high praise of his many good qualities.

'Now, should not you think, Miss Morison,' said Mrs. Handy, 'that when my husband had got home to his own comfortable house, he would be inclined to stop at home, and not to wander to the ends of the earth again to seek for gold?'

'I am sure,' said Clara, 'that such a pleasant tea-table as this should make you very reluctant to go through as much discomfort and privation as you must have suffered in California.'

'The tea is very well in its way, Miss,' said Mr. Handy, 'particularly in such pleasant company as we are favoured with this evening; but when a man comes home, and cannot get work at his trade, he feels quite lost. I should like to take a turn at Bathurst, till things work themselves right in Adelaide. I am a builder by trade, and that business is very slack just now. It is all very fine talking about the hard life in California, but that only makes me inclined to try if I could not take it easier in New South Wales. And *that* hundred-weight of gold!—I cannot get over that. Suppose I were to pick up such a bit, Betsy, would not you set up for a lady directly? Oscar, Brown, and the rest, would have to march in double-quick time, and we would buy a place in the country, and live in peace and quietness.'

'You don't seem to value peace and quietness much, Handy, or you would remain where you are now. He had not been

Clara Gets a 'Sunday Out'

home a week, when he began to talk of going off again. It is not fair to me; is it, Miss Morison?'

'Well, Betsy, if I had brought you anything back from California besides myself I should have liked to stop; but whatever I made there by hard work went to feed a parcel of sharks that cheated folk right and left.'

'But the Sydney people will cheat you quite as cleverly as the others. You know that most of the diggers are old convicts,' said Mrs. Handy.

'I am sure they are better than the Californian rascals; if they were not convicts before they came, they deserved to be every day of their lives that I had anything to do with them. An honest man has no chance among them; but there is more law and justice in New South Wales. There is a settled responsible government there, and not so much of Judge Lynch's authority.'

Clara asked some questions about the state of California, and the methods of obtaining the gold, but Mr. Handy was too sore upon the subject to tell anything but how he had been overreached; he would give no general information, but was copious concerning his personal experiences.

Mr. and Mrs. Handy promised to see Clara home, so she was in no hurry to go, and sat chatting happily till near ten o'clock. She parted with her friends at the corner of the street, got in quietly, and was not found fault with for being too late.

CHAPTER XIV

MRS. BANTAM AND MINNIE LAY A PLOT TO GET QUIT OF MISS WITHERING

As Miss Withering would not go to chapel upon any consideration, and disliked to go to church by herself, Minnie, though in general a chapel-goer, felt obliged to accompany her, and was entertained with lectures on the ignorance and vulgarity of the great proportion of dissenting teachers, both in the way to church and on her return. In the afternoon, Miss Withering yawned over a volume of sermons, which she complained were rather superficial, and took the book into her bed-room, thinking she might be able to fix her mind upon her studies if she were undisturbed.

Mrs. Bantam and Minnie canvassed Miss Withering's character in her absence, and found themselves of one mind on the subject.

'I think I know now why newcomers are called Griffins in India. It has not been adopted here, but it is very appropriate to Miss Withering. She is a Griffin,' said Minnie.

'I wish I could tell her to go away,' said Mrs. Bantam; 'but I cannot do such a thing even to a servant without its disturbing me for a week; and she is such a clever woman that I know I should feel ten times worse if I quarrelled with her. Could you not do it, Minnie?'

'I have said more rude things to Miss Withering than I ever thought I could say to any one, but it has no effect upon her except to make her say more disagreeable things.'

'What does she say to you? I think she is more polite to you than to me,' said Mrs. Bantam.

'Oh, it is not what she says, but her spiteful way of saying it, that makes me so uncomfortable,' said Minnie. 'Would not Mr. Bantam quarrel with her if you asked him? I think he grows thinner every day she is here.'

'I could not trust Mr. Bantam; if he could be roused to say anything he would say a great deal too much, and then

Mrs. Bantam and Minnie Lay a Plot

she will spread such reports about us. She says such things about people she knows, it makes me quite afraid to give her a handle. I do not know how I can manage it.'

'I have got an idea that may do,' said Minnie. 'You know she is always asking Clara to do unreasonable things for her; let Clara refuse, and you can take her part. I think that may make a breach wide enough to get Miss Withering out of the house through.'

'It is really a capital thought, Minnie. Well, two heads are better than one; I never should have contrived such a plan by myself. I will tell Clara about it as soon as she comes home. I am quite thankful for your suggestion.'

And Mrs. Bantam began to read with some composure, while Minnie's thoughts wandered no further than next door. She must go and see the Elliots again to-morrow, and try to get George to be once more friendly.

Reginald returned from North Adelaide about eight o'clock in the evening, and told Mrs. Bantam that he found he must return to his station immediately.

'I am sorry you are leaving us so soon,' said Mrs. Bantam, 'and still more distressed to see that you have derived no benefit from the change of air. You look quite as ill as when you came. Could you not stay another week to see what that would do for you?'

'You seem to be in a great hurry, Reginald,' said Mr. Bantam. 'I understood the visit was to be for a month, and unless you give us good and sufficient reasons, I shall not be inclined to let you go. I feel quite disappointed in my visitors. Here is Reginald, who came here looking ill, now going away worse; and poor Minnie, who came blooming like a rose, looks more like a lily now; and——'

'What of me, Mr. Bantam?' said Miss Withering, with a very stern expression.

'Oh!' said Mr. Bantam, shrinking into himself, 'I do not see much change upon you. Your constitution seems not to be affected by the air of Adelaide, which has told so sadly on poor Minnie, and even the servant girl seems to suffer from it too. But I must drive you down to the sea-side some fine day this week, Minnie, and see if I cannot bring back your roses.'

'By-the-bye, Mr. Reginald, I think you are fond of reading manuscript,' said Miss Withering. 'Read this aloud, and guess where I found it.'

It was not a large piece of paper that she handed to him. The writing was in a plain round hand, and appeared to be only a fragment, for it terminated abruptly. He saw it was in verse, and after glancing down a line or two to get into the rhythm read as follows:—

'Lords of creation! how I envy you!
What in these stirring times can woman do?
Shut up each avenue, close-barred each gate,
Every approach forbid her to the Great!
Even if Ambition does not fire her soul,
If Independence merely is her goal,
Scarce can her head and hands, however good,
Earn that small pittance, even a livelihood.
The pleasure, too, of giving is forbid;
How much good will lies in her dormant, hid!
The power to bless, relieve, protect, maintain—
Her nature longs for—struggles for—in vain.
Thus the sad teacher, or domestic slave,
Feeling her toil but drag her to the grave,
Looks for a refuge from her war with life
Even as a loveless and indifferent wife;
Dashes the tear-drops from rebellious eyes,
Veils the heart's image of Love's happy skies,
Stifles the proud thoughts that across her come,
And marries—not a husband—but a home.

'But surely *I* shall never stoop so low,
I shall not tamely yield to Fortune's blow—
Not necessary is it to be great,
Or rich or honour'd, 'tis the chance of fate;
Or loved or even happy;—wise men say
Life was not meant to be a holiday.
Through many pangs the soul shakes off the dust;
I *must* do right,—that is the *only* must.
Shake off——'

Reginald had not read far before he was as certain that Clara had composed and written these lines as if she had told him so. But though he was sure that Miss Withering had come unfairly by them, and shrank from making the inmost thoughts of the poor girl public, he could not stop without betraying her secret, and he accordingly read all the verses.

'Where did you get this?' said he, almost fiercely. 'It is not your own writing, is it, Miss Withering?'

'No, indeed! I do not write like a charity-school girl. This is my writing,' said Miss Withering, showing her name on the fly-leaf of her book of sermons, in which the letters were all length and no breadth, and formed a complete contrast to poor Clara's business-like hand.

'Is it written by any friend of yours?' asked Minnie.

'I knew that none of you would find it out. It is some of Clara's scribbling. She seems fond of copying poetry, or she would not have taken the trouble to write out such stuff; but perhaps it is for the improvement of her hand.'

Mrs. Bantam and Minnie Lay a Plot

'How did you come into possession of it? I am sure she did not give it to you to criticize,' said Reginald.

'Why, I missed my brooch this afternoon, and I thought I would just look if Clara had not picked it up by mistake. Girls do such things sometimes, you know. And there, between the leaves of Longfellow's poems (that was the odd name of the author), I found this slip of paper sticking out. I thought I should like to see what was in it, and then that you would like to see it too, for Miss Hodges has such an idea of Clara's taste in poetry, that perhaps she will admire this precious fragment.'

'I wonder at you,' said Minnie. 'I am ashamed of you, Miss Withering. Your brooch is safe. I put it away this morning in its proper place. You know I have arranged the room ever since I came here, and you should not have been going up like a spy into Clara's garret, until you had asked me if I had seen the brooch, and Mrs. Bantam if she would give you leave to do such a thing. English ladies may think this sort of conduct right, but colonial people think differently.'

'Ah! you have a great deal to learn yet, Miss Hodges,' said Miss Withering. 'It is quite a customary thing in England, and I have heard so many strange tales about Australian servants, that I did not think it necessary to stand upon ceremony with Clara. But are you sure my brooch is safe? I should be quite grieved to lose it.'

Mrs. Bantam would fain have taken Minnie's side of the question, and rebuked Miss Withering's over-suspicion; but she could not hit upon the exact words to say, and her courage died during the hesitating delay.

'You will oblige me, and I am sure Mrs. Bantam too, by taking this piece of paper and putting it exactly where you found it. I will go with you and carry the candle,' said Minnie, resolutely.

Mrs. Bantam wished the manuscript to be replaced; Mr. Bantam agreed that they had no right to keep it; and Reginald was relieved to see Minnie mounting guard, and insisting that it be done.

'Though these lines are not half so pretty as what Clara repeated to me last night,' said Minnie, when she returned to the parlour, 'perhaps that was the reason she copied them, for she might not think them pretty enough to learn, and yet be unwilling to lose them altogether. Is it not strange, Mr. Reginald, that Clara should have such a taste for poetry, and her reading aloud is the most beautiful I ever heard. None of the Elliots have such variety in their tones, though they are admirable readers too.'

'I should like to know the Elliots,' said Reginald. 'I hear that they are such a fine family altogether.'

'I wish you knew them,' said Minnie. 'I know which of them you would like best. Margaret is exactly to your taste, I should think. She is so clever, and knows so much, but yet has no pretension about her; you really must get introduced to them—don't you know George or Gilbert?'

'I know George a little, from seeing him in Ainslie's store; I must fish for an invitation the next time I meet him. He seems a fine, intelligent young man.'

'They are all intelligent,' said Minnie; 'but though Gilbert is very clever, I consider Margaret the genius of the family.'

Reginald had rather a horror of 'the genius of the family' in general, and he doubted Minnie's ability to judge of what would suit his taste; but yet he did wish to know a family whom every one respected, and a good many people loved, and he had had his curiosity raised with regard to the second Miss Elliot years ago.

'Margaret, is not that the young lady I used to hear Dent talk so much about?' said Reginald. 'He used to come to my station, and talk in the evening of his fair lady.'

'Yes, it was Margaret that he admired so much, though they were very unlike each other,' said Minnie.

'I cannot think what made the man confide so much in me,' said Reginald. 'He struck me as being a close, reserved man, and yet he unbosomed himself regularly every time he came to Taringa, until he had actually proposed. He never could bring himself to confess the refusal.'

'He was certainly close and cautious in money matters,' Minnie said, 'but this love seemed to be a thing he could not keep to himself. He told papa all about it in the same way, and papa, as in duty bound, told it over again to mamma and me. What Mr. Dent admired in Margaret I cannot conceive; he did not think her pretty, and I am sure he did not appreciate her talents.'

'Perhaps her manners were frank, and that to a man like Dent is a great attraction,' said Reginald.

'No—Margaret's manner is cold, and to him was particularly so. She had no money, no position, and few accomplishments, and yet he liked her notwithstanding; and in spite of his money, his position, and his perseverance, Margaret could not like him.

'My taste is so diametrically opposed to Mr. Dent's, that I cannot think of admiring Miss Margaret Elliot. I never can be his rival.'

'Oh, you don't know till you see,' said Minnie; 'don't be too sure.'

When Reginald saw Clara in the morning, he was pleased

Mrs. Bantam and Minnie Lay a Plot

to see how much better she looked. 'Have I not prescribed well for you?' said he. 'You look quite a different being to-day—you must go to see Mrs. Handy whenever you are afraid of being ill. I am going to my station again this morning, and I feel relieved to see that I have not killed you outright.'

'There is a great deal of vitality left in me yet,' said Clara, smiling, 'and I think even Miss Withering will not succeed in crushing it out of me. While Miss Minnie remains here, I shall not mind the other much.'

She looked straight into Reginald's face while she said this, to see if he really cared much for Minnie.

'Yes, that young lady is a visitor among a thousand. Without great abilities or much cultivation, she has a steady, fearless uprightness and truth in her that are very delightful to see.'

'She is very pretty,' said Clara.

'Do you think so, Miss Morison? I consider her pleasing in her appearance, but I do not think her pretty.'

'Hush! I must go now; I hear Miss Minnie coming out of her room.'

'Good bye; do not forget my address.'

'Good bye; I am much obliged to you,' said Clara, as she hurried out of the room.

Reginald left Adelaide immediately after breakfast, leaving no one to regret him much but Clara, who, though she had been miserable when he was near, felt now that she missed him, and scolded herself for being so very unreasonable. Mrs. Bantam proposed that Minnie should take the room which he had occupied, which Minnie would gladly have done, to escape, for some part of her time, from her tormentor; but Miss Withering would not part with her, and assured Mrs. Bantam that, in Miss Hodges' present state of health, it would be highly dangerous for her to change her sleeping-room. So, as they trusted soon to get rid of Miss Withering herself by following Minnie's ingenious plan, of which they had made Clara cognizant, they thought she might as well remain in the same room while she stayed in Adelaide.

But as if by some instinctive knowledge of the snare laid for her, Miss Withering seemed determined to ask Clara to do nothing so unreasonable as to justify opposition. Clara could not refuse to brush her dresses, though it took up a great deal of valuable time; nor to fetch her pocket handkerchief from the next room, though Miss Withering could easily have done it herself; so things remained *in statu quo*.

Minnie would not take Miss Withering's hints of her curiosity to see the Elliots, and as Mrs. Bantam could not go without her incubus, she went by herself in the afternoon. She went early enough to have a good talk with Annie, and

she hoped that when George came home she should not be too flurried to speak comfortably to him.

Annie was alone, and delighted to see her. 'I have been wondering if you would come to-day, for I feel so dull,' said she. 'Grace and Margaret have gone an hour ago to spend a long evening with Mrs. Plummer, and have left me to keep the house. Gilbert is going to dine with the Plummers, and will bring them home in the evening, so George and I shall be much the better for your company. How is Miss Withering?'

'Oh, the griffin! She gets worse and worse. She has driven Mr. Reginald out of the house, and I should gladly follow. In time she will send Clara away too, and then we shall see Mr. and Mrs. Bantam slowly taking leave of their paradise, and leaving her "monarch of all she surveys." You will have an observing neighbour then—I advise you to keep your blinds down as it is. But I was much comforted the other night by the servant Clara reading aloud to me, and repeating poetry so softly and so sweetly, that it really felt like a balm to my ears and nerves, after they had been irritated by Miss Withering's sharp, inquisitive, mischief-making voice. I cannot help thinking that Clara must be a lady, her accent is so beautiful.'

'It is rather strange,' said Annie, 'but perhaps she might have been a shop-girl in some fashionable milliner's establishment. Those girls pick up the accent from the people they serve, you know. But you must see Gilbert's letter to the newspaper, if you promise not to tell whose it is, for of course it is anonymous. Margaret helped him with it, and George criticised their joint production, so you must really read it all through. I think it is very clever myself.'

Minnie read it all, and admired it as much as her friend expected.

'Why does not George write something of his own?' said Minnie.

'Oh! you know George is not half so clever as Gilbert, though, *entre nous*, Minnie, I like him the best. Besides, poor George seems very dull and out of spirits lately. I think Mr. Ainslie is very unreasonable in making him go back to work at the office in the evenings. You know his hours are long enough through the day. But he told me he should not need to go back to-night, and that is pleasant. And now, Minnie, we must try over the new songs Mr. Harris has lent me. They belonged to his sister; you see the name, Maria Harris, at the beginning of the book, in her own hand, I suppose, and a beautiful hand it is. I really wish I did not write such a scrawl myself; but you don't write any better, and that is one comfort.'

Mrs. Bantam and Minnie Lay a Plot

They tried over several songs, and were sure that George would be able to take a part in some of the prettiest, when he came home.

'I suppose Grace and Margaret will spend a duller evening at Mrs. Plummer's than we shall do at home,' said Annie; 'for Mrs. Plummer never thinks of inviting anybody to meet them, as Grace is engaged, and Margaret has so much sense. Mrs. Plummer is very prosy, and she never talks on any subject but the state of baby's teeth—I am *so* tired of those eye-teeth! As I am volatile, and like to talk, I am sometimes favoured with a strange face; and I have several times met a certain Mr. William Bell lately; such a strange fellow he is, Minnie; I should like you to see him, and to tell me what you think of him. He contradicts everybody, and me in particular, a great deal more than I like; he would argue every point with George and Gilbert, instead of concurring with them, or letting the thing pass, as Mr. Harris does. Mrs. Plummer says he is an admirer of mine, but it must be an odd sort of admiration; I don't think I could win a compliment from him if I were to try for a month. And, strange enough, George has taken quite a fancy to this Mr. Bell, and says he thinks he shall make a fast friend of him. He is a brother of the James Bell who died a short while ago—you saw the death in the papers; he was in business in Hindley-street; I don't know whether William means to carry on the concern. But, bless me! Minnie, here comes George, and I have quite forgotten his dinner; the potatoes will be soup by this time, for we have sung six songs since I put them on. Do talk to him, and keep him in good humour while I try to make them presentable.'

Minnie blessed these potatoes from the bottom of her heart, for it is so seldom that young people in the middle ranks of society have an uninterrupted moment together, to make up any little misunderstanding, that the opportunity was as rare as it was desirable. A frank look and smile to George when he came in, an expression of her pleasure that there was no stranger with him to-day, and that he did not need to go back to his work, seemed to make her peace, for he never thought of jealousy again. There was no Mr. Harris to eclipse him at home, and the relieved manner in which Minnie mentioned Reginald's departure, convinced him that his suspicions in that quarter were unfounded.

Minnie exhausted part of her grudge against Mr. Harris by talking slightly of him all dinner time, which made her friend warm in his defence. She began to fear that Annie's heart was in danger; but if he liked George, and would follow his advice, Mr. Everard Harris might make a tolerable husband after all. George's hoarseness, which had been

brought on in a great measure by shouting for unsuccessful candidates at the elections, was quite gone by this time, and he sung with the girls with great success. He begged Minnie to listen to a really fine article from the 'Edinburgh Review,' which had struck him when reading by himself; he showed her some drawings which he had just finished, and hoped she would like them; in short, he was delightful, and Minnie did not think it near time to go when she heard the gate open and saw the other members of the family come in.

'We have had such a delightful evening!' said Annie. 'I have been pitying you three sadly, for you have been where you had neither books, nor music, nor conversation, and we have been revelling in all of them.'

'Neither books nor music, certainly, but enough of conversation,' said Margaret.

'Of course,' said Annie, 'you had the progress of the teeth brought down to the latest date, and Mr. Plummer has been lording it over Gilbert because he is a government officer, while Gilbert is only a lawyer's clerk, who has not even got articles; and talking magniloquently of 'our department of the public service;' but surely you do not call that conversation, Margaret?'

'No, I do not; but we had other speakers and better subjects; at least another speaker,' said Margaret. 'We met one of the most brilliant birds of passage I ever saw—a Mr. Staynes, on his way to Sydney. He has seen all the great writers of the day, and does not point out their faults or disagreeable peculiarities, but admires them after seeing them quite as much as we do unseen. Your friend, William Bell, was at Mr. Plummer's, too, quite eclipsed, but resigned; and he listened without contradicting very much.'

'He asked for you, Annie,' said Grace; 'and Mrs. Plummer looked quite sly on the subject. Gilbert asked him to come in, but he said it was too late, and promised to spend an evening with us some other day.'

'He walked home with me,' said Margaret, "and really, Annie, he is quite agreeable when you have him, as we Scotch say, to a 'two-handed crack'.'

I suppose you mean *tête-à-tête*, Margaret,' said Minnie.

'I mean nothing so tender as that,' said Margaret.

'And were you sewing all the evening?' said Annie. 'Mrs. Plummer has always a nice piece of work for her young friends when they come to visit her.'

'I had something in my hands,' said Margaret, 'but it got on very slowly.'

'What was this Mr. Staynes like, Gilbert? It is of no use asking Margaret,' said Annie.

Mrs. Bantam and Minnie Lay a Plot

'Much plainer than even William Bell,' said Gilbert, 'and not so tall. Grey eyes, fair hair, and a dull complexion, but he speaks pure English, and choice English, and seems to know everything. However, he must be at least five years older than I am, and I do not mean to remain stationary; though we are ill-provided with the means of improvement in the colonies, I shall surely be able to make something of myself by that time.'

'I must go now,' said Minnie, 'it is surely very late.'

'Only twelve o'clock,' said George. 'Time flies swiftly when we are among friends.'

Minnie found George ready to escort her home, and in the tone of his voice in wishing her good night, and the pressure of his hand at parting, she felt an assurance that she was loved by him. She did not care whether Miss Withering was up or not, she was indifferent now to either her talk or her silence. All the family had gone to bed but Clara, who opened the door for her, but she did not want to go to bed just then. She sat for an hour and a half by the parlour fire, which went out while she thought how happy she was.

George was poor, but time would amend that; he was only a merchant's clerk, while she was the daughter of a wealthy stockholder, and a justice of peace for the province besides. But she felt that there was really no disparity between them, and that by and bye her father would see that he could have no son-in-law so good and suitable in every way as George Elliot. There was no hurry for the marriage. Minnie must remain at home at any rate for several years to come, to educate her sisters, and by the time the youngest was out of the school-room, George would be thirty-one, and Minnie herself twenty-five, a very proper age, just the ages of her father and mother when they were married; and surely George would be rich enough to begin life with her in a quiet way then. Minnie recollected a thousand little words and looks which convinced her that she was not mistaken, and that George had liked her for a long time, when she had never dreamed of such a thing. Even his sulkiness last Friday was confirmation strong. How delightful it is when a girl's first intimation of the love she feels is awakened by the consciousness that she is beloved! Minnie wanted no declaration, no engagement; she rested in her present happiness with perfect satisfaction.

Minnie looked so well and cheerful next day that Miss Withering was convinced that she must have entered into a clandestine engagement with one of the Elliots. She had no faith in human nature, and could not fancy a girl's looking happy unless she had done something wrong. She determined to watch Minnie narrowly, and if she had her convictions

strengthened by observations, to communicate with Mrs. Bantam, and even if she found it necessary, with Mr. Hodges. These things should be taken in time; Mr. Hodges had evidently no desire for an increased intimacy on his daughter's part with this low family, and he would feel very much shocked and very grateful for her timely discovery. He was a man whom a clever woman could turn round her finger, and he was very likely to engage Miss Withering on handsome terms to look after the education and right training of his family, which Minnie by her duplicity would have shown herself quite incapable of doing.

These were pleasant thoughts for Miss Withering, and made her more than usually polite to every one, and even to Clara, to whom she presented an old gown with great condescension. How Clara longed to refuse it! but she swallowed down her proud heart, and heroically said, 'thank you,' determining to give it to the first black woman who might come to chop wood. It was old and oddly made, but her acquaintance, Black Mary, would make no objection, and would be very much the better for a gown, for she had nothing at present but an opossum skin rug, and an old drawn silk bonnet, which had once been white. The dress was a morning wrapper, and drew in with strings, so that it would be sure to fit; and it had also a capacious pocket, which would charm Mary's heart. Mary occupied a considerable part of Clara's next letter to Susan, which she now mustered courage enough to write; she described Minnie at great length, slightly touched upon Miss Withering's character, but did not mention Mr. Reginald's name. She described the delightful visit to Mrs. Handy's, chronicled the weather, the appearance of the country, and the political news, so far as she had gathered them from broken scraps of conversation when she was waiting at table. It was what Mr. Morison would have called a good letter, for it contained a great deal of information clearly expressed, but Clara knew that Susan would be disappointed with it, for it was empty of those delicious personalities which sister expects from sister. 'Any other person might have written this,' she said to herself, bitterly, when she laid it aside, 'but I cannot make a better one. I cannot write how I feel, for it would only make Susan miserable.'

In her journal she felt at liberty to write without reserve. She wrote how absurd it was in her to regret Reginald, for it would be the best thing that could happen that she should never see him again; noting it first in short-hand; then not feeling much relieved, repeating it in long-hand; and at last burning it lest any one by any chance might see and be able to read it. She then imagined herself in the parlour, and wrote down a fanciful conversation, in which she bore a

Mrs. Bantam and Minnie Lay a Plot

principal part. She differed from Miss Withering on every point, supported Miss Minnie, and contradicted her master and mistress most unscrupulously whenever she put any absurdity into their mouths, which was not seldom. Nor had she said half she intended, when Mrs. Bantam roused her from her interesting employment by bidding her bring in supper, as Miss Withering had got very hungry over a keen discussion.

CHAPTER XV

CLARA HAS AN OPPORTUNITY OF SEEING HER FELLOW-PASSENGERS

The discussion which had occasioned Miss Withering's hunger, had been on the subject of marriage, and the motives which should induce thereunto; and Miss Hodges had advanced such dangerous and heterodox opinions with regard to this important matter, that her benevolent friend was certain that there was something very wrong going on.

'There can be no excuse for marriage but love,' said Minnie. 'I am sure I never could bring myself to marry for friendship, because I should have to leave so many dear friends, that I should be the loser if my husband did not love me as much as all of them together, and if I did not love him quite as much.'

'You do not mean to say that circumstances, position, and connexions are to be overlooked,' remarked Miss Withering. 'I think it a very impertinent proposal when a young gentleman offers a young lady an inferior home, fewer comforts, and a lower position, all merely to gratify a selfish feeling, which he dignifies by the name of love.'

'There is some truth in that, Minnie,' said Mr. Bantam. 'I think, unless a man is her equal, that he has no right to urge a union with a young lady. Don't *you* marry to be worse off than you are, for marriage brings so many cares and toil upon you that you do not need poverty to aggravate them.'

'Indeed,' added Mrs. Bantam, 'young people are very apt to think too lightly of the advantages of a comfortable home. They fancy that if they are only fond enough of each other, the butcher's and baker's bills will be paid somehow; but there is nothing like poverty coming in at the door for making love fly out of the window.'

'Debt is indeed a wretched thing,' said Minnie, 'and even the most affectionate pair could not be considered happy if they owed money which they could not pay. And I should

like always to have enough to eat; but I have not many wants, and should not break my heart because I wore gingham while my neighbours wore silk.'

'But when people are poor, and have much drudgery to do, they get so very coarse-looking,' said Miss Withering; 'and in a climate like this, if ladies have toil and cares, even when in comfortable circumstances'—and here she glanced at Mrs. Bantam—'sufficient to plant wrinkles in their cheeks before their time, what must poverty superadded bring a poor young wife and mother to? I had heard in England that people faded very fast here, and so I was in some measure prepared; but I must confess that those ladies you took me to call on the other day, looked so miserable and careworn, that I was quite shocked at their appearance. And the neglected children, who were in everybody's way, must be a great drag upon their unfortunate mothers. I have quite made up my mind to remain single unless I could marry a gentleman worth at least eighteen hundred a year—and even then I think I should be thrown away upon such specimens as I have yet seen.'

Mr. Bantam looked his intense pity for the gentleman whom Miss Withering would take, even in fancy—it would be, indeed, a take in.

'Can't you say ten thousand a year at once?' said Minnie, scornfully. 'But, to be sure, I do not think there is a gentleman with so much as ten thousand a year in the colony. There are a few who have eighteen hundred, but I have never seen a rich man who was half so agreeable as the poor men are in general. He seems always in such fear of being caught, that one is obliged to look cold and distant out of self-respect; and it is quite a penance to me to be cold or distant to any one.'

'I should think it is,' said Miss Withering. 'Your manners are certainly very much the reverse in general. But you show no stiffness to Mr. Reginald, and yet I have been told that his circumstances are good.'

'He does not come up to your mark by a long chalk,' laughed Minnie.

'What *did* you say?' exclaimed Miss Withering, in a tone of utter amazement.

'I meant that he has not nearly eighteen hundred a year,' said Minnie, blushing at having been led into speaking colonial slang.

'Oh! is that what you meant? I understand *English*, but I see you colonists are corrupting the language sadly. It is a pity, for the purity of their diction marks the lady and gentleman. Mr. Bantam quite puzzles me sometimes with novel phrases, and even Mrs. Bantam makes me feel at a loss to apprehend

her meaning occasionally. But to return to our original subject, though Mr. Reginald is tolerably rich, you still think him agreeable, Miss Hodges?'

'He is rather slow,' said Minnie, who now was determined to defy Miss Withering, 'but I think he is really a good fellow; he does not seem afraid of being taken in and done for, so that I feel at ease with him. But I suppose he is engaged to some cousin or other at home, for he has just the cut of it.'

Miss Withering seemed to be greatly shocked, and said, coldly, 'I see I must get you to explain the unintelligible words and phrases I meet with in the Adelaide newspapers, Miss Hodges. What is a *nobbler neat,* for instance?'

'Don't you know what a nobbler is, Miss Withering? Your education must have been neglected! Why, you are quite as ignorant as the judge, who positively asked once in full court what a nobbler was—and it was considered a capital joke all over the colony. A nobbler is half a glass of spirits, generally brandy; and when it is taken neat, it means that it is undiluted.'

'I am glad to find that my ignorance is sanctioned by such high authority, for I suppose that his honour the judge is at least a gentleman,' said Miss Withering.

'But he has not got eighteen hundred a year,' answered Minnie, maliciously. 'Though, perhaps in consideration of his high standing in the colony, you may place him in the list of your 'eligibles.' I advise you not to refuse the judge if he asks you.'

'I must say I feel surprised at your mode of expressing yourself, Miss Hodges; and it is odd that you seem to think yourself competent to give advice to me, who has seen so very much more of the world than you have done. Perhaps I may be allowed to hint, that it is not considered ladylike to talk of love in the manner you do.'

'It is ladylike to laugh at love, and even to despise it, I suppose,' said Minnie.

'Certainly, that is quite admissible, even in the best society,' replied Miss Withering.

'But,' said Minnie, 'it is unladylike to feel it, to honour it, or to speak of it with earnestness. We are only to be unbelieving spectators of such things, if we are to be considered worthy of the world's respect or admiration. Well, I don't care for being thought to be a lady; I would rather be considered a genuine character, which I will try to deserve by saying always what I think, without distressing myself about how it will sound in the nice ears of society.'

Miss Withering looked infinitely more shocked than before, and addressed herself to Mrs. Bantam, speaking at Minnie,

who was quite callous to her disagreeable remarks, and ate her supper as carelessly as possible; choosing to be deficient in politeness, rather than let Miss Withering fancy she cared for being considered ladylike or vulgar.

Minnie was engaged on the afternoon of the next day in trimming a new bonnet, which she meant to wear to pay a visit with Annie Elliot. Miss Withering advised her to trim it fashionably by only giving it a deep curtain and strings, leaving the bonnet bare of ribbon elsewhere; but Minnie was determined not to take any advice from the griffin, and, out of a spirit of contradiction, put on even more ribbon than she would naturally have done. She had triumphantly crossed the ribbon over the bonnet, and made a large knot at one side, when she found that she should not have enough left for strings. Mrs. Bantam, seeing that she looked mortified, suggested that Clara should be sent out to get an additional yard, and Minnie went herself into the kitchen to ask the favour. Clara was very willing to oblige Minnie, and even the information that she must match the ribbon at Macnab's did not damp her zeal. Miss Withering took the opportunity to get Clara to execute two or three little commissions for her at the same time, and gave her orders with great exactness. It was to get two yards and a half of white blond, with a tolerably rich edge; and three yards of peach blossom gimp, to match a piece of silk which she gave her; also half a yard of pea-green satin ribbon, about an inch and a half in width, and three quarters of a yard of wiredrawn black tulle.

Clara set off to execute these commissions, and rejoiced that the roads were not muddy; for there had been a keen, dry north-east wind, blowing strong for the last two days, which had made the footpaths dry, though they were hard and uncomfortable, being, as it were, baked into shoe moulds and irregular excrescences. She was sorry that she had not closed her letter to her sister, for she would have liked to have put it in the post office as she passed; but she had omitted to mention Mr. Campbell's name, and as she felt grateful to him for the interest he had taken in her, she did not like to despatch it without taking some notice of him; and there was too little daylight remaining for her to have ventured to write anything additional before she went out.

She found Renton looking well, but could not see Macnab, with whom she would rather have transacted her little business, for he generally sat in a little back crib, dignified by the name of the counting-room, whence he might see, but in which it was hard to get a sight of him.

Renton was in his element, talking an old woman into the purchase of a set of red cotton pocket-handkerchiefs for her husband.

'Twenty pence apiece, young man! I think that is a most unconscionable sum,' said she. 'I can get as good as these anywheres for fourteen pence, and I don't see no call on me to give you such a price.'

'We could show you an article at one and two, ma'am,' said Renton, 'but it would not give you satisfaction. These are the genuine Turkey red; all dyed with turkey's blood, ma'am. It makes a fast colour, but you know, my good lady, that it comes expensive. Ah, Miss Morison, you are giving us a call at last. What shall I have the pleasure of showing you?'

'I want this ribbon matched,' said Clara.

'Was it bought here?' said Renton, 'for I can't pretend to match things that have been got in other shops.'

'Yes; it was bought in this shop last week,' said Clara.

'Oh, yes, very true; I know the article now. A tall young lady who came from the country bought it, and you want three yards of it, I suppose.—I assure you, Mrs. Higgs, that these handkerchiefs are worth double the money I ask for them. They are the real adamantine touch—you may put them on in the pot, and boil them ever so fast, for the colours are faster still.'

'Only a yard of ribbon for me,' said Clara.

'Phil,' said Renton, 'make up a dozen of these pocket-handkerchiefs for Mrs. Higgs, and put them along with the shawl and gown-piece, and take them home for her.'

'I have not bought the gown-piece,' said Mrs. Higgs, who had yielded upon the other counts of the indictment, but was determined to make a stand there.

'It is the most genteel thing in the shop,' said Renton. 'The Governor's lady got a dress of it just last week, and I am sure if you once saw it on her, you would confess that a thing does not show what it is till it is hanging on a lady.'

Mrs. Higgs was completely overcome, and saw Phil put the dress into the parcel with pleased resignation. Renton made out her little bill, received payment, and then turned to Clara, who told him her other commissions.

She had felt her eyes ache a good deal during her walk, and now, in the dubious glimmer of a newly-lighted lamp struggling with the setting sun, she endeavoured to get Miss Withering's silk matched. Mr. Renton left her to attend to a young milliner who was choosing a variety of materials for her trade; Phil had left with Mrs. Higgs' parcel, the other shopman had gone to his tea, and Mr. Macnab kept to his books, so that Clara could get no assistance. Her eyes grew dazzled over the varieties of peach-blossom; then she looked over a box of ribbons to find a right pea-green; and after turning over all the black tulles in Mr. Macnab's shop, she

found out that there was none of the kind that Miss Withering wanted. So she went into three other shops, with no better success; and as the shopmen were all sure that they had the article she wanted, she was obliged to turn over all their stock of the description before she found out their mistake.

Renton had offered to send home her small parcel, in the hope of getting her address, but Clara had declined his courtesy. She now returned unwillingly to ask him if he knew where she was likely to get the wiredrawn tulle. He directed her to a large shop at a considerable distance, where he said she was sure to find the article; and as he was then at leisure, asked if there was any news of Miss Waterstone. Clara told him of that lady's intended marriage, and Renton received the intelligence with his usual nonchalance.

'So, the fair Elizabeth has charmed another, and thought it of no use waiting for me. I wish the marriage had taken place here instead of Melbourne, for it would have been a good thing for the shop. It would have taken twenty yards of white satin to make a proper wedding-dress for her; and I know she would have everything of the best for such an occasion.'

'You take a great interest in the shop, Mr. Renton, and yet you say that you are going to leave it soon,' said Clara.

'Not so sure of that now, Miss Morison. Mac has behaved very handsome, and I think I'll stick by him. I expect soon to get a footing in the business, now that Mac knows my value. Times are rather dull in Adelaide just now, but the premises are central, and we have never felt custom slack, so I think I shall let the Turon alone. I could not blarney the gold out of the quartz as I did Mrs. Higgs out of her sovereign with that tale of the turkey's blood. Besides, I never was fond of hard work in my life, and I have a notion that it won't agree with me, so I'll stick to the counter and Mac —Mr. Macnab, don't you see Miss Morison here?'

Mr. Macnab now emerged from his den, looking very much as usual, grunted that he did see Miss Morison, and hoped she was well, and that she liked the colony; then, without waiting for an answer, he made his way into the back shop.

'A sad bear, is he not?' said Renton, compassionately; 'but I bear with him *for a consideration,* you know. I hope you will give us a more extensive order next time you look in our way. Good evening, Miss Morison.'

It was quite dark before Clara had completed her purchase of tulle; and the walk home was miserable for the cutting east wind entered into her eyes, and made them ache dreadfully.

Minnie was of course quite pleased with her ribbon, and attached it to her bonnet with great satisfaction.

'It will look quite nice to-morrow when I go to see Mrs.

Beverly. I used to go to school with her when she was Miss Watts, and she expects me to spend one day with her while I am in town; Annie Elliot is going with me. Mrs. Beverly has got a little boy now; Annie says he is quite a beauty, so I long to kiss him.'

'Where can Clara's eyes have been?' said Miss Withering. 'She has brought me sky-blue ribbon instead of pea-green, and if she calls this gimp peach-blossom, I call it puce. The things are of no use whatever; it is a downright picking of my pocket to buy such things for me.'

'Clara shall go and exchange them to-morrow,' said Mrs. Bantam, apologetically. 'It is not a good plan in general to give commissions to servants, they execute them so badly; but I did not think Clara would be so stupid. By the bye, Mr. Campbell sent across a letter for her while she was out; I will give it to her now, and tell her she must rectify her blunders to-morrow.'

CHAPTER XVI

DARKNESS AND SORROW

At the sight of a letter from Susan, Clara forgot the pain in her eyes; she devoured every word of the long, closely written epistle, and then sat down to add a postscript to her own, with the view of posting it to-morrow, when she had to rectify her blunders with regard to Miss Withering's commissions. While reading and writing, she wiped her eyes frequently, for the tears came very fast, hot, and scalding; and when she had signed her name and addressed the letter, she became conscious of an insupportable pain shooting through her head. She had heard that weak eyes were quite common in Australia, and knowing that Mrs. Bantam had a lotion which she used when she suffered from them herself, she requested some for hers; and her mistress, without looking at Clara's eyes carefully, gave her the lotion, telling her to apply it frequently, for it never failed to do good. But it was rather of a stimulating nature, and was very unsuitable to the violent inflammation which Clara was suffering from, and as all through the long night she kept applying it, in the hope of relieving the pain, she grew gradually worse, and in the morning she could open neither of her eyes.

No one has ever had ophthalmia without feeling apprehensive that it will terminate in total blindness; and as Clara, alone and friendless in a strange land, contemplated the loss of her sight as probable—nay, almost certain—it is no wonder that her mental agony should increase the real physical pain she felt. Her pulse was high, and her skin parched and burning; but in a sort of despair she got out of bed, groped to her clothes, and dressed herself. She went down stairs, but found she could do nothing, not even light the fire; so she sat down on the single kitchen chair, and waited till she should hear either Mrs. Bantam or Miss Minnie getting up. Minnie was the first to move, and Clara, tapping at her door,

entreated her to speak to her for a moment. She was shocked at Clara's miserable condition.

'Go to bed directly, Clara,' said she; 'you are not fit to be up; you are going to have a sharp attack of ophthalmia, and must take care of yourself, or you may find it a serious affair. Keep out of any draughts, for it is very sensitive to cold. It must have been going on my message yesterday that brought it on, and no wonder that you matched Miss Withering's silk so badly with this hanging about you. Mrs. Bantam and I must do all that there is to be done for two or three days; but keep yourself quiet and easy, Clara; it will do you no good to fret.'

'Had you ever eyes like these, Miss Minnie?' said Clara.

'No, nor any of our family; but I remember seeing Mrs. Elliot when she had ophthalmia, and I saw how it should be treated.'

So Clara returned to her room, with no other company than her miserable thoughts. She thought of going home blind to her uncle, and being a burden upon him, and feeling that she was of no use to anybody. It was hard that, now she had learned the use of her hands, all the labour should be thrown away from want of eyesight. She thought how grieved Susan would be to see her so helpless, and how she would overwork herself to make up for her sister's inability to do anything to serve her generous uncle. Then she thought that she should never see Mr. Reginald again; and that it was well that he was gone, for she could not bear him to see her. She envied everybody who could see, and even Miss Withering, for the time; for though her eyes had a disagreeable expression, they seemed to be very strong, and never failed her.

Minnie brought her up some breakfast, which she could not eat, and shortly afterwards came up with Mrs. Bantam and Miss Withering, to hold a council as to what was to be done.

'I say leeches,' said Miss Withering, oracularly; 'and as Miss Hodges is going out, at any rate, she might get half-a-dozen.'

'Yes, Clara,' said Minnie, 'there is nothing so good or so safe as leeches in inflammation of the eyes. I am sure they will do you good, and I shall be very glad to get them for you.'

'But who is to put them on, for I cannot touch a leech?' said Mrs. Bantam.

'I will see that they are put on,' said Miss Withering. 'I have a great turn for all branches of medicine and surgery, and rather like the employment than otherwise. And, Miss Hodges, you will exchange the ribbon and gimp for me, as you are going to the chemist's next door.'

Darkness and Sorrow

This arrangement was agreed to, for though Minnie pitied Clara for having such a nurse, she had no doubt that she would be the better for her skill.

Miss Withering really enjoyed the task she had imposed upon herself; she compelled her patient to remain quite still, and rebuked every moan she made, while she recounted dreadful stories of the French and English soldiers in Egypt, and many other cases of ophthalmia, which she had read of in her favourite medical books; dwelling upon the frequency of the disease in Australia, and on the liability of a person who has had it once to have it again.

Though Clara could see nothing with her eyes, she seemed to see a great deal in them; a sort of morbid vision had taken the place of the natural sight, and while lying in Mrs. Bantam's attic, she saw around her her own lost home: every little adjunct was there—her father's spectacles were lying beside him on the round table; she imagined that she had put them on, and was trying to read the debates in parliament to him; her sister's drawing portfolio was open, and she was putting the finishing touches on a favourite landscape; her mother was stitching a shirt-collar—it was two-threads-stitching, and Clara found herself compelled to count the threads as the needle went in and out. This picture she could not shut out; her mind intently examined it, while it as intently listened to Miss Withering's spoken pictures of sufferings which she was likely to endure, and was as sensible of every throb and sting that shot through her own head as if nothing else occupied her attention.

At last the leeches were tired, but not Miss Withering. She brought hot water, and made Clara foment her eyes, remarking how frightful she looked, and that very likely she would not be able to see for a month.

'You can scarcely expect Mrs. Bantam to keep you when you are such an object. You should go home to your friends, Clara; it does not suit mistresses to have their servants laid up and giving trouble, instead of doing work. Would you like me to write for you to your parents, that they may know what a state you are in, or would you prefer the hospital? I thought at first that you might get better in a few days, but I see now that the inflammation is very violent, and will not be so soon cured. If Mrs. Bantam approves, I should say blisters on the temples, and perhaps a dozen more leeches would be beneficial; but I must go down to lunch now; keep the hot cloths on your eyes, and do not moan so childishly—to think of a grown woman having so little fortitude! I will make you up a dose of medicine when I am down stairs, and I will see it swallowed, too; for I am sure you are too much of a baby to take it unless you are looked after.'

Clara's eyes partially opened upon Miss Withering's return with her potion, and the sight of her cold, inflexible face did not by any means sweeten the dose; but she swallowed it, and tried to feel grateful for what was really good service on Miss Withering's part. That lady had no contemptible amount of skill in matters like this, and had Clara's feelings been less acute, and her sense of desolation less crushing, she might possibly have benefited more by her deeds than she suffered by her words and manner. She tried to be brave, and to show Miss Withering how much she could endure without flinching, but the effort only increased the fever and reduced her strength. Miss Withering was satisfied that she had done a world of good to Clara, by standing firm and not allowing her to give way like a baby; and went down to dinner in a state of self-glorification at her condescension, for which also she received high praise from both Mr. and Mrs. Bantam.

Minnie had spent the day with Mrs. Beverly, and the evening with the Elliots. She had met Mr. William Bell, and had paid as much attention to him as she could spare from George, who had a great deal to say to her. She had again promised to go with the Elliots to the conversazione, if she was in town so long; and Mr. Bell had been trying to ask if he might accompany the party, for ten minutes, without success, when George put an end to his abortive attempts by asking if he had any objection to join them.

Minnie would not allow that Mr. Bell was plain-looking; he could not be so with such expressive eyes, and such a good-humoured smile. She was too grateful to him for not coming between her and George, to consider that his manners were defective; and if he was a little contradictory, why, it served to bring other people out. And he seemed to understand Margaret, and not to be afraid of her, so that, on the whole, she assured Annie that he was very agreeable, with more satisfaction to herself than in the praises which had been extorted from her in favour of Harris.

With sunshine in her heart, and comfort on her lips, she hurried up to Clara's cheerless attic as soon as she came home. Miss Withering had left the invalid by herself since dinner, and Clara's heart leaped to hear the light step of the young guest breaking upon the dreary solitude.

'Well, Clara, how are you getting on? I think the eyes look better to-night. Do I hurt them by putting the candle so near you?'

'A little; but I really think the pain is not so violent now,' said Clara.

'Don't be afraid of losing your eyesight,' said Minnie. 'I fancy Miss Withering has been croaking to you on that text,

for she never could resist such a favourable opportunity of prophesying evil. The lady I saw (who was the mother of the young ladies next door) had ophthalmia quite as severely as you have it, and she was able to go about the house in a week, and in a month she could read and sew by candle-light; and though she lived for three years afterwards, she never had another attack. So you must keep up your spirits, and trust to my friends the leeches—wonderful little doctors they are—but did not they bite sharply?'

'Very sharply, indeed,' said Clara. 'I thought they were almost taking out my brains. But what does Mrs. Bantam say about me, for Miss Withering spoke of my going home to my friends or to the hospital. I have no friends here—I am quite alone; so do, Miss Minnie, try to persuade Mrs. Bantam not to send me away. I shall feel so grateful if she will only keep me till I get well.'

'Miss Withering is a humbug,' said Minnie. 'Mrs. Bantam has no idea of sending you away, and if Miss Withering tries to put such a notion into her head, I will take your part against her, and be quite glad of the pretext for a quarrel. I suppose that you think I might offer to read to you to-night, in return for your kindness to me on Saturday; but you are too feverish, and it would do you more harm than good. You look thirsty; shall I give you a little water? There now—you only want a tolerable night's sleep to give you the turn; sleep and quiet will do you more good than all the medicine in the world.'

And Clara felt so soothed by Minnie's kind voice and cheerful words, that she really fell asleep, and though her dreams were wild and uncomfortable, she felt better when she woke. Miss Withering, however, insisted on completing her cure, and infallibly prevented a relapse by the application of six more leeches, and two small blisters on the temples. The eyes were then certainly cured, and Miss Withering considered herself entitled to Clara's everlasting gratitude. By the time that Minnie was sent for, Clara was able to do her house-work as usual, but was forced to sit with vacant hands when that work was done, and to content herself with turning over and over again the confused chaos of her thoughts.

Miss Withering had given Minnie several hints that she expected an invitation to her father's house, because she was very anxious to study colonial subjects and colonial manners, and thought that the bush was the best place for arriving at a right conclusion as to the real merits of the land she had adopted. Mrs. Bantam, though desirous of being freed from her guest, had too much conscientiousness to give any encouragement to these suggestions, and Minnie herself heard the hints as if she heard them not. She would as soon have

invited a boa-constrictor to her home as the formidable griffin. Clara was quite sorry when Minnie was borne away by her father, though she was pleased that the custom of the colony, as well as Minnie's natural delicacy of feeling, prevented any offer of money in the shape of vails when she went away. She took a cordial farewell of every one but Miss Withering, to whom she was very stiff, and left that lady as firmly rooted in Mrs. Bantam's house as she had been on her arrival. But Miss Withering had not succeeded in collecting any such chain of evidence with regard to the conjectural clandestine engagement, as she thought would justify her in making known her suspicions to Mr. Hodges. Minnie had been several times at the Elliots', and had talked of them all frankly enough, but had not been betrayed into confusion by Miss Withering's insinuations. She was so comfortable now in her own mind, that she did not heed what anybody said; it was only after that miserable evening when Mr. Harris's star was in the ascendant, that Miss Withering's words had stung her, and made her show her agitation. If she had gone to the conversazione with her friends, Miss Withering would have gone there by one means or another, and have watched her behaviour; but Mr. Hodges came into town for his daughter before the day fixed for that mild species of dissipation.

She had hinted her fears with regard to Miss Hodges to Mrs. Bantam, but that lady had expressed such a horror of meddling and mischief-making, and declared so decidedly that the Elliots were as well-born and as well-educated as the Hodges, and that in time it would be a very likely and suitable thing if Minnie could make it up with one of the young men, that Miss Withering was convinced Mrs. Bantam would be a very bad coadjutor.

When Minnie was gone, Mr. and Mrs. Bantam felt how invaluable she had been to them, for they were again burdened with the whole of Miss Withering's tedious dogmatism; but though her bright idea had not benefited herself, it did not fall to the ground for about a week after she had gone, it was acted upon, and the Bantams and Clara were delivered from their unwelcome guest.

Miss Withering was somewhat of a 'gourmet,' and had a partiality for hot suppers, which was contrary to all Mrs. Bantam's ideas of health and economy; and she had accordingly resisted that encroachment with all her power. But Miss Withering, having made a poor tea on Thursday evening, had taken a violent fancy for something nice for supper, and had talked of what was customary in England for a long time in vain.

'What has Clara to do now, when she can neither read nor sew in the evenings, but to get supper for the family in a

civilized manner? I am quite tired of bread-and-cheese, and I am sure so is Mr. Bantam; besides, cheese is indigestible, and apt to occasion troublesome dreams. Would you not relish a nice pork chop to-night, Mr. Bantam?'

'I assure you, Miss Withering,' said Mrs. Bantam, 'that there is not a morsel of anything in the house that could be made warm for supper. There is cold roast beef, but nothing else.'

'I saw such beautiful pork chops in a butcher's shop in Rundle-street this afternoon. Can you not send Clara for a dish?'

'*I* certainly shall not send her on such an errand,' said Mrs. Bantam. '*You* may do as you please.'

So Miss Withering asked Clara to go out at nine o'clock to buy pork chops for supper; and Clara said she would rather not. Miss Withering was determined to carry her point, and called on Mrs. Bantam to support her; but she was sadly disappointed, for she only said the girl was quite right not to do such an unreasonable thing.

The griffin saw that her hold on Mrs. Bantam was lost, for in spite of her conviction that she was born to rule, she knew that if she submitted to one act of rebellion, others would follow; so she retreated to her room, packed her trunks, and made her preparations for departure on the morrow.

Mrs. Bantam could scarcely believe she was serious when she announced her determination to go. She made no polite objection, fearing that the slightest hint would be sufficient to induce her tormentor to remain, but bade her good-bye with an agitation which certainly had no grief in it. She stretched herself out on the sofa when the door closed on Miss Withering, and indulged in a comfortable lounge for nearly two hours; then she went into the kitchen, and raised Clara's wages to five shillings a-week on the spot.

CHAPTER XVII

MR. REGINALD'S LETTER TO ENGLAND IS RECEIVED AND ANSWERED

Miss Marston was reclining on a sofa, reading an interesting French novel, when the letter of her suitor in Australia was delivered to her. She had come up with Mrs. Reginald to London for a fortnight, to see the Great Exhibition; but Mr. Bisset, who was to take them under his escort, had been delayed from unforeseen causes for three days, and Miss Marston felt impatient of a stay in town which she had not yet enjoyed. However, Mr. Bisset was positively coming this very day, and Julia was filling up the hours which must intervene with a very exciting tale, which she could not leave till she had finished; so she put the letter unopened into her escritoire, saying to herself, that a letter from Charles would suit her better when she was weary of pleasure, than when she was anticipating it; and returned to see what answer Celestine gave to poor Armand. When Mrs. Reginald came in from her own apartment to sit with Julia, she rose and placed a chair for her in the most pleasant part of the room, and bringing her the newspaper and her spectacles, she settled herself again to her novel. It was by such little attentions as these that she had made herself so dear to Mrs. Reginald, and convinced her of the amiability and genuine goodness of her disposition. The mother was very fond of talking of her son, and Julia listened with patience, if not with interest. Mrs. Reginald read every description of colonial news, from the Adelaide newspapers which her son sent her, to the shorter notices of the colonies given by the London journals, and drew from all she read the deduction that Charles was quite lost at a sheep station in South Australia, and that it was only a feeling of duty which made him say he liked it. While Julia, for her part, was sure she should be miserable there, and talked so much and so feelingly of the pain it would give her to part from all her dear, dear English friends,

Mr. Reginald's Letter to England

that Mrs. Reginald thought it would be blameable in even her own son to wound so tender a heart, and condemn so brilliant a girl to such a limited sphere.

Mr. and Mrs. Bisset, as soon as they arrived, were of course all eagerness to set off to see the world's wonder, and Julia having finished her novel, and Mrs. Reginald read every word of the colonial news, they too wished to lose no time, and were very soon ready. What they saw I need not describe, for of course my readers have either seen it for themselves, or read all about it in the newspapers, according to Miss Waterstone's plan; and even we in the colonies are getting tired enough of that Great Exhibition and its appendages. Of course Mr. Bisset's party were charmed with everything they saw; but there was one part to which Mrs. Reginald's motherly heart turned with peculiar interest; this was to the South Australian division. There was not much to see in it—wool, wheat, and mineral specimens being almost the only articles exhibited; but Mrs. Reginald gazed at and admired the wool, long and intently. A knot of gentlemen were talking together close to this department; one of them, a tall, thin gentlemanly man, who was dressed with peculiar care, seemed to look on the pieces of ore as if he remembered every one of them.

'Fine specimens these,' said he to the person next him; 'the Burra malachite is not to be despised even in the world's fair, Langton.'

'The Russian beats it hollow,' said Mr. Langton, 'but I care more about the wool. That is Escott's; I should know it among a thousand. You can see that he has still got Humberstone with him. I fear my old master's will not look so well this year.'

'Can there be any of Charles's wool in the Exhibition?' whispered Mrs. Reginald to Julia; 'this gentleman seems to recognise some of the specimens.'

'Nonsense!' said Julia; 'he would have written to us that he meant to exhibit if he had sent anything home.'

'The Port Phillip specimens of wool are much better than the South Australian,' said the tall gentleman; 'but in the matter of minerals none of the Australian colonies have anything to show, except South Australia.'

'True,' said Mr. Langton, a short, thick-set man, who had been an overseer in the north, and had returned to England to gratify a feeling of home-sickness after ten years' absence, but who meant to return to the colony. 'I wish I had done as you did, Mr. Dent, and bought Burras with my capital before I left; I might then have been drawing my dividends here and cutting a figure. You bought cheap; but I suppose you mean to hold for one cannot get more than three per cent. in this old country.'

147

'Pshaw!' said Mr. Dent, 'I don't trust to my Burra dividends altogether, though they are pleasant things when they come, and I certainly do not mean to sell out any of my shares.'

'Come with me, Mrs. Reginald,' said Julia, 'Mr. and Mrs. Bisset are on before us.'

'Mrs. Reginald!' said Mr. Dent, coming forward, 'I have no doubt, from the locality in which I find you, that you are the mother of my friend, Charles Reginald, of Taringa, in the north.'

'I am very glad to see any friend of my son's,' said Mrs. Reginald, 'and so I am sure is Miss Marston and Mrs. Bisset. Alice, this is a friend of your brother's.'

'I ought to have given you a letter of introduction before this time, which Reginald was good enough to give me,' said Mr. Dent, 'but I have never been in ——shire since I came to England. I do not deserve this pleasant meeting, but I hope you will permit me to wait on you in town while you remain in it. My name is Dent; probably Mr. Reginald has mentioned me in some of his letters. I shall be proud to make the acquaintance of his family.'

As Mr. Dent had no party of his own to accompany, he was easily prevailed on to join Mr. Bisset's; and, giving Julia his arm, he felt quite happy. Miss Marston was so strikingly beautiful, that he wondered at his ever having admired Margaret Elliot, and the elegance of her deportment made him reflect with incredulity on the time when he had fancied Margaret ladylike. Mr. Dent had been in the colonies from his childhood, and had grown up to manhood in the bush, where he had rarely seen a female face; and the death of his father put him into possession of considerable property in the shape of flocks and herds when he was about four-and-twenty. He had taken cattle and horses overland to South Australia, and sold them well; he had disposed of his sheep with their stations at a good time, and realized prices beyond his expectations; and when he settled in Adelaide to look out for investments for the capital he had realized, he naturally began to look out for a wife at the same time.

He had looked very keenly to his own interest in all the bargains he made, indeed, too keenly for Margaret's taste, despising as she did the great colonial sin—an overweening love of money. Mr. Dent had been at first incredulous of Margaret's contempt for riches, but when he saw that it was borne out by her whole behaviour, and that it was in no way allied to extravagance, his affections fixed themselves on her in preference to prettier and more fashionable girls, whose fathers and mothers flattered and invited him, and who were very much more gracious to him themselves. Besides, Margaret's good sense, her varied information, and her lofty self-

Mr. Reginald's Letter to England

respect, gave her in Mr. Dent's eyes the appearance of a lady. Her few accomplishments she did not parade; her face, though he did not think it pretty, was expressive; he knew that she was religious without being tiresome, and that she would certainly make a good wife. He himself stood very high in the world's opinion—it is surprising how easily a man can gain a good character. Mr. Dent was free from the more vulgar vices; he was not extravagant, neither could he be considered mean; he was fond of ladies' society, and had great ideas of propriety in his intercourse with them. So every one said, 'What fault has Margaret Elliot to find with Mr. Dent?' But if Margaret had seen no positive vices, neither had she seen any virtues in her persevering admirer. He had no greatness of soul, no highminded generosity; nothing, in fact, to look up to; and she had given him his dismissal as soon as he afforded her an opportunity, which was not till half Adelaide was fixing the wedding-day.

Mr. Dent never paid another visit to the cottage after he had been refused; if he was not to be Margaret's husband, he cared little to be her friend. The death of an uncle soon obliged him to go to England, in order to convert into money a quantity of miscellaneous property which had been left to him, and there he resolved to obtain a handsome, accomplished English wife.

Mrs. Reginald was pleased to see Julia so friendly with her son's friend, and asked him to come home and dine with them. Mr. Dent was, of course, most happy, and accepted the invitation with many thanks.

'Now tell me how Charles looks,' said Mrs. Reginald, after dinner, to her guest. 'It is long since this likeness of him was taken; does he look much older?'

'Considerably older,' replied he, 'and not so animated—but of course he cannot be so lively at a dull place like Taringa, as he must have been in such a delightful family circle as this.'

'Is Taringa very dull? He writes as if he liked it,' said Julia.

'Wretchedly dull, in winter especially. In summer Reginald has a few visitors, but some of them are queer characters, though all meet with a welcome from him. I always called on my way to and from the Burra, and I think he was glad to see a gentleman for a change.'

'He keeps his health, however,' said Mrs. Bisset, 'and that is a great point. We hear from all quarters that the climate is very fine.'

'Very middling,' said Mr. Dent; 'nothing to equal either Van Diemen's Land or New Zealand, and even Port Phillip

is cooler and pleasanter. The hot winds in Adelaide used to lay me up altogether.'

'Are there many snakes in the colony?' asked Julia.

'There are none in the town, and for some distance out of it; but in the bush they are pretty numerous. A lady of my acquaintance used to be dreadfully alarmed by seeing one pop its head through a cranny in the back of her parlour chimney. She had a great horror of snakes, and this creature's occasional appearance quite preyed upon her spirits. You know that snakes are fond of being about old walls, and I suppose the wall of her house had not been well built (few colonial houses are), and the snake had found a nest there to live in.'

Julia looked shocked, and whispered to Alice to ask Mr. Dent how Charles was dressed now; for she did not like to inquire herself. Alice did so, and Mr. Dent willingly gave the information.

'In town, he dresses tolerably well; but in the bush he is quite different. You should see him, Miss Marston, in an old shooting-coat, often out at the elbows, a blue striped shirt, moleskin trowsers, and a leathern belt round his waist; a cabbage tree hat, with a black ribbon round it sometimes— the whole affair not worth a shilling—and a short black pipe in his mouth; no waistcoat, no gloves, and very thick boots. I always made a point of dressing very particularly when I visited him, for I thought my example might do him good; but I think nothing but a visit to England will improve him. The sheep farmers who live round him dress no better than himself; and that encourages him in his carelessness.'

'Does Mr. Reginald really smoke—and smoke such a thing as a horrid black pipe?' asked Julia.

'He takes a cigar in Adelaide, but in the bush he sticks to the short pipe. He sits in that long, low room of his, close to the wide open fireplace, smoking and reading alternately, and sometimes both together, for the entire evening, unless any visitors happen to be there, when he will make an effort, and be very agreeable. I always came provided with a pack of cards, and we used to play piquet together. There was no man in the colony I liked so well as Reginald; there was no nonsense about him.'

'What are the characteristics of colonial ladies?' said Julia. 'Do they dress as wretchedly as poor Mr. Reginald?'

'Some do dress shockingly. Ladies are always so ill supplied with servants in the colonies, and have to do so much with their own hands, that it would be unreasonable to expect them to be handsomely dressed.'

'I suppose that we shall hear of Charles marrying a colonial young lady some day soon. I should like to hear a description

Mr. Reginald's Letter to England

of the wife he is likely to get from a gentleman who has seen so much of South Australia,' said Julia.

Mr. Dent could think of no one as a colonial lady but Margaret Elliot, and he accordingly gave her portrait.

"I will describe one to you whom I used to consider a very favourable specimen of the class. She was tall and fair, with a slight stoop; her voice was rather loud than soft, and her manner would have been ladylike if it had not been too abrupt. She was very well informed, and particularly fond of posing people with puzzling questions. She danced tolerably, and played and sung a little; her hands were neither small nor white, but yet they would have looked well if she had not spoiled them with washing dishes and scrubbing floors. I mention this lady in particular, for she is more likely than any in the colony to take Reginald's fancy, unless, indeed, he returns to England, and sees how superior ladies are here to those half-polished, half-educated colonial girls.'

'You are describing a lady whom you admire,' said Julia, 'but you do not flatter her. Could you really consider a girl who did such drudgery a lady? I think washing dishes is a very singular accomplishment.'

'Ladies are forced to practise strange accomplishments in the colonies. There are many who could afford to keep enough of servants, who cannot get them, and the mother of a young family, in particular, is greatly to be pitied. The houses are all so small, that there is rarely a nursery, and not always a nursemaid; and the children are always under people's feet in the single sitting-room.'

All this talk was no good preparation to Julia for the reading of her lover's letter; and when she saw that he would not yield to her wishes, but required her to go with him to the miserable colony which he said he liked, she felt very indignant. She drew in her mind's eye a picture of him equipped as Mr. Dent had described, and could not bear the idea of spending her life with such an object. The dull home, where every corner was welcome, and the picture of a colonial lady's toils and cares, made her long to break off an engagement which never could result in happiness to either party. But what would Alice and Jane say, and, above all, how bitterly Mrs. Reginald would feel her conduct! And Julia was entirely dependent on her brother James, who was warmly attached to Reginald. She thought how foolish she had been to have engaged herself at all. She put away Reginald's letter without letting any one see it, and made up her mind not to answer it till she had returned home.

Miss Marston had observed that Mr. Dent admired her, and she rather liked him, though he had told her so many disagreeable things. She had led him to believe that she was

very young when Charles left England, and as she did not look more than twenty, Mr. Dent had no suspicion of the engagement; though he was certain that, if Reginald came home for a visit, he would undoubtedly be enslaved by her beauty and talents.

If Mr. Dent was not very polished, he was evidently desirous of pleasing; and as he had scarcely any English acquaintances, he would have been inclined to cultivate this, even if Julia had not been of the party. He was anxious to buy a property in the country, and Mr. Bisset recommended him to Thorns, which was offered at a moderate price, and which was within two miles of Ashfield. There were many improvements to be made on the house and grounds, but he rather preferred it on that account, and showed both taste and discrimination in the remarks he made on the subject.

Julia was to return to Ashfield when their short stay in London was over, and she thought with complacency on the probable new neighbour, whom she laughingly told Mrs. Bisset she should like to civilize.

'Don't you think, Alice, that if I could get him to fall desperately in love with me it would do the poor man an infinity of good?'

'You take people at an unfair advantage, Julia,' said Mrs. Bisset, 'for there is no chance of his love being reciprocated. And what a miserable neighbour you would have if he fancied you had used him ill. I am sure his face could look remarkably unhappy; it is rather a hatchet face at best.'

'It is rather thin, and I am sure a hopeless passion would make Mr. Dent look quite *distingué*. I assure you I mean to try, so don't any of you drop a hint of my engagement to Charles. I hate being laid on the shelf so summarily.'

Mr. Dent always happened to meet with Mr. Bisset and his party in their frequent visits to the Exhibition, and as he had been there from the first time it was opened, he was at first valuable as a cicerone, and subsequently the whole family grew accustomed to his presence, and would have felt disappointed if he had not accompanied them. When Mrs. Reginald was leaving town, Mr. Dent spoke of going to look at Thorns, and was invited to spend a week or two at Ashfield, that he might have every opportunity of inspecting the property he desired to purchase. His attentions to Julia were not marked, for he was only feeling his way; but he was thoughtful of her comfort, and spared no pains to amuse her. When she sang, he listened with pleasure, but he preferred her talk, for she was lively and amusing, and succeeded in making him shine in conversation as he was conscious he had never done before. With Margaret he had felt nervous and embarrassed, and neither party had been felicitous in

Mr. Reginald's Letter to England

selecting topics for discussion. Margaret liked to get a thorough insight into whatever chanced to be mentioned, and always succeeded in convincing him that he knew nothing about the subject; but Julia lightly skimmed over the surface, and was infinitely better suited to Mr. Dent's cast of mind.

Mr. Dent liked Thorns very much, and succeeded in getting the price still more reduced; then having consulted with an architect and ornamental gardener, he proceeded to establish himself there as an independent country gentleman, with an income of three thousand a-year. He went very frequently to Ashfield, and consulted Julia's taste upon the improvements he was making; but yet he was so unobtrusive, and had always such admirable reasons for asking her advice on this particular point, that even Julia was puzzled as to his feelings. When they met at parties, Mr. Dent did not dance with her; indeed, he did not dance with any one, for he did not dance well enough to venture on such an exhibition; but he paid Julia a shade more attention than any other lady in the room, which pleased Mrs. Reginald much, as he was such a friend of Charles!

Julia did not answer Reginald's letter till she was thoroughly ashamed of herself for her delay, nor till she had got another as uncompromising in the main point as the first. She did not take Mrs. Reginald into her confidence with regard to these letters or her answer; but only said that she had insisted on his giving up smoking, and dressing like a gentleman, otherwise she would not go to South Australia with him. She wrote thus:—

'MY DEAREST CHARLES,

'I am quite shocked at your cruel language, and the doubts you cast upon me. After all the sacrifices I have made for you, can you really expect me to leave all my beloved friends here, and live so miserably as people do in Australia?

'Dear Charles, I have seen a friend of yours, a Mr. Dent, who says that you go with your coat out at elbows, and smoke a short black pipe constantly. I thought I should have fainted when I heard of it, and Alice too was greatly shocked. It is not what your friends in England would have expected from you. And I cannot learn to wash dishes and scrub floors, as Mr. Dent says all colonial ladies must do. And the idea of snakes peeping out of the fireplace is too much for my nerves altogether.

'Mr. Dent has bought Thorns, and is consequently a near neighbour of ours. We met him first at the Exhibition, where your mother could not help fancying that some of the specimens of wool were from your flocks; I did not fancy anything

so absurd, for my love is not so blind as your mother's. If you make yourself agreeable to me I shall always like you; but if you will not I must and shall grumble.

'Alice is very much stronger since her tour on the continent, and was equal to a great amount of sightseeing. I have grown to love her more dearly than ever. Independently of her being your sister, she is very loveable for herself. I should not like her so much if she were not more gentle and forbearing with me than you are; she never reproaches me as you are so often doing. Indeed, Charles, it is cruel of you to write so unkindly to me. Alice wished me to go to Carrington with her for the autumn and winter, but your mother had set her heart upon my staying with her, and as she has the best claim upon me, I remain at Ashfield for some months. James has got accustomed to my absence, and Jane says she does not miss me so much as she expected; they have complimented me by making me godmother to their beautiful baby, and I can assure you that little Julia promises to eclipse me altogether.

'Your mother is very well this summer. She is going to write under the same envelope, so I may close this by hoping that you will not be unreasonable with your very affectionate,
'JULIA MARSTON.'

'P.S.—Mr. Dent says that you are very likely to fall in love with a young lady, who, though well enough connected, is very much reduced, and is obliged to do things which are left to servants here; but he said she was well informed, and fond of asking questions. I felt quite jealous, and longed to ask her name; but though I was desirous of information, I could not bring myself to ask any questions except from you. Your taste must have deteriorated from what it was when I knew you, if you can admire this lady, supposing Mr. Dent's description of her to be correct. Yours ever,

'J.M.'

'I wish I knew whether Mr. Dent likes me or not,' said Julia, half aloud to herself, when she had finished this letter. 'It would be better to be happy with him than miserable with Charles, who can easily get a wife in the colony willing to go to the bush with him. But then what would my friends say to such a thing? I should like him to be more explicit, but I cannot bring him to the point. He always looks at me, and seems to value my opinion more than that of others; but I suppose that my face is a pleasing object to most people, and I have sense and taste sufficient to give weight to what I say. Thorns will be a beautiful place when it is completed; perhaps

Mr. Reginald's Letter to England

he is waiting till then before he speaks out, and then I *ought* to refuse him.'

Months passed, and Mr. Dent slowly but surely found his way to Julia's heart: his face grew handsomer every day, and his manners more polished; his taste in books and music echoed her own; and her influence made him too delightful for her own peace. But still Mr. Dent would not speak without more encouragement than Julia felt she ought to give, and which the very yearnings of her heart made her backward in giving.

Mrs. Reginald looked forward to her son's coming home soon to relieve the flutter of spirits which Julia evidently suffered from; and she had planned that if Charles could not remain in England, she would accompany him to Australia, and brave the long voyage and all the hardships of colonial life, for the sake of her son and her daughter, Julia.

CHAPTER XVIII

MR. REGINALD MAKES THE ACQUAINTANCE OF THE ELLIOTS

We return to Mrs. Bantam's kitchen in Adelaide, where Clara sits listless and weary, suffering from the stagnation of mind which generally succeeds to great excitement. The routine of her daily duties did not rouse her; she seemed to be unable to struggle against what she knew to be a wrong state of mind. Her thoughts, on every subject but one, were vague and indistinct; while, on that subject, every idea was sharp in its outline, and painful in its intensity. She tacitly acknowledged that she was not strong enough to struggle with her love; she must let it wear itself out, and as it had no encouragement, it was sure to die. Now she longed to be with Susan again, and tell her all her sufferings, for her sympathy might compensate for the coldness of all the world beside; then again she shrank from going where she could never see Reginald more. She despised herself for giving away her affections when they were neither asked nor cared for; but yet love had become so identified with her nature, that she thought she should be nothing at all without it. Her only amusement was a dangerous one; it was journalizing. She had nothing to be interested in but herself, and her mind was constantly turned inwards, so that every shifting cloud or shadow was observed and magnified. She had found so much pleasure in writing imaginary conversations when she could share in none real, that she indulged herself in it till it became necessary to her; and she said many brilliant things on paper to her uncle, to Mr. Bantam, and Mr. Reginald. She introduced herself in the same way to the family next door, and gave a distinctive character to each of them, corresponding to the expression of their faces. From the first she had liked them, but she did not win their friendship until two long conversations had passed between them.

Mr. Reginald Makes the Acquaintance of the Elliots

Two or three months passed before Reginald came again into town, or at least to Mrs. Bantam's. She wondered if he meant to make any stay in the house, and looked into the little room he had occupied, to see if it was in fit order to receive a guest. But he had only come to call, and though Mrs. Bantam invited him to make a longer visit, she did not press the matter. A feeling that if Mr. Reginald was staying with them, Miss Withering might be induced to return, though perhaps it was unreasonable, influenced her in not insisting upon his accepting her hospitality.

But, in truth, her dread of the griffin's return was a continual trouble to Mrs. Bantam; she used to plan what she would do if she met her in the street, and what if she called, without ever coming to a distinct idea of the right conduct to be pursued. Miss Withering had never been at the house since her exit; Mrs. Bantam had heard that she had got a situation at Mrs. Denfield's with a salary of thirty pounds a-year; and that she ruled the household with a rod of iron. Strong as Mrs. Denfield's will was, it succumbed to Miss Withering's, which was stronger. By adroit flattery of the children, and still more skilful management of Mrs. Denfield's own peculiarities, she succeeded in commanding a respect and consideration which no governess had ever obtained in the family before. Mr. Denfield certainly hated her; but as, in her opinion, the master of the house was a mere cipher, she took little pains to ingratiate herself with him—she could hold her ground without him.

The children were forced to learn unreasonably long lessons, as they had such fine abilities; they were punished severely if the tasks were not well learned, for there was nothing like decision in the management of such remarkable children; and the servants were kept running at Miss Withering's beck and call, that they might feel a proper respect for the lady whom Mrs. Denfield entrusted with the office of instructing her prodigies of genius. Caroline Denfield did not love her governess, but she stood in awe of her; and she loved her mother better every day, which was a result exactly suited to Mrs. Denfield's views. Her love for her father was also increasing, but that neither of the ladies in authority paid any attention to.

But Mrs. Bantam had no confidence that this state of things at Langley would continue, and was nervously afraid of Miss Withering's coming back with some good excuse, such as so clever a woman could not fail to find. She started quite alarmed at a strange knock at the door, particularly if it was a loud one, and Clara was instructed that she was particularly engaged in case Miss Withering asked to see her. Clara would not say 'not at home,' which was likely to be more effectual,

for the pretext of an engagement would be but a flimsy protection from such a dauntless invader.

Clara saw that, as Mr. Reginald left their house, he met George Elliot going into his. They seemed to exchange a few words together, which probably resulted in an invitation on George's part, for Reginald accompanied him into the cottage. Clara was bringing in water from the butt which stood in the yard when she observed this; she tried to go on quietly with getting the dinner forward, but she experienced the old feeling, which resembled envy of the Misses Elliot, coming upon her more strongly than ever.

Mr. Bantam did not come home at his usual time, and her mistress came into the kitchen to see if dinner was not getting spoiled.

'Did you not think that it was Miss Withering, when Mr. Reginald rapped at the door to-day, Clara? The two people, though so different, having been here at the same time, I naturally think of the one when I see the other, and his rat-tat on the knocker is nearly as decided as hers. What should I have done if it had been really she? I have not such a good way of managing as poor Mrs. Campbell had. She was quite infested with 'consignments,' as Mr. Campbell had so many Edinburgh connexions and acquaintances, but she used to get quit of them very cleverly.'

'I have heard that Mrs. Campbell was very kind,' said Clara.

'Oh, yes! she was remarkably kind and obliging to her friends and equals; but when people are forced upon one, as Mr. Dillon forced Miss Withering on me, one cannot stand upon ceremony. I remember one young girl whose father had been at school with Mr. Campbell for three months, and who founded some claim upon him through that, whom Mrs. Campbell did not like, but whom she could not get rid of for more than a month. But it chanced that a young gentleman who visited at the house took some notice of Miss Ker, and flirted with her a whole evening, with which the young lady was very much pleased, and got into high spirits; so Mrs. Campbell was very much shocked at the impropriety of her conduct, and dismissed her the next day with a great deal of good advice. By the bye, you had some recommendation to Mr. Campbell, Clara, as a needlewoman, or something of that kind; but I can tell you that you are much better off in a comfortable place like this, than if you had been a *protégée* of poor Mrs. Campbell, for she would not have paid you as much as the current rates for your work, and would have made you feel dependent besides; though nobody could be more attractive or delightful in society than she was.'

'Do you know what became of Miss Ker, ma'am?' asked

Mr. Reginald Makes the Acquaintance of the Elliots

Clara, sympathizing in a fate which might have easily been her own, for what would Mrs. Campbell have thought of the way in which she had talked to Mr. Reginald?

'Miss Ker, poor girl! she met a wretched fate. She married a man whom she knew nothing about; but, poor little thing, she had no home, and could not get a situation. This man had a good deal of property; she was pretty and inexperienced, and thought anything that would give her a shelter would be comparative happiness. He had a shocking temper, and was very unsteady; but that was not the worst of it, for about six months after he married Miss Ker, he went on some pretext to Sydney; and shortly afterwards, his wife and four children came out to Adelaide to join him. Of course the true wife took possession of all his property here, and poor Miss Ker was left penniless with a sickly baby, and was forced to apply to the Destitute Board. She gets rations from public charity in this way, and takes in plain sewing; but her constitution is quite broken up, and the doctor says she cannot live over another winter. Girls should be very careful who they marry in a place like this, for there are many men who have a wife in each of these colonies, besides one in England. I am glad to see that you are contented without any followers, Clara, for you have a chance to draw a bad lot; and even at the best, you will never be so comfortable as you are here. You have no care, no trouble, your work is not hard, and your hours are regular; you have nothing to do but draw your wages and buy your clothes, and you are clear of the world. Don't marry the baker if he asks you, for I have heard that he is dissipated and extravagant, and you would lead a wretched life with him.'

Clara disclaimed all intention of taking the baker, who besides had no desire to ask her. He thought her genteel in her manners, and rather pretty, but she was not tall enough to come up to his ideas of a fine woman, and he was afraid she wanted style. He had asked her once if she was going to a tradesman's ball, and had generously offered 'to stand treat if her missis would let her come'; but she had refused so haughtily, that he was offended, and took Plummer's Betsy instead.

Mr. Reginald liked all the Elliots better than he had generally liked people whom he had heard so much praised. He differed from Mr. Dent with regard to Margaret, for he thought her positively pretty, particularly when she smiled; but he did not feel at all inclined to fall in love with her. He compared her in his own mind, not with Julia Marston, but with Clara Morison, and thought her infinitely less charming. Margaret Elliot was full of what she herself called *elbows*, —salient points which people who did not know her very well

were apt to find inconvenient. She had been accustomed to take the lead in conversation at-home, and being more reflecting than observant, she was not skilful in adapting what she had to say to the tastes and prejudices of those whom she addressed. If a subject did not interest her, she could not feign an interest, and either sat silent, or expressed her disapproval; but when a subject did interest her, she was completely possessed with it, and could not be prevented from enlarging upon it with warmth and vehemence. Her mind was not poetical, nor imaginative; if she was silent, she seemed always to be thinking, never dreaming. Her eyes were never timidly cast down, but bravely looked the whole world in the face, with a steady truth in them which demanded nothing less than truth in return.

Grace was more loved by common acquaintances, and Annie more indulged and humoured by the family at-home; but Margaret was the life and soul of the circle. She studied mathematics with George and law with Gilbert; she read the driest books, and made extracts from them in an old ledger which she called her album, and was fond of singing something wise and stirring to the tunes of love-songs. She read all the newspapers she could get hold of, and was as well acquainted with current history as with Magnall's Questions. In general she preferred the company of gentlemen to that of ladies, though this preference was not reciprocated, for gentlemen did not like a girl who thought for herself, and spoke as boldly as she thought, without desiring to be led by their superior judgment. From all these characteristics, it is not surprising that she won for herself from the public voice of South Australia the reputation of being a blue, which she bore very philosophically, but sheltered her sisters from any imputation of the kind, for she knew they disliked it.

She rather liked Reginald at first, though his character was scarcely marked and rugged enough to come up to her idea of manliness. She knew he had been a friend of Robert Dent's, and was afraid he was of the same calibre. Reginald agreed with her about Dickens and Thackeray, but they differed on Tennyson and Carlyle. She admired what was clear, and thought many of Tennyson's poems were incomprehensible, and therefore valueless; Carlyle's style was so unnatural and affected, that if he had as much sense as Reginald gave him credit for, he should reform it forthwith; and when she was met by the assertion that the gift of language is not bestowed upon all men in equal measure, and that it is often as easy a task to change one's character as one's style, she declared that if what a man writes is not clear, he must either think indistinctly, which is a radical error, or mystify his clear thoughts by involving them in a

Mr. Reginald Makes the Acquaintance of the Elliots

complexity of words, which is a contemptible practice, merely followed to make people wonder what the meaning really is, and fancy that as it is incomprehensible, it must needs be deep and wide.

'Macaulay writes very differently, and very much better,' said she.

Reginald admired Macaulay too, but insisted that he felt more improved by reading Carlyle than Macaulay; which Margaret wondered at, but believed that he really thought so. 'None of those dreamy Germanized minds ever have much strength in them,' thought she; then said aloud, 'I dislike German philosophy, for it leads to nothing.'

'That is a sweeping charge,' said Reginald, 'yet I think it is not altogether an unfounded one. There is a friend of mine who studies Kant and Fichte, and talks admirably on all subjects connected with the mind and the will; but he really does nothing with his knowledge, and finds it as difficult to resist temptation as the most ignorant ploughman in the colony. He has been long attached to a lady in his own country whom he has known from childhood; but he could not resist the fascinations of a pretty milliner in Grenfell-street, and he is going to be married to her to-morrow. He feels very much ashamed of himself, and made as many apologies to me as if I had been his conscience-keeper, because he had told me previously of his love for the other lady. He begged me to be present at the ceremony, that I might see how very pretty and captivating the girl was, and I have agreed to go. After the honeymoon is over, he means to go to Ballarat, to try the diggings there; for he does not seem able to settle down comfortably. Do you know of any party who will start from Adelaide about that time, Mr. Elliot, for Haussen is desirous of meeting with one?'

'I know of one party consisting of two shopmen, a bricklayer, and a gentleman, who start in ten days,' said George; 'but very few people take a month to think of the matter. Have any of the shepherds in your neighbourhood gone off yet?'

'A few,' said Reginald, 'but the chief migration has been from the mines. Several parties have left the Burra and the Kapunda, and all the unprofitable mines are getting fast deserted. I hear that a good many young gentlemen are leaving Adelaide for Ballarat—have you no idea of trying your luck yourselves? The distance is not so formidable as to California or the Turon; you can get to Geelong in two or three days, with good winds, and sixty miles is nothing of a land journey.'

'We have no intention of leaving South Australia,' said Gilbert. 'I have no inclination to give up my home and

situation for gold washing, and our sisters would never hear of such a thing.'

'I am grieved that gold has been found in these colonies,' said Margaret. 'We were avaricious enough before the discovery, and I fear it will only feed the restless desire of our population to make money as easily as possible—we meet with so many men who think it quite a virtue to be worldly-minded. I wish we could find coals in the colony, for we should see how many gentlemen would fancy digging for them; though they are really far more useful, and look beautiful, too, when they burn; and though the work is not a whit dirtier or more disagreeable, I think we should have a very poor turn-out. People are fonder of unearned money than of what they give a real, fair proportion of work for.'

'I should not like to burn coals,' objected Annie; they make so much dust, and have a disagreeable smell. There is nothing so cheerful as a blazing wood-fire.'

'The Sydney coal, which is the only kind you see here, is not nearly so good as what we burned in Scotland,' said Grace. 'I hope that if we were to get coals here, they would be of better quality.'

'But it is their application to machinery that would make them so valuable to us,' observed Gilbert. 'Once give us coals, and we should not be long in having railroads.'

'You are going to be a lawyer,' said Reginald to Gilbert, 'and I suppose it would be very ill-advised in you to give up good prospects to dig for anything, even for coals.'

'I have not got my articles yet,' answered Gilbert, rather gloomily, 'but I study as hard as if I could be admitted. I hope to make myself so useful to my employer, that he will give me my articles to retain my services. I like law very much, and Margaret and I help each other on. We mean to be Mr. Sampson Brass and Miss Sally, by and bye.'

'I think Dickens wrote that sketch to frighten ladies from law, which, besides, is a thing he never can resist hitting hard. How well he describes Doctors' Commons in David Copperfield! Do not you find law a very dry study, Miss Margaret?' asked Reginald.

'Nothing is too dry for Margaret,' said Annie. 'She has an idea that what men can understand should be comprehensible to women, but I think law very dry indeed; and as for mathematics, they are frightful.'

'I do not understand why the piano should be kept shut,' said Reginald. 'It is quite a cruelty to me, for I never hear such a thing in the bush, and very seldom even when I visit Adelaide. I know that Miss Margaret Elliot can both play and sing, and feel extremely anxious to hear her.'

Mr. Reginald Makes the Acquaintance of the Elliots

'How do you know that I play or sing, when you never saw me in your life before?' demanded Margaret.

'Mr. Dent used to expatiate on the subject of your accomplishments once a fortnight at my station,' Reginald answered. Margaret did not look at all conscious.

'Do you know what has become of Mr. Dent?' asked Annie. 'Somebody told me last week that he was travelling on the continent, and had married a Parisian lady; but I did not believe it.'

'He has not written to me since he left the colony, though he promised to do so, so I know nothing of what he has been about. I gave him a letter of introduction to my mother, which he does not appear to have delivered, for she takes no notice of either it or him when she writes. But his friendship for me was merely one of convenience; it suited him to call at Taringa in his frequent visits to the Burra, and he consequently took every opportunity of doing so; but I never expected his liking to outlive change of scene and circumstances.'

Margaret was delighted at this hit at Mr. Dent, for she scarcely expected it from such a quarter. She opened the piano with alacrity, and Reginald, who would not lose the rare opportunity of cultivating his fine second, volunteered to take a part. Grace busied herself with a piece of crochet, while Annie came up close to her sister, wondering very much in her own mind whether Reginald was to turn out the paragon that Margaret could fall in love with. She thought her sister everything that was beautiful and excellent, and was afraid that this sheep farmer, though his talk was certainly not so dreadfully sheepish as that of the generality of his class, was not quite good enough for Margaret.

When he had gone, Margaret was sorry that she had not talked more with him, instead of wasting so much time in singing; for, as she said to Grace, 'he is a new character to me, and I should like to understand him better;' but Annie thought his singing was better than his conversation, for it was in perfect harmony with Margaret's, while there were jars and discords in their spoken expressions. Grace settled the matter by trusting to see a great deal more of Mr. Reginald, for Henry Martin had said that no man in the north bore so high a character, and that his acquaintance was well worth cultivating.

CHAPTER XIX

MR. AND MRS. BANTAM RETREAT BEFORE THE ENEMY

Mrs. Bantam, in the course of a morning call on Mrs. Townley, a mutual acquaintance of herself and Mrs. Denfield, was alarmed to hear that Miss Withering had been inquiring very particularly about her, and had spoken of calling on her the next week, and bringing Mrs. Denfield with her. Some words had fallen from her lips about spending a week in town, as the children had petitioned for holidays, and Miss Withering had thought it advisable to allow them a short respite, in order that they might engage in their studies with renewed ardour at its termination.

Mrs. Bantam consulted with her husband as to what should be done, and they came to the resolution that they should go out of Adelaide for a fortnight, so that Miss Withering might be met by a true 'not at home' from Clara. There was not much doing in the commission line of business at the time, and Mr. Bantam thought that he might take a holiday, and spend a week or two with Mr. Hodges. Mrs. Bantam was charmed with the arrangement, and communicated her intention to Clara in an overflow of spirits.

'You will have an easy time of it when we are gone,' said she. 'I do not care for anything extra being done; only keep the house clean and tidy, and if any friend comes to call, ask her to walk in and rest, and give her a glass of wine; for it is a long way out of town, and people are always tired before they get here. I leave you the keys of the wine-cupboard, for I can trust you with them, Clara. If Miss Withering comes, you must not let her in on any account. Have you any message to Miss Minnie, whom you liked so much, and who was so kind to you when she stayed here? Yes, you send your respects; well, I will deliver them. I assure you I am quite thankful that you are so steady, for I feel comfortable in leaving you in charge of the house.'

Mr. and Mrs. Bantam Retreat

Clara did not feel quite so comfortable in being left to a fortnight's utter solitude, and looked at the gig which conveyed her master and mistress to the country with a regret which she could not conquer.

She tried to write to her sister, and to Miss Waterstone; she journalized till she was weary of writing, and read some of Mrs. Bantam's books, hoping that they would be more interesting than her own. She considered herself fortunate in a visit from black Mary, one day in the first week of her solitude, and bribed her, by crusts of bread and an old gown of her own, to relate to her what she remembered of her history. It was uninteresting enough, but yet it did not seem true, so that it was unsatisfactory in all respects. Mary had no way of recording time except by moons, and no power of counting more than ten; after that they were called many moons; and when she told Clara about the piccaninny she had had many moons ago, who had wasted away and died, she did not weep as an English mother would do, nor did her voice sink to sorrowful pathos; but she talked of it with indifference, till she had finished her recital, and then burst out into a long expostulatory whine, which terminated in a request for medicine, for she felt very bad. Almost all the natives are fond of medicine, particularly of castor oil; and if you keep a good medicine chest in the country, they will besiege you for it, or for salts, senna, or any other nauseous drug you choose to give them, which they swallow without a grimace, and always profess to feel much the better for. Clara indulged Mary with a dose, which she swallowed with a horrible relish, and took her departure forthwith.

After a week had been passed, sadly enough, Clara wrote a note to Mrs. Handy, requesting her to come and see her for an hour or two, for she herself could not leave the house; and next day, at about eleven o'clock, Mrs. Handy knocked at the kitchen door. Clara opened it with agitation, and falling into the arms of her only friend, sobbed as if her heart would break.

'What is the matter, Miss Morison?—what distresses you, my dear Clara?' asked Mrs. Handy, puzzled to know what could occasion such violent distress.

'I am very foolish, but this does me so much good! Don't be angry at me for crying like a baby; I thought I should lose my senses altogether from being left so long alone, but the sight of your kind face is bringing me to myself again, though in a strange way.' And Clara set a chair for Mrs. Handy, close to her own, and clasping her hand in both of her own, looked in her face steadily, as if to sun herself in a human smile. Mrs. Handy waited till she was more composed, and then opened a budget of news.

'Handy goes off next week,' said she. 'I persuaded him past the Turon scheme, but he has set his heart on going to Ballarat, which we hear such great accounts of now; and indeed I prefer it greatly to the other, for it is pretty close at hand, and the people are more respectable there. And who do you think is going with him, but Haussen—you remember him, the German gentleman, who was so polite, but said so little—and Samuels, who used to wear so many rings? They want a fourth, and Mr. Oscar has offered to go with them; but they fight shy of him, for they don't think he'll work hard. I wish they would make him cook to the party, for it would just serve him out for all his grumbling, and the trouble he has given me these many years. Both Samuels and Handy are very particular about their food, and would not spare him. And do you know that Mr. Haussen has got a wife now—a silly pretty little thing that used to work as a milliner's girl in Grenfell-street? She is to live with me while her husband is gone; and I shall do the best I can for her, as I know Mr. Haussen will do by Handy at the diggings; but she does give herself airs to be sure, just as if nobody had ever been married before. Mr. Haussen was married when Mr. Reginald was in town last, and he got him to go to the wedding, and be groomsman. And Mr. Humberstone was in town a few days ago, and says that Mr. Blinker makes a first-rate hut-keeper; but that he suits that place so well, that he has no chance of promotion to be a shepherd. He fries chops to perfection, and his dampers are the best to be seen for fifty miles round —quite famous, in fact; and he has ventured on some attempts at puddings, which have given great satisfaction. I told Mr. Humberstone about his old flame being Mrs. Fleming now, and he seemed quite vexed, for, as he said, she would have suited him to a T. He quite looked down on Mrs. Haussen, when he met her at table; for, as he said to me, with a sort of sigh, 'she was not half so fine a woman as Miss Waterstone'.'

Clara became more cheerful during this recital, and was smiling and laughing, taking an interest in the tattle of the boarding-house, and telling the most insignificant things to Mrs. Handy, when Miss Withering and Mrs. Denfield knocked at the door. She knew the rap and the voices, and entreated Mrs. Handy to go and open it, for her face was stained with tears, and she could not bear the idea of seeing and being recognised by Mrs. Denfield.

Mrs. Handy was good-natured enough to do what Clara wanted; she hastily threw off her bonnet and shawl, and put on a large apron, and then went to the door courageously.

'Mrs. Bantam is at home, I hope,' said Miss Withering.

'No, ma'am; she is not at home,' said Mrs. Handy.

'I suppose she will be in presently; I will wait till she returns.'

'She has gone to the country, and will not be home again for a week.'

'I am sorry to hear that,' said Miss Withering, 'for I had promised myself the pleasure of spending this very week with her; but as I am an old friend, I need stand upon no ceremony; so I'll stay here, notwithstanding, as I have been accustomed to do when in Adelaide. James, bring my box from the carriage. I know my room.'

'I beg your pardon, ma'am,' said Mrs. Handy, 'but I was left in charge of the house, and got no instructions to receive visitors. I am sorry it has happened so unfortunate, but I cannot go beyond my orders. I wish you a good morning.'

Miss Withering, astonished at this rebuff, requested James to replace her box on the carriage; and, loudly complaining of the woman's insolence, proceeded homewards.

'I shall enjoy my holidays more at Langley than at poor Mrs. Bantam's, for indeed pity alone induces me to visit her,' said Miss Withering. 'She is so weak, that she lets herself be imposed upon by everybody, and is the better for having a strong-minded friend by her side. I am sure that vulgar woman who opened the door is cheating her during her absence. You keep your servants in very different order from poor Mrs. Bantam's. I never need to give you any advice; everything is done just as it ought to be at Langley. All that I can give you is sympathy, and that you may be assured I feel for you. I regret that certain parties scarcely appreciate you, and that all your sacrifices and toils are not sufficiently considered.'

'It is too true,' said Mrs. Denfield; 'I have all along felt this great want of congeniality; but still in all great points agreement is preserved; it is only in trifles that I feel the jar.'

'Nothing can be called trifling that wounds the feelings or cramps the genius; consideration should be shown to the slightest wish of one so thoroughly a lady as yourself. But gentlemen are so very deficient in those delicate sympathies which are felt by us, that I fear little is to be hoped.' And here Miss Withering applied her handkerchief to her eyes, and gave two little sighs.

Mrs. Handy stayed with Clara till four o'clock, and as she left, asked a favour from her.

'Will you copy out for me in a legible hand a few of the songs and poems that Miss Waterstone said you knew so well? I have brought you a blank book for you to write them down in. It would be a great acquisition to me, for I have lost my 'Little Warbler.' Mr. Oscar says that poor Mr. Blinker took it, but that I do not believe, though I am sure

if he had wanted it he might have had it and welcome. But you cannot think how much I miss it. You need not try to recollect exactly what was in my book, but write what you yourself think pretty, and I assure you I shall prize it very much. Now good bye, my dear child; don't get so miserable again, for you have a friend in the colony, though neither a great nor a strong one.'

Clara's pen was a quick one, and the blank book filled fast. Mrs. Handy had shown a woman's tact in the request she had made, for nothing could have relieved the poor maid-of-all-work more than this delightful task. She first repeated the songs and poems aloud, that she might be sure she had them perfect; and then wrote them where they would be seen and prized by a friend.

Grace Elliot observed that Clara was left all alone, and thought that the poor girl must feel miserably dull. She exchanged a few words with her over the fence, asking her if she was afraid to sleep in the house when there was no one else in it, and assuring her that Adelaide was very little infested with robbers, and that she need not be afraid of them.

The second week was not so long as the first, but yet Clara felt unspeakably relieved when she saw her master and mistress return. Mrs. Bantam's first question was as to what had been seen or heard of Miss Withering; and Clara told her that though she had called, she had not seen her, but the person with whom she had lived when she first came to the colony, who had happened to be in Mrs. Bantam's house at the time, had gone to the door instead, and passed herself off as a woman left in charge, completely discomfiting Miss Withering, though the griffin had done her utmost to effect an entrance.

'I do not think I could have managed the thing half so well myself,' said Clara, 'so I hope you are not displeased.'

'Displeased! no, I am delighted, for nothing could have happened better,' said Mrs. Bantam, glorying in the success of her retreat. 'And she brought Mrs. Denfield with her too, and her box—the impudence of that woman is really beyond everything. I may be glad that I was safe enough thirty-five miles off, thanks to Mrs. Townley's information. I will never accuse her of being a gossip or tattler again, now that I have gained so much by her telling all she hears to everybody. Well, I suppose I am safe now from Miss Withering till Christmas, and may keep my mind easy till then.'

CHAPTER XX

SOUTH AUSTRALIA UNDER AN ECLIPSE

But, before Christmas, changes came upon the colony, from which neither Mrs. Bantam, nor the family next door, nor any other family in town or country, could escape.

There had been for some months, as has already been hinted, a stagnation of business, and a great want of money in South Australia. Over-speculation in building and in mines had prevailed for some years, and though the mines which were every now and then discovered, and paraded as likely to rival the Burra or Kapunda, undoubtedly contained copper ore, it was neither of rich quality nor in great quantity; while the high prices of labour and freight demand both these requisites to make mining pay in South Australia. But speculators had bought the mines, and puffed the mines, selling shares at an enormous profit, and commencing in many instances expensive workings, which produced ore not worth the freight, till every one that had dabbled in shares felt a painful tingling come over him at the very name of 'indications.' The gold interest in New South Wales had not been shaken into its place; the exchanges were so much against England there, that the banks in all the colonies were forced to sell bills on England at a discount. The Burra dividends had been stopped, and though there was every prospect of a speedy resumption, still it prevented money from being in circulation during the scarcity from other causes. There was a general want of employment, particularly in Adelaide. No one had courage to build, and all trades, connected with the erection of houses, were suffering. Clerks were getting miserable salaries, and every situation that was open was besieged by dozens of applicants. Shops were empty of customers, but overflowing with goods; for a market so small as that of Adelaide is easily glutted; and the colony had over-imported, trusting to the large profits of retail business. Under all these

circumstances of depression, it is not at all surprising that when the wonderful gold-diggings of Mount Alexander were discovered, so many times richer and more productive than those of Bathurst or Ballarat, the rush from Melbourne was followed by a similar rush from Adelaide.

Labourers, tradesmen, shopkeepers, clerks, and gentlemen, all caught the gold-fever, and there was no business doing in Adelaide but the sale of outfits to the diggings. You could have no better account of the state of Adelaide about Christmas, 1852, than is contained in a letter from Annie Elliot to her friend Minnie:—

'MY DEAREST MINNIE,

'I promised to write you soon after my last, to detail all that happens in Adelaide, but I have nothing to write about but the all-engrossing gold-fever. I suppose you see plenty of drays going overland in your quarter, but here most people go by sea. The clerks out of employment, supernumerary shopmen, failing tradesmen, parasol-menders, and piano-tuners, went first; but now everyone is going, without regard to circumstances or families. Married and unmarried, people with lots of children, and people who have none, are all making up their minds and their carpet-bags for Mount Alexander. Those who are doing nothing here fancy they will do something at the diggings, and those who are doing something are sure they will do more; so that there is no security against any one's leaving dear South Australia.

'We hoped that our dear family circle would have been spared, and that we should have shown an example of moderate contentment; but, oh! Minnie, George and Gilbert are both making preparations, and will sail in ten days at furthest. And yet, you know that neither of them is avaricious, but they have been in a manner forced to go. When Mr. Ainslie told George that he had no more need of his services, for he could keep his books himself in future, George looked out for a party to join, but could not meet with one that suited him; and as Gilbert was threatened with a reduction of his salary, both Margaret and Grace advised him to give up his situation and accompany George, so that in case of sickness one brother might take care of the other. I cried a great deal about losing them both, for we shall be all so anxious and miserable while they are gone; and we hear such dreadful accounts of the bad health that the diggers suffer, with no protection from the changes of the weather in this variable climate but a tarpaulin, or a tent at best. And the water they have to drink is as thick with mud as pease-soup, which must be as bad as poison.

'But Margaret and Grace are busy making things as com-

fortable for the poor dear fellows as they can. I am sure Grace has thought of many things that will agreeably surprise them. Well, as I was saying, we were making up our minds to their leaving, when dear Grace got a letter from Henry Martin, saying that he had got his dismissal too (he called it '*the sack*,' but that was only his fun), and hoped he was not too late to join George's party. Henry is expected in Adelaide to-morrow, and will spend a week with us before he starts for the Mount; and I hope he will cheer dear Grace a little, for she feels so sad to think of us three girls being left without a protector in the colony.

'Margaret is the bravest of the whole of us; she has promised to Gilbert that she will make extracts for him, and go through Chitty systematically in his absence; for though Adelaide just now looks as if it was knocked completely on the head, she has confidence that it will revive again, and that Gilbert will find both his own and her knowledge of law useful to him yet.

'I wish, Minnie, you were here to see how our parlour is confused with the purchases they make; it is now a lot of Guernsey shirts, then a collection of pannikins, that are displayed and commented on. The cradle stands in one corner, for they all admire it so much that they will not allow it to be turned into the kitchen; and George actually put their pickaxes and shovels, and crowbars, and fossicking knives under the piano, till Grace remonstrated with him on the impropriety.

'Grace and Margaret have been sewing over again the strong shirts they have bought ready-made, which Grace says are only *blown together*. I have done nothing but make a housewife-case, and stick needles and pins, and tapes and buttons in it; but my head is not fit for such a bustle. I have promised George to keep the garden in order, and see that the dollicas grows well over the verandah, to shade us from the west sun, which comes in so dreadfully in the afternoon. The seeds you gave me have come up, though I did not scald them with hot water.

'Henry writes that Mr. Harris says he must turn over a new leaf, and save enough of money to take him to the Mount; for he does not like the idea of staying at the Burra when all the men have left it; besides, he thinks that it will be bad for him—he will be made too much of.

'William Bell says he shall probably go in a few months, but he has his brother's affairs to wind up, and they were left in a very involved state. I like him now better than I did, though he does not flatter me at all. By the bye, Mr. Plummer took it upon him to lecture Gilbert about leaving his situation to go to the diggings. Mr. Plummer is appre-

hensive of a reduction in his own salary, for the government are cutting down every description of expenditure in their panic; but he valiantly resolves to stick to the public service of South Australia, for he knows that nothing could be done in his department without the aid of his experience. So he wonders at Gilbert's being dissatisfied with a diminished salary; but a reduction of ten shillings from two pounds a week is rather severe.

'Things are cheap enough in Adelaide now, but people are afraid to buy the greatest bargains, for they do not know where the money is to come from for future necessities. We are perfectly besieged by women offering to do washing and needlework for us, saying that they are in great distress; but, of course, we are less able than ever we were to pay for labour which we can do ourselves.

'Has your papa lost anything through Mr. Campbell's stopping payment? George says that there are enough of assets, but that it is impossible to turn them into money in Adelaide at this time; so Mr. C. has got permission from his creditors to go to Melbourne to sell his goods, and six months' time to do it in; and I hope he may be able to clear off all his debts soon.

'I hear that our next-door neighbour, Mr. Bantam, is going to Melbourne, some time next month; he lost sadly by Menkoo and Mount Remarkable shares. He has advertised the house for sale, but I see nobody looking at it. I wonder what will become of your pretty friend, Clara; perhaps Mrs. Bantam will take her to Melbourne, as it is impossible to get servants there. I hear that Mrs. Bantam is in great distress at leaving Adelaide; I never see her over the door, but poor Clara looks very woe-begone.

'Our butcher's man has dwindled into a small boy, who tells us that he is the only man at the shop. Our baker drives his own cart, and you see women driving about quite independently now. If you go up into the business part of town, you hear men in knots talking of going by the 'Hero' or the 'Queen of Sheba'; and the words nuggets, ounces, gold-dust, cradles, and diggings, are in everybody's mouth. The chief streets are still very full of a most unsettled-looking population; but the outskirts of Adelaide are greatly thinned, and the villages round about are almost deserted.

'George and Gilbert hope to have your best wishes for their success. George has a favour to ask of you; he knows that you have three copies of Shakespeare in the house, which nobody reads but you, and even you seldom; and he asks if you would let him have the old one, with the absurd woodcuts, to read at Mount Alexander. He does not like to deprive Margaret of her beautiful copy, and is sure that the quaint

old-fashioned one will be more delightful at the diggings than any he could buy; besides that, everybody is buying up Shakespeare in Adelaide. I know that you will sent it in by the dray on Tuesday, along with an answer to this long letter. I hope you have more cheerful things to write about than I have, and that the gold fever has not cost you so many tears. All the family unite with me in love to yours and you; so I must remain, as ever, your very affectionate

'ANNIE.'

The dray which was to bear Minnie's answer and the Shakespeare did start, as Annie expected, on the Monday, so as to reach town on the following day; but the driver, going into an inn on the road for a glass of ale, met with a party of diggers going overland, who were much in want of a man who had been used to drive bullocks or horses; for they were all shopmen, and got on very badly. They told the man that they would take him with nothing, that he might live with them, get to Mount Alexander without spending a shilling, and share equally with the party when he arrived. This temptation was too strong for Ben Hardy; he joined the party, and telling the landlord of the inn to send in the dray for Mr. Hodges, who would pay any one handsomely for his trouble, he cracked his new whip over his old bullocks by way of farewell, and left them.

Several days passed before anybody found it convenient to take the dray into town, and it was not till the party were on the eve of sailing that the parcel was delivered. When Annie opened her note she found that Minnie had been very anxious for its speedy delivery; for Charley had taken a violent desire to go to the diggings, and her father and mother were afraid to trust him alone, or among strangers. They therefore begged George and Gilbert to take him with them for the sake of old friendship between the families; offering to pay a full share in all the expenses they had incurred or might incur. Nothing could make them feel so easy in letting Charles go to the diggings at all, as the knowledge that he was with such a steady set of young men, to whom also he had been in the habit of looking up; for Charley was only seventeen, and though he was a fearless rider, and knew how to deal with wild cattle, and could shoot kangaroos and wild turkeys in the bush, he was utterly ignorant of the world, and his parents and Minnie were afraid that if he got among bad companions now, he might be ruined for life.

'It is too late now,' said George. 'We have taken out our passages, and cannot afford to forfeit them; but if Charley has set his heart on going, he had better wait till we can inform him as to our whereabouts, and join us at the Mount.'

'He will be of no use,' said Martin. 'A raw lad of seventeen will be rather an encumbrance. Don't you think we should get on better without him?'

But Annie and George would not hear of such an ungracious refusal, and George's proposal was considered the proper way of treating their friend.

It was a very sorrowful parting; for Adelaide was in such a state that those who left it were uncertain as to their ever seeing it again. Grace, calm as she generally was, could not see the three dearest objects on earth leaving them for a life of hardship and danger without most unwonted tears. Annie cried a great deal, but that was nothing so uncommon. Margaret shook the tears from her eyes as she bade them good-bye, and said, without much faltering—

'Don't forget that there are other things better than gold, wherever you may be. God bless you, and keep you, and send you back to us with the same hearts, and we shall not mind whether you are any richer or not. Write soon, and write often. Good-bye—good-bye!'

Clara saw the party set off on their way to the port, in their Guernsey shirts and belts, with green veils tied round their cabbage-tree hats, and wished them success with all her heart. She felt the young ladies next door drawn closer to her in their sorrow and solitude than they had ever been before, and determined to apply to them for advice as soon as she could get an opportunity. Mrs. Bantam was in miserable spirits, and her temper was not so even as it had been; so that Clara shrank from asking her where or how she was to get another place, when her master had gone to Melbourne.

The only conversation she heard was about the universal distress in Adelaide, and how this man had failed, and that stopped payment,—how one lady had parted with her governess, and another dismissed her servant; so she supposed that it would be impossible to get a place without strong recommendations, and Mrs. Bantam was not likely to give her a high character. Sorrow is often selfish, and Clara felt that she was now regarded by her mistress as a mere appurtenance to her house, which did not interest her half so much as the house itself.

Clara fancied, after her long course of suffering, that her uncle must surely relent, and that his letter would be kind. Perhaps, if Adelaide were ruined, it would be excusable in her to go home, even at his expense; but she was startled one day to hear Mr. Bantam tell his wife at dinner that Mr. Campbell had sailed for Melbourne. Of course he had been too much engrossed in his own affairs to have thought of hers at all; but to whom could she apply now in her threatened destitution? She had thought of Mrs. Handy, but

her husband had been very unlucky at Ballarat, and by the last accounts he and Haussen had left the diggings there for Mount Alexander, with only ten shillings between them; Mrs. Handy's house was almost empty, and her spirits much depressed by difficulties of many kinds, particularly the task of managing Mrs. Haussen, who was either very merry and flighty, or in the depths of woe.

The only person in the colony who was at once willing and able to assist her, was Mr. Reginald; but her heart beat too strongly to allow her to ask even advice from him; and the idea of applying to the Elliots seemed more natural and pleasant to her than any other.

CHAPTER XXI

CLARA IS OFFERED A HOME

'Clara,' said Mrs. Bantam one day, 'has the waterman gone to the diggings, that he has never been to fill our cask?'

'I don't know, ma'am,' said Clara; 'but he seems to have forgotten us. If he meant to go, he ought to have told us, that we might apply to some one else. We have no water for tea, and this is miserable weather to be without it.'

'Will you give my compliments to Miss Elliot, and ask her if she would be good enough to lend us some for the present; and to tell her man to bring us a load the first opportunity; but perhaps, though he is a German, he may be off too.'

Here was an opportunity for Clara to speak to one of her neighbours; and when Margaret opened the door, and said Mrs. Bantam was heartily welcome, and that they would let their waterman know as soon as they saw him, she took courage, and asked if she knew any one that wanted a servant.

'Then you do not go to Melbourne? We all thought you would accompany Mrs. Bantam,' said Margaret.

'Oh no, ma'am, though I almost wish I were going, for I like my mistress, and I have one friend there.' Poor Miss Waterstone was now looked on as a friend.

'You are a Scotchwoman. What part of the country do you come from?' asked Margaret.

'I was born and educated in Edinburgh, and have not been quite a year in the colony,' said Clara.

'Yes, I thought you had a smack of Auld Reekie about you,' said Margaret. 'Were you ever at service before you came out here?'

'No, Miss Elliot, I was brought up very differently; but I can work very tolerably now. Could you not take me? I do not mind about wages; I only want a home, till I can hear from my friends, which must be soon now.'

Clara is Offered a Home

'What is your name? I don't mean your Christian name, which I know is Clara, but your surname.'

'It is Morison,' said Clara.

'Morison!—and your mother's name before she married, what was it?'

'My mother's name was Agnes Somers,' Clara answered, wondering at Miss Elliot's questions.

'And your father's name was William Morison, and you lived in Inverleith-row, did you not?'

'How do you know so much about me?' asked Clara, with increasing surprise.

'A friend of ours in Edinburgh wrote to me to befriend a Miss Morison, who had gone to Adelaide as a governess; and I suppose you are the person I was requested to take an interest in,' said Margaret, kindly; 'which I do the more willingly, now that I have seen you, as you are a second cousin of my own, and have a resemblance to my dear mamma. Her name was Agnes Robertson, and her mother was a Somers, and therefore she was a cousin-german of your mother's. I supose you never heard of us, because there was a quarrel between our grandfathers about some money that was left to them by our great-grandfathers; so there was no intercourse between the families. But we must forget old quarrels in this new country, and be glad to find relations. Grace!—Annie! come and find a cousin; this is the Miss Morison whom we have been puzzling ourselves to find out, who has been living next door to us for all these many months.'

'She has quite a look of mamma's family,' said Grace Elliot.

'No wonder Minnie said she thought you must have been a lady; and I, like a silly thing, would not listen to such an idea,' said Annie. 'I must write to her how good a judgment she had. How hard it must have been to you to go service, and to be tormented by Minnie's griffin, as she told me you were!'

'My worst misfortune is not in having had to go to service,' said Clara; 'it is in having to seek another place, and not knowing where or how to get it in these dreadful times; and Mr. Campbell has gone out of the colony, so that I cannot go home, at least till I hear from my uncle—'

'That is, Mr. James Morison,' answered Grace. 'I wonder at a man who has such a high character sending you out here, so young and friendless; for a recommendation to Mr. Campbell was a very insufficient introduction.'

'I had a recommendation to Mrs. Campbell, too; but from all that I hear, that would have done me very little good,' said Clara.

'I understand it all perfectly,' said Margaret; 'Mr. Morison

is a respectable man of the world, and so is Mr. Campbell, and you have had but a poor chance between them. But what has become of your sister—despatched to Melbourne or America, I suppose?'

'No, Susan stays as a governess to my uncle's family. She is so much more accomplished than I am, and has a better temper,' said Clara.

'So it was convenient to keep her, but not you, poor child! There is very little generosity among those respectable people,' Margaret said. 'And of course you kept your name and position as secret as you could, that nobody might be able to ask at Mr. Morison's evening parties how his niece likes being a maid-of-all-work in South Australia. However, we need not disturb his sleek repose, and it would do you no good either. You see, Grace, that Clara is losing her place, and wants another. I hope she may find one more suited to her rank and education when the colony has shaken itself into some kind of order; but in the meantime she need only leave Mrs. Bantam's to live next door; and, poor as we are, we can surely afford food and house-room to so near a relation; and warm hearts too, which I suppose she will prize still more.'

Clara could not thank her cousins in words, but her face was sufficiently expressive. Though Margaret had made the proposal, it was evident that all three were of one mind in the generous offer; and Clara was almost thankful for her late distress, since it had impelled her to take a step which resulted in so much good.

'Now, Clara,' said Grace, 'Mrs. Bantam wants her tea, for this is dreadfully hot thirsty weather; so you must not delay taking home your bucket of water. Tell her that you have found relations in us, and keep your spirits up, for as the old Scotch proverb says, 'Tine heart, tine a'.' And Clara was kissed by the three cousins she had so unexpectedly found, and told to come again soon, if Mrs. Bantam would let her.

Clara could scarcely wait till she had filled the kettle, before she told her mistress the joyful news. She burst into the parlour, and started to find Reginald talking earnestly to Mrs. Bantam.

'What has come over you, Clara, that you look so happy?' said Mrs. Bantam. 'I think everything is miserable now, and your mirth is surely very ill-timed.'

'I have found friends,' Clara answered, 'and cannot help looking pleased. The Misses Elliot are cousins of my own, and have been so very kind as to ask me to stay with them till I can get a situation. It has relieved my mind greatly, for I really did not know where to turn.'

Clara is Offered a Home

'The Miss Elliots your cousins? Why, they are ladies, Clara,' said Mrs. Bantam.

'And so was I once,' said Clara, 'and had quite as good a position as they had at home; but I was sent out here with very little money, and preferred going to service to going into debt; so, of course, I am no lady now.'

'I met Miss Morison at Mrs. Handy's,' said Reginald, coming to the rescue, 'and I assure you that I was very much surprised to find her in the position she holds here. If it had not been that I have heard you say that you never had a day's comfort while you had a Miss Gibb, who wanted to unite in her own person the incompatible offices of lady and servant, I could have told you that your maid of all work was both educated and refined.'

'But Miss Gibb made me wait upon her,' said Mrs. Bantam, 'and flew into a passion with me, because I happened once to call her Mary. Clara, to be sure, was the most helpless creature I ever saw when she came to the house; but she gave herself no airs, and dressed so plainly, that I never thought of her being used to anything higher. Well, I have taught her a good many useful lessons, and now I am obliged to part with her; but really, Clara, I rejoice in your good fortune. There is no home that could be so safe or comfortable, or where you would have a better chance of getting a better situation than you have had with me.'

'I never could have met with a kinder or more patient mistress,' said Clara, 'and I run no risk of ever forgetting you. Not an article of furniture or cooking utensil, but will remind me of how much you taught me.'

'Well, Clara, I hope you were not too overjoyed to fill the kettle, for I feel quite parched. Do get me my tea as soon as possible, there's a good girl.'

When Clara brought in the much wished for tea, Mrs. Bantam made a heroic effort, and roused herself to say, 'Since you are an equal of Mr. Reginald and the Elliots, I cannot consider you beneath me, so you must sit down and make tea to-night; and for this week, the last week I have to remain in Adelaide, let us be friends, and nothing more distant.'

Clara saw that her mistress was in earnest, and did as she was bid. Mr. Bantam was at the port, choosing a cabin in a vessel bound for Melbourne, and his wife did not know whether to expect him home or not that night. She was very dull, and could scarcely speak at all, so that Clara, uncertain of her position, felt much embarrassed when she found that all the conversation must lie between herself and Reginald. At first she could scarcely raise her eyes to his, to make the most common-place remark with regard to her tea-making duties, but when he began to speak frankly and cheerfully to her,

and to tell her all he had seen and heard of her cousins, she soon felt at ease. They began to talk as they had done at Mrs. Handy's, and Clara, seeing no disapproval in Mrs. Bantam's face, threw herself into the various subjects which Reginald started, with an enjoyment that was so keen as almost to be painful. She displayed so much information and such various reading, as well as fluency in expressing her thoughts, that Mrs. Bantam could not help staring at her servant, and wondering what Mr. Bantam would say. When tea was over, and the tea-things cleared, Clara asked Mrs. Bantam for a piece of needlework, which that lady provided for her speedily and gladly, as she was then busied with a sort of outfit for Melbourne. And while she sewed she listened. How pleasantly the needle went through now, when Reginald was recounting his troubles with his shepherds, and the absurd shifts he had been put to when ten of his men gave notice in one week, and how he had been compelled to come into town to supply their places, if possible.

'I mean to get men with wives and large families,' said he, 'for it will surely be hard for them to go off as the single men do.'

'Shall you not find that an expensive plan,' inquired Mrs. Bantam, 'with so many useless mouths to feed?'

'I do not mind that, if I can retain their services, for unless these diggings raise the price of provisions very much, the rations will not cost a great deal. If there is a boy of twelve in the family, he could take out a small flock of sheep; the wife might act as hut-keeper, though sometimes shifting hurdles is heavy work for a woman; and we should gladly feed the younger children for the sake of three available labourers. Digby has got five children who can do nothing, and Escott four, without grumbling about it at all. Wheat is very cheap yet, for the farmers are all so eager to raise money to take them to Mount Alexander, that they will not wait for a rise in price. I have got enough to last all my stations for twelve months, and I hope the millers will condescend to grind it for fifteen pence the bushel.'

'The colony is ruined, that is clear enough,' remarked Mrs. Bantam. 'To be sure I am going out of it, but I know I shall never like Melbourne as I have liked Adelaide, or ever have a house I shall be so fond of as this cottage. My children have been born here and buried here, and you cannot think, Mr. Reginald, what a wrench it gives me to leave the place where my darlings' graves are.' And Mrs. Bantam eyes swam in tears.

'The colony may revive yet, and you may return,' said Clara; 'let us hope that this panic is but temporary. With a fine climate, a good soil, and inexhaustible copper mines, I

Clara is Offered a Home

cannot believe that South Australia has received its death-blow.'

'I have always had quite a contempt for the Swan River settlement, but we are sinking even lower than it, when everybody that can raise a few pounds leaves the colony as if the pestilence was in it,' Mrs. Bantam complained.

'I am an exception,' said Reginald; 'for I intended to go to England this New Year, and what has driven so many people away has kept me here. Sheep farmers dare not leave their flocks, if they mean to save any property at all. My neighbour Escott was saying to me yesterday that, whatever property we reckoned ourselves to possess a month or two ago, we must reduce the value of by one-half; but I am glad that we trust to an English market for our produce, for it is not so fluctuating as these times show colonial markets to be. How Miss Withering would delight to enlarge upon the dreadful uncertainty of all things in this wretched colony if she were among us now; there would be enough of truth in her remarks to make them doubly bitter.'

'I may be thankful for one thing,' exclaimed Mrs. Bantam, 'and that is, that I am going out of that woman's reach, for in my state of mind she would drive me crazy. Mrs. Denfield has kept her much longer than I could have expected; she must have been four months at Langley, and luckily has not thought of giving me a visitation these Christmas holidays.'

'What is Mrs. Denfield's character?' asked Reginald. 'I suppose she must be very yielding, to have borne so long with Miss Withering?'

'Not at all yielding; no, Mrs. Denfield is far from that; but I suppose she has made such an idol of firmness all her life, that she cannot help admiring and worshipping it when it comes to her in a bodily shape. I wonder how Mr. Denfield's affairs are standing, for if he has difficulties about money, and Miss Withering in the house, I should not be surprised at his going mad or blowing his brains out.'

'I suppose nobody's affairs are very flourishing just now,' Reginald said; 'the Gazette is full of bankruptcies, and three are tottering for one that has fallen. I do not remember the first Australian panic, for I was not in the colony at the time; but does this strike you as being worse, Mrs. Bantam?'

'I think it is a great deal worse,' was the answer; 'for though people were poor then, they had no inducement to leave, and accordingly they worked hard in the colony, and brought it to rights again; but now there is no chance of our doing any better in South Australia, so I must leave along with others. I hear that the markets at Melbourne are brisk enough, and the prices at the diggings shameful. What a pity that we have not succeeded in finding gold here! The thousand pounds

reward offered by government has not been claimed yet, but it would have saved the colony.'

'I am not so sure of that,' said Reginald; 'let our neighbours dig for gold in Victoria, but if we supply them with food, we may make that as profitable as the other. If our farmers are rational enough to return to put in their crops in time, I feel sure that they will get higher prices for their produce than they have got these seven years I have been in the colony.'

Clara began to fancy that the colony was not in such a very hopeless condition; and though one might suppose she had very little reason to like South Australia, she still rejoiced when she thought of its revival.

When Mr. Reginald took leave of Mrs. Bantam and Clara, he promised to come again on the following evening, as he wished much to see Mr. Bantam before the latter sailed for Melbourne. He also determined in his own mind that he must call on the Elliots; ostensibly to see how they were now they were left without their brothers, but really to discover if Clara would be happy with them, and to express his interest in her welfare. He left Mrs. Bantam and Clara sitting at the open window, with no light but that of the moon, for it was a hot night, and they had given up sewing, and were talking of the preparations that must be made for the voyage. Clara was willing to do anything, and spoke so gently and cheerfully, that Mrs. Bantam gladly threw the whole matter on her hands, and proposed that she should make all necessary purchases next day; 'for,' said Mrs. Bantam, 'I cannot bear to go out, when I may meet people who will only vex me with questions; perhaps I might even see Miss Withering. By the bye, Clara, is not the attic upstairs very hot to sleep in? Miss Withering went up one day, and called it a miserable hole.'

'Yes it is very hot indeed; my ears tingle and smart when I go up to dress in the middle of the day, and when there is a hot night I feel suffocated in it.'

'It is dreadful to-night, so don't go up; take the little room downstairs so long as you stay in the cottage.'

'I shall write to my sister to-night, before I go to bed,' said Clara. 'My last letter was so gloomy, that I must not delay communicating good tidings.'

So Clara sat down in the little room to write to Susan. Among all the miserable letters that were dropped into the Adelaide post-office next morning, hers, if it could have been seen, would have shone like a sunbeam. Had not the bad times and the general distress given her a home and friends, and hope and sympathy again? and, as she scarcely whispered to herself, had they not kept Mr. Reginald in the colony?

Clara is Offered a Home

She had seen him once more as an equal; she had a prospect of seeing him again, for he knew and liked her cousins, and he would visit them when he came to town; his eyes had lighted up as she spoke, and there had been a smile in them whether his lips had smiled or not; his voice had grown animated when he addressed her; they had agreed on all matters of taste and opinion, and Clara suffered herself to hope that if they met often, she might become nearly as dear to him as he was to her. Who could sleep with such thoughts? And as she sat remembering all that had been said, and thinking on what might have been said, she saw the red and grey streaks in the east promising as hot a day as the preceding one. She roused herself from her reverie, and putting on her morning dress, proceeded with a light heart to do her ordinary work. It seemed to be done in half the usual time; and she surprised Mrs. Bantam shortly after breakfast by saying she was ready to execute all her commissions. She asked leave to call on Mrs. Handy, and explain her new prospects; and no objection being made, she dressed herself with particular care, and set out.

When her shopping was accomplished, she went up to Mrs. Handy's front door, and knocked without much timidity. Mrs. Handy was busily preparing lunch for Reginald and Humberstone, who were both going down to the port in quest of shepherds.

'I tried the labour office this morning, Miss Morison,' said Humberstone, 'but there is nobody there worth their salt. A parcel of old weavers and factory men, who don't know a sheep from a cow, and who would lose the sheep in the scrub if you trusted them in their charge—to ask employment from me! The most senseless blockheads I ever saw!'

'How does Mr. Blinker get on?' asked Clara. 'I hope he has not deserted you in this emergency.'

'Blinker is a trump,' said Humberstone. 'Not a word from him either of going or asking for more 'screw'. He goes on with his dampers and puddings as if there was no turning the world upside down. Escott is going to raise his wages upon principle, but I don't think he will be any the happier for it. But these are ticklish times, Miss Morison; it does not do to be so very short of hands. I wish, Mr. Reginald, we could get those lazy natives to mind the sheep; they will do it by fits and starts, but there's no stability about them.'

'In the Tatiara country,' said Reginald, 'they are very serviceable; and it is a good thing, for that is the district of South Australia which lies nearest the diggings, and which is sure to be soonest deserted by white men. A friend of mine has a flock of three thousand under a black man and his two wives; they camp out with them all night, and never need

to put up the hurdles. He gives them plenty of food, blankets, and tobacco; but is obliged to get white men to cook for them, for not even the women are fit for hut-keepers.'

'It would be too bad to make poor Mr. Blinker cook for natives,' said Clara.

'Yes, Miss Morison,' said Humberstone, 'good fellow as he is, there is a pitch beyond which he would not go. But that plan of having native shepherds is much better than Stone's plan of making a man on horseback take care of so large a flock as three thousand. The sheep are driven too fast, and have not room to disperse or time to feed.'

'Time to feed!' exclaimed Mrs. Haussen, who now entered the room. 'I am sure that you always take time enough to do that, whatever else you neglect.'

'I was not speaking of myself, ma'am,' said Humberstone, 'but of a very different set of animals—sheep, in fact.'

'I do not see so much difference between you,' returned Mrs. Haussen. 'You are both very rough to look at, and as for manners, one is quite as good as the other.'

'That is the unkindest cut of all,' said Humberstone.

'Shakespeare!' said Mrs. Haussen. This was her favourite joke, whenever any quotation was made.

'I don't know where it came from at first, but I found it on a jug in the bush,' said Humberstone.

'I have told Mrs. Handy,' said Reginald to Clara, 'of your finding cousins in the Elliots; but, of course, you have a great deal to explain to her yourself. Is not this your writing, Miss Morison?' continued he, taking up the blank book which Clara had filled. 'I opened it last night, and read it through before I slept; for besides many old favourites which I never tire of reading over again, I met with many new poems which were quite as beautiful. I received a book the other day which I had written to England for, of which I want your opinion, and your cousin, Miss Margaret's, too. It is Mrs. Browning's poems—have you seen them?'

'Not her whole works,' answered Clara, 'only copious extracts, and I should like to see all that such a woman has written. What do you think of them yourself, sir?'

'You wish to entrap me into giving my opinion of a woman's writings, before I know the decisions of her own sex. I think the poems feminine without being feeble, and musical without being over smooth, and really admire them more than any I have read for years. But you must not tell your cousin Margaret what I think; for she is so fond of contradicting, that she will take a prejudice against them, because they please me. I will send you the two volumes by the first opportunity, and I hope they may give you as much pleasure as this little book has given me.'

Clara is Offered a Home

'That is Reginald all over,' said Humberstone. 'He can't talk of anything else but books; do not you think he might find other subjects to entertain young ladies, Mrs. Haussen?'

'You read nothing yourself,' was the answer, 'and don't understand a refined taste. I am *so* fond of reading myself; I have just finished Valentine Vox and begun Mortimer Delmar, and I find them very interesting indeed. I need something to keep up my spirits now. Heigho!'

'Those books have not names like Christians at all,' said Humberstone. 'I should like to see books called John Smith or James Watson, or even such a respectable name as William Humberstone. I like a thing to be real and natural. I was induced to read a book about Pisistratus Caxton, for they said there was something about Australia in it; but I would advise the man who wrote it to take his passage for one of these colonies as soon as possible, if he means to write any more about us; for in all the sixteen years I have been in them I never heard of a damper being *turned* till I read it in that precious book. And after reading through hundreds of pages of rigmarole, to find such ignorance on the only subject I cared about; it was a shameful imposition—in fact, too bad.'

'Really,' said Clara to Reginald, 'could any one go through a work so full of wisdom, of kindly feeling, and of poetical fancy, with the impression that it was only a rigmarole; and blame a man who knows the human mind by heart, because he does not know how a damper is baked?'

'We must be off now,' Humberstone said. 'Good bye, Miss Morison. You must tell your friend, when you write to her, that I did not expect her to go and marry, before the year and day I promised to wear the willow for her were expired.'

Mrs. Haussen was decidedly very pretty; she had a pretty face and a pretty figure, and she was very prettily dressed; but Clara did not think the German gentleman's English wife was either clever or sensible. Her manner wanted repose, and she spoiled the effect of her good looks by her restless endeavours to make the most of them. Mrs. Haussen talked of her husband's absence and her anxiety about him with tears in her eyes, and immediately afterwards began to laugh at Humberstone's clownishness and Reginald's grave airs. Clara managed to get a few minutes to tell Mrs. Handy of her good fortune, and that lady sympathized as heartily with her in joy as she had done in sorrow.

'It is a good thing for you, Miss Morison, to get among friends who are not such great people as to hold themselves above you, and disown you on account of your having gone through so much; and yet who are so respectable and well thought of, that they can carry you through anything. If that

uncle of yours had given you letters to them, instead of Mr. Campbell, you would not have needed to go to service.'

'Better go to service than meet with such a dreadful fate as that of poor Miss Ker,' said Clara. 'I cannot get her story out of my head, and I am very anxious to know where she lives and how she is. Mrs. Bantam has lost sight of her for some months; if you could find out, I should feel much obliged to you.'

'I will try what I can do,' said Mrs. Handy. 'I have more time to go about now, for there is very little doing in the house. All my old stagers are gone but Mr. Brown and Mr. Green, and I do not think they will stay long. I expect two birds of passage from the ship that came in from England on Tuesday last, but they wont stay more than a week or two; and you know that Mr. Reginald and Mr. Humberstone are but chance people. As for Mrs. Haussen, I shall never get any board for her, unless her husband is lucky at the diggings; and then I shall not need it so much, for, of course, Handy will have got gold too. Just now I am at my wit's end for money; but I should not like to give up the house, for things may take a turn.'

'I am sure they will,' replied Clara, 'but I must really go now, or Mrs. Bantam will think I have been unreasonably long. Good-bye.'

CHAPTER XXII

SWEET AND BITTER

Mr. Bantam was not much surprised to hear that Clara was superior to her station, but took the news very pleasantly, and was glad to have her in the parlour to cheer his wife and help her preparations; and she showed such foresight and quickness, that her aid was invaluable. She seemed to fall into her proper place in the household at once, and was a strong-minded as well as a kind-hearted friend to her late mistress. When Mr. Reginald came in the evening, Mr. Bantam told him all his plans, and relieved his mind of a good many floating ideas, which he had not liked to tell even to his wife, but which looked very feasible when they were fairly expressed. Reginald gave him a letter to an old friend and school-fellow of his, who was doing well as a merchant in Melbourne, which he said he hoped would benefit him more than letters of introduction in general.

'I will give you a commission, too, to begin with,' continued Reginald. 'If Campbell settles in Melbourne, and gets his head up again, you will be able to recover the three hundred pounds he owes me, and charge me the commission current there upon it. I hope that you will have more important business soon, but you must not scorn small things.'

'Have you any message to Mr. Campbell, Clara?' asked Mr. Bantam. 'He was a sort of patron of yours.'

'I have no message, except that I can do without him; but I am very wrong to say so, for he certainly got me the very best place in Adelaide, and gave me a great deal of good advice,' said Clara.

'Mr. Campbell is a very worthy man,' said Reginald; 'but I do not think him very well qualified to give advice to you. He was always so conscious of his position, and so condescending, that it must have been painful to have felt under obligations to him. Was it not so, Miss Morison?'

'I did not feel it so; I was only *comfortably* grateful; but lately I was inclined to forget all he had done for me, in my disappointment at his leaving the colony without inquiring at all about me, when he knew that he was the only channel through which I could get any assistance from my uncle, and that I was likely to need it in the universal distress.'

There was something so delightful to Clara in having her imaginary conversations realized—in being actually speaking on equal terms with her master and mistress and Mr. Reginald —that she felt unusually placid and contented. Mr. Bantam seemed quite pleasant; opinions, from which he had dissented when she stood behind his chair, she readily adopted now that they sat side by side; Mrs. Bantam's commonplaces appeared new and startling; and, of course, Reginald, always delightful, seemed now to surpass himself. As Clara's needle went through her work with outfit rapidity, the sparkle in her eye, and the flush on her cheek, made up for the effects of months of slow suffering, and she looked lovelier than ever. She caught Reginald's eye resting occasionally on her face, and saw in its expression something that might well give new life to her half-conceived hopes.

Mrs. Bantam's spirits had gradually risen from the time that she had discovered a friend in Clara, and she was beginning to look upon her departure from Adelaide with tolerable resignation; and even talking of the time when, if they prospered, she would send for Clara to join them, not as a servant, but as a cherished guest. Mr. Bantam liked her very much, and as they were sadly afraid that society in Melbourne was in a wretchedly disorganised state, it was the more necessary to make a society for themselves.

The morning after Reginald's farewell visit, Mrs. Bantam and Clara were both busy with needlework, when a short, decided double knock was heard at the door.

'That is Miss Withering—shall I say that you are particularly engaged?' asked Clara.

'It is useless to say it,' Mrs. Bantam answered, 'for she is determined to come in to triumph over me; but as it is the last time, we had better submit with a good grace;—but stay with me, Clara; I need all the help you can give me.'

'And that is but little; I wish you had Miss Minnie instead,' said Clara, as she went to open the door.

Miss Withering, who, to Mrs. Bantam's great joy, was alone, sailed into the parlour with more than her usual importance, and was greatly surprised to see Clara follow her, and taking a seat near Mrs. Bantam, quietly resume her work.

'I could not let you leave the colony, my dear Mrs. Bantam, without coming to bid you farewell; and I have hurried Mrs. Denfield sadly, that I might get to town in time to see you

before you sailed,' said Miss Withering. 'Mrs. Denfield and myself were very much shocked to hear that you were actually going to accompany Mr. Bantam; we anticipated your remaining here until Mr. B. had in some measure settled himself, for, as you have not sold your cottage, you might as well occupy it, as house-rents are enormous in Melbourne, I understand.'

'So I believe,' said Mrs. Bantam; 'but wherever my husband goes, I must go too, and of course I am glad to go, even to Melbourne, with him.'

'Of course,' answered Miss Withering. 'Mrs. Denfield was saying to me this very morning, when we were talking about you and your affairs, that she was thankful Mr. D. had no intention of leaving South Australia, for she should have been so divided between her duty to her husband and her duty to her children, that even her strong mind must have had a long and painful struggle. But Mr. Denfield is determined to see this colony through its difficulties; and indeed his property is so valuable that it would be folly to leave it without a master's care. He purposes having a great breadth of wheat sown this year, even though he and his boys have to put it in themselves; for he is sure more is to be made in that way than by gold-digging or gold-broking. Does Mr. Bantam go to the diggings, or does he mean to settle in town?'

'It depends entirely on circumstances; I think our prospects are tolerably bright,' was the answer; but the tremor in the speaker's voice belied her words.

'Will you be good enough to hand me the scissors, ma'am,' said Clara; 'I am ready to begin the sleeves now.'

'I see that you are preparing for Melbourne in many ways, and are initiating yourself in the general levelling of ranks which pervades that town,' observed Miss Withering.

'When people are quiet and agreeable, there is no hardship in having their company; if they are not, it is indeed a penance,' said Mrs. Bantam.

'You cannot look for much quiet in Melbourne,' remarked the visitor; 'but I suppose you take Clara with you. It is just the place for a girl like her; she will be very soon marrying some fortunate digger, and leaving you in the lurch.'

'I do not take Clara with me at present,' replied Mrs. Bantam; 'she is going home to her friends for awhile; but if we succeed, as we expect to do, I may send for her to join me; for she has been quite a comfort to me, now that I know her value; and perhaps I may want a friend.'

'That is indeed a sad want,' said Miss Withering, pathetically. 'Mrs. Denfield can never feel the want of a friend in future, for, as we often say, we were formed for each other. She half reproached me to-day for leaving her to the care of

servants, as she has not been confined above ten days, and has not yet been up. She has got a most lovely boy—so large and strong, and so like his papa! I have taken the whole charge of the house during her illness, as well as my ordinary scholastic duties; this, I hope, will serve as my excuse for not paying you a visit at Christmas; we have thrown the holidays a month forward, and as I fear that then you will be out of the colony, I must delay my visit till you return to Adelaide.'

'I see that you have no intention of going to Melbourne, Miss Withering,' observed Mrs. Bantam, hopefully.

'Certainly not,' answered Miss Withering. 'I have seen one Australian colony, and I have no desire to see any other, particularly Victoria, where vulgar wealth is so completely in the ascendant, and where talents, education, and refinement are trodden under foot. I think that Melbourne seems to have all the evils of Adelaide, without any one of its advantages.'

'There is more money and more prospect of doing business in Melbourne than in Adelaide at present,' Clara said, quietly.

Miss Withering stared; but made no remark for a minute or two.

'I should like to know how I could serve you in any way, Mrs. Bantam,' she then said. 'Mrs. Denfield is of opinion that you might find keeping a boarding house very profitable; and, as I know your active habits, I think it would suit you. If any advice from me could benefit you, you are most welcome to it; and I understand how these things are managed, for I lived a long time at an establishment of the kind in Liverpool, and was the landlady's right hand. I should, indeed, be glad if you would point out how I can serve you in your present difficulties.'

Mrs. Bantam could make no reply to this impertinence; but Clara said—

'Since you are so kind as to offer assistance, I wish you could put this dress together; for Mrs. Bantam and I have been puzzling ourselves over it all this morning, and cannot get it to come right. Do you think it can have been properly cut?'

'I know nothing whatever about dressmaking,' said Miss Withering, 'and think time too valuable to be frittered away on the adornment of the person.'

'I beg your pardon, ma'am,' said Clara; 'but I really thought you could do everything, and that your time was at the service of your friends.'

Miss Withering turned round to address herself to Mrs. Bantam.

'I think I saw Mr. Bantam in King William-street to-day; but he is so changed that I scarcely knew him. He looks very

much thinner and older than he used to do. Are you sure that he is well enough to undertake a sea voyage? He did not recognise me at all; but he is always so absent that I did not mind. Mrs. Denfield gives me this character, which I am proud to think I deserve—that I do not take offence at trifles. Miss Hodges would have frequently offended me, and Mr. Reginald still oftener, if I had not been very lenient to their *étourderies*. But I had made up my mind that such a thing as good society was not to be found out of England, and consequently was surprised at nothing. Ah! here is my old friend,' continued she, taking up the book of chips. 'I have ransacked Mr. Denfield's library in vain for this valuable work; and he has endeavoured, without success, to procure a copy at Platt's, and other booksellers' in town. But really the supply of books is shamefully limited in Adelaide. Such a work as this ought to be procurable wherever books are sold at all. Where was the copy purchased, may I ask, Mrs. Bantam?'

'It was bought by auction many years ago. But you are heartily welcome to it, for no one in the house ever reads it,' answered Mrs. Bantam.

'It is not attractive to people who read only for amusement; but to those who are desirous of information it is invaluable. As a text book, I shall find it of the greatest service; and Miss Denfield will thank you as well as I do for it. Did I leave a pocket-handkerchief and a silver thimble about my room, Clara?'

'No, ma'am,' was the answer. 'There was nothing left in the room belonging to you. I found some knitting-needles, which Mrs. Bantam has in her work-box now; but I think they belonged to Miss Hodges.'

'Then they must have been picked up by the servant at the boarding-house I went to from here. The girl denied it flatly; but I suppose she must have been guilty, nevertheless. There is very little truth in colonial servants, as I have found out by sad experience. Mrs. Denfield always keeps them at a distance; but yet she watches them narrowly; and I think she manages them much better than any one I have yet seen in Australia.' And Miss Withering looked as if she was determined to drive Clara out of the room; but Mrs. Bantam's appealing face kept her in her seat.

'Was not Christmas week excessively hot?' continued Miss Withering. 'I never felt anything so prostrating as such a continuation of hot winds. I suppose we must expect a great deal of such weather before summer is over. You will not like being boxed up in the miserable cabin of a coasting vessel for three weeks, Mrs. Bantam, with the thermometer at 100 degrees, or higher. I believe it is no uncommon thing to be

three or four weeks on the way to Melbourne, unless the winds are favourable.'

Here there was a knock at the door; and Clara was glad of the interruption, for she hoped that a new comer might divert the current of Miss Withering's eloquence. It was Grace Elliot, who thought she would call to see if she could do anything for Mrs. Bantam.

'I do not like to force myself upon people, Clara,' said she; 'but Mrs. Bantam is in trouble, and if I offer to assist her, I can, at the most, only be refused. I can, at least, show my good will.'

Clara came in with Miss Elliot, who immediately seemed to change the aspect of affairs. She asked the name of the vessel Mrs. Bantam was to sail in, and praised it highly, saying that both the captain and his lady were considered attentive and agreeable. She offered to put the dress to rights, and took her thimble out of her pocket in a business-like manner that was delightful to behold; spoke of Melbourne as a wonderful place, where people with talents and energy could not fail to get on well; was sure that Mr. Bantam would get into a first-rate business as a bullion-broker; and thought there was no doubt that Mrs. Bantam would at once take her place in Melbourne good society, which every one knew was reckoned superior to that of Adelaide by English people.

Grace talked in a continuous stream, which Miss Withering could not interrupt, till it had made a pleasant way to Mrs. Bantam's heart. Miss Withering felt greatly shocked at the very low people Mrs. Bantam was associating with; and, as she told Mrs. Denfield when she got home, felt it due to herself to leave the house. When she was fairly gone, Mrs. Bantam sighed, Clara smiled, and Miss Elliot laughed outright.

'Is not she a dreadful woman, Miss Elliot?' said Mrs. Bantam. 'Though she did not say much while you were here, you could see by her face what a disagreeable creature she is. Your friend Minnie used to fight regular battles of words with her; and I must say that, clever as Miss Withering may be, she never had the best of it.'

'I understand she is quite a character,' Grace answered. 'She did not think it worth while to open upon me, and I am afraid I shall never have an opportunity of seeing her again. Minnie will be quite disappointed that I have not seen her griffin to advantage.'

'Be thankful, Miss Elliot, that she takes no notice of you, for she has nearly upset me to-day,' said Mrs. Bantam.

'Well, I dare say, she might have made me very uncomfortable by talking of midnight robberies and bowie-knives at the diggings, and about the slight chance we have of seeing

our dear friends again,' said Grace. 'How glad you may be that you are going with your husband to Victoria; for I can assure you, that all the widows I know are inconsolable. There is poor Mrs. Reid, with her five children, whom I never see smiling; and Mrs. Brown has only been married three months, and Mrs. Trueman five, and they are all so anxious and miserable. They fancy every gale is going to wreck their husband's vessel; and if the wind is still and the sun hot, they can think of nothing but sun strokes. We ourselves are far from comfortable in the absence of our brothers and poor Henry; and if the diggings were not a very unfit place for single ladies, we should have been strongly tempted to accompany them. Any hardship or sorrow is endurable if it is shared with those we love; but when our friends are so far away, and the post-office so ill conducted, that we cannot trust to receiving the letters they write, we cannot feel at all easy about them. I hope, Clara, that you be able to enliven us a little, for you have no dear friend at the diggings to pine after.'

Mrs. Bantam began to perceive that her situation was comparatively enviable, and thought Miss Elliot was a most sensible girl. Clara lifted her eyes from her work occasionally, and examined more minutely than before her cousin Grace's appearance. The features were not regular, nor their expression very intellectual, and the first bloom of youth was over; but still, Grace Elliot, at eight-and-twenty, was a very comely and joy-giving woman. Her eyes were very gentle, and her voice soft; and though she was tall, and rather stout, her step was light as a fairy's. She was what every one called the best creature in the world, and was applied to in times of sickness and distress by all her acquaintance. Mrs. Bantam reproached herself for never having called, and thanked Miss Elliot again and again for having overlooked etiquette in this well-timed visit.

The days went swiftly by, which intervened before the vessel sailed. All preparations were completed on the previous evening, and Mr. Bantam had gone to bed, leaving his wife sitting with Clara, and telling her all she meant to do or try to do in Melbourne.

'I felt quite pleased at Mr. Bantam's single commission from Mr. Reginald, for it may lead to more, and he is so admirable in this line of business, that he cannot fail to succeed if he only gets a fair start,' said she. 'It was very friendly in Mr. Reginald to put a little work in his way. What do you think of Mr. Reginald, Clara? I am very anxious to know your opinion of him.'

'I esteem him very much,' answered Clara, hesitatingly.

'I knew you must esteem him, for he is just the sort of

man whom one would like to see always, and not merely now and then,' said Mrs. Bantam. 'It is plain that he takes a great interest in you, Clara, from all he has said to me—you must feel quite flattered by his good opinion.'

Clara's eyes were turned away; her heart fluttered; but she gave a silent assent to what was said, and fell into a pleasant reverie.

'I have been wondering,' Mrs. Bantam continued, 'how to account for what he said to me the other day, before you came in with your joyful face. You must know he asked me if I meant to take you with me to Melbourne, and I said that I did not think of doing so, and he said with some emphasis, that perhaps you would be more happy and comfortable here. I thought at the time that his idea was that Melbourne was an unfit place for such a young and pretty girl as you are, but now I think he meant something more than that.'

Mrs. Bantam here subsided into silence; Clara dared not make any inquiry, but wondered if her mistress was ever going to tell what she conjectured. The lady proceeded.

'Now, Clara, I had a letter a month or two ago from a Miss Leicester, in England, which told me a piece of news as a secret. Of course, I have told nobody about it; but I think, for the sake of all parties, I had better read you some part of the letter, and you will see if my idea about Mr. Reginald is not borne out by it. Miss Leicester lived for several years in Adelaide, and was a fellow-passenger of Mr. Reginald, as well as an intimate friend of Mr. Bantam's and myself; so you must feel an interest in her.'

'Was she young?' asked Clara.

'Oh, no! she was ten years older than I am, I dare say, but a delightful creature; and though she was fond of a gossip, she never exaggerated, or told what was not true; so I trust entirely to what she says. I have the letter here, so you must listen.'

'MY DEAR MRS. BANTAM,

'You will see that I have not forgotten you or old days in Adelaide when you open this, for it requires some courage in me to commence a correspondence, and I have not heard from you yet. Don't wish to come back to England, for you have forgotten how fearfully cold it is; and after being twice as long in South Australia as I have been, you are likely to suffer still more from the change. I overwhelmed myself with clothes, and kept quite close to the fire all last winter, but I never could keep myself warm.'

'Well,' said Mrs. Bantam, interrupting herself, 'after some more of the same gossip, Miss Leicester goes on to say how

she went to the Exhibition, and also to a ball in the country, and how at the last she met a gentleman formerly of this colony.

' 'Who,' she writes, 'should be leaning over the sofa I sat upon but Robert Dent? He did not dance, but looked very well as a wallflower. He paid me a few compliments, not quite so stiffly as of old, and introduced me as an Adelaide lady to Mrs. Reginald, an old lady, and Miss Marston, a young one. Of course, I knew Mrs. Reginald at once, and I had no sooner seen Miss Marston than I was convinced Charles Reginald had very good reasons for his coldness to all the young ladies I ever saw him in company with. I never beheld a lovelier creature; her hair and eyes are very dark, and her complexion brilliant; and she is so tall and elegantly proportioned, that she moves like a queen among her subjects. I fancied Dent was smitten, but my hints did not seem to affect him, and soon I learnt the truth from the old lady. She told me that Julia Marston had been engaged to her son since the summer he left England, and that she expected him to come home in the course of a year, if things went rightly in the colonies; but that Julia did not like it talked of, as was very natural. Mrs. Reginald seemed to love her as a daughter, and assured me she was the most amiable and affectionate of girls. I judged for myself of her talents, for I talked a good deal to her, and found her remarkably intelligent and well informed. She asked me some questions about the colony, and, wishing to teaze her, I told her it was a horrid place, and that I never meant to go back again, at which Miss Marston looked delightfully annoyed.

'Dent told me that she was very highly accomplished; and I, remembering that he did not care much about accomplishments when you and I knew him, gave him a slight hint of his more humble tastes, which he did not like at all. One has only to remind him of the existence of a certain Miss Margaret, to make him look quite miserable yet. How silly she was after all, for he has a clear three thousand a-year, and a beautiful house and grounds; and I am sure it will be long before she has such another offer.

'You must address me . . .'

'But the rest is of no consequence,' said Mrs. Bantam, folding up the letter. 'The Miss Margaret mentioned here is your cousin, who was foolish enough to refuse Mr. Dent with three thousand a-year. I am sure the elder girl has far more sense. But what has struck me, Clara, in putting what Miss Leicester says and what Mr. Reginald says together, is, that his sheep station being a very dull place for his beautiful young wife, he thinks you would make a cheerful companion

for her, and will be able to do many things which, of course, a lady brought up as she has been knows nothing about. It is a great compliment to you, and I hope that what I have told you will quite set you at your ease with Mr. Reginald, who is all the same as a married man; and any favour he may wish to do you, you need have no scruple in accepting, for you can thank his wife for his kindness, and return it to her in some way or other. Still, Clara, if I can make you as comfortable as they can, remember I have a prior claim upon you. And now good night, child; for it is twelve o'clock, and we must be up early to-morrow.'

Mrs. Bantam left the room, but it was some time before Clara could move. When she had recovered in some degree from the stupor occasioned by this unexpected news, she rose languidly, and went to her bedroom.

> 'She pitied her own heart
> As if she held it in her hand.'

Reginald was then altogether out of her reach—all the same as a married man, Mrs. Bantam had said—and she felt sure that Miss Leicester's intelligence was true, from many little incidental expressions she had heard him let fall, which memory called up sharply before her again. His betrothed was so beautiful, so accomplished, and so amiable. Clara looked herself all over in the mirror, and quite scorned her pretensions to beauty. She took a mental inventory of all she could not do, and thought she must have been mad to hope ever to win the regard of one accustomed to qualifications so much higher than her own.

'I have only seen him in company with Miss Waterstone, Mrs. Handy, and Mrs. Bantam,' thought she. 'He finds me more agreeable than they are, but that is no criterion; for, oh! how inferior I am to Miss Marston, and how completely I should be neglected if she were in his company! If he expects me to become a companion to his wife, he will be disappointed; for I could not live with them and be a constant spectator of her happiness and his love. I am not good enough to wish only for his happiness; I cannot see my own life withered, and only smile over the wreck of hope and happiness. Why—why did I regard him, when he could not care for me? Did he not himself say of our first meeting that it was a pleasant passage, which led to nothing—nothing, alas! to him, but much—how much!—to me.

'A week ago, and the prospect of a restoration to my own position, and the discovery of such kind and excellent friends, would have seemed like a fairy vision, too bright to be realized; now I overlook all in the certainty that my affection is hopeless, as I might always have known it would be.

'How Mrs. Bantam would despise me if she knew the suffering caused by the news that was to set me at my ease with him, she thought, for ever! And he would scorn me, too, for he never gave me any reason to think he cared at all for me. He was merely finding out if I should be a suitable companion for his lovely Julia; and I fancied that he was interested in my opinions and pleased with my tastes.

'Oh! why did I come to this miserable Australia?—to be forced into love from utter vacuity of heart and life, and to find now that no good fortune, no employment, no friends, can ever compensate for the pang of having my love thrown back upon me as a thing valueless and vain. I am glad that I wrote cheerfully to Susan; she will not get such a joyous letter again, and I hope it may make her happy for months. God grant I may overlive this blow in time!'

Volume 2

CHAPTER I

CLARA LOOKS AT ADELAIDE MORE PLEASANTLY THAN BEFORE

If Clara appeared somewhat nervous and distraught when she went to her new home, her cousins attributed her agitation to her recent parting with a kind mistress, and to her being thrown among strangers. They exerted themselves to please her, and certainly even a lovelorn damsel could not but feel somewhat comforted by intercourse with three new minds, all genuine and kind. Margaret's *elbows* were of infinite service to Clara; for an occasional knock from one of them reminded her that there were other opinions in the world besides Reginald's, and other people who were worth studying and thinking about. The carpet was faded and the piano old, but the hearts in that little cottage were warm, and the minds unwarped by prejudice or ostentation; and Clara felt that if she had not gone through so much, and braved the world's estimation by accepting of a servant's place, she would not have been so much loved and honoured by Margaret, or so much sympathized with by Annie.

Margaret asked her what she could do, and was quite pleased at her list of accomplishments. An Edinburgh girl who could neither play, nor draw, nor pretend to do either, was a delightful novelty. She wanted to go on with Latin during her brother's absence, and Clara knew just about as much as herself, and would spur her on. Annie expressed a strong desire to learn short-hand, that she might write long letters to George on small sheets of paper, which nobody could read if they chanced to fall into wrong hands (a most likely thing at the diggings' post-office); but, after all, George could not read it himself, unless he had been taught, and it would be labour lost; but Margaret had an idea that if by labour the art could be acquired while Gilbert was away, she should like to surprise him by her skill when he returned. Gilbert had often thought of learning some system of stenography, but

201

was deterred by hearing that the task was equal to the acquirement of at least three languages.

'Dickens calls it 'savage stenography,' and quite appals me about it,' observed Margaret.

'My system is the phonetic, and is beautifully simple,' said Clara. 'I took lessons when it was fashionable, and my father wished me to learn it thoroughly for many reasons; particularly for taking notes from books and sermons. His health was so bad for the last two years of his life, that he rarely went to church; and I used to take down the sermons I heard, and read them when I came home. Our clergyman was a man of great and varied talents, and it gives me great pleasure now to read over my notes, and recollect how eloquently they were delivered.'

'Can you read them after years have passed?' asked Margaret; 'for I have often heard that reporters find difficulty in deciphering their own notes.'

'I can read mine quite easily now,' said Clara. 'I will read you a sermon or two some day soon, and you will see how simple it is. At first I felt very much flurried from trying to keep pace with the preacher; but as our pew was curtained round, and no one knew I was taking notes, I soon overcame that nervousness.'

'Don't you keep your journal in short-hand? It must be delightful to write what nobody else can read,' said Annie.

'I shed many tears over my secret correspondence with myself,' answered Clara; 'and I mean to give it up henceforward, for I think it hurts the mind to be always looking into itself.'

'You did not keep a journal on board ship, I hope,' said Margaret. 'A man of genius would have enough to do to make such a journal interesting, from the monotony of his subject; but to find a man chronicling what he had to eat at breakfast, luncheon, dinner, tea, and supper; counting the albatrosses and flying-fish killed every day; detailing every petty squabble for precedence; and then expecting you to consider him quite a literary character, is too much for my small stock of politeness.'

'I kept no journal on board the *Magnificent*,' replied Clara. 'I had no fancy then to write that I was miserable, miserable, miserable; and my room-mate chattered so much and so constantly, that I had not time, even if I had had the inclination.'

'I think that if you teach Margaret short-hand, Clara, you must learn something from me; for I am too old to be a scholar, and yet want something to occupy my mind,' said Grace. 'Margaret and Annie may say that they are glad you know nothing of music; but you will find your ignorance of

Clara Looks at Adelaide

that essential accomplishment a great drawback to your success here, and you really ought to make an effort and master the first difficulties. I will give you a lesson every day; and though I am not at all a fine musician, I can qualify you for giving the first lessons, at least.'

'Oh, thank you! I shall indeed be very glad to learn; but I fear I shall be very stupid.'

'None of us play superlatively, so you need not be afraid to make mistakes,' said Annie.

'Is there nothing I can do for you in return for your great kindness to me?' asked Clara. 'I wish you would let me be your servant.'

'You are a silly little thing,' said Margaret. 'Don't you see that we are very dull here just now, and are glad to have something to do that will interest us. You will take your part in the work of the house, and help Grace with the set of shirts she is making; for I am not in a sewing humour, and Annie is too busy with the slippers she is making for our diggers, to give any assistance.'

'You will tell us how things are done at home,' added Grace, 'without insisting that everything colonial is radically bad. You will read our books, and we shall read yours; you will visit with us, and help us to comfort the poor widows; and when Mrs. Bantam sends for you, or you meet with a desirable situation, we shall quite miss our dear little cousin.'

Thus Clara was made one of the family, and if she was not happy, it was not from any fault on the part of her cousins. They saw that she had been over-fatigued during the last week or two at Mrs. Bantam's, and allowed her to rest even from amusement till she was capable of exertion; and then Annie took her out to see all the prettiest spots round about Adelaide. They were both excellent walkers, and thought nothing of going four or five miles in search of a running stream or a romantic glen. They found their way up the range of steep hills which lie within walking distance of Adelaide; as long as flowers were to be found, they brought home nosegays; and when the advancing summer withered them all, they gathered green boughs instead. They would sit together under a gum-tree with a book, which they never read much of, but listened to the screaming of the paroquets and cockatoos, or the more musical chirping of the smaller birds. No one ever molested them in their rambles; there was scarcely a man to be seen, for at that time South Australia was in a very extraordinary position for a colony: there were far more women in it than men. Almost all the boys whom they met driving cows or sheep, were talking about the diggings, and how father got gold the very first spadeful he dug up, and how they were going themselves next month.

The very young children were all busy with pannikins, making believe to wash for gold, and feeling convinced if they only had a cradle they should find plenty. Or sometimes Clara and Annie would wander through the quietest streets of Adelaide, and admire the beautiful irregularity of the buildings. Annie would point out a short-waisted, broad-paling house, of which the bright red door and windows marked it as incontestably a German edifice. Next to that would be a two-story brick-house; then again, a low clay cottage, with dilapidated thatch; and close to that, a large iron-store, looking like a petrified tent.

'Is not Adelaide a delightful place?' said Annie, one day, when they had been across the river by the little wooden bridge, and round by the back of North Adelaide, and then having re-crossed the river by a fallen tree and stepping-stones, were returning home by the terraces. 'I do not remember Scotland distinctly, and my recollections of Edinburgh are merely of a wilderness of houses, without any open spaces; so that I love Adelaide like a native.'

'Don't you think it would be pleasanter if there were less dust?' asked Clara.

'Perhaps it might; but, you know, the dust is quite a boon to Grace; for if it did not keep her so busy cleaning, she would be quite miserable. And you know, Clara, that it is not the fault of the town that it is so dusty, for it is all owing to the climate being so dry. Sydney and Melbourne are both very dusty, and I don't suppose that they can be cured any more than Adelaide.'

'Then I suppose it is the fault of the climate,' said Clara. 'It does not look like rain yet, and we have not had a drop for six weeks.'

'I am sure, Clara, that the climate is beautiful,' answered Annie. 'We get so much rain in winter, that it would be unreasonable to expect it in summer. An old Scotchman, whom papa knew at home, was so struck with the invariable beauty of our weather, that he exclaimed—'I never saw onything to equal this! It is just ae fine day after anither!' But who is this coming towards us? Mr. Harris, I declare! Why, Mr. Harris, I thought you were going to the diggings. Are you *en route?*'

'My route is a tedious one, Miss Annie; but I hope that it will, in the end, land me safe at Mount Alexander,' said Harris. 'I am going, like the gold I mean to get, through the Assay Office.'

'What is the use of that? You don't want to be tested, surely,' said Annie. 'You look as if you could dig any quantity of gold.'

'Perhaps I could if I were on the spot; but as I have no wings to convey me to the diggings, and as my father will

not allow me to fly any kites in his direction, I have taken a billet in the Assay Office; where I hope, by strict economy, to save enough to let me off in two months. It is hard upon a genius like mine to be condemned to look at gold continually; but envy is an evil passion, and ought to be repressed. This young lady is not one of your sisters, surely?'

'Oh, no! it is our cousin, Miss Morison, lately come from Edinburgh, who is kind enough to stay with us in these dull times.'

'Have you heard from your brothers or Martin yet; and what do they say?' asked Harris.

'We have had one letter, written at Melbourne, from Henry Martin,' said Annie. 'They had been dreadfully crammed on board ship; the three were in one cabin, and there were only berths for two, so they took their turns of the beds; but the first night not one of them could sleep at all, for the 'row' their watches made. They had each a watch, and very properly wound them all up at night, but the miserable ticking kept them awake. Henry says that none of the watches were wound up next night. They got lodgings in Melbourne at most exorbitant rates, for one night, and next day they were to set off on foot, throwing their luggage into a cart. How brown they will be when they come back!—and what beards they will all have!'

'I hope to see them when I go,' said Harris; 'but they will have got so much gold then that they will quite despise me!'

'I am sure they will not,' said Annie; 'but I do not want them to stay more than three months at the Mount, so that one of us must be disappointed. Margaret will be quite glad that you are in the Assay Office, for she is enthusiastic about the good it must do. Money seems a little more plentiful already.'

'I am glad to hear it. I hope I may get some of my debtors to pay me as the times get better. Martin owes me five shillings. No, by-the-bye, it is the other way; but it does not signify much among friends. I must come to see you soon. I hope you will make me welcome.'

'I am sure we shall all be glad to see you—Grace especially, as you were a friend of Henry's. I have tried all your sister's songs, and I think I know a great many of them. You have not missed the book, I hope?'

'Not at all! And talking of songs puts me in mind of your friend Minnie. She has a powerful voice, though it is not so sweets as yours. How is Miss Hodges?'

'She is quite well, but a good deal distressed about her brother Charley going off to the diggings. If he had gone with George, they would have been quite satisfied; but he was too late in applying, and would not wait till he heard

where our party was located, but started off last week with a party of working men. Minnie writes to me quite unhappily, for he is her favourite brother, and has never been from home before.'

'What a lucky dog he is to get away at all!' said Harris. 'I suppose your visiting acquaintance is thinned considerably now!'

'Plenty of ladies,' answered Annie, 'are still left, who will not come to see us, but expect us to visit them once a week; and we have had a few gentlemen bidding us good-bye; but that is all, I think, except Mr. Bell, who comes occasionally.'

'William Bell, I suppose. Is not he an odd fish?'

'Margaret likes him because he does not flatter, and is not obtrusive,' said Annie. 'I think Clara likes him too, because he is a study for her. Grace finds his services useful, and, I am sure, I ought to feel grateful too.'

'Grateful for being bored!' exclaimed Harris. 'It is certainly great benevolence on his part to bestow his tediousness on you. Where does he live, for I am in search of lodgings?'

'At Mrs. Brown's,' replied Annie. 'I believe there are vacancies there, and you would be comfortable, I dare say.'

'Then I go to Handy's,' said Harris. 'I only asked, that I might avoid him. Good-bye, young ladies. I may be expected at your house this evening; so tell Miss Margaret that she must not be too political!'

'What do you think of this gentleman, Clara?' asked Annie, when he was out of hearing. 'Don't you think him very amusing?'

'I have not made up my mind what to think of him. I will tell you when I know myself.'

'But you said you liked William Bell the first day you saw him, and I have noticed that you are remarkably quick in seeing through people.'

'Mr. Harris is not so easily seen through as Mr. Bell,' said Clara. 'His temper and manner seem very flighty.'

'Yes, of course; he is far cleverer than the other,' Annie observed.

'A parcel for you, Clara, with Mr. Reginald's compliments,' said Margaret, on their return. 'It feels like books, and I have had a great desire to open it, but have honourably refrained.'

'Yes,' said Clara, unwrapping it. 'He promised me a reading of these poems; but you must recollect they are sent as much to you as to me. Take you one volume, and Annie the other. I cannot read to-day; so, Grace, do give me some work, and tell me what has happened while we were out.'

'The pigs have been in the garden,' answered Grace, 'through the hole in the fence, between us and Mr. Bantam's

cottage; and those schoolboys have broken another window of the empty house. I wish we could get somebody to live there to take care of it, for they don't mind me at all,' said Grace.

'I will go and stop up the gap in the fence,' said Clara; and she went.

'Clara is rather ungracious about these books,' remarked Margaret. 'Not even to open them when they have been sent so far!—and so fond of poetry as she is in general!—one wonders at her preference of hammer and nails to-day!'

Clara took a long time to mend the fence, for she was very awkward at the work. She bruised one of her fingers, and ran a splinter into her thumb; but she contrived to hammer herself out of her excitement, and was more inclined to accept Reginald's compliments coolly after her little bit of fencing.

She even took up one of the volumes when she came in, and read aloud to her cousins, making Margaret admire what she admired from the earnestness with which she read it. But the book opened naturally at the finest passages, and reminded her of traits of a character which she wished to forget.

'Really he has fine taste!' said she to herself. 'In these matter-of-fact days, how rare it is to see a vein of poetical feeling running through a man's nature, as this does through his.'

William Bell came in to tea, and was quite pleased at the idea of seeing Mr. Harris again.

'I have not seen him for a year and a half, and I suppose he will be changed as well as myself,' said he.

'You cannot think how insufferable I was then, and for several years before, Miss Annie. I thought I had seen all that was worth seeing, and knew a great deal more than was worth knowing. Harris used to show me up amazingly, while I despised his capabilities of enjoyment then, but which I envy now, and hope to acquire; for I grow younger every day. I have shaken off a good many wrinkles in this room, and I hope the sight of Harris will rid me of the few grey hairs I have still about me.'

'You are in a transition state,' said Margaret. 'I have observed you casting your slough, and am sure you will come out quite a butterfly soon.'

'After my absurd affectation of old age at one-and-twenty,' said Bell, 'I got into another state—a sort of doubting, wrangling, disputing humour seized me. I began to see that there was something in the world worth living for, and was anxious to prove all things, and hold fast by what was good; but disputing about the truth is not always the best way to

get at it, for I think I learn more from quiet listening, or reading and reflection afterwards, than from the keenest altercation.'

'I remember how well you listened to Mr. Staynes, when we met him at Mr. Plummer's,' said Margaret; 'I had good hopes of you from that day. Was he not very delightful?'

'He was indeed the very best talker I ever heard,' answered Bell.

'Do you know,' whispered Annie to Clara, 'Mr. Staynes told Mrs. Plummer that Margaret was the most intelligent young lady he had seen in the colony. 'Don't you think, Mr. Bell,' she added, aloud, 'that ladies are generally very bad talkers?'

'Certainly not, Miss Annie; of course I know that ladies talk a great deal.'

'Yes, in quantity; but what do you think of the quality?' said Annie.

'The quality depends on the speakers,' was the answer.

'Did you not think there was some one besides Mr. Staynes who talked well on that particular evening,' asked Annie.

'Yes; I thought the little I said myself was very much to the purpose,' said Bell.

'You are incorrigible,' cried Annie; 'but here comes Mr. Harris, who will teach you better than I can.'

Clara was curious to discover the footing on which these gentlemen stood towards Margaret and Annie, and particularly the latter. Her youngest cousin was prettier than the other two, and her manner more winning. Clara liked Bell, because she thought there was a sturdy uprightness about him that would make him a suitable support for gentle Annie, who had been accustomed to lean on other people all her life. But she did not like Harris, considering him full of affectation; and she did not like the attentions which he paid to Annie, and which seemed to be well received. She watched them narrowly, and saw that her cousin drank in all he said with delighted ears; while William Bell was evidently uncomfortable, and took refuge with Margaret. Harris supposed his flattery could do no harm, because everybody knew that he could not afford to marry. But he did not consider that a girl, brought up as Annie Elliot had been, thought nothing of poverty, and knew that a steady young man might easily earn a livelihood sufficient to maintain a wife. He had as good a salary as George had, or William Bell; he had no lack of abilities, and if he was only in love, sufficient motive would be given for exertion. And his constant appeals to her taste, his earnest manner of looking at and addressing her, were making Annie believe that he did love her.

Clara Looks at Adelaide

'I will find out, through Mrs. Handy, what sort of man this Mr. Harris really is,' thought Clara; 'she will let me know many traits of him in her incidental remarks. I hope poor Annie will not give her heart away, as I have done, only to repent of it in bitterness all her life.'

CHAPTER II

A NEW NEIGHBOUR COMES NEXT DOOR

Mrs. Handy was not known to the Elliots, but when they heard how kind she had been to Clara, they had desired her to invite her to visit them. Mrs. Haussen was not included in the invitation, at which she was surprised, but consoled herself by making a very pretty bonnet in the absence of her hostess. She did all her needlework in her own room, with the blinds drawn, for she could not bear to be seen working; yet she was very fond of society, so that there was often a severe conflict between her desire to have everything very smart, and her wish to be amused. Now that Mr. Harris had come to Handy's, she particularly wished to look well, and as flirting was a necessity of his nature, she received more compliments from him in the course of the first half hour, than her husband had paid her during all his courtship and the honeymoon. His letters were in broken English, and in a German hand, which she could not read; and she could only conjecture from their frequency that he had not forgotten her, trusting to his reading them to her when he returned. (Annie Elliot thought it was very perverse that such useless letters should come all right, while the news that they were pining for at home seemed to be buried in the post-office). Mrs. Haussen was very anxious for the oblivion of the fact that she had been a milliner, and talked of 'her relatives in England' with as much importance as if they had been members of parliament at least; so she thought she had convinced Mr. Harris that she had been born and educated a lady.

Such was the substance of what Mrs. Handy said; but she could not help expatiating on the cleverness and good-humour of her new boarder.

'I wont say that he is as good as Mr. Reginald, but he suits a house like mine better, for he keeps everybody merry. We have had two Melbourne gentlemen, who have come

A New Neighbour

across to buy flour, staying with us, and they were delighted with Mr. Harris, and have invited him to come and see them on his way to the diggings. As for Mrs. Haussen, she is not like the same person since he came; she is as blithe as a lark, and my own spirits have got up too; and that was before I heard from Handy from Mount Alexander. He is doing better now, and will send me some gold when he can find a safe way.'

'We are going to have an Adelaide escort to bring the gold here,' said Margaret. 'I hope we shall hear from our brothers when it comes down, for we are sick with hope deferred. It will be some time before we can be sure of that; for the escort has not yet started, and must be several weeks going and returning. I hope they may find water all the way, and a tolerable road, for it will be a great thing for our people to get the yellow dirt direct.'

'Have you heard from Mrs. Bantam yet, Miss Morison?' asked Mrs. Handy.

'Not yet,' said Clara, 'but I am in daily expectation of a letter, for I hear that the vessel has arrived, and she promised to write to me immediately. I wish we knew what to do about the house, for it is getting quite pulled to pieces.'

'Do you know, I found out Miss Ker yesterday, living in a room of a miserable house in a lane,' said Mrs. Handy. 'She goes by the name of Mrs. Smith, and seems very ill indeed, as well as the baby. She is not in want of anything but decent society, and a kind word now and then; for she gets rations and medical comforts from the Destitute Board. The person she lives with is a noisy, quarrelsome Cornish woman, and the sound of her voice is enough to make a person ill of itself; if the poor thing could be taken away from the set of people she is among, she might get better, or at least die more comfortably.'

'What do you think of getting her to occupy Mrs. Bantam's house till it is sold or let,' said Grace. 'It is a nice healthy situation, and we could look in now and then; and even a woman living in the house would save it from destruction. My remonstrances from our yard are of no use.'

'What a good idea,' said Clara, 'particularly as Mrs. Bantam seemed to feel a great sympathy for her wretched fate. I must go to see her as soon as possible; will you come with me, Grace?'

'No, I am in such bad spirits that I should do no good; I would rather that Margaret went with you.'

'If you will come with me,' said Mrs. Handy, 'I will take you to the house she lives in. It is in a low neighbourhood, but I shall be a sort of protection.'

Clara and Margaret were glad of Mrs. Handy's offer, and

accompanied her to Mrs. Smith's wretched lodging. There was noise and dirt all around; and the sight of the thin wasted young woman, of whose beauty scarcely a trace remained, and whom no one would have taken to be a lady, fallen as she was very much to the level of the people she was among, excited great pity in both the cousins.

She did not care for being removed—she was very well where she was—her baby was fond of the noisy Cornish woman, and would go to her when he was cross with herself —and as she had no furniture but a bed, a chair, and a small table, it would be nonsense to go into a large house. But her objections were all over-ruled by the doctor, who happened to call when the visitors were in, and ordered her to accept the kind offer.

'You are getting into such a low nervous state,' said he, 'that you want a little rousing, and the exertion of moving will do you good; besides that, this is not a fit place for an invalid.'

'I will get our waterman to call with his cart to-morrow to bring you over,' added Margaret; 'and you will find that your boy will be much the better for having a little garden to run about in.'

'He can't walk yet, and he is eighteen months old,' Mrs. Smith said, despondingly.

'He will soon learn,' said Clara.

'He has been a very troublesome thing ever since he was born,' continued the mother—'and I did not know how to manage him, and I dare say I have done him a deal of mischief, but it can't be helped. Don't scream so, Bobby, my darling—Shall I give you to your own Tregillian? You will break your heart to part with her to-morrow.'

This was rather an ungracious return for substantial kindness; but our three friends were not easily daunted, and went away, quite pleased at doing the poor thing good against her will. When they parted from Mrs. Handy, Clara told her cousin that at first she had considered her a commonplace talkative woman, without any refinement or delicacy of feeling, but that gradually she had shaken off the landlady, and shown herself a true gentlewoman.

'The most brilliant genius,' Clara said, 'could not have comforted me so much as Mrs. Handy did in my desolate kitchen, when I sent for her; and the way she asked me to do her a favour then, not even yourself could have improved upon.'

'I am not good at doing things of that kind,' said Margaret; 'Grace and Annie are more delicate. But with regard to first impressions, I am very apt to judge of people from them, and

often find myself mistaken; but I thought you were so quick-sighted you could read people at a glance.'

'I leave that to my friend, Miss Withering. When I look into my own heart, and reflect that I have been studying it for twenty years, and do not half understand it yet, I should be diffident in my judgment of others. But, Margaret, is it not delightful to think that the more you know people the better you like them? Surely poor human nature cannot be so bad as it is called, or that would not be the case. I disliked Miss Waterstone at first, but grew to see that she had many good points. Mrs. Handy I looked down upon, and now I love her dearly. Mrs. Bantam taught me a great deal; and Mr. Bantam has twenty times more sense than I gave him credit for at first.'

'You did not learn to like Miss Withering, however,' said Margaret.

'I did not know her, even at the last,' answered Clara. 'Poor woman! what a misfortune it must be to be afflicted with such a disagreeable temper, and to have nobody to love her. But she really knew well how to manage leeches, and was a painstaking nurse.'

'What did you think of me when you saw me first?' asked Margaret.

'I was first envious of you, then afraid of you, and now I am going to try to be like you,' replied Clara. 'If I had had as much courage and strength of mind as you have, I should have got better through my troubles.'

'You would have done no such thing,' Margaret said. 'My mind is strong when it is employed on suitable objects; but I could not bring myself to take a situation, even as governess, in the best family in South Australia. I must and will speak out my mind wherever I am, and I know I should have quarrelled with Mrs. Bantam the very first week of my servitude.'

'And yet you do not mind hard work or tedious work,' observed Clara, 'and have resolution enough to go on with dry and unprofitable studies without encouragement from any one.'

'I pursue these things because they please me,' was the answer; 'but I cannot bear the idea of selling my time, my mind, my identical self, for so much a-year. I think I could get a situation if I tried; but though it would be very proper in present circumstances, I cannot bring my mind to such a thing.'

'Could not I get a situation?' Clara inquired; 'for I am a burden to you.'

'No; for I cannot spare you,' replied Margaret. 'If our brothers do not succeed, and we are forced to live on our

own very scanty means, will you submit to a dry morsel, and quietness therewith, in preference to a better style of living where there is not so much love? You have made me quite interested in your phonetic short-hand, and I must go on with it till I conquer it entirely; you sit and talk with Grace while I am engaged with law; and you take long walks with Annie, which do her a great deal of good; so I beg, as a favour to myself, that you will not think of leaving us till our brothers return. I have now more leisure than I ever had in my life before, and I am anxious to make the most of it.'

'Carlyle says:—'Find your work, and do it,' remarked Clara; 'I wish I could find out what is my proper work; for though I have some good theoretical ideas on education, I do not think I should make a good teacher; and I never felt that the work I did at Mrs. Bantam's was the work I was sent into the world to do.'

'Your vocation is marriage,' said Margaret. 'You are formed to make some good man very happy, and I hope ere long to see you do it. All your little talents are pleasure-giving; you have feeling, and taste, and tact, and I can fancy your husband finding new charms in you every day.'

'Many people mistake their vocation when they marry,' said Clara; 'and if I were to meet with the one man in a thousand that I should like for a husband, how many chances there are that he would not like me for a wife. I suppose the poor girl we have just seen fancied she should be happy when she entered into her new state; and yet it has brought her into a depth of misery, which I hope, even at service, to escape. Is there a prejudice here against old maids? for it is a very mischievous one?'

'Of course, old maids are laughed at here as elsewhere,' Margaret answered, smiling herself; 'and though all our married friends advise us never to marry, as we are so much happier single, I fancy that when I get gray and wrinkled, they will change their tone. They are always complaining of the trouble and care of children, till I often feel angry with them for it.'

'Perhaps it is a delicate way of expressing their sense of their responsibility,' observed Clara.

'You are charitable, Clara; but I believe they do think too much of the trouble,' Margaret persisted. 'And as for the fathers, they seem to look upon their children as pleasures, not as duties. They keep them beside them while they are amusing; but as soon as they begin to be naughty or tiresome, they hand them over to their mothers.'

'My father never did so,' Clara said, 'but I have observed it in others, and have felt as angry at it as you can do.'

'I am glad you did,' said Margaret. 'Different as we are,

A New Neighbour

Clara, we agree on all great points; you despise what is petty, and hate what you think wrong, just as uncompromisingly as I do. People think me hard and cold; but you know me better.'

There was not 'an elbow' Margaret had that Clara did not love her the better for. There were many endearing points about her, and one true soul always recognises another. It was pleasant to have something again to learn, and to associate with people who were not so engrossed with the petty concerns and cares of the present, as to neglect preparation for the future. Margaret's religion was not kept for Sunday use only; it was a continual up-looking—an habitual conscientiousness; and Clara felt that she grew stronger and happier under her cousin's influence. She knew that in religion alone she could find consolation under her trials; and in the comparative leisure she now enjoyed, she found sermons more interesting, and religious meditation more profitable than she had done at Mrs. Bantam's; when she was often too weary to listen to what was preached, and too anxious lest any piece of work should be forgotten or neglected, to pursue any connected train of thought. One requires time to think; and Clara now sometimes laid down her work, and would sit for a quarter of an hour endeavouring either to subdue her idle reveries, or to induce something more profitable, without her cousins, either by words or looks, reproaching her for her idleness. She often saw one smile chasing another on Annie's face, or heard an occasional little sigh escape her, as she worked diligently at the slippers, and wondered what she was thinking of, without daring to ask.

Annie took quite as much interest in Miss Ker as any of the others, and was the first to offer to take the baby for an hour or two, while his mother rested from the fatigue of the removal. He was not nicely dressed; but Clara rummaged out something, and got Grace to show her how to cut a new frock for him, and set about making it as fast as possible. Bobby was crying in Annie's arms when Mr. Harris called, and he looked annoyed to find her so much engrossed with the cross little monkey, as he called it, when he had expected her to be both ready and able to amuse him, either by music or badinage.

Clara related the history of the unfortunate mother, as far as she knew it, with earnestness; but her enthusiasm called forth no correspondent feeling from him. Perhaps it was too much to expect a man to sympathize in a woman's wrongs; but he seemed flippant.

'How very heroic you all are,' said he, 'to venture on benevolence to such a questionable object! I was reading, in a silly novel, recommended to me by Mrs. Haussen, that very serious imputations were cast upon a young lady of rank,

who deigned to visit a person who had been entrapped into a mock marriage, like your friend Miss Ker; but that the angelic creature was superior to all such considerations. Certainly, Miss Margaret has courage enough for anything; but I did not expect Miss Annie and Miss Morison to be so quixotic.'

'I do not think you like children,' said Clara.

'They are horrid pests when they are babies,' he answered; 'but I like them when they begin to talk, and are amusing. I believe there is a great deal of affectation in the fuss ladies make about them. It looks amiable, does it not, Miss Annie?'

Annie kept rocking the child in her arms, and singing monotonously to it; but she felt grieved that Harris should think her affected.

'Have you heard from your brothers, Miss Elliot?' continued he. 'There is a vessel in from Melbourne to-day, and we are getting a great deal of gold into the office.'

'We have not heard yet,' said Grace; 'but we get such accounts of the miserable state of things at the diggings, that we are quite unhappy. Nobody dares to go out at night for fear of being robbed and murdered, and the health of the generality of the diggers is very bad. Annie, give me the child; you cannot pacify it.'

'No, Grace, let me keep it. I promised his mother to nurse him myself, and I will keep my promise,' said Annie.

Mr. Harris talked to Margaret and Grace for half an hour, and then went home to Handy's to dinner; where he was pleased to see that he could make Mrs. Haussen nearly forget, that her husband had sent her thirty ounces of gold by the newly arrived ship.

The Elliots found their new neighbour rather exacting, liking some one to talk to, and being always glad to get rid of the baby, which cried so much that it made her ill; so that they were almost constantly encumbered with it. Adversity had changed Miss Ker from a lively, good-humoured girl, into a miserable and selfish woman. She liked to see the new frocks her neighbours made for Bobby, but wanted energy to do anything for him herself. The doctor begged the Elliots to bear with her, telling them it was impossible either mother or child could live many weeks. Miss Ker talked about her husband with bitterness, and was fond of recounting all the falsehoods he had told her. She also dwelt on the appearance of his true wife, saying how much she hated her, and what pert, ugly things all the children were. But not even of her husband did she speak so bitterly as of Mrs. Campbell; for, she said, 'If it had not been for her, I am sure I could have married Mr. Johnson, and I should have been rich and comfortable, instead of being trodden upon

A New Neighbour

by everybody. If he had only seen more of me, I am sure he would have made me a proposal. Do you know him, Miss Annie, for I should like to see him again?'

'I have met him once or twice,' said Annie. 'He is at the diggings now.'

'Just let me see him when he returns,' said Miss Ker, 'for I may have some hold on him yet.'

William Bell was authorised to take in the letters for the Elliots and Miss Morison, and to bring them to their house. Their hearts used to beat quick in anticipation when they saw him walking hastily to the house, but the first letter he brought was a great disappointment to the Elliots, for it was from Mrs. Bantam to Clara. The first pang over, they were anxious to know if Clara was to leave them, and as there were no secrets in it, she read it to her cousins. It ran thus:—

'MY DEAR CLARA,

'I promised to write to you when we got settled, and as we are as much established here as we can hope to be for some time to come, I take up my pen to tell you my adventures.

'Our voyage was rather a quick one, as we got across in a week; but the ship was so crowded, and the people in the next cabins were so disagreeable, that I was quite glad when it was over. I did not want to stay in the vessel after Mr. Bantam had left it, so we landed together, and began the difficult search for lodgings. We were directed first to one house, then to another, and another; but every place was full to overflowing. Then we tried the inns, and though I offered to wait upon myself, and to give no trouble if they would only give us house-room, it was of no use. The streets were crowded with noisy men and women driving about furiously in gigs; I counted five diggers' weddings while I was going about; the women were prodigiously smart, but the bridegrooms had only those horrid tartan things, like short smock-frocks—they call them jumpers here—which all the returned diggers seem to wear, and which looked very shabby beside white satin and lace veils. I was footsore and miserable, but still was determined not to go back to the ship if I could help it, when at the last public-house Mr. Bantam inquired at, we were directed to go up a narrow lane, where there were apartments to let.

'For the first time that day, we got an answer of 'Yes' to our inquiries. I was so glad that I sat down, but was vexed to hear that we could not have a room to ourselves. I could have a bed in a room where there were three ladies already, and Mr. Bantam was to have a sofa in the parlour. However, there was no help for it, and Mr. Bantam went back to see

about getting our most necessary luggage brought to our lodgings, and left me staring at the six sofas, that were ranged all round the room, with an idea that each of them was slept on at night. I begged to be shown into my room, that I might arrange my dress before dinner; and the landlady, who was a red-faced, vulgar woman, made a sort of apology for Mrs. Tomkins, who was in bed, as she felt poorly. The bedroom was wretchedly dirty, and there was such a smell of spirits and tobacco in the house, that I felt quite sick. I had not got myself fairly tidy when I was summoned to dinner; but oh! what a scene met my eyes. Dirty, unshaved men, who were swearing at everything and nothing, and women who seemed unsexed altogether. It was a ship-load of convicts from Van Diemen's Land, with or without a ticket-of-leave; none of them deserved to be let loose on society, I was sure; the people who kept the house were old convicts; Mrs. Tomkins was intoxicated; and there was I without my husband, exposed to every kind of insolence.

'I thought Mr. Bantam would never return; when he did, I begged him to take me back to the ship. Of course, we forfeited the three pounds ten shillings we had advanced, and got a great deal of abuse besides from the people in the house. I was obliged to go into the bedroom for my bonnet and shawl, and found that Mrs. Tomkins had got well enough to help herself to my handsome cameo, which I had left on the dressing-table. She used such dreadful language, that I did not dare to complain, but went off with Mr. Bantam as fast as I could.

'We stayed on board ship for a few days, paying for the accommodation, till Mr. Bantam could get the house we live in now. We pay a hundred a year for it, and it only consists of two small rooms; but it is in a nice situation in Collingwood, which may be called the North Adelaide of Melbourne. It is more crowded than North Adelaide, and there are scarcely any gardens or vineyards to be seen, nor any villages round about the town; but yet it is better than Melbourne itself. Mr. Bantam has to walk between two and three miles every day to his business, but he does not seem to mind it. Melbourne is a much finer town than Adelaide in many respects, but it is not a nice place to live in. The streets are alternately broad and narrow, such as Great Collins-street and Little Collins-street, Great Bourke-street and Little Bourke-street; but all these are well built on. The lanes are horrible; and there are so many of them, and they are tenanted by such low people, that it is a wonder they do not bring a pestilence on the town. I miss the park lands very much here, and also the fruit, so abundant at this time in Adelaide, but here extravagantly dear. Vegetables, too,

are unattainable; milk is four shillings a quart, and butter as much per pound. Water is four shillings a hogshead, though we are quite near the river. I see quite respectable-looking women, with handsome dresses, drawing water from the river in pailsful.

'Melbourne is a wonderfully stirring town, and Mr. Bantam thinks his prospects are good. I have seen a good many Adelaide people, and you cannot think how my heart warms to them. There is a nice family living near us; that I am grown quite attached to. Mr. Hallam is a pleasant old gentleman, and his wife is very clever, but never disagreeable, as Miss Withering used to be. Two of the young men are at the diggings, and the girls are always talking about their cleverness; so I hope the Hallams would make up to you for the Elliots, in some measure. They used to live in North Adelaide, but I never saw them before.

'Mr. Reginald's letter did Mr. Bantam good, for Mr. Harringdean has shown us great kindness. Your friend, Mr. Campbell, is getting into first-rate business here, and has paid the three hundred pounds to Mr. Bantam, who has since remitted it to our friend, Mr. Reginald.

'I cannot think of asking you to come across here, while we are in such a small house, but depend upon it, that whenever we can find room we shall want you. Write to me how things go on in Adelaide, and if our poor cottage has been inquired about, and if the garden has gone to ruin. Have you seen or heard anything of Miss Withering? Mr. Bantam told Mr. Dillon his mind about her when he announced our removal: he called her an insufferable incubus. I hope to goodness she will not change her mind, and come here.

'I trust you get on nicely with your cousins, and that the young gentlemen are doing well at the diggings. There seems to be no falling off, but rather an increase in the quantity of gold brought down weekly. Give the Misses Elliot my kind regards, and remember Mr. Bantam and myself to Mr. Reginald, when you see him; and believe me, ever yours truly,

'E. BANTAM.'

After Clara had told Mr. Bell what might be considered the public news of this letter, Annie showed Bobby to him, saying:—

'This is one of the present occupants of poor Mrs. Bantam's cottage. Even his sick mother prevents the mischievous children from pulling it to pieces.'

'Will you do us a favour, Mr. Bell?' said Grace. 'We have no small wood, and should be glad if you would take George's place, and chop us a little.'

The visitor at once complied, and went into the yard, while Annie followed with the child, who wanted to be out of doors. She sat down on a log, and pleased Bobby by letting him watch the chopping; while William secretly admired her gentle face and soft brown eyes, as they turned tenderly on the helpless object on her knee.

'What a sad story that is of Miss Ker,' said he; 'I heard of it at the time it happened. I think there is nothing so dastardly as to deceive a woman, as Smith deceived her. There she is, or at least the wreck of what she was, coming up to us.'

'Are you tired of Bobby?' the mother asked.

'Not at all,' answered Annie. 'I think he is beginning to be fond of me, and to forget his old landlady. Don't you think he looks better since he came here?'

'I don't expect I shall be able to rear him at all,' said Mrs. Smith. 'But, however, you are more able to nurse him than I am, for I have such a pain in my side, I cannot do it.' And Mrs. Smith returned to her cottage.

'She is not very grateful,' said Bell; 'but I am glad to see you do not expect too much. She has had much to try her temper, and we who have been more fortunate should make allowances. Look! Bobby, here is a famous stroke coming down!—There is a lady just come to Mrs. Brown's, who seems to hate children; pushing little Amy about, and scolding Fred. It is not good to see a woman without a kind heart for children, and I am sure I shall never like this Miss Withering.'

'Miss Withering!' cried Annie. 'Has she left Mrs. Denfield's, or is she only on a visit to town?'

'It is no business of mine, and I made no inquiries; but when ladies whisper very loud, one cannot help hearing,' said Bell. 'I heard Miss Withering telling our hostess what a very superior person Mrs. Denfield was, and that the family were excellent, with one exception; but, as she said, 'one bitter drop is sufficient for me, I would not remain to create disunion in the family; and I hope Mr. Denfield will reflect seriously on the sacrifice that has been made to him'.'

'I shall write Minnie Hodges all about it,' said Annie; 'she was staying at Mrs. Bantam's while Miss Withering was there, and was made quite wretched and ill by her; and indeed so was Clara, all the time Miss Withering was in the house.'

Here Annie stopped short, and blushed. She had tried to keep Clara's situation at Mrs. Bantam's secret from everybody, and had presented her as a fashionable cousin from Edinburgh; insisting on her sewing on all her flounces again, and wearing her best dresses.

'I knew what your cousin was before she came to you,' said William; 'but you do not fancy I should think the less

A New Neighbour

of her for what she did; or the less of you, because you had been kind to Mrs. Bantam's servant.'

'Why, Mr. Bell, that is but a negative compliment,' Annie answered; 'as I get no positive ones from you, I must treasure this up.'

William looked rather sadly in her face, and began to chop very hard indeed; and Annie thought it was a great pity Harris and he could not divide each other's good qualities between them, for they would make two delightful men, if better balanced.

CHAPTER III

MR. HARRIS'S PROSPECTS OF GETTING TO THE DIGGINGS
LOOK BRIGHTER

As the weeks and months passed away without any letters arriving from their brothers, the Elliots felt very unhappy, and Clara found she must throw aside her own griefs in order to try to mitigate theirs. Grace would cry over her needlework, Margaret could no longer fix her attention on her books, and poor Annie found the slippers very trying to her eyes, and used to walk with Bobby every day towards the Flagstaff, to see if any vessels were coming in from Melbourne. William Bell told them to blame the post-office, which was wretchedly managed; and assured them that if anything seriously bad had happened, they would certainly have heard of it. Everything that he could hear about the diggings that was at all cheerful, he told them; he advised them not to judge of the state of things at the Mount by what was reported of Melbourne, for, as he said, people who were digging for gold were far more orderly than those who were spending it.

'You are sure to hear from them by the Escort at any rate; and when I go, I will deliver your letters into their own hands. I wish I had this concern fairly wound up, but I cannot leave Adelaide till I have disposed of my brother's premises, and Mr. Macnab is a cautious Scotchman, who is very slow in coming to terms. He has been five evenings at Mrs. Brown's already to talk to me about it, and gave Miss Withering an opportunity of displaying her eloquence. He seems to think her a clever, sensible woman, and I am afraid she will enslave him.'

'I do not think it,' said Clara; 'for I never saw a man so afraid of female fascination as he is.'

'But Miss Withering is not fascinating, and there lies his danger,' answered Bell; 'if she were young and pretty, and seemed amiable, he would be on his guard; but she is none of these, and makes no secret of her real love of money.

Mr. Harris's Prospects

She talks at great length on the importance of wealth, on the weight it gives its possessor, and the miserable condition of those who have it not, and Mr. Macnab cannot help agreeing with all she says. She tells him of her engagement as a daily governess, does not disguise that she has only a paltry salary, but boasts that she can make as handsome an appearance on a little, as other people on a great deal. Really I hate the woman.'

'Because she slights you, and prefers Mr. Macnab,' said Annie, laughing.

'No, it is not for that; it is because she is so unfeminine; she seems to lower the character of the sex by ignoring everything good and gentle.'

'I am glad she did not come to Handy's,' said Harris, who had also dropped in this evening, 'for though Mrs. Haussen is intensely silly, she tries to be agreeable even to a penniless dog like myself; and she is both young and pretty, which would make me overlook a host of faults.'

'So it would not me,' exclaimed Bell; 'for if a person is not good or amiable when young and pretty, when can she be? I think it is much harder to be amiable when one is old and ugly; don't you think so, Miss Annie?'

'People always reckon youth and beauty as temptations, but I suppose that is only to comfort those who have not got them,' replied Annie.

'I think it is very hard to be good when one has nothing to attract the liking of other people,' said Bell; 'it is a mistake in novels to represent the neglected child growing up beautiful and amiable, for coldness is a bad atmosphere for the virtues to thrive in. Many whom we find it difficult to love, would be made more amiable by a little affection, than more attractive people are by a great deal.'

'Like all your countrymen, Bell, you are fond of getting metaphysical,' remarked Harris.

'Like all your countrymen, you are fond of having nothing said that you cannot say better yourself, I might retort,' said Bell.

'What countryman do you suppose me to be?' Harris asked.

'Irish, of course,' was the answer.

'I am English by extraction; but I was born in Scotland and educated in Ireland. You are all Scotch here, so I choose to be considered a Caledonian.'

'*I* am not Scotch!' said Annie; 'I am colonial!'

'Then I, too, am colonial. An adept in all colonial phraseology, skilful in compounding colonial beverages, unrivalled in enlivening colonial public dinners, and drawing all I have to live upon from the colonial treasury!'

'I suppose you will not do the last long, for you intend to be at the diggings before Mr. Bell,' said Clara.

'I intended to do so, Miss Morison, but really Adelaide is a more expensive place to live in than Kooringa; and at my present rate of saving, it will take me three years and four months to get to Mount Alexander, according to an elaborate calculation which I made last night.'

'Is there any necessity for your spending so much money?' Margaret asked, gravely. 'Setting aside your desire to go to the diggings, you should think of the possibilities of sickness and accidents, and provide against them.'

'I don't think you are very anxious to go to the diggings,' observed Bell. 'You lead a pleasant enough life here, and are not driven out of the colony by necessity, as so many of us are.'

'And if you were in my place you would stay,' said Harris; —'you would be quite contented with a hundred and thirty pounds a-year, while so many fellows were making their thousands gold-digging? Why, even if my salary were ten times what it is, I should want to see the gold fields just the same. It shows a great lack of spirit to stay quietly boxed up in an office, when all the adventurous young men in the colony are camping at Mount Alexander!'

'Then you really wish to go?' said Bell, emphatically.

'Yes, I do;—but what is the use of tantalizing me about it? It only makes me miserable! Pray, Miss Elliot, play something that we can dance to, to put me in good humour.'

Grace played a polka; Harris asked Clara to dance with him, and William Bell took Annie. Harris had never danced with Clara before; and when he saw how graceful she was, he thought Annie must feel jealous, particularly as Bell was a very second-rate performer. He talked to Clara, and tried to make himself agreeable; while Clara, willing on her part to draw him out, kept up the conversation with spirit. William Bell very soon became tired, and set his partner down.

'Don't you think my cousin very pretty?' then whispered Annie to him; 'and does not she dance much better than we poor colonial girls do?'

'Yes, I dare say she does,' answered he. 'But I hope you do not let Harris know all about her, for he might make her feel uncomfortable.'

'I don't think he would, Mr. Bell. You do not do Mr. Harris justice,' replied Annie, not liking Bell's attempt to take advantage of his rival's neglect.

Singing soon followed. William Bell begged Annie to sing 'The Flowers of the Forest.' She tried it, but soon broke down; for she could not overcome the feeling of its applicability to their present case; all the flowers of South Australia being

Mr. Harris's Prospects

indeed gone, and no one knowing when they would return. Mr. Harris almost regained the ground he had lost, by praising the air very much, and requesting Annie to copy it for him, to take to the diggings, and sing there, which she promised to do.

When the young men were on their way home, Bell said to his companion, 'I could lend you enough money to take you to the Mount, if you do not need much; and I dare say you will be able to pay me in nuggets when I get up there myself.'

'Oh! twenty pounds is all I want, and you really are a good fellow to make the offer. You shall be paid, principal and interest, whenever I have it; but take care not to give it to me till I am on the point of starting, or I may lose sight of it; I am the worst fellow in the world to take care of money.'

'I do not want any interest, but of course I should like my money again, for I have had much ado to save the little I have.'

'You are a brick!' said Harris, 'and you will lose nothing by me, I assure you. I shall give notice at the office to-morrow, and then, hurrah for the diggings!'

The attention of the Elliots was diverted from their personal anxieties by the alarming illness of poor little Bobby, who, as his mother had anticipated, was not strong enough to cut his double teeth. The little fellow fretted and pined for two days, and then, on the third, became so quiet and peaceful, that Clara and Annie were sure he would win through it; but Grace shook her head. Grace had had great experience amongst her married friends' families, and turned out to be in the right; for Bobby died in Clara's arms late on the third night. Though the mother had talked with apparent indifference of the probability of his death, the reality awoke all her maternal instinct, and her grief was violent. The only thing she had on earth was taken from her—her own dear pretty boy! How she longed now to hear his querulous cry, and felt that she could never weary of watching over and working for him! She thanked her friends for all their kindness to her poor child, but would not trouble them any more, she said; she only wanted to die, and be with her boy. She looked at the dress she wore, which was old and faded, saying something about not having anything black; but it was no matter; and then begged them all to go away, and leave her to weep by herself.

Next morning, the family held a sort of council about providing her with mourning: 'For it is evident,' said Grace, 'that it would comfort poor Mrs. Smith to have a black gown to wear for her boy.'

'It is an absurd custom,' observed Margaret, 'to wear mourning at all. It gives people gloomy ideas of death, and is a very expensive thing at a very expensive time. The Society of Friends wear no mourning, and I think they are right.'

'You wore mourning yourself for our father and mother,' said Annie, 'and I think it is a graceful custom; and if I were Mrs. Smith, I should not like wearing coloured clothes.'

'I wore mourning, first, because my mother wished me to do so, and afterwards to please George and Grace, but not because I thought it either necessary or right; still, I make no objection to Miss Ker having mourning, and if I had the money, I should think it well bestowed on any comfort to her.'

'Do you think she would be too proud to wear an old dress?' asked Clara; 'I have two tolerably good, which I threw off when it got so hot on board-ship.'

The dresses were brought out, and Mrs. Smith was pleased with them, and laid them down, saying that when she got up next morning, she would try on one of them. But they lay untouched for days and days; the bereaved mother never grew strong enough to rise; she became weaker and weaker, and one or other of her neighbours was constantly with her.

'Have you any relations in Scotland?' asked Clara, wishing, in case of her death, to know to whom to write.

'Only some brothers and sisters by the half-blood, and a step-father, whom I never could bear. My mother has been long dead, and her husband married again. I was at school all my life till I came out here.'

'Did you like your teacher?' asked Clara, remembering the love and gentleness of her own dear instructress.

'Oh! yes, when she was not cross; but I was quite glad when they told me I was to come here, for I thought I should have my own way; but you see it has been a very miserable way.'

'I was sent out with a letter to Mr. Campbell, like you,' Clara said; 'and with a strong recommendation to Mrs. Campbell's motherly care; but she had been dead a year when I came out, and Mr. Campbell was quite surprised that I did not know of it. I regretted it exceedingly at the time, for I found myself compelled to go to service; but, after all, it was not a bad thing for me. So you need not be surprised that I take a great interest in you.'

'I dare say Mr. Campbell fancied you were sent out to be his second wife,' said Mrs. Smith; 'he was always rather suspicious, though not so bad as Mrs. Campbell.'

It flashed across Clara's mind that this was true, from a singular expression which she had sometimes observed in Mr. Campbell's face; and she wondered if her uncle had really

been so regardless of her character and comfort, as to send her out with so questionable an object. But here we will do Mr. Morison justice. He did not trouble himself to read the Adelaide papers, which Mr. Campbell occasionally sent to him, and was consequently ignorant of the death of his friend's wife. He remembered that the Campbells were kind, hospitable people in Edinburgh, and trusted that Clara's connexion with himself, her orphan condition, and her odd accomplishments, might ingratiate her with his friends, and that they would push her into society where she might settle in life. People in India are always glad to have a pretty girl to bring out, and he expected no less in South Australia.

When Mrs. Smith once began to talk of Mrs. Campbell, she was apt to continue the subject till she was quite exhausted; and on this occasion she brought on such a violent fit of coughing, that Clara was dreadfully alarmed, and called in her cousins. Margaret went for the doctor with all possible despatch; but when he came, he said that nothing could be done; he had been expecting his patient to be carried off in this way for some time back; and he assured Clara, who reproached herself for exciting Miss Ker by talking of past events, that nothing could have prolonged her life for a week, while the most trifling exertion might have killed her before.

'Poor Miss Ker!' said Margaret; 'this has been an unfriendly land for her; here she has lost name and fame, and joy and hope.'

'Let us trust that she leaves this world for a better,' said the doctor, as he closed her eyes, and told the Elliots that all their cares on her account were over.

They were sitting talking of their late neighbour, and almost forgetting that there was such a thing as a Flagstaff, when Annie exclaimed,—

'Here is William Bell; he is bringing us letters, I am sure, by his face.'

She opened the door for him with a radiant smile, and he lost no time in delivering three letters—one for each of the Elliots—saying, that the escort was coming in with the gold in the afternoon, but that the mail had been sent forward for delivery first.

He was going away to let them read their letters in quiet, but he looked very anxious to hear the news; and Margaret insisted on his staying till they had picked out what might interest him.

'Well,' said William, 'then I shall ask Miss Morison to come into the garden with me, for I am afraid I may otherwise look inquisitive while you read.'

Clara stepped out of the French window with him, and told him the sad tale of the death of their neighbour.

'I wonder how Smith feels now,' said he; 'I should not be surprised if I meet him at the diggings, for he was always a roving character; if so, I will tell him what has happened, and I hope he may have the grace to be sorry. I looked hard at the addresses of these letters, and I think they seemed healthy enough. How I long to get beside George and Gilbert again! You do not know them yet, Miss Morison; but I am sure you will like them when you do. They have had the advantage of being always in ladies' society, and though they are not very polished, they are never so awkward as I am.'

'They are not so accomplished as Mr. Harris, but I cannot say I like him much,' observed Clara.

'I thought all ladies liked him,' said Bell.

'Oh, no!' exclaimed Clara. 'Women are not so simple as you think them. A man can very rarely sing or dance himself into a woman's heart; I think we understand the beauty of truth and uprightness as well as you.'

'I am glad you say so, for unless I have these, I have little else to recommend me,' Bell answered.

'And you really wish to please us,' said Clara; 'you need not then doubt of success. Do you expect to start soon?'

'Yes; Macnab has come to terms at last, and I hope to go in a fortnight. I fear Miss Withering will miss her swain, for he will hardly come to Mrs. Brown's except on business. His assistant has left him, which the lady considers a great hardship; 'for,' says she, 'though Mr. Macnab's mind is eminently a commercial one, it is not fitted for the petty details of the counter, and it must be ruinous to his constitution to have no relaxation and no congenial society'.'

'Then Mr. Renton has gone?' said Clara; 'I must go into the shop some day, and see how Mr. Macnab comes on by himself.'

'I think Renton was foolish to go to the diggings, when Macnab offered him a share of the business; but it was in dull times, and he thought there was little prospect of things looking up again. However, the place is open for him when he returns.'

'Mr. Harris goes on Wednesday, does he not?' said Clara. 'I cannot think where he found the money, unless he only makes a parade of extravagance, while secretly saving. Margaret is beginning to suspect the latter, and you know she is more lenient to extravagance than to avarice; but she does not know what to think of this sudden change.'

William Bell felt reluctant to tell even Clara that he had lent the requisite money to Harris, for he was not sure that it was right either to lend it or to talk of it. He began to twist the creepers round the twine that Annie had nailed and

tied to the pillars of the verandah, while Clara snipped off the withered roses which disfigured the bushes.

When they were called in to hear the news, Grace in the first place gave Bell an escort-receipt for five ounces and a half of gold, which had been enclosed to her.

'Is it not a poor thing for these three dear fellows to have been working for so long and so hard? You must try to dispose of it for us, for little as it is, we need it greatly; and indeed, Mr. Bell, we shall miss you very much. They have written often to us, but these are the first letters that have come safe, and Henry says he has only received one of mine, though I wrote regularly once a fortnight.'

Margaret read her letter from Gilbert straight through, but Grace and Annie left out great pieces of theirs. However, we will give them entire, as we have no secrets with our readers.

CHAPTER IV

LETTERS FROM THE DIGGINGS

From Henry Martin to Grace Elliot.

'Forest Creek.

'My Dearest Grace,—

'If I were not sure that you write to me, and that your affection is unchanged, I should have been miserable indeed, for I never received a letter till last Sunday, and that was written about ten days after we sailed.

'We are accustomed to be separated, but I used to go once a week to the post-office at Kooringa, as certain of a letter as I was of my dinner,—indeed, more so, for Mrs. White sometimes disappointed me, but you never did. Now, Sunday after Sunday, I dress myself as well as circumstances will permit, at least putting on a clean shirt, but of course not shaving—for a man would be quite a Guy here without a beard—and sally to the tent which serves as a post-office, which is three miles off, but can hear nothing either good or bad. How thankful I was to see Tolmer and his band come up the other day, for I feel sure that what I write now will reach you, and that the next escort will bring an answer. There is a great deal of jealousy of Adelaide men amongst the Victoria and New South Wales people, and they are making rather a row about our police coming through their country, to fetch away the gold we have dug, without its passing through their city and port of Melbourne. But I was glad to see Tolmer sitting in the Chief Commissioner's tent; they were drinking wine together, and the Commissioner seemed quite gracious, so I hope it is all right. It is intended to erect a house for the Commissioner soon; at present he is in a tent handsomely fitted up, and lined with black velvet.

'Though we have all written often, I suppose I must take it for granted that you have received none of our letters, and begin at the beginning. We stayed only one night at Mel-

Letters from the Diggings

bourne, in a miserable lodging-house, where we three slept in the same room with three other queer customers. There was a lame man, a very deaf man, and one subject to fits, all bound for the diggings. It cost us thirty shillings for the day and night, food and accommodation for three, which is not so bad as California used to be.

'Next morning we set out on our eighty miles walk, and putting our traps on a dray, we walked by the side of them, and camped every night. We might have got up in three days easily if we had not been obliged to stay with our goods; but the roads for vehicles are horrible. The streets of Melbourne are highly praised, and are really better than those of Adelaide; but once out of the town, there is not a mile of made road in any direction. So we took six days to reach Forest Creek, where we pitched our tent. It is entirely occupied by Adelaide men, as the South Australians are all called here, whether they come from Mount Remarkable or Encounter Bay. They are wonderfully friendly among themselves, and we were glad to hear familiar voices amongst them when we came up.

'It is a perfect lottery here; we have sunk nine holes already, and have got nothing, while from holes close by us fellows have taken pounds upon pounds of gold. I saw one party take eighteen pounds' weight of gold from a hole that touched ours, in a day and a half. We can only say, 'Better luck next time'; but I must confess, my dear Grace, that I am ashamed of our first remittance, for it *is* the first,— we have sent nothing before, either *viâ* Melbourne, or by private hand. Here have we paid two months' licence—that is nine pounds for three—we have worked like slaves, and send you five ounces and a half of gold, worth here only two pounds fifteen per ounce.

'However, we have cleared our expenses hitherto, for we bought a lot of stuff from a party who were so busy nuggeting, that they would not take the trouble to wash for the smaller particles, and we hired a horse and cart, and took it four miles to wash it in the creek. Such dust we had to drive through! Adelaide is a joke to it, and even the Burra road is, comparatively speaking, a pure atmosphere. Oh, Grace! if you could have seen me there, with such a dirty face and hands, and looking as cross as the policemen do when they catch a chap working without a licence, I fear you would neither have known me when you saw me, nor liked me when you knew me. But it always did me good to remember your dear, gentle face, and I can tell you that one thought of you used to make me relax the muscles of my begrimed countenance, and give an afflicted sort of smile.

'Five ounces and a half! This does not look like our getting

married soon; but don't think I despair. If people will only persevere long enough, they will be successful in the end, and if we cannot raise the money for our licences next month, we shall go into some employment, and not be too proud to work for wages, till we can raise the thirty shillings a piece, and start afresh. If we could just clear two hundred each, and come back to find Adelaide so far recovered as to give us employment again, I think we need delay matters no longer. It is two years and a half now since we were engaged, and though I have been very patient hitherto, the thought that a lucky stroke may enable us to marry at once, makes my heart beat very restlessly, and sends my pickaxe down with double force. Now, write to me, dear Grace, to tell me how little you would be satisfied with, and also how things are going on, for we hear such confused accounts. It is of no use sending newspapers through the post-office, but if William Bell comes, make up a packet for him to bring us.

'I have turned out a capital cook — decidedly the best of the party — so you will know who to apply to on an emergency. No doubt I made mistakes sometimes; the first plum-pudding we made was a singular production. I made George stone the plums, and Gilbert chop the suet, while I put on the pot to boil the pudding in, and made a damper. There was a pannikin full of plums, and another of suet; with this I mixed up five pannikins of flour, and kneaded it up as stiff as the damper. It was in vain that George told me puddings were made in a basin, and stirred with a spoon. I told him that these were delusive puddings, and not the substantial fare which working men required; so I tied it in a cloth, and boiled it for five hours. And was it not a stiff piece of work? We took three days to get through it; and the jokes that were perpetrated, as I chewed away at the cold pudding, were very aggravating. However, I am now quite a proficient in the art, and some of our hungry neighbours like to drop in on a Sunday to take a share of Martin's pudding; for there are many here worse off than ourselves, who live in a sort of scrambling way upon chance hospitality; and they do clear everything before them. Many a time we have thought ourselves provisioned for two days, and half-a-dozen fellows would drop in, sometimes altogether, but generally by two and two, and polish off everything we had in the house, so that we were obliged to bake fresh damper for tea, and eat it without mutton; for it is only in the morning that the butchers will serve you, and then you must buy a whole quarter, or you will get none.

'And, oh! Grace, the washing has been a dreadful business; we should have taken lessons from you before we went away, but we had a conceited idea that all women's work was easy,

and could be done by instinct. And I had passed myself off to your brothers as completely up to the thing, and was entrusted with the management of the first washing. I took the clothes, and cut up half a bar of soap, and put them into the pot with a lot of stones and pebbles, thinking that the friction would be beneficial, and boiled all together for two or three hours. Then I took them out, saying that if they were not clean, they ought to be by this time; but the stewed shirts and trousers looked horrible; even diggers were ashamed to wear them, for the dirt was completely boiled into them, —fast colours, and no mistake; and I felt so completely discomfited, that I let George and Gilbert wash by themselves next time; but their exploits were very little better than mine, which consoled me in some measure. However, one day I saw an old woman drawing water from a deserted hole, (these holes are all the wells we have here,) which was very hard work for her; she was the first woman I had seen on the diggings, and I was glad to have it in my power to help her. She was profuse in her thanks, and I insinuated that I should be more than repaid by a few plain directions about washing; these she gave me at considerable length, and my success has been brilliant ever since, though we find it very hard work. We are all very much shocked at the idea of your having to wash, now that we know how disagreeable it is, and hope that if we are successful, you will not need to do it in future.

'We have a lot of Burra miners here, who have a bad trick of undermining other people's holes, and taking the gold out of them, so that when you fancy you are striking into the real good stuff, down comes your crowbar upon disappointing emptiness. They have not been uniformly successful, and I have seen a good many who regret their comfortable billets under the South Australian Mining Association.

'We send you the escort receipt for the gold; it is in a chamois-leather bag, marked with your name. Next time you will have to pay two per cent. for its safe conveyance to Adelaide, but this Tolmer says is a labour of love; so you will have it all; and a miserable lot it is. It is part of what we washed out of Jones' party's rejected stuff; I believe it is likely to be published in the Adelaide newspapers, so there will be plenty of chaff flying about touching Elliot's party's large remittance.

'I know it was you that put up the portfolio for us to write upon, and we are very glad of it; for it is unpleasant to write on one's knee, or even on the top of one's hat; I must now resign it to George, who looks volumes at me, and will, no doubt, write a voluminous letter to Annie.

'And now, dear Grace, I must bid you farewell; you cannot think how reluctant I am to cease, when I think that you will

really get my letter. God bless you, my dear girl, comfort you in all your troubles, and make me worthy of you, is the constant prayer of

'Yours more than ever,
Henry Martin.'

George Elliot to his sister Annie.
Forest Creek.

'My Dear Little Sister,—

'I hope you have given up crying for us by this time, though I do not wish you to give up missing us. It was a comfort to receive one letter from you, though a very old one, in which you said something about finding a relation in whom you are interested, for anything that diverts your mind will also relieve it. I feel curious to see this new-found cousin, whom you call so pretty. I fear she will become a formidable rival to Minnie in your friendship, if she stays long with you. We have seen nothing yet of Charley Hodges, but as we are not sure that you have been able to tell him where we are, perhaps he has not started. You can let him know that we are at Forest Creek, three miles from the post-office, and next tent to Esdaile's store. When you write to Minnie, tell her that we have all been very glad of her 'Shakespeare.' Perhaps it is as well that Charley did not join us, for we have been by no means lucky, and I should have been vexed to have taken him into such a poor affair.

'I think you would laugh to see what a fierce-looking fellow I am now, 'bearded like a pard.' Of course Henry and Gilbert are bearded too, but they are recognisable. Tom Dennis, who was working in the next hole, knew Harry by his voice, and found out Gilbert after a good look, but was obliged to ask who t'other chap was; and I could not help laughing to think that a fellow who had been for years in the same store with me, should not know me; but my laugh betrayed me, and he slapped me on the back, and asked me what I meant by disguising myself so. But the voice is the great means of recognition all over the diggings.

'I have not seen anything of Harris yet, and as I hear he has got a situation in the Assay Office, we can hardly expect him now. He promised to teach me to sing the Standard Bearer, and he should be just the man to enliven poor diggers. Should Wiliam Bell come over, I hope he will join our party, supposing we become more successful, for he is really a capital fellow, though not so amusing as Harris. William acts upon principle, and Harris upon impulse; and though the impulses are generally good, one places more dependence upon principles.

'Both you and Minnie would be delighted to hear the Adelaide men talk of their own colony with pride and affection. Victoria is not to be compared with it, and all our diggers mean to return and spend their gold at home. Tell Mrs. Trueman that her husband is looking very well; he cannot get his coat on, he has got so much stouter. His party are doing more than ours, but nothing great. I have not seen Mr. Brown, but I hear he is doing better. Mr. Reid means to go home soon, having got very tired of the diggings; but, of course, they will all have written by the escort. However, this will show that we diggers know something about each other.

'Do you remember Tom Barnes, who used to be so very particular in his dress at Adelaide? I saw him yesterday, looking such an object. He had on a blue serge shirt, with a leathern belt, broken in several places, and sewed together with twine; knee breeches, with blue worsted stockings, each of them torn down the leg; a boot on one foot, and a shoe on the other; a hat, torn out of all shape, tied down with a piece of string; and a black pipe, sticking, I don't know how, through a rent in the straw. He certainly had a most Hibernian appearance, but laughed so heartily at his own accoutrements, that I quite envied his good-humour. I myself have a fidgety uneasiness if I have any holes about me, and apply to your huswife-case more frequently than the others. I manage everything better than the stockings, for I always make my darns into a hard knot, which is ugly to look at, and uncomfortable to wear.

'I have not many adventures to tell you, but perhaps you may elicit something from me when I get home, by judicious cross-questioning; or you may walk me up and down the verandah, and get me to remember many things, which now, without any prompting but Gilbert's evident desire to have the portfolio, I cannot call to mind. I thought I should have one tale of midnight robbery to relate the other night, when Harry started out of bed, crying 'Thieves!' I heard a rustling outside, and began to try to recollect what valuable property was in danger, when Gilbert said, sleepily, 'We have nothing to steal, Harry; there is not an ounce of gold in the tent.'

'Nothing to steal!' cried Harry, 'didn't I leave a pail of water outside? and now there is some rascal making off with it.'

'However, it turned out to be only a horse who wanted a drink, and had emptied the pail; and Harry did not much mind the loss of the water, so long as the pail was extant. We are obliged to get the water in very early, if we want to have it pure; for it settles during the night at the bottom of the holes, and when taken before it is disturbed, it is as good as most of the well water down in the south; but it has not

the delicious flavour of wood that you admire so much in the Torrens water. I thought of throwing a log or two into the holes we frequent, but laziness prevailed, and I did not.

'We have shifted our tent three times, in the hope that, by changing ground, we should change the luck, but hitherto without success. I saw the drayman who was the cause of our not taking Charley with us, about a fortnight ago. I told him the mischief he had done, and he had the grace to look rather ashamed; but he condescendingly said, that if Charley would come to him, he could let him have a few ounces if he was hard up, for he had done a very snug thing, and though his mates were soft at first, they did not want for pluck, and he would like to see a party who had done better. 'I seen Hodges' overseer here,' said Ben Hardy, 'and I fancy he wants Charley at home to lend a hand with the cattle, and look to the stations; so Hodges will be glad enough I did not take the letter in time, and it's all for the best. George,' continued he, with great affability, 'I am sending my old woman three pounds weight of gold, just to spruce her up a bit afore I go home, but I am taking the bulk of my booty to Adelaide myself.'

'Mr. Reid, whom you know to be rather a timid man, was very nearly robbed the other night; but was saved by his extreme cautiousness, which had been laughed at. He had a good deal of gold, which he had put in his trousers' pocket, and his trousers under his head, according to the ordinary custom here; but for additional security he put a tin dish just over his head, and was awakened by hearing it rattle down over his ears. He started up, saw that his money was safe, and, looking out, detected a man running away as fast as he could; after which he found a great slit cut in his tent, just at the back of his head. The thief meant to have put his hand under Mr. Reid's head, and walked off with the trousers, but the tin dish gave the alarm; and Harry says he means to take the same precaution whenever he has anything worth stealing.

'Tell our minister that we hear a sermon every Sunday, and are not becoming heathens altogether. Grace had better pay our landlord his rent, if you can afford it out of our miserable remittance. I hope you have had the interest paid upon your own little mortgages, for you must be sadly put about if you have not. I left the matter with William Bell, but I think when he goes, that Mr. Plummer might be kind enough to look after it. I fear it is but 'water-brose and muslin-kail' hospitality that you can give to your cousin, Miss Morison; but if, as you say, she is in want of a safe home, she must overlook the poverty of it.

'Now, my own little sister, I must bid you good bye, with

the hope that we may be united soon again, as loving and happy as ever we were in old times; and believe me, ever your affectionate brother,

'GEORGE ELLIOT.'

Gilbert Elliot to his sister Margaret.
Forest Creek.
'MY DEAR MARGARET,

'I can fancy Chitty thrown aside at the sight of this letter, and that it will drive musty law out of your head for at least twelve hours. I have got out of the habit of thinking of my old studies, and though I often long to be at home again, I fear that my enthusiasm for Blackstone and the rest of his fraternity has gone for ever. However, we were to bring home the same hearts, and that I think we shall all do, for I never felt how dear you all were till now.

'An Anglo-Saxon has always had the character of adapting himself better to new countries than one of any other race, and where he can make a home he grows attached to it. We cannot make a home in this sort of vagabond life at the gold diggings, and our affections cling to the home we have made for ourselves in Adelaide, with an earnestness which could not be exceeded by the people of any old country in the world. I have not met a South Australian who did not mean to return, and really at present there are few inducements to settle in Victoria. I say at present, because by judicious legislation much might be done to improve the great natural advantages of this wonderful colony; and when the news of the gold discoveries reaches the mother country, it may bring out such an immense number of people, that the gold fields may be exhausted, and civilization and cultivation take the place of the present nomadic system.

'This is not such a democratic colony as our own; society has been divided into two classes, the great sheep farmers and their servants, but the body of hard headed yeomanry is wanting. Our working farmers, struggling for and obtaining comfort and even opulence, buying section after section, and making the value of their land ten times greater by their labour, have a much stronger attachment to the soil than the squatters here, who have only a lease of their runs, or the shepherds, who are not connected with the land at all.

'Land cannot be bought here in sections of eighty acres, as in South Australia; nothing less than a square mile is sold by government; and the squatters are so jealous of interference with their runs, that they keep fine agricultural land out of the market, even within a few miles of Melbourne. So you see the reason why the Port Phillip people have imported

wheat from us and from Tasmania, is, that they have never grown enough for their own consumption. Of course, they grow still less now, and flour is likely to be very high before next harvest comes in. All our farmers whom I have met here, mean to go home, whether they are successful or not, to put in their crops; for they see what a number of unproductive mouths there are to feed, and the more abundant the gold is, the higher will be the price of wheat.

'The country around Melbourne looks very different from that near Adelaide; there are not the scattered villages nor the fine gardens and vineyards that make our suburbs so beautiful. And when we remember that people could go nearly forty miles on the south road, between fenced sections generally cultivated, and that there were so many houses, that one could have as many drinks of water as one wanted along the road on the hottest day in February, the contrast is very striking. Once out of Melbourne, you are in the bush. There are no roads made, and it looks desolate to see a sheep or cattle station within two or three miles of town.

'We are among friends here; for the Adelaide people keep together, partly from choice, and partly because the people from the other colonies are so bitterly jealous of us. We consider ourselves as by far the most respectable part of the digging community, and are as sociable as the engrossing nature of our employment will permit. I think this bout of rough country work and country life is a capital thing for my health, for I was thrust into an office very young, and had got pale and nerveless; but now I am as brown as Charley Hodges, and nobody laughs at my strokes, however they may laugh at the feeble results of them. It is well that none of you had very extravagant ideas of our gold digging success, for you would have been all the more disappointed at the sight of our poor five ounces and a half. Here, as elsewhere, the working men carry the day, partly from their greater strength and skill, but really mostly from luck. I think I may call myself a working man now, and require to be legislated for, like our friends of old. If we can only weather it, we shall not regret going, unless you have suffered a great deal in our absence; for this change must do us good in many ways, and it makes us feel how much you always did for us. I suppose no party at the diggings misses their sisters so much as we do; when we sit down to sew on a button, or set about our miserable washings, we remember whose hands were always ready to work for us, and whose good nature never complained of the trouble we gave.

'I am growing extremely anxious to find a good hole, and bring you home pockets full of gold, because I know you would make a good use of it. At first, I fancy your proposing

some Utopian scheme to do everybody good but yourself; but I think my practical wisdom would overrule you; and we should settle down comfortably on a property of our own, and have plenty of books, which we need not study unless we were in the humour. It would be delightful to see your restless energy tamed down to a life of philosophic and literary ease; and only think what weight your opinion would have, if you were an independent woman of fortune. But I am more Utopian than you, and your practical common sense will point to the five ounces and a half as rather a narrow superstructure for such extensive castles. But I have hopes still that we shall make something before we leave, and so turn the laugh on our side.

'I hope people have not been frightening you with absurd tales of the insecurity of life and property at the diggings, for if one behaves with ordinary prudence, one is as safe here as in Adelaide. If you go into a stranger's tent at night he is at liberty to shoot you, but then you have no business there. Summary justice is executed on those who are guilty of theft or assault, but here it is absolutely necessary. No wines or spirits are allowed to be sold on the diggings, and if any one is discovered keeping a sly grog shop, his tent is burnt to the ground with all that it contains. Nevertheless, a good deal of this illicit trade goes on, as it is very profitable. They sell a miserable compound which they call wine, at one shilling the glass, and another which they dignify with the name of brandy, at two shillings and sixpence. The diggers are generally very sober while they are digging, but I suppose when they are in Melbourne or Adelaide, they are as bad as English sailors.

'You would be surprised to see what a medley of people we have here. Gentlemen, whom you remember seeing in professional black, are now digging in Guernsey shirts and moleskin trousers; those who used to drive about in gigs, with hands that looked too genteel to hold the reins, are now handling the pickaxe; and those who bowed across the counter are now hallooing from the bottom of a hole. You recollect Dr. Endell, that respectable old gentleman, whom our father used to hold up as the very pink of medical practitioners—he is digging with such blistered hands, that it is grievous to look on them. I advised him to get a pair of hedger's gloves to protect his hands, but he said he could not, for he should be laughed at by his party, as they were a very rough lot.

'We get for our thirty shillings a month a block of land eight feet square, which we may change as often as we like; but a hole abandoned for twenty-four hours (Sundays excepted) is no longer ours. Any one who likes may take it, and we were provoked to find that a hole we had deserted

as useless, had been seized upon by another party, who took forty ounces out of it. The process is very simple, but very dirty; we take the stuff to the river, and generally puddle it down in tubs to get off the bulk of the clay, before we put it into the cradle. We use no quicksilver to separate the precious metal from the clay, as they do at Bathurst and in California, but trust to washing alone. The dirtiness of the work has earned for it the sobriquet of Jack the Painter; and for the last three weeks we have given up the more aristocratic employment of sinking, for the certain though small gains of Jack the Painter's mob. People can always clear their expenses washing, but the great gains are when you sink a good hole, and pick out nuggets with fossicking knives. Many lucky parties never think of washing, at least, at this season of the year; if they stay over winter, they cannot do anything else. It is cheerless to come home after a hard day's work, and have to cook, and bake, and wash; but our party is too small to afford a hutkeeper. Nobody digs on Sundays, though there is more cooking and eating than you would quite approve of. We go to hear a sermon while the pudding boils; Mr. Henderson, who is cook to a party, preaches under a spreading gum-tree; and I was shocked to hear that his mates complain of his neglecting them, in order to study and preach his sermons. No clergyman has as yet been sent up to the diggings by government, though the voluntary principle is not predominant in the Victorian legislature, and there is a grant for the clergy of all denominations who will accept of it. Victoria has almost no country churches, no district being sufficiently settled to maintain one; but if these diggings go on as they have begun, both clergymen and schoolmasters must be sent up; for we would hope that the example of South Australia, in considering government as a mere system of police, will not be followed in such critical circumstances as society is placed in here.

'They threaten to send us soldiers to preserve order, and mean to double the licence fee in order to pay them; but they will find out their mistake. If the licence fee is doubled, the most respectable people will leave the gold fields, and no soldiers can keep order if there is no salt left in society to purify it. Write to me if the constitutional party are making any head in Adelaide, or if they excuse themselves from exertion on account of the bad times.

'We hear that going to the post-office on Sunday is soon to be stopped, which I suppose you will approve of; but I must say, that the general gathering of diggers round that tent on that day has rather a civilizing effect upon us. We are clean enough to be recognisable by our friends, whom we recognise in turn. However, we have had very little encourage-

ment to go to the post-office, for we have only had one letter each, and we know that you have written at least six by this time. Register your letters in future, that we may have some chance of having them returned to you if we do not get them; for I cannot bear the idea of strangers reading what is meant for us, and perhaps laughing at anxious Grace, romantic Annie, or your dear blue self.

'It is now very late, as I have been the last indulged with the writing materials, so I must bid you good-bye. Ever, my dear Margaret,

'Your most affectionate brother,
'GILBERT ELLIOT.'

'It is well that they have kept their health so well,' said William Bell, 'and have not lost heart with their indifferent success. I shall be off in a fortnight, and if they will take me on with them, we shall see if I do not turn the tide of luck. You must make me up a packet of letters and newspapers, that I may deliver them, and win a welcome for their sake, if not for my own. Will any of you ladies turn out to see the Escort come in this afternoon? I cannot stay to talk now, for I have a deal to do with that slow Macnab yet. I will come over again in the evening; but you must not expect more than three pounds five or six for your gold, for it is too small a lot to go into the assay office, and you must submit to something short of the three eleven. Good-bye.'

CHAPTER V

MR. HUMBERSTONE'S THEORY AND PRACTICE WITH
REGARD TO LONG ENGAGEMENTS

The Elliots were wonderfully cheered by the news they had got, and though Clara grieved that she was a burden upon them when they were really so poor, the frank manner in which George had spoken of it was a consolation to her. The funeral of poor Miss Ker was to take place the next day, and Annie was looking depressed when she saw the undertaker coming to make preparations for it, so Clara proposed that they should all go out to see the Escort come in. Neither Grace nor Margaret cared to go, and perhaps if the younger girls had anticipated the crowd that was collected, they too would have stayed at home. They got squeezed between a stout German woman and two Irishmen, who were shouting, 'Hurrah for Tolmer;' and they were becoming very uncomfortable, when at a short distance they saw Mr. Harris, with Reginald on one side and Humberstone on the other. The three gentlemen came up to the girls, and took them into Handy's, from whence they could see the Escort pass.

When they were settled comfortably at the window, Mr. Harris took the opportunity of introducing Annie Elliot to Mr. Humberstone.

'A phoenix, a *rara avis*, Miss Annie. A gentleman who declares he has no intention of going to the diggings.'

'Mr. Reginald has no intention either,' said Annie; 'so your *rara avis* is not so rare, after all.'

'But Reginald cannot go, if he were ever so willing; whereas it is only a principle of fidelity that keeps Humberstone constant to Escott,' said Harris. 'I am sure that your sisters would admire his conduct, and that Miss Margaret would put his name down in her album as a bright example to all South Australian overseers. Yours has gone, I suppose, Reginald?'

'Yes,' answered Reginald, 'and I cannot get another, so I

have to work double myself. But here come Tolmer and the Escort.'

'How brown and dusty they look, and how their teeth shine through between the thickets of moustache and beard,' exclaimed Annie. 'It is quite delightful. The men look fresher than the poor horses, which want the excitement of being admired and cheered.'

And Annie waved her handkerchief from the window, as also did Mrs. Handy and Mrs. Haussen. But Clara sat back, and ventured upon no sign of applause.

'Miss Morison does not share in the general enthusiasm, or perhaps she is stunned by the Adelaide band, playing their three tunes with more force than elegance,' said Harris.

'I feel a stranger here; I have no brother at the diggings,' answered Clara.

'Nor any gold coming by the Escort,' continued Harris. 'How much have you got, Miss Annie? Mrs. Handy and Mrs. Haussen have got two pounds' weight between them, and I suppose your party will have sent you more, for it is their first remittance.'

'We have got five ounces and a half,' replied Annie. 'Don't laugh now, Mr. Harris, for I am sure they have worked hard enough to get it.'

'I mean to do things famously when I go,' said Harris. 'Now, Reginald, don't you envy me? There you are, tied to a parcel of sheep, and unable to pursue adventure at the mouth of a hole.'

'How do you like Adelaide now, Miss Morison?' asked Reginald. 'You must find it dull now there are so few gentlemen in it.'

'Indeed, my cousins leave me nothing to wish for, and I am beginning to get quite attached to the dear, dusty town, as Annie calls it,' Clara answered.

'Oh! we have still a few gentlemen,' said Annie, 'but they are all going this month or next, and one gets sad at so many leavetakings. Mr. Bell goes in a fortnight, and I suppose you go in a day or two, Mr. Harris?'

'Alas! it is even so,' said Harris. 'I am coming down this evening for a preliminary farewell, just to break it off by degrees; for unless I practise bidding good-bye, I shall never be equal to the final parting. I am sure your sisters will be glad to see Reginald and Humberstone, so I will bring them over with me. Bell is sure to be with you, and we shall positively muster a gentleman to every lady, which will put you in mind of old times.'

Mrs. Handy wished the young ladies to stay and take tea with her, but they declined, and went home to tell what they had seen and whom they had met.

Clara wondered whether Mr. Reginald's question about the dullness of Adelaide was intended to discover how she would like Taringa. How often a little previous knowledge sets one wrong, and the merest commonplace is invested with important meaning! Reginald had really meant very little by his question, and had never fancied that Clara would suit Julia, from the time he had seen her at Mrs. Bantam's. She was too sensible to worship her as she would expect, and too clear-sighted not to find out her faults, which, though he saw them himself, he would fain conceal from all the world besides.

Mr. Humberstone, the overseer, was delighted at the idea of encountering no less than four young ladies, more particularly as he had had first one rise in his salary in January to a hundred and fifty pounds a-year, and again this month to two hundred, which, with rations, and a wandering kind of accommodation, was quite a large income. He was a first-rate overseer, and Mr. Escott, his employer, had offered him every inducement to remain; while Humberstone's commonsense told him that a good income in a situation he liked, and for which he was better fitted than any other man in the colony, was a better thing than wandering to the ends of the earth to handle the pick-axe and rock the cradle, and perhaps get nothing, after all. Escott, in the hope of making his stay more permanent still, had said to him, when he was starting for town:—

'I wish, Humberstone, that you could pick up a wife in Adelaide; one who could keep things in order at the home-station, where these Shetland people are so horridly dirty and careless; a pleasant, active woman, not too young, with a cheerful face and a good temper. We would make everything comfortable for her, and with tolerable sense and prudence, she would be quite a queen among us. I know you have a very soft heart, and can fall in love whenever you think it convenient.'

Humberstone gave a sigh to the memory of Miss Waterstone, and tried all the way into Adelaide to recollect who among his female acquaintance would suit both him and Escott. There was Mrs. Archer, the widow of a publican on the road, but she had too many children, and was also too old; Miss Morison was too young and far too little; besides, she could know nothing of housekeeping. Then there was Miss Hartop, but she had a bad temper, while Ellen Casey was not genteel enough. He had thought of taking Mrs. Handy into his confidence, but when he was invited to the Elliots', and heard from Harris that the two eldest sisters were tall and sensible girls, who could do everything about a house, he thought that he had better judge for himself as to whether

Mr. Humberstone

one of them would suit him, before consulting his hostess. Harris easily saw through the transparent Humberstone, and thought what fun it would be if he fell in love with either Grace or Margaret. So he instigated him to buy gloves, and a new and surprising waistcoat, in order to make himself agreeable; and talked much as they went along of the good gifts and great poverty of the family; while Reginald thought over the letter he had just received from Julia, and chafed at being compelled to stay in the colony, instead of going home and discovering how she really felt affected to him.

Nothing escaped Clara that evening, for love had quickened all her perceptions, naturally very acute, to a painful degree. She heard all that Humberstone said to Grace, and all that Harris whispered to Annie; she lost nothing of the side talk between Margaret and Bell, while at the same time she carried on a conversation with Reginald, which she had thought would be constrained, but was agreeably disappointed to find the reverse; for, indeed, when two minds are tuned to perfect harmony, it is not easy to strike jarring notes. Besides, Reginald was not aware that Clara knew his secret. They canvassed Mrs. Browning's poems, and quoted what pleased them; they appealed to Margaret for a share of admiration, which she did not bestow so lavishly as Clara, for never having herself been in love, she did not quite understand love poetry, and discovered faults which Clara could not perceive.

'What do you think on the subject, Mr. Harris?' asked Annie. 'Here is Mr. Reginald saying he prefers Mrs. Browning's 'Eve' to Milton's.'

'Treason!' said Harris. 'Nothing can possibly surpass Milton's 'Eve,' so beautiful, so clinging, and so tender; with the idea that her husband has God to serve, while he stands in the place of God to her.'

'But,' observed Reginald, 'such entire dependence of a wife upon her husband, though it would be well if men were angels, does not suit a world like ours. I think, in general, that a woman's conscience is less warped than her husband's; and that she has a great duty to perform in giving him unworldly counsel, and telling him how things look to her less sophisticated mind. Besides, I do not say that Mrs. Browning's 'Adam' is so fine as Milton's. Women describe women best; I hear great complaints of the monsters they make for men, but I dare say that we make as great blunders in describing them. Is it not so, Miss Morison?'

'You make us so absurdly amiable, and so dazzlingly lovely, that we do not recognise ourselves at all,' Clara answered. 'Is not Jane Eyre, who is neither handsome nor what is called good, a much more interesting and natural character than you will find in men's books?'

'I think so,' said Bell; 'for I never can fancy that any of these super-angelic beings would smile on a plain fellow like myself; and, after all, how little effect has beauty on the heart!'

'I do not agree with Bell; beauty has always irresistible charms for me,' murmured Harris to Annie, in a low, emphatic whisper, which sent the blood up to her face.

'Poor Mrs. Smith died this morning,' said Annie, wishing to start another subject, 'and she is to be buried to-morrow. She only survived poor little Bobby a fortnight.'

'Oh! then, the house will be vacant; I think I have heard of a tenant, perhaps a purchaser for it; but I did not like to disturb the sick woman,' Harris replied.

'We would have taken Mrs. Smith here, rather than that Mr. Bantam should have suffered from her staying in his house,' said Grace.

Mr. Harris gave an almost imperceptible shrug.

'Oh! no time has been lost yet,' said he; 'for Pengarvon only told me of it the other day. He was a miner at the Burra, and did very well at the diggings. We have got three hundred pounds' worth of gold of his in the office, and his two sons have each as much; so they want to cut a dash, and get a house in town. They took a fancy to the cottage because it looked quiet and genteel. They had also seen a young lady twining the creepers up the verandah next door, and thought they should be all right in such a good neighbourhood. Pengarvon wants to settle before his eldest son is married; for the last wedding was celebrated in a two-roomed cottage, where there was scarcely room to turn. I think I told you, Miss Annie, that I was invited to a digger's wedding last week; one of the Miss Pengarvons', who was united to a certain Bill Weston, who had also done well at the diggings. Truly, the talk was much of sinking, and surfacing, and nuggets, and such things; but everything was done in style: the bride, in a white silk dress, with a blue drawn bonnet; and her mother rejoicing in a grass-green satin, and an amethyst-coloured bonnet with a scarlet feather. The dejeuner, or collation, or dinner, was very splendid, but very long in being produced. There was a turkey at one end, where the clergyman presided, and a pair of fowls graced the other, where I had the post of honour; and the worst of it was, that nobody would carve but the parson and myself. For, as it was half-past four before we sat down, and the company had assembled at eleven, you may imagine we were all pretty sharp-set. The parson's wife looked very hungry, so I helped her first; but there was one voracious old gentleman, for whose sake the dinner had been delayed, who was dressed entirely in black, with a massive gold watch, and chain and seals corresponding, who sent in

his plate again and again; while half a dozen hungry lads beside him stared on their empty platters in vain desire.'

'How very ill-bred!' said Annie. 'Surely he could not have been a gentleman, in spite of his costume!'

'A gentleman!—oh, no, not within a hundred degrees of one! I heard him ask the clergyman's wife, while her husband was saying grace, 'D'ye see that lad o' mine down there? 'D'ye see that lad o' mine down there?' three or four times, while she in vain pretended not to hear; and when, at last, she answered—'Yes, I see him;' he replied, in a stentorian voice, 'Well, that lad o' mine that ye see, every hole he dug he took goold out o't.' There was a pie opposite to him, and it was hinted that he might relieve the exhausted carvers, and cut it up. 'No, indeed, Mrs. Kedslie, I'll do no such thing; I dunna consider myself qualified to cut up that pie.' 'It is quite a simple matter,' said she; 'and you see all those lads, including your sons, are getting nothing to eat, while Mr. Harris and Mr. Kedslie are starving in the midst of plenty.' 'I'll trouble you for another slice of turkey, said the inexorable man, whose name I discovered to be Ruggles. 'As for these lads, I fancy they are no more used to them sort of things than I am myself; and they may just wait, for I do not consider myself qualified to cut up that pie.' And he resumed his process of devouring. I quite pitied Mrs. Kedslie, for he only talked of very vulgar subjects, in a very rough way, and never would take a hint to hold his tongue.'

'I don't think they would be nice neighbours at all,' said Annie. 'So noisy and disagreeable, they would make us remember you very unpleasantly.'

'I do not wish to be forgotten,' Harris answered; 'and I do not think Mrs. Pengarvon will annoy you further than by passing your door, arrayed in all sorts of incongruous colours; but you must make allowance for defective taste. Every one has not *your* eye for harmonious colouring, Miss Annie;' and he looked at her simple but becoming dress with evident admiration.

William Bell saw how prettily Annie blushed at this compliment, and wondered if he could ever learn to make himself agreeable. He thought he might venture on a small tribute to Margaret.

'You are never guilty of such a solecism as wearing amethyst and green, Miss Margaret,' he said, and looked quite pleased with his attempt, but only for a moment; for both Harris and Annie laughed, and assured him that those colours were the finest contrast imaginable; wondering, also, that any one could think of complimenting Margaret on her dress, a subject about which she was perfectly indifferent.

'It is no matter what a lady wears,' said Humberstone.

'One always knows her; and some people look better in gingham than others in satin. Mrs. Haussen buys a new bonnet every letter she gets from her husband, and she must spend quite a fortune in silk dresses. I have seen her in three since I came to town this time; a black satin, a sky-blue silk, and one the colour of a pigeon's neck; but though they are all handsome, and fit her, and she puts them on well enough, she don't look the lady in them, in spite of all.'

'There is a great deal of the grisette about her,' said Harris. 'But you must allow that she is pretty and coquettish enough to turn the head of a fellow like Haussen.'

'I don't know what he means by a grisette! Will you be so good as explain it to me, Miss Elliot? asked Humberstone.

Miss Elliot explained; and Humberstone could not help thinking she was just the person for him. She was evidently not far from thirty, but yet she looked very well; her house was in beautiful order, yet she kept no servant; she talked to him without quizzing him, and allowed him to make himself agreeable; for Grace, happy in the thought that Henry was well and cheerful, had sunshine to spare even to this under-educated man, and listened to his 'facts' and broad compliments without either weariness or dislike.

Harris begged that they might be indulged with a dance; and as Humberstone could dance nothing more modern than country dances, he contented himself with standing over the piano, and admiring Grace's unwearied fingers as she supplied music for the party. Clara could scarcely believe that she was awake when Reginald asked her to waltz with him, and went through it in a kind of dream. Harris preferred the polka and schottische, and would not dance with any one but Annie; for he saw that William Bell was anxious for an opportunity to speak to her, and was determined to prevent it. Very soon he should be obliged to leave her altogether, and, while still in the colony, he was resolved to be first with her. He had never admired her so much as now; she had so much knowledge of some things, and such delightful ignorance of others; there was a tinge of sentiment in her thoughts, and a charming candour in admitting the merit of other people; and, altogether, Harris thought that, if he ever could afford to marry, she would be exactly the wife for him. He insinuated that he should be glad if she would make him a needle-book, or something of the kind, for he had lost that which Maria had made him; and Annie promised to do it. An earnest whisper, that it would be preserved as a precious memento, produced quite as great an effect as the whisperer intended.

Now, though William Bell had done so much for them all, and only recently had exerted his influence with a friendly shoemaker to induce him to make up the slippers for the dear

diggers—a task of no small difficulty in Adelaide in those times—Annie did not feel so grateful for what he had done as for what Harris had asked: and she almost smiled at a joke of the latter's about his rival's vulgar acquaintances.

'I hate long engagements!' said Harris, aloud, suddenly. 'What is the use of two people setting themselves for months and years to find out each others faults?'

Clara could not help looking at Reginald. His lip quivered, but he said nothing; and she thought he was indignant at Harris for speaking against what was right and proper.

'But suppose people only find out virtues,' said Grace, with a frankness which made Harris think Humberstone would take the alarm: 'it is delightful to see one good point after another developing itself!'

'Would it not be as well to find out the virtues after marriage as before?' asked Reginald, with some constraint.

'I don't know,' answered Grace. 'But it gives such confidence of happiness when you are thoroughly acquainted.'

'I think,' said Humberstone, ' 'Happy's the wooing that's not long a doing.' If a fellow has made enough to keep a wife, and admires a girl, let him ask her at once, and have the thing over, that they may settle down to be perfectly happy —in fact, comfortable.'

'But if a fellow has not made enough,' suggested Harris; 'what would the oracular Humberstone advise him to do?'

'Wait till he has, and leave both parties free. A long engagement is, in point of fact, a millstone tied round a man's neck.'

Clara saw Reginald shrink a little further into the corner of the sofa at this expression of Humberstone's opinion, and wondered what he could be thinking of; when Annie asked him to sing with Margaret. Clara had never envied the power of singing before; but this evening she did, when she heard Margaret's clear voice aided by Reginald's second. Then Harris sung with Annie; while William Bell, who only liked a Scotch ballad now and then, and could not turn a tune any more than Clara, looked remarkably uncomfortable. Humberstone was delighted with so much music, and sang a ballad which had been popular sixteen years ago, with much applause from Harris.

Shortly afterwards, all the four gentlemen took leave; and Humberstone was profuse in his thanks to Harris for introducing him to such a delightful family. On their way, they passed an inn, which was brilliantly lighted up for a ball, and Harris proposed they should adjourn thither.

'I shall miss the government ball through going to the diggings,' said he; 'but I daresay we shall get quite as much fun here. Come, Reginald, tickets only five shillings, and a

select ball. Bell shakes his head, but you other two will come with me.'

'Not I,' said Reginald. 'I suppose the company cannot be very select.'

'You will find as good gentlemen as yourself, and you see so few female faces in the bush, that you should be glad to dance with green-grocers' daughters, and pretty servant girls. I know two or three good dancers among them, and will find you a partner.'

'I am not going. It is neither good for them nor for me to mix together at public-house balls,' said Reginald.

'As if you have never danced with servant girls before!' exclaimed Harris, at random. 'You are inclined to be priggish, because Bell is here, and you want to show me up before him; but I wash my hands of you. You will come, Humberstone, though I don't expect you will see any one to equal Miss Elliot here. Good-bye, Bell and Reginald. 'Do ye think, because ye are virtuous, there shall be no more cakes and ale?'

'I think,' said Reginald to Bell, as they walked on, 'that the home we have just left is too sacred a place to exchange for amusement such as this; and there has been so much to-night for my mind to rest on with pleasure, that I feel quite a horror of any inferior entertainment.'

'So do I,' was the answer; 'but Harris, who has just been bidding good-bye, and appearing so sorry at parting, will dance as merrily at this affair as anybody there.'

'I have always admired the Elliots from report,' said Reginald, 'but I admire them still more, now I know them. I suppose that, if they were in similar circumstances in England, in these days of absurd pretensions, one, or perhaps two, of these girls would go out as governess, in order that the third might be able to keep her brothers' house, with a servant and a few showy luxuries. How much more independent and happy they are living all together; able to help one another, and to show substantial kindness to those who need it!'

'You mean Miss Morison. Do you know, I like her, though she is not quite colonial? I think Gilbert will like her too, when he comes back, particularly if he does well at Forest Creek.'

In the meantime, Harris and Humberstone were making their way into the ball-room. The first was a great favourite at everything of this kind, for he threw himself into the pleasure of the moment with careless enjoyment, and descended easily to the level of the company, unlike the affected government clerks. He brushed against a gentleman in a polka, and recognised Mr. Beaufort, of the North, whom

he addressed at the end of the dance in these words:—

'I never expected to see you here, Beaufort, for I fancied you had turned over a new leaf since you married. I wanted Reginald to come in with Humberstone and myself, but the milksop declined; and it is as well for you, for he would have been sure to tell Mrs. Beaufort.'

'Mrs. Beaufort be hanged!' said the gentleman. 'I am on my way to the diggings, and want one night's fling to put me in mind of merry bachelor days.'

'Then you, too, are going to the Mount!' said Harris. 'So am I. I start the day after to-morrow; but I leave nothing behind me, except a few small debts, not worth mentioning; while you leave a young wife, a fine farm, and a lot of sheep and cattle to look after themselves.'

'The fact is, Harris, that I am sick of the place,' answered Beaufort. 'I am tired of seeing nothing new, and hearing my wife talk of nothing but the comforts of domestic life; so I am going to try a little change. As for farming, I am too far out of town to farm with any profit, and I lost heavily on my crop last year, so I shall put none in this season. There are thirty acres of self-sown stuff, and Mrs. Beaufort must get some one to harrow it in; and as for the sheep and cattle, I have given them in charge to my neighbours—put them out to board, as it were; and I hope they will thrive better with them than they have ever done with me. How long has Humberstone been in town, Harris?'

'He came in the day before yesterday.'

'All right,' said Beaufort. 'I shall hope to see you again, Harris, at the diggings. I set sail to-morrow, and mean to go to Adelaide Gully in the first place, to join my friend Turner. If you want a party, we should be glad to take you.'

'I'll think about it,' replied Harris, who had grudged the time occupied in this conversation, and now began to dance again with a certain Miss Selina Barnes, nearly as good a dancer, he thought, as Annie Elliot, and one not so soon tired. A country-dance gave Mr. Humberstone an opportunity of coming out; and though both Miss Barnes, and her friend, Miss Price, voted it low at first, they nevertheless enjoyed it very much. Harris was evidently considered the best partner in the room; and Miss Barnes was mortified to see him leave her for a pretty young woman, who was just newly married, but whose husband was at the diggings.

'Upon my word, Emma Price,' said she, 'there's far too many grass widows at this ball; quite half of the ladies has wedding-rings on. I think when girls get married they should leave the beaux to them as is single.'

'Hard up, now, I suppose,' said Beaufort to Harris, when they met again. 'Well, I can't say I am; it is merely a roving

disposition that takes me to the diggings, and I could make it worth your while to join me, for I have got everything in first-chop style. Mrs. Beaufort took care that I should be comfortable, and I have no end of biscuits, and preserves, and hams, and cheeses in my kit.'

'Well, that is tempting, and I do not think I can resist your offer,' answered Harris. 'I say, Humberstone, how do you feel by this time? Have you danced your heart into its right place?'

'I can't tell whether I have a heart or not, I have been whirled about so. I must have a nobbler or a spider to put me to rights. What will you take, Miss Amelia?'

'Nothing at all; I leave you to the error of your ways. I am a teetotaller.'

'So are all the ladies I have danced with,' said Harris; 'I suspect for this occasion only.'

After a very long polka, and Sir Roger de Coverley for a finale, the ball broke up at five o'clock, and Harris and Humberstone walked home with their partners, and reached Handy's about six.

It was impossible for Humberstone to sleep in daylight, even if his mind had been at ease; and now, though he had danced so much, and tried to forget his love in excitement, his admiration of Grace Elliot was stronger than ever. Not one girl at the ball was fit to hold the candle to her. So while Harris lay down to get a little sleep, the restless overseer walked about Adelaide, wondering how early he might call upon the Elliots to have another look at Grace.

It was washing day, and Clara, Annie, and Margaret were busy in the kitchen, chatting so pleasantly, that Clara wondered at the dislike she used to have to this piece of work. In fact, in good company, and with a tolerable subject of conversation, washing is really far from disagreeable. They were talking over Henry's distresses with his stewed clothes, while Grace, housemaid for the day, was busy with a duster, and taking an occasional share in the conversation, when Humberstone knocked at the door. Annie laughed a merry little laugh when she heard his voice, and conjectured that he had come to pay a morning call.

Here was an opportunity for Mr. Humberstone — Miss Elliot was alone, and now was the time to speak, for he really admired her very much, and he could afford to marry. After a few stammering common-places, he began to describe the home-station with great minuteness; then he diverged to tell how long he had been with Escott, and how comfortable he had always been; how he had obtained a great rise in his salary since the bad times came, and at last how there was only one thing now wanting to make him perfectly happy.

Mr. Humberstone

Then he made a long pause, and Grace wondered what could make him so communicative.

'I am in want of a companion,' said he, after much hesitation, 'in fact, a wife.'

'Indeed!' answered Grace; 'then why don't you try to find one?'

'Am I not trying all I can?' asked he, in return. 'Will you have me? I am sure you are just the woman—I beg pardon, I mean the lady—for me, and I would make you a good husband.'

'I thought everybody knew I was engaged?' said Grace, scarcely less amused than astonished.

'Engaged—whom to?' asked Humberstone, eagerly.

'To Henry Martin, who is now with my brothers at the diggings. We have been engaged for two years and a half, and I never dreamed of your not knowing it.'

'Two years and a half! Henry Martin of the Burra! Why, bless my soul! who would have thought of such a thing? And you don't think you could like me better. I am rich enough, and would cross you in nothing, and Escott is so anxious to have a lady about the place.' Grace shook her head. 'Could you speak a good word for me to your sister?' said Humberstone. 'If I cannot have you, I should like her next best. *She* is not engaged to anybody, I hope.'

'Which sister do you mean, for it would be awkward if I recommended you to the wrong one?' Grace answered, with comic gravity.

'I mean your tall sister, with the clear blue eyes; the one that sung with Reginald. I think she would suit me nearly as well as yourself.'

'Well!' said Grace, almost laughing outright, 'I will mention the thing to Margaret.'

'Will you beg her to come and see me now?' quoth the impatient suitor. 'Only don't let her know that I asked you, for she might not like to wear your old shoes, you understand.'

All Grace's command of countenance was needed to announce to her sister, that Mr. Humberstone wished to see her immediately, and to offer her his hand.

Margaret did not dress herself, but went in her morning gown, looking so dignified, that Humberstone, whose courage had been oozing out at his finger ends from the moment Grace left him, and who began to suspect he was making himself ridiculous, could only falter out:

'I thought—that is, I hoped—but it is all nonsense, I suppose; in fact, no go.'

'Certainly not,' said Margaret.

'Then I must bid you a good morning,' said the forlorn

swain, and he hurried out of the house, internally vowing vengeance on his friend Harris for betraying him into such a position, and feeling conscious it was not the thing to propose to one lady, not to say to two, after sitting up all night at a public-house ball, and drinking more than enough. Without much delay he started on his return to the north.

CHAPTER VI

DEPARTURES

When Harris came again to say good bye, he found that Annie Elliot had the needle-book ready for him, as well as the song he had asked, and he really felt very sorry to leave her. What between recent want of sleep and present grief, he looked quite dull; and though he tried to quiz Grace about Humberstone's sudden departure, he failed in eliciting a laugh even from himself. When he bade Annie farewell, the last of them all, he grasped her hand, gazing long and earnestly into her face, and repressing a sigh, said that he should see her again in a few months, and hoped her brothers would let him join them at Forest Creek.

Clara's quick eye saw that Harris had made great way in her cousin's heart, and hoped that time would mend all, for it was not likely to be a happy love. She had given away her own, but then she had never doubted that it was on a worthy object; and though she had been very miserable in her hopelessness, it had not made her querulous or ungenerous. But Annie's uncertainty as to whether she was loved or not, and as to whether Harris deserved her love, was affecting her temper as well as her spirits. Margaret sometimes made harsh remarks about Mr. Harris, and Annie's own judgment told her that William Bell was a better man, and more likely to please all the family. Even Minnie had preferred Bell at the first; and Annie vainly tried to picture to herself all his good qualities, in the hope of changing her sentiments.

'If Harris really loves me,' thought she, 'I have no right to say he is not good enough for me, when I have so many faults myself; and I am sure that either Margaret or Clara would make William far happier than I could. But then he has never avowed his affection, and I shall never find out what he thinks, unless he gets rich at the diggings, and so can afford to marry; which is very right, I dare say; but I

like Henry's way best. How happy Grace is, compared to me! She has something fixed, instead of this hateful uncertainty.'

William Bell was disappointed to find that he gained nothing by Harris's departure. It grieved him to see Annie so dull and spiritless, and he longed to begin his hard work, and to serve her brothers as much as he could, that she might hear good accounts of him. He begged Margaret to allow him to write to her, for, as he said, he was alone in the world, and should feel wretched, when George and Gilbert were writing, to have no correspondent himself. 'I do not expect,' said he, 'that you will open my letter till you have read all the others, but promise to read it some time.'

Margaret promised both to read and answer, and Annie thought that what she had so long wished was in train, and that Bell was transferring his affection to her sister; but she scarcely found the idea so pleasant as she had expected. When he was fairly gone, she was surprised to find how much she missed him; there was nobody to fetch them a new book now, or to read it aloud, or to talk it over; there was no one to keep up Grace's spirits, or to be good-natured enough to submit to ridicule for the benefit of her own. And William had not asked her for the slightest favour; he had gone away, leaving her immeasurably in his debt.

Clara received a letter from her uncle before Bell went, very characteristic of the man. He told her he was shocked at the selfishness Mr. Campbell had displayed in making no exertion in her behalf, and in allowing her to demean herself so much; but that he had always heard people grew very avaricious and ungenerous in colonies, and that now he fully believed it. He wondered that she should have failed in getting a situation in a colony where, by statistical returns which he had been at the pains to examine for himself, there were so few teachers and so many scholars; feared that her manners would be ruined, and that it would be impossible for her to take any position in society, even where the dreadful fact was unknown; hoped that she had either risen above the sphere she had chosen, or else brought down her mind to its level; and concluded with a very guarded invitation to return to Scotland, where he would do his best to procure her some kind of situation.

Susan wrote, entreating her to come back, and deploring the sad fate she had met with in that miserable Australia; but blaming no one,—not even Mr. Campbell.

Clara read the letters to her cousins, and they advised her to stay where she was, for some months at least, till either a situation opened for her in Adelaide, or Mr. Morison should see that, even for Susan's sake, he ought to do more for her sister.

Departures

Clara had expected more kindness from her uncle, and her spirits fell below their usual level, so that she felt unable to comfort Annie in her evident suffering.

'Don't you think, Annie,' said she, one morning, 'that it would do us good to make a round of calls to-day? We have been quite neglectful of the widows since the Escort came in, and surely they will be in better spirits now that they have heard from their husbands.'

'Well,' Annie said, 'let us start early, and go through all that are within walking distance. We shall have the two extremes,—Mrs. Brown at eighteen and Mrs. Fielding at sixty; and we must find out whether the young or the old wives bear the parting best. I have never been at Mrs. Fielding's since the old gentleman started overland, and I dare say she feels anxious; but perhaps we are too young to attempt to condole with her. Will you come with us, Grace?'

'I think two are plenty to go abroad,' answered Grace, 'and you know how fond Mrs. Fielding is of young people.'

So the two girls set out by themselves, and paid their first visit to Mrs. Brown, whom they found in tears. She had heard from somebody that somebody else had told him that he had seen one of Brown's party, who said that he was very ill. Clara tried to comfort her, by saying that George Elliot had written he was quite well; but Mrs. Brown's intelligence was a fortnight later, and she feared it was too true.

'And oh!' said she, 'to think of his being ill—perhaps dying—and I that was to be with him in sickness and in health, can do nothing for him! Dear, dear, it seems all a dream that I am married at all,—just three bright months, and then to be parted thus! If I could do anything at all, it would ease my mind; but there is nothing to be done but to sit and pine for letters, which perhaps may never come.'

'Brown is a very common name,' Clara said; 'I know another Mr. Brown at the diggings.'

'And I know of four besides your Mr. Brown,' added Annie.

'But Stroker is not at all a common name, and he was of poor James's party, and it is from him the information came,' Mrs. Brown persisted.

The visitors sat nearly an hour with the poor young wife, without improving either her spirits or their own, and then proceeded to Mrs. Fielding's; where they found another widow of the same order, her daughter Mrs. Whiston, who had come into town to stay with her while their husbands were at the diggings. Mrs. Whiston had four young children, and the youngest was very ill; while Mrs. Fielding was grieving herself about her husband's rheumatism, which walking four hundred miles and camping out every night was sure to

bring on; and she reproached herself for letting him go without accompanying him herself.

'You could never have borne such a journey, mother,' said Mrs. Whiston. 'If you could have kept my father at home, that would have been of some use; but fancy what I should have felt if you had gone with him, particularly now Agnes is so ill.'

'A wife's first duty is with her husband,' Mrs. Fielding answered; 'and as she cannot command him to stay with her, she should go with him; not that I think you should have gone, for you would have been a burden instead of support, and with those four helpless babes.'

'I can tell you, young ladies, that you are fortunate, for people never know what anxiety is till they are married,' said Mrs. Whiston.

Both Annie and Clara rather doubted the fact in their own minds, but assented to the proposition mechanically; for they had heard it so often of late, that they saw it would not do to contradict it.

'We will try Mrs. Reid's next,' said Annie, as she and Clara departed, 'for I know she had some gold by the Escort, and surely her husband is not ill, too.'

But Mrs. Reid thought the quantity of her gold very small for the toil and misery it had cost; Mr. Reid had been once in danger of his life; he had written that the diggings were a dreadful place; and then, after recounting with great minuteness two short illnesses he had had, he wound up by declaring that he was very miserable, which of course made his wife still more so. The children were all quite well except the baby, but she could not expect baby to be well while she fretted so much herself.

'My brothers have done very little,—much less than Mr. Reid,' said Annie, 'but they write in good spirits.'

'Depend upon it, they are not so cheerful as they make out. My husband's first letters were written much more cheerfully than this last, but he says he finds it impossible to keep up the deception any longer, and tells me all he feels, which I am thankful to know, though of course it gives me great distress. How many are there in your brother's party now?'

'Only George, Gilbert, and Henry at present, but Mr. Harris and Mr. Bell both talked of joining them.'

'Harris will never do any good,' said Mrs. Reid; 'he can't work, and he has no notion of saving what he may make. Bell might do better, but your brothers should get a Cornish man—Martin must know hundreds of them—to sink the holes. It would be worth while to give him a double share, for Mr. Reid gained much by the hard-working miner he took in his party, though now that he is ill, he will find him an

inattentive nurse and an uncongenial companion;' and here Mrs. Reid's eyes filled again.

'Shall we go home now?' asked Clara, as they left Mrs. Reid's, 'or shall we go to Mrs. Trueman's? We heard her husband was doing tolerably well; so never fear, Annie, let us make another attempt to get up our spirits.'

Mrs. Trueman was sewing when they came in, but she thrust her work under the sofa-mattress, and exclaimed:—

'Where have you been all this while, you two girls? You have not been near me these three weeks, and you know how few acquaintances I have in the colony, and how solitary my life is.'

'We have been very busy at-home, and the weather has been very hot; but we will call sooner next time,' replied Annie.

'Do, like dear girls, for I sit moping so that I cannot write cheerfully to John at all; and I am sure it is very ungrateful, for he writes so often, and his letters are all so kind, that I am sure I ought to feel quite happy.'

Here Mrs. Trueman began to cry.

'After all he is doing for my sake and for —— I should be quite cheerful, you know ——'

'No, indeed! that would be paying him a poor compliment,' said Annie; 'all you can do is to be resigned, which you are; and I quite admire you for it.'

'I think we should mourn less for those that go away than for those left behind,' observed Clara.

'I am sure our sufferings are nothing compared to theirs,' said Mrs. Trueman.

'Your husband has active work,' urged Clara; 'he has the hope of gaining a good sum of money, which will prevent you from being separated again; he sees new faces, and hears new adventures every day, while you sit alone over the dreariest of occupations, and have nothing to break the monotony of your life.'

'Then you think Mr. Trueman is happy away from me?'

'Of course he grieves to be parted from you, but that only makes him work the harder,' was the answer.

'Come home with us, and see Grace and Margaret,' said Annie; 'they will comfort you better than I can, for I always begin by crying out of sympathy.'

'I can't leave the house, but you two shall stay the evening with me.'

This invitation was accepted, and Mrs. Trueman took off the young ladies' bonnets, and made them sit down with her to an early tea, emptying her mind of all its most distressing thoughts, and professing to be much relieved by their visit;

but Annie and Clara walked home in the twilight very sad indeed.

'Mr. Plummer has been here,' Margaret told them, when they reached home, 'and has asked us all to tea with him to-morrow, to meet Mrs. Brown, and Sarah Attwood, and Jane Rivers, and several other ladies. He does not promise us any gentlemen, but will make an effort to secure Mr. Dalton, a clerk in his department, who affects to be shy of parties now, he is made so much of.'

'Now, you will see a specimen of under-educated colonial girls, Clara,' said Annie, 'and if Edward Dalton is there, of the most insufferable of colonial coxcombs, ignorant and assuming. So different from *our* style of young men. But who of us are to go, Margaret?'

'We will lock up the house,' answered Grace, 'and go altogether. There is nothing here worth stealing, as poor Henry says; and Adelaide has not yet lost its character for honesty.'

CHAPTER VII

MISS WITHERING'S MATRIMONIAL SCHEME
IS CROWNED WITH SUCCESS

It certainly was enough to turn any young man's head, to find himself the only single gentleman among such a bevy of ladies as were assembled at Mr. Plummer's; and it was all the more dangerous to Mr. Dalton, because he was a very old colonist, and had often been cast into the shade by pleasanter men when young ladies were in an important minority. The present party would, perhaps, have been more agreeable without him, in the opinion of most of the ladies.

'And what is your opinion of things in general, Miss Margaret Elliot?' said he.

'Things are too unsettled at present for me to venture on an opinion,' she replied.

'For my part,' said Dalton, 'people may say this and that, and prophesy great results from these gold discoveries; but I would fain retire from this miserable world to a hermitage, or any such secluded spot, if it were not that society claims me as the invaluable Edward Dalton!'

'Mr. Dalton,' replied Margaret, 'God has not made this beautiful world for you to get tired of, or pretend to get tired of, at thirty; and if you cannot mix in society with pleasure to yourself, or with profit to others, I, for one, think you may leave it when you please.'

But Mr. Dalton appealed to Miss Attwood and Miss Rivers, and obtained a more favourable judgment; the latter young lady pointing sarcastically to a blue riband which Margaret wore round her neck, and asking if she were not particularly fond of that colour. Margaret answered, simply, that it was thought to suit her complexion; when Mr. Dalton followed up the attack with some reflections upon learned ladies, which put her upon her mettle.

'Yes,' said she, 'I believe it is the rule that, though a lady may strain all her accomplishments to the utmost, singing

her very loudest, and playing her very strongest before gentlemen—though she may display her masterpieces in drawing, in painting, in embroidery, and even in crochet, to the most mixed society;—yet, if she has thought out a subject, she must be silent on it—if she has gained a fact, she must not communicate it,—she must let her faculties rust from want of the brightening which mind exerts over mind;—and must habitually talk below herself, lest she should be supposed to arrogate either equality to the lords of creation, or perhaps superiority over them.'

Mr. Plummer, who was rather slow of apprehension, began to discover about this time that Margaret Elliot was not complimentary to his single gentleman and subaltern in office, and put in a word for him:—

'You must not induce Mr. Dalton to go into a hermitage, or to the diggings either, Miss Margaret,' said he; 'for I don't know how we should get on without him. He writes decidedly the best hand in the office, and is the most punctual in the mornings. Indeed, the head of our department observed to me the other day, "So long as you and Dalton remain, we can get through business creditably; but, were either of you to leave, I could not answer for the consequences!"'

'When did you hear last from Mr. Watson, Miss Rivers?' asked Mr. Dalton, endeavouring, at last, to recover from Margaret's sarcasm.

'Oh, Mr. Dalton, I wonder why you should ask me about him,' was the answer. 'I know nothing at all about him. I suppose he is digging with the rest of them. What business is it of mine? You had better ask Miss Attwood how Mr. Williams is, for I am sure she knows more about him than I do about Mr. Watson.'

Hereupon ensued a perfect war of friendly recrimination between the two girls, during which Mrs. Plummer, who was telling Clara how much Johnny had suffered with his teeth, 'though, thank God! they were well through now,' could scarcely keep up the stream of her narration, when, suddenly, Miss Denfield came in.

'Am not I very late?' she cried. 'I am quite ashamed of myself, Mrs. Plummer; but I have been at Miss Withering's wedding, and we have had a most delightful day. We went all round by Glen Osmond; and then mamma and I had some shopping to do; and now I have leave to stay all night, as you promised me a bed, and am to walk to Langley in the morning. Oh! Miss Morison, I did not expect to see you here. I wish you had come to us, instead of that cross old Miss Withering, that ma' thought so much of. I can tell you, Mrs. Plummer, that I was thankful to see her fairly married, for I was always afraid she would come back, in pa's teeth.

Ah! Sarah Attwood, I could tell you who was asking particularly after you last week, but I won't.'

And then Miss Denfield, who was just coming out, and liked it very much, sat down beside Miss Attwood, to tantalize her concerning this unknown admirer. But she was not long quiet.

'I vote,' she exclaimed, aloud, 'that we have a dance, even with no music but singing. And I am sure that Mr. Dalton can whistle, supposing he has no instrument to play on!'

'Whistle!' said Dalton, scornfully, 'I wonder at any one presuming to say I could do such a thing!'

'I see an accordion, Mr. Plummer. Can any one play on it?' asked Caroline.

'I can play 'God Save the King' and 'Old Hundredth;' but these are not dancing tunes,' answered Mr. Plummer, ruefully.

'What is to be done?' urged Caroline; 'I never could fancy I had been at a wedding unless I had a dance in the evening; and only think what it would be to fancy Mrs. Macnab Miss Withering still. I shall sing a polka. Come, Sarah, will you dance with me?'

'I think I could play a slow waltz on the accordion, if Miss Denfield would like it,' said Grace Elliot.

'Oh! thank you, Miss Elliot. Won't you dance, Sarah?'

'No, I don't like making a show of myself,' replied Miss Attwood.

'Won't you, Miss Rivers?' But Caroline was again answered in the negative.

'I know that Miss Morison will be good-natured enough to go two or three rounds with me, just to let me say I have had a dance;' and, so saying, Caroline looked intreatingly in Clara's face.

Mrs. Plummer, who feared the party was rather dull, begged Clara to comply, and not in vain. Caroline had never had so delightful a partner; she had never fancied a slow waltz could be so charming. By degrees, chairs and sofas were crowded into corners, and all the ladies rose and waltzed, leaving Mr. Dalton, who could not, talking largely to Mr. Plummer upon the absurdity of the proceeding.

The rest of the evening was spent over a round game of cards; and Mr. Dalton, after protesting, at least six times, that cards were an intolerable bore, and standing aloof for five deals, at last sat down between Miss Denfield and Miss Attwood, begged the richest ladies for counters, and grew keener in the game than any other of the company.

'Are you staying with the Elliots, or are you in a situation?' asked Miss Denfield of Clara, who was sitting on the other side of her.

'I am with my cousins at present.'

'We have got such a good-natured girl for a governess now,' continued Caroline. 'She lets me do whatever I like; but I should have liked you better, because you dance so nicely. However, mamma likes the one we have, and it is a capital change for me, for I had no pleasure while Miss Withering was with us; and at last complained to pa'; and he told mamma that he would go to the diggings, and take my two eldest brothers with him, if Miss Withering was not sent away. So I got rid of her; and though mamma says we do not make half the progress now, I can eat my dinner, and laugh when I please. This one never minds whether I laugh at her or not, she is so very good-natured. But I quite pity Mr. Macnab. Do you think she will set him tasks?'

'I should think it very likely,' said Clara; 'for it is her vocation, you know.'

'Well, it is a vacation to me, at all events, and this has been a delightful day. Young Mr. Hastie, who was a fellow-passenger of Mr. Macnab's, was groom's-man; he called himself *best man,* and really, for a Scotchman, he is quite agreeable. I have seen him several times before, but neither of us thought of meeting each other at a shopkeeper's marriage. You know that mamma does not like mixing with tradespeople at all, but Miss Withering had sent her *such* a note!—begging that I might honour the ceremony by being her bridesmaid, and humbly soliciting mamma to be present at the trying occasion, in order to communicate courage to her own palpitating heart, and to invest with her sanction the step she had been overpersuaded to take,—all strongly underlined. I learned the note by heart, in case I should ever need to ask Lady Young to my own marriage, and might want a model. Is not your cousin Margaret a frightful quiz? I never saw her before, for mamma has only just made the acquaintance of Mrs. Plummer. But see, the deal is with you now, Miss Morison.'

'You have lost your two beaux lately,' said Miss Attwood to Annie Elliot; 'I hope you will be able to make up your mind which to take before they come back.'

'There is no doubt about that,' added Miss Rivers; 'Bell is so awkward, and Harris so agreeable.'

'Only think of Bell lending Harris twenty pounds to take him to the diggings;' said Dalton; 'Harris told me so himself. How simple Bell must have been!'

Nothing that could have been said against Mr. Harris by people whose opinion she valued, would have annoyed Annie so much as to hear him praised by persons she despised. And to think of poor William Bell being so generous, and getting no credit for it! She tried to laugh at the sallies pointed

against her, but made a sad failure; and was glad when Mrs. Brown gave the signal, and they rose to go. She would not stay to listen to the half hour's gossip which Sarah, Jane, and Caroline liked to keep up in the bed-room; but hurried her sisters and cousin away. Mr. Plummer escorted them home, leaving Mr. Dalton under the painful necessity of accompanying the other ladies, which he told the clerks in the office next day was the most disagreeable part of the duties he owed to society, but as they all lived near each other, he was spared the dangers of a *tête-à-tête*.

Mr. Plummer was a slow man, and a pompous man, but he was kind-hearted and upright; and Annie was soothed by his praising William Bell, and hoping he would succeed at the gold fields. Then he reverted to the old subject, that Gilbert should never have gone, for it would unsettle him, and there would soon be openings for young men in Adelaide.

'You will be sorry you did not take my advice, Miss Margaret,' said he, 'and keep him at home; for one of our old hands who started off and came back unsuccessful, cannot settle to his desk again at all. However it can't be helped now.'

And Mr. Plummer sighed as he showed the ladies in at the gate, and bade them 'good night.'

CHAPTER VIII

MORE LETTERS FROM THE DIGGINGS

'The Escort is coming in again,' said Annie, one morning; 'the milk girl tells me, and she expects to hear from her father; and so in her joy, I think she has put a double dose of water in the milk, for it looks remarkably blue this morning. Whom shall we get to sell our gold for us, now William Bell is not here?'

But Annie might have spared her anxiety on this score, for though four letters arrived, every one was shaken for an Escort receipt, but none appeared; and they had merely to suppose that no good luck had attended their party.

'And see,' said Annie, 'the date is not Forest Creek, but Bendigo. They must have shifted quarters again.'

The letters were as follows:—

From Henry Martin to Grace Elliot.
Bendigo, 1852.

'MY DEAREST GRACE,

'Don't be very much disappointed at our wretched success, but bear the news that we have nothing to send you as well as you did our recent small remittance; for we are now in hopes of better things. Since William Bell came up a week ago, and put us both in funds and in spirits, so that we could move to these new diggings, we are getting our hopes up amazingly. We had sunk hole after hole, but we never chanced upon the right thing, and we saw that we could not raise the four pounds ten for our licences. If William had not come the day he did, we should have gone as storekeeper's assistants or day-labourers, getting the licence fee as an advance on our wages. But he insisted on paying all for us, and being at the expense of moving our goods to Bendigo, between thirty and forty miles from our old location. The roads are not very

bad yet, but in winter they are sure to be horrible. We are now sinking two holes; Gilbert and I working at one, and George and William at the other; and are expecting great things, but have got nothing in time for the Escort.

'Your letter sent by Harris has never reached me, nor Annie's to George. He might at least have put them into the post-office, if it was not convenient to bring them himself; but perhaps he did—for that post-office is a gulf, a Maelstrom, which sucks in all our letters, and never delivers them up. It was well you wrote me a few lines by Bell, for they came safe enough; and the newspapers with Margaret's marginal notes, which make them more valuable to all of us, were most welcome. We have scarcely had time to read them yet, having been so busy with the removal, and other things. William prophesies that we shall bring back most of them unread, for we mean to find such quantities of gold, that all our spare time will be employed in washing it. And when people are very lucky, they dare not desert their holes through the night, but are obliged to watch by turns, lest any unprincipled fossicker should make off with their treasure.

'All the married men are getting very sick of the life here. I, who am next thing to a married man, but who have never known the comfort of a home of my own, bear up better; but I know that you, my dearest girl, are with your sisters, and that you believe we are doing our best, and trust in Providence to bless our endeavours. Bell tells us your cousin, Miss Morison, is a great acquisition to you all, although he had always thought the family complete before; but she, he says, seems to form one side of a symmetrical square—a mathematical compliment quite worthy of William Bell.

'There is abundance of wood here for a slab hut, in case we should want to stay over the winter; but we shall not do so if we can help it, for it will be miserably wet, and we should rather gain a little and return home soon, than be separated much longer, even for a great deal.

'We have no sermons yet at Bendigo, but hope to have some soon. There is a post-office here, to which you must address your letters; but really I cannot mention the post-office at all without getting angry, a very bad frame of mind in which to conclude a letter to my gentle, loving Grace. Farewell, and God bless you. Ever most faithfully yours,

'HENRY MARTIN.'

From George Elliot to his sister Annie.
Bendigo, 1852.

'MY DEAR ANNIE,

'You cannot think how delighted we were to see William,

and to hear about you all from him. He wrote his letter to Margaret last night, that we might all have time to write to-day, and I suppose he has told her of the good prospects he might have taken advantage of in Melbourne; but he preferred trying his luck with us, and we now feel confident of success. There is nothing like trying new ground at these diggings.

'We found Charley Hodges to-day, but you will be grieved to hear that he is very unwell. I do not think there is anything serious the matter with him, but his party had neglected him, and had taken possession of all the comforts which his mother and Minnie had provided for him. The man that possessed the horse and cart quarrelled with the other man on the road, and Charley took the side of the man without property; so he was in the wrong box, for you cannot think how tyrannical the keeper of all your eatables can be. Then both of the men always took Charley's gun to amuse themselves on the road; and when they killed a turkey, or a lot of teal, grudged giving the poor fellow a share. When they came to dig they only allowed him a seventh, though he had furnished half of the provisions, and they had brought over three months' supply. There was one share for him as a boy, two for each man, one for the horse, and one for the cart; and he thinks they cheated him besides, for they always seemed to have plenty, while he scarcely ever got anything. They made him cook on Sundays, telling him he must learn to rough it, while they went out shooting or amusing themselves; and they wanted him to wash for them too, but he would not submit to that. When he was taken ill, they were on the point of going to Bendigo, and proposed to leave him at Forest Creek; but Charley insisted on their taking him with them, and, as an invalid, he was allowed to ride on the top of the cart. Then the heat of the weather and the long journey quite overcame him. He was lying in bed, without a drop of water in the tent, when William and I happened to pass on our way from our hole, and as the tent was open we could see in. 'There's a poor fellow that wants his mother by him,' said William; 'he looks quite young. Let us see what is the matter with him.' So we went in, and you may guess how glad Charley was to see friends. William would not hear of our leaving him in the hands of the Philistines, so after scrawling in chalk on a box in the tent that Charley had been taken away by Elliot's party, we managed to bring him here.

'Is it not good in William to encumber himself with a useless hand? Charley has dictated a few lines to Minnie, and I shall write as much to his father, to let them all know he is in safe hands, and that I expect him to recover soon.

It is all very well at the diggings while you keep your health, but to be ill among strangers is a dreadful thing.

'Mr. Brown had a sunstroke about three weeks ago, that nearly killed him; but he is slowly recovering, and means to go home when he is able to walk. He looks very queer, for his mates cut off all his hair and his whiskers in their fright. Mrs. Brown will expect him to return with a superabundance of hair, instead of none at all. I fear all he had made will have vanished in this expensive illness. In general, the gentlemen have been unsuccessful, and the married gentlemen most unlucky of all; but often the weakest and the worst worker gets a great deal, for, as you hear everywhere, it is a lottery.

'I cannot imagine what Harris is about. His ship arrived in Melbourne ten days before Wiliam's, and the latter heard there he had gone to the diggings directly, so that as he knew where we lived, we might have expected to see him before William; but neither he nor the letters you sent by him have yet made their appearance.

'Bell tells me that, in spite of the bad times, you had your quarter's interest paid, and that you said you had enough to live on till this Escort should come in; but I am vexed and puzzled to think how you can hold over till the next, in these days of shaken credit, for we have nothing to send now. I wish I had left you my watch to sell, for it is of no use to me here. I stupidly left my Euclid, which would have been ten times more valuable; but William has brought his; and in spite of all his anticipations that we shall have no time for mathematics, I believe we shall get far beyond Margaret before we return.

'Henry has been trying, by boiling his puddings for a very long time, to make up for the paucity of plums, and insists they are as good as the old ones. We had a famous one last Sunday, in honour of Bell's arrival; you would have stared at the amount of fruit in it,—quite enough for a Scotch bun.

'Trueman has done very little more than clear his expenses, and is becoming anxious to get home again. I hope you go pretty often to see that sweet little wife of his, for his heart is very sore about leaving her so long.

'I have nothing more to say, except that I hope you will keep up your spirits in spite of dull times and continued disappointment. Love to all at home, and compliments to my cousin, unknown, in whom William has made me feel quite interested. And believe me,

'Your very affectionate brother,

GEORGE ELLIOT.'

Gilbert Elliot to his sister Margaret.

Bendigo, 1852.

'MY DEAR MARGARET,

'I feel angry and disgusted at myself and the whole affair here, when I find that after so many months of hard work the result is nothing. 'Money,' as Charles Lamb says, 'is not dross; but books, pictures, wines, and many other pleasant things;' and when I see so many here getting more gold than they know what to do with, and which will probably be a curse to them, and then think of the comfort and independence such gains would bring to us, I can only take refuge in the German book I am studying, which rails at the unprofitableness of all human pursuits, and which would no doubt rail at gold-digging if the writer had tried it. I know that you want money at home; I feel ashamed of the drudgery you have to do, and the miserable hospitality you have to offer; and when that fellow Tom Collins—whom you may remember a dirty stable-boy, that could neither read nor write—told me the other day he had sent word to his sisters to leave their places, and take a house, and dress smart, and see company, and that he had sent them plenty to do it upon, I felt the contrast so much, that I could scarcely help knocking the fellow down. In these diggings we hear of nothing but how a man is doing,—well, ill, or middling, as the case may be, but as to what he is or what he knows, that is a matter of perfect indifference.

'I was surprised to hear that you were learning short-hand and Latin with your cousin. What singular accomplishments for a young lady! I am afraid she is bluer than you. But I am sorry you are taking so much trouble, as I have felt quite a disgust for law since I came here, and I fancy it is principally on my account that you are prosecuting these studies. You are hard at work with the laws of real property, while we are shifting about from one block of eight feet square to another, looking for the real precious metal. I fancy you have found out nothing about our tenure in all your reading.

'Your account of the political world with you is just what I expected. No effort made in the right direction, but every one looking with feverish impatience to the shifting clouds in the mercantile horizon, to see whether South Australia is to be a nation, before any effort is made to benefit it.

'One good thing is, that your governor, if powerless for good, is also powerless for evil. If he gave up the Church grant to the clamours of faction, he has also yielded to the popular voice in establishing the assay office, and sending the Escort. We hear that the reduced salaries of all the officials are to be made up to their full amount, as the Treasury is

More Letters from the Diggings

able to bear it; so our friend Mr. Plummer's disinterested attachment to government will be rewarded.

'The government here is very unpopular, and much more obstinate than that of South Australia; there is an exclusive attachment to old interests, and a blindness to the mighty new ones that are arising, which in times like these, when difficulties should be met with promptitude, is a grievous injustice to the colony.

'If land is to be withheld from sale in order to please the squatters, while for want of a right and safe investment for his money, the successful digger squanders or gambles it away, it is not to be expected that the people will be satisfied.

'South Australia gains by this deficiency in Victoria, for so long as land is sold by auction in convenient blocks, it will be an attractive investment, and will besides tend to keep people at home to improve it. A great many of our farming friends are leaving us with the view of getting in their crops, and I hope the season will be favourable.

'I suppose George has written all about Charley to Annie; he is the only friend we have seen here, though we hear that this part of Bendigo is the Adelaide district. I fear that we shall not find it so orderly as Forest Creek. There is very little chance of finding a horse here if once you lose him; for many parties find horse stealing much more profitable than digging; and you may see columns of advertisements for horses lost and stolen at the diggings in the Melbourne papers.

'I think, if I had been Bell, I should have stayed in Melbourne—two hundred and fifty pounds a-year is a handsome salary for a clerk, even in Melbourne. But you see that steady as Bell is, there is a touch of romance about him, and being forced out of Adelaide, he has no idea of giving up the diggings thus. Believe me with love to my sisters, and respects (nothing more familiar) to my learned cousin,

'Your very affectionate brother,

GILBERT ELLIOT.'

From William Bell to Margaret Elliot.
Bendigo, 1852.

'MY DEAR MISS MARGARET,

'I have chosen the evening before the last day of letter-writing to write to you, for I should not like to be hurried in opening a correspondence with so good a judge. Henry has fortified me with a good supper; Gilbert has given me the portfolio and the best pen in the tent; and George has promised not to ask me any questions while I concoct my epistle, so you may see with what consideration I am treated.

'I can give you no account of the diggings so good as you

have had from your brothers; but as I stayed three days in Melbourne, while they came in at dusk and left next morning, I have the advantage of them there. Do not elevate your eyebrows, and say impatiently, 'What kept the idle fellow so long in that wretched town?' till you read my reasons. I had a small bill to settle with Mr. Campbell on my brother James's account, and like an honest man went to his place of business in Melbourne to pay it. He received me graciously, was glad I had remembered my debt, which he had forgotten completely, and begged me to sit down while he gave me the receipt. Then he told me in a good many words that he wanted a trust-worthy young man as clerk, for his last had gone to the diggings; and concluded by offering me a salary of two hundred and fifty, if I would promise to stay out the year. This was twice as much as I ever had before, and I promised to think over it, and give him an answer in two days.

'So these two days I poked about from street to lane, and from lane to street. I inquired the price of lodgings, and what sort of accommodation I could get for thirty-five shillings a-week, the sum named by Mr. C., but in no case could I have a room to myself, and in every instance the parlour was full of those symptomatic sofas Mrs. Bantam liked so ill. Where I actually was I had the fourth part of a room; the inmates were all noisy and quarrelsome, and I had good reason to believe, from the broad arrow on the night-cap of my nearest neighbour, that he was an old convict. Now, that is not at all my idea of comfortable lodgings, and though Miss Withering used to complain of the state of matters at Mrs. Brown's, you cannot think how superior Mrs. B.'s is to anything you could find in this Babel of a town. The houses are finer and the shops more splendid; there is a sort of centralization in Melbourne, which your scattered irregular town cannot boast of; but it seems to me that rich and busy as it is, there is very little enjoyment or happiness in it. It is uncomfortable, and indeed dangerous, to be out at night, and that to a man shut up in an office all day is a great deprivation. One had better remain in Adelaide with one hundred, where one had a room to oneself, and where it was perfectly safe, at least in a physical point of view, to walk over to your cottage of an evening, and chat with you and your sisters, than dwell in troubled Melbourne with two hundred and fifty.

'It is true that the best society in Melbourne has always been considered by Scotch people superior to its counterpart in Adelaide; but how was a stranger and a clerk, with such very slender social talents as you know I have, to get into it? Where should I find a place in the universal overturn of

society which is taking place in Victoria? The aristocratic members of the community are retreating when they can to England, to keep out of the crowd and discomfort; the mercantile are turning over money with unexampled rapidity, large profits and quick returns being the order of the day; and there is the same keen money-making look about them, which you used to observe in the frequenters of your Exchange, but with more feverish anxiety about the Melbourne men.

'The town is densely crowded; places built in narrow lanes for stables are filled by human occupants, who live in dirt and discomfort, injuring the general health of the town. Owing to the stringent Building Act there have been many good streets built, because every man in buying his piece of land got the plan of the house to be erected towards the front; but as there was nothing to prevent the back being divided into lanes, the profit of the speculation has induced many to do it. It is shameful that with an unlimited extent of country, and in such a new town, people should be living in rows of houses only ten feet apart. You know a few such places in Adelaide; you know them to be nests of fever and sickness; and when I tell you that there are no fewer than two hundred and ninety of these private alleys in Melbourne not subject to the street regulations, you will not believe it can be a healthy city. Nor will you think so the more when you consider that a great proportion of the people are the sweepings of British jails, who have just made their way to a place where almost every description of crime may be committed with impunity. A feeble government, which is now led by a clique of squatters, a wretched police, and incompetent courts of law, is a great obstruction to the course of justice. I heard a gentleman say it was no bad thing for the colony that Melbourne was not a desirable place of residence; for that in a new state comfortable and luxurious cities impede the spread of the people and the subjugation of the soil. And there is some truth in that, but the only subjugation people think of now, is getting the gold out of the land; and every other description of industry is for the time paralyzed. I did not see much gambling in my peregrinations, at least not nearly so much as I expected, from our knowledge of its extent in California; but I suppose that the great medley of nations who find a common language and common sympathies over the gambling table, have not yet come to an understanding. But of drinking and swearing I saw more than enough. I thought Adelaide was not particularly moral, but it is infinitely better than this. Even gentlemen make a boast of swearing in Victoria, while few, except bullock-drivers, do so in South Australia.

'I happened to look into a shop when an Irish orphan, who had come to the colony with scarcely a shoe to her foot, was buying white satin for a bridal dress at twelve shillings a yard, and scornfully rejecting any shawl under ten guineas. Marriages are very frequent, and on a few days' acquaintance. The disproportion of the sexes was always great, for Melbourne was peopled chiefly by independent emigrants and people from the other colonies; and not so much from free emigration, paid for out of the colony's land fund, in which case pains are taken to equalize them. The high upset price of crown lands has on the whole been a great benefit to South Australia; for when half the price was devoted to bringing out labour to improve the land it benefited both the mother country and the young colony.

'Scarcely any wages will tempt a girl to remain in service, when she sees the foolish finery in which the foolish brides go off; and the ladies of Victoria are forced to do the meanest drudgery, even occasional assistance not being to be had. To them it is a special hardship, for they never were so independent of servants as the Adelaide ladies. I met Mr. Bantam in Great Collins-street one day, and he took me home to see his wife. Their cottage is nicely situated but very small. He is doing a good business as a commission-agent; but his wife seems to pine after Adelaide yet, and was pleased to hear that things were looking up a little when I left. They were both glad that Miss Morison had not found a situation, for they still hoped she would have no objection to join them at some future time.

'So after my two days' researches, I determined to refuse Mr. Campbell's offer of a situation, and to set off immediately to join your brothers, and deliver your letters and messages. Mr. Campbell shook his head, called me a rash young man, and gave me back my money with some hesitation, seeming to fear that I could not be trusted with it. And thus I quitted Melbourne, with the conviction, that if the discovery of gold in South Australia would bring such characters there as I had seen poured into this devoted city, we ought to pray daily that God would not send such a curse upon us, as a punishment for our colonial sin of worldly-mindedness.

'I lost no time on the road; and did not Elliot's party give me a shout of welcome! I consider myself remarkably fortunate in joining a party which has been unlucky hitherto; for I shall share all the good fortune they may justly expect in return. Our change of quarters also gives a prestige of success. I do not need to buy a cradle or a tent, and I am benefited by the experience of my comrades. Your brothers and Martin are all looking well, and seem to have excellent

health. I hope that you will answer this long epistle, and remain,

'Yours very faithfully,
WILLIAM BELL.'

'I like this letter,' said Margaret, after reading both of her letters aloud; 'it is written in a better spirit than Gilbert's.' And she sunk into silent thought, leaning her head on her hands.

Annie wanted to say something about Gilbert's having been so long disappointed, but her tongue refused to speak. She thought how happy William would be with Margaret, but she felt wretched herself.

'Can we retrench our expenses any further, since we are not likely to get any money for a while?' enquired Grace.

'We can do without the newspaper and the library subscription,' suggested Margaret.

'We must buy no more fruit,' added Annie.

'I must go away,' said Clara; 'I cannot be a burden to you any longer, and Mrs. Trueman would take me as a servant, I dare say.'

'And do you think we would let our cousin go to service there?' exclaimed Annie. 'No, Clara; do not leave us in our sorrow; I cannot do without you.'

'I think you are making a rash proposal; let us wait a day or two and see what is to be done,' said Margaret. 'If you can get a comfortable situation as a governess, I shall not be selfish enough to make any objection; but I feel confident that there is good luck in store for our party at Bendigo; and if in a month we are to set up for as great ladies as Mrs. Pengarvon next door, you had better not affront us by taking a place. I hope that prosperity may find us all in frame of mind to profit by it. Hand me down Chitty, Clara; and look over the short hand I wrote this morning, to see if it is all right. I have not put any vowels, so you must exercise your ingenuity. If you talk of leaving us, I may as well get as much good out of you as possible.'

And Margaret fixed herself at her book, making notes and extracts as she went along, while Annie's trembling fingers endeavoured vainly to get through a simple piece of crochet.

CHAPTER IX

SIGNS OF COLONIAL PROSPERITY!

'Annie is not well,' said Clara to Margaret, as they went out walking together on the day after they had the letters. 'She wants change of air and scene. Do you know any friends in the country, who are not particularly doleful, to whom you could send her?'

'She might go to the Hodges', though they have been sad enough about Charley, and Minnie has written in wretched spirits lately; but perhaps now that they have heard of him, they will be more cheerful. What do you think is the matter with Annie, for I am a very bad judge? I suppose Adelaide is very dull for her; and then she was so wrapped up in George, that she cannot bear the long separation. I am sure I am quite as anxious about Gilbert; but I can settle myself to more engrossing occupations than Annie, who sings sad songs, and draws dreary pictures from her own cheerless imagination; so that her very amusements aggravate her complaint. Don't you think I might write to Mr. Hodges, asking him to take Annie for a while to the south? Not a hint, but an honest request.'

'I think you might; but will not Mr. Hodges be in town himself soon, to hear more about Charley?'

'He may, but he has been rather shy of us lately; and he may be sure that Annie will give him all the information he wants in her letters to Minnie.—Do you see the woman who is standing at the door of the 'pizé' cottage before us. She was our washerwoman long ago, and initiated me into the mystery. Let us go and ask for a drink of water. How do you do, Mrs. Tubbins? My cousin and I would be obliged to you for a drink of water.'

'You are welcome hearty, Miss Marget,' answered the person addressed, who had on a smart cap, but a dirty gown, with rather a slipshod appearance about the feet; 'come in

and chat with me a bit, for I am lonesome now my master is off to them diggings again.'

Never had such an incongruous-looking abode greeted the eyes of the cousins. Into one room, which had a clay floor, and was indeed the only room in the house, there was crammed so much furniture, that there was scarcely standing room. A piano, by Collard and Collard, stood in one corner; a cheffonier, with a great array of decanters and glasses, graced another; there were two chests of drawers, wedged between a common stretcher and a heap of bedding, which seemed intended for a nightly shakedown. There was, in truth, an abundance of everything but chairs, and that deficiency was made up by a number of three-legged stools, which the children liked to lift on to the drawers, and, climbing by the handles, to perch themselves where they could reach the rafters of the unceiled house. A very small piece of matting lay under the table, but the legs of the piano and of all the valuable furniture rested on the earthen floor.

'Rather a change of days for us,' said Mrs. Tubbins, glancing complacently from her furniture to her visitors. 'Aint we snug now, Miss Marget? This is a prettier piany than yours, and cost more money too, I expect, for my master gin sixty guineas for it the week before he left me, that I might have something cheerful in the house; but the children are for ever strumming on it, and broke three of the prettiest of the brass wires no further gone than last night. They tear at the wires with their fingers, and scrape across them with an iron hoop they picked up, which aint doing justice to the piany. Just play us a tune, Miss Marget, to let them see how it should be done.'

Margaret found that the piano had suffered very much from the course of treatment which the young Tubbinses had pursued; she played very softly, in order to spare her own ears.

'Just try now, Fanny, if you can play like that,' said Mrs. Tubbins.

Fanny struck the notes at random, more gently than her wont, and her mother smiled approvingly, and said she knew she would come on if she had any one to tell her how to play. Then Clara was asked to give a tune, and as she was but a tyro, she could not moderate her style to the piano, but played as hard as she did on her cousin's.

'Your cousin beats you, Miss Marget; but if she would just put her foot on the stick below, it would make a wonderful improvement. It sounds quite grand, and booms in your ears; but I think there ought to be two sticks, one for each foot, that folk may have all their limbs helping the music; but yours had only one. Do you know anybody who would

come in for a few hours every day to teach me and Fanny, for it would be grand to able to play to Mr. Tubbins when he comes back?'

'Have you any music?' asked Clara, wondering at the extraordinary tones of the handsome and apparently new piano.

'Oh! I beg your pardon, Miss. I should have given you the books. I never play without them myself.' And Mrs. Tubbins handed her a leaf of Jeannette and Jeannot, and another which had formed part of the overture to Tancredi, saying that she really ought to buy another book or two. 'I went to Platts' last week, and they wanted to sell me an instruction book, as they called it, and asked a guinea for it, but I saw they thought me green, for the book was more words than music; so I told the young man as served me that I knew chalk from cheese, and that was not the book for my money, and did not spend a brass farthing in the shop after all. You'll stop and have a glass of wine with me, Miss Marget? Fanny, run across to the public-house for a pint of sherry, the best they have got.'

'I wish Annie had been with us,' said Margaret, unable to repress a smile. 'She has not been well or in good spirits lately, and it would have done her good to have seen you in the midst of all your splendour.'

'I expect her young man is at the diggings, and she is pining about him; but it's far worse to have to pine after one's old man;' and Mrs. Tubbins heaved a sigh, but controlled her feelings at the sight of her piano.

'All our young men are at the diggings—George, Gilbert, and Henry Martin,' observed Margaret.

'That's the young man Miss Grace has married,' said Mrs. Tubbins.

'Only going to marry.'

'Dear, dear! how long you two misses have been in settling for yourselves! But here's Fanny with the wine and biscuits.'

'Give me my fourpenny, mother, for going your message.'

'I only said I'd give you twopence, and I can see you have been nibbling, and don't deserve a brass farthing, you little good-for-nothing! Oh, how I wish I had not lost my keys!'

'Bob has planted them somewhere, mother, to get at the plums and sugar. I've got my fourpenny, so I don't mind how soon you find them.' And Fanny ran away to the nearest lolly shop, and all her brothers and sisters followed her.

'Don't you send the children to school?' asked Margaret. 'It is very bad for them to be running about idle.'

'I did send them a bit, but Fanny got scolded, and Bob got thrashed; and the little ones were kept in, and got no

dinner at all one day; so they just hate the school, and won't go to it no more.'

'You should make them go, whether they will or not,' said Margaret. 'You will ruin your children if you allow them to do as they please, and all the gold and all the fine furniture in the world will never make up to you for the misery disobedient children will give you. I speak seriously to you, Mrs. Tubbins; for I see great evils coming on this colony from money being thrown into the hands of people who, instead of teaching their children the uses and duties of wealth, indulge them in everything they ask for. Send your children to school regularly, and insist upon their obeying you at home, that their father may be proud of them when he returns, and may find, after all his toil and hardships, a happy fireside and an orderly family.'

'What you say is all very true, Miss Marget, but you are over hard on the likes of us, who never got no learning, and don't quite see the use of it.'

'If you don't see the use of their learning, make them work as they used to do.'

'They ain't got no call to work, for I have lots of clothes for them, and a silk gown for myself to go to town with; and where is the use of them slaving just as if we had not a penny.'

'I have not seen you at church for a long time,' said Margaret. 'Do you go to chapel now?'

'Indeed, I ain't got a sitting anywheres just at present, and I don't like getting my religion for nothing now, when I can afford to pay for it. Your church is not ours, and I am just wondering which one to join; but, after all, I never get time to go to church, for there is the dinner to make ready in the morning, and the children to put to bed at night, so it is ill convenient for me to get away.'

'But don't the children go to church or Sunday school? I remember your telling me how fond Fanny was of learning hymns and catechism.'

'So she was then, and I was glad to get an old frock of yours to make down for her, to look decent to go to school in; but we are much smarter now.'

And Mrs. Tubbins took from a very miscellaneous lot of things Fanny's pink satin bonnet and dress of green and lavender silk, saying that she thought them very genteel, and that they took her fancy in the shop at first sight. Then her own gorgeous attire for Sundays was brought out for Margaret's inspection and admiration; and she was busy telling how much every article had cost, when her two nieces, Sarah and Lucinda Hagget, came in.

'Oh, aunt, how vain you are of your finery!' said Miss

Lucinda. 'You never let anybody miss the sight of it if you can help. I fancy you are prouder of that fine silk dress than you are of your piany, though it's the piany I envy,'—but the speaker looked very hard at the gown too.

'Have you left your places, girls, that you are both here at this time of day?—and such good places you had too,' said Mrs. Tubbins.

'I hadn't enough of wages,' said Sarah. 'How do people expect one to dress on seven shillings a-week? I sha'n't take a place again under eight, if I have washing to do. Lucinda had no washing, so she might have stopped.'

'Stopped at such a place! Why, it was so dull that you could hear the grass growing, for want of anything else to hear. If I could get a good cheerful place, I shouldn't mind taking six shillings a-week till we hear from father.'

'I know a lady who wants a girl; she would give you an easy place, and she is a good mistress—Mrs. Trueman,' said Margaret.

'A grass widow!—I won't go there,' cried Lucinda. 'It is enough to pull down any creature's spirits, to live with such whining people. You, aunt, are the cheerfullest of the lot, and me and Sarah have come to stop with you till we get suited.'

'Where are you all to sleep?' asked Margaret.

'Oh! I make up a bed on the piany every night,' replied Mrs. Tubbins; 'and it holds a good many of the little ones, and Sarah may go beside them. It is quite handy for a bed. I can manage, I warrant.'

Miss Lucinda meanwhile was busily engaged trying to make out a nigger melody, but could not manage it. She was just going to ask Margaret to tell her what notes should be struck, when the cousins rose to depart. Clara could not get over the idea of the handiness of the large square piano, and its being strummed on and raked with hoops all day, and slept on all night: she hurried out of hearing of the people inside, and indulged in a long and hearty fit of laughter.

'It is all very well for you to laugh,' said Margaret; 'but I must say it is no laughing matter. I remember Mrs. Tubbins a hard-working honest woman, who brought up her family better than the average of her class; and now this suddenly-acquired wealth is ruining them all. When his gold is spent, I suppose Tubbins will set off for more; and until the diggings are worked out, South Australia is none the better for that family.'

'Are you longing to see the end of the gold, Margaret?'

'Heartily!' was the answer; 'I do long for it, though my brothers get none. Indeed, I do not wish them to get much,

though it is hard for poor Grace and Henry to be disappointed.'

'Do you know, I had an idea of offering to give your old friend and her daughter lessons on the piano,' said Clara. 'They seemed to admire my playing more than yours, and it would have brought in a little money.'

'You are an absurd girl, Clara. Tubbins was tipsy, I am sure, when he bought the instrument, and you would be mad to go to such a place. I do not know what sort of characters you might meet there. And besides, I thought you despised quackery—you are not an accomplished musician, and I hope you will not pretend to be what you are not.'

'You need bring forward no further argument, Margaret; I am not qualified to give music lessons, even to a digger's wife. But why does not Mrs. Tubbins get a better house, when she has so much finery to put into it?'

'Oh, the house is their own property; I remember her borrowing five pounds from my father to make up the purchase-money, and coming back proudly to pay it, and inviting me to come to see her in her own house. Besides, she likes the situation of the place; it is close to the shop where she makes her daily purchases, and enjoys her daily gossip; then three of her children were born in it; and small and mean as it is, I do not wonder at her being attached to it. But a nice bedroom could have been added for the price of the piano; while the cheffonier and its appurtenances might have put up a back kitchen. Still, the poor woman is proud and pleased, and her nieces are envious; and I suppose she has great enjoyment in the midst of her heterogeneous property. But the children—ah! Clara, I am grieved about the children. You cannot be expected to care much about the colony or the character of the colonists here; but such things affect me keenly and deeply. Do you remember Gilbert at all, Clara? Did you know one brother from the other?'

'Gilbert was the younger, and slighter and handsomer, I think,' Clara answered.

'Just so; and he has finer abilities than George. He can do anything he sets himself to do. I wish he were back with us again. Did you ever try anything in the way of original composition, Clara?'

'Sometimes. I used to write imaginary conversations, in which I gave myself greater latitude than I had any right. I once made you call me a miserable little coward; but that was before I knew you.'

'I have no turn that way—not the least in the world,' said Margaret; 'but Gilbert writes well. I must show you some of his essays when we go home. You must spur him on, for it is a gift he should not allow to go to rust.'

281

After calling on one or two friends, they returned home, and Clara told Annie about the piano, and all Mrs. Tubbins' possessions, as grotesquely as she could; not minding Margaret's theory, that it was really very deplorable, but glad to see Annie laugh again.

Though Mr. Hodges had been shy of the Elliots for some time, as Margaret said, the news of the kindness received by his son at the diggings from his old friends, made him come into town on purpose to thank them through their sisters. Minnie begged to come with him; and was pleased to think that all her time would be spent with Annie this visit. Neither Mrs. Bantam nor Miss Withering could come between her and her friend now. She knew, too, that Annie would show her George's letters; so she arrived at the Elliots' in great spirits.

'I cannot tell you how much we feel obliged to your brothers for their kindness to Charley. We feel sure that he is as comfortable as he can be under the circumstances, and both his mother and myself are comparatively easy about him now.'

'You should thank William Bell, too, for it is more his doing than theirs,' said Margaret. 'Of course they have all the good-will in the world; but, poor fellows, they have very little power.'

'Oh yes, we are very grateful to Mr. Bell, too,' said Mr. Hodges; 'but we can thank you young ladies for your brothers, —whereas we must delay showing our gratitude to Bell till he returns, unless one of you will take the onus of receiving it for him. Eh, Miss Margaret, you take a great interest in that young man! I see what it will end in.' And Mr. Hodges looked positively sly. 'But now tell me what I can do for you, by way of returning, in some trifling degree, your brother's kindness to my boy.'

'I have two favours to ask of you,' replied Margaret. 'One is, the loan of ten pounds till our brothers come back; and the other—'

'Stop,' said Mr. Hodges, taking out his pocket-book, 'till I give you the first. Would you not be the better for twenty? No! very well, ask for more when you want it, and in the mean time here are the notes—count them, Margaret; you should never take money, even from your father, without counting it. And now for your second request?'

'Which is, that you would take Annie with you for a fortnight or three weeks. She wants a change—she is not well.'

'Delighted to do such a thing! Indeed, poor Minnie has been moped to death, and had made me promise to take

Annie out at all events; so that request goes for nothing; you must make another.'

'I have nothing more to ask,' said Margaret.

'Not even on William Bell's account?' hinted Mr. Hodges. 'I'll pay my debt to Bell in a white satin dress, or something of that sort, when you consent to give up your dearly beloved will, and love, honour and obey.'

'You are talking nonsense, and you know you are,' said Margaret.

'I know nothing of the kind,' retorted Mr. Hodges; 'I can see quite as far into these things as my neighbours. Ah! Annie, there are very few young fellows down our way now. Even the sheep farmers stick so close to their sheep that they can very seldom come over to amuse us; and all the agriculturists are off to the diggings. But the change of air and riding on horseback with Minnie will do you good, though we are so stupid.'

'I am sure it will do me a great deal of good to be with Minnie,' replied Annie.

'And I shall be delighted to have you,' said Minnie, 'for the only young ladies in the neighbourhood are so busy with their accomplishments that they are but dull company. First Miss Forbes plays, then Miss Jemima, then Miss Rose, then little Miss Jane; and at last the governess winds up with a thundering piece. Then out come the drawings and the fancy work; and this with complaints of bad servants and neglected gardens, forms all our amusement. But with you, Annie, there will be an inexhaustible variety of amusement.—Do you know I want to see how poor Mr. Macnab looks after his marriage? And I am going to do a great deal of shopping, and shall encourage him in the first place. And you will come with me, Annie, I know.'

'Of course I will,' was the answer.

'Clara will come, too,' said Minnie, 'as she is an old friend of both parties.'

'No, excuse me!' exclaimed Clara, 'I cannot go where I have the faintest chance of seeing Miss Withering.'

Annie and Minnie asked Mr. Macnab to show them several troublesome articles, in order that they might have a good look at the poor victim; and he certainly seemed uncomfortable and awkward enough. He was trying to drill a small boy and a raw though middle-aged man, into the duties of serving customers, but apparently without much success; for neither of them understood either the names of the goods, or the marked prices; and they were continually applying to him as to what was barége and what was chintz, and what was the price of each.

'I wonder that you do not have a lady in the shop,' said

Minnie, maliciously. 'There are many girls who wait upon customers much better than young men, and you know they would be cheaper.'

'No! no!' said Macnab; 'silly things that go on giggling at every body! I would not have such creatures behind my counter if I were paid for them. Is it thread buttons or pearl buttons you want?'

'I want both, Mr. Macnab; just let me choose for myself. Here is another customer coming, a digger, I see.'

And a man, in one of those plaid jumpers which have so long been the characteristic dress of returned diggers, with a bushy beard and way-soiled aspect, shouted out, 'Well, mate, what have you got in my line, eh?'

'What would you see, sir? silks or parasols?' asked Mr. Macnab, looking somewhat puzzled. 'Or perhaps ready-made shirts? We have them of every quality, and at every figure.'

'You are out altogether, Mac, my old chuff,' said Renton, for it was he; 'I want to see the shop and you, but I am going to buy nothing—cleaned out, d'ye see!' and he turned his pockets inside out in testimony of the fact.

'If ever you catch me going to the diggings again, I give you leave to put a strait waistcoat on me. I have come back to my old quarters, and you'll give me a slice of the business, as you promised before.'

'Well, Renton, I am glad to see you again,' answered Macnab. 'Go to your own room, where your box is; take your beard off, and make yourself decent. Then you may come and take that blockhead Sims' place; and when I have consulted with Mrs. Macnab, I will speak to you about your share in the concern.'

'Hooked at last!' said Renton, laughing. 'That is jolly! Why don't you get your wife to wait on the ladies? You know you make a very poor hand of it yourself.'

'The fact is,' Macnab answered, in a low emphatic whisper, 'that Mrs. Macnab has not been used to that sort of thing; and though she said she should be serviceable to me in my business, and I thought she would be just the person to take the fancy department, she won't do it. She says she can help in the counting-house, and superintend the domestic arrangements, but she has no notion of the counter.'

'The counting-room you could always manage yourself; and you let domestic matters take care of themselves; so I don't see that you are much the better for such an expensive supernumerary as a wife. However, I am a host in myself, and will make things ship-shape presently.'

And so saying Renton withdrew to make himself present-

able, while Sims, anticipating the loss of his place, looked after him with ineffable disgust.

Mr. Macnab really stood in awe of his wife; for having battled an entire week to persuade her to serve in the shop, and having not only failed signally, but also been compelled to give her a handsome dress as a peace-offering, he felt it was best to let her have her own way. She was always wanting something from the shop, to give a cheerful appearance to her little parlour; but after all it was a dreary place, and already she had begun to teaze her husband for a house in the country. Every person of property and standing, she would say, had a country-house; and the confinement of town would kill her; for she could not get out of doors at all, except through the shop, and that was so disagreeable. So many diggers and vulgar diggers' wives frequented it, that it was unfit for a lady to pass through; and she had always been accustomed to have plenty of fresh air, and the doctor declared that confinement would ruin her constitution.

Mrs. Macnab was quite aware, if nobody else was, that she had thrown herself away in marrying a tradesman; and she wore an air of quiet dignified resignation, which charmed people who did not know her. But it was a puzzle to those who visited her, to find out how she got rid of the days as they passed. She gave her servant no rest, yet still complained of her laziness; she sent out all her needlework, and grumbled at the expense; she neither sewed nor read, but sat in a comfortable easy chair; lamenting that there was nothing to be seen from the window; and telling her husband that if she was in the country she would rise with the lark, and work in the garden; and attend to his buttons too, which were a perfect bore in town.

Mr. Renton was not likely to be a favourite with Mrs. Macnab; she thought him low, and was thunderstruck at his impudence in asking for a share of the profits, without having a penny to put into the concern. But Macnab had suffered too severely from the absence of his shipmate and shopman, to part with him lightly again. A rival house on the other side of the street endeavoured, by the offer of a very large salary, to secure the services of the irresistible Renton; and, in spite of his wife's entreaties and remonstrances, Mr. Macnab took him into partnership, and added his name on the sign over the door.

It was in vain he told his wife that the salary the new partner had been offered, was equal to more than the sixth of his own profits; it was the degradation that she disliked; and the idea that Renton would rise as they rose, and that every one would consider the late shopman their equal. And when Mr. Macnab brought him in to dinner, and asked her

to see that he was comfortable, she fairly took ill, and persuaded the doctor to insist that she should get out of Adelaide as soon as possible.

She read the newspapers to see what properties were advertised to sell or let; and made her husband drive her out so often to look at them one after another, that at last he began to think he should lose less time and money by yielding to her wishes, and to muse seriously on becoming a purchaser.

CHAPTER X

A SITUATION TURNS UP FOR CLARA

When Annie returned from her three weeks' stay in the south, she looked much better than when she left Adelaide. Two letters from her brothers, of marvellously old date, sent by private hands, and telling of hopes quite as brilliant as their present chance at the Bendigo, but which had since been contradicted by the Escort letters—were not forwarded to her, lest she might be depressed by new forebodings of disappointment. She had ridden about with Minnie and her brother John, had had an occasional dip in the sea, and had recovered her appetite; so that she looked once more like the Annie Elliot of old times.

Reginald had passed an evening with the Elliots while Annie was in the south, and as usual, had enjoyed the society of girls who were so much like what he thought young ladies should be. His pleasure was less mixed than poor Clara's; who was apt to fancy that if he looked sad, he must be pining for his beautiful Julia; or if he seemed happy and animated, that he was in hopes of being soon united to her. But she rejoiced in a conviction which forced itself upon her, that he was himself interested in her character and opinions; and that though he might wish his wife to like her too, it was not merely or even chiefly with a view to her, that he drew her out.

She was pleased when Grace gently rallied her on Mr. Reginald's attentions; the thought that her cousins considered her his equal on all points, seemed to justify, or at least to excuse, the vain hopes in which she had indulged for one happy week. But she was determined, that if ever she met another man who loved her, and who was worthy of being loved, she would do her utmost to foster a prepossession in his favour; for she had no idea of dying for love, or of shutting up her heart for ever because the first time she had

287

opened it, it had been in vain. Even her friendship for William Bell had done her good; and when she looked forward to the return of two pleasant and clever cousins, she was determined to like them both very much, so as to try whether friendship for three would not inflict a death-blow on her love for one.

Margaret liked to talk to her about Gilbert, and showed her his essays; pointed out to her his peculiar marks and jottings in books; and was pleased to find that Clara's opinion of his abilities was equal to her own.

'Gilbert, however, is not poetical,' said Margaret one day to her cousin; 'he could not repeat verses by the hour together like our friend Reginald, much less compose them, as I strongly suspect Reginald does when he is left by himself. For so young a man Gilbert has not much imagination; but he has strength and clearness of thought, whereas, begging your pardon, my dear cousin, Reginald is apt to be misty. Do you always understand him yourself, Clara?'

'I never have any difficulty whatever in making out his meaning. You always understand me, Margaret, and I am often in a kind of dreamy mood. I am sure you understood all he told you about Mr. Dent, at any rate.'

'Yes, I certainly understood that,' answered Margaret. 'Mr. Dent has settled as an English country gentleman, making improvements in his own property, enlivening the neighbourhood by his occasional visits, charming Reginald's mother and sisters by his agreeable manners, and in short conducting himself with exceeding propriety. Was I foolish to refuse to share such a respectable position, cousin Clara?'

'Not at all! for Mr. Reginald has a contempt for him, even when he tells us how other people respect him.'

'Well, Clara,' said Margaret, musingly, 'I have had two offers in my life. One man fancied that I was ladylike, and another that I should make a good stepmother; they were both mistaken, for I do not pretend to be a lady, and I never will be any man's second wife. I wonder if I shall ever be loved for what I am; for it is mortifying to find oneself only loved by mistake. Well, at any rate, I can love my brothers as much as I please, and I hope they will love me nearly as much in return. But here is Mrs. Plummer coming to call. What can bring her here to-day? for though she considers us bound to visit her at least twice every month, the cares of her family, and of Johnny in particular, quite exonerate her from returning our visits.'

When Mrs. Plummer came in, she complained that it was a very headachy day; took out her smelling bottle, and asked where Grace was.

'I am sorry she has gone out with Annie to see Mrs.

A Situation Turns Up for Clara

Trueman, but she will be back in time for tea. You had better stay till she returns,' said Margaret.

'Stay three hours here, and my Johnny so ill of the croup! You could not ask me to do such a thing, Margaret.'

'I am very sorry to hear it. When was he taken ill?'

'Only last night, and we had such a fright with him. Mr. Plummer was for turning up the cyclopedia for croup, but I insisted on his going for the doctor, and when he came he gave the boy something that relieved him greatly. He is lying now in Betsy's arms, quite spiritless, poor little angel, and I have just stept across. I am sorry Grace is not at home.'

'Did you want her to go home with you?' asked Margaret; 'I will tell her when she returns, and I think I may promise that she will be with you to-night. She is always glad to be of service to her friends.'

'Oh, no! it was not that,' replied Mrs. Plummer, 'but I think it strange that Grace should be out the only day I have called for months.'

'You may say years,' said Margaret, smiling.

'Well, perhaps it may be years, but you girls cannot fancy how tied a wife and mother is. However, my business to-day is with Clara. Did you not say that she would be happy to get a situation either as a governess or companion?'

'Oh, yes,' said Clara, 'have you heard of anything for me?'

'Dr. Bennet asked me if I knew of a cheerful pleasant young lady who would go as companion to a lady in the country who was in delicate health; and I said I thought I did; and promised that you should be at my house in the afternoon, when he was to call again. So I hope you will put on your things, and come at once with me. Don't make yourself too smart, for the doctor is an oddity, but he has wonderful skill with children.'

Clara lost no time in dressing herself suitably, and went out with Mrs. Plummer, after receiving Margaret's injunctions on two points; first, that she was not to be made a mere sick-nurse of, for it would kill her; and secondly, not to go for nothing, for she would gladly keep her on those terms herself.

Dr. Bennet was a middle-aged man, with a pair of very sharp eyes, an abrupt way of speaking, and a habit of nodding his head from side to side, as if he gained—or at any rate fixed—a great deal of information by that means. Mrs. Plummer had unbounded confidence in him, and though he had called her a nervous fool many times in her various alarms about Johnny, he had accounted for it satisfactorily by saying, that with her head and her temperament she could be nothing else. Clara had naturally a great deal of courage, or she would have disliked the sharp glances that seemed

determined to see into her and through her; but the expression was kindly though inquisitive, and she felt that the doctor had a duty to perform towards his patient. Just fancy his taking such a person as Miss Withering to wait upon a sick lady, and not closely questioning her, and scrutinizing her answers.

'Temperament—nervous-sanguineous—it will do,' said Dr. Bennet. 'Mrs. Beaufort's is bilious-sanguineous—the two will suit tolerably well. Hope, large—benevolence, full—keep your comparison and causality to yourself young lady, and you will get on very well. Language, very full—mirthfulness, fair—yes—— How old are you?'

'Twenty,' answered Clara.

'Yes. Yes, you are just twenty; I could have told you so myself, but I am pleased you don't call yourself seventeen. Do you know anything about nursing invalids, young lady?'

'I nursed my father in his last illness,' she replied.

'What was the matter with him?' asked Dr. Bennet.

'He had had a paralytic shock, and had lost the use of one side. He did not want much nursing, but he liked to be amused.'

'And how did you amuse him? sing and play, and all that sort of thing, eh!'

'No, I cannot sing,' Clara said. 'I read and talked to him; I wrote for him; I sat beside him and looked at him, and whether he answered me or not, I know he was never weary of hearing my voice.'

'Never had anything to do with diseases of the lungs?'

'A very little, sir,' said Clara, feeling alarmed. 'Mrs. Smith, who died in a decline next door to where I live with my cousins, sometimes had me to sit up with her, and Grace said I did pretty well; but really, sir, I should be afraid to have the charge of a lady in a consumption out in the bush, where there is no doctor near. I fear I must decline the situation.'

'Nonsense!' cried Dr. Bennet. 'While there is hope, you have only to follow my directions, and write to me frequently to let me know if any change takes place. And if the case is hopeless, what can all the faculty of physicians do, more than you? But I must tell you that Mrs. Beaufort is not at all aware of her danger, and would not hear of such a thing as a professional nurse being sent to her. She would stay alone in the house with her baby and a miserable, faithful servant of hers, and never fancy she wanted anything more. I might have preached to her for hours on the necessity of her having a cheerful young companion to enliven her till her husband returns (here Dr. Bennet thrust his stick into his mouth), and she would never have allowed it was needed;

A Situation Turns Up for Clara

but when I hinted that little Lucy would grow dull and sad if she had not a smiling face to look at, she, after trying in vain to laugh and look cheerful, begged me to look out for a young lady to come to stay with her; telling me that she would give her thirty pounds a-year, and would make the Barn as comfortable for her as it was in her power to do. What fools women are after all!' and the doctor sucked his stick and stared very hard at Clara.

'Philoprogenitiveness full, I see; but do you know anything about children?'

'Not much, but I like them; how old is the baby?'

'Only five weeks; the mother wanted to nurse it herself, and so commit a double murder; but I would not hear of it—on the child's account, of course—and it is brought up by hand—rather a troublesome business for you, young lady.'

'I never had anything to do with so young a baby. Can you trust me with it?'

'Of course I can,' said Dr. Bennet. 'We may trust to instinct in such cases, for it is marvellous how naturally women learn how to manage babies. Light sleeper, eh?'

'I am easily aroused, but I like a good deal of sleep.'

'Right—of course you do. Sleep is the best thing in the world. Take as much of it as you can, young lady, when you can get it. But, Miss Morison, Mrs. Beaufort, though not your ostensible charge, must be your principal one. You must frame all manner of excuses for the non-arrival of letters from the diggings; you must take her out to walk with you and Lucy in sunny days, but beware of letting her out of doors if it is at all damp. You must keep faithful Dorothy as much as possible in the kitchen, for the woman is enough to pull down the spirits of a rhinoceros; and you must, if you see it is advisable, take the management of the household.'

'Do you think I can do all these things? I am inclined to hesitate about my being competent,' said Clara.

'I know you can do them. You have a good head, and you have been in a good school.'

'Did you know anything about Miss Marshall or me, that you are so sure I have been in a good school?'

'I don't mean boarding-school education,' answered Dr. Bennet; 'but Mr. Plummer says that you have been for some months with the Elliots, and you can learn nothing but good from those girls. Well, Miss Morison, I shall write to Mrs. Beaufort to-night that I have engaged you, and that I know you will suit her exactly; so hold yourself in readiness to go out when you are sent for.'

'How far is it from town?' asked Clara.

'A good long journey; you will be tired enough before you

291

Clara Morison

get out in a shaky spring cart. I never counted the miles, but it is somewhere between Adelaide and the Burra. You can go out in a day, so you need not make preparations for bushing it at night.'

'How far is this place I am going to from the post-office?' asked Clara, thinking what delightful letters Margaret would write to her.

'Why, I don't know, but I should not think it is more than ten miles off—nothing at all for the bush. And the house is roomy enough, though ill laid out. I really think houses here are contrived to make people catch cold. If the colonial houses were built like English houses we should not have so much business, Mrs. Plummer.'

'I am sure,' said Mrs. Plummer, 'that our back-door is enough to kill Johnny sometimes; but it is useless to talk of altering it now, when there is not a carpenter or a bricklayer to be had for almost any money.'

'Things are still worse with people in the country,' said the doctor. 'Last time I was out at the Barn, I found Dorothy pasting up the broken windows with brown paper. They had plenty of glass panes, but nobody to put them in; however, as I have the use of my hands, and utterly detest brown paper, I managed to make the windows tidy before I left.'

'Mrs. Beaufort is an English lady, is she not?' asked Mrs. Plummer. 'Her husband went home for her two years ago, or thereabouts. I suppose it was an old engagement?'

'No, I rather think it was not,' replied the doctor.

'She had a fine fortune, to be sure. I have heard it called ten thousand pounds,' observed Mrs. Plummer.

'It was only five thousand,' said Dr. Bennet. 'But I must be off now, so good bye. Hold yourself in readiness to go to the bush when Mrs. Beaufort sends for you, Miss Morison.'

Clara was anxious to get home to tell her cousins what had happened, and also to learn something about the place, and the people to whom she was going. It was somewhere on the Burra-road; surely Grace would be able to give her some idea of the locality.

'I am fixed, Margaret,' said she, when she got home. 'I must be ready to start at a day's notice.'

'Are you going to be a sick-nurse?'

'I rather think I am; but I am to get thirty pounds a-year, and a comfortable home; so don't be angry with me, and don't pity me.'

'Who is the lady you are going to nurse?' asked Margaret.

'Mrs. Beaufort; she is an Englishwoman, and has not been long here. She lives at a place called the Barn, and Dr. Bennet says she is a most amiable woman.'

'Milk-and-water, you may depend upon it, Clara, my dear.

292

A Situation Turns Up for Clara

I shall sadly miss you, for you have been a great help to me, particularly this last month.'

'If I have, you have repaid me tenfold,' said Clara. 'I was very wretched when I came here, and now I am myself again —or nearly so,' she added to herself.

Grace and Annie were of course very much surprised at anything so sudden and energetic as Clara's new engagement, being brought about through Mrs. Plummer; but none of the family knew anything about Mrs. Beaufort. Each of them promised to write often and fully to her; and she was to come home to them if she was uncomfortable. How delightful it was to Clara to think that she had now a home in the colony, and that instead of being tossed from one situation to another, she might occasionally rejoin a loving circle of friends.

CHAPTER XI

THE RETURN OF THE DIGGERS

Next morning came a letter, which had been sent by private hand. It was from George to all his sisters, and it was very short, but remarkably pleasant, for it told them the party had had good luck at last, having got about twelve pounds weight a-head, from the holes they had sunk at the Bendigo; they would tell all about it when they got home, which might be expected every day, as they should lose no time on the road. Charley was well, though he had never been able to dig, and they were all jolly. Gilbert wanted to stay another month or two, but the others thought it would be better to start while the roads were passable, besides that they pined for Adelaide, and all dear friends there.

'We must air all their clothes, and give their room a thorough look up,' said Grace.

'I can do nothing but dance,' cried Annie. 'What good luck William Bell has brought them!—but we shall lose you very soon, Grace, I am afraid.'

'It is likely enough, if Henry can get employment, that he and I shall wait no longer; but Annie, you must not be sorry about what you have expected so long, and wished for too.'

'What a pity that you are going away so soon, Clara!' observed Margaret. 'We shall all be so happy, and I should so like to show you a brighter phase of Adelaide life than you have yet seen.'

'And Grace would like you to help with her needlework; you had better write to Dr. Bennet, and tell him that you cannot go.'

'I cannot do that now, Annie, though I should very much like to see and know your wonderful brothers. You must let me make a cake before I go, that Gilbert may see that I can do other things as well as write short-hand.'

'You shall make a cake this very day,' replied Annie. 'I

294

The Return of the Diggers

won't help you a bit with it, for it must be all your own. Oh! dear George is coming back, and Gilbert, and Henry, and Charley!'

'And William Bell,' said Margaret. 'You surely do not mean to leave him out of the list of expected friends, for he is one of the best we have in the world.'

Margaret helped Grace with her employments, and Clara worked in the garden with Annie all the morning. There were still a few roses on the bushes, but there was little promise of more; however, Annie was sure her friends would be back before they were over. After dinner, Clara began to think about her cake, and by the time the fruit was picked and the eggs beat and everything ready for baking, it was getting late. It was twilight when she put the cake in the camp oven, and covered the lid with the hot red embers. She raised her glowing face from her work, and shook a live coal from the large apron she wore, and saw entering the kitchen a host of bearded men.

'I thought they would be in the kitchen at this time of day, looking after tea, but instead of them we have Mrs. Bantam's Clara,' said George.

'They must have heard of our good luck,' said Gilbert, 'and have lost no time in getting a servant. But here they are. . . .'

William Bell hung back to allow the brothers and sisters, and Grace and her lover, to meet without restraint; but Charley Hodges had no such delicacy, and walked into the parlour with them.

'You have not been long at the diggings, Mr. Bell,' said Clara. 'Are you tired of the work?'

'Not at all; but I am disinclined to stay over the winter,' said he. 'Besides, George and I think that a small capital may be made something of now; whereas money will soon be too abundant in Adelaide to be valuable. If I cannot get on here, I shall go back in September, but I would rather not.'

'Have you heard anything of Mr. Harris?' asked Clara.

'George met him in Melbourne ten days ago. He had quarrelled with his party somehow, and had got disgusted with the diggings; so he returned to Melbourne, where he has got a good billet under government. But, Miss Morison, you know nothing about managing the camp oven. You have not half enough of ashes in the hearth. You will never be able to make a bush damper in your life. You have left a gap for the air to get in to cool the oven. Take my word for it, the loaf will be raw.'

'It is a cake,' said Clara, 'and I am sure it will be an admirable one.'

295

Clara Morison

'Not without my help,' said William Bell. 'I suppose you have observed that everybody thinks he can manage a fire better than anybody else, and I am no exception; I must and shall remodel that fire.'

And William Bell took the tongs and filled up the gap, while Clara laughed at his fancy that smothering the fire would improve it.

'We used to dry the gold in the camp oven after it had been washed,' continued he; 'I can't tell how many uses it was put to, but we should have done very ill without it. The only woman who had any fowls in the neighbourhood used to sell eggs at eighteen pence a-piece to invalids, and how do you think she got them? When I went to buy one for Charley, she bade me rest a bit, while she caught a hen and put her under the camp oven. In about half an hour I had my egg, and there was no mistake about its being a fresh one.'

'Where are you, Clara?' asked Annie, coming joyfully into the kitchen. 'My brothers want to see their blue cousin; but you look red enough now—perhaps I am *de trop* here.'

'You have not spoken to me since I came,' said Bell.

'Did you expect me to see or think of anybody but my brothers? It was only when Margaret asked eagerly where you were, that I thought I might find you here. How glad I am that you are not gone to that stupid Mrs. Beaufort's, Clara! I would not have had you miss the sight of our joy for a great deal. But I wish they would shave themselves, for they are all frights but Charley; and he sighs for a beard, as if it would improve him.'

'Then you do not like the hirsute appearance of a returned digger, Miss Annie?' said Bell.

'Not at all; I never can tell what a man is thinking about, if I cannot see the changing expression of his mouth, which those thickets quite conceal,' said Annie.

'You cannot, then, tell by the eyes; your cousin can—at least I fancy so, by some remarks she has made to me,' said Bell.

'O yes! Clara is very quick sighted,' Annie answered, coldly.

'And this is Miss Morison, or rather our cousin Clara,' said George Elliot, taking her hand. 'I am quite sorry you are going away so soon, for I wished very much to become acquainted with so dear a friend of all my sisters; but we shall have time for that by and by, I hope.'

'This is the learned lady, who is equally skilled in short-hand and shortbread,' added Gilbert. 'I certainly did not think you looked very alarming in the kitchen, but now I see you are rather formidable. You don't know German, I hope?'

'Not at all,' answered Clara, smiling.

296

The Return of the Diggers

'I am glad to hear it. I have one tower of refuge from you in that,' said Gilbert. 'Have you had tea, Grace?'

'I don't know,' said Grace. 'Perhaps we have. I am not sure. Do you remember, Margaret, whether we have had tea?'

Margaret was talking to William Bell, and did not hear; Annie was listening to what they were saying, and could not attend to anything else; but Clara settled the matter.

'Nobody has had tea in the house this evening. Grace and I will get it directly; but my cake is not ready for eating yet.'

In ten minutes, Clara brought in tea, and sat down to make it, invading Grace's privilege for once; and, amid all the bustle and noise of so many people talking at once upon all imaginable subjects, she managed to give sugar to those who liked it, and to commit no blunder with regard to the quantity of milk.

'Ah, Grace!' said Henry Martin, 'it is such a pleasure to drink from a teacup again, with you at my side! I won't deny that tea is good at all times, and that by pouring it quickly from one pannikin to another, we raised a froth upon it, and made believe there was cream in it, pretty successfully; but still it was nothing to compare to this.'

'I have never got reconciled to a pannikin yet,' said George; 'it is always hotter or colder than what you drink out of it. Have you got any new furniture, Grace, that the room looks so bright and pretty?'

'No; we leave buying furniture to our friends, Mrs. Tubbings and Mrs. Pengarvon. Indeed, I thought you would think the carpet very dingy after the dust and wear of another summer.'

'It is positively beautiful!' said George.

'I am glad you like home again,' Annie said; 'and I hope dear George; that you will never think of leaving us again; for I have been very miserable and ill while you were away.'

'I see you look thin, my little sister; but don't be alarmed. I am going to set about looking for employment to-morrow.'

'Poor Charley has done nothing!' said Annie.

'Oh!' exclaimed Gilbert, 'Charley means to go to the Bendigo with me in September, and we intend to make our fortunes.'

'Yes, we shall astonish the natives then,' said Charley.

'You don't mean to go again to the diggings, Gilbert?' Margaret asked, anxiously. 'Mr. Hastings will be glad to get you back again. Mr. Plummer thinks it a great pity you ever left, for though you may have made a little more at the Bendigo, you have lost much time.'

'I did not think you attached so much weight to Mr. Plummer's opinion, Margaret,' he answered.

297

Clara Morison

'It is very unkind in you to talk of leaving us again so soon,' said Annie. 'You have quite taken away my appetite. And after bringing home far more gold than I ever expected you would.'

'Four hundred pounds!' said Gilbert. 'Your ambition is very moderate, Annie. This is not the competence that was to procure for Margaret her life of literary and philosophic ease, nor for me the position I wish to hold in the colony.'

'But are you sure that a life of ease is a life for me?' asked Margaret. 'I prefer a life of labour and activity; and the position you ought to hold is one you will have risen up to by slow and painstaking steps, and not one that you can mount to on the back of a bag of nuggets.'

'Give me another cup of tea, if you please, cousin Clara,' said Henry Martin; 'and let me tell you all what a sight I saw at the Port to-day. A wholesale diggers' wedding!—twelve couples started at once in the matrimonial race! One man had told his mates he meant to get married on such a day, and they had a good mind to do the same; so they tried among all the loungers at the Port, and actually made up a round dozen, which, with a bridesmaid for each lady, and a groomsman for each gentleman, grew to quite a large party. The forenoon was spent in driving about through the streets of Port Adelaide. At last, they tired of it, and alighted; and then the four-and-twenty ladies walked all round the Port arm-in-arm; while the twelve happy bridegrooms adjourned to a hotel, where they treated all who came. The landlord told me he had a notion some of them had wives before; and that there had been instances of men being married twice over to different parties at the Port—by licence, of course.'

'It is an absurd system,' observed Margaret. 'People ought to be married by proclamation of banns, or by advertisement in the newspaper, or posting the intention in a public part of the town, for three weeks before the marriage takes place. The secrecy and despatch of the licence system is a great encouragement to deception.'

'Would you like to have your own banns proclaimed in church three times, Miss Margaret?' asked Bell.

'If I could make up my mind to marry a man,' answered Margaret, 'I think I should not feel ashamed, even though the whole world knew of it. I certainly will never countenance by my example so great a mockery of a public marriage as the licence is. It is a branch of the ecclesiastical law—a relic of Doctor's Commons. How rotten all that part of the law seems to be! Does it not want reform, Gilbert?'

'I daresay it does; but I wrote to you that I was sick of law, and though I may find my knowledge of it useful to

298

The Return of the Diggers

me in enabling me to keep out of it, I have not much desire to be useful to *it*.'

'What Gilbert says about law reminds me of what Mr. Brown says about the diggings,' remarked Grace. 'He tells me he has learned wisdom there; the most important part of which is, never to go back to them on any account.'

'Well, Grace,' asked Henry, 'have you any objection to being married by banns? or will you try the rotten licence system, in confidence that I am not deceiving you in any way?'

'I think registration would be a good compromise,' Grace answered.

'It is a quiet way, but not secret or hurried,' said Bell.

'And it is not so expensive as the licence, which is another recommendation,' added Gilbert, with a laugh, that Margaret did not like.

'I am going home to-morrow,' said Charley to Annie. 'Shall you have any letter for me to take to my sister?'

'I do not think I can write, in my joy to-night; but give her my love, and tell her how very happy we all are.'

But Annie's restless eyes and throbbing pulses scarcely showed the happiness she spoke of.

'I have a message for you all from Harris,' said George. 'He did not like the diggings, or, at least, he did not like his party. Both his mates were lazy. He could have borne Beaufort's want of push; but Turner's sulkiness was too much for him. You know what a good-humoured fellow he is himself. And, indeed, if a man does not work hard at the diggings, there is no getting on with him at all; and I must say that, for a good-tempered, hard-working mate, William Bell is a paragon. There was not such a thing as sulking ever seen or heard in our tent. I can promise you, Grace, that if Henry preserves his good humour under all the trials of domestic life, as he has done under the hardships, disappointments, and annoyances of Forest Creek and Bendigo, you are likely to lead a happy life.'

'But,' said Clara, 'this has nothing to do with Mr. Harris. We are all dying to receive his message. We have been hating him so much for not forwarding your letters, that unless you can deliver it with his own insinuating voice and irresistible smile, I fear we shall not be melted.'

'Oh, yes—the letters. I felt quite angry and spoke fiercely about them to him in Melbourne; but he told me he had sent them by a chap that was going our way, but that he had found out afterwards the fellow was not to be trusted. It is a scoundrelly thing to promise and not perform, particularly in the matter of letters.'

'But we have not yet heard the message,' said Clara, who

299

Clara Morison

saw the intense interest with which Annie was listening, while George was leisurely and digressively telling his story.

'Oh, yes; it is not much of a message after all, but I thought you would like to hear something about him. He has got a government appointment in Melbourne, and has taken a house, in conjunction with two others in the same department. You know one of them, Tom Davis, that used to be in the same office with Gilbert. Harris is getting into good society, and was going to a party the evening I met him. He sent his compliments to all the young ladies at home, and wished them to persuade me to settle in Melbourne without delay; for there was no place like Victoria for getting on. He said the Melbourne young ladies were not so clever or amusing as those in Adelaide. I hope you take it as a compliment, for Harris is a good judge. I told him I had no intention of leaving Adelaide again if I could make a livelihood there; and that, particularly on my sisters' account, I disliked the idea of living in such a disorganized town as Melbourne. He said it was a thousand pities I had any scruples, for they would be sure to take a good position there. He seemed very sorry to part from me, particularly as there was little chance of our meeting again. He was looking remarkably well. I never saw him look better.'

'Did he pay you back the money he borrowed from you, Mr. Bell?' asked Margaret.

'Oh yes! I got it all, and in sovereigns too,' said Bell. 'Harris was perfectly honest, though thoughtless and forgetful.'

'And how did you like Melbourne the second time you passed through it?' asked Margaret.

'It is a strange place,' replied he; 'so full of noise and confusion; money flying about as it never did anywhere before, and nothing thought too much to ask for anything. The Melbourne people look upon us with pity; consider us as completely eclipsed; laugh at our Bullion Act, despise our copper-mines, smile at any suggestion that an Adelaide man may offer; but I really think that, as a whole, the Adelaide folks are more intelligent. They are not such great readers in Victoria as we used to be; but of course the gold discoveries will bring out clever men as well as diggers; and let a country once have good leaders, it is in a fair way to go right.'

'True,' said Margaret; 'very true. We want some great men here now more than ever.'

'There are strange scenes to be witnessed in Melbourne occasionally,' said Bell. 'I wish you ladies had been with me in the shop I went to for a coat, because you would have enjoyed the absurdity of the thing more than I could do. The master was waiting upon the governor's lady; and the only

The Return of the Diggers

assistant was supplying the wants of a digger and his wife, who looked as if they were going to buy the whole stock of goods. The man had a huge roll of notes in his hand, and insisted on paying for each thing as he chose it, and getting his change; for he said his head got confused with figures, and he always preferred paying cash on the nail. They had spent about sixty pounds, and were looking at the distinguished lady on the other side, as if to take the cue from her for their next purchases, when the shop-keeper showed her some superb silks. 'What is the price of this?' said she, holding one of them to the light. 'Twenty-five pounds the dress, ma'am; it is a magnificent article.' The lady smiled, as if she thought it an exorbitant price; but the digger crossed over and laid his hand on her shoulder. 'Put up that one for me, mate,' said he; and then looking in the lady's face with a knowing wink, added, 'If my old woman wasn't a-looking on, I'd treat you to any one of them gowns you took a fancy to!' '

'Did you sell your gold in Melbourne?' Annie asked.

'No; we have brought it all with us,' answered George. 'I hope you won't be afraid to sleep in the house with so much valuable bullion in it. You must take your choice of a nugget from my lot, Annie, and buy something prettier with it. Take the biggest you can find, there is nothing above an ounce and a half.'

'And here is my best nugget for you, Grace,' said Henry. 'An ugly misshapen thing it is, but it nearly cost me my life. You know what a famous hole we sunk at Bendigo. We excavated pretty extensively, and had only a pillar to keep the soil from falling in. I was sitting in the bottom of the hole with the candle, which I turned round to show off the bits of gold as they shone in the light. The pillar was right in the vein of gold, and I was too greedy; I picked at it with my fossicking knife; and when I saw the end of this large nugget sticking out, I thought I must have it for you, and made a desperate thrust for it. I had just put it safe in my pocket when I saw the pillar shake; and before I could move, down came a ton of earth on my legs. Luckily my head was thrown well back at the time, so it escaped. I thought it was all over with me, Grace; but Gilbert, who was at the top, came down and dug me out, very much bruised, but with no bones broken.'

'I don't think I should like to have that nugget; give me another,' said Grace.

'But I really wish you to have this particular one; take another besides, but I can't keep your nugget, the one I got especially for you.'

Margaret chose what she liked from Gilbert's bag; and Wiliam Bell asked, with rather a rueful countenance, if

301

Clara Morison

nobody would accept of a specimen from him. None of the Elliots seemed to like to take any; but Clara frankly came forward and chose an odd looking little bit; which she said she would keep in remembrance of the slights the donor had put on her management of the camp-oven.

'Where are you going, Miss Morison!' asked William Bell. 'If to the bush, you will need some lessons before you can make a damper.'

'I am going to the Barn, to a Mrs. Beaufort's. Do any of you know where it is? Dr. Bennet did not seem to have a clear idea himself.'

'It is in the north,' answered Henry Martin. 'Beaufort was with Harris and Turner at Adelaide Gully, and had done nothing when Harris left the party. He only settled in the north when he returned from England with his rich wife. I have not heard much about him, except that he was very unsettled, and that Mrs. Beaufort was too stupid to amuse him.'

'That does not promise you a very pleasant life, Miss Morison,' said Gilbert. 'You will wish yourself back in Adelaide before a week is over; for to be shut up with a stupid woman in the bush is the most miserable of all fates.'

'You should not try to depress me,' Clara replied. 'I am to cheer and support a delicate lady; and I dare say I shall have too much to do to feel it very dull.'

'Hard work is the dullest thing of all,' remarked Gilbert; 'particularly women's work.'

'Clara is right, and you are wrong,' said George. 'Making up your mind so bravely, you are sure to do well, Clara. I am not afraid for you.'

The family sat up to a very late hour; William Bell talking almost all the evening to Margaret and Clara; for Annie was so shy towards him, and apparently so wrapped up in her brother George, that even if he had wished, he could scarcely have spoken to her. Margaret seemed to look in William's eyes with delighted confidence; and Annie groaned inwardly when she thought of the true heart she had rejected for a mere trifler like Mr. Harris. Harris's compliments fell like ice upon her heart; his wish that the family should settle in Melbourne seemed almost an insult, for of course he only cared to be amused; while every service William had done, every sacrifice he had made, rose up in judgment against her. When, at last, he reluctantly went home to his lodgings, she could not even wish him a good-night; she seemed quite indifferent, and she felt that he thought her so. All his party began to praise him directly he was gone; Grace and Margaret joined warmly with the diggers, while Annie could not say a

302

The Return of the Diggers

word in his favour, and Clara would not, for fear of paining Annie.

It had often and often been declared bed-time before the family party finally broke up; and then Clara and Annie, who slept together, had not a word to say to each other after all their exciting day. Clara lay so still, that her companion thought her asleep, and rose to give vent to the grief which was choking her as she lay.

'Annie,' then said Clara, rising also to console her, 'I do not care for William Bell. If you would only smile on him a little more, he would be as devoted to you as ever. Don't let yourself get miserable, but hope for better things.'

'I am not jealous of *you*, Clara—at least, not very. But I cannot bear to see William so fond of Margaret, who has done so much for me, and who would make him such a good wife. Do not you hate me for it, Clara?'

'No; for love is the most tyrannical of all things; but I think your fancy is mistaken.'

'Oh, Clara, I have often imagined what a glorious thing it would be to give up the man I loved to my sister! I have read of such things, and thought of imitating them. But—but—'

'But it is hard to see yourself neglected for your sister—to see no chance for showing such magnanimity,' said Clara. 'Of course it is; but my opinion is, that Bell still prefers you.'

'Do you think so? Oh, no, Clara. I know I have treated William ill; I have been blind, blind, for a long time, and now I see too well.'

'I will try to find out the truth,' said Clara, 'if I do not go to the Barn very soon; and I shall be a cooler observer than you. But do not repel William as you did to-night. If he likes you, as I believe, he must have been miserable to see you so distant.'

'He did not look at all miserable,' replied Annie. 'And Margaret was more excited, and looked more beautiful to-night than ever I saw her before. You know how restless she has been ever since she had that letter from him.'

'*Those* letters,' said Clara. 'I believe Gilbert's was the one which affected Margaret so much, and that now her anxieties are chiefly about him.'

Annie was somewhat tranquillized by her cousin's suggestions, and, to her own surprise, fell asleep, and did not wake till daylight.

CHAPTER XII

THE DIGGERS SETTLE DOWN

In the morning the young men appeared at the breakfast table, looking civilized; and Annie said she knew them all now, and was sure that when Gilbert had relinquished so substantial a token of the diggings as his beard, he could not think of going again. Gilbert laughed, but said that his mind was made up on the subject; and sitting beside Clara, seemed determined to let her see that his late rough life had not lessened his politeness. Clara thought she had never seen a handsomer young man than her attentive cousin, but yet his appearance was not, to her, prepossessing. A very high forehead, dark, keen grey eyes, an aquiline nose, and a thin-lipped but well-formed mouth, gave her an idea of his energy and decision; his sentences were well put together, and his language more choice than either George's or Henry's, who had both a large infusion of colonial colloquialisms in their talk. For so young a man, he had read a great deal, and whatever he read, his memory never lost; he did not positively quote, but he turned other people's ideas to good use, and had an original genius which invested even borrowed thoughts with force and novelty.

Margaret listened with delighted attention to Gilbert's remarks on the convict system, its evil influence throughout all the Australian colonies, and the large proportion of expirees and escaped criminals that had found a way to Victoria.

'You must write out your ideas on this, and send them to one of the newspapers,' said she.

'What good would that do me?' asked Gilbert. 'The editor would make quite a favour of inserting it, and I should not get even thanks for my trouble. I remember how my contributions were treated before I went to the diggings.'

'Newspapers here are merely meant to give news,' said

304

The Diggers Settle Down

George. 'It is of more consequence to the sale of the paper that the shipping reports should be brought down to the last moment, and that the public should be informed how many men were fined five shillings for drunkenness, than that it should contain the most brilliant and powerful leading articles, or the most amusing and interesting letters.'

'That is not my idea of a public instructor,' said Margaret. 'Gentlemen may say that they do not read the editorial matter, but the working classes do; they take their political creed in a great measure from the journal they read, and it behoves those who write for it to write with honesty and talent. More good is to be done by improving the tone of our newspapers, than by all the public libraries that could be established in South Australia, for there are thousands who never open a book who faithfully read the local papers. Let us make all the papers wiser and better, and the people will improve with them.'

'But a good paper will not pay,' said Gilbert. 'Any trash suits the working man better than a style too high for him.'

'And must we do like the Americans,' asked Margaret— 'write down to our readers, instead of raising our readers with us? Oh, Gilbert, something must be done for our people! This convulsion has unfixed everything. Religion is neglected, education despised, the libraries are almost deserted; nobody is doing anything great or generous, but everybody is engrossed by the single object of making a great deal of money in a very short time. I know that you can write the truth clearly, Gilbert; and you have ability enough to make it agreeable, if you choose. Put it to the good sense of our people and our government if, in circumstances like these, this colony is to be trusted to *supply and demand* for its moral and religious regeneration.'

'I really did not expect to be set to task so soon, Margaret. I am going to Mr. Hastings to-day to see if he will take me into the office for the winter; surely that is doing a great deal for the first day in Adelaide, my energetic sister?'

'I think you could get your articles now if you asked for them,' said Margaret.

'And be tied to Hastings' desk for five years,—unable to take advantage of any turn of fortune—unable to go to the diggings again when I choose—in order to learn from him what I know quite as well as he already!'

'There is a form in all things,' said Margaret. 'The wisdom of our ancestors has fixed a five years' apprenticeship as proper and necessary. If you think otherwise, you may agitate the matter when you have undergone the probation, and are considered a competent judge.'

'I thought that you despised forms, and the wisdom of our

Clara Morison

ancestors, too. But I know you admire prudence and caution. I must see what prospects I have out of the law before I bind myself to be its slave for five years. As for the newspaper article, you had better write it yourself. I have given you all the facts, or, as it is technically called, crammed you.'

'You know, I cannot write, Gilbert. I wish I could, but I can only think,' replied Margaret.

'And I'm not sorry for it. I was only joking. Only fancy *my* sister scribbling for the Adelaide press. People would have quite a horror of you, Margaret, if you did such a thing.'

Charley Hodges set off homewards immediately after breakfast, bearing many kind messages from the Elliots. Charley felt a great admiration for Annie, and thought she looked prettier now than ever. He wished he was two or three years older, or that he had been successful at the diggings; it would have been so charming to have brought her a bag of gold, and told her he had dug it for her sake. He looked forward eagerly to going back with Gilbert in September, when he would surely be more fortunate; perhaps, too, by that time his beard would have made its appearance; and, though Annie had said she did not admire that addition, he feared his smooth chin was a terrible drawback.

The three other young men went up to town, and found there would be no difficulty in obtaining employment; for business was getting brisk, and the tide of labour had been setting out of South Australia so constantly, that there was a scarcity of hands in almost every department. George came home in great glee; for when he had gone up to his late employer's store, Mr. Ainslie had asked him eagerly how he had succeeded; and hearing that he had cleared about four hundred pounds, said to him:—

'You are the very man I wanted to see, Elliot. I am going to Melbourne in a fortnight. I have succeeded in securing premises in a central situation, and I am sure to make my fortune.'

'You don't wish me to go to Melbourne with you, I hope?' George answered.

'No. I want you to take this concern in Adelaide off my hands. I leave some goods in the store, and expect consignments regularly to come here, part of which you will forward to me as I advise you. You will have to watch the Adelaide markets, and correspond with me. You will buy flour to send across, and hay, and such like farm produce; and I shall buy English goods before they are landed at Melbourne, and ship them back to you. Do you understand? We shall thus save the tremendous expenses of lighterage, and heavens knows what, which will double the price of goods Adelaide must get from Melbourne. In this way we shall play into each

306

The Diggers Settle Down

other's hands, and each make a good thing of it. Advance me the money you have got, and I will give you time for the remainder; for you are a steady fellow, and certain to do well.'

'I will consult with my brother and sisters,' answered George; 'but I think I shall be glad to accept of your offer, if your valuation of the property is not too high.'

'Oh, very moderate, indeed," said Mr. Ainslie, sitting down to make a list of what he would leave. 'You see there what price I put upon the concern, and you may consult with any friend as to whether I ask too much. Remember, you may never have another chance of setting up on your own account. A good situation and an established business; if a young man so steady and industrious as yourself cannot make a handsome income out of it, call me a Dutchman!'

As Mr. Ainslie had really been moderate in his valuation, the Elliots were delighted at the opening for George.

'I know you will do well,' said Margaret, 'for you will never try to overreach anybody. But I fear I shall not like you so well if you starve us, and send away all our flour to Victoria; though, to be sure, the poor diggers must have something to eat. I wish a regulation could be made that the diggers should send us a large detachment, chosen by lot, to assist at seed-time and harvest; for I am really apprehensive of a famine.'

'It could not be done. There would be a public meeting of the diggers to protest against such tyranny,' replied George. 'But how have you got on, Henry?'

'I went to the Burra Office,' was the answer, 'and found they had a vacancy at the mine for a good book-keeper. I am to get sixty pounds advance on my old salary, and a cottage at a low rent, or, if I like to buy the lease of a cottage, the price would be moderate. I told the secretary I had some thoughts of getting married; and he said I had better look sharp, for I must be up at Kooringa in a fortnight if the Board appointed me, which he had no doubt they would. What do you say, Grace? Could you make up your mind for better and worse, by that time?'

'I think I could,' said she; 'for I suppose you don't care for my being very splendid in my attire?'

'Distinction is on the other side,' answered Henry. 'I have been dazzled to-day by all the colours of the rainbow. I never saw so few pretty faces in Adelaide, or so many handsome bonnets.'

'I have seen creatures in silks of every varied hue,' added Gilbert, 'whose feet were cased in thick, strong boots this fine day!'

'Thick boots are very dear, Gilbert,' said Annie, 'and,

307

Clara Morison

consequently, must be worn in all weathers. People give a pound or twenty-five shillings for them, if they are very clumsy.'

'But what have you been doing, Gilbert?' asked Margaret.

'I have done very little,' he replied. 'Mr. Hastings inquired if I had come to stay. And when I told him I only meant to remain over the winter, he said he did not like being made a convenience of; but as he was short of hands, he would give me two pounds ten a-week. So I go to work to-morrow. And what has my task-mistress been doing herself all this morning?'

'I have been looking out some things that must be made for Grace. We must be very busy at needle-work all this fortnight, and neither read nor write at all. But what has become of William Bell?'

'He has gone part of the way with Charley, to see about a section belonging to him, which he had let, and which his tenant threw up to go to the diggings, where William met him. Bell has a notion of taking it into his own hands, though it will be hard to get people to plough and sow; and as for the reaping, we must trust to the machine.'

'And very likely, after being at great expense, and growing a crop that will only pay at seven shillings the bushel, the Yankees may inundate the colonies with flour, and bring the price down to a losing point,' observed Gilbert.

'But American flour is very bad,' said Annie; 'it is not to compare with ours, and will never fetch such a high price.'

'American flour is the best in the world,' answered Gilbert. 'It imbibes more water than any other, and is therefore more economical.'

'But it is horribly sour,' urged Annie.

'Only when ill packed; good American flour is a splendid article.'

'I never heard of any of that description in South Australia, and until I see it, I will not believe it,' Annie persisted.

'You are absurdly patriotic, Annie,' said her brother. 'Everything South Australian is the best in the world with you. I suppose now you will not believe that the soil and climate of Victoria are better than ours.'

'No, I will not; for why are our people so willing to return? besides, it is no good sign of either soil or climate, that the colony has never grown enough of food for itself.'

'That is accounted for by the monster interest of sheep-farming being followed by the other monster interest of gold-digging,' Gilbert replied; 'and by the folly of the legislature in not encouraging agriculture; but the soil is really much better; a fine black loam for hundreds of square miles, which would grow thirty-five or forty bushels of wheat to the acre,

308

The Diggers Settle Down

and the climate is a little cooler than ours, and not quite so dry. The scenery too is remarkably fine; I never saw anything in this colony to compare with the romantic views all round the Bendigo. George was always meaning to take sketches, but, poor fellow, he had no time.'

'What a shame,' said Annie, with tears in her eyes, 'that you should praise that horrid Victoria above our own dear colony, where we have all grown up together, where we have had joy and sorrow, where all our remembrances turn, and all our hopes are fixed!'

'Not all our hopes; for I hope to get a great deal of gold at the Bendigo in September,' returned Gilbert.

'But the people! Surely you don't like the people there as you do those that are here?' said Annie.

'Certainly not,' Gilbert answered, putting his arms round his sister, and kissing her fondly. 'There are no people in all the colonies to compare with Adelaide people; that I grant you, Annie.'

CHAPTER XIII

A VISITOR INQUIRES FOR MR. HAUSSEN

Clara wondered, as day after day passed, that she got no message from Mrs. Beaufort. She began to think that Dr. Bennet had not been authorized to engage her; and, though sorry in one sense, she was pleased to think she should be present at Grace's marriage. But one day when the four girls were sitting in the parlour sewing, and there was a great litter of dress-making, and all kinds of making, Dr. Bennet walked in unceremoniously.

'A marriage!' said he; 'glad to see such good signs! Which young lady or ladies? Not you, I hope, for you can't marry anybody so long as you are engaged to me.' And he shook his stick at Clara.

'Certainly, you will not be disappointed, for I am not going to be married. It is my cousin Grace's wedding we are preparing for.'

'Well, Miss Grace going off at last. A good wife you will make, I am sure. Not too young, but as blooming as ever. I wish you joy. I expect to see all you girls going off before the new year; there is nothing like a good example in such cases. It is a long time since I have seen you, Margaret. I think you have grown taller, have you not?'

'I think I have been past growing ever since I knew you,' said Margaret.

'But what am I to do about Mrs. Beaufort?' Clara asked, 'She has sent me no message.'

'That is the very thing I came about,' answered the doctor. 'She has written to me that one of her neighbours has offered to bring the young lady out. A very steady gentleman he is, and a very careful driver, so you need be in no alarm. He will probably come into town to-day or to-morrow; and so I came to give you a reminder; for bush gentlemen don't like to be kept waiting, even for a young lady. I have no time

310

A Visitor for Mr. Haussen

to stay to-day, though I should like a chat with Margaret Elliot, of all things. Good bye, young ladies, I must be off.'

In the evening Clara was surprised to see Reginald stop at the door; he was in a spring cart with a pair of horses.

'I called to see your brothers, Miss Elliot; I heard they had come home; how have they succeeded?'

'Oh! very well indeed, as times go,' answered Grace; 'they have made quite a little fortune. But what brings you into town so soon again? not to inquire after my brothers, I suppose?'

'Not entirely that, though I was very anxious to know their fortune; but I have to see about procuring servants; and Mrs. Beaufort has desired me to call on Dr. Bennet, concerning a young lady coming out as companion to her.'

'That is Clara. Mrs. Beaufort has sent an old friend for you, Clara.'

'Dare you trust yourself with me, Miss Morison,' asked Reginald, 'and the respectable married woman I am going to engage to look after things at Taringa? The place has got into such a state of confusion for want of a woman's care, that I have made a vow not to leave Adelaide without taking one out in the cart; by which also I make sure that her husband will keep his engagement. I want them both.'

Clara was much obliged to Reginald for his trouble, and thankful in her heart that she should not have to drive *tête-à-tête* with him that long way. Reginald promised to come back to tea after putting his horses in the stable, and looking in at Mrs. Handy's.

He found Mrs. Handy much excited.

'Oh, Mr. Reginald!' she exclaimed, 'I never was so glad to see you in my life.'

'Has your husband returned?' asked he.

'No, it is not that. Don't you speak German? There is a German lady just come here to inquire for Mr. Haussen, and my mind misgives me that all is not right. She speaks very little English, but she looks like a gentlewoman by her dress and manner, though she is very foreign looking too. Mrs. Haussen is out spending the evening at North Adelaide. I am thankful she was not in when this lady called, for I might have made some dreadful blunder.'

Reginald sighed deeply, and desired Mrs. Handy to let the lady know that a friend of Mr. Haussen's, who could speak German, would be glad to see her. He was instantly admitted to her room, and shut the door fast after him.

'Miss Sophie Werner, I presume?' said he, in German.

'Then Max has told you he expected me, though till lately there was little prospect of it? Where is Max Haussen—he

311

Clara Morison

used to live here? Do you know where he has gone, Mr. ——?'

'Reginald is my name. I have known Mr. Haussen ever since I came to the colony. He is now at the gold diggings, at Mount Alexander.'

'I hope he is doing well,' said Miss Werner, nervously.

'He was doing very well by last accounts,' answered Reginald; musing how he could break the fact of Haussen's marriage.

Sophie was tall and pale, with high features, and a profusion of magnificent brown hair. Her air was unquestionably ladylike, and though she seemed fluttered, it did not look like her habitual demeanour.

'When is Max expected home?' she asked, with more anxiety.

'In a month or two—in a month or two,' he repeated. 'But, madam, I have bad news, which it is my duty to tell you. Mr. Haussen told me of an attachment, but never of an engagement. He has married in this colony.'

Sophie's features grew rigid; she sank back in her chair, and though she neither groaned nor shrieked, Reginald saw how much she suffered.

'I assure you that he did not forget you; but he thought his position was hopeless; and—and the girl was pretty—'

'And *young*,' said Sophie, with a sad look in her eyes, which spoke of thirty.

'Yes, she was young, but he did not love her as he had loved you. He had told me much of you, and he despised himself for his inconstancy; but you cannot tell—no woman can tell—what a temptation it is to our fidelity, to be so far apart, with so faint and distant a hope of being united.'

'And I dare say he thought my letters were cold,' poor Sophie said; 'for I could not leave my father while he lived, and dared not tell Max all I felt in being so long separated. We were not positively engaged, because my father objected to our betrothal; but we have always corresponded, and I was resolved that as soon as I was left at liberty, no scruple, no coquetry on my part, should prevent my coming out to join Max. If Max was disappointed in my appearance, if his affection had died out, or if he could not afford to marry, I meant to take a situation; for among so many of my countrymen as are here, I surely could find employment. But since he is married, I will return home, and earn my bread among my own people. I have been accustomed to tuition for ten years.'

Reginald's heart bled for the woman who had been wearing out her life and soul teaching tiresome children, and nursing an invalid father, for ten years, in the hope that Max Haussen

A Visitor for Mr. Haussen

would make her happy at last; and all only to find that hope disappointed.

'Do you know his wife?' Sophie asked.

'I do a little; she is silly and conceited, but I think she likes Haussen.'

'Silly and conceited!' said Sophie; 'but she is young, and if her heart is good, all may be right for him and her. But for me! Could I see her without her suspecting anything? You could introduce me as a cousin of Mr. Haussen's (which I am, through a distant one), who has come out on a long sea voyage for the benefit of her health; I shall return in the vessel I came in, for the captain and his lady were both very kind to me. Can I see Max's wife?'

'She lives in this house, and you will be able to see her to-morrow, if you please. But do you think your chances of success in your own country are greater than they are here? German ladies are well thought of as governesses here, so that if you remain in Adelaide, I have no doubt you could get a good situation.'

'It would not be happy for either Max or myself if I remained. We cannot forget each other—that is impossible; a ten years' attachment is no such light matter. But in time we may, if we are separated, remember without such pain as we feel now; whereas, if I were exposed to meet him and his wife any day, it would kill me; and if, as you say, Madame Haussen is silly, perhaps he might feel vain regrets. No, I must go home, and never see him more! I should like to be left alone this evening; good night.'

'This is a lesson and a warning for me,' said Reginald, as he walked to the Elliots' to keep his appointment. 'I must see a great deal of Clara Morison when she is at the Barn, for Mrs. Beaufort will miss me if I do not come as often as usual, and she needs all the comfort I can give her, poor woman! And what were Haussen's temptations to mine? But now I see what suffering Haussen's weakness has brought on that poor Sophie, I must be doubly cautious. And she says she wrote coldly; could she have written such letters as I get from Julia?'

'When do you go out of town, Mr. Reginald?' asked George, when the visitor came in. 'I hope not for a week, for we want to keep Clara till Grace leaves us.'

'I mean to leave town the day after to-morrow, if I can get servants,' was the answer; 'and Miss Morison will please be ready at seven o'clock precisely, for it is a long way, and the days are getting short.'

'What a comfort it is that you are going, Clara,' said Gilbert laughing, 'for with you aiding and abetting my sister Margaret, I really get no will of my own at all. I can manage

313

Clara Morison

Margaret by herself, but there is no withstanding two. Don't you think, Mr. Reginald, that a man who has been at the diggings, should be allowed to do as he pleases?'

'Not to go back again, however,' said Margaret; 'but we had better drop this subject. We are all very anxious to know something of Mrs. Beaufort, on Clara's account. You know the lady, Mr. Reginald?'

'Yes, and I like her,' he replied. 'She is not handsome, nor clever, nor active; but she is gentle and feminine, and bears up against very bad health with great patience.'

'It must be very miserable for her to be ill when her husband is away; she must weary for him sadly.'

'She does weary for him, but she has great comfort in her baby; I do not generally admire young babies, but I am greatly interested in little Lucy.'

'Then you visit pretty frequently at the Barn,' said Grace.

'Yes; she is the only married lady I know in the neighbourhood, though you town ladies would scarcely think her within visiting distance.'

Reginald seemed dull and out of spirits, and Clara for once was right in her conjecture that he was thinking of Julia. He talked to the young men, and asked them many questions about the diggings; but with both Margaret and Clara he was unusually shy and silent.

'I don't know what is the matter with Charles Reginald to-night,' said Margaret, when he was gone; 'he used to talk so much to Clara; I expected him to go over his month's reading with her as usual; but to-night he scarcely opened his mouth.'

'He will have plenty of time to talk to her in the long ride to the Barn, and in his frequent visits there,' observed Gilbert; 'and in the meantime, he leaves her to us, for which I am bound to thank him. Well, I have some copying to do, and must finish it before I go to bed, though I know it is three hours' work.'

'I hope it is not engrossing,' said Clara; 'for if it is not, I could take part of it off your hands. I can write quite like you.'

'Thank you, Clara. I shall be very glad of your assistance,' he answered. And they sat up writing after the rest of the family had gone to bed. When the task was finished, they compared it with the copy.

'Thank you, Clara,' then said Gilbert; 'it is very nicely done—not a single blunder in it all through. You could make a good income at threepence a folio; and I suppose you like it better than women's work.'

'I do. I am very fond of using the pen, even to copy such

314

A Visitor for Mr. Haussen

stupid involved sentences as these; but I prefer writing according to my own fancy, and in short-hand.'

'Capital!' said Gilbert; 'I got hold of a book of your writing the other day, not one word of which I could read. Why, you should have been a lawyer, or a reporter, and not a governess.'

'I suppose that if I had not happened to be a woman, I could have been taken on the staff of one of the newspapers here as a reporter.'

'No doubt of it; but it is not a very enviable employment, nor very well paid. What a deal of despicable twaddle your fingers would have had to chronicle, if you had taken notes in Adelaide this last year or two! But, as a lawyer's clerk, you could get a tolerable livelihood, though it is a drudging business you would soon have tired of.'

'I should not like it without the prospect of rising; but with your abilities, and with the turn of your mind for hard study, I think nothing could be so delightful as threading the mazes of the law, in order to make it clearer and more intelligible to others.'

'It is not delightful to work with such a faint prospect of success. Even if I were to go through five years' articles, and read hard with Margaret all the time, I should never make a popular lawyer. Any sharp microscopic-eyed pettifogger would succeed better in Adelaide than I could do. George is fortunate. He has got a start; and he will undoubtedly succeed in business. Henry is happy; for he has not much ambition; and Grace is satisfied with humble competence. William Bell will get on well here; for everybody places confidence in him; and he is ready to take advantage of any opening that may present itself. But I am young and unsettled, and chafe a good deal more at being ordered about by a master than any of them. I don't even like Margaret's way of telling me what I ought to do. Harris used to say I was under petticoat government; and I think it is time now that I were free.'

'I think you mistake Margaret,' said Clara. 'It is because she has such a high opinion of your ability, that she is fearful you may not make a good use of it; and no brother was ever more loved than you are by her.'

'But yet she would tie me down to Hastings' desk; and then, thinking she has done her duty, she would marry William Bell, and leave me to go on by myself.' And Gilbert's handsome face looked dark, as he bent his eyes searchingly on Clara.

'Are you not perfectly able to go on by yourself? I thought you were impatient of leading-strings; and yet you seem unable to go without them. Besides, I do not think Margaret cares for William Bell. He is scarcely so old as she is.'

315

Clara Morison

'But he has so much sense and steadiness, that he might pass for thirty,' said Gilbert; 'and she is always bringing forward his opinions and conduct as an example to me. I grow quite to dislike him, in spite of all his kindness.'

'Sleep off all these mistaken notions, Gilbert: I must bid you good night.'

Sophie Werner was very much struck with the extreme prettiness of Mrs. Haussen, and overlooked her silliness; which, indeed, as it was expressed in English, she could not understand; while her ignorance of English manners made her think that the little creature's restlessness might, in the eyes of her country folks, be perfect good-breeding.

Mrs. Haussen was vain of her youth, and was pleased to see how faded her husband's cousin looked beside her. But Reginald secretly admired the lofty refinement of Sophie, and felt disgusted by the absurd pretensions of the uneducated and slip-slop milliner; while, on the other hand, both the ladies were thoroughly convinced, Sophie from ignorance, and Mrs. Haussen from vanity, of the wife's superiority.

'I must go back to the vessel immediately, Mr. Reginald,' said Sophie in German, 'for this is painful to me. I have seen her; and I find her very charming, and that is enough.'

'Permit me to accompany you on board,' he answered. 'I have business at the port, and my escort may be useful.'

The offer was gratefully accepted. The two ladies bade each other farewell; one with tearful earnestness, and the other with self-conscious indifference. And Sophie took leave for ever of the land of Max Haussen's adoption. Reginald saw her safe on board, and received a message and letter for Haussen, which he promised to deliver in person. He then visited a newly-arrived vessel, and succeeded in engaging an Orkney man and his wife, with five children, the youngest of whom was three years old. Having explained that the woman, with her youngest child, was to go out with him in his spring-cart early on the ensuing day, while the husband and the others were to follow by the dray, and having seen them all on a port cart to come up to Adelaide, he returned himself to transact the rest of his business in town. All was accomplished in time; and in the evening he called to know if Clara would be ready in the morning.

'We have everything in readiness,' said Annie, 'except willingness to part with our cousin; but, Mr. Reginald, if she is not happy at the Barn, or if the air of the place does not agree with her, you must bring her back, or we will never forgive you.'

'I willingly promise to bring her back when she asks me,' he answered. 'I know what a treasure she will be to Mrs.

316

A Visitor for Mr. Haussen

Beaufort; and I think it likely that Miss Morison will be very comfortable at the Barn, at least till Mr. Beaufort returns. I would not advise her to stay any longer than she feels comfortable.'

'Do you think the lady is dangerously ill?' asked Clara.

'She has a bad cough, and has no strength; but I do not think she is in immediate danger. If her spirits were good she might rally. A long letter from the diggings would do her a great deal of good.'

'How much of our happiness depends on the post-office,' said Henry Martin. 'That was the worst of the diggings: we were never certain of our letters.'

'You will not write much in future,' observed Margaret; 'for you never cared to correspond with anybody but Grace. And now that you are going to have her always beside you, you will turn over all the letter-writing to her.'

'Grace is an admirable letter-writer; you could not have a better hand to trust to.'

'I believe Clara can write beautiful letters,' said Annie; 'and she is going to write alternately to Margaret and me.'

Here William Bell came in to see Clara before she went to the country; and Reginald could not help admiring the way in which all the family, and all the friends of the family, seemed to include Clara as one of its members; and how thoroughly she understood the peculiarities of each, and never jarred against any. When he had seen her at Mrs. Handy's, she had been fluttered at a casual remark, and annoyed at a glance: here she was perfectly at her ease, and seemed to smooth down everything and everybody before her.

'What are you thinking of?' asked Reginald of Annie, when he saw her looking very earnestly at Margaret and Clara.

Annie started, and said, 'I was wondering whether casual observers would prefer Clara's pretty little hand to Margaret's handsome large one, for I do not know which of them I admire most myself.'

'Neither do I,' said he; 'they both suit their possessors, and look well on them, but would look very ill if exchanged.— What prospect do you see of farming to advantage, Mr. Bell?' he asked, in a louder voice.

'I can do nothing this year but let the land grow a crop of hay. The man I let it to has got the ground so full of wild oats and drake, that I don't see any other way of clearing it.'

'Hay will be up to a tremendous price in Melbourne next year,' said Gilbert; 'but surely you are not going to settle in the country to look after your self-sown hay, William?'

'No, I mean to start on the Exchange as a bullion-broker and commission-agent. I am pretty well known in Adelaide, and I think I have a good chance of success.'

Clara Morison

'I am going to speculate with my little capital,' Gilbert said; 'buy cheap and sell dear. I have the offer of a group of cottages at a reasonable price, which I shall be able to sell again for double the money in a few months' time, for rents are sure to rise.'

'They are not nice cottages,' observed Annie; 'and I advise you to have nothing to do with them.'

'They are in an unhealthy part of the town, too,' added Margaret. 'You ought to do something to improve them if they become your property.'

'It will not pay to make improvements at the present rate of wages,' replied Gilbert.

'I think we should have a building act passed soon,' Margaret said, 'for now that no building is going on, nobody will make any objections, and wise regulations may be made without any one raising a cry of vested interests, which is always such a bar to progress. No houses should be permitted to be built back to back, and lanes should be of a certain prescribed width. In our hot climate, ventilation is of the greatest importance. The Germans seem to have a great fancy for crowding their building-ground. You will know a German acre in Adelaide by seeing the wood laid down at the front door, and being carried painfully through the house, sometimes through the windows.'

'Melbourne is far worse than Adelaide in these respects,' observed Gilbert, 'in spite of its Building Act; for though that compelled the proprietor to put up a good house in the front street, there was nothing said about the background.'

'And it lies in a hollow,' added William Bell, 'so that it is very difficult to get thorough ventilation.'

'Adelaide is on a rising ground, and though we get dust with it, there is no want of circulation of air,' said Annie.

'There is no place like the bush for fresh air,' remarked Reginald. 'Miss Morison is going to see how much pleasanter the country is than the town, and will bear me out when she returns.'

'If I like the country better than the town, I shall like it quite as well as Scotland, for I have got singularly fond of Adelaide and Adelaide people.'

After a long, discursive conversation, Reginald and William Bell left the Elliots, and Clara sat up late with Margaret, forgetting how early she was to rise next day. They had many things to talk about, and Clara was anxious to know what chiefly engrossed her cousin's thoughts, and so far as she could judge, it was Gilbert, and the difficulty of getting him to take an interest in his old pursuits. What she said of Bell was in high commendation, but she neither blushed nor hesitated when she mentioned him.

318

A Visitor for Mr. Haussen

'You will see a great deal of Charles Reginald when you are at the Barn, Clara,' said she; 'you must write to me if you find out any new point in his character. There is a great deal of good in him, but he would be improved by a conversation with you once a week. These sheep-farmers let their minds rust sadly.'

'Do you think that I can polish his at all?' asked Clara.

'You can bring him out, and that is all he wants, for he has plenty in him, but is backward in displaying it. Do you think him handsome, Clara?'

'His face pleases me,' Clara answered.

'But Gilbert is handsomer,' said Margaret, 'and he has more information for his age. Besides, he is ten years younger than Reginald, I should think; if he would but apply, what a splendid figure he could make in ten years! Write always some message to him, that he may see that others expect much from him as well as I. I am twenty-five to-day, Clara; I do not in general keep birthdays, but now you must drink my health, and wish with all your heart that another year may find me happier than I am now. So I have lived a quarter of a century! I may now expect to fall off in my looks, but not I hope in other respects.'

'I am sure you will not fall off for many years to come, either in looks or in mind,' replied Clara. 'You are very lovely to all who have eyes to see you.'

CHAPTER XIV

A RIDE TO THE BUSH

May is always a lovely month in Australia, and as Clara drove along the fine level road that leads out of Adelaide to the North, she felt her heart lighter, and her hopes of happiness at the Barn rose brightly. Everywhere the fresh grass and new shoots seemed starting up as at the touch of spring; the air was cool and bracing; and Mr. Reginald knew all about the road, and could tell Clara who lived in every house; and by this time she took so great an interest in the colony, that she liked to hear the names of all who were in it. Mrs. Duncanson and her little boy were sitting behind; she was a decent-looking Scotch-woman; and both herself and her child were well and warmly clothed, though their apparel presented rather an antediluvian air.

'I can scarcely understand a word she utters,' said Reginald to Clara; 'for though I can read and understand Scotch poetry, the spoken language puzzles me sadly; and I have taken most of her qualifications for granted. She looks as if she could work, and be civil.'

'How do you think you will like the colony?' asked Clara of the woman.

'There's a hantle bonnie trees, and the grass is braw and green, but oh, sirs! we're gaun a lang way frae the sea. We wunna hae a fish frae ae year's end to anither, I'm thinking.'

'I suppose your husband went to the fishing at home?' said Clara.

'Aye, and to the whale fishing in the season,—and I minded the hairst, and had the corn tight under thack and rape, or ever he cam hame. There's a hantle left to the women-folk our way, ye ken.'

'Is your husband used to mind sheep?' Clara asked.

'Oo aye! we had nae less than five sheep of our ain, and a cow forbye; and I span a' the woo' in the winter nichts,

320

A Ride to the Bush

and braw stockings an' flannen coats I made o't; but the gudeman is a canny man as weel.'

'A canny man!' echoed Clara; 'I am at fault here. Do you mean that he is gentle?'

'Oh, we're no gentle—we're simple bodies; but he is canny, ye ken.'

'You mean that he is quiet,' Clara said, 'and not quarrelsome; or that he is nothing out of the common, nothing 'unco,' in fact?'

'We are na unco, for we hae been on the mainland for twal generations; but Sandy is canny;—he can mak shoon, and shape and sew his ain claes.'

'Ah, I understand now; you mean he is canning, skilful. —You see the word is from the same Saxon root from which we get our word king, Mr. Reginald.'

'We hae nae kings in the Orkneys, and never had ony,' said Mrs. Duncanson. 'There was naething grander than yerls in the Orkneys.'

'If your husband can make shoes, he will be invaluable in the bush,' said Clara, 'and I have no doubt that a little tailor's craft will be useful too.'

'Can do is easy carried aboot wi' ane,' observed Mrs. Duncanson, sententiously.

'What can you do?' asked Clara. 'This gentleman does not well understand what you say, and I am a countrywoman, and can interpret.'

'I can bake, an' milk, an' kirn, an' mak cheese; an' wash an' dress claes, an' soop the hoose; an' scrub, an' spin, an' knit; an' mind swine an' hens, an' pickle herrin; but we needna' speek aboot fish in this unkent land, an' I misdoot we're far frae ony preachin, too.'

'We have no church within thirty miles,' Reginald said; 'and I am afraid many of Mrs. Duncanson's accomplishments will be lost upon us at Taringa; for we have neither cows, nor hens, nor pigs.'

'Dear me! this is a queer country,' remarked Mrs. Duncanson. 'I heard that folk a' eat oot o' tins here, like we did on boord-ship, sae I dinna wunner at the want o' pigs; but cows, an' hens, an' swine are things that canna be dune withoot.'

'I will get them for you,' said Reginald, 'if you can manage them, and do not mind the trouble; but remember this, that if you leave me the cows will be allowed to go dry, the hens will lay away or be seized upon by the hawks, and the pigs will be starved; for I never can get hut-keepers to do any extra work, even to make themselves comfortable.'

'We have appointed to bide wi' you a towmont, sir, an' we are nae gangrel bodies, Sandy or me; we hae nae will to leave a gude place when we find ane. There's just twa

321

Clara Morison

things I dinna like—nae kirk, an' nae schule for the bairns, puir things!—but Sandy micht gie them a lesson at an orra time, at nicht, when there is na muckle thrang?'

'Certainly,' said Reginald. 'Your husband will find his education of use to him here, for he may be promoted to an overseer's place if he deserves it. I have a very clever young Englishman, Miss Morison, who has been a shepherd for many years in the colony, whom I would gladly make an overseer, but he cannot write or cast accounts, and I cannot dispense with these qualifications. Your countrymen, however poorly they may have been brought up, have always some book-knowledge.'

It was past sunset when they reached the Barn, which was a large low building, thatched with reeds, with a broad verandah all round it, and French windows with green venetian blinds in great abundance. A somewhat neglected looking garden surrounded the house, with some tolerably large fruit trees and a number of young vines, now shedding their leaves and looking dejected. There were still a few flowers blooming on the borders, but the evergreens which covered the verandah seemed to darken the house too much for the season of the year. The stables were large, but there was no man-servant in the place to look after the horses, which were all turned out into a paddock, and were the plague of Dorothy's life; for they had grown so wild that she scarcely durst go near them, and they were every now and then getting into the garden, or lifted the slip-panels of the paddock and running away; requiring to be advertised, with rewards for their recovery. Besides, as Dorothy often told her mistress, drawing water for five horses, or driving them two miles to the creek, was not woman's work; and though she would do a great deal for Mrs. Beaufort, flesh and blood could stand it no longer. But the horses were Mr. Beaufort's favourites, and his wife had promised they should be well cared for in his absence, and had now given Reginald carte-blanche to procure her a man-servant.

The cart drew up at the door, and Reginald told Dorothy that Miss Morison was the young lady whom Dr. Bennett had engaged to stay with Mrs. Beaufort. Dorothy, who hated the doctor, and thought her mistress wanted no companion while she was with her, received the new-comer with a mournful smile, and introduced her into the parlour, where Mrs. Beaufort was lying on a sofa, with an untasted cup of tea beside her.

'This young lady is an old friend of mine,' said Reginald; 'and I am sure that Dr. Bennet could not have made a better

322

A Ride to the Bush

choice. I know, Mrs. Beaufort, that you and Miss Morison will be excellent friends.'

'I am glad you know the lady,' Mrs. Beaufort answered, in a low, weak voice, 'for any friend of yours must be welcome at the Barn. Have you been able to get me a man-servant?'

'Yes; at twenty-seven shillings a-week, with board and lodging; it is too much, but you told me not to mind expense.'

'I am very much obliged to you; I don't mind the wages, and only hope he will not quarrel with Dorothy; for, good creature as she is, she is very touchy, and has much to try her. Will you call her as you pass through the hall, Mr. Reginald?'

Dorothy came when she was summoned; she was rather deaf, and though she came close up to her mistress, Clara could see that it was only with a great effort that the invalid could make herself heard.

'Show Miss Morison into the little room next mine, Dorothy; and see that Mr. Reginald's room is in order for him; make his servant and her child as comfortable as you can in the kitchen, and bring in tea-things for three.'

'Shall I make tea in the parlour, ma'am?' asked Dorothy.

'No, I thank you, Dorothy; if Miss Morison does not like to do it, you know Mr. Reginald will. There is Lucy waking —give her to me.'

The baby was lifted from the basket where she lay by the side of the sofa, and given to her mamma; and Clara, who had thought Mrs. Beaufort a remarkably plain-looking woman, saw her face light up with such a beautiful smile as she looked on the pretty little creature, that it reminded her of her sister Susan's, and she knew she should love her. Mrs. Beaufort was certainly upwards of thirty; she had bad teeth, and her hair and eyes were too light for her complexion; her figure was not good, and her hands were large and clumsy; but yet Reginald could see a great deal that was lovely in her, and Clara was disposed to agree with him. While taking off her bonnet and cloak, she scrutinized a picture that hung over the chimney-piece, and hoped it was not the portrait of Mr. Beaufort; for though it represented a young and handsome man, the expression of the face was so disagreeable, that Clara would fain have turned it to the wall, to avoid the mean, searching eyes, which seemed to follow her wherever she moved.

'I expected you to-night,' said Mrs. Beaufort, when they had sat down to tea, 'and stayed up a little longer than usual. What do you think of your charge, Miss Morison?'

'She is a little darling, and I am sure I shall teach her to like me soon,' Clara answered.

323

Clara Morison

'I wish papa were here to see her,' said Mrs. Beaufort, sighing. 'I suppose there are no letters yet, Mr. Reginald?'

'I have heard something of Mr. Beaufort,' said Clara. 'He was then digging in Adelaide gully with a Mr. Turner and a Mr. Harris. I believe Mr. Beaufort was quite well at that time, but the party had not found much gold. My cousin George met Mr. Harris in Melbourne, and he supposed the others were still at their old quarters.'

'I am glad to hear anything of Beaufort, when I can hear nothing from him,' said Mrs. Beaufort.

'The post-office is wretchedly conducted,' remarked Clara. 'My cousins have had letters four months old, and there were many they never got, and never will get; and everybody says the same thing.'

Mrs. Beaufort put a number of questions relative to the diggings to Clara, who found herself established as quite an authority on the subject; and by telling everything cheerful and amusing that she had heard, and treating the hardships as lightly as her cousins had done, she made Mrs. Beaufort's mind more comfortable than it had been since her husband had gone. But she was not strong enough to sit up long; and, soon after tea, she said that she would leave Mr. Reginald to amuse Miss Morison, and retired to bed.

'Is this the portrait of the master of the house?' asked Clara.

'Yes; and it is very like him,' replied Reginald.

'I feel disinclined to stay after he returns,' she added.

'I should not advise you; for though I am very sorry for it on Mrs. Beaufort's account, I cannot disguise the fact that he is a worthless person, and the less you know of him the better.'

'She loves him truly, however,' said Clara.

'Yes; love is blind, and it would be death to her to have her eyes opened,' Reginald answered. 'She is older than he. I often have thought, Miss Morison, that people love most strongly when they have the least chance of winning love. The attachment of a woman of thirty-two must be a stronger feeling than that of a girl of seventeen, and probably it is the same with our sex too.'

'I dare say it is,' Clara said. 'But tell me, if you can, how I shall best please Mrs. Beaufort, for this is a *terra incognita* to me.'

'You will please her most by admiring her baby, and talking about her husband. You must act as a sort of telegraph between her and Dorothy for the servant's deafness is a sad trial to Mrs. Beaufort's weak lungs. And, if possible, keep Dorothy from talking so much against the perfidy of our much-abused sex; the poor woman's husband deserted her

324

A Ride to the Bush

shamefully, and she hates and distrusts all mankind in consequence. You know it is not good for a nervous invalid to hear philippics of any kind; and the misconduct of a truant husband is a very tender point with a grass widow.'

'There are very few books in the house, apparently,' said Clara.

'And the piano is out of tune, and has not been opened for six months, to my certain knowledge,' observed Reginald. 'You will have no lack of employment here, but you will want amusement. You will miss your cousin Margaret sadly.'

'I do not expect to be so happy here as at my cousins',' Clara answered; 'but I hope to be more useful; and, at any rate, I shall be less miserable than at Mrs. Bantam's. My life there seems like a painful dream, which I would fain shake from my memory; while my voyage out, and the few weeks I spent at Mrs. Handy's, have a vague dreaminess about them, too. I seem, indeed, sometimes not to have lived at all in the interval between leaving Scotland and coming to the Elliots.'

Reginald turned the conversation from these reminiscences; and he and Clara talked about books, and things colonial or otherwise, till it was time to retire.

CHAPTER XV

LIFE AT THE BARN

'I must tell you, Miss Morison,' said Mrs. Beaufort to Clara, when Reginald had gone next day, 'that I might have sent Mr. Chaloner, or Mr. Digby, or Mr. Stones, or Mr. Ree for you, and I am sure each would have been happy to be honoured with the commission; but I thought Mr. Reginald was the oldest and the steadiest of my acquaintance, and as you knew him before, it is as well I fixed upon him. I have very kind, obliging neighbours, and I expect that now I have a young lady staying with me, they will be still more attentive in coming to inquire for me and Lucy. Mr. Chaloner is very handsome, Mr. Stones is very witty, Mr. Ree is clever, and Mr. Digby has fine manners; but I think Mr. Reginald has the best heart of them all, and he takes most notice of baby. Don't you think Lucy very like her papa, Miss Morison?'

Clara checked the 'no,' which rose to her lips, and said, 'I think that her nose will be like his, and the shape of her face is similar. We must go out for a walk, now, baby; and I hope, ma'am, you will accompany us into the garden.'

'Well, I should like to see how my poor flowers look to-day. How I wish I was strong enough to work among them! I will walk beside you and Lucy, that she may not feel strange with you, though she really seems to know you already.'

Clara was at once domesticated at the Barn; and though Dorothy was jealous of her influence, and disliked Scotch people, she felt relieved from a great deal of trouble by the companion; and when the man came, and she could order him to bring in the cows, to water the horses, and mend the fences, she felt her life so much easier, that she did not grumble half so much as she had done before. Clara waited on Mrs. Beaufort, took care of the baby, and was always a pleasant object for the invalid to look upon; and though to her the Barn was very dull and silent after the continual

326

Life at the Barn

talking she had been accustomed to in town, she saw that the same quietude was favourable to her patient.

Mrs. Beaufort would never allow there was anything the matter with her, and complained bitterly to Clara of Dr. Bennet's cruelty in not allowing her to nurse her baby. It was difficult, also, to induce her to attend to his prescriptions. She could not, she said, be expected to be well or strong when Beaufort was away, and it was of no use employing remedies; but when he returned, she was sure she should change all at once.

Clara chanced one day to mention the sermons she had taken down in short-hand in Edinburgh; and on the first Sunday after her arrival, Mrs. Beaufort begged to hear one. So Clara chose a discourse which had always been a great favourite with her sister, and read it to Mrs. Beaufort and Dorothy. They both expressed themselves very much pleased; but Clara thought it rather too hard a sermon for an invalid, and observed that Mrs. Beaufort seemed a good deal excited by it. Sermons are prepared for people in health; and that is one reason why the sick are often made worse by going to church; for the strong meat which suits the general congregation is not the best food for a nervous and delicate patient. Many times during the week Clara glanced over her notes, in the hope of finding something more gentle and soothing; but the clergyman whom she had attended was what is called a rousing, powerful preacher, and none of his discourses seemed suitable to her principal auditor. So Clara thought she would try to write a sermon herself; and on Saturday night, when everybody had gone to bed, she wrote what reflections occurred to her, on part of the twenty-second verse of the fourteenth chapter of Luke, 'And yet there is room;' with the intention of trying how it would sound when read aloud on the following day:—

'You must read me another of your short-hand sermons to-day,' said Mrs. Beaufort on the Sunday afternoon; 'for I have read everything in the house so often, that makes no impression on me, and it is next to hearing a sermon preached, to hear you read those odd hieroglyphics so well.'

Clara had settled herself to her discourse, and had read the first two sentences, when Mr. Reginald came in.

'Just in time to hear a good sermon,' said Mrs. Beaufort; 'and if you would be so good as read prayers first, and allow Clara to act as clerk, it would remind me pleasantly of England.'

Clara got through her share in the unfamiliar service without much blundering; but she could not help thinking how her sermon would pass muster before the new listener. She had begun it, and could not change it now; but she thought

327

Clara Morison

Reginald would consider it a curious specimen of Scotch pulpit eloquence.

'What a beautiful sermon!' exclaimed Mrs. Beaufort, when it was finished. 'I like this better than the last you read, though I admired that very much, too; but this seems so full of promise and encouragement. What do you think, Dorothy?'

'I liked the last one the best, for it was more of a trimmer,' said Dorothy.

'Well, I feel the better for this,' Mrs. Beaufort said. 'I wish you could sing a hymn now, Clara, for then we should have had all the forms of public worship, as well as the spirit.'

'I cannot sing,' Clara answered; 'but there is baby singing now. Has she not been good, to sleep all this time?'

Mrs. Beaufort always took a siesta after dinner, and Reginald and Clara were entrusted with the baby, while she was out of the room. Clara saw by the smile that was rising on Reginald's lips that she had not escaped detection.

'You never heard that sermon preached in Edinburgh, or anywhere else, Miss Morison,' said he.

'I knew that you would find me out; but I hope you don't think it was wrong in me to do it; for though it was not exactly the sermon for you, it pleased Mrs. Beaufort, without exciting her too much. I did it for the best.'

'I know you did,' he answered; 'and I advise you to continue the experiment, for you really made a charming little discourse, and I felt the better for your mild theology myself. Yes; we must all enter the kingdom of heaven as little children. But I am apt to grow hard and dogmatic in my solitary readings and reflections, and to fancy this point of faith, and that line of conduct, imperatively necessary to our salvation; whereas you only insisted on two things—humility and love. There was a freshness in your views and your phrases which one rarely finds in sermons by regular preachers. Is this your first attempt?'

'It is,' replied Clara; 'but I was once acquainted with two ladies, in straitened circumstances, who wrote sermons for their livelihood, and sent them to London for sale—Edinburgh not being a place in which to dispose of such things. They were very pious women, and wrote very good, sound discourses; so let us hope that they did good. If ministers are too lazy or too stupid to write their own sermons, I hope they at least know a good sermon when they read it. These ladies used to ask me to criticise their sermons, for I had the reputation of being a judge, and they were afraid that, writing so many, they might unconsciously write themselves out. Women are generally sadly underpaid, and get into a hurried way

328

Life at the Barn

of executing their work, which makes people think they cannot possibly do anything so well as men.'

'Do you think they can, under equal circumstances, Miss Morison?' asked Reginald.

'I admit our general inferiority in matters of ability and skill, though there are brilliant exceptions,' she replied; 'and you know you own to our general superiority in a moral point of view, though you can produce still more brilliant exceptions. It is a glorious thing to see a man unspoiled by the world.'

'We are interrupting an interesting conversation, we fear,' said a voice strange to Clara, as a very curly head popped in at the French window, followed closely by a head covered with straight shining black hair. The new comers were introduced by Reginald as Mr. Chaloner and Mr. Digby, two sheep-farmers in the neighbourhood.

Mr. Chaloner was of a very good family; he visited at Government House, was made much of among the exclusives of Adelaide, and for a partner at a ball was well enough to look at; for he was tall, and he danced nicely, and his hair had a beautiful curl; but he was very dull in conversation. He had a few stock phrases, which did duty on all occasions; but though his vocabulary was so limited, he never could master it completely, and his words were oftener misapplied than otherwise. If he told an incident twice over, it was always in exactly the same words; but he made a little variation by raising his tone every repetition. He was good-natured, but vain; he thought that his family, his appearance, and his position should command universal respect, and he would let Mrs. Beaufort's companion see and feel that he condescended to her.

Mr. Digby was different, yet the same; he had many words at command, and paid many little attentions; but after hearing and receiving them all, you felt that there was absolutely nothing in them. He, too, was of an unexceptionable family, and had received a good education; but he seemed to have taken pains to forget all he had ever learned, and made a parade of having entirely given up reading, and of knowing everything without taking the trouble to study anything. He never confessed to ignorance of any subject, though often to indifference about it; and used to laugh at Reginald, who was always reading and plodding, but whom he had heard confessing one day that he knew nothing whatever of the differential calculus, and giving a very timid and hesitating opinion with regard to the constitution of Mexico; while Digby would have made a bold guess, likely enough to pass for correct, and which, even if proved to be erroneous, would not disconcert him at all. Fluent and flippant, Mr. Digby

329

Clara Morison

was considered a delightful and clever young gentleman by all the half-educated girls he met in polite society; but Margaret Elliot would have taken him to pieces in half an hour, and have entailed on herself his undying hatred.

'Charming day, Miss Morison,' said Mr. Chaloner. 'And how is Mrs. Beaufort?'

'She feels fatigued, and is resting a little,' answered Clara.

'Baby quite well?' asked Mr. Chaloner.

'Very well indeed, I am glad to say. You would not have me disturb Mrs. Beaufort now. She will be up to tea, and I suppose you will stay till then.'

'Certainly,' said Mr. Digby. 'We poor bachelors are so happy when we can catch a glimpse of the fairer part of the creation, that we could wait for hours in patient expectation.'

'I suppose there are not many ladies in the neighbourhood?' Clara said.

'You are the only single lady for a circuit of twenty miles,' Mr. Digby replied, 'and of course have only to command to be obeyed.'

'This is quite a delightful phase of country life,' said Clara, 'for in Adelaide the ladies form so great a majority, that they have lost their importance.'

'And we can't get into Adelaide for a few months now-a-days to cut a dash,' observed Chaloner. 'It is a confounded shame.'

'Business must be attended to, my dear fellow; and now that Miss Morison honours the Barn with her presence, we shall not feel so completely out of the pale of civilization,' said Digby.—'Have you heard of the new partnership in the neighbourhood, Reginald? Stones and Ree have joined their flocks and their shepherds, and are living together at Stones' home station. How do you think they will pull together in these queer times?'

'It will be a good arrangement for Stones, for his flocks are not so large nor in such good condition as Ree's; but I do not know how they will agree, for they are of very opposite tempers,' answered Reginald.

'Well,' said Chaloner, 'I wonder at a gentleman like Stones taking on a fellow who has kept a retail shop in Adelaide. Sheep-farming will be spoiled altogether if a parcel of petty tradesmen are allowed to mix in it.'

'Nobody cares for such things now, for cash is the universal solvent. I myself, nephew of Sir Henry Digby, would take any man into partnership who would give me pecuniary advantages to counterbalance his want of gentility or reputation. Money is not so plentiful among us sheep-farmers as to let us be scrupulous where it comes from.'

Life at the Barn

'I think that Mr. Ree has mistaken his vocation in giving up his shop,' said Reginald; 'for he understood his business thoroughly, and I fear he will not improve his position by this partnership with Stones, who wants steadiness.'

'Beaufort never cared who he mixed with,' said Chaloner; 'I thought he would have cut Ree when he brought out his wife; but he did not; and Mrs. Beaufort is gracious to everybody.'

'What a beautiful specimen of female submission we have here,' said Digby, pointing to his pipe, tobacco-box, and cigar-case, that lay always on the chimney-piece, to be ready in case Mr. Beaufort should come home. 'Very few ladies are so considerate to their husbands' little pleasures as Mrs. Beaufort is.'

'I am considered qualified to dust the mantel-piece now,' said Clara; 'Dorothy used always to arrange this corner with such ill-will, that Mrs. Beaufort could not bear to let her meddle with it, and did it herself when she was able; but as I touch every article tenderly, and lay it down with no impatient noise, I am invested with full power over the pipe and its appurtenances.'

'Would you allow a fellow to smoke, now, if you were married to him?' asked Mr. Chaloner.

'Not unless I liked him very much indeed,' answered Clara, laughing; 'and I don't think even then that I could submit to it in the house.'

'Then we dare not take one of Mr. Beaufort's cigars?' said Digby.

'You may take it if you please, and if you can answer to Mrs. Beaufort for the theft, but you must not smoke it,' Clara said.

'Tyrannical already,' cried Digby. 'Reginald, you must aid me and Chaloner in the defence of our favourite pipe.'

'I am trying to give it up, for I am quite aware that it is a very silly custom,' said Reginald; 'but you must excuse bushmen, Miss Morison, for making a companion of their pipe when they have no other company.'

'Certainly,' said Digby; 'under present circumstances we should be inexcusable if we annoyed Miss Morison in any way; but she may rest assured that all of us indulge in the 'pernicious weed,' as Byron calls it, when uncheered by the smiles of the arbiters of our destiny.'

'Anything stirring in town, Reginald, when you were in last?' asked Chaloner.

'A good many diggers have returned,' said he; 'but almost all of them talk of going back to the gold-fields in September, so how we are to get our wool off this year, I cannot tell;

Clara Morison

and I fear that though the prices will rise, they will not be at all in proportion to our increased expenditure.'

'Any parties in Adelaide—not digging, but dancing parties, I mean?'

'Why, I am not in the way of knowing anything about such things; but I did hear something of a ball and an 'at home' at Government-house.'

'It is a confounded shame,' said Chaloner, 'that my shepherds know nothing about their business, and want as much looking after as if they were a parcel of babies; and that stupid of a new overseer is a humbug altogether; so I could not go when I was invited. How do your new people get on at Taringa, Reginald?'

'I think they will suit me very well,' was the answer. 'The man takes a pretty large flock of sheep, and the eldest boy a small one, and I think the second boy may soon be made useful; while Mrs. Duncanson cooks for us all in an odd fashion. They are so astonished at the abundance of provisions, that they will not make use of them, and I am in a fair way of being starved amongst them. I happened to be out for three days among the stations, and when I returned as hungry as possible, asking for supper, Mrs. Duncanson said she could give me fine bread and wealth of tea, but they had not thought it worth their while to kill a sheep when I was awa'.'

'To offer a fellow who had been riding sixty miles fasting, bread and tea!' said Chaloner, in a tone of the greatest disgust and horror. 'The woman must have been cranky!'

'But Mrs. Duncanson assures me that, if she had but hens, she could kill me a chuckie ony day, or boil me eggs; an' I maun hae swine, too, and then there would be aye a bit o' bacon to ready for the maister; and if we had a cow to milk, there would be butter to kitchen my bread. I think I must indulge her, for she seems to think she has not got enough to do. Don't I manage the Scotch famously now, Miss Morison? My knowledge of German helps me a good deal.'

'There is a foreign accent about your Scotch still, but you will soon get over it,' she answered.

Mr. Digby now became very attentive to Clara; he told her whose parties were considered the best in town, and regretted that the best musicians had left the colony; hoped that the races would be kept up in Adelaide, for there was always a good deal of amusement to be found in them; asked her what she thought of the Bloomer costume, and ventured on an opinion that the waistcoat would be very becoming to her; hoped that some lady of influence in Adelaide would show the example, that it might be followed; talked eloquently

332

Life at the Barn

of the misery gentlemen suffered from wearing black hats in this hot climate, and asked her opinion of his own wide-awake; while Mr. Chaloner displayed his broad-leaved pana-ma, and begged that she would only try it on, that she might see what a becoming thing it was to a lady.

When Mrs. Beaufort came in to tea, she found that Mr. Chaloner and Mr. Digby had been amused for the whole afternoon without giving her any trouble; and perceived that her new companion would be useful in many ways. She saw that very few words of her own were required, and by this time she found speaking much very wearisome. When she got well, and Mr. Beaufort came home, she hoped Clara might marry one of her nearest neighbours; for she was much in want of female society, and Clara was really a dear, good girl.

Mr. Stones called a few days afterwards, accompanied by his partner: and Clara, remembering the character Mrs. Beaufort had given them, hoped they would be more agree-able than the other gentlemen; but Mr. Stones was so loud, and Mr. Ree so nervous, that for some time she could make nothing of them. The retired shopkeeper had a much more intelligent countenance than his gentlemanly partner, but there was an irresolute expression about his mouth; and, possibly from not being at ease in ladies' society, he seemed unable to give an opinion about anything, except that sheep-farming was a very poor trade indeed—a remark which he repeated several times with much emphasis.

Mr. Ree was looking back with regret to his deserted counter, where money was to be made, and where, after all, he was much more influential than he could be in the bush. He had a talent for buying and selling; he understood the wants and tastes of the colonial population; and having always had the command of money, he was able to be first in the market, and to keep up his prices, and hold his own with firmness and success. But out of his shop his resolution was gone; he read, but formed no fixed opinion on any subject; he was lukewarm in politics, and vague in his ideas of right and wrong. Without a single relation in the colony, and keeping up no correspondence with those whom he had left in the mother-country, his domestic affections had not been called out; he had been accustomed to make no sacrifices for others, and was quite ignorant of the minor morals of life.

Clara might have brought any of the other gentlemen to her feet by going half-way to meet them; but with the retired shopkeeper she must have gone a good deal further. There is nothing so dangerous to a bushman as the idea that a girl prefers him to all the world besides; and an unscrupulous coquette, by feigning a little love, can drag them in her fetters

333

Clara Morison

for years. But none of these gentlemen, or of the other casual visitors who looked in occasionally at the Barn, were men to captivate Clara, even if her heart had been unoccupied. She began to think that, in general, poor clerks in Adelaide were a superior race to the independent gentlemen of the country; but perhaps, if she had remembered Mrs. Handy's young gentlemen, she would have been more merciful in her comparison. However, she offended none of Mrs. Beaufort's friends, and only indulged in her dissection of character in her letters to her cousins. Margaret wrote that her letters were common property, and that Gilbert, in particular, was delighted with her lively descriptions and sharp observations.

Reginald came to the Barn pretty frequently—generally on a Sunday—and criticised Clara's sermon; always ending by saying that hearing it had done him good; and maintaining a style of conversation which, without being gloomy, or dogmatic, or disputative, was still very well suited for Sunday. Clara felt that she could say what she liked to him; and was so happy in his presence that she forgave herself for her wish to see him oftener and longer; while every new interview convinced Reginald that Clara was a very dangerous neighbour. But he felt improved by her society; he had been in danger of losing sight of his religious principles and feelings, from utter want of any one to sympathize with his difficulties and deal kindly with his doubts. Clara's mind was of much the same cast as his own, but more gentle and hopeful; and his horizon brightened as she looked upon it. She threw a clearness and beauty over every subject which they discussed together; and the cold-mannered and reserved Charles Reginald thawed and grew genial under her influence.

But how lonely and dull did Taringa seem to him now! how moodily he sat over the fire in the long winter evenings, trying to read, and longing for a listener; raising his eyes now and then to look on blank walls, or to start at the sound of his own breath when he involuntarily sighed. The black pipe, formerly his only consolation, had been sacrificed to Julia's request; and when month succeeded month, and he heard nothing from her, he chafed at the bondage which prevented him from making a bold effort to secure happiness, and soliciting Clara to share all he had, including even his solitude. There was much for the master to do during this long, dull, wet winter; and when he returned from his long journeys, tired and drenched, fancy would paint how bright his dwelling would look if Clara stood on the threshold, and welcomed him to their home. Her light step, her pleasant voice, would make all the house musical, without either piano or harp; the books would be more delightful if they could be read

Life at the Barn

together; all things would work for good, if they could journey hand-in-hand through time to eternity.

But Sophie Werner's sad eyes haunted him; and not seldom made him wake with a wide start from such delicious day-dreams. And besides, Clara herself would despise him if he was so base as to forget a solemn engagement; and would think such love as he had to offer a very mockery.

CHAPTER XVI

THE MASTER'S RETURN

When Dr. Bennet came again to visit his patient, he found her considerably worse than before Clara went out; for never hearing from her husband was such a constant source of distress to her, that even Clara's care and gentleness could not counteract its bad effects. But Dr. Bennet chuckled over the choice of a companion that he had made, when he saw how useful and how dear she was to the invalid.

'Now, Mrs. Beaufort,' said he, 'you must believe in phrenology; for I fixed upon Miss Morison solely on account of her head.'

'I like her heart better than her head,' Mrs. Beaufort answered; 'and that you could not see in a quarter of an hour!'

'I could form a very good idea of her heart from the moral organs being so well developed. You had better get Miss Morison to sleep in the room with you, for it is cold for baby to be where there is no fire. And, Mrs. Beaufort, you must not worry yourself about the harrowing; for I am sure Miss Morison knows as much about it as you do, and can direct the men quite as well. And as to the house-keeping, I suppose Dorothy likes as little to be interfered with as ever; but she ought to take her orders from Miss Morison; for you must save your voice to speak to Mr. Beaufort when he returns. And, by-the-bye, I have heard that Mr. Beaufort had made up his mind to leave the diggings, for he has never got any gold; and if he has favourable weather, he will be here in a few weeks. So you must try to get up your strength, and eat a little more than you have done. Baby gets on well, I see, and can give us a smile now. Don't you think I was right about having a cheerful nurse?'

'You were very kind and thoughtful,' said Mrs. Beaufort; 'and Clara is a great comfort to us all. What do you think of her putting in two panes of glass for us the other day?'

336

The Master's Return

'Clara is a good girl,' said Dr. Bennet, giving her three hearty pats on the back, 'and must not let any of the young men about here take possession of her heart, and seduce her away from the Barn; for you and baby would get on very ill without her. Besides, my dear,' said he, gravely, 'there is not a man within ten or a dozen miles with half as much brains as you, and it does not do for a clever woman to marry a fool, even if she governs him, which is the best arrangement.'

'It is too much for a poor girl to do, to rule her house, and her husband as well,' Clara said. 'I intend to obey—that is to say, I will do anything in reason that my husband wishes.'

'But if he is a fool, and asks unreasonable things, of course you will not; nobody could expect it of you,' observed Dr. Bennet.

'There is a pleasure in giving up one's own will to a husband,' said Mrs. Beaufort. 'I am sure that if Mr. Beaufort were here, I could do anything in reason, or out of it, for his sake.'

'The chief thing you have to do,' said the doctor, 'is to take care of yourself, my dear madam. Don't you feel this winter colder than the last, for it really is, you know?'

'I used to complain of the heat of this climate,' Mrs. Beaufort answered; 'but really, I cannot keep myself warm now. What must it be for the poor diggers at Mount Alexander and the Bendigo? My poor husband will have nothing but a tent to protect him from the inclemency of the weather.'

'My dear Mrs. Beaufort,' said the doctor, 'I have often told you your husband's constitution is very hardy; and his temperament, which is bilious-sanguineous, is one which suffers very little from changes of weather, or of mode of life. When I say bilious, I use a wrong phrase; but it is a vulgar error. I know you have been always afraid of his having jaundice, or some such illness, from the time when I first mentioned what his temperament was; but the correct nomenclature is fibrous, which expresses endurance.'

Clara received her directions for the management of the patient in private. And the doctor shook his head when she asked what chance there was of Mrs. Beaufort's ultimate recovery.

'I fear, Miss Morison,' said he, 'she cannot possibly get over this; the disease is making very much more progress than I expected. I must write to Beaufort again, telling him to return immediately, if he wishes to see his wife alive; but I fear that even the sight of her husband will not lengthen her life many weeks. But, my good girl, be as careful and

337

Clara Morison

painstaking with her as if there were hope; and let her last days be as easy as you can make them.'

'My greatest difficulty is with Dorothy,' Clara said. 'She places no confidence in me, and is always talking against interlopers. I never could manage servants.'

'And Dorothy is a most impracticable specimen of her class,' said Dr. Bennet. 'But you must make the best you can of her. I know that no salary can remunerate you for your many toils and cares; but if you have a consciousness that you are doing your duty, that will be your reward. And do not leave Mrs. Beaufort while she lives. Promise me that,' said the doctor, earnestly.

'I will not leave her,' Clara answered.

'That is what I expected from you, my little pearl of a sick nurse,' said Dr. Bennet. 'And now tell me all about your cousins; for, of course, you hear from them often; and where your cousin, Grace Elliot, has settled, and how the wedding went off.'

'Grace is now Mrs. Henry Martin, and she lives at the Burra,' replied Clara; 'and the wedding went off beautifully. The only things to disconcert the party were, that Mr. Bell, who was present, wore a remarkably ugly coat, and that my cousin Annie cried a great deal.'

'Margaret is my favourite,' said the doctor. 'I should insist on coming to her wedding, whether invited or not. I hear she is going to marry William Bell, and I dare say they will do very well, for he is an excellent young man. I attended his brother in his last illness; and if you had seen how tenderly William nursed him, and how patient he was with all his whims, you would have been surprised at such gentleness from such a plain, rough fellow. God orders everything for the best. It was a great blow to William to lose his brother; and, for a while, he felt isolated and wretched; but still, it is better as it is; for his brother was a misanthropic and disappointed man, who required William to love him, but would not allow him to like any one else. Now, he bids fair to gain a good wife, and to be taken into a kind family, and all his fine qualities will be brought out by sympathy. There are many things in life, my dear child, that at the time we would like to have altered; but afterwards, we see the good we get from them, and would no more have them changed or erased than we would disturb the plot of a well-constructed tale.'

'There are some things in my life that I wish had never happened,' Clara said, sadly.

'You wish it now, but ten years hence tell me if your opinion is the same,' said the doctor. 'Yes, it is a mingled tangled thread, but One higher than we holds it in his hands; and if we submit at first, we may rejoice afterwards. I am

338

pleased to see how William Bell has brightened up by getting to know the Elliots; and that his life seems now to have a purpose. Margaret is a jewel worth winning too; I remember the Adelaide folks' indignation at her refusing a fellow with such a little head; but that she could ever have married such a dolt, was absurd and impossible.'

'So,' thought Clara, 'then perhaps, after all, Annie has really lost her suitor. No wonder that she writes so sadly—but Margaret's letters are by no means cheerful either—I wish I could get into town for a few days.'

But Clara kept these thoughts to herself, and laughed aloud at Dr. Bennet's characteristic way of decrying Mr. Dent, and began to ask him questions with regard to phrenology. Dr. Bennet rode his hobby to his heart's content, and was charmed with his attentive and intelligent listener.

'I tell you what it is,' said he, in conclusion; 'I see you believe all you understand on the subject; but you must study the thing and make yourself master of it; for with such observing faculties as you have (I have rarely seen such a fine development,) phrenology will be invaluable to you in the choice of your friends, and of your husband too, which is of more consequence than all. If Mrs. Beaufort had had your eyes, and my knowledge, she would never have given herself and her fortune to such a paltry scoundrel as Beaufort. Take warning, my dear child.'

Mrs. Beaufort's man, after harrowing in the wheat, became restive under Dorothy's rigorously exercised authority, and intimated his desire for a change.

'And indeed, ma'am,' said Dorothy, 'now that the wheat is put to rights, and there is plenty of water in the water-holes for the horses and cows, I don't see what earthly use we have for Thomas; and it would be a relief to my mind to have no more growling in the kitchen. I can't ask him to do the least thing, but he comes down on me with his impudence, or begins to sulk directly; but men are all alike. They are smooth and pleasant enough for a month or six weeks, and you think you are in paradise with them; but they are all false and fickle. I wish Mr. Beaufort may ever find his way back to the Barn at all, for I am getting very doubtful about it.'

'I should like Thomas to stay, for we shall have nobody to send to the post-office, and Dr. Bennet told me I was sure to hear from Mr. Beaufort soon.'

'Of course Dr. Bennet puts the best face on the matter, and stands up for his sect,' said Dorothy. 'I dare say Miss Morison could get Mr. Digby or Mr. Ree to go for *her* letters, and I don't see any use in our keeping a man to go for letters

to us when there never is one. What business have young women to get letters from their sweethearts every week, when us poor wives never get a line from our husbands?' and Dorothy began to cry piteously.

'Clara gets letters from her cousins, and often reads parts of them to me, so she does not deserve your insinuation; but tell Thomas I should like to speak with him; I want to know why he wishes to leave the Barn.'

'If he does not go, I must,' said Dorothy, who knew her power, 'for nothing can make me submit to his temper.'

'Well, do as you like; but you know that you will have more to do when he goes, for we cannot get another man-servant,' observed Mrs. Beaufort.

Dorothy joyfully acceded to this, and hastened to tell Thomas that her mistress saw how useless he was, and was very glad to get quit of him. For some days after his departure she enjoyed her triumph, and congratulated herself on the quiet tidy kitchen she could keep now Thomas was not there. But she made a very wry face the next week, when the woman who lived at the end of the large paddock, and who had taken in the family's washing, brought back the clothes as they went; saying that her husband had returned from the diggings with a hundred and fifty pounds; and that he would never let her wash any more; and she was going to be a lady for the future;—utterly forgetting who had given her and her children bread, when six months before they had been left with only a bag of flour and two shillings and sixpence in the house.

'The ungrateful hussy!' said Dorothy to Clara; 'they would have been all starved if it had not been for Mrs. Beaufort and me—the very gown on her back was a present from the missis—and now that we are in such trouble, the missis ill, and the master away, and no man-servant about the place, she comes here with her sauce. She is just as bad as if she was a man; but I told her a bit of my mind. A fine lady *she* will make, the slatternly creature, with her shoes down at the heels, and her hair flying about her face like a mop. I very near offered her an old cap to cover her head. I wish I had, for it would have made her pretty mad, I expect. But now, Miss Morison, I make free to tell you that though I will wash for my missis and her baby, I won't bargain to do your things, for it is more than I am able; and all servants object to wash for governesses and such like.'

'I would pay you for it,' replied Clara; 'but as you say you cannot do it for love, it is not likely you can do it for money.'

'You are just right there, Miss Morison,' said Dorothy, grinning.

'Then all I can do is to help you when baby sleeps in the

day or at night. I *can* wash;—I have not been a year and a half in South Australia for nothing.'

'That is speaking like a sensible woman,' said Dorothy, who was delighted to have brought Clara to know her level.

Thus Clara's duties grew heavier every day; the baby slept less, and required more nursing and dandling; and Mrs. Beaufort, though she gave as little trouble as possible, now became so ill that she needed a great deal of attendance. The gentlemen who visited at the Barn perceived that the new inmate fell off sadly in her appearance, and Mr. Digby pretended to believe she had fallen a victim to his fascinations; but Reginald, who knew how Clara looked when she was overworked, attributed her pale cheeks and weary eyes to their real cause. Dr. Bennet had advised Mrs. Beaufort to get more help, but the difficulty of finding any one who would submit implicitly to Dorothy, and the probable annoyance of continual quarrels, prevented Clara from pressing the matter. Certainly, nobody could be more grateful than Mrs. Beaufort; but still Clara's post was a difficult and painful one. Her only comfort was in Reginald's occasional visits. She asked his advice, and took it; and availed herself of his offer to call at the post-office for her letters, being disinclined to ask such a favour from any of her nearer neighbours.

'Mr. Ree knows a good deal,' said she one day to Reginald. 'In talking with him the last time he was here, I found that he had a great deal of information, but it lies dormant in his mind, and produces no fruits.'

'Could not you apply a torch, and kindle him to action?' asked Reginald. 'It is a pity that a mind like his should be of no use to the world.'

'I do not think I could, for he does not see the worth of action,' answered Clara; 'he is contented to be nothing, and to do nothing, and I suppose considers his indifference philosophy. Margaret would get out of all patience with his indolence, while his nervousness in the presence of ladies would make her despise him; for you know how brave she is herself, and how much courage she expects from your sex. She does not think that you have enough of courage; but I think that you are improving, and will soon come up to her standard.'

'The first remark you made to me which caught my attention as striking,' said Reginald, with a half-sigh, was on the admiration with which women regard moral courage in men; and I shall not easily forget it. Do you remember what I said to you as well?'

Clara commanded her countenance with an effort, and did not blush.

'You know,' she replied, 'that I have a very good memory,

and forget nothing that I hear which is worth hearing; I could repeat every conversation I have had with Margaret, or Gilbert, or you, almost word for word. I like to remember anything delightful.'

'To me the pleasures of memory are far from unalloyed,' said Reginald. 'How many things I would fain forget! But what do you think of Mr. Stones, Miss Morison?'

'If he used less slang, he might be called witty; but I do not see the point of the greater part of his jokes. My cousin George and Mr. Martin indulged sometimes in popular corruptions of the vernacular, but not disagreeably; but really Mr. Stones never speaks a sentence of English. Then he is always taking me up if I utter a Scotticism, and making his partner laugh at me in an uncomfortable, nervous way,—not heartily, but in a manner under protest; so I don't like him at all.'

'I think you speak very well, Miss Morison,' said Reginald. 'After hearing my Scotch family at Taringa talk, your dialect seems to me English undefiled. Beaufort is nearly as vulgar as Stones, and when they are together, I fancy their conversation would be quite incomprehensible to you. But I suppose there is little chance of your being so indulged, for Mr. Beaufort seems to be in no hurry to return home.'

'Dr. Bennet seems to expect him soon,' Clara said; 'he has written to him so pressingly. But Dorothy assures me he will never come again unless he wants money. She does not see that her mistress is in any danger, though Mrs. Beaufort seems to be getting gradually aware of it, and has not left preparation for eternity to her death-bed. Nobody could be in a more humble and pious frame of mind, and from all I can gather from what she relates of her past life, this piety has been habitual from childhood. You cannot think what a relief it is to me to know all this.'

'You should try to get out of doors a little, Miss Morison,' Reginald said, 'or you will lose your own health, and be unable to take care of Mrs. Beaufort's.'

'I really should be glad of some fresh air,' Clara answered, 'but Dorothy leaves me no time.'

'I will speak to her,' said Reginald, 'and tell her how unreasonable ——'

'Don't, I beg of you, unless it be to find fault with me, and then perhaps she would indulge me, from the spirit of contradiction,' said Clara.

A few days after this conversation, Clara succeeded in getting an hour's respite in the afternoon, and walked out in the direction of Adelaide, rejoicing, rather irrationally, in the idea that she was diminishing the distance between herself and her cousins. All seemed quiet along the road, so she sat

The Master's Return

down on a little grassy hillock, and took out Margaret and Annie's last letters, and read them again. Margaret's was filled with politics; she told Clara what Council ought to do during the session, but what they would not do, and gave her own ideas of what would actually be done; quoted some speeches in Parliament on colonial questions, and enlarged on the ignorance of the British public with regard to their dependencies; deprecated the policy of the Governor of Van Diemen's Land in writing home for more convicts, and hoped that the Home Government would not consent to such a suicidal request. These topics so filled her letter, that she scarcely left herself room for 'Yours in haste, Margaret Elliot;' and as she was unladylike enough never to cross her letters, or to append a postscript, it seemed to Clara a very unsatisfactory epistle. Annie enlarged upon the high price of boots, described how she had made the new winter dress George had given to her, said that George was getting on very well in his business, and that he would soon be able to marry, and was sure that Minnie would not refuse him, for she had confessed her partiality for him when they were in the country together last April; then she complained of a nervous headache, and closed her letter abruptly.

Clara was wondering how matters really stood with William Bell, when she heard the tramp of horses, and saw three gentlemen riding towards her quickly. One she recognised as Mr. Beaufort, from his resemblance to the portrait at the Barn; another was certainly Mr. Dalton, whom she had met at Mrs. Plummer's; and the third gentleman was a stranger.

'A young lady reading love-letters on the sly,' said Beaufort to Dalton. 'Would you like to hear anything from the diggings, ma'am? I have just returned, and have got lots of letters for different parties—quite a small post-office, in point of fact. If you would tell me your name, I will see if I have anything for you.'

'You are Mr. Beaufort, of the Barn,' answered Clara. 'You must not go home so abruptly, for the shock will be too much for Mrs. Beaufort. You will allow me to prepare her for seeing you.'

'And who are you who know me so well,' asked Mr. Beaufort; 'and are so ready with your advice, though I never cast eyes on you before?'

'My name is Morison; I have been staying with Mrs. Beaufort for some time,' was the answer.

'Any relation of Morison's Pills, I wonder,' said the stranger, who was the Mr. Turner of Beaufort's party at the diggings.

'Mr. Dalton knows me, for I met him one evening at Mrs. Plummer's.'

'Really I cannot say,' said Dalton; 'but I will take your word for it, Mrs. Morison, and believe that I *have* met you.'

'She does look like a grass widow, after all,' observed Beaufort to Turner. 'Your husband is at the diggings, I expect, Mrs. Morison?'

'I am not married; Mr. Dalton is mistaken in supposing so. I am Miss Morison.'

'Well, Miss Morison, make haste and tell my wife that I have got back safe and sound, and have brought out two friends with me to enliven the Barn, for you must have spent a very dull winter.'

'Mrs. Beaufort has not left her bed for a week, and only wants quiet,' said Clara, with emphasis, indignant at two disagreeable strangers being brought upon them thus, to double everybody's work, and to make Dorothy ten times crosser than ever.

'Her spirits will rise when she sees me, and she was always pleased to see my friends; so, make haste, Miss Morison.'

Clara lost no time in getting home, but was tormented with doubts as to how the news could be broken to Mrs. Beaufort, and how these gentlemen could be made aware that their presence at the Barn would be exceedingly inconvenient.

Gently as she made the announcement, it was very sudden and surprising.

'I must get up, Clara,' Mrs. Beaufort exclaimed; 'help me to dress, and I will get across the hall into the parlour. I have been saving up my strength all this week, just as if I knew he was coming. And put a prettier cap on Lucy. How pleased papa will be to see his little beauty! Oh, Clara, this joy will either kill or cure me! I cannot help thinking that, now I have so much to live for, strength will be given me to live. But poor Beaufort is tired, and I am so cruel as to keep him within a mile of his own house; run out and tell him to come—I can dress myself. No, I see I cannot; so send Dorothy, and stay you here to help me. It was kind in him to bring out visitors, for of course he does not know how ill and lazy I have grown.'

Clara would have advised Mrs. Beaufort to remain in bed, but she could not prevail over her anxiety to meet her husband.

Mr. Beaufort certainly was shocked to see how changed his wife looked from what she was when he started for the diggings; and his two companions deemed themselves badly treated in being ensnared to such a miserable place as the Barn. Little Lucy was much admired by her father, partly because he thought her very like himself; and Mrs. Beaufort

The Master's Return

felt so happy, that she forgot how long and how much she had suffered.

'I never have received a single letter from you, Beaufort,' she said, 'all the time you have been away.'

'It is such an abominable post-office,' he answered. 'I wrote to you four times, and it is really shameful that none of the letters reached you.'

Dorothy, who was setting down the tea-things at the time, gave an almost imperceptible but very unbelieving shake of the head, and went out of the room to shake it to her own satisfaction.

'Did you receive mine, dear? I wrote eight, but the last you could not possibly have had.'

'I had one, in which you said you were complaining a little, but that baby was very well. I did not expect to find you so ill.'

'Did you receive any letters from Dr. Bennet?' Clara asked.

'Well, I think I did,' replied Beaufort, slightly colouring; 'but he is such a croaker that I did not believe him. I see our Dorothy is as cantankerous as ever; she began to scold me before she came within hearing, and all the way along she has been laying the blame of the man going away, and the horses breaking the fences and destroying the garden, and old Mother Dawson giving up washing for the Barn, and Miss Morison's high airs, and God knows what beside, upon my shoulders. I expect I have faults enough of my own to answer for, without being burdened with those of the whole neighbourhood.'

'Poor Dorothy!' said Mrs. Beaufort; 'she certainly is cross; but don't be very angry with her, for if she leaves us we shall never get another. And tell me, Beaufort, how did you succeed at the diggings?'

'I just made nothing, and have had work enough to get home. We consumed everything we took away with us. All we dug would not cover my expenses, and I expect I am fifty pounds out of pocket by the trip; but Turner is more savingly inclined, and has positively got an ounce and a half of gold in a bag in his pocket.'

'I have never seen any Australian gold,' remarked Mrs. Beaufort. 'Would you let me look at yours, Mr. Turner?'

Mr. Turner took out his bag, displayed his gold, and put it up again very carefully.

'You had better have stayed at the Barn, Beaufort, than have left home so long, for less than nothing. And you look thin, too,' said Mrs. Beaufort.

'I have had a hard life of it, and somehow I don't suit with so much discomfort. We spent five miserable days in Melbourne, on our way home, when the town was crowded

more than it had ever been before. The ballroom of our hotel was turned into a bedroom, and twenty-one stretchers put in it; and there Turner and I were fixed with nineteen others.'

'And the only way to know our own beds,' added Mr. Turner, 'was by counting from the door to the chimney. I had the sixteenth stretcher, and Beaufort the seventeenth. And at dinner time, it was only the first comers that could get a seat at the table; those who were late had to stand round it like beggars or waiters.'

'How miserable it must have been for you, Beaufort!' said his wife.

'Well, I think the voyage home was more miserable still,' he answered. 'We took cabin passages, and thought we had a respectable captain; but such a set of fellows we got amongst! Six hundred dozen of ale and porter were sold during the voyage, at half-a-crown the bottle, and four hundred dozen of bad sherry, at six shillings, besides brandy and gin. But you are tired now, Mary, and I fancy you would like to go to bed. Miss Morison will go on making tea, for I am inclined to make a comfortable meal for once.'

When Mrs. Beaufort had retired, her husband forgot how ill she was. Pleased to be in a house where he was lord and master, and comfortable in the thought that an upper servant like Clara would not dare to resent anything he said, he began to talk to her with impertinent familiarity. Turner was rude, and Dalton supercilious; and Clara's cheeks burned, but she could not trust herself to speak. When Dorothy removed the tea equipage, Clara saw her looking inquisitively and maliciously both at herself and at Beaufort, who was sitting close beside her, and asking her indifferent questions in a manner quite the reverse.

'Did our neighbours ever come to see you when I was absent?' he inquired. 'I should think that you would prove an attraction to the Barn.'

'Yes,' answered Clara.

'Miss Morison says she was an attraction,' interposed Mr. Turner, with a loud laugh; 'that is candid, at least.'

'I mean that visitors did come to see us sometimes,' said Clara, quietly.

'Who came?' asked Beaufort. 'Not Henryson, for I quarrelled with him about the run; nor Roberts, for ever since he jockeyed me with a worthless mare, he has never shown face; nor Escott, for he has had a bad bargain with my sheep —they are not sound, and I expect they will have infected his own, in spite of all Humberstone's care. Has Escott been here, Miss Morison?'

'He called once in passing, and appeared very much dissatisfied; but when I told him Mrs. Beaufort was so ill, he

did not annoy her, and only complained to me, which was a great comfort.'

'I admire the cool way in which you take the matter, Clara (it is a pretty name, and I like it better than Miss Morison.) But did no one else come here either to grumble at or flatter you?'

'Mr. Ree and Mr. Stones, Mr. Chaloner and Mr. Digby did neither the one nor the other; nor did Mr. Reginald. They called to see Mrs. Beaufort, and to inquire after her health.'

Clara saw that Mr. Beaufort was bringing out wine and spirits, and felt uneasy at what might ensue.

'I must go to see how Mrs. Beaufort is now,' she said. 'I have been in the habit of sitting with her constantly, and I know she cannot do without me.'

'Neither can I,' answered Beaufort; 'you must sit with us, and drink to my safe return. We saw very few ladies at the diggings, and are glad of such society now. I have brought out a lot of new 'Punches' you shall look at—get them out of my portmanteau, Turner; we must not let Clara slip away.'

But Clara would not be detained, and went to her patient. She found Mrs. Beaufort too much excited to think of sleeping, but so happy in her husband's return, that she needed no company.

'Really, Clara,' said she, 'I think I am quite well now, but not strong, you know; go back and entertain Beaufort and his friends; since I cannot do it myself, I must provide a substitute. And, by the bye, tell him I should like him to come here and chat half an hour with me, that I may be sure I have not merely been dreaming that he has come home; and ask Dorothy to make my gruel to-night; it is too much for you to have to do it always.'

Clara did as she was desired, but Dorothy grumbled at everything, and felt quite injured by her mistress's request.

'I knew how it would be,' muttered she; 'Miss Morison will be having it all her own way now Mr. Beaufort has come home. Faithless wretches all men are, and *he* is as bad as *him.*'

Clara did not hear these words, as she moved reluctantly to return to the parlour. She sat down and endeavoured to get absorbed in the 'Punches.' The gentlemen had just looked at the wood-cuts, and fancied they had seen all that was worth seeing; and they wondered at Clara's slow progress, the letter-press being to her the most attractive part. She was reading one of those serious articles which are sometimes to be found in the witty periodical, and had almost forgotten her company, when Beaufort snatched the paper from her, and said it was treating him very cavalierly, to neglect answering his last question.

'What was it?' said Clara, wonderingly. 'I beg pardon, sir, but I did not hear.'

'Sold!' exclaimed Mr. Turner. 'Mr. Beaufort did not ask anything; but you looked so taken up with what you were reading, that he ventured to say so, and you were caught.'

'I ask you a question now. Will you sing us a song?' Beaufort said.

'I cannot sing, and if I could, I would not, when Mrs. Beaufort is so ill. The noise would certainly make her worse,' Clara answered, wishing to put a veto on singing by any of the party.

'She could not hear through two deal doors and a large hall, unless her ears are double million magnifiers, like Sam Weller's eyes,' cried Beaufort.

'I beg of you,' said Clara, earnestly, 'not to think of such a thing. Mrs. Beaufort has been very much excited by seeing you again; she asked me if she had not dreamed it all; and she would like to talk with you for half an hour when you are a little rested after your journey.'

'Then I will go now; pass the bottle, you two, while I am away, and keep Clara in order; I see well enough she wants to rule the roost.'

Clara, however, managed to keep the gentlemen in better order than before. A young lady, if she chooses, can generally silence impertinence, unless, indeed, her situation be as peculiar as Clara's was at Mrs. Handy's. She gave Messrs. Turner and Dalton to understand that they ought not to make a long stay at the Barn, and they quite agreed with her.

'I shall go and see Chaloner to-morrow,' said Dalton; 'he will be very glad to hear the news of Adelaide; and I shall spend my fortnight's leave of absence with him and Digby, for I have no notion of staying where I am unwelcome.'

'How is Mr. Plummer?' asked Clara. 'You are in the same department of the public service as he is, Mr. Dalton; are you not?'

'He was very well when I left him, but I suppose he will look differently before I return, for nothing can go on rightly in my absence; and the young fellow under me has his heart in the highlands, or at the diggings, for he is never there when he is wanted. I remember you now, Miss Morison; you are a cousin of Margaret Elliot's. I suppose you have heard that Annie has lost both of her admirers; Harris has settled in Melbourne, and is very sweet upon a young lady there; and William Bell has shifted his quarters, and pays all his clumsy attentions to Margaret. After refusing Dent and Somerset, I suppose the blue-stocking will accept Bell as a *pis-aller*. I say, Turner, I should like to see you and Margaret Elliot together; she is such a Tartar. She always pounces upon

me fiercely whenever she sees me;—not that I care; it is very good fun. But I fancy Bell will get very little of his own way, or any peace in his own house, if he marries her. And she is neither pretty, nor rich, nor young.'

'She is all those things to me,' said Clara; 'and whomsoever she marries, she will do her duty by.'

Beaufort returned, and the evening slowly wore away. Clara escaped before the gentlemen were inclined to leave their wine, and gladly sought her bed to obtain rest of body, though not peace of mind. Weary of the perplexing thoughts that haunted her, she rose in the night, and wrote to Margaret for advice; and then, somewhat relieved, dropped to sleep for an hour or two.

'Dorothy,' said Mr. Beaufort the following day, at dinner-time, 'what do you mean by giving us no tea at dinner, when you know I cannot do without it? Mr. Turner is accustomed to it too; and Miss Morison looks as if she would be the better for it.'

'It is a deal of trouble, sir, on a washing-day,' answered Dorothy, tartly; 'and Mrs. Beaufort and Miss Morison never asked for it all the time you were away. They contented themselves with a glass of fair water;—and it's quite good enough for any one of you,' she added, within her teeth.

'I insist on it,' said Beaufort. 'Did you ever hear of a house in the country, where the teapot was not brought in regularly with dinner? You have been very badly treated, Miss Morison, if Dorothy's laziness has prevented you from seeing what bush-life really is.'

Dorothy brought in tea most reluctantly, and when Clara began to make it, thought it was all her fault, and hated her accordingly. Patience and good humour were quite thrown away upon Dorothy. When Clara left her dinner almost untasted, to take up the little Lucy, who was crying to be nursed, and sat with the babe upon her lap, while every one else was being attended to, Dorothy could only see an artful creature endeavouring to attract attention by prétending fondness for Mr. Beaufort's child, and complaisance to his guests. She had not much *esprit de corps*; she hated all men, but she liked few women; her sympathies were confined to wives afflicted with brutal or faithless husbands; and all young women and widows she looked upon with suspicion, as mere traps to lead astray. There was something in the turn of Clara's head which reminded her of the girl to whose arts her own happiness had been sacrificed, and she had always resolved to watch her narrowly whenever Mr. Beaufort should return.

She was glad when the strangers departed, and there was

no object to divert Mr. Beaufort's attention. Her eyes followed Clara's movements with an unkindly and uncomfortable gleam in them, which cost Clara many tears when she could shed them unseen. But Mrs. Beaufort always insisted on her sitting with her husband as much as possible, for, poor man! it was such a dull thing for him to be left in that solitary parlour without a soul to speak to. Beaufort himself could not object to the arrangement; pale and reserved as Clara was, he thought her both pretty and clever; and it was worth his while to make her agreeable, particularly as for several days heavy rain prevented him from getting out of doors. He found that Clara liked him best when he talked about his wife and child, and that he could not make himself more agreeable than by nursing and taking notice of little Lucy. He promised that a nursemaid should be procured for her; for, said he, it was really too much for Clara to have the charge of an invalid and a young baby, and when the weather cleared, he would go to the nearest German village and obtain one. But Clara would have hoped more from the proposal, if Dorothy's ominous brows had not distinctly pronounced her disapprobation.

CHAPTER XVII

CLARA TAKES COUNSEL WITH HER FRIENDS

Owing to the badness of the weather, some time elapsed before Reginald heard of Beaufort's return. He learnt it from Dalton and Chaloner, who rode up to Taringa on the first fine day, being somewhat at a loss what to do with themselves. Mr. Dalton hinted that Beaufort finding his wife so ill, thought her companion infinitely more agreeable.

'Yes,' added Mr. Chaloner, 'Beaufort will monopolize the only girl in the neighbourhood, and marry her too, before the year's mourning is out. I just give him six months to have it all over.'

'It is a shame in you, Chaloner,' said Reginald, 'to talk of Beaufort, heartless as he is, marrying again in six months—and his poor wife alive when you say it,—or that Miss Morison would take Beaufort, even if he were free to ask her.'

'She won't be able to help herself if she stops there long,' replied Dalton; 'with Beaufort so attentive, and that horror of a servant watching her like a wild cat. Besides, Beaufort is young, handsome, and has a good deal of property through his wife, if not of his own; and I think that Miss Clara Morison will snap at such an offer, and, indeed, do her utmost to bring it on.'

'I believe you are very much mistaken,' Reginald said; 'Miss Morison has a happy home in Adelaide, and need not stay, except from her attachment to Mrs. Beaufort.'

Reginald determined to go to the Barn on the next day, which was Sunday; and when his visitors left him, to make a run across to the Burra, pretty early in the morning, he mounted his horse, and rode as fast as he could. Within half a mile of the Barn he met Clara, walking as if to meet him, looking so sad, so wan, and so hopeless, that he stared at her appearance.

'I wished to speak to you by yourself,' said she; 'and as I had a presentiment that you would be here to-day, I begged Mrs. Beaufort to take care of Lucy, while I had a walk.'

For once, Clara felt thankful that Reginald was engaged; for she could never have brought herself to tell him how miserable she really felt, or to ask him what he thought would be her wisest policy, if she had not known that his faith was pledged to another. Reginald dismounted, threw his bridle over a post, and sitting down beside Clara on a fallen tree, gave his earnest attention to what she had to say.

'You are the only friend here to whom I can speak; for, of course, I cannot complain to Mrs. Beaufort,' she began. 'Dorothy went away yesterday, after assailing me with every sort of insinuation and calumny. She said that no girl who was worth anything at all, would submit to such language as Mr. Beaufort used to me; declared she would tell Mrs. Beaufort how basely her husband and pretended friend betrayed her, and threatened to publish my conduct all over the colony. Now judge for me, Mr. Reginald, if I can quarrel with Mr. Beaufort, or say one word to his wife, when I know well that she cannot live more than a few weeks at most. But Dorothy said that her mistress was not dying, as we pretended; and that she would live to find out how deceitful I was; and she was just rushing into Mrs. Beaufort's room to tell her all, when I interrupted her, and entreated her to spare her mistress's feelings, however much she might choose to wound my own. So she went off directly to Mrs. Dawson's, to go with her husband to town; and has left me alone with her master and mistress. I cannot make a satisfactory excuse for her to Mrs. Beaufort; and she keeps repeating that it is cruel, cruel, in Dorothy to leave when she is so ill. Mr. Beaufort has engaged a German and his wife and daughter, and they are coming home to the Barn to-morrow. But in the meantime my position is worse than ever. I cannot tell what to do or think. I have written to Margaret for advice, and asked Mr. Beaufort to post my letter, but he forgot it, and has it in his pocket now. So I have come to you as an old friend, and one on whose judgment I can rely, to ask you if you think I should leave the Barn, or remain.'

Never had Reginald felt his real interest in Clara so strongly as now, when, with her pale cheeks and tearful eyes, she looked up to him as her only friend and adviser. Never had he felt so powerful an inclination to shake off his bondage, and ask her hand; for if, as his affianced bride, he approved of her remaining at the Barn, and told Beaufort of his intentions with regard to her, nobody could say anything against her; and even Dorothy's slanders would fall harmless to the ground. And Clara, he thought, would not refuse him:

Clara Takes Counsel

she could not, for her friendship was of such a nature, that a word from him might change it into love. And she was so wretched now, that the acknowledgment of his feelings might be to her as light out of darkness; but then what would she not suffer when she discovered that he had no right to ask her, and no right to love her?—he could never keep the secret from her, for she was so true herself that it would be impossible to have any concealment from her when they were married. And to give up all this for Julia, who cared so little for him!

But he commanded himself sufficiently to say, with tolerable calmness, 'You have taken counsel from One wiser than me, Miss Morison; and after such counsel, what do your own instincts say on this matter?'

'They tell me to remain,' Clara answered; 'I feel that it would be base and ungenerous to leave so helpless a sufferer without a friend beside her; but I am fully aware of the extent of the sacrifice I make, and it overpowers me. Do not think me a coward, Mr. Reginald.'

'I do not,' said he; 'but are you sure that you can go through with what you have undertaken? I think you are right in your views of your duty, as you always are; and surely no one can blame you for remaining with your friend as long as you are of service to her.'

'And I promised the doctor that I would not leave her,' said Clara.

'Beaufort is a scoundrel, but he is not a villian,' observed Reginald. 'He has neither talent nor boldness enough to be dangerous.'

'I can keep him at a greater distance now that Dorothy has gone, than I could before; but I certainly dislike and despise him very much. He has such a mean soul, and is so thoroughly selfish!—but I believe he is a little afraid of me. Still I should like much to know what Margaret would advise me to do; will you post a letter for me?'

'I can do better,' was the answer; 'I will ride into Adelaide myself with your letter, and explain how matters stand at the Barn; and if your cousins think you must stay here no longer, I will take you back with all possible expedition.'

'Thank you—thank you a thousand times!' said Clara; 'but is it not very inconvenient for you to go just now into Adelaide?'

Reginald looked reproachfully into her eyes, and she felt that she should have said nothing about the inconvenience. The blood rushed to her finger tips, as a strange and sudden surmise crossed her mind, that he was not absolutely indifferent to her, in spite of his engagement to Miss Marston.

'I must return home now,' she continued, after a pause.

'My mind is greatly relieved by your kindness—I asked for advice, and you have given me assistance, which I needed still more.'

Reginald felt greatly inclined to start for Adelaide there and then; but Clara interposed—

'You must not go without your instructions. I have to get my letter from Mr. Beaufort, and to add a postscript to it; and I rather think that you will have to call at the doctor's for some medicine; and very likely Mr. Beaufort will have other commissions for you. You are so willing to take trouble for your friends, that we have no mercy upon you. I am very doubtful as to your chance of getting any dinner here, for Mr. Beaufort is cook, and his success hitherto has been sadly disproportionate to his exertions. Only think of his milking the cow this morning! I said plainly that I could not do it, and that, besides, I could not leave Mrs. Beaufort so long; so he set out heroically with the pail, and contrived to fill it tolerably well.'

Beaufort was not particularly partial to Reginald, whom he considered unsocial and priggish; but when he heard that he was going into town, he remembered twenty things that he should like him to do for him there.

'I wish I could get my trap mended and fresh stuffed,' said he; 'but I suppose you could not take it into town through such roads. The weather will soon be fine, and I should like to drive Mrs. Beaufort and Clara out to see a bit of the country. You won't forget to call at the saddler's, and ask if he has finished the saddle I ordered the other day. And just get me a good case of cigars—you are a judge; and bid my wine-merchant send me out something better than the last. And you can look in at any sale of horses that may be going on, and ask what I could get for 'Priam;' and you may bid for a half-broke thing for me—one that would suit a lady; for Clara, poor thing, cannot get out at all; and I could soon make it fit for her riding. And then get me some powder and shot, like a good fellow as you are. You must tell Reginald what is to be said to the doctor yourself, Clara; for I do not understand symptoms; but I think Mary's cough is not so bad as it was—is it, Clara?'

'No, it is not quite so bad,' said she; 'but Mr. Reginald has undertaken to deliver my letter, and I will thank you for it, as I have a postscript to add. And in the meanwhile you may get on with your cooking.'

'Oh yes! Reginald, by the bye, you must stay to dinner, and see if diggings experience has not made me a first-chop cook. I have soup, a joint, and a pudding, in a state of progress just now, and flatter myself that they will all be famous.'

Clara did not take long to finish what writing she had to

do, and was glad to return to Mrs. Beaufort, with a mind comparatively easy. She tried to divert Mrs. Beaufort's thoughts from Dorothy's desertion, using a little excusable dissimulation in supposing that perhaps the old dame had heard something of her husband.

'I never thought of that, Clara,' said Mrs. Beaufort; 'and of course if she had good news she would be very unwilling to tell it, for she dealt chiefly in the gloomy. Perhaps Mr. Reginald may see or hear something of her in town. I have such an absurd question to ask you, Clara, I hope you won't laugh at me. Don't you think baby is beginning to feel her teeth?'

'Yes, I think she is,' Clara answered; 'but there is nothing absurd in that question.'

'No, but that is not it. I am naturally very anxious about Lucy, and of course would like her to get her teeth easily.'

'You wish Mr. Reginald to ask Dr. Bennet about it,' Clara suggested.

'But that is not it either,' said Mrs. Beaufort. 'Do you think Mr. Reginald could be trusted to buy a coral for Lucy? There—the murder is out at last.'

'I think he might,' replied Clara, laughing. 'Will you ask him yourself to bring it out?'

'I feel half ashamed to trouble him about such a thing; but you can ask for me; he likes to do anything for you.'

'He likes to do any good he can,' Clara said; 'and I am sure, my dear Mrs. Beaufort, he will attend to your slightest wish.'

'Yes, I am very grateful to him. But still, Clara, I think he likes you, and a good husband he will make, I am sure. At first, I thought I should like to see you settled nearer to the Barn; but it is plain none of the gentlemen about here will suit you. And if you are at Taringa, the distance is not so very great but that you could come to see poor Lucy now and then. If I am taken away from her, who will love her as you do?—and we are having strangers among us now. Dorothy was often cross and unreasonable, but still she loved both me and Lucy, and what can I ask for more?'

'Perhaps she may come back again,' Clara suggested.

'Pray God she may, for my poor child's sake. I must trust Lucy to God. Don't tell Beaufort how doubtful I feel now about my recovery, for it would only grieve him.'

Reginald chafed at the familiar manner in which Beaufort spoke to Clara; his eyes flashed, his colour rose, and his voice trembled. Clara felt that this arose from his generous nature, and thanked him in her heart for his interest in her comfort and happiness. Beaufort thought that if Reginald admired

Miss Morison, he would surely speak out; and as he did not, he felt quite at ease with regard to his intentions.

Clara pined for Reginald's return, and felt quite angry within herself at the absurd and troublesome commissions Beaufort had given him to execute. The German people, who came when they were expected (for a wonder), were very stupid-looking, and neither spoke nor understood English. Their master knew a smattering of German, and was skilful in gestures of command, so that he managed to explain his wants; but Clara could not make herself understood; and little Lucy would not look at the new nurse, whose queer, quaint dress, round face, and elaborately braided and plaited hair, were strange to her; and whose foreign accents frightened her out of her usual good behaviour.

At last, late one evening, Reginald returned, and while Beaufort eagerly inquired concerning his various commissions, Clara was devouring her letters from Margaret and Annie; there was another, too, from her uncle, but it was not the first read.

Margaret could not think of such a thing as Clara leaving Mrs. Beaufort in her last illness, merely from a fear of what the world would say; advised her to rely on Mr. Reginald's promise to bring her back to Adelaide whenever prudence might require; and assured her she would always be welcome to their house and their hearts, whatever Dorothy might say or Beaufort either. Then Margaret praised Charles Reginald for his kindness and his good sense, and confessed that he had no lack of courage or decision, in spite of his understanding German and admiring Carlyle; after which she branched off into an account of a discussion she had had with a Melbourne gentleman on the subject of the colonial currency, which he considered to be in an unsound state, because Adelaide notes were at a discount in the other colony.

'I am doubtful,' she wrote, 'whether it will do us any good to have a local coinage at all, but I am sure that it will not suit the wants of the colony if the coins are made overweight. You know that the Californian gold coins are eagerly bought up by speculators for a profitable investment, and if the currency is not to circulate through the country in which it is coined, but to be sent out of it in order to be re-coined, it is a complete waste of time and labour to pass it through the Mint at all.

'To the best of my recollection, these were my principal arguments; but, as usual, my opponent was not convinced. I ran over the heads of our discussion to Charles Reginald last night, and he agreed with me on every point. It has quite raised him in my opinion, to see what a sensible view he takes of this matter. He said what I thought very true, that it

would be well for the colony if all other things were in as sound a state as the currency.

'Gilbert still proposes to go to the diggings again next month. He is working very hard with Mr. Hastings; but he has no inclination to study. Mr. Plummer reminded me, last Tuesday, that he had disapproved of his going at all, but that I advised it. I felt it keenly; but I do not think Mr. Plummer observed it.

'Thank God, George has no thought of going again. He is getting on very well in his business; and it appears that he could not have started at a better time; for whatever sort of goods you may have on hand are sure to sell in the present scarcity. George is protected from becoming too absorbed in money-getting, by his attachment to Minnie, who cares very little whether he has two hundred a-year or two thousand. I expect him to settle down soon; and Annie can live with him and his wife, and will be perfectly happy when she sees George happy. At least, I hope so. She is in a fidget now to get the declaration and acceptance over; and seems to be more nervous than the occasion demands; but you know she was always an excitable little thing.

'I think of shifting for myself, now that Gilbert has made up his mind to give up law, and that I can be of no use whatever to George. I have a project in my head with which I will not trouble you now, but upon which you will perhaps advise me when you come to town. Till then, I remain,

'Yours faithfully,
M. ELLIOT.'

Annie's was a sadder letter. It was full of pity for Clara, of anger at Beaufort and Dorothy, and of hopes that Clara would not kill herself outright. And it gave a long extract from Grace's last letter, in which Clara was very kindly mentioned; but there was very little of Annie Elliot in it.

Her uncle's letter was kinder than she expected. He had, at length, found an opening for her in Scotland; in fact, he had become acquainted with a family who wanted a governess like Clara, and who were in no hurry. The children were young; and it was not till next year, when they would leave Edinburgh for the Highlands, that they required a governess at all. Mr. Morison described the lady as a most superior and sensible woman, who never said anything that was not worth remembering; and who had taken a great fancy to Mrs. Morison and her eldest daughter at first sight. Clara would receive a moderate salary, and would be able to see her sister once a-year. Her uncle then empowered her to draw upon him for her passage money, in a style of such grandiloquent generosity, that Clara felt great repugnance to do so. She sat

with the three letters in her hand, wondering why it was she felt so little desire to return to Scotland.

Charles Reginald was sitting opposite to her; and when she looked up and met his eyes, her heart detected the cause of her irresolution at once; she could not bear to leave the country which was his home. It was not without a certain scorn that she acknowledged it to herself; but she felt that it was true.

'Did you see Mr. Bell when you were in town?' she asked, to escape from her thoughts.

'Yes; I met him one evening at the Elliots', and next day on the Exchange. He is getting into business slowly, but, Miss Elliot says, surely.'

'How are my cousins looking?' Clara inquired again.

'George looks very well indeed. Gilbert seems dissatisfied with something or other; but appears in good health.'

'And Margaret and Annie?' said Clara. 'You do not fancy it is only the young men I am interested in.'

'Depend upon it,' said Beaufort, 'you have gone the right way with your answer, in spite of what she says.'

'Well, Miss Morison, I do not think either of the young ladies looks as she used to do,' said Reginald. 'They seem thin and anxious; and complain of the winter being long and dull, and of having so much to do that they can find no leisure. Margaret—she will excuse my freedom: I do like to call her Margaret—had been much interested in a long discussion with a gentleman from the Victoria side, on the subject of the currency; and told me how the argument went. I agreed with her, for I thought she had decidedly the best of it.'

'What in the world have ladies to do with the currency?' cried Beaufort. 'Don't take a leaf out of your cousin's book, Clara, or set yourself down as an old maid at once. Currants are more in your line. I wish you could manage to make us some cakes to-morrow; perhaps my wife might take a fancy to them. She used to be fond of such things.'

'By-the-bye,' said Reginald, 'I have acquitted myself of Mrs. Beaufort's commission. I have got a coral for Lucy.'

'Come, then, into her own room and deliver it. She is very much better to-day; and I know she would like to see you.'

Reginald accompanied his host to Mrs. Beaufort's room and received her thanks for his attention. He was pleased to see her looking so well; and she spoke more cheerfully than he had expected.

'I do not know why people should all be so kind to me,' said she. 'I shall get well soon, now that I have my husband near me, and you to fetch and carry things from Adelaide for me; and Clara, too. I cannot tell you what a comfort she

358

Clara Takes Counsel

has been, and is still, to me. I wish I was not so troublesome to her, and engrossed less of her time; she is such pleasant company for Beaufort when I can spare her.'

'Oh, yes! Clara and I get on nicely; though she is rather saucy sometimes,' Beaufort said.

'I am sure I have never found her so. She must have learned it from you.'

'I suppose she knows I like a little spirit, and shows it, in order to please me,' observed Beaufort. 'I can see I am a prodigious favourite of hers.'

'I wish we could have the little tea-table brought in here; for if you gentlemen will excuse my dressing-gown, I should be glad of your company to-night. Though I am so much better, Clara will not let me out of my room yet; but I hope to be released on Monday, if I improve as I have done these last two days.'

The table was brought in; and when tea was over, Beaufort challenged Reginald to a game of back-gammon; and as his wife said she should rather enjoy the noise than otherwise, Reginald made no objection. Clara sat with little Lucy on her knee, who would not go to sleep on any consideration, and watched the faces of the two players. Beaufort was rather the younger man of the two, but that was all the advantage he had, at least in Clara's eyes.

'You have had letters, Clara,' observed Mrs. Beaufort. 'Have you good news from England—Scotland, I mean?'

'My uncle wishes me to return home; and I am inclined to think that I ought to go,' was the answer.

'Not to leave me!' exclaimed Mrs. Beaufort. 'Ah, Clara, do not follow Dorothy's cruel example! Though, to be sure, your uncle is your natural guardian, and in the place of a parent to you, and so you ought to obey him. And really there are so many trials and annoyances in this colony, that, I dare say, England looks very tempting to you. If I were not married, I should certainly wish to go home to England; but my husband's country is mine, and will always be.'

'Clara must get married,' Beaufort said; 'and then she need not mind what her uncle says. Deuce—ace. Confound the luck!'

'Well, I must say, I don't wish Clara to marry yet awhile,' remarked Mrs. Beaufort. 'You must try to excuse yourself to your uncle, my dear; and stay here with me and Lucy.'

'You always leave *me* out,' said Beaufort; 'and you know what a favourite I am of Clara's, and Clara of mine. Don't take me up, Reginald. Your hands are tied, my boy; and the game's my own.—Did you ever play draughts with Humberstone?' he continued, as the game ended in his favour. 'He is a very keen player.'

359

'Draughts is the dreariest of games, in my opinion,' Reginald answered; 'and whenever I have played with Humberstone, it has been against my will. He knows I cannot play, yet exults greatly over my defeat, and is fond of boasting that nobody in the colony can beat him except one.'

'That is myself,' said Beaufort. 'He tells me I am the only man in the province that can do it.'

'I have heard three other gentlemen lay claim to the honour, however,' said Reginald.

'By-the-way,' remarked Beaufort, 'Humberstone must be getting rich; for he was always of a saving turn, and I fancy he has a famous billet under Escott.'

'Yes; he is in fair circumstances,' said Reginald. 'He told me, the other day, Miss Morison, that he had had rather a painful meeting lately. He had gone up to the Burra, with some sheep for the butcher, and he met your cousin, Mrs. Martin, in the street. He was dreadfully confused for a minute of two; but recovered himself, and asked for an invitation to dinner, which she good-naturedly gave him. He told me all about it next day, and how well Miss Elliot that was, looked; and how kind she was, and what an orderly house she kept, and how comfortable she made her husband. Then he began to rail at Mr. Harris for leading him into such a scrape with Miss Margaret, or, as he called her, the tall, blue-eyed one. Did Harris ever talk about him at the diggings, Beaufort?'

'Oh, yes; by-the-bye, I did hear all about it from him. How poor Humberstone rode straight off to the north, immediately after receiving three or four refusals.'

'Harris has been exaggerating as usual,' said Reginald.

'He was a strange companion, was Harris,' observed Beaufort. 'He used to take such furious fits of work, and look quite black at both Turner and me, because we were not so keen about it as he was; and, by-and-bye, when our courage was up, his would be down; and he would stand beside us idle, and dispirit us completely by telling us he knew *that* hole was no good.'

'Harris wants perseverance sadly,' said Reginald.

'It was well for him that he did not persevere in digging, for he has a good billet in Melbourne. We made up our difference there, over a couple of bottles of wine, and a tolerable allotment of cigars. One can see with half an eye that he lives up to his income there, as he always did; so I fancy he will never be rich. But he says he is always happy, and always admired, and therefore is all right,' said Beaufort.

'That will do well enough so long as he is young,' observed Reginald; 'but when his animal spirits fail, and he is too old to be flattered and caressed, he will feel how his talents were thrown away—how he 'beggared his autumn to enrich his

May.' That is not the correct quotation, Miss Morison, is it?'

'Not literally,' Clara answered; 'but true in its application to Mr. Harris. I always felt sad in his company; for I could not help thinking how much better and more useful he might be.'

'I hope, Clara, you don't think such things of me,' said Beaufort. 'I am in the habit of thinking that I cannot be improved.'

'I dare say Miss Morison sometimes despises the sort of vegetable life I lead,' Reginald said, 'in the midst of my sheep. But I had a living to make; and, having been brought up to no profession, and considerably spoilt at home, I thought it rather heroic to start as a sheep-farmer in the wilds of Australia. At first, when everything was to be done, there was enough to excite all my energy; but afterwards I fell into a lazy and monotonous sort of life, and have been rather glad at being roused to action again, since the gold fever tempted away so many of my hands. I am naturally rather a dreamer, Mrs. Beaufort; and my dreams are more rational and healthy, after riding sixty miles, and setting right what was going wrong, than while sauntering about my homestation, and wondering over the disorder of my garden. I wish somebody would scold me about the state of my place, for I really ought to keep it more comfortable.'

'It is a jolly place enough for a bachelor,' Beaufort said. 'It will be time to make improvements, when you are looking out for a wife, and I don't see much chance of that just now.'

'But Mr. Reginald wishes to be scolded,' remarked Mrs. Beaufort; 'and when I get well, I will go up to Taringa for change of air, and scold him well then if everything is not in apple-pie order.'

'And Clara will help: she has quite a genius that way,' added the husband.

'Well, Mrs. Beaufort,' said Reginald, 'I shall beg some seeds and cuttings of you, and try to brighten the garden with a few flowers in time for your visit.'

'Let us try another hit, Reginald,' said Beaufort. 'You play worse than Clara, and I'm sure to beat you; but it does pass the time.'

So a few more games were played, to the discomfiture of Reginald, and the consequent delight of his host. The former had often before found Beaufort a bore; but now he felt him more tiresome than ever; for he interrupted all conversation, and prevented him from enjoying the society of Clara.

CHAPTER XVIII

GRIEF UPON GRIEF

Reginald quitted the Barn early on the following morning, leaving Clara disappointed to have had no opportunity of telling him that Mrs. Beaufort was not really better, but that this apparent change was merely a transient flicker. However, he had promised to repeat his visit soon; and her mind had been greatly relieved by the letters from her cousins, and even by the thought that, if the worst came to the worst, she might go home to her uncle without the risk of displeasing him, or making Susan uncomfortable; so that, though her duties were as numerous and laborious as before, she worked more hopefully. She begged that Dr. Bennet might be sent for. But Mrs. Beaufort thought it would be absurd to make the poor man ride so far through such roads, and perhaps catch his death of cold, merely to see how much better she was getting; and Mr. Beaufort was easily persuaded to his wife's opinion. But very few days elapsed before a great and alarming change took place in the symptoms of the invalid; and Clara felt herself obliged to communicate her fears to the hitherto unsuspicious husband. He was greatly shocked, and much softened. He had never contemplated danger—at least, immediate danger; and he began now to think he had been to blame for his wild trip to the diggings;—he hung over his wife, and entreated her to forgive him for that and all his many other faults; and promised that, if she were only spared to him, he would be more observant of her wishes, and more grateful for her love.

'I am sure I have nothing to complain of in you, Beaufort,' she answered, at the same time visibly sinking. 'You have always been kinder to me than I deserved. But oh! it is hard to die, when one is so happy;—it is hard to submit to the will of God in this matter—to leave my husband, my child, and my friend. Do you really think me so very ill, Clara? Must I die?'

Grief upon Grief

'Cannot Fritz go for the nearest doctor?' Clara inquired, aside, of Mr. Beaufort. 'He would know so much better than I can pretend to do.'

'Fritz is an idiot, and would make some silly blunder,' replied Beaufort, in a louder tone. 'But I will go myself. Bid him saddle my horse directly.'

'You don't mean to ride off in this pouring rain, Beaufort?' said his wife, feebly. 'Besides, no one would be any good but Dr. Bennet; and he is too far—too far,' she murmured.

'But, Mary, I must go. I cannot leave a stone unturned——'

'No, no—you must not. I shall die if you leave me. It is a fearful night. So cold!' she moaned. 'Surely the fire is out.' She had seized her husband's hands, and held him beside her, fixing her eyes on his face with an intenseness of expression which gradually wore off, though the grasp seemed to grow firmer.

Before morning she was dead. And Clara sat weeping, with little Lucy on her knee, wholly unable to meet the child's unwitting mirthfulness with any of her usual encouragement.

Mr. Beaufort showed great grief for a day or two, and was very gentle and quiet; but when the funeral was over, he seemed to find relief, and to relapse into his old manner. Mrs. Beaufort was buried under a fine old tree in her own garden, where she had expressed a wish to have her grave made in case of her death. The funeral took place on a very wet and stormy day; and but few of the neighbours were present. Clara expected Reginald to be there; but he did not come, though Fritz had gone to Taringa to ask him. He had not been at home, but was expected back immediately; and Beaufort was rather offended at his absence.

When all was over, and the guests departed, Beaufort thought he might as well seek comfort and amusement from Clara; and accordingly he asked her to join him in the parlour while he smoked his pipe.

'I am busy,' she answered; 'I cannot come.'

'What are you about now? You can have nothing particular to do.'

'I am getting my things ready to go to Adelaide.'

'To Adelaide!—you are not going to Adelaide! I don't mean you to go away from the Barn.'

'But I desire to go back to my own relations. I cannot stay here any longer, now that I have lost my friend.'

'But what, in the name of wonder, can Lucy and I do without you? You know there is no getting her to go to that dismal German girl; and as for myself, I have no intention of parting with you at all—at any rate, so soon. It would be ungrateful in you to leave your friend's child to strangers,

and poor Mary would never have expected you to desert me in my affliction. She trusted in your being always our friend, and would have been shocked to hear you talk of getting away as soon as possible, and sooner too, for this is no weather for long journeys. What do you mean to do in Adelaide?—look out for a situation as a governess? A nice life you would have of it! If you don't think your salary high enough, I will raise it. And you will not have half so much to do now—only to see after those idiots in the kitchen, look to Lucy a bit, and sit at meals and in the evenings with me. Nothing disagreeable in any of these duties, Clara; you may be quite the lady here, if you have any sense.'

'I cannot stay,' persisted Clara; 'you must know very well that it is out of my power.'

'It is not at all out of your power, and the Barn will be unbearable if you leave it. I shall positively start off for the diggings again, and put the child out to nurse. And you best know who will be to blame if any harm comes to it.'

'You are cruel, Mr. Beaufort, to speak so. I would do anything in my power to serve Lucy, but this is impossible.'

'It is out of your power to go till I choose to drive you, at any rate, you stubborn thing; and I hope you will be reasonable before I find it convenient. You had better make up your mind to be comfortable at once. Come, sit down here, and read me something while I smoke. That request is too much after your own heart to be refused.'

Clara set her teeth together, and whispered to herself, 'This cannot last long; Reginald will surely be here to-morrow: I may as well keep terms with him, while I am so much in his power; and there can be no harm in reading to him.'

It was a sporting magazine which Beaufort gave her to read, and she read mechanically, without observing the meaning; but he seemed to understand it, and expressed himself much obliged to her. But she found it a most tedious occupation.

'I do not like reading this just now,' she said, in a weary voice, after finishing two long articles. 'It tires me, and I feel very nervous to-day.'

'Oh, you have done vastly well for one day,' Beaufort answered. 'I dare say you are tired, for you have read more than an hour. Now, what say you to a game at back-gammon?'

'I say, I won't play,' said Clara, shocked out of all her resolutions of acquiescence.

'That is rather strong,' cried he. 'Why, where is the harm? You are fond of the game, and you play it well, and you have often played with me before. Come, Clara, get the box.'

'Not to-day. By-and-bye—perhaps—'

'Then you are going to stay, after all? I feel so much obliged for that kind 'by-and-bye,' that I quite forgive your

cruel 'I wont play;' and I wont ask you to do anything for me again till to-morrow. Let us have tea.'

When Clara had made tea to his liking, he declared there was nothing so miserable as having it alone; and Clara, remembering her own solitary meals at Mrs. Bantam's, felt some sympathy with him. But when she saw that he was determined to forget his late loss, and was angry with her for any allusion to it, telling her he was miserable enough when alone, and wanted her cheerful conversation to sustain his spirits, she could scarcely restrain her tears.

'Don't be a fool, Clara,' said he, on seeing them; 'you know it is both foolish and sinful to mourn over those who are happier than we could make them.'

A week had elapsed since Mrs. Beaufort's funeral, and still Reginald had not made his appearance. Mr. Beaufort had not announced the death of his wife in any of the Adelaide papers, and Clara's letter, communicating the news, had never been posted, so that her cousins were ignorant of her situation. The weather was wretchedly bad, and Fritz had never been told by his master to go to the post-office, while all that Clara herself could say to him was utterly unintelligible. How she longed to be able to speak German!—she would have given every accomplishment she possessed for the power of telling Fritz's wife that she wished to get away from the Barn— for she was very unhappy—and of asking her advice and assistance. But the two German women seemed to consider her as their mistress, and she saw them several times exchange significant looks with each other, which she trembled to think were aimed at her doubtful position. She tried to speak to them in broken English, and then again in broad Scotch, as Reginald had said there was some affinity between Scotch and German; but all in vain—she was never understood.

'What can have become of Reginald?' she asked herself every hour of every day. Was he ill, or was he changed? Had Miss Marston come out to Australia to marry him, and was she forgotten in his happiness? Fritz had not learned where he was when he went to the station, but only that he was not at home. Beaufort often abused him for not coming to inquire after the family, but knew nothing of the extent of Clara's disappointment. He began to think she was now so completely in his own hands, that she must of necessity listen to reason, and stay to keep house at the Barn. He was not very sure himself how matters would end; she was undoubtedly pretty, and if she were only a little less obstinate and more complying, it would perhaps be her own fault if she ever wanted a house of her own; but these were too early

days to talk of such things. At any rate, he was bound to detain her to take charge of the baby for the present, and by-and-bye she would be at his mercy. Reginald, if he cared for her at all (which was very doubtful), had lost his opportunity, and would not be inclined to interfere. Mr. Beaufort was rather amused than otherwise at Clara's restlessness, her frequent and anxious looks at the weather, and her repeated inquiries whether he would drive her in the next day. All this, he thought, would soon subside; and while Clara sat silent at breakfast or dinner, scarcely able to utter the necessary phrases of the table, he congratulated himself that she was taming down amazingly well.

She was in her own room one morning, thinking of walking herself to the post-office, or of calling on some neighbour who could speak English, and would understand what she wanted, when she heard a visitor on horseback ride up to the door, and Beaufort's voice welcoming him.

'It must be Reginald at last,' said she, and she sat down for a few minutes to calm herself sufficiently to meet him.

'Come in near the fire,' she heard Beaufort say; 'you must be half frozen. You are just in time, for we are going to have rain, and no mistake.'

Clara could not hear the answer, but she heard the rain rattling against the roof and the windows.

'How good of him to come through such weather!' thought she. 'I could not have got to the post, even if I knew the road, while it rains so hard. But I must go to see him,' and she went into the hall, and perceived Fritz leading a horse to the stable. It was not like any of Reginald's horses, but she knew that he had a great many, and this might be a new one, so she did not doubt that the visitor was her friend. She was on the point of turning the handle of the parlour door, when a voice, unmistakably Chaloner's, drawled out:—

'You thought it a confounded shame that Reginald was not here last week, Beaufort, did you not? But you see the poor fellow could not help it.'

'How so?' asked Beaufort; 'I know nothing about him.'

'Have you not heard what has happened to him?'

'Not I, indeed.'

'He was crossing the river that very day; and as sure as I sit here, Beaufort, he slipped in; and it is all up with him.'

'You don't mean to say he is drowned?' Beaufort exclaimed.

'No mistake about it; I sent two days ago to borrow some tobacco of him for my men, and those Scotch people were all in a fluster. The man had gone off to see the body, and the woman was wringing her hands, and wondering what was to be done. Phil Blake had brought the news, but he had gone off again before my man went up, so he could give me no

particulars. The woman would lend nothing, for she said the master would surely have somebody to leave his possessions to; and so I have been obliged to give away my first-rate tobacco. Have you any to spare, Beaufort?'

'Not a bit;—but this is a strange story about Reginald. He used to have more sense than to cross a dangerous river during the floods.'

'So he did,' said Chaloner; 'but Phil said he was bent on getting home, and had also said something about going to town, and would not be prevented. The woman told my fellow that her master must have been 'fey;' I suppose she meant cracked. He has left a fine lot of sheep and a famous run. If I can raise the wind, I'll make a bid for it.'

'Who will be heir or administrator, I wonder?' asked Beaufort. 'He has two good horses and ——'

Clara could hear no more;—she hurried back into her own room, and sat with dry eyes and burning brain, remembering all Reginald had been to her, and how very much she had loved him. She recalled her first meeting with him; how they had understood each other from the beginning; how kingly he had looked among Mrs. Handy's young gentlemen; then how kindly he had spoken to her when she was at service; how delightful he had been when he visited the Elliots; and, above all, how, since she had come to the country, he had been her only adviser and friend. He had been anxious to serve her, he had braved the swollen river for her sake; she had cost him his life, and now she cared nothing for her own.

Then she began to piece together his history from the little he had told her of his life in England. She was imagining the grief of his mother at this dreadful misfortune, when the thought struck her like a blow that to Miss Marston it would bring a real and legitimate sorrow. His last thought would be given to Julia; though it was for Clara's sake he died, he would not feel that any one but Julia was left hopeless and desolate. His mother would try to comfort Julia: she would encourage her to talk of him; Julia's bereavement would be no secret, and all the world would sympathize with her who had lost her betrothed. A momentary thought flashed upon her;—she must go and tell everybody how much she loved him; she, too, must claim a right to weep for him; but a laugh—positively a loud laugh—from the parlour, fell with sudden discord upon her ear, and chilled the ardour of her heart.

'Home!' she thought; 'I need not care to go home now; I may die here as well as there. It is here that I have seen most of him, and I need not care now what people may say of me.—Dead!—Charles Reginald ——'

She sat with her door bolted; little Lucy, who was asleep

on her bed, woke up and began to cry. Clara called Carolina to take her, regardless now of her screams; she pointed to her head, and sighed, to make the girl understand she was ill, and again secured herself in her solitude.

She had sat so a considerable time, when some one knocked at the door.

'Come in to dinner, Clara,' said Beaufort; 'Mr. Chaloner is here.'

'I cannot come; I am very ill.'

'Do come, Clara!—there is dreadful news of Reginald;—drowned crossing the river, on his way to his home-station. You would like to hear all the particulars, and Chaloner knows all that is known.'

'I am too ill to hear anything; you can tell me by-and-bye.'

'What can I send you for dinner, Clara?' he asked.

'Nothing,' she answered; 'I want nothing.'

'You will surely take a cup of tea?'

'No, no,—I want nothing.'

'Clara is in her tantrums to-day,' said Beaufort, on returning to Chaloner, 'and pretends she is ill, and wants no dinner; so we must do without her. There is the child squalling, too, but she pays no attention to it. I believe that girl Carolina pinches it slily, just to get quit of it.'

CHAPTER XIX

ESCAPE

The rain ceased in the afternoon, and Chaloner started homewards. His host was so loth to part with him, that he accompanied him as far as Digby's, where he was going to try to get a little tobacco. They were both away before Clara knew of it; and she blamed herself for not requesting Mr. Chaloner to post her letter, though, to be sure, it was of very little consequence now. She left her room, and wandered through the house. She took Lucy in her arms, and though she could not speak to her, the child grew quiet at the sight of her familiar face; and Clara, carrying her into the parlour, tried to warm her own frozen hands and feet, but in vain.

A slight clatter sounded outside;—it must be Beaufort returning. Clara wished to avoid him, and rushing through the hall, beheld Charles Reginald entering at the door, wet and pale, with a scar across his temple, but still indisputably alive.

She stared at him for a few moments, threw the child into Carolina's arms, seized Reginald's hands, drew him into the parlour, and burst into tears.

'Thank God! thank God!' said she, when she could speak, 'you have come at last. But are you really safe? Oh! oh! how I have wearied for you!' and half unconsciously she kissed his brown hands.

'Clara,' said he, 'I have come as soon as I could; I know you have been reproaching me for my delay, but I have had a slight accident, and did not come rightly to myself till yesterday.'

'I heard to-day that you were drowned; but you are not,—I see that you are not. But how did you get this dreadful scar?'

'A snag in the river struck me, I suppose; but I don't exactly know what happened, for I lost my senses; and the

first thing I remembered afterwards was that you depended on me; so I left the people that saved me, without learning anything. There will be time enough for that by-and-bye.'

'You thought of me first!' Clara said, dreamily; 'and I have looked and listened for you till my eyes and ears were weary. Mr. Beaufort will not let me leave; but you will take me away, in spite of him.'

'Will you be ready to go to Adelaide with me to-morrow? Mrs. Duncanson will come with me, which will make it more comfortable for you, and deprive Beaufort of any feasible excuse for detaining you. The old dame thinks it unsafe for me to go anywhere by myself, having at first taken me for a ghost, then for a 'wraith,' and now, I believe, considering me 'non compos;' but you see that I am sane enough.'

'I believe I am scarcely sane myself,' said Clara, now at last relinquishing the hand she had so long held; 'but I am ready to go away from this place whenever you will take me; and I cannot tell—I never can make you understand how grateful I feel to you. But how came they to say you were drowned? I overheard Mr. Chaloner telling Mr. Beaufort about it; he had sent his man up to borrow something.'

'Oh! a story told by an Irishman to a Scotchman, and then to another Irishman, was likely to be somewhat distorted. I suppose Phil told them I was kilt, for I was stunned, and Duncanson and his wife thought it was all over with me. You look faint, Miss Morison; can I get you a glass of wine? No;—then water?'

'I am more able to wait on myself than you on me,' said she, smiling, as she rose trembling, and obtained a glass.

'What have you thought of me all this week?' asked Reginald.

'I thought you were ill—I thought a thousand things—I don't know what I thought.'

'You did not think that I had forgotten you, or my promise.'

'Sometimes, but not often.'

'I fear you will hardly be able to travel to-morrow,' Reginald said, observing her falter.

'Of course she will not,' said Beaufort, entering at the moment. 'Where do you think of going, Miss Clara?'

'Mr. Reginald is going to drive me in to Adelaide,' Clara answered.

'Reginald! Adelaide! Clara, too ill to-day to eat any dinner, and looking like a ghost, and now going with a drowned man to Adelaide! Am I in the land of the living myself?'

'Pray give your ghosts some tea,' Reginald said; 'and let your man take the harness off my horses. I have had a shake, though I am not quite drowned. I should be all the better for dry clothes, too, for I have had more than one shower since leaving Taringa.'

'All that looks life-like, but I am not quite sure about you yet. Let me see Clara making tea, and you drinking it, and perhaps I shall be convinced. I'll go and see if your horses look as ghost-like as yourself.'

'Those brutes of yours won't take you to Adelaide to-morrow,' said Beaufort to Reginald at tea. 'You must give them a rest for a few days, and keep me company the while.'

'I expect you to lend me a fresh pair—the best you have got.'

'There are two words to that bargain,' Beaufort said. 'Besides, I don't see why Clara should go at all, or why she should go with you rather than with me. I always meant to take her home if she was not comfortable here, and I think it looks very ill to see her setting off in this way with a stranger. You may well blush, Miss Morison.'

'Mr. Reginald brought me here, and promised to take me home whenever I wished it,' Clara answered; 'and Mrs. Duncanson is going in with us.'

'And you really *wish* to go,' said Beaufort, bitterly. 'I am sure I don't know what I am to do with the baby. Unfeeling —ungrateful,' he muttered.

'I promised your cousins to bring you back safe and sound; but you do not look as you used to do. You must try not to shock your cousin Margaret by those pale cheeks to-morrow.'

'Margaret will never observe they are pale, though Annie will; but the drive will revive me, I do not doubt.'

Clara quitted the room after tea, to finish her preparations for starting at the first peep of dawn. She then went into the kitchen, and inquired of Mrs. Duncanson whether she should be ready, and was answered in the affirmative.

'I'm thrifty of the mornings,' said the old dame, 'and never cared muckle for sleep a' my days; sae I'll hae a cup o' tea ready for the maister and you afore ye gang. But oh! sirs! he's far frae weel. Do you think he's fit to gang the length?'

'Oh! I think he is,' said Clara; 'but perhaps that is because I am so anxious to go myself. Oh! how grateful I feel to both him and you.'

'Deed it was na' for your behoof that I came, though I daur say it's no' a place for you to bide here when the mistress is ta'en awa, puir thing, and ye'll be a' the better o' a 'sponsible body like mysel' to see ye safe to your freends. But the maister looks sae queer an sae wild that I thocht I maun e'en gang to tak' care o' him, and he said I micht gang to the preaching on Sabbath, and see my freends in the toun forbye; but it's a lang road an' a rough one.'

'And how do you like Taringa? Can you live without fish?'

'Oh, brawly! it's a bonnie bit, an' when ane has a gude

maister ane can pit bye wi' a hantle o' things. An I hae gotten a' I wanted to mak' the place wiselike, sae there's only ae want noo, an' that I'm thinking wunna be lang o' getting filled up neither, for it's mair his want nor ours.'

'Is that a church?' asked Clara.

'To be sure there is nae kirk, an' nae chance o' getting ane; but that wasna what I meant,' said Mrs. Duncanson, looking somewhat sly. 'We would be nane the waur o' a mistress, an' Maister Reginald would be muckle the better o' a wife, for it's dull an' lonesome for him to sit by his-sel' at nichts wi' naething but buiks; an' it's queer for him to be living in sic plenty, and hae nobody to tak' pairt wi' him. Weel, it is a wunnerfu' place this! I was just saying to Sandy, nae further gane than last week, that if ony body had telt me in the Orkneys that we should come to siccan a land o' Goshen beyond the sea, where we could get for oursels' an' our bairns as muckle wheat breed an' grand mutton as we could set our faces to, wi' tea by neive-fus an' the will o' the sugar bag, and fifty-six pounds by the year forbye, I would hae called it just senseless havers. And as for the work we get to do, it's just bairn's play to what we had to do in the Orkneys. I'm thinking that if we do get a mistress she'll mak' us stir our shanks a bit faster. But here comes the maister—I ken his fit weel.'

'You'll be ready in time, I hope,' said Reginald, as he came in.

'Nae fear of us,' answered Mrs. Duncanson; 'but ye maun gang to bed yoursel, sir, for ye look sair dune out, and want a gude nicht's rest.'

'I'm just going to bed now,' said he. 'I see you have got my clothes drying; you never need to be reminded of anything. Good night, Miss Morison.'

Clara was so glad to talk with a woman who understood her, that she would willingly have sat up half the night with Mrs. Duncanson, but she was very soon ordered off to bed by her. As she passed the parlour, she heard Beaufort rattling the dice by himself; and soon afterwards she heard his foot treading up and down the hall with heavy, impatient steps, until at length he knocked at her door.

'You are not gone to bed yet, Clara—you have not bid me good night. Come out and speak to me; you know we have business to settle together. Just come and speak to me for ten minutes.'

She opened the door, and Beaufort took her hand and led her across to the fire. The candles were out, but he heaped several logs of wood on the fire, and sat silent till they blazed.

'You look quite unearthly by this light, Clara. Where is

my cheque-book? I must write you out a cheque for what I owe you—but hang me if I can part with you like this.' He threw down the pen and ink. 'I tell you, Clara, I never meant you harm. What are you afraid of, that you cower from me like that? Come now; let us be friends. Why don't you speak? What are you going to do in Adelaide? not marry Reginald, I hope?'

'Certainly not; I think of going home to Scotland by the first opportunity,' and Clara sighed.

'You sha'n't go to Scotland, on any account. I should never see you again if you did. What is there to hinder you from staying here as Lucy's governess and my housekeeper for the present? By and bye I can put the matter on a better footing. Hang it, Clara, you don't want me to offer you marriage just directly; but if you won't listen to me without, I will marry you whenever you please.'

'I never can marry you,' replied Clara. 'We should be miserable together. And how can you think of it so soon after——'

'You compel me to think of it, Clara. I thought you had more courage. You leave your friend's child to neglect and misery, perhaps to death, because you do not like to be talked about.'

'You should send Lucy to her mother's sister in England. Mrs. Beaufort told me that was her wish.'

'Yes; to a woman who hates me like poison, and who will bring up my child to do the same. Do you think I care so little for her as that? Now, you love my child, you loved her mother, say that you will love me—say that you don't hate me. Clara, give me an answer.'

'I can never love you. I could not do my duty by you, nor by Lucy either. . . . But I am tired; let me go to bed.'

'If this is the last time we are to talk together, I have a great deal more to say; if you will give me another opportunity, I will let you off now. Besides, I must write you out your cheque, and not fly into a passion with it again.' He succeeded in writing it this time, and handed it to her. 'You would be offended if I offered you more than I owe you, or I would have made it double. I am sure you worked hard enough for this paltry sum. Now say, 'thank you,' and give me one smile. That looks a little better. You always thought my wife was too good for me, did you not?'

'Yes, I did,' Clara answered.

'Perhaps she was. I never cared much for her, and I dare say she would have found it out soon; so it is as well that she is taken away. You are different. I would give you far more of your own way than I gave to Mary. And don't fancy

that I should make a bad husband. You have only seen me in a wrong box—I mean, in a false position.'

'Mr. Beaufort,' said Clara, solemnly, 'you would have preferred to keep me here against my will, until you thought I had no alternative but to accept you, whenever you might choose to make me an offer. I consider that you have treated me ungenerously, and I despise you for it. Now that I can escape, you try to move my pity for you and Lucy, and it is selfish. I despise you for that. And, for my own part, I will never marry any man whom I do not love.'

'You must be in love with some one already, or you never would be so scornful. If it is Reginald, I can tell you, he won't have you now. I sounded him to-night; and if he had cared two straws about you, he would have spoken out. And our Dorothy's tongue won't help you to a husband in Adelaide. Why, even these German people are not over nice in their remarks. There will be a pretty tale among the villagers hereabouts.'

'Is this all you have to say to me, sir?' Clara demanded, haughtily. 'I wish you a good night.'

'I am mad,' said Beaufort, intercepting her retreat, and taking her hand. 'Good night, do you say? It is a very bad night to me: to be refused and despised is not good for such a temper as mine.'

'Release me then, sir, while you are tolerable. I may else provoke you again.'

'Then we are friends,' said Beaufort, kissing her hand. 'Let this little conversation be kept quiet, for it is awfully mortifying to me. Good-bye, Clara. I hope you may be happy with some one else. That is the style, is it not? But hang me if I mean it.'

Clara made her escape, as he muttered these words, heartily thankful that her last interview with him was over. She was too engrossed with her own varied excitement on this eventful day, to think of poor little Lucy, till she got into bed, and felt her nestling in her arms. On the morrow, she must leave her to strangers. There was no alternative; but surely even these German people would be kind to the little motherless child; and when she herself was away, Lucy would take to them more kindly. Clara did not believe Mr. Beaufort's account of the English aunt; for his wife's description was very different; and it was probable his story was invented, in the hope of persuading her to stay with him. Still, her heart grieved for the baby; and, amidst her broken and restless slumbers, she had visions of its mother entreating her to remain at the Barn, and take care of Lucy; and when she tried to explain to the phantom why she was obliged to go, the effort to find words always awoke her.

Escape

Mrs. Duncanson had breakfast ready before daylight, and Beaufort was up to see Clara away. He sat sulkily beside the travellers, and would neither speak himself, nor allow them to speak with any degree of freedom.

'Mr. Reginald,' Clara said, 'I wish you would tell Fritz's wife and Carolina how anxious I feel about Lucy, before we go. Carolina must sleep with her at nights now, and take great care to keep her warm, for she is naturally of a cold temperament.'

'Caught that of you, I expect!' cried Beaufort. 'Fritz, saddle grey Bess for me, and give Mr. Reginald the two gig-horses. Don't you understand? I suppose I must go to the stable myself. What an idiot the fellow is!'

'Where can Mr. Beaufort be going?' asked Clara. 'I hope not into town with us.'

'I hope not, too,' answered Reginald; 'but he seems in a strange humour, and you look quite afraid of him. You will be safe with your cousins to-night. It is a promising morning, and these brown horses of Beaufort's are famous ones to go. We shall be in town before sundown.'

When Beaufort returned with the horse, Reginald asked him where he was bound for.

'As far as the gate with you, at any rate; afterwards I shall be guided by circumstances. You have not bid Lucy good-bye, yet, Clara; and I don't think you will before me.'

'God bless you, darling,' Clara said, kissing her late charge fondly, while her tears fell on its face.

'Now let *me* hand you in,' said Beaufort. 'Look in my face, girl. I am not going to eat you. There are two roads when we come to the gate—north and south. Which direction do you take?'

'South, of course,' Clara answered.

'And shall I take the same road?'

'You have no business in town.'

'None, but to see you safe there.'

'Mr. Reginald and Mrs. Duncanson can do that, without taking you away from your home and your child. I do not need—I do not desire your escort.'

'Then I go north. Good-bye, Clara. Reginald, you must call as you return for your own horses. I do not mean to spare Bess to-day.' And so saying, Mr. Beaufort rode off at a furious rate.

Clara drew a long breath, and composed herself. The last peep at the Barn was sad; but in a short time the fresh air, the spirited horses, and the prospect of returning home to Adelaide, made her heart light and her voice cheerful.

'You have left the north without ever seeing Taringa,' said Reginald. 'It was an old promise of poor Mrs. Beaufort's,

that she would take me by surprise some day, and, of course, you would have accompanied her.'

'I suppose I have missed a great treat,' said Clara. 'Mrs. Duncanson calls it 'a bonnie bit.''

'It has little artificial beauty to boast of, for I have been too lazy to improve it; but it is prettily situated, and might be made a very beautiful place. I fancy that at present lady-visitors would consider it desolate enough. I dare say, you conceive yourself as having been fairly in the bush, and knowing all about it; but, as you have never been at a sheep-station, or seen what wretched lives stock-holders who are not blessed with wives, lead in their lonely huts, you really cannot say that you have been in the bush at all.'

'I have been quite far enough out of town surely—farther than any of my cousins, although they have been so many years in the colony; for they have never been beyond Mr. Hodges' farm.'

'By-the-bye, is there not some talk of a marriage between George Elliot and Miss Hodges?' asked Reginald.

'I think nothing is yet settled; but it is very likely. I know he is attached to her, and I fancied more than twelve months ago that she liked one of the brothers. How Miss Withering used to watch her in those days!'

'What a dreadful woman that was!' said Reginald. 'Poor Mr. Macnab! I think his cup of life must be intensely bitter.'

In spite of the badness of the roads, good horses and a good driver made Clara feel as confident and secure as if she had been in a first-class railway-carriage at home. In her present frame of mind the jolting was rather agreeable than otherwise; but the occasional interruptions of conversation caused by a bad gully or an awkward piece of 'Bay of Biscay ground,' gave her time to remember how strangely she had received Reginald on the preceding day, when he had come upon her as if from the dead; and the recollection brought some internal confusion.

'What could he think of me?' she asked herself. 'Could he suppose it was only joy? I certainly told him I was beside myself at the time, and I hope and trust he believed me.'

CHAPTER XX

THE ECHUNGA DIGGINGS

'I suppose you have heard the news, sir,' said the host of an inn where they stopped to rest for an hour; 'it is going over the country like wildfire.'

'The only news I have heard lately is, that I was drowned,' Reginald answered; 'and I should advise you not to believe that. Is there anything else more trustworthy?'

'The diggings, sir!—the new diggings at Echunga, on the Onkaparinga, sir! The Colonial Secretary has been up with a party to see if it was not all a hoax, and every hole they dug they found gold in—yes, every single individual spadeful, sir. The place is nice and handy to town, and a made road all the way; so we may yet beat the Port Phillip folks hollow, and see them coming over in thousands to have a look at our gold fields, sir. It don't do me any good, for here I am in the wrong direction altogether; but there will be nice pickings for my brother host at Echunga, sir. But here comes a gentleman from Adelaide; you'll excuse me, sir; but I must go and get the latest particulars of this grand discovery, sir. Would you not like to inquire for yourself, sir?'

'I have heard enough for the present,' replied Reginald. 'I am on my way to Adelaide myself, and shall hear all about it there. We want dinner as soon as possible. These new diggings will not suit me, Miss Morison; where are we poor sheep-farmers to find servants, when one gold field is discovered after another, and now in such a tempting proximity to town?'

'There have been many hoaxes already,' suggested Clara; 'perhaps this is one, too, though our host talks very positively.'

'Well, the news need not take away our appetites, at all events,' said Reginald. 'Mrs. Duncanson, I have done an ill thing in bringing you to town; your head will be turned with

this excitement, and you will turn Sandy's too when you get back.'

'We appointed to bide out the year, sir,' answered Mrs. Duncanson; 'an' it would be queer diggins that turned us frae our solemn engagement. Na, na, I hae nae broo o' leaving a gude place an' a gude maister, just because a hantle fule-bodies sets off wi' tin milk-pans an' shules, saying they're gaun to mak their fortunes howking holes.'

The country did not look quite so beautiful as it had done when Clara went out to the north; there were too many muddy lagoons and long marshes, where the points of the grass were alone visible over the surface of the water; and the road itself was deep in mud; but Clara was going home, and was satisfied with everything.

'There is Adelaide,' said Reginald, suddenly; 'do you see the church on North Adelaide hill?—does not your heart warm to the dear dirty town, Miss Morison?'

'Yes, indeed;' and Clara gazed on the still distant church with delighted eyes. 'Yes, indeed; and to the people there, too.'

'Where do you wish to be landed, Mrs. Duncanson?' continued Reginald, as they drew nearer.

'At my gude-brither's, where ye cam' for me to tak' me oot; he's been langer settled in the place, an' he'll be glad to hear news o' Sandy an' the bairns.'

'That is near the stable where I put up my horses, so I will take Miss Morison home first.'

Clara's heart beat violently when at last she alighted; she stood at the French window for a minute before she could open it or knock. She saw Margaret walking up and down the parlour in a state of high excitement, while George, sitting on the sofa, was apparently endeavouring to pacify her, but to no purpose.

'Don't tell me, George,' Margaret was in fact saying, 'that if they turn out productive it will be all for the best. What do I care about its being good for business? You must be degenerating yourself, or you would not bring forward such an argument.'

'Margaret!' said Clara, here opening the door, 'will you give me a home again, now I need one?'

'Clara! you!'—and the cousins were locked in each other's arms. 'Where are you from?—how have you come?' Margaret asked quickly, after the first embrace.

'Mr. Reginald has brought me; he is at the door.'

'And Mrs. Beaufort?'

'She died ten days ago.'

'Poor thing!—poor thing! And the poor little baby! But

why have you been so long? Mr. Reginald promised to bring you home as soon as you wished it, and that must have been a week ago.'

'Yes; but Mr. Reginald has had an accident, and is still far from well.'

George was out of the house before this was said, to invite Reginald to come in; but the latter said he must take Mrs. Duncanson to her brother's.

'George will do that for you,' said Margaret, following to the door; 'and also put up your horses. Call at Mrs. Plummer's as you come back, George, and bring home Annie; she will be quite overjoyed to hear who has come.'

Clara seemed to recognise every trifle at a glance, and was struck by one novelty.

'Does the kitchen fire smoke,' she asked, 'that you have got the black kettle on in the parlour?'

'No, Clara, not at all; it is all these Echunga diggings,' answered Margaret, with reviving excitement. 'You will find cold comfort here, after your long drive.' And Margaret gave a hasty blow with the bellows, and began to walk about the room as before. 'But I will not pay five pounds ten for a load of wood to any man. What need had we of diggings here, in the name of all that is rational? Our people were just beginning to settle down for the winter; carpenters and shoemakers were busy at their trades; and now they are all seized with the gold fever again, and are leaving us to whistle for the necessaries of life. I counted twenty people passing this window to-day, with pannikins, and shovels, and milk-pans; all of whom I knew to be tradesmen earning easily ten shillings a-day. Wood has been more than double the old prices all this winter, and we thought it very dear at two pounds the load; but only yesterday I was asked five pounds ten, for some no larger than we got for fourteen shillings when you were with us, and quite green besides.'

'It is an enormous price,' said Clara.

'George was saying we could as well afford the high price now, as we could the fourteen shillings when they were at the diggings; but I know how many families who cannot, and I will not pay it, on principle. We have a few large logs in the yard; George and Gilbert must just warm themselves in the morning with splitting them; and we may warm ourselves with blowing the bellows; for it is the 'dourest' wood to burn I ever saw in my life.'

'How do you think your cousin is looking, Miss Elliot?' Reginald asked. And Margaret then observed that Clara was very pale.

'But she is tired now,' she said; 'and I have been forgetting to make her take off her bonnet. You must rest on the sofa

while we are away, Mr. Reginald, for you look worse than Clara.'

'Now, Clara,' said Margaret, when they were alone together, 'I know you have a great deal to tell me, but I will not let you say anything till you have answered a question of mine. Can you tell me what is the matter with Annie? I thought she would be all right when her brothers came home, but instead of that, she seems to get worse; and yet I cannot get her to say what ails her.'

'You wrote me you meant to shift for yourself, Margaret, and not live with the rest. Did you mean you were going to be married to the gentleman rumour gives you to?'

'Gives *me* to! What do you mean, Clara? No, I never thought of marriage. My project was to open a school for the poorest children in the colony, and settle myself as the teacher; and I thought of asking you to join me; but then I reflected that it would be almost like taking the veil, and that you might have some entanglement to prevent it.'

'And so *you* have no entanglement at present, Margaret? In short, you are not engaged to William Bell?'

'William Bell! my very good friend, William Bell! Why, Clara, he is three months younger than I am, and —— indeed it is too ridiculous altogether. I have helped to train the boy, and I never could promise to obey him,—nor, in truth, would he ever ask me.'

'Then you must tell Annie so, for I believe her bad health and spirits arise from a struggle between her affection for him and for you.'

'I will tell her so to-night,—I will tell her as soon as she comes home. Oh! Clara, what a weight you have taken from my mind! I am sure William Bell likes her, and if she were to search over all Australia, she never could find a worthier or a better husband. I wish you could relieve my other anxiety about Gilbert as satisfactorily. If he would only settle down to be comfortable with us, I should have nothing more to desire; I would give up my project of the ragged school, and go on with what is perhaps not so useful, but which suits my disposition better.'

'I think Gilbert has the same idea about William Bell, for he hinted as much to me the last night I sat up copying with him.'

'What can have come over my brother and sister to make them fancy I have any concealment with them? I told them at once about Mr. Dent and the widower; when Grace accepted Henry Martin, she came straight to us, and told us all; and now here are Gilbert and Annie finding an absurd mare's-nest, which one question would have exposed. And you think Annie is really fond of William? Well, she must

let him see it, and not be so dreadfully shy. There, you look better now, Clara, with your curls about your face. I hope you have not quite cried your eyes out, or blunted your wit at that wretched Barn, for I want you very much to help me keep Gilbert at home. I have never been able to understand him since he came from the diggings, and I am constantly making blunders. Try, Clara, for my sake, to please him, and to find out what arguments are likely to prevail with him. Add your influence to mine, for it would indeed be a pity if Gilbert Elliot should find no better field for his talent and energy than the gold-fields.'

'What can my influence do if yours fails?' said Clara; 'but I will try.'

Reginald had taken up Margaret's album in her absence, and found in it some very curious notes and abstracts, legal and statistical. Still he did not think her at all unfeminine; there was a basket of stockings which she had been mending, lying on the side-table, the piano on which she had been playing was still open, and when she came in, she put down the tea-things, and cut bread-and-butter with a housewifely air, in which there was nothing alarming.

It was not long before Annie came home with another warm greeting for Clara, in the midst of which Gilbert also arrived.

'Here he is,' Annie cried, 'with the usual papers under his arm. But there shall be no writing done to-night, Gilbert, for Clara has come home; Mr. Reginald has brought her back safe at last.'

'And she is welcome,' said Gilbert. 'I shall soon make you useful again, Clara; you will help me like you used with my copying, for I must go through a great deal of work before I start for the Bendigo again.'

'You will have time to do it all for yourself before then,' Clara answered. 'So you don't think of trying the Adelaide diggings?'

'I may possibly look at them, but I am told it is all puddling work there, and that no great prizes are offered. Besides, one cannot call it going to the diggings to move only twenty miles from home. There is a certain adventure in a trip to Forest Creek, or even to Ballarat, which is utterly wanting in a journey to Echunga.'

' "Far fowls have fair feathers," ' said Margaret. 'But indeed I wish these new diggings were further from town. If they turn out productive, Adelaide will be intolerable, as a residence. If Melbourne, eighty miles from the nearest goldfields, is made so disagreeable and dangerous by them, what will this town be when the diggers can come down in a day,

and will probably favour us with their company every Sunday?'

'Well, Margaret,' said George, 'I have just learned for your satisfaction, that there is not much chance of Echunga rivalling even the Turon. It will be well for us in that case, for it was a respectable thing to say of South Australia, in addition to 'No convicts here,' 'No gold found here.' '

Tea had been but a short time over, when Reginald rose to take leave. They wished him to accept a bed, but he had business, he said, at Handy's. Mr. Haussen was returned, he had heard, and he had a message for him. He must bid them good night.

'Then come and spend to-morrow with us,' said Margaret. 'Come to church with us, and dine here afterwards.'

'That I shall be most happy to do. At present I feel too weary to be good company for such a happy party. Good night, Miss Morison; you look wonderfully well after so long a journey. Good night—good night.'

'I must go to bed,' said Clara, when the door closed after him. 'I am more fatigued than I appear.'

And she retired with Annie, after a repeated 'good night' to the others.

'I want sleep, Annie dear,' she said, when they were together, 'and so I will not sleep with you to-night, for if we begin to talk, we shall lie awake all the night.'

'Yes, you shall be by yourself to-night.—But do you know what Margaret has been telling me? Do you really think Margaret will feel no pain if William ——'

'Nothing but pleasure, Annie. Irresistible as he appears to you, you must not fancy other people have exactly the same taste.'

'But he is so true, so upright, so generous, that one would think even Margaret could wish for nothing more. How good Margaret has been to me!'

CHAPTER XXI

MR. REGINALD DELIVERS SOPHIE'S LETTER

Both Handy and Haussen had been, on the whole, fortunate at the diggings, and brought home about two hundred pounds' worth of gold with them. Handy was lavishing his money in presents to his wife, and in treating his friends; but Mrs. Handy was still doing her best to keep her boarders together, for she saw that her husband's habits of steady industry were completely broken up, and that she must depend henceforward on her own exertions. Haussen was seeking employment, but with very little encouragement from his helpless little wife. She had forgotten all about the cousin who had spent a night in the house, and only remembered, for her husband's information and entertainment, the pretty speeches and compliments which had been paid to her by Harris and other gentlemen. Mrs. Handy was prevented by a certain foreboding from mentioning the visitor, and left it to Reginald to tell the news. It was not till the next morning that he found an opportunity to deliver the letter, and to explain how he had received it. Haussen was much agitated by the tale.

'If I had known—if I could have imagined that I was so near happiness, nothing could have made me swerve from my fidelity,' said he. 'Poor dear Sophie! how did she look? I have not seen her for many years. She is just my own age, and I dare say her appearance may have changed, but her heart is the same—so true, so warm, so unselfish. And I have left her to pine out her life in solitude, toil, and poverty. She waited for me till her youth was over, and she has but a poor chance of settling in life comfortably at thirty-two. You saw her down to the vessel she says, and you showed her kindness. Thank you for it, my good friend. Do you think she will get over this blow?'

'I think she may in time; she, at least, has nothing to reproach herself with.'

'But how did she speak to Maria?' Haussen asked. 'How did they look beside each other?'

'She spoke gently and kindly, and seemed to think Mrs. Haussen pretty and fascinating; but, to my eyes, Miss Werner was much the more attractive of the two; for though she does not look young, she is a very handsome woman, and has a fine manner.'

'I hope she may marry some one better than I am,' said Haussen, sighing, 'and be happier. But, Reginald, I cannot stay here spending money, and doing no good. I must either go out to the country and farm, or go to Melbourne. I should prefer the farm, but Maria has a horror of the bush, so I must set off as soon as possible for Victoria. I think I shall go by the *Sea-bird* on Tuesday.'

'This is a very sudden resolution,' Reginald said. 'Have you consulted your wife about it?'

'It just came into my head this minute; but what good would it do to consult my wife?'

'Will you come to church with me, Mr. Haussen?' said the lady spoken of, tapping at the door of Reginald's room, where he and Haussen were talking German together.

'No, my love, you must pray for me to-day. She has got a new bonnet and mantle, and wants to show them off, Reginald. I am going into the fields with Sophie's letter, and hope I shall not feel savage when I come back.'

'I don't like you to talk that horrid German, Mr. Haussen; it looks as if you did not want me to understand what you say. Well, good-bye, I am off to church; Mr. Bradshaw will only be too glad of the chance of escorting me.'

'I think it will be good to take her to Melbourne, Reginald, away from these foolish people who flatter her too much. So, you are going to church too; but I shall see you at dinner?'

'I am engaged to dine with George Elliot, so I shall not see you again till night.'

William Bell was also dining with the Elliots on this day, and was agreeably surprised at Annie's coming, of her own accord, to sit beside him, asking him questions, and looking to him for attention and conversation. There was a mixture of frankness and timidity in her manner which gave him great encouragement, and made him think that she had quite forgotten Mr. Harris. Annie wished she could forget him, for she felt ashamed of herself whenever a thought of him crossed her mind.

As for Margaret, she would scarcely speak to William at all, and rather overdid her little piece of management. She desired to throw together Gilbert and Clara, and William and Annie; and thus it fell to her to entertain Reginald. But he

was not one to flatter himself that her questions as to the working of the voluntary system in the north, her regrets that there was no church near Taringa, her sympathy with his difficulties in getting shepherds, and her interest in the rising price of wool, expressed any personal feeling. He saw what was in her mind with regard to Clara, and he thought there was no doubt of her success.

'Is there any vessel going home to Britain soon?' asked Clara.

'Yes, there is one expected to sail in a fortnight,' George answered; 'but it is of no use to write by it, when we expect the first steamer in every day.'

'My question did not relate to writing, Clara said; 'but I think of going home to Scotland.'

'Nonsense, Clara,' exclaimed Gilbert; 'don't break our hearts by talking so. I have plenty of writing for you to do, and Margaret has a month's work in store in deciphering her hieroglyphics. And, besides, you cannot mean to leave the colony the same Clara Morison you came.'

'My uncle has written for me, and Susan is very anxious that I should be with her again. I have authority to draw, George; I suppose it can be done through one of the banks?'

'Exchanges are very heavy against England now, Clara,' observed Gilbert. 'Wait till the current of gold flows back upon us coined, and you may get the bill done at par. Your uncle will excuse your delay, if you save him seven per cent. discount.'

'That is an odd reason for staying where I seem unable to earn my living.'

'You are perfectly able to earn your living here,' said Gilbert; 'and you know that when I go to the diggings, you will be wanted to keep Margaret company. I wish you would teach her something new next trip; I have a famous study for her.

'What is that?' asked Margaret, eagerly; 'what would you like me to learn?'

'I want you to learn that graphic style of describing people and characters which Clara excels in. She hit off the people of the north to a nicety, Mr. Reginald; the whole bevy of sheep-farmers who visited at Mrs. Beaufort's, and who, I dare say, thought they made themselves vastly agreeable to her, have been dissected in masterly style. I do not suppose I have escaped myself; and as for you. . . .'

'Stop, Gilbert,' said Clara. 'You may imagine my opinion of yourself, if you please; but you have no right to meddle with other people. I really think I ought to go back to my uncle; he has a situation ready for me in the Highlands.'

'You will not like Scotland after being here nearly two

years, Clara,' Gilbert urged. 'You may shake your head, and fancy you have had misery enough in Australia; but by-and-bye you would be sorry you ever left the colony of colonies, as Annie calls it.'

'Why, then, are you so anxious to leave it yourself, Gilbert?' Clara asked.

'Oh,' was the answer, 'you know that I only go in the hope of returning with gold enough to increase my influence, and to improve my prospects.'

'But that is very commonplace,' said Clara. 'Everybody looks for advancement by means of money: it would be much more distinguished—much more striking—to trust to prudence and talent. And I am sure it would be pleasanter, when you grow old, to have people date your rise from the time when you made an eloquent speech or an important reform, than from the day when you brought home a large bag full of nuggets from the gold-fields.'

'What makes you always throw law in my teeth, Clara? Have you ever looked through my books?—I am sure, if you have, you must have been shocked at the amount of rubbish you found in them.'

'Which a clever man might do something towards clearing away,' Clara said. 'A colonial lawyer has great advantages in that respect, for antiquated abuses cannot be looked on with the same reverence here as in the mother country.'

'Would you like to learn to engross, Clara? We want a good hand, and I could find you employment; I hate the thing myself, I am so very slow; but you are clever with the pen, and I have no doubt that you would very soon do it in first-rate style.'

'I have a fancy for everything unladylike, and of course should like to learn it. And there is another thing I wish to learn—that is, to speak German; for I have suffered from my inability.'

'I have nearly forgotten the little I ever knew,' said Gilbert; 'but I think it is pretty clear, from all this, that you are not going away to Scotland.'

'And you, Gilbert, I hope, are not going to the Bendigo either,' observed Margaret, who had been delighted with the force of Clara's arguments.

'You are much too strong for me, now you have Clara to back you,' Gilbert answered. 'I must own that at present I have very little desire to go to the diggings; I must fortify myself with an hour's solitude, and consider how ill used I am, how little I am appreciated, and how slowly I can rise, before I am fit for another battle.'

'Does he look like an ill-used man?' said Annie to William

Bell. 'He has his own way far more than George has, and I am sure he does not deserve it.'

'Annie upon me, too!' said Gilbert, trying to make round eyes. 'The first time she has condescended to notice me to-day, and now *so* severe.'

'I fancy you must be in the wrong,' observed Reginald, 'for you seem always apprehensive of an attack.'

The conversation now turned upon the requisites of sermons, and Reginald saw that Gilbert and Clara differed in respect to what constituted a good one. The poetical element in her mind had no counterpart in her cousin's, and the discordance seemed to give Gilbert all the more to say, and increased spirit to say it well; so that the good-humoured contest served to show them both to advantage. Gilbert treated Clara's opinions with respect and tenderness, even while he dissented from them; he seemed to remember all she had said in the week after his return from the diggings; and he appeared to know her letters by heart. Clara herself thought him improved since they parted; he was more frank and agreeable, though he certainly talked too much to her, and did not treat Reginald with sufficient attention.

After tea, Reginald accompanied the rest to church, but was not able to offer Clara his arm, as Gilbert was before him, and walked with her far in advance of the others. His conversation with Margaret flagged sadly, and yet she talked well—it was better Sunday conversation than he had heard all day—but an idea that his interest with Clara was declining, a fancy that even her friendship might cool under the new influences around her, made him so absent and blundering that Margaret wondered why Clara had ever called him the best of Sunday companions.

CHAPTER XXII

A RELEASE

Reginald went out to his station on the following day. Little dreaming that Clara was agitated by a struggle very similar to his own—a struggle between affection and duty—he hoped that the solitude of Taringa would calm down the fever of his mind. Months had now passed since he heard from Julia; he no longer doubted her indifference; he had written twice to her since he received her last letter, explaining that, in the position of the colony, it was impossible for him to go home even for a short time; and also telling her that owing to the rise in wages, and all other expenses, he was now a much poorer man than he had been. But at that time every body in the colony was complaining of the non-arrival of letters, for the sailing vessels all went round by Melbourne, where their seamen deserted for the diggings, and they were often detained for months; while the government steamers varied in their passages from three months to five, and thus made things very little better. So on the present occasion the *Australian* had been long overdue; and when at last it arrived, Reginald had subsided into such a state of gloomy indifference, that he let several days pass before he sent for his letters.

'The *Australian* is in, sir,' said Duncanson, when he came back; 'an' I ha'e gotten a muckle letter for ye, an' paid just the dooble price for it. It's no like at hame, where sic a letter would only cost tippence, but to be sure it comes a lang way. There's a little ane forbye.'

Reginald tore open the little letter first, for it was from Julia; and read thus:—

'SIR,—I beg to set you free from an engagement which I can easily see makes you miserable. It has given me no happiness either, and though your mother is grieved, and your

sisters are indignant, I think you owe me thanks for this decisive step.

'I wish you happy with some one better suited to you than I am, and remain,

'Your sincere friend,
JULIA MARSTON.'

Reginald could not help smiling at this curt little note, and wondering if any one had dictated it to the writer; it was so unlike her usual style. But, relieved and amused as he was, the cavalier manner of the dismissal was still somewhat mortifying.

The other letter was partly from Alice, and partly from Jane; and there was also a short letter from Reginald's mother, which he read first, but which, though full of pity for his disappointment, and of wonder at Julia's conduct, explained nothing. 'Alice puts most news into her letters; I will see what she says.' Alice did not extenuate what had occurred.

'You are not only rejected,' she wrote, after some preliminary lamentation, 'but rejected in favour of another; and that other, your friend, Mr. Dent! It was partly our own fault, for we liked him and encouraged him to visit us; and our mother was so pleased at his settling in the neighbourhood—all on your account;—but had we known how it was to turn out, I am sure we should never have spoken to him.'

* * * * * * *

'I believe he never declared himself till he heard the news of the gold discoveries; and then he went and told Julia that everybody in South Australia, and the sheep-farmers in particular, were utterly ruined; and that the colony was being deserted as fast as the ships could convey people away. I believe he told her also that his own income was materially lessened by the stopping of the Burra mine in the crisis. I suppose she looked concerned; but at any rate, somehow or another, he managed to make a proposal; and what do you think was her answer? she told him that if she had not been entangled in a childish engagement to you, she would have been happy to accept him even with half his former means! A childish engagement, indeed!'

Reginald, reading the letter in a vein wholly different from that of the writer, hurried rapidly over the rest of the story —how Mr. Dent applied to Julia's friends; how they protested against the proposed breach of faith; and how the suitor only became more pressing in consequence; until he read that the matter ended in an elopement—when he almost clapped his hands, and tossing the letter on the table, called eagerly to Duncanson for the newspapers.

'Walth o' papers, sir, half a pokefu. There's a lot o' the

picture papers amang them; I put them a' aneath the book shelves.'

The 'Illustrated London News' was however tossed heedlessly aside; even the 'Evening Mail' was not looked at; while Reginald sought hastily for the insignificant-looking Adelaide papers, and glanced eagerly over their shipping news.—'The *Petrel* has taken all her cargo and passengers on board, and will clear out to-morrow.'—But to-morrow was yesterday, and no list of passengers was given.—Could Clara have gone to Scotland without letting him know? had he been treated as a common acquaintance, and left to glean the intelligence from the newspapers?—And now he was free.—Why had not Julia released him months ago? why did she wait for a better offer before she told him her engagement was a bondage?— Why had not the steamer kept its time, that he might have declared himself to Clara when her heart was softened to him by gratitude and hope, when her kisses were on his hands, and her blessings rising to Heaven for him?— Then the thought of Gilbert flashed across his mind; then again he recalled Clara's apparent determination to leave the unfriendly colony; thinking, with a sigh, that he himself had not urged her to stay. He was wondering if it would still be of any use to go into town and try his fate; and imagining his feelings if he should find that Clara had gone off in the hateful *Petrel;* when he heard a vehicle of some kind approaching his house. Hurrying to the door, he saw Mr. Hodges alighting from his gig; Minnie was with him, but waited to know if Reginald could give tired travellers a night's lodging.

'Minnie and I meant to have reached the Burra to-night,' said Mr. Hodges; 'but the roads are too heavy; and so we are come to ask you for some sort of bush accommodation.'

'I shall be too happy,' Reginald answered. 'We have plenty of room, but Miss Hodges must not expect elegance.'

'Oh! I am so tired!' exclaimed Minnie, when she was seated in the easy chair by the fire. 'It was a silly thing of me to come with papa, but he had business at the Burra, and I had such a wish to see Grace. Why, this is a palace of a sheepstation, Mr. Reginald. Books, pictures, fire-irons, why you only want paper-hangings and a carpet, to be equal to us, who do not consider ourselves bush people at all. I shall never allow again that you bachelor sheep-farmers deserve any pity; you can sit here and smoke your independent pipe; you have a pretty cat and two handsome dogs for company; and what can you want more?'

'Well, some few things,' Reginald said, smiling; 'but you have brought a little sunshine with you, and my poor station looks all the brighter for it. Have you come across the country?'

A Release

'Oh no! we came by Adelaide,' replied Mr. Hodges. 'Minnie does not mind tiring the horse, and she has so many dear friends in town, she will not miss any opportunity of seeing them. I expect her to cut her country connexions altogether very soon.'

Minnie blushed, and said something about the absurdity of saving five or ten miles, at the expense of having worse roads and no bridges. Reginald, who was very anxious to know all about her dear friends in town, tried to speak indifferently, as he asked how they had left the Elliots.

'All well,' answered Minnie; 'everything going on delightfully; William Bell has at last summoned resolution to propose to Annie, and she has not said 'no.' I never saw her looking so well; she was always a very pretty creature, but now she looks so happy that I think her positively beautiful; and as for him, he is really the pleasantest fellow I ever saw.'

'Except——' said her father.

'Don't interrupt me, papa, please; it is to be at least a twelvemonth's engagement, as William wishes to be more settled in business before he marries. Our poor Charley is sadly cast down, and declares he will not go to the marriage, even if he is asked; but I expect that before a year has passed, master Charley will have got over his disappointment, and be very glad of an invitation.'

'And how is— Miss Margaret making up her mind to——' Reginald hesitated.

'To 'wearing green stockings?'' said Minnie. 'More than philosophically, delightfully. She knows Annie will be happy, and she has been rather anxious about her of late. Clara has done them all good. I rather think she poked up William Bell to make the offer; and now she is teasing Gilbert out of his determination to go to the diggings. She has learned to engross, and is beginning to teach him short-hand; Margaret will be able to keep it up when Clara has gone.'

'Gone!' exclaimed Reginald, 'gone where? Not to Scotland, I hope!'

'Oh no! the Elliots will not spare her, though her poor sister at home has written for her quite piteously. And Mrs. Bantam has written to her too, offering her a handsome salary if she will go over to Melbourne to be her factotum; but to that Margaret objected, saying that the position of half-servant, half-companion, is not at all comfortable.'

'Where is she going, then?' asked Reginald, with the greatest impatience.

'Minnie takes a long time to tell a plain story,' said her father; 'but it is evident enough that self-willed Maggie Elliot does not wish her pretty little cousin to leave the colony, and anybody, with common penetration, can easily see why. She

and all of us are anxious that Gilbert should not go back to the diggings again, and take my Charley, when I want the boy so badly at home; and so if Miss Morison can help Maggie to fix him to the law—and he is sure to make a figure there, for I never saw such a clear head for business in so young a man; and he has a good memory, and great quickness both in speaking and thinking, so that I think his success may be looked on as certain—if Miss Morison can help to do this, it will be a very good thing for everybody. And I for one think it likely enough she will be Mrs. Gilbert Elliot, shortly after Gilbert is out of his time.'

'Papa is a great deal more tedious than I am,' said Minnie. 'The fact is, that we have prevailed upon Clara to come out as governess to us; and as papa thinks he shall be able to part with her in five or six years, he good-naturedly gives her to Gilbert, as soon as it is convenient for himself. I think it likely enough myself, but it is rather premature to speak of it. Who would have thought, when we first saw the quiet little servant-girl at Mrs. Bantam's, that she was by-and-bye to become such an important person in our eyes?—at least in mine; I must beg pardon for including you.'

'I thought that you taught your brothers and sisters yourself,' Reginald said, vainly trying to suppress a sigh.

'Oh, they have got much too clever for me, now,' cried Minnie.

'That's a good joke,' said her father; 'a fine excuse for your deserting them! It is no secret Reginald—and I rather enjoy telling it—that my girl is going to marry George Elliot in six weeks; and though, of course, I shall miss her, I don't think I shall ever repent giving her to one we have known so long, and never heard anything against. He is getting into an excellent business, and will by-and-bye take a lead in the colony, I expect.'

Reginald acknowledged that he had already had his suspicions of an attachment between the young people; congratulating Mr. Hodges on his son-in-law elect, and wishing Minnie every happiness. Minnie was proud of her lover, and looked more radiant than ever. Her father and Reginald began to talk over the English news, and to find the last quotations in the previously despised papers; and then to discuss the expense of their respective sheep-shearings; while she looked through the 'Illustrated News' for the fashions, to see if she could hit on something pretty for her wedding-dress. But she soon laid down the papers, and sat gazing at the cheerful fire, pondering over her old random supposition that Reginald was engaged to some lady at home, of which she had been reminded by the hurried and agitated manner in which he crumpled his letters into his pocket when she entered with her father. This idea,

A Release

however, did not engross her long; she soon let her thoughts turn to their habitual subject, which, of course, was George Elliot; and drew pictures in her imagination far finer than any either painted or engraved.

She made tea for the party; and Reginald could not help thinking how well Clara managed it, and how pretty she would look sitting in that place as mistress of the house. Minnie's praises of Taringa were encouraging; and, after all, there had not been many weeks for Gilbert to make his way with Clara, and he, Reginald, was a much older acquaintance. Clara had asked his advice, she had trusted to his protection. He would go to town as soon as his guests left him, and see how she looked, at any rate. And if unable to obtain a private interview with her, he would write his proposal, and explain why it had been so long delayed.

Mr. Hodges and Minnie retired in good time, so that about ten o'clock Reginald found himself alone, trying to concoct a letter to Clara, but long failing to satisfy himself. His sixth attempt proved no better than his first, but he adopted it in despair.

Breakfast at Taringa was early enough to please even Mr. Hodges; and as Minnie was anxious to get to Mrs. Martin's in good time, they started immediately it was over. Reginald said that he must go into Adelaide, as he was short of wool-bags, and also wanted to hire two additional hands; so he set off at the same time with his guests.

'Papa,' said Minnie, as they drove away on their separate roads, 'I am afraid you will have to advertise for a governess, for I am rather doubtful about Clara Morison.'

CHAPTER XXIII

BROTHER AND SISTER

On the afternoon of that same day, it happened that Annie Elliot had appointed to take a walk with William Bell, who was to come for her at four o'clock. Gilbert declared he must have a walk, too, for he felt completely smoke-dried, with being so much in-doors all winter, and the weather was now so beautiful that it almost made him feel romantic. Would his cousin Clara favour him with her company? But Clara had a letter to write to her sister, announcing her change of destination, and the *Petrel* was positively to sail to-morrow. So Margaret offered to accompany him, saying she should like it above all things, as she had never been out with Gilbert since he came from the diggings.

William Bell came punctually to his hour, and both Margaret and Clara were delighted to see Annie's happy face turned up with confidence towards his, as they went arm-in-arm out of the gate towards the hills. But Margaret soon became impatient for the arrival of Gilbert.

'I have not had a walk with him for many months,' she said to Clara; 'and I have a great deal to say to him that I cannot say before these foolish lovers, or even before you, Clara. I hope you do not mind being left by yourself, and indeed, I daresay you will like the quiet to write in. I suppose you find it easy enough to write home to your sister, having left her so recently. But I find it hard work to write to people who remember me a mere child, and of whom my own recollections are rather dim. I am obliged to put a great deal of politics into my letters, Clara, for want of anything else to say; but that is a common habit of mine. Those letters I wrote to you at the Barn were a very poor exchange for yours; but then I was so unhappy, so uncertain, so diffident of everything, that I could not write home news. I will write better letters to you at the south, particularly if Gilbert does not go to the diggings——Ah, here he comes at last! I think

you know where my parasol is, for I certainly do not;—thank you. I will meet him at the gate.'

And Margaret took her brother's arm, and walked silently with him till they were clear of the town.

'Now, Margaret,' then said he, 'I know you have something on your mind, but you seem to want words. Don't be afraid to scold me, for I know I deserve some blame for my absurd jealousy of William Bell's influence with you. That cloud is cleared away now, and I think I can quite appreciate all his good qualities.'

'Gilbert,' Margaret answered, 'I have a great deal to say to you, but I must have time, and you must have patience with me. I know that often, when I have the best intentions in the world, I notwithstanding give offence, because I want tact and discernment; but surely there need be no half-hints or beating about the bush between brother and sister; particularly between such a brother and sister as we are. I have always thought that such a family as ours forms a valuable element in colonial society; we came here not to make our fortunes and leave the colony forthwith, but to grow up and settle in it; we have all rather more than average abilities; we have had good principles instilled in us from early youth; we have all a deep feeling of our accountability to God for both our private and public conduct; we have all, I think, a love for the country of our adoption, and a wish to serve it; and we are not eager about money—we do not care to make haste to be rich, at least we used to show moderation on this point, though lately I have been grieved to see this passion growing upon you.'

'It is not love of money, Margaret,' said Gilbert, eagerly; 'it is because wealth is the only lever by which we can move our little world. It is because money brings distinction, influence, and authority, and because nothing else can do so. We have no patronage in the colonies; even supposing I became a first-rate lawyer, as I could if I tried, should I ever have a chance of rising to the bench, or even of being advocate-general? I am aware that an equal amount of study in the colony would make a better colonial lawyer or colonial judge than the same study in England; but how few would believe this. Every office is filled by some needy hanger-on of Downing-street; by second or third-rate middle-aged men, who never understand our wants, and never learn to care for our interests. And as for private practice, I am not pettifogging enough or sharp enough about technicalities to succeed well in Adelaide. I admire broad principles, and cannot stoop to a mere ferreting out of verbal errors.'

'But before you are a first-rate lawyer, I expect that things will be changed here. I think that the discovery of these gold-

fields will throw us at once into a more advanced state; I do not mean of morals, but it will bring us improvements in arts and sciences: we shall have steam and railways; towns will grow suddenly into cities; population will increase at an unexampled rate; and not only diggers and speculators will come to our shores, but men of intellect and enterprise. The English government will find out that the surest way to keep her colonies, is to leave them very much to act for themselves. It was the want of patronage, more than the Stamp Act, that lost her America. And, Gilbert, we shall soon be an important nation; you must get into council by-and-bye, and help to clear away the cumbrous and expensive trappings of justice. It is likely that transportation to these colonies will soon be abolished; but the effect of so many criminals having been poured into them wholesale for so many years must be long felt in every part of Australia. If you can make any improvements in our criminal law—if you can make our prison discipline reformatory—if you can do something towards raising our moral standard of education, so that we may not sink in the scale of nations through having been deluged with thieves and pickpockets—you will have lived to a great and useful purpose. Yes, Gilbert, you must get into council, and I must live to see it.'

'As a delegate!' exclaimed Gilbert, scornfully. 'Shall it be mine to implore the most sweet voices of the lieges, with bowing and cringing? to represent all men as naturally equal? and—reckoning the most ignorant mechanics or day-labourers as wise as myself—humbly to beg them to accept of me as their mouth-piece, and return to my constituents every session for instructions what to say, and how to vote?'

'No, you must be a representative, not a delegate,' Margaret answered; 'you need not cringe to the people, but, on the other hand, you must not despise them. They certainly have a right to some courtesy and consideration. You must speak the truth, and deal honestly, and I believe that you will inspire confidence. I was not satisfied with the manner in which the candidates on both sides conducted their electioneering affairs last year. Votes ought to be solicited respectfully by the candidate in person, and not left to an unscrupulous comittee, who are ready to promise anything, but whose promise does not bind the returned member. First deserve public favour, and then ask for it. Be careful now of your reputation; let no one say that you were ever mean or grasping; let no one say that you ever were insincere or dishonest; and by-and-bye your country will be nearly as proud of you as I am. I am glad it is ambition that has made you so restless, and not avarice, for ambition can be turned towards noble objects, while avarice is always of the earth, earthy.'

Brother and Sister

'If I were to go to the diggings, would you stay contentedly with George?' Gilbert asked.

'No; I have thought of opening a school in the most populous part of the town. I suppose I might expect a grant from government, and that even our liberal legislators would not prevent me from teaching religion, as far as a human teacher can instil it. I could afford to teach for very low fees, if I had not a high rent to pay for my school-room, for my wants are very few. The very poorest children I would teach for nothing, for you know, Gilbert, that there is a great lack of labourers in this harvest, and girls are tempted by the high wages offered them, to go to service before they can read their Bibles, and before they have any distinct principles of right and wrong to guide them through life. They are exposed to many dangers and temptations, cast amongst strangers with empty minds and uncultivated consciences; they marry young, and often imprudently; and when children come, they do not know how to teach them anything. 'Religion can be taught only at the mother's knee,' say our liberal members; but if the mothers know nothing of it, what is to become of the children; I suppose it is better that they should perish for lack of knowledge, than that government should lift its finger to save them. But so long as the same government will let me work on sufferance in a cause which it disowns, I suppose I may do so.'

'But you do not like teaching, Margaret,' said Gilbert.

'I can't help my likings or dislikings, Gilbert,' she replied.

'But do you think you will ever make a good teacher, without some natural taste for the occupation? It is dreadful drudgery to teach such ignorant and tiresome children as you propose to instruct. You will meet with nothing but ingratitude from your pupils and their parents, and you will perhaps hear the inspector say, that Miss Elliot is in great want of training, and that she has apparently taken up the business for a livelihood, as she has neither the acquired skill nor the natural talent requisite to success. To think that *you,* who have never been found fault with in your life—*you,* who are so admired and honoured in your own family, should be subjected to such remarks! The man might recommend you to go to a normal school!'

Margaret's colour had changed several times during her brother's speech. She put her hand to her heart, as she answered—

'Perhaps the best thing I could do would be to go to a normal school, but there is none within reach. I must do something more interesting than washing dishes and sweeping floors,—very good occupations in their way, but not enough to fill my mind. I have been grieved at my distaste to teaching, and that at twenty-five I am not so pliant as I was at eighteen;

but since I have lost the labour of the last few years,—for it is only through you that my legal knowledge can be of any avail—I must bend myself to the only career now open to me, and undertake a sort of ragged school.'

'Have you spoken to Clara of this strange resolution?' Gilbert asked.

'Yes; I thought at first of her joining me, but as it might hurt her prospects of settling in life, I have recommended her to go to Mrs. Hodges' instead.—I thought Clara might have influenced you, Gilbert; she is very averse to your going back to Bendigo. You are fond of Clara; are you not?'

'Yes; she is a very nice girl.'

'Are you not in love with her, Gilbert? Look into your heart, and tell me truly; she is a sister to me already, and my most earnest wish is, that by-and-bye she should be your wife.'

'Why, Margaret, I thought that you disapproved of cousins marrying.'

'But you are once removed on both sides of the house; so that is a very trifling objection.'

'But really I am not in love with her at all. She is a very clever girl, and a very charming girl, but she is too clear-sighted for me. She sees all my faults far better than you can do, and will never love me half so well. Besides, I have no idea of entangling myself in a long engagement.'

'Ah!' said Margaret, in a disappointed tone, 'I have been mistaken; I see. I am very sorry, for I thought you would take Clara's advice if you loved her.'

'And cannot I take yours, when I love you, my dear sister? Did you really think that a little chit of a cousin, whom I have only known for a few weeks, could do more with me than the sister I am so proud of? I have news for you, Margaret; Mr. Hastings offered me my articles to-day; I suppose he does not want me to go just now, because he begins to find my head useful, and two of the other clerks have given notice to leave next week. I said that I would give him an answer to-morrow; and I wish to consult you about it. It is really a consideration to me, that in throwing law overboard, I throw away the fruits of your years of patient study; and though five years is a long time to wait before our knowledge becomes available, we shall be all the more thorough lawyers when we do begin. Now, in the first place, we must consider our ways and means; we must make sure that we have enough to live on during our probation. Interest is coming down, and all the necessaries of life are rising, so that my four hundred pounds is a very poor thing to depend on, and the interest you can expect for your own money will not nearly keep you even in dress.'

'I am not a bad manager,' Margaret said; 'but I think we must live by ourselves, and leave George and his wife here;

for if you are to study hard, it will be dull for them. We must have a small cottage to ourselves and our books. Oh! Gilbert, how happy you make me! I have nothing now to wish for.'

'Except that I should marry Clara; perhaps in time, when I can afford it, I may foster a little attachment, for she is really a pretty creature, and you love her so much. But do you never think of marrying yourself?'

'I think I am past all danger of falling in love now, and certainly I will not desert you while you are in your articles. Poor Clara!'

'What are you pitying her for? Do you think she likes me? How much you are mistaken! Did you not observe how miserable I made Reginald when he brought her into town, by talking and flirting with her? How I did enjoy it!'

'It was heartless in you, Gilbert. You mean me to understand that you thought he was in love with Clara, and that you tried to wound him. You shock me.'

'It served him right,' said Gilbert. 'There had he been visiting constantly at the Barn, listening to Clara's sermons, and praising them, going to the post for her, asking her opinion about books, quoting poetry, very likely opening to her his religious opinions and his religious difficulties, till poor Clara came home with her heart considerably touched, and all the while he, Mr. Charles Reginald, had never dreamed of proposing to a girl who had been once at service. I quite enjoyed making him wretched.'

'Cowardly—unmanly!' exclaimed Margaret, indignantly; 'I thought better things of Charles Reginald; but Carlyle and German philosophy only make men lip-valiant. Clara is his equal in every sense; she is superior to him in tact; she has youth and beauty in her favour; and yet, because circumstances once forced her to earn her bread by honest labour, he considers it would be stooping too low to ask her to make him happy. And happy she would make him! He could not have been in love with her, or so slight an obstacle would not have prevented a declaration.'

'You seem to know more about love than I do,' said Gilbert. 'I merely speak from my own observations, which I think are correct.'

'I am afraid they are correct,' answered Margaret. 'But I must open Clara's eyes, and show her that Reginald is only a creature of conventionalism after all. And I have been praising him so much to her lately—he understands the currency, is not lukewarm in his politics, is a member of the church of England without being either indifferent or bigoted, agrees with me on the voluntary question, likes a good sermon, is a kind master, a good neighbour, and a valuable friend. Oh!

Gilbert, surely you must be mistaken; he could never be so cruel to Clara as you say.'

'Well, let us hope so,' said Gilbert. 'But it is getting late, we must go home now.'

Margaret's mind was confused between joy and sorrow; joy that Gilbert had been so reasonable and kind, and that he was restored to her still dearer from the temporary alienation; and sorrow that Reginald was so unworthy of her friendship and poor Clara's love.

CHAPTER XXIV

CONCLUSION

Clara had scarcely settled to her letter after Margaret had gone, when Reginald arrived. He was surprised to find her alone, and though they had often been *tête-à-tête* before, he felt this meeting to be at once most embarrassing and most happy. He took a few wild flowers from his button-hole and offered them to Clara.

'They are the first of the season,' he said. 'I picked them on that sunny bank near the Barn. I looked in and saw Lucy; and the blue flower was gathered under poor Mrs. Beaufort's bedroom window. You remember the bush.'

Clara tied the flowers together with a thread, and fastened them in her bosom.

'How is little Lucy?' she asked.

'Quite well; Carolina seems to have got very fond of her now; and she has taken more kindly to Carolina. I did not see Beaufort; I believe he is in town.'

'I am glad to hear such good news of Lucy,' said Clara; and she could not think of anything else to say. Reginald, too, looked at her without speaking, which was very strange, for they had always had topics enough and to spare, to discuss. After a long pause he inquired to whom she was writing.

'To Susan, my sister. The *Petrel* has been delayed for want of hands, and thus I have had time to change my mind about going home, and shall send my letter by the ship I thought of going in myself. I am going as governess to Mrs. Hodges. Minnie is to be married to George in six weeks, and I hope to be at the marriage before I go.'

'Are you sure that teaching is your vocation?' Reginald asked. 'I have heard you say that you were more theoretic than practical, and that you doubted your capacity for teaching.'

'How can I ever be practical if I have no practice? Do not

throw cold water on my projects when I mean to be so good, Mr. Reginald. If teaching is not my vocation, what else can I do? I am so unfortunate as to be a woman, and my sphere is very limited. Surely you would not have me to go to service again.'

'No,' said Reginald, in an agitated voice; 'but you have such admirable qualities for a delightful companion, that it seems like throwing your gifts away to go among children.'

'The lady is coming,' thought Clara; 'but I will be no companion of hers. I do not like,' said she, aloud, 'to go to a situation where I have no tangible services to perform; and if I had not been also sick nurse and nursemaid at the Barn, I would not have gone as companion to Mrs. Beaufort. I do not think I should be at all a pleasant companion to healthy people.' And Clara pouted her pretty mouth, and tried to look cross.

'Clara,' said he, 'I really want you for a companion at Taringa.'

'No. Mrs. Reginald ought to be enough for you, and you for her. I will be a governess.'

'Yes; and teach me many things. Mrs. Reginald would indeed be enough for me if you were she. Tell me, Clara, should I be enough for you? I am in earnest—Clara, will you marry me?'

'What would Miss Julia Marston say to such a proposal, sir?' said Clara, haughtily.

'Julia Marston is now Mrs. Dent, and has no right to give any opinion as to my affairs. I have been jilted, Clara. My handsome bride has been too happy to accept your cousin Margaret's rejected suitor, and, thank God, I am free. This declaration would have come long ago, but that I was bound to an indifferent and unloving woman. It is not from any caprice I ask your hand; it is from the deep conviction that you only, of all women in the world, can make me happy; and if you will trust me with your happiness, I will guard it as my own. You may find younger, and handsomer, and better men in the world, but I am sure you can never find one who loves you more. Do not refuse me, Clara.'

Clara put her hand in his. 'I am very proud of your love, sir,' she said; 'and I will try to deserve it. You are young enough, and handsome enough, and good enough for me. I can trust myself entirely to you.' Her eyes were full of tears, but she shook them off.

'Have you thought me cold, Clara? Have you thought me indifferent? Have you ever guessed at my struggles? I have suffered a great deal when I could not speak. I only heard of my freedom last night, and you see I have lost no time.'

'I do not wish to conceal anything from you now,' answered

Conclusion

Clara. 'I must confess that I have loved you for a long time; and when I heard of your engagement, on the night before Mrs. Bantam went to Melbourne, it was a dreadful blow to me. I have tried to conquer this attachment, for I knew it was not right; and I have done all I could since I came to town to please Margaret by putting Gilbert in your place, but without any success.'

'Poor Gilbert!' said Reginald.

'Oh! do not pity him; he does not care for me.'

They sat silent for a few minutes.

'I suppose you think me a voiceless lover, Clara. But I was just thinking how differently I feel towards you than I ever did to Julia. I was determined to humour her—to exact nothing from her—to bend my tastes to hers—and to obtrude none of my peculiar idiosyncrasies on her. And now, loving you incomparably more and better than ever I loved her, I feel that I shall be an exacting husband. I shall want a very great deal of your time and attention; I shall tell you every thought as it arises, without asking myself if it is likely to be agreeable to you; I shall insist on your going over old reading and thinking ground with me; I shall bore you with the price of wool, with the health of my sheep, and the conduct of my shepherds; and all because I love you so very much.'

'And I was thinking, Charles, that I was rightly punished for my unwillingness to make sacrifices, by not having one to make to you. Minnie must give up riding, and her beautiful large country garden when she marries; Annie's music and drawing will be laid aside, for her husband will take no interest in them; Grace had to leave all her relations and friends, and banish herself to the Burra;—while I have not a single taste to give up. There is only one little sacrifice that I can make: you may have your pipe whenever and wherever you please; but that is nothing.'

'And you do not consider that you will be banished from your friends and acquaintances when you go to Taringa. Besides, you give me a first love for a second, or perhaps a third;—there is a great sacrifice at once.'

'That was done long ago. And, besides, who cares about being loved first? All I want is to be loved best and longest; and that I know I shall be. But do not expect perfection from me, for I shall want to be humoured sometimes. And, above all, if I do not manage your servants well, do not be angry with me, for you know that is my weak point.'

'Do you think you can manage Mrs. Duncanson?' Reginald asked, smiling.

'I cannot be too confident even of that. And, besides, she may not stay more than the year she engaged with you.'

'But by that time we may get a better manager than my

little Clara. Write to your sister to come and live with you, to help you in this difficult business with her experience. Believe me, your sister will be mine, and my house will be a home to her till she finds one for herself. I will write to her, too, to introduce myself to her as her brother. I am not rich, but matters are looking up with us now; and I do not think I have got an extravagant little wife.'

Clara could not speak her thanks; she was more pleased than surprised at Reginald's kindness.

'I quite grudge to tell my uncle of my happiness,' said she; 'for he will think it is all owing to his excellent management. Now, there were ten thousand chances to one against my making either a comfortable or a happy marriage; and I do believe that if I had not found my cousins, I should have married any one only for a home. I tried hard to steel myself against it; but time would have worn away all my resolutions. And yet my uncle will congratulate himself on his admirable foresight in his views for Clara.'

'I suppose they told you, when you came out, that you were sure to marry to keep a carriage.'

'Of course they did,' said Clara, laughing.

'Then dwell on the fact, that my only vehicle is a spring-cart; that I have only one sitting-room, and that it has no carpet; that we are going to live without any pretensions to style; that you will have to do a great deal of work, and will never go out into company. But when you write to your sister, tell her that we mean to be very happy; and that some improvements can be made at Taringa before she comes; though, when I once see you in it, I shall think it paradise already. Now, Clara, what is the use of delay? We love each other,—you have no parents to make objections,—why should we not be married this week, and go home quietly?'

'That is too sudden,' said Clara. 'I have not made up my mind that I am not dreaming yet. Besides, your busy season is coming on; and if you leave me long by myself at first, I shall be sure to cry a great deal, and that will be a bad beginning. Your shearing will be over in six weeks. Minnie is to be married then; and I would rather be married on the same day.'

'I am sure the shearing need not take six weeks; but your will is sufficient for me.'

'And you must write me little scraps of notes as you find time; and let me get better acquainted with you in that way. But what am I to say to Mrs. Hodges? for this is treating her very ill.'

'Marriage is a sufficient excuse for any breach of contract,' said Reginald.

'But how could Miss Marston prefer Mr. Dent to you?'

Conclusion

'Absence does not make the heart grow fonder, Clara; and he was richer than I was, and saw her often. Here are a few of her letters. And look at my sister Alice's; see how she pities me, and recommends another lady.'

Clara glanced at the letters and defended Miss Marston.

'I dare say,' she concluded, 'Margaret's old admirer will be very happy with your lovely Julia.'

'Not so happy as I am,' said Reginald, pressing Clara's hand.

It reminded her of a passage in her life that happened a few weeks ago, and she blushed deeply. The return of Margaret and Gilbert relieved her from embarrassment.

'I suppose the clergyman can marry two couples at once,' said Reginald; 'for I have prevailed on your cousin to trust herself to me; and I hope that you will make no objection to a double marriage, Miss Elliot?'

'None at all,' said Margaret, looking triumphantly at Gilbert. 'Clara, I wish you happiness both in this world and in the next. I am glad to see that you are not ashamed to be looked at. I wonder if Minnie and you will have courage to let yourselves be proclaimed three times in church. It is not genteel, Mr. Reginald, but it is really the right way of getting married, and we ought to set our faces against those absurd licences.'

'I am completely cut out, after all,' said Gilbert. 'Could you not have broken the news to me by degrees, Clara? You really cannot fancy what I suffer. Well, I am wedded to the law for five years at least, and must submit to my fate.—By the way, I want that indenture, Clara; come and show me where you put it, if you are not too confused. But I fancy you are likely to look in the fireplace, or the teapot.'

'No I am not,' said Clara; 'come and see.'

So they went. Margaret fixed her eyes on Reginald's.

'Why was not this declaration made before, Mr. Reginald?' she asked; 'it would have relieved Clara's mind very much when she was at the Barn.'

'Clara will explain the reason,' he answered. 'Believe me, it was not voluntary on my part.'

'Now, I have really nothing more to wish for,' said Margaret, who seemed far more excited than Clara, and was getting tea in a very confused manner.

'Except the failure of the Echunga diggings,' said Reginald; 'and as I hear that they are turning out very poorly, perhaps that wish will be gratified too.'

When the family party collected for tea, everything was told over and over again. Margaret made a great many blunders, and called everybody by wrong names, but was very happy. Reginald was no longer stiff or reserved, and

he began to think he had been labouring under a delusion in fancying himself a grave man; but Clara knew that his natural character would soon assert itself again. She never could have loved him so well if he had not been so grave and so quiet.

The notes that were written by the lovers somehow expanded into long letters, and were of course very delightful to both parties. The double marriage went off very pleasantly; William Bell's coat fitted him pretty well, and Annie did not cry very immoderately. Mrs. Handy put on the handsomest dress her husband had given her, to do honour to the ceremony, and was firmly persuaded that Clara's marriage was one of her making.

Mrs. Macnab ferreted out that 'Clara, second daughter of the late William Morison, Esq., of Edinburgh,' was the identical Clara who had been at Mrs. Bantam's, and was very much astonished and shocked at the strange marriages that took place in the colonies. 'Gentlemen marry people who are not ladies, and ladies frequently marry persons who are not gentlemen,' she said, looking at her husband in a dissatisfied manner.

Although both Mr. Macnab and Mr. Renton said that Miss Morison was really a lady, she did not think that they knew anything about the subject, and kept her own opinion. Her life is still embittered by the name of the firm—Macnab and Renton—and by the impossibility of getting into good society. She says she has discovered that it is best to keep oneself to oneself at Adelaide, and has got a gloomy place in the country, which she calls 'The Retreat,' where she sits in stately solitude, and whence she would fain drive forth in her gig for a daily airing; but no man is obtainable to drive, and Mr. Macnab goes to his business at such unreasonably early hours, that it is impossible for a lady to be ready to accompany him. However, she makes him drive her about all Sunday, when the poor man would rather rest at home. He has not become at all polished, but is growing rich, in spite of his insatiable wife.

Mr. Renton is on the point of marrying a wealthy widow, but means to 'stick to Mac. like a good one,' even when he is independent.

Mr. Beaufort set off again for the diggings, when Reginald brought his wife to the north, but did not get any further than Melbourne. He returned, bringing a tall, dashing lady as Mrs. Beaufort, who gave herself out to be the widow of a British officer. But it is strongly doubted whether her tale is true; and though she rides about and visits all the unmarried sheep-farmers in the neighbourhood, and is visited by them in return, Reginald will not allow his wife to call

Conclusion

upon her, though both of them long to see the child they loved so well. The German girl has got very fond of the little Lucy, and takes more interest in her than the careless father and step-mother; and it is expected that the English aunt will not be opposed if she offers to bring up her unknown niece.

Mr. Dent's losses on his Burra shares have been more than made up to him by the rise in value of a small property near Melbourne, which he had sold, but which the buyer repudiated as too dear. This land has since been sold out in small allotments, and is becoming a populous little village; while the purchase-money will enable Mr. Dent to hold his head higher than ever; and Julia will have no reason to regret accepting him in his comparative poverty.

When Margaret went up to the north some time after the marriages, to see Clara and Grace, she found that whitewash and paper-hangings had quite divested Taringa of the gloomy appearance Reginald used to ascribe to it. It was really a cheerful, pretty place; the garden was thriving, and under Mrs. Duncanson's able management, the sheep-station began to look like a comfortable farm-house, for the domestic animals were her pride and her pleasure.

Clara was industrious without being a drudge, and it was evident to Margaret that she had all that her heart desired. She was the companion, the friend, the counsellor of her husband, and his life seemed to him but newly begun. All his vague wishes were satisfied, and he rested in the consciousness of entire happiness. Margaret thought his life was too inactive, and his ambition too low; but it suited Clara, though it would not have suited her.

And Grace, too, was happy with her upright, good-humoured husband, who laughed at every annoyance, and was never known to be out of temper. 'Marriages are surely made in heaven, otherwise I might have been allotted to Reginald or Henry, and I never could have made them happy,' thought Margaret.

So, after spending some weeks with those happy married people, and seeing daily how well George and Minnie were suited to each other, Margaret settled herself down with her brother in their cottage, and studied with all the energy of her active nature; without ever fancying that such a home was in store for herself, or that she ever could be anything but an independent old maid. She rejoices over the almost total desertion of the Echunga diggings, and is in hopes that the Victoria gold fields will soon yield nothing more than good wages for hard work; so as to offer no very powerful inducement for South Australians to desert their agricultural and mechanical pursuits. Even Victoria is getting into a

wonderfully orderly state; and Margaret's alarm about the demoralization of the colonies has greatly subsided. The abundance of money has raised the price of almost every description of property, so that Humberstone triumphantly tells Mr. Escott, that if last year he was inclined to halve the value of his property, he must this year double it; for sheep and cattle are now worth looking after in such markets. Still there is a continual ebb and flow of the population to and from Melbourne and the gold fields; and some of the discomforts which afflict Victoria, are now felt pretty severely in South Australia; so that many who have the means, are retreating to England, where people can live for so much less, and where civil and cheap servants are obtainable. Margaret is of opinion that it is cowardly to leave the colony, merely because it is a little uncomfortable; but though she will not acknowledge it, her notion on that point is quite as transcendental as any of those of her pet aversions—Carlyle and the German philosophers. Still, to her and her brother Gilbert, it is the country they are happy to live and work in; and Mr. Plummer has at last perceived that it is time to drop his old reproaches on account of Margaret's letting Gilbert go to the diggings; for he is now as industrious and methodical in his own business, as any member of Mr. Plummer's department of the public service, or of any service, public or private, in the colony.

THE END.

4/10/54.
A.G.

2
Autobiography

EDITOR'S NOTE

Catherine Helen Spence: An Autobiography appeared in the columns of the Adelaide *Register* after Catherine Spence's death in 1910. It was reprinted in book form in the same year and in facsimile form in 1975. The manuscript was unfinished when Spence died, and the account of the years from 1887 until 1910 was completed, in first person form, by her close friend Jeanne F. Young. The diary which Spence had consulted during the writing of the *Autobiography*, and which Jeanne Young had used as the basis of her book *Catherine Helen Spence: a study and an appreciation* (1937), has been lost, and in the absence of many other private papers, the *Autobiography* assumes prime importance for biographical information.

The Register, which had published most of Spence's journalism throughout her long life, had serialized two of her novels in its weekly counterpart *The Observer* (*The Author's Daughter*, then titled "Hugh Lindsay's Guest", in 1864; *Gathered In*, in 1881–82). The newspaper's first issue appeared in London on 18 June 1836, and resumed publication in Adelaide on 3 June 1837 as the *South Australian Gazette and Colonial Register*, thereafter becoming the *South Australian Register*. The newspaper was absorbed with *The Advertiser* on 21 February 1931.

This section contains excerpts from the *Autobiography*, reproducing some sixty per cent of the original. Asterisks indicate where material has been omitted.

Excerpts from Catherine Helen Spence: An Autobiography

I EARLY LIFE IN SCOTLAND

Sitting down at the age of eighty-four to give an account of my life, I feel that it connects itself naturally with the growth and development of the province of South Australia, to which I came with my family in the year 1839, before it was quite three years old. But there is much truth in Wordsworth's line, "the child is father of the man", and no less is the mother of the woman; and I must go back to Scotland for the roots of my character and ideals. I account myself well-born, for my father and my mother loved each other. I consider myself well descended, going back for many generations on both sides of intelligent and respectable people. I think I was well brought up, for my father and mother were of one mind regarding the care of the family. I count myself well educated, for the admirable woman at the head of the school which I attended from the age of four and a half, till I was thirteen and a half, was a born teacher in advance of her own times. In fact, like my own dear mother, Sarah Phin was a New Woman without knowing it. The phrase was not known in the thirties.

I was born on 31 October 1825, the fifth of a family of eight born to David Spence and Helen Brodie, in the romantic village of Melrose, on the silvery Tweed, close to the three picturesque peaks of the Eildon Hills, which Michael Scott's familiar spirit split up from one mountain mass in a single night, according to the legend. It was indeed poetic ground. It was Sir Walter Scott's ground. Abbotsford was within two miles of Melrose, and one of my earliest recollections was seeing the long procession which followed his body to the family vault at Dryburgh Abbey. There was not a local note in *The Lay of the Last Minstrel* or in the

novels, *The Monastery* and *The Abbot*, with which I was not familiar before I entered my teens. There was not a hill or a burn or a glen that had not a song or a proverb, or a legend about it. Yarrow braes were not far off. The broom of the Cowdenknowes was still nearer, and my mother knew the words as well as the tunes of the minstrelsy of the Scottish Border. But as all readers of the life of Scott know, he was a Tory, loving the past with loyal affection, and shrinking from any change. My father, who was a lawyer (a writer as it was called), and his father who was a country practitioner, were reformers, and so it happened that they never came into personal relations with the man they admired above all men in Scotland. It was the Tory doctor who attended to his health, and the Tory writer who was consulted about his affairs.

I look back to a happy childhood. The many anxieties which reached both my parents were quite unknown to the children till the crisis in 1839. I do not know that I appreciated the beauty of the village I lived in so much with my own bodily eyes as through the songs and the literature, which were current talk. The old Abbey, with its 'prentice window, and its wonders in stonecarving, that Scott had written about and Washington Irving marvelled at — "Here lies the race of the House of Yair" as a tombstone — had a grand roll in it. In the churchyard of the old Abbey my people on the Spence side lay buried. In the square or market place there no longer stood the great tree described in *The Monastery* as standing just after Flodden Field, where the flowers of the forest had been cut down by the English; but in the centre stood the cross with steps up to it, and close to the cross was the well, to which twice a day the maids went to draw water for the house until I was nine years old, when we had pipes and taps laid on. The cross was the place for any public speaking, and I recalled, when I was recovering from the measles, the maid in whose charge I was, wrapped me in a shawl and took me with her to hear a gentleman from Edinburgh speak in favour of reform to a crowd gathered round. He said that the Tories had found a new name — they called themselves Conservatives — because it sounded better. For his part he thought conserves were pickles, and he hoped all the Tories would soon find themselves in a pretty pickle. There were such shouts of laughter that I saw this was a great joke.

We had gasworks in Melrose when I was ten or eleven, and a great joy to us children the wonderful light was. I recollect the first lucifer matches, and the wonder of them. My brother John had got sixpence from a visiting uncle as a reward for buying him snuff to fill his cousin's silver snuffbox, and he spent the money in

buying a box of lucifers, with the piece of sandpaper doubled, through which each match was to be smartly drawn, and he took all of us and some of his friends to the orchard, we called the wilderness, at the back of my grandfather Spence's house, and lighted each of the fifty matches, and we considered it a great exhibition. My grandfather (old Dr Spence) died before the era of lucifer matches. He used to get up early and strike a fire with flint and steel to boil the kettle and make a cup of tea to give to his wife in bed. He did it for his first wife (Janet Park), who was delicate, and he did the same for his second wife until her last fatal illness. It was a wonderful thing for a man to do in those days. He would not call the maid; he said young things wanted plenty of sleep. He had been a navy doctor, and was very intelligent. He trusted much to Nature and not too much to drugs. On the Sunday of the great annular eclipse of the sun in 1835, which was my brother John's eleventh birthday, he had a large double tooth extracted — not by a dentist, and gas was then unknown or any other anaesthetic, so he did not enjoy the eclipse as other people did. It took place in the afternoon and there was no afternoon church. In summer we had two services — one in the forenoon and one in the afternoon. In winter we had two services at one sitting, which was a thing astonishing to English visitors. The first was generally called a lecture — a reading with comments, of a passage of Scripture — a dozen verses or more — and the second a regularly built sermon, with three or four heads, and some particulars, and a practical summing up.

Prices and cost of living had fallen since my mother had married in 1815, three months after the battle of Waterloo. At that time tea cost 8s a pound, loaf sugar, 1s.4d, and brown sugar 11½d. Bread and meat were then still at war prices, and calico was no cheaper than linen, and that was dear. She paid 3s.6d a yard for fine calico to make petticoats. Other garments were of what was called home made linen. White cotton stockings at 4s.9d, and thinner at 3s.9d each; silk stockings at 11s.6d. I know she paid 36s for a yard of Brussels net to make caps of. It was a new thing to have net made in the loom. When a woman married she must wear caps at least in the morning. In 1838 my mother bought a chest of tea (eighty-four pounds) for £20, a trifle under 5s a pound; the retail price was 6s — it was a great saving; and up to the time of our departure brown sugar cost 7½d, and loaf sugar 10d. It is no wonder that these things were accounted luxuries. When a decent Scotch couple in South Australia went out to a station in the country in the forties and received their stores, the wife sat down at her quarter-chest of tea and gazed at her bag

of sugar, and fairly wept to think of her old mother across the ocean, who had such difficulty in buying an ounce of tea and a pound of sugar. My mother even saw an old woman buy a quarter ounce of tea and pay 1½d for it, and another woman buy a quarter pound of meat.

We kept three maids. The cook got £8 a year, the housemaid £7, and the nursemaid £6, paid half-yearly, but the summer half-year was much better paid than the winter, because there was the outwork in the fields, weeding and hoeing turnips and potatoes, and haymaking. The winter work in the house was heavier on account of the fires and the grate cleaning, but the wages were less. My mother gave the top wages in the district, and was considerate to her maids, but I blush yet to think how poorly those good women who made the comfort of my early home were paid for their labours. You could get a washerwoman for 1s or 1s.6d a day, but you must give her a glass of whiskey as well as her food. You could get a sewing girl for a shilling or less, without the whiskey. And yet cheap as sewing was it was the pride of the middle-class women of those days that they did it themselves at home. Half of the time of girls' schools was given to sewing when mother was taught. Nearly two hours a day was devoted to it in my time.

* * *

[In April, 1839] I went with [my sister] Jessie to Wooden, to Aunt Mary's, to hear there that my father was ruined, and had to leave Melrose and Scotland for ever, and that we must all go to Australia.

As I said, I had a very happy childhood. The death of my eldest sister at sixteen, and of my youngest sister at two years old, did not sink into the mind of a child as it did into that of my parents, and although they were seriously alarmed about my health when I was twelve years old, when I developed symptoms similar to those of Agnes at the same age, I was not ill enough to get at all alarmed. I was annoyed at having to stay away from school for three months. When the collapse came Jessie had a dear friend of some years' standing, and I had one whom I had known only for some months, but I had spent a month with her in Edinburgh at Christmas, 1838, and we exchanged letters weekly through the box which came from Edinburgh with my brother John's washing. It was too expensive for us to write by the post. Well, neither of our friends wrote a word to us. With regard to mine it was not to be wondered at much — she was only thirteen — but the other was more surprising. It was not until 1865 that an old woman told me that when Miss F. B. came to return some books

and music to her to give to my aunt in Melrose, "she just sat in the chair and cried as if her heart would break". She was not quite a free agent. Very few single women were free agents in 1839. We were hopelessly ruined, our place would know us no more.

The only long holidays I had in the year I spent at Thornton Loch, in East Lothian, forty miles away. I did not know that my father was a heavy speculator in foreign wheat, and I thought his keen interest in the market in Mark Lane was on account of the Thornton Loch crops, in which first my grandfather and afterwards the three maiden aunts were deeply concerned. My mother's father, John Brodie, was one of the most enterprising agriculturalists in the most advanced district of Great Britain. He won a prize of two silver salvers from the Highland Society for having the largest area of drilled wheat sown. He was called up twice to London to give evidence before Parliamentary committees on the corn laws, and he naturally approved of them, because, with three large farms he'd on nineteen years' leases at war prices, the influx of cheap wheat from abroad would mean ruin. He proved that he paid £6,000 a year for these three farms — two he worked himself, the third was for his eldest son; but he was liable for the rent. On his first London trip, my aunt Margaret accompanied him, and on his second visit he took my mother. That was in the year 1814, and both of them noted from the postchaise that farming was not up to what was done in East Lothian.

My grandfather Brodie was a speculating man, and he lost nearly all his savings through starting, along with others, an East Lothian Bank, because the local banker had been ill used by the British Linen Company. He put in only £1,000; but was liable for all, and, as many of his fellow shareholders were defaulters, it cost £15,000 before all was over, and if it had not been that he left the farm in the capable hands of Aunt Margaret, there would have been little or nothing left for the family. When he had a stroke of paralysis he wanted to turn over Thornton Loch, the only farm then had, to his eldest son; but there were three daughters, and one of them said she would like to carry it on, and she did. She was the most successful farmer in the country for thirty years, and then she transferred it to a nephew. The capacity for business of my Aunt Margaret, the wit and charm of my brilliant Aunt Mary, and the sound judgment and accurate memory of my own dear mother, showed me early that women were fit to share in the work of this world, and that to make the world pleasant for men was not their only mission.

* * *

The only cloud on my young life was the gloomy religion, which made me doubt of my own salvation and despair of the salvation of any but a very small proportion of the people in the world. Thus the character of God appeared unlovely, and it was wicked not to love God; and this was my condemnation. I had learned the shorter catechism with the proofs from Scripture, and I understood the meaning of the dogmatic theology. Watt's hymns were much more easy to learn, but the doctrine was the same. There was no getting away from the feeling that the world was under a curse ever since that unlucky apple-eating in the garden of Eden. Why, oh! why had not the sentence of death been carried out at once, and a new start made with more prudent people? The school in which as a day scholar I passed nine years of my life was more literary than many which were more pretentious. Needlework was of supreme importance, certainly, but during the hour and a half every day, Saturday's half-holiday not excepted, which was given to it by the whole school at once (odd half-hours were also put in), the best readers took turns about to read some book selected by Miss Phin. We were thus trained to pay attention. History, biography, adventures, descriptions, and story books were read. Any questions or criticism about our sewing, knitting, netting etc., were carried on in a low voice, and we learned to work well and quickly, and good reading aloud was cultivated. First one brother then another had gone to Edinburgh for higher education than could be had at Melrose Parish School, and I wanted to go to a certain institution, the first of the kind, for advanced teaching for girls, which had a high reputation. I was a very ambitious girl at thirteen. I wanted to be a teacher first, and a great writer afterwards. The qualifications for a teacher would help me to rise to literary fame, so I obtained from my father a promise that I should go to Edinburgh next year; but he could not keep it. He was a ruined man.

II TOWARDS AUSTRALIA

Although my mother's family had lost heavily by him, her mother gave us £500 to make a start in South Australia. An eighty-acre section was bought for £80, and this entitled us to the steerage passage of four adults. This helped for my elder sister and two brothers (my younger brother David was left for his education with his aunts in Scotland), but we had to have another female, so we took with us a servant girl — most ridiculous, it seems now. I was under the statutory age of fifteen. The difference between

steerage and intermediate fares had to be made up, and we sailed from Greenock in July 1839, in the barque *Palmyra*, four hundred tons, bound for Adelaide, Port Phillip, and Sydney. The *Palmyra* was advertised to carry a cow and an experienced surgeon. Intermediate passengers had no more advantage of the cow than steerage folks, and except for the privacy of separate cabins and a pound of white biscuit per family weekly, we fared exactly as the other immigrants did, though the cost was double. Twice a week we had either fresh meat or tinned meat, generally soup and boudle, and the biscuit seemed half bran, and sometimes it was mouldy. But our mother thought it was very good for us to endure hardship, and so it was.

There were 150 passengers, mostly South Australian immigrants, in the little ship. The first and second class passengers were bound for Port Phillip and Sydney in greater proportion than for Adelaide. There was in the saloon the youthful William Milne, and in the intermediate was Miss Disher, his future wife. He became President of the Legislative Council, and was knighted. There was my brother, J. B. Spence, who also sat in the Council, and was at one time Chief Secretary. There was George Melrose, a successful South Australian pastoralist; there was my father's valued clerk, Thomas Laidlaw, who was long in the Legislative Council of New South Wales and the leading man in the town of Yass. "Honest Tom of Yass" was his soubriquet. Bound for Melbourne there were Mr and Mrs Duncan, of Melrose, and Charles Williamson, from Hawick, who founded a great business house in Collins Street. There were Langs from Selkirk, and McHaffies, who became pastoralists. Our next cabin mate, who brought out a horse, had the Richmond punt when there was no bridge there. All the young men were reading a thick book brought out by the Society for Promoting Useful Knowledge about sheep, but they could dance in the evenings to the strains of Mr Duncan's violin, and although I was not fourteen, I was in request as a partner, as ladies were scarce. Jessie Spence and Eliza Disher, who were grown up, were the belles of the *Palmyra*. Of all the passengers in the ship the young doctor, John Logan Campbell, has had the most distinguished career. Next to Sir George Grey he has had most to do with the development of New Zealand. He is now called the Grand Old Man of Auckland. He had his twenty-first birthday, this experienced surgeon (!) in the same week as I had my fourteenth, while the *Palmyra* was lying off Holdfast Bay (now Glenelg) before we could get to the old Port Adelaide to discharge. My brother saw him in 1883, but I have not set eye on him since that week in 1839.

Autobiography

We have corresponded frequently since my brother's death. In his book *Poenama*, written for his children, there is a picture of the *Palmyra*, with an account of the voyage and the only sensational incident in it. We had a collision in the Irish Sea, and our foremast was broken, so that we had to return to Greenock for repairs, and then obtained the concession of white biscuit for the second class for one day in the week. Sir John Campbell's gift of a beautiful park to the citizens of Auckland was made while my brother John was alive. Just recently he has given money and plans for building and equipping the first free kindergarten in Auckland — perhaps in New Zealand — and as this includes a training college for the students it is very complete. These *Palmyra* passengers have made their mark on the history of Australia and New Zealand. It is surprising what a fine class of people immigrated to Australia in these days to face all the troubles of a new country.

The first issue of *The Register* was printed in London, and gave a glowing account of the province that was to be — its climate, its resources, the sound principles on which it was founded. It is sometimes counted as a reproach that South Australia was founded by doctrinaires and that we retain traces of our origin; to me it is our glory. In the land laws and the immigration laws it struck out a new path, and sought to found a new community where the sexes should be equal, and where land, labour, and capital should work harmoniously together. Land was not to be given away in huge grants, as had been done in New South Wales and Western Australia, to people with influence or position, but was to be sold at the high price of twenty shillings an acre. The price should be not too high to bring out people to work on the land. The Western Australian settlers had been well-nigh starved, because there was no labour to give real value to the paper or parchment deeds. The cheapest fare third class was from £17 to £20, and the family immigration, which is the best, was quite out of the reach of those who were needed. The immigrants were not bound to work for any special individual or company, unless by special contract voluntarily made. They were often in better circumstances after the lapse of a few years than the landbuyers, and, in the old days, the owner of an eighty-acre section worked harder and for longer hours than any hired man would do, or could be expected to do.

* * *

People came out on the smallest of salaries with big families — H. T. H. Beare on £100 a year as architect, for the South Australian Company, and he had eighteen children by two wives.

Towards Australia

I do not know what salary Mr William Giles came out on with nine children and a young second wife, but I am sure it was less than £300. His family in all counted twenty-one. But things were bad in the old country before the great lift given by railways, and freetrade, which made England the carrier for the world; and the possibilities of the new country were shown in that first issue of *The Register* in London in the highest colours. Not too high by any means in the light of what has been accomplished in seventy-three years, but there was a long row to hoe first, and few of the pioneers reaped the prizes. But, in spite of hardships and poverty and struggle, the early colonial life was interesting, and perhaps no city of its size at the time contained as large a population of intelligent and educated people as Adelaide.

Mrs Oliphant, writing in 1885 at the age of fifty-seven, says that reading the *Life of George Eliot* made her think of an autobiography, and this was written at the saddest crisis of her life. She survived her husband and all her children, and had just lost the youngest, the posthumous boy. For them and for the family of a brother she had carried on the strenuous literary work — fiction, biography, criticism, and history — and when she died at the age of sixty-nine she had not completed the history of a great publishing house — that of Blackwood. Her life tallies with mine on many points, but it is not till I have completed my eighty-four years that her sad narrative impels me to set down what appears noteworthy in a life which was begun in similar circumstances, but which was spent mainly in Australia. The loss of memory which I see in many who are younger than myself makes me feel that while I can recollect I should fix the events and the ideals of my life by pen and ink. Like Mrs Oliphant, I was born (three years earlier) in the south of Scotland. Like her I had an admirable mother, but she lost hers at the age of sixty, while I kept mine till she was nearly ninety-seven. Like Mrs Oliphant, I was captivated by the stand made by the Free Church as a protest against patronage, and like her I shook off the shackles of the narrow Calvinism of Presbyterianism, and emerged into more light and liberty. But unlike Mrs Oliphant, I have from my earliest youth taken an interest in politics, and although I have not written the tenth part of what she has done, I have within the last twenty years addressed many audiences in Australia and America, and have preached over one hundred sermons. My personal influence has been exercised through the voice more strongly than by the pen, and in the growth and development of South Australia, to which I came with my parents and brothers and sisters when I was just fourteen, and the province not three years old, there have

been opportunities for usefulness which might not have offered if I had remained in Melrose, in Sir Walter Scott's country.

III BEGINNING AT SEVENTEEN

My mother, from her own intimate relations with her grandmother, Margaret Fernie Brodie, who was born in 1736, and died in 1817, knew how two generations before her people lived and thought. So that I have a grasp on the past which many might envy, and yet the present and the future are even more to me, as they were to my mother. On her death in 1887 I wrote a quatrain for her memorial, and which those who knew her considered appropriate —

> HELEN BRODIE SPENCE
> Born at Whittingham, Scotland, 1791.
> Died at College Town, Adelaide, South Australia, 1887.
> Half a long life 'mid Scotland's heaths and pines,
> And half among our South Australian vines;
> Though loving reverence bound her to the past,
> Eager for truth and progress to the last.

Although my mother had the greatest love for Sir Walter Scott, and the highest appreciation of his poems and novels, she never liked Melrose. She liked Australia better after a while. Indeed, when we arrived in November 1839, to a country so hot, so dry, so new, we felt like the good old founder of *The Adelaide Register*, Robert Thomas, when he came to the land described in his own paper as "flowing with milk and honey". Dropped anchor at Holdfast Bay. "When I saw the place at which we were to land I felt inclined to go and cut my throat." When we sat down on a log in Light Square, waiting till my father brought the key of the wooden house in Gilles Street, in spite of the dignity of my fourteen years just attained, I had a good cry. There had been such a drought that they had a dearth, almost a famine. People like ourselves with eighty-acre land orders were frightened to attempt cultivation in an unknown climate, with seed wheat at twenty-five shillings a bushel or more, and stuck to the town. We lived a month in Gilles Street, then we bought a large marquee, and pitched it on Brownhill Creek, above where Mitcham now stands, bought fifteen cows and a pony and cart, and sold the milk in town at a shilling a quart. But how little milk the cows gave in those days! After seven months' encamping, in which the family lived chiefly on rice — the only cheap food, of which we bought a ton — we came with our herd to West Terrace, Adelaide. My

Beginning at Seventeen

father got the position of Town Clerk at £150 a year twelve months after our arrival, and kept it till the municipal corporation was ended, as the City of Adelaide was too poor to maintain the machinery; but £75 was the rent of the house and yards. We sold the cows, and my brothers went farming, and we took cheaper quarters in Halifax Street.

The Town Clerkship, however, was the means of giving me a lesson in electoral methods. Into the Municipal Bill, drawn up under the superintendence of Rowland Hill (afterward the great post office reformer, but then the Secretary of the Colonization Commissioner for South Australia), he had introduced a clause providing for proportional representation at the option of the ratepayers. The twentieth part of the Adelaide ratepayers by uniting their votes upon one man, instead of voting for eighteen, could on the day before the ordinary election appear and declare this their intention, and he would be a Councillor on their votes. In the first election, November 1840, two such quorums elected two Councillors. The workmen in Borrow and Goodear's building elected their foreman, and another quorom of citizens elected Mr William Senden; and this was the first quota representation in the world. My father explained this unique provision to me at the time, and showed its bearings for minority representation.

* * *

The years at Brownhill Creek and West Terrace were the most unhappy of my life. I suffered from the want of some intellectual activity, and from the sense of frustrated ambition and religious despair. The few books we had, or which we could borrow, I read over and over again. Aikin's *British Poets*, a gift from Uncle John Spence, and Goldsmith's complete works, a school prize of my brother William's, were thoroughly mastered, and the Waverley novels down to *Quentin Durward* were well absorbed. I read in Chamber's *Journal* of daily governesses getting a shilling an hour, and I told my friend, Mrs Haining, that I would go out for sixpence an hour. Athough she disliked that way of putting it, it was really on that basis that I had made my beginning when I reached the age of seventeen. In the meantime I had taught my younger sister Mary (afterwards Mrs W. J. Wren) all I knew, and in the columns of *The South Australian* I wrote an occasional letter or a few verses.

* * *

It was not till 1843 that I went as a daily governess at the rate of sixpence an hour, and gave two hours five days a week to the families of the Postmaster-General, the Surveyor-General, and the Private Secretary. Thus I earned three guineas a month. I

don't recollect taking holidays, except a week at Christmas. I enjoyed the work, and I was proud of the payment. My mother said she never felt the bitterness of poverty after I began to earn money, and the shyness which, in spite of all her instructions and encouragement, I had felt with all strangers, disappeared when I felt independent. When a girl is very poor, and feels herself badly dressed, she cannot help being shy, especially if she has a good deal of Scotch pride. I think mother felt more sorry for me in those early days than for the others, because I was so ambitious, and took religious difficulties so hard. How old I felt at seventeen. Indeed, at fourteen I felt quite grown up. In 1843 I felt I had begun the career in Australia that I had anticipated in Scotland. I was trusted to teach little girls, and they interested me, each individual with a difference. I had seen things I had written in print. If I was one of the oldest feeling of the young folk in South Australia in my teens, I am the youngest woman in feeling in my eighties; so I have had abundant compensation.

IV LOVERS AND FRIENDS

It is always supposed that thoughts of love and marriage are the chief concerns in a girl's life, but it was not the case with me. I had only two offers of marriage in my life, and I refused both. The first might have been accepted if it had not been for the Calvinistic creed that made me shrink from the possibility of bringing children into the world with so little chance of eternal salvation, so I said "No" to a very clever young man, with whom I had argued on many points, and with whom, if I had married him, I should have argued till one of us died! I was seventeen, and had just begun to earn money. I told him why I had refused him, and that it was final. In six weeks he was engaged to another woman. My second offer was made to me when I was twenty-three by a man aged fifty-five, with three children. He was an artist, whose second wife and several children had been murdered by the Maoris near Wanganui during the Maori insurrection of the forties, and he had come to Adelaide with the three survivors.

* * *

If the number of lovers had been few, no woman in Australia has been richer in friends. This narrative will show what good friends — men as well as women — have helped me and sympathized in my work and my aims. I believe that if I had been in love, especially if I had been disappointed in love, my novels would have been stronger and more interesting; but I kept a watch over

myself, which I felt I knew I needed, for I was both imaginative and affectionate. I did not want to give my heart away. I did not desire a love disappointment, even for the sake of experience. I was thirty years old before the dark veil of religious despondency was completely lifted from my soul, and by that time I felt myself booked for a single life. People married young if they married at all in those days. The single aunts put on caps at thirty as a sort of signal that they accepted their fate; and, although I did not do so, I felt a good deal the same.

* * *

The South Australian Institute was a treasure to the family. I recollect a newcomer being astonished at my sister Mary having read Macaulay's *History*. "Why, it was only just out when I left England," said he. "Well, it did not take longer to come out than you did," was her reply. We were all omnivorous readers, and the old-fashioned accomplishment of reading aloud was cultivated by both brothers and sisters. I was the only one who could translate French at sight, thanks to Miss Phin's giving me so much of Racine and Molière and other good French authors in my school days.

But more important than all this was the fact that we took hold of the growth and development of South Australia, and identified ourselves with it. Nothing is insignificant in the history of a young community, and — above all — nothing seems impossible. I had learned what wealth was, and a great deal about production and exchange for myself in the early history of South Australia — of the value of machinery, of roads and bridges, and of ports for transport and export. I had seen the four pound loaf at 4s and at 4d. I had seen Adelaide the dearest and the cheapest place to live in. I had seen money orders for 2s.6, and even for 6d, current when gold and silver were very scarce. Even before the discovery of copper South Australia had turned the corner. We had gone on the land and become primary producers, and before the gold discoveries in Victoria revolutionized Australia and attracted our male population across the border, the Central State was the only one which had a large surplus of wheat and hay to send to the goldfields.

Edward Wilson, of *The Argus*, riding overland to Adelaide about 1848, was amazed to see from Willunga onward fenced and cultivated farms, with decent homesteads and machinery up to date. The Ridley stripper enabled our people to reap and thresh the corn when hands were all too few for the sickle. He said he felt as if the garden of Paradise must have been in King William Street, and that the earliest difference in the world — that bet-

ween Cain and Abel — was about the advantages of the eighty-acre system. Australia generally had already to realize the fact that the pastoral industry was not enough for its development, and South Australia had seemed to solve the problem through the doctrinaire founders, of family immigration, small estates, and the development of agriculture, horticulture, and viticulture. We owed a great deal in the latter branches to our German settlers — sent out originally by Mr G. F. Angas, whose interest was aroused by their suffering persecution for religious dissent — who saw that Australia had a better climate than that of the Fatherland. We owed much to Mr George Stevenson, who was an enthusiastic gardener and fruitgrower, and lectured on these subjects, but the contrast between the environs of Adelaide and those of Sydney and Melbourne were striking, and Mr Wilson never lost an opportunity of calling on the Victorian Legislature and the Victorian public to develop their own wonderful resources. When you take gold out of the ground there is less gold to win. When you grow golden grain or ruddy grapes this year you may expect as much and as good next year. My brother David went with the thousands to buy their fortunes at the diggings, but my brother John stuck to the Bank of South Australia.

V NOVELS AND A POLITICAL INSPIRATION

It was the experience of a depopulated province which led me to write my first book, *Clara Morison — A Tale of South Australia during the Gold Fever*. I entrusted the MS to my friend John Taylor, with whom I had just had the only tiff in my life. He, through his connection with *The Register*, knew that I was writing in *The South Australian*, trying to keep it alive, till Mr Murray decided to let it go, and he told this to other people. At a subscription ball to which my brother John took me and my younger sister Mary, she found she had been pointed out and talked of as the lady who wrote for the newspapers. I did not like it even to be supposed of myself, but Mary was indignant, and I wrote an injured letter to my friend. He apologized, and said he thought I would be proud of doing disinterested work, and he was sorry the mistake had been made regarding the sister who did it. Of course I forgave him. He was the last man in the world to give pain to anyone, and I highly admired him for his disinterested work on *The Register*. He reluctantly accepted £1,000 when the paper was sold. He must have lost much more through neglect of his own affairs at such a critical time. He was taking a holiday with his

Novels and Political Inspiration

sister Eliza in England and France, where the beautiful widowed sister was settled as Madam Dubois, and I asked him to take *Clara Morison* to Smith, Elder and Co.'s, in London, and to say nothing to anybody about it; but before it was placed he had to return to Adelaide, and in pursuance of my wishes, left it with my other good friend, Mr Bakewell, who also happened to be visiting England with his family at the time — 1853-54. I had an idea that, as there was so much interest in Australia and its gold, I might get £100 for the novel. Mr Bakewell wrote a preface from which I extract a passage:

> The writer's aim seems to have been to present some picture of the state of society in South Australia in the years 1851-52, when the discovery of gold in the neighbouring province of Victoria took place. At this time, the population of South Australia numbered between seventy and eighty thousand souls, the greater part of whom were remarkable for their intelligence, their industry, and their enterprise, which, in the instance of the Burra Burra, and other copper mines had met with such signal success. When it became known that gold in vast quantities could be found within 300 miles of their own territory, they could not remain unmoved. The exodus was almost complete, and entirely without parallel. In those days there was no King in Israel, and every woman did what was right in her own sight.

Another reason I had for writing the book. Thackeray had written about an emigrant vessel taking a lot of women to Australia, as if these were all to be gentlemen's wives — as if there was such a scarcity of educated women there, that anything wearing petticoats had the prospect of a great rise in position. I had hoped that Smith, Elder and Co. would publish my book, but their reader — Mr Williams, who discovered Charlotte Brontë's genius when she sent them *The Professor*, and told her she could write a better, which she did (*Jane Eyre*) — wrote a similar letter to me, declining *Clara Morison*, as he had declined *The Professor*, but saying I could do better. J. W. Parker and Son published it in 1854, as one of the two-volume series, of which *The Heir of Redcliffe* had been most successful. The price was to be £40; but, as it was too long for the series, I was charged £10 for abridging it. It was very fairly received and reviewed. I think I liked best Frederick Sinnett's notice in *The Argus* — that it was the work of an observant woman — a novelist who happened to live in Australia, but who did not labour to bring in bushrangers and convicts, and specially Australian features. While I was waiting to hear the fate of my first book, I began to write a second, *Tender and True*, of which Mr Williams thought better, and recommended it to Smith, Elder and Co., who published it in two volumes in 1856, and gave me

£20 for the copyright. This is the only one of my books that went through more than one edition. There were two or three large editions issued, but I never got a penny more. I was told that nothing could be made out of shilling editions; but that book was well reviewed and now and then I have met elderly people who read the cheap edition and liked it. The motif of the book was the jealousy which husbands are apt to feel of their wives' relations. As if the most desirable wife was an amiable orphan — if an heiress, so much the better. But the domestic virtues which make a happy home for the husband are best fostered in a centre where brothers and sisters have to give and take; and a good daughter and sister is likely to make a good wife and mother. I have read quite recently that the jokes against the mother-in-law which are so many and so bitter in English and American journalism are worn out, and have practically ceased; but Dickens and Thackeray set the fashion, and it lasted a long time.

While *Clara Morison* was making her debut, I paid my first visit to Melbourne. I went with Mr and Mrs Stirling in a French ship consigned to him, and we were twelve days on the way, suffering from the limited ideas that the captain of a French merchantman had of the appetites of Australians at sea. I intended to pay a six weeks' visit to my sister and her family, but she was so unwell that I stayed for eight months. I found that Melbourne in the beginning of 1854 was a very expensive place to live in, and consequently a very inhospitable place. Mr Murray's salary sounded a good one, £500 a year, but it did not get much comfort. His sister was housekeeper at Charles Williamson and Co.'s, and that was the only place where I could take off my bonnet and have a meal. From the windows I watched the procession that welcomed Sir Charles Hotham, the first Governor of the separated colony of Victoria. He was received with rejoicing, but he utterly failed to satisfy the people. He thought anything was good enough for them. One festivity I was invited to — a ball given on the opening of the new offices of *The Argus* in Collins Street — and there I met Mr Edward Wilson, a most interesting personality, the giver of the entertainment. He was then vigorously championing the unlocking of the land and the developing of other resources of Victoria than the gold. It had surprised him when he travelled overland to Adelaide to see from Willunga thirty miles of enclosed and cultivated farms, and it surprised me to see sheepruns close to Melbourne. With a better rainfall and equally good soil, Victoria had neither the farms nor the vineyards nor the orchards nor the gardens that had sprung up under the eighty-acre section and immigration system of South Australia. It had

Novels and Political Inspiration

been an outlying portion of New South Wales, neglected and exploited for pastoral settlement only. The city, however, had been well planned, like that of Adelaide, but the suburbs were allowed to grow anyhow. In Adelaide the belt of park lands kept the city apart from all suburbs. Andrew Murray was as keen for the development of Victoria agriculturally and industrially as Mr Wilson, and they worked together heartily. Owing to the state of my sister's health I was much occupied with her and her children; but in August she was well, and I returned with Mr Taylor and his sister in the steamer *Bosphorus*, when it touched at Melbourne on the way home. He brought me £30 for my book, and the assurance that it would be out soon, and that I should have six copies to give to my friends. Novel writing had not been to me a lucrative occupation. I had given up teaching altogether at the age of twenty-five, and I felt that though Australia was to be a great country, there was no market for literary work, and the handicap of distance from the reading world was great.

My younger sister married in 1855 William J. Wren, then an articled clerk in Bartley and Bakewell's office, and afterwards a partner with the present Sir James Boucaut. Mr Wren's health was indifferent, and caused us much anxiety. My brother John married Jessie Cumming in 1858, and they were spared together for many years. As the Wrens went on a long voyage to Hongkong and back for the sake of my brother-in-law's health, my mother and I had the charge of their little boy. But in that year, 1859, my mind received its strongest political inspiration, and the reform of the electoral system became the foremost object of my life. John Stuart Mill's advocacy of Thomas Hare's system of proportional representation brought back to my mind Rowland Hill's clause in the Adelaide Municipal Bill with wider and larger issues. It also showed me how democratic government could be made real, and safe, and progessive. I confess that at first I was struck chiefly by its conservative side, and I saw that its application would prevent the political association, which corresponded roughly with the modern Labour Party, from returning five out of six members of the Assembly for the City of Adelaide. But for blunders on ballot papers the whole ticket of six would have been elected. They also elected the three members for Burra and Clare. I had then no footing on the Adelaide press, but I was Adelaide correspondent for *The Melbourne Argus* — that is to say, my brother was the correspondent, but I wrote the letters — he furnished the news. I read Mill's article one Monday night, and wrote what was meant for a leader on Tuesday morning, and went to read it to my brother at breakfast time, and posted it forthwith. I

knew *The Argus* had been dissatisfied with the recent elections, and fancied that the editor would hail with joy the new idea; but I received the reply that *The Argus* was committed to the representation of majorities; and, though the idea was ingenious, he did not even offer to print it as a letter. About two years later Mr Lavington Glyde, MP, brought forward in the Assembly Mr Fawcett's abstract of Hare's great scheme, and I seized the opportunity of writing a series of letters to *The Register*, signed by my initials. Mr Glyde, seeing the House did not like his suggestions, dropped the matter, but I did not. I was no longer correspondent to *The Argus* — the telegraph stopped that altogether. My wonderful maiden aunts made up to me and my mother the £50 a year that I had received as correspondent, and did as much for their brother, Alexander Brodie, of Morphett Vale, from £1,000 they had sent to invest in South Australia. It was as easy to get ten per cent then as to get four per cent now; indeed I think the money earned twelve per cent at first. My brother John was accountant to the South Australian Railways, then not a very great department — I think the line stretched as far as Kapunda to the north from Port Adelaide. He was as much captivated by Mr Hare's idea as I was, and he said that if I would write a pamphlet he would pay for the printing of one thousand copies, to be sent to all the members of Parliament and other leading people in city and country. I called my pamphlet *A Plea for Pure Democracy*, and when writing it I felt the democratic strength of the position as I had not felt it in reading Hare's own book. It cost my brother £15, but he never grudged it.

* * *

I had been both amused and annoyed with the portraits I was supposed to have drawn from real people in and about Adelaide — often people I had never seen and had not heard of. "But Harris is Ellis to the life," said my old Aunt Brodie of Morphett Vale. "Miss Withing is my sister-in-law," said another. Neither of these people had I seen. Of course, Mr Reginald was Mr John Taylor, the only squatter I knew, but I myself was not identified with my heroine Clara Morison. I was Margaret Elliott, the girl who was studying law with her brother Gilbert; but my brother and my cousin Louisa Brodie were supposed to be figuring in my book as lovers. In a small society it was easy to affix the characteristics to some one whom it was possible the author might have met; but I shrank from the idea that I was capable of "taking off" people of my acquaintance, and for many reasons would have liked it if the book had not been known to be mine in South Australia. There must, however, have been some lifelike presentment of my

characters, or they could not have been recognized. About this time I read and appreciated Jane Austen's novels — those exquisite minatures, which no doubt her contemporaries identified without much interest. Her circle was as narrow as mine — indeed, narrower. She was the daughter of a clergyman in the country. She represented well-to-do grown-up people, and them alone. The humour of servants, the sallies of children, the machinations of villains, the tricks of rascals, are not on her canvas; but she differentiated among equals with a firm hand, and with a constant ripple of amusement. The life I led had more breadth and wider interests. The life of Miss Austen's heroines, though delightful to read about, would have been deadly dull to endure. So great a charm have Jane Austen's books had for me that I have made a practice of reading them through regularly once a year.

As we grew to love South Australia, we felt that we were in an expanding society, still feeling the bond to the mother-land, but eager to develop a perfect society in the land of our adoption.

VI A TRIP TO ENGLAND

I have gone on with the story of my three first novels consecutively, anticipating the current history of myself and South Australia. There were three great steps taken in the development of Australia. The first was when Macarthur introduced the merino sheep; the second when Hargreaves and others discovered gold; and the latest when cold-storage was introduced to make perishable products available for the European markets. The second step created a sudden revolution; but the others were gradual, and the area of alluvial diggings in Victoria made thousands of men without capital or machinery rush to try their fortunes — first from the adjacent colonies, and afterwards from the ends of the earth. Law and order were kept on the goldfields of Mount Alexander, Bendigo, and Ballarat by means of a strong body of police, and the high licence fees for claims paid for their services, so that nothing like the scenes recorded of the Californian diggings could be permitted. But for the time ordinary industries were paralysed. Shepherds left their flocks, farmers their land, clerks their desks, and artisans their trades. Melbourne grew apace in spite of the highest wages known being exacted by masons and carpenters. Pastoralists thought ruin stared them in the face till they found what a market the goldfields offered for their surplus stock. Our South Australian farmers left their

holdings in the hands of their wives and children too young to take with them, but almost all of them returned to grow grain and produce to send to Victoria. It was astonishing what the women had done during their absence. The fences were kept repaired and the stock attended to, the grapes gathered, and the wine made. In these days it was not so easy to get eighty acres or more in Victoria; so, with what the farmers brought from their labours on the goldfields, they extended their holdings and improved their homes. For many years the prices in Melbourne regulated prices in Adelaide, but when the land was unlocked and the Victorian soil and climate were found to be as good as ours it was Mark Lane that fixed prices over all Australia for primary products. After the return of most of the diggers there was a great deal of marrying and giving in marriage. The miners who had left the Burra for goldseeking gradually came back, and the nine remarkable copper mines of Moonta and Wallaroo attracted the Cornishmen, who preferred steady wages and homes to the diminishing chances of Ballarat and Bendigo, where machinery and deep sinking demanded capital, and the miners were paid by the week. These new copper mines were found in the Crown leases held by Captain (afterwards Sir Walter) Hughes. He had been well dealt with by Elder, Smith and Co., and gave them the opportunity of supporting him. At that time my friends Edward Stirling and John Taylor were partners in that firm, and they shared in the success. Mr Bakewell belonged to the legal firm which did their business, so that my greatest friends seemed to be in it. I think my brother John profited less by the great advance of South Australia than he deserved for sticking to the Bank of South Australia. He got small rises in his salary, but the cost of living was so enhanced that at the end of seven years it did not buy much more than the £100 he had begun with. My eldest maiden aunt died, and left to her brother and sister in South Australia all she had in her power. My mother bought a brick cottage in Pulteney Street and a Burra share with her legacy — both excellent investments — and my brother left the bank and went into the aerated water business with James Hamilton Parr.

We made the acquaintance of the family of Mrs Francis Clark, of Hazelwood, Burnside. She was the only sister of five clever brothers — Matthew Davenport, Rowland, Edwin, Arthur, and Frederick Hill. Rowland is best known, but all were remarkable men. She was so like my mother in her sound judgment, accurate observation, and kind heart, that I was drawn to her at once. But it was Miss Clark who sought an introduction to me at a ball, because her uncle Rowland had written to her that *Clara*

A Trip to England

Morison, the new novel, was a capital story of South Australian life. She was the first person to seek me out on account of literary work, and I was grateful to her. I think all the brothers Hill wrote books, and Rosamund and Florence Davenport Hill had just published *Our Exemplars*. My friendship with Miss Clark led to much work together, and the introduction was a great widening of interests for me. There were four sons and three daughters — Miss Clark and Howard were the most literary, but all had great ability and intelligence. They were Unitarians, and W. J. Wren, my brother-in-law, was also a Unitarian, and had been one of the twelve Adelaide citizens who invited out a minister and guaranteed his salary. I was led to hear what the Rev. J. Crawford Woods had to say for that faith, and told my old minister (Rev. Robert Haining) that for three months I would hear him in the morning and Mr Woods in the evening, and read nothing but the Bible as my guide; and by that time I would decide. I had been induced to go to the Sacrament at seventeen, with much heart searching, but when I was twenty-five I said I could not continue a communicant, as I was not a converted Christian. This step greatly surprised both Mr and Mrs Haining, as I did not propose to leave the church. The result of my three months' enquiry was that I became a convinced Unitarian, and the cloud was lifted from the universe. I think I have been a most cheerful person ever since. My mother was not in any way distressed, though she never separated from the church of her fathers. My brother was as completely converted as I was, and he was happy in finding a wife like minded. My sister, Mrs Wren also was satisfied with the new faith; so that she and her husband saw eye to eye. It was a very live congregation in those early days. We liked our pastor, and we admired his wife, and there were a number of interesting and clever people who went to the Wakefield Street church.

It was rather remarkable that my sister's husband and my brother's wife arrived on the same day in two different ships — one in the *Anglier* from England, and the other in the *Three Bells* from Glasgow — in 1851; but I did not make the acquaintance of either till 1854 and 1855. Jessie Cumming and Mary Spence shook hands and formed a friendship over Carlyle's *Sartor Resartus*. My brother-in-law (W. J. Wren) had fine literary tastes, especially for poetry. The first gift to his wife after marriage was Elizabeth Browning's poems in two volumes and Robert Browning's *Plays and Dramatic Lyrics* in two volumes, and Mary and I delighted in them all. In those days I considered my sister Mary and my sister-in-law the most brilliant conversationalists I knew. My elder sister, Mrs Murray, also talked very well — so much so that her

husband's friends and visitors fancied she must write a lot of his articles; but none of the three ladies went beyond writing good letters. I think all of them were keener of sight than I was — more observant of features, dress, and manners; but I took in more by the ear. As Sir Walter Scott says, "Speak that I may know thee". To my mind, dialogue is more important for a novel than description; and, if you have a firm grasp of your characters, the dialogue will be true. With me the main difficulty was the plot; and I was careful that this should not be merely possible, but probable. I have heard scores of people say that they have got good plots in their heads, and when pressed to tell them they proved to be only incidents. You need much more than an incident, or even two or three, with which to make a book. But when I found my plot the story seemed to write itself, and the actors to fit in.

When the development of the Moonta Mine made some of my friends rich they were also liberal. Edward Stirling said that if I wanted a trip to England I should have it at his cost, but it seemed impossible. After the death of Mr Wren my mother and I went to live with my sister, and put two small incomes together, so as to be able to bring up and educate her two children, a boy and a girl. My brother John had left the railway, and for nine years had been Official Assignee and Curator of Intestate Estates; and in 1863 he had been appointed manager of the new Adelaide branch of the English, Scottish, and Australian Bank. My friend, Mr Taylor, had helped well to get the position for one he thought the fittest man in the city. He had lost his wife, Miss Mary Ann Dutton, when on a visit to England, and at this time was engaged to Miss Harriet McDermott. His sisters both were very cold about the engagement. They did not like second marriages at all, and considered it a disrespect to the first wife's memory, even though a decent interval had elapsed. When he wrote to me about it I took quite a different view. He said it was the kindest and the wisest letter I had ever written in my life, and he knew I had loved his late wife very much. He came to thank me, and to tell me that he had always wished that I should be in England at the time he was there, and that he was going in a P & O boat immediately after his marriage. Although Mr Stirling had promised to pay my passage, I hesitated about going. There were my mother, who was seventy-two, and my guardianship of the Duvals to think about. I had also undertaken the oversight of old Mrs Stephens, the widow of one of the early proprietors of *The Register*. These objections were all overruled. I still hesitated. "I cannot go unless I have money to spend," I urged. "Let me do that," was the generous

reply. "I have left you £500 in my will. Let me have the pleasure of giving you something while I live." I was not too proud to owe that memorable visit to England to my two good friends. John Taylor had put into my hands on board the *Goolwa*, in which I sailed, a draft for £200 for my spending money, and in the new will he made after his marriage he bequeathed me £300. I said "Goodby" to him, with good wishes for his health and happiness. I never saw him again. He took a sickly looking child on his knee when crossing the Isthmus of Suez — there was no canal in 1864 — to relieve a weary mother. The child had smallpox, and my friend took it and died of it. He was being buried beside his first wife at Brighton when the *Goolwa* sailed up the Channel after a passage of fourteen weeks — as long as that of the *Palmyra* twenty-five years before — and the first news we heard was that Miss Taylor had lost a brother, the children a favourite uncle, and I, a friend. It was a sad household, but the Bakewells were in London on business connected with some claims of discovery of the Moonta Mines, and they took me to their house in Palace Gardens, Kensington, till I could arrange to go to my aunt's in Scotland. All our plans about seeing people and places together were, of course, at an end. I was to go "a lone hand". Mrs Taylor had a posthumous son, who never has set foot in Australia. She married a second time, an English clergyman named Knight, and had several sons, but she has never revisited Adelaide, although she has many relatives here. So the friend who loved Australia, and was eager to do his duty by it — who thoroughly approved of the Hare system of representation, and thought I did well to take it up, was snatched away in the prime of life. I wonder if there is any one alive now to whom his memory is as precious. *The Register* files may preserve some of his work.

VII   MELROSE REVISITED

Of the twelve months I spent in the old country, I spent six with the dear old aunts. How proud Aunt Mary was of my third novel, with the sketch of Aunt Margaret in it, of the *Cornhill* article, and the request from Mr Wilson to write for *The Fortnightly*. I introduced her to new books, and especially new poets; she had never heard of Browning and Jean Ingelow. She was so much cleverer than her neighbours that I often wondered how she could put up with them. How conservative these farmers and farmers' wives and daughters were, to be sure. These big tenants considered themselves quite superior to tradesmen, even to merchants, unless

they were in a big way. There was infinitely more difference between their standard of living and that of their labourers than between theirs and that of the aristocratic landlords. James Barnet, the farm steward, said to me — "You have brought down the price of wheat with your Australian grain, and you do big things in wool, but you can never touch us in meat". This was quite true in 1865. I expected to see some improvement in the farm hamlet, but the houses built by the landlord were still very poor and bare. The wages had risen a little since 1839, but not much. The wheaten loaf was cheaper, and so was tea and sugar, but the poor were still living on porridge and bannocks of barley and pease meal instead of tea and white bread. It was questionable if they were as well nourished. There were 100 souls living on the farms of Thornton and Thornton Loch.

* * *

I can never forget the look of tender pity cast on me as I was sitting in our old seat in church, looking at seats filled by another generation. The paterfamilias, so wonderfully like his father of 1839, and sons and daughters, sitting in the place of uncles and aunts settled elsewhere. They grieved that I had been banished from the romantic associations and the high civilization of Melrose to rough it in the wilds, while my heart was full of thankfulness that I had moved to the wider spaces and the more varied activities of a new progressive colony. My dear old teacher was still alive, though the school had been closed for many years. She lived at St Mary's with her elder sister, who had taught me sewing and had done the housekeeping, but she herself was almost blind, and a girl came every day to read to her for two or three hours. She told me what a good thing it was that she knew all the Psalms in the prose version by heart, for in the sleepless nights which accompany old age so often they were such comfort to her in the night watches. I had sent her my two novels when they were published, *Clara Morison* and *Tender and True*. She would have been glad if they had been more distinctly religious in tone. Indeed, the novel I began at nineteen would have suited her better, but my brother's insistence on reading it every day as I wrote it somehow made me see what poor stuff it was, and I did not go far with it. But Miss Phin was, on the whole, pleased with my progress, and glad that I was able to go to see her and talk of old times. How very small the village of Merose looked! How little changed! The distances to the neighbouring villages of Darnick and Newstead, and across the Tweed to Gattonsville, seemed so shrunken.

* * *

There was an absurd idea current in 1865 that all visiting Australians were rich, and I could not disabuse people of that notion. Of all the two families of Brodies and Spences who came out in 1839 there was only my brother John who could be called successful. He was then manager of the Adelaide branch of the English, Scottish, and Australian Bank. If it had not been for help from the wonderful aunts from time to time both families would have been stranded. I had the greatest faith in the future of Australia, but I felt that for such gifts as I possessed there was no market at home. Possibly I should have tried literature earlier if I had remained in Scotland, but I am not at all sure that I could have succeeded as well. For the first time in my life I had as much money as I wanted. I am surprised now that I spent that £200 when I had so much hospitality. In fact, except for a week in Paris, I never had any hotel expenses. I had got the money to enjoy it, and I did. This was what my friend wished. I made a few presents. I bought some to take home with me. I spent money on dress freely, so as to present a proper appearance when visiting. I was liberal with veils, though I hate the practice. To a woman who had to look on both sides of a shilling since 1839 this experience was new and delightful.

VIII I VISIT EDINBURGH AND LONDON

My return to London introduced me to a wider range of society. I had admissions to the Ladies' Gallery of the House of Commons from Sir Charles Dilke, Professor Pearson's friend, and I had invitations to stay for longer or shorter periods with people various in means, in tastes, and in interests. To Mr Hare I was especially drawn.

* * *

My *Plea for Pure Democracy* had been written at a white heat of enthusiasm. I do not think I ever before or since reached a higher level. I took this reform more boldly than Mr Mill, who sought by giving extra votes for property and university degrees or learned professions to check the too great advance of democracy. I was prepared to trust the people; and Mr Hare was also confident that, if all the people were equitably represented in Parliament, the good would be stronger than the evil. The wise would be more effectual than the foolish. I do not think any one whom I met took the matter up so passionately as I did; and I had a feeling that in our new colonies the reform would meet with less obstruction than in old countries bound by precedent and prejudiced by

vested interests. Parliament was the preserve of the wealthy in the United Kingdom. There was no property qualification for the candidate in South Australia, and we had manhood suffrage.

South Australia was the first community to give the secret ballot for political elections. It had dispensed with Grand Juries. It had not required a member of either House to stand a new election if he accepted ministerial office. Every elected man was eligible for office. South Australia had been founded by doctrinaires, and occasionally a cheap sneer had been levelled at it on that account; but, to my mind, that was better than the haphazard way in which other colonies grew. When I visited Sir Rowland Hill he was recognized as the great post office reformer. To me he was also one of the founders of our province, and the first pioneer of quota representation. When I met Matthew Davenport Hill I respected him, because he tried to keep delinquent boys out of gaol, and promoted the establishment of reform schools; but I also was grateful to him for suggesting to his brother the park lands which surround Adelaide, and give us both beauty and health. To Colonel Light, who laid out the city so well, we owe the many open spaces and squares; but he did not originate the idea of the park lands. Much of the work of Mr Davenport Hill and of his brother Frederick I took up later with their neice (Miss C. E. Clark), and their ideas have been probably more thoroughly carried out in South Australian than anywhere else; but in 1865 I was learning a great deal that bore fruit afterwards.

I fear it would make this narrative too long if I went into detail about the interesting people I met. Florence and Rosamund Davenport Hill introduced me to Miss Frances Power Cobbe, whose *Intuitive Morals* I admired so much. At Sir Rowland Hill's I met Sir Walter Crofter, a prison reformer; Mr Wells, editor of *All the Year Round*; Charles Knight, who had done so much for good and cheap literature; Madame Bodichon (formerly Barbara Smith), the great friend and correspondent of George Eliot, who was interesting to me because by introducing the Australian eucalyptus to Algeria she had made an unhealthy marshy country quite salubrious. She had a salon, where I met very clever men and women — English and French — and which made me wish for such things in Adelaide. The kindness and hospitality that were shown to me — an absolute stranger — by all sorts of people were surprising. Mr and Mrs Westlake took me on Sunday to see Bishop Colenso. He showed me the photo of the enquiring Zulu who made him doubt the literal truth of the early books of the Bible, and presented me with the people's edition of his work on the Pentateuch.

Edinburgh and London

In all my travels and visits I saw little of the theatre or concert room, and some of the candid confessions of Mrs Oliphant might stand for my own. I had read so many plays before I saw one that the unreality of much of the acted drama impressed me unfavourably. The asides in particular seemed impossible, and I think the more carefully the pieces are put on the stage the more critical I become concerning their probability; and when I hear the praise of the beautiful and expensive theatrical wardrobes which, in the case of actresses seem to set the fashion for the wealthy and well-born, I feel that it is a costly means of making the story more unlikely. I seem to lose the identity of the heroine who in two hours wears three or four different toilettes complete. As Mrs Oliphant did not identify the "nobody in white tights" who rendered from *Twelfth Night* the lovely lines beginning "That strain again; it had a dying fall" with the Orsino she had imagined when reading the play, so I, who knew *She Stoops to Conquer* almost by heart, was disappointed when I saw it on the stage. I was taken to the opera once by Mr and Mrs Bakewell, and heard Patti in *Don Giovanni*, at Covent Garden, but opera of all kinds is wasted on me. I liked some of the familiar airs and choruses, but all opera needs far more make-believe than I am capable of. It is a pity that I am so insensible to the youngest and the most progressive of the fine arts. I am, however, in the good company of Mrs Oliphant, who, speaking of the musical parties in Eton, where she lived so long, for the education of her boys, writes in words that suit me perfectly:

> In one of these friends' houses a family quartet played what were rather new and terrible to me — long sonatas and concerted pieces which filled my soul with dismay. It is a dreadful confession to make, and proceeds from want of education and instruction, but I fear any appreciation of music I have is purely literary. I love a song and a "tune"; the humblest fiddler has sometimes given me the greatest pleasure, and sometimes gone to my heart; but music, properly so called, the only music that many of my friends would listen to, is to me a wonder and a mystery. My mind wanders through adagios and andantes, gaping, longing to understand. Will no one tell me what it means? I want to find the old unhappy far off things which Wordsworth imagined in the Gaelic song of the "Highland Lass". I feel out of it, uneasy, thinking all the time what a poor creature I must be. I remember the mother of the sonata players approaching me with beaming countenance on the occasion of one of these performances, expecting the compliment which I faltered forth, doing my best not to look insincere. "And I have this every evening of my life," cried the triumphant mother. "Good heavens, and you have survived it all" was my internal response.

IX MEETING WITH J. S. MILL AND GEORGE ELIOT

... Stuart Mill's wife was the sister of Arthur and of Alfred Hardy, of Adelaide, and the former had given to me a copy of the first edition of Mill's *Political Economy*, with the original dedication to Mrs John Taylor, who afterwards became Mill's wife, which did not appear in subsequent editions; but, as he had two gift copies of the same edition, Mr Hardy sent it on to me with his most illegible handwriting: "To Miss Spence from the author, not, indeed, directly, but in the confidence felt by the presenter that in so doing he is fulfilling the wish of the author − viz., circulating his opinions, more especially in such quarters as the present, where they will be accurately considered and tested." I had also seen the dedication to Harriet Mill's beloved memory of the noble book on *Liberty*. Of her own individual work there was only one specimen extant − an article on the "Enfranchisement of women", included in Mill's collected essays − very good, certainly, but not so overpoweringly excellent as I expected. Of course, it was an early advocacy of the rights of women, or rather a revival of Mary Wollstonecraft's grand vindication of the rights of the sex; and this was a reform which Mill himself took up more warmly than proportional representation, and advocated for years before Mr Hare's revelation. For myself, I considered electoral reform on the Hare system of more value than the enfranchisement of women, and was not eager for the doubling of the electors in number, especially as the new voters would probably be more ignorant and more apathetic than the old. I was accounted a weak-kneed sister by those who worked primarily for woman suffrage, although I was as much convinced as they were that I was entitled to a vote, and hoped that I might be able to exercise it before I was too feeble to hobble to the poll. I have unfortunately lost the letter Mr Mill wrote to me about my letters to *The Register*, and my *Plea for Pure Democracy*, but it gave him great pleasure to see that a new idea both of the theory and practice of politics had been taken up and expanded by a woman, and one from that Australian colony, of which he had watched and aided the beginnings, as is seen by the name of Mill Terrace, North Adelaide, today. Indeed, both Hare and Mill told me their first converts were women; and I felt that the absolute disinterestedness of my *Plea*, which was not for myself, but only that the men who were supposed to represent me at the polling booth should be equitably represented themselves, lent weight to my arguments. I have no axe to grind − no political party to serve; so

J.S. Mill and George Eliot

that it was not until the movement for the enfranchisement of women grew too strong to be neglected that I took hold of it at all; and I do not claim any credit for its success in South Australia and the Commonwealth, further than this — that by my writings and my spoken addresses I showed that one woman had a steady grasp on politics and on sociology. In 1865, when I was in England, Mr Mill was permanently resident at Avignon, where his wife died, but he had to come to England to canvass for a seat in Parliament for Westminster as an Independent member, believed at that time to be an advanced Radical, but known to be a philosopher, and an economist of the highest rank in English literature. I had only one opportunity of seeing him personally, and I did not get so much out of him as I expected — he was so eager to know how the colony and colonial people were developing. He asked me about property in land and taxation, and the relations between employers and exployes, and I was a little amused and a little alarmed when he said he was glad to get information from such knowledge; but he said he knew I was observant and thoughtful, and what I had seen I had seen well. He was particularly earnest about woman's suffrage, and Miss Taylor, his stepdaughter, said she thought he had made a mistake in asking for the vote for single women only and widows with property and wives who had a separate estate; it would have been more logical to have asked for the vote on the same terms as were extended to men. The great man said meekly — "Well, perhaps I have made a mistake, but I thought with a property qualification the beginning would awake less antagonism." He said to me that if I was not to return to London till January we were not likely to meet again. He walked with me bareheaded to the gate, and it was farewell for both.

Wise man as Mill was he did not foresee that his greatest object, the enfranchisement of women, would be carried at the antipodes long before there was victory either in England or America. When I received, in 1869, from the publisher, Mr Mill's last book, *The Subjection of Women*, I wrote thanking him for the gift. The reply was as follows:

Avignon, November 28, 1869

Dear Madam

Your letter of August 16 has been sent to me here. The copy of my little book was intended for you, and I had much pleasure in offering it. The movement against women's disabilities generally, and for the suffrage in particular, has made great progress in England since you were last there. It is likely, I think, to be successful in the colonies later than in England, because the want of equality in social advantages bet-

ween women and men is less felt in the colonies owing, perhaps, to women's having less need of other occupations than those of married life.

I am, dear Madam, yours very truly,
J. S. Mill

I have always held that, though the Pilgrim Fathers ignored the right of the Pilgrim Mothers to the credit of founding the American States — although these women had to take their full share of the toils and hardships and perils of pioneer and frontier life, and had in addition to put up with the Pilgrim Fathers themselves — Australian colonization was carried out by men who were conscious of the service of their helpmates, and grateful for it. In New Zealand and South Australia, founded on the Wakefield system, where the sexes were almost equal in number, and the immigration was mainly that of families, the first great triumphs for the political enfranchisement of women were won, and through South Australia the women of the Commonwealth obtained the Federal vote for both Houses; whereas even in the sparsely inhabited western states in the United States which have obtained the state vote the Federal vote is withheld from them. But Mill died in 1873, twenty years before New Zealand or Colorado obtained woman's suffrage.

In treating of my one interview with Mr Mill I have carried the narrative down to 1869. With regard to my single meeting with George Eliot, I have to begin in 1865, and conclude even later. Before I left England Mr Williams, of Smith, Elder and Co., offered me an introduction to George Henry Lewes, and I expressed the hope that it might also include an introduction to George Eliot, whose works I so admired. Mr Lewes being away from home when I called, I requested that the introductory letter of Mr Williams should be taken to George Eliot herself. She received me in the big Priory drawing room, with the grand piano, where she held her receptions and musical evenings; but she asked me if I had any business relating to the article which Mr Williams had mentioned, and I had to confess that I had none. For once I felt myself at fault. I did not get on with George Eliot. She said she was not well, and she did not look well. That strong pale face, where the features were those of Dante or Savanarola, did not soften as Mill's had done. The voice, which was singularly musical and impressive, touched me — I am more susceptible to voices than to features or complexion — but no subject that I started seemed to fall in with her ideas, and she started none in which I could follow her lead pleasantly. It was a short interview, and it was a failure. I felt I had been looked on as an inquisitive

J.S. Mill and George Eliot

Australian desiring an interview upon any pretext; and indeed, next day I had a letter from Mr Williams, in which he told me that, but for the idea that I had some business arrangement to speak of, she would not have seen me at all. So I wrote to Mr Williams that, as I had been received by mistake, I should never mention the interview; but that impertinent curiosity was not at all my motive in going that unlucky day to The Priory.

Years passed by. I read everything, poetry and prose that came from George Eliot's pen, and was so strong an admirer of her that Mr W. L. Whitham, who took charge of the Unitarian Church while our pastor (Mr Woods) had a long furlough in England, asked me to lecture on her works to his Mutual Improvement Society, and I undertook the task with joy. Mr H. G. Turner asked for the MS to publish in the second number of *The Melbourne Review*, a very promising quarterly for politics and literature. I thought that, if I sent the review to George Eliot with a note it might clear me from the suspicion of being a mere vulgar lionhunter. Her answer was as follows:

> The Priory,
> North Bank, Regent's Park,
> September 4, 1876.
>
> Dear Madam
>
> Owing to an absence of some months, it was only the other day that I read your kind letter of April 17; and, although I have long been obliged to give up answering the majority of letters addressed to me, I felt much pleased that you have given me an opportunity of answering one from you; for I have always remembered your visit with a regretful feeling that I had probably caused you some pain by a rather unwise effort to give you a reception which the state of my health at the moment made altogether blundering and infelicitous. The mistake was all on my side, and you were not in the least to blame. I also remember that your studies have been of a serious kind, such as were likely to render a judgment on fiction and poetry, or, as the Germans, with better classification, say, in "Dichtung" in general, quite other than the superficial haphazard remarks of which reviews are generally made. You will all the better understand that I have made it a rule not to read writing about myself. I am exceptionally sensitive and liable to discouragement; and to read much remark about my doings would have as depressing an effect on me as staring in a mirror — perhaps, I may say, of defective glass. But my husband looks at all the numerous articles that are forwarded to me, and kindly keeps them out of my way — only on rare occasions reading to me a passage which he thinks will comfort me by its evidence of unusual insight or sympathy. Yesterday he read your article in *The Melbourne Review*, and said at the end — "This is an excellently written article, which would do credit to any English periodical", adding the very uncommon testimony, "I shall

keep this". Then he told me of some passages in it which gratified me by that comprehension of my meaning — that laying of the finger on the right spot — which is more precious than praise, and forthwith he went to lay *The Melbourne Review* in the drawer he assigns to any writing about me that gives him pleasure. For he feels on my behalf more than I feel on my own, at least in matters of this kind. If you come to England again when I happen to be in town I hope that you will give me the pleasure of seeing you under happier auspices than those of your former visit.

I am, dear madam, yours sincerely,
M. G. Lewes

The receipt of this kind and candid letter gave me much pleasure; and, although on the strength of that, I cannot boast of being a correspondent of that great woman, I was able to say that I had seen and talked with her, and that she considered me a competent critic of her work. Mrs Oliphant says that George Eliot's life impelled her to make an involuntary confession — "How have I been handicapped in life? Should I have done better if I had been kept, like her, in a mental greenhouse and taken care of? I have always had to think of other people and to plan everything — for my own pleasure, it is true, very often, but always in subjection to the necessity which bound me to them. To bring up the boys — my own and Frank's — for the service of God was better than to write a fine novel, if it had been in my power to do so." There might have been some points in which George Eliot might have envied Mrs Oliphant.

X RETURN FROM THE OLD COUNTRY

I returned to Australia, when this island continent was in the grip of one of the most severe and protracted droughts in its history. The war between Prussia and Austria had begun and ended; the failure of Overend and Gurney and others brought commercial disaster; and my brother, with other bankers, had anxious days and sleepless nights. Some rich men became richer; many poor men went down altogether. Our recovery was slow but sure. In the meantime I found life at home very dull after my interesting experiences abroad. There was nothing to do for proportional representation except to write an occasional letter to the press. So I started another novel, which was published serially in *The Observer*. Mr George Bentley, who published it subsequently in book form, changed its title from *Hugh Lindsay's Guest* to *The Author's Daughter*. But my development as a public speaker was

more important than the publication of a fourth novel. Much had been written on the subject of public speaking by men, but so far nothing concerning the capacities of women in that direction. And yet I think all teachers will agree that girls in the aggregate excel boys in their powers of expression, whether in writing, or in speech, though boys may surpass them in such studies as arithmetic and mathematics. Yet law and custom have put a bridle on the tongue of women, and of the innumerable proverbs relating to her use of language. Her only qualification for public speaking in old days was that she could scold, and our ancestors imposed a salutary check on this by the ducking stool in public, and sticks no thicker than the thumb for marital correction in private. The writer of the Proverbs alludes to the perpetual dropping of a woman's tongue as an intolerable nuisance, and declares that it is better to live on the housetop than with a brawling woman in a wide house. A later writer, describing the virtuous woman, said that on her lips is the law of kindness, and after all this is the real feminine characteristic. As daughter, sister, wife, and mother — what does not the world owe to the gracious words, the loving counsel, the ready sympathy which she expresses? Until recent years, however, these feminine gifts have been strictly kept for home consumption, and only exercised for the woman's family and a limited circle of friends. In 1825, when I first opened my eyes to the world, there were indeed women who displayed an interest in public affairs. My own mother not only felt the keenest solicitude regarding the passing of the Reform Bill, but she took up her pen, and with two letters to the local press, under the signature of "Grizel Plowter", showed the advantages of the proposed measure. But public speaking was absolutely out of the question for women, and though I was the most ambitious of girls, my desire was to write a great book — not at all to sway an audience.

When I returned from my first visit to England in 1866, I was asked by the committee of the South Australian Institute to write a lecture on my impressions of England, different from the article which had appeared in *The Cornhill Magazine* under that title, but neither the committee nor myself thought of the possibility of my delivering it. My good friend, the late Mr John Howard Clark, editor of *The Register*, kindly offered to read it. I did not go to hear it, but I was told that he had difficulty in reading my manuscript, and that, though he was a beautiful reader, it was not very satisfactory. So I mentally resolved that if I was again asked I should offer to read my own MS. Five years afterwards I was asked for two literary lectures by the same committee, and I chose as

my subjects the works of Elizabeth Browning and those of her husband, Robert Browning. Now, I consider that the main thing for a lecturer is to be heard, and a rising young lawyer (now our Chief Justice) kindly offered to take the back seat, and promised to raise his hand if he could not hear. It was not raised once, so I felt satisfied. I began by saying that I undertook the work for two reasons — first, to make my audience more familiar with the writings of two poets very dear to me; and second, to make it easier henceforward for any woman who felt she had something to say to stand up and say it. I felt very nervous, and as if my knees were giving way; but I did not show any nervousness. I read the lecture, but most of the quotations I recited from memory. Not having had any lessons in elocution, I trusted to my natural voice, and felt that in this new role the less gesticulation I used the better. Whether the advice of Demosthenes is rightly translated or not — first requisite, action; second, action; third, action — I am sure that English word does not express the requisite for women. I should rather call it earnestness — a conviction that what you say is worth saying, and worth saying to the audience before you. I had a lesson on the danger of overaction from hearing a gentleman recite in public "The Dream of Eugene Aram", in which he went through all the movements of killing and burying the murdered man. When a tale is crystallised into a poem it does not require the action of a drama. However little action I may use I never speak in public with gloves on. They interfere with the natural eloquence of the hand. After these lectures I occasionally was asked to give others on literary subjects.

XI WARDS OF THE STATE

Land was bought and plans were drawn up for an industrial school at Magill, five miles from Adelaide, when Miss Clark came to me and asked me to help her to take a different course. She enlisted Mrs (afterwards Lady) Davenport in the cause, and we arranged for a deputation to the Minister; Howard Clark, Neville Blyth, and Mr C. B. Young joined us. We offered to find country homes and provide lady visitors, but our request was simply scouted. As we did not offer to bear any of the cost, it would be absurd to give us any share in the administration. Children would only be given homes for the sake of the money paid, and Oliver Twist's was held up as the sort of apprenticeship likely to be secured for pauper children. So we had to play the waiting game. The school built to accommodate 230 children was on four floors,

though there were forty acres of good land. It was so popular that, though only 130 went in at first, in two years it was so full that there was talk of adding a wing. This was our opportunity, and the same men and women went on another deputation, and this time we prevailed, and were allowed to place out the overflow as an experiment; and not only the Boarding-out Committee, but the official heads of the Destitute Department, were surprised and delighted with the good homes we secured for five shillings a week, and with the improvement in health, in intelligence, and in happiness that resulted from putting children into natural homes. What distinguishes work for children in Australia from what is done elsewhere is that it is national, and not philanthropic. The state is *in loco parentis*, and sees that what the child needs are a home and a mother — that, if the home and the mother are good, the child shall be kept there; but that vigilant inspection is needed, voluntary or official — better to have both. Gradually the Magill School was emptied, and the children were scattered. Up to the age of thirteen the home was subsidized, but when by the education law the child was free from school attendance, and went to service, the supervision continued until the age of eighteen was reached. For nearly fourteen years, from 1872 to 1886, the Boarding-out Society pursued its modest labours as auxiliary to the Destitute Board. Our volunteer visitors reported in duplicate — one copy for the official board, and one for the unofficial committee. When the method was inaugurated, Mr T. S. Reed, chairman of the board, was completely won over. We had nothing to do with the reformatories, except that our visitors went to see those placed out at service in their neighbourhood.

XII PREACHING, FRIENDS, AND WRITING

It was through Miss Martha Turner that I was introduced to her brother and to *The Melbourne Review*. She was at that time pastor of the Unitarian Church in Melbourne. She had during the long illness of Rev. Mr Higginson helped her brother with the services. At first she wrote sermons for him to deliver, but on some occasions when he was indisposed she read her own compositions. Fine reader as Mr H. G. Turner is he did not come up to her, and especially he could not equal her in the presentment of her own thoughts. The congregation on the death of Mr Higginson asked Miss Turner to accept the pastorate. She said she could conduct the services, but she absolutely declined to do the pastoral duties — visiting especially. She was licensed to conduct marriage ser-

vices and baptized (or, as we call it, consecrated) children to the service of Almighty God and to the service of man. During the absence of our pastor for a long holiday in England Mr C.L. Whitham, afterwards an education inspector, took his place for two years, and he arranged for an exchange of three weeks with Miss Turner. She was the first woman I ever heard in the pulpit. I was thrilled by her exquisite voice, by her earnestness, and by her reverence. I felt as I had never felt before that if women are excluded from the Christian pulpit you shut out more than half of the devoutness that is in the world. Reading George Eliot's description of Dinah Morris preaching Methodism on the green at Hayslope had prepared me in a measure, but when I heard a highly educated and exceptionally able woman conducting the services all through, and especially reading the Scriptures of the Old and New Testaments with so much intelligence that they seemed to take on new meaning. I felt how much the world had been losing for so many centuries. She twice exchanged with Adelaide — the second time when Mr Woods had returned — and it was the beginning to me of a close friendship.

Imitation, they say, is the sincerest flattery; and when a similar opportunity was offered to me during an illness of Mr Woods, when no layman was available, I was first asked to read a sermon of Martineau's, and then I suggested that I might give something of my own. My first original sermon was on "Enoch and Columbus", and my second on "Content, discontent, and uncontent". I suppose I have preached more than a hundred times in my life, mostly in the Wakefield Street pulpit; but in Melbourne and Sydney I am always asked for help; and when I went to America in 1893-94 I was offered seven pulpits — one in Toronto, Canada, and six in the United States. The preparation of my sermons — for, after the first one I delivered, they were always original — has always been a joy and delight to me, for I prefer that my subjects as well as their treatment shall be as humanly helpful as it is possible to make them. In Sydney particularly I have preached to fine audiences.

* * *

For one of my sermons I wrote an original parable, which pleased my friends so much that I include it in the account of my life's work.

> And it came to pass after the five days of Creation which were periods of unknown length of time that God took the soul, the naked soul, with which He was to endow the highest of his creatures — into Eden to look with Him on the work which He had accomplished. And the Soul could see, could hear, could understand, though there were

neither eyes, nor ears, nor limbs, nor bodily organs to do its bidding. And God said, "Soul, thou shalt have a body as these creatures that thou seest around thee have. Thou art to be king, and rule over them all. Thy mission is to subdue the earth, and make it fruitful and more beautiful than it is even now, in thus its dawn. Which of all these living creatures wouldst thou resemble? And the Soul looked, and the Soul listened, and the Soul understood. The beauty of the birds first attracted him, and their songs were sweet, and their loving care of their young called forth a response in the Prophetic Soul. But the sweet singers could not subdue the earth — nay, even the strongest voice could not. Then the Soul gazed on the lion in his strength; on the deer in his beauty. He saw the large-eyed bull with the cow by his side, licking her calf. The stately horse, the huge elephant, the ungainly camel — could any of these subdue the earth? He looked down, and they made it shake with their heavy tread, but the Soul knew that the earth could not be subdued by them. Then he saw a pair of monkeys climbing a tree — the female had a little one in her arms. Where the birds had wings, and the beasts four legs planted on the ground, the monkeys had arms, and, at the end of each, hands, with five fingers; they gathered nuts and cracked them, and picked out the kernels, throwing the shells away — the mother caressed her young one with gentle fingers. The Soul saw also the larger ape with its almost upright form. "Ah!" sighed the Soul, "they are not beautiful like the other creatures, neither are they so strong as many of them. But their forelimbs, with hands and fingers to grasp with, are what I need to subdue the earth, for they will be the servants who can best obey my will. Let me stand upright and gaze upward, and this is the body that I choose." And God said, "Soul, thou hast chosen well, Thou shalt be larger and stronger than these creatures thou seest; thou shalt stand upright, and look upward and onward. And the Soul can create beauty for itself, when it shines through the body." And it was so, and Adam stood erect and gave names to all other creatures.

* * *

[In] the seventies I wrote *Gathered In*, which I believed to be my best novel — the novel into which I put the most of myself, the only novel I wrote with tears of emotion. Mrs Oliphant says that Jeanie Deans is more real to her than any of her own creations, and probably it is the same with me, except for this one work. From an old diary of the fifties, when my first novels were written I take this extract: "Queer that I who have such a distinct idea of what I approve in flesh-and-blood men, should only achieve in pen and ink a set of impossible people, with an absurd muddy expression of gloom, instead of sublime depth as I intended. Men novelists' women are as impossible creations as my men, but there is this difference — their productions satisfy them, mine fail to satisfy me." But in my last novel — still unpublished — I felt quite satisfied that I had at last achieved my ambition to create

characters that stood out distinctly and real. Miss Clark took the MS to England, but she could not get either Bentley or Smith Elder, or Macmillan to accept it.

On the death of Mr John Howard Clark, which took place at this time, Mr John Harvey Finlayson was left to edit *The Register*, and I became a regular outside contributor to *The Register* and *The Observer*. He desired to keep up and if possible improve the literary side of the papers, and felt that the loss of Mr Clark might be in some measure made up if I gave myself wholeheartedly to the work. Leading articles were to be written at my own risk. If they suited the policy of the paper they would be accepted, otherwise not. What a glorious opening for my ambition and for my literary proclivities came to me in July 1878, when I was in my fifty-third year! Many leading articles were rejected, but not one literary or social article. Generally these last appeared in both daily and weekly papers. I recollect the second original social article I wrote was on "Equality as an influence on society and manners", suggested by Matthew Arnold. The much-travelled Smythe, then, I think, touring with Charles Clark, wrote to Mr Finlayson from Wallaroo thus: "In this dead-alive place, where one might fire a mitrailleuse down the principal street without hurting anybody, I read this delightful article in yesterday's *Register*. When we come again in Adelaide, and we collect a few choice spirits, be sure to invite the writer of this article to join us." I felt as if the round woman had got at last into the round hole which fitted her; and in my little study, with my books and my pigeon holes, and my dear old mother sitting with her knitting on her rocking chair at the low window, I had the knowledge that she was interested in all I did. I generally read the MS to her before it went to the office. What is more remarkable, perhaps, is that the excellent maid who was with us for twelve years, picked out everything of mine that was in the papers and read it. A series of papers called "Some Social Aspects of Early Colonial Life" I contributed under the pseudonym of "A Colonist of 1839". From 1878 till 1893, when I went round the world via America, I held the position of outside contributor on the oldest newspaper in the state, and for these fourteen years I had great latitude. My friend Dr Garran, then editor of *The Sydney Morning Herald*, accepted reviews and articles from me. Sometimes I reviewed the same books for both, but I wrote the articles differently, and made different quotations, so that I scarcely think any one could detect the same hand in them; but generally they were different books and different subjects, which I treated. I tried *The Australasian* with a story, "Afloat and Ashore", and with a social article on "Wealth,

Waste, and Want". I contributed to *The Melbourne Review*, and later to *The Victorian Review*, which began by paying well, but filtered out gradually. I found journalism a better paying business for me than novel writing, and I delighted in the breadth of the canvas on which I could draw my sketches of books and of life. I believe that my work on newspapers and reviews is more characteristic of me, and intrinsically better work than what I have done in fiction; but when I began to wield the pen, the novel was the line of least resistance. When I was introduced in 1894 to Mrs Croly, the oldest woman journalist in the United States, as an Australian journalist, I found that her work, though good enough, was essentially woman's work, dress, fashions, functions, with educational and social outlooks from the feminine point of view. My work might show the larger questions which were common to humanity; and when I recall the causes which I furthered, and which in some instances I started, I feel inclined to magnify the office of the anonymous contributor to the daily press. And I acknowledge not only the kindness of friends who put some of the best new books in my way, but the large-minded tolerance of the editors of *The Register*, who gave me such a free hand in the treatment of books, of men, and of public questions.

XIII   MY WORK FOR EDUCATION

I was the first woman appointed on a Board of Advice under the Education Department, and found the work interesting. The powers of the board were limited to an expenditure of £5 for repairs without applying to the department and to interviewing the parents of children who had failed to attend the prescribed number of days, as well as those who pleaded poverty as an excuse for the non-payment of fees. I always felt that the school fees were a heavy burden on the poor, and rejoiced accordingly when free education was introduced into South Australia. This was the second state to adopt this great reform, Victoria preceding it by a few years. I objected to the payment of fees on another ground. I felt they bore heavily on the innocent children themselves through the notion of caste which was created in the minds of those who paid fees to the detriment of their less fortunate school companions. And again, education that is compulsory should be free. Other women have since become members of school boards, but I was the pioneer of that branch of public work for women in this state. It is a privilege that American women have been fighting for for many years — to vote for and

to be eligible to sit on school boards. In many of the states this has been won to their great advantage.

* * *

It had been suggested by the Minister of Education of that period that the children attending the state schools should be instructed in the duties of citizenship, and that they should be taught something of the laws under which they lived, and I was commissioned to write a short and pithy statement of the case. It was to be simple enough for intelligent children in the fourth class; eleven or twelve — it was to lead from the known to the unknown — it might include the elements of political economy and sociology — it might make use of familiar illustrations from the experience of a new country — but it must not be long. It was not very easy to satisfy myself and Mr Hartley — who was a severe critic — but when the book of 120 pages was completed he was satisfied. A preface I wrote for the second edition — the first five thousand copies being insufficient for the requirements of the schools — will give some idea of the plan of the work: "In writing this little book, I have aimed less at symmetrical perfection than at simplicity of diction, and such arrangement as would lead from the known to the unkown, by which the older children in our public schools might learn not only the actual facts about the laws they live under, but also some of the principles which underlie all law." The reprinting gave me an opportunity to reply to my critics that "political economy, trades unions, insurance companies, and newspapers" were outside the scope of the laws we live under. But I thought that in a new state where the optional duties of the Government are so numerous, it was of great importance for the young citizen to understand economic principles. As conduct is the greater part of life, and morality, not only the bond of social union, but the main source of individual happiness, I took the ethical part of the subject first, and tried to explain that education was of no value unless it was used for good purposes. As without some wealth, civilization was impossible, I next sought to show that national and individual wealth depends on the security that is given by law, and on the industry and thrift which that security encourages. Land tenure is of the first importance in colonial prosperity, and consideration of the land revenue and the limitations as to its expenditure led me to the necessity for taxation and the various modes of levying it. Taxation led me to the power which imposes, collects, and expends it. This involved a consideration of those representative institutions which made the Government at once the master and the servant of the people. Under this Government our persons and our prosperity are pro-

tected by a system of criminal, civil, and insolvent law — each considered in its place. Although not absolutely included in the laws we live under, I consider that providence, and its various outlets in banks, savings banks, joint stock companies, friendly societies, and trades unions, were matters too important to be left unnoticed; and also those influences which shape character quite as much as statute laws — public opinion, the newspaper, and amusements. As the use of my little book was restricted solely to school hours, my hope that the parents might be helped and encouraged by its teaching was doomed to disappointment. But the children of thirty-years ago, when *The Laws We Live Under* was first published, are the men and women of today, and who shall say but that among them are to be found some at least worthy and true citizens, who owe to my little book their first inspiration to "hitch their wagon to a star". Last year an enthusiastic young Swedish teacher and journalist was so taken with this South Australian little handbook of civics that he urged on me the duty of bringing it up to date, and embracing women's suffrage, the relations of the states to the Commonwealth, as well as the industrial legislation which is in many ways peculiar to Australia, but although those in authority were sympathetic no steps have been taken for its reproduction.

Identified as I had been for so many years with elementary education in South Australia, my mind was well prepared to applaud the movement in favour of the higher education of poorer children of both sexes by the foundation of bursaries and scholarships, and the opening up of the avenues of learning to women by admitting them to university degrees. Victoria was the first to take this step, and all over the Commonwealth the example has been followed. I am, however, somewhat disappointed that university women are not more generally progressive in their ideas. They have won something which I should have been very glad of, but which was quite out of reach. All opportunities ought to be considered as opportunities for service.

* * *

But one exception I must make to the aloofness of people with degrees and professions from the preventible evils of the world, and that is in the profession that is the longest and the most exacting — the medical profession. The women doctors whom I have met in Adelaide, Melbourne, and Sydney have a keen sense of their responsibility to the less fortunate. That probably is because medicine as now understood and practised is the most modern of the learned professions, and is more human than engineering, which is also modern. It takes us into the homes of the poor more

intimately than even the clergyman, and it offers remedies and palliatives as well as advice. The law is little studied by women in Australia, but in the United States there are probably a thousand or more legal practitioners. It is the profession that I should have chosen when I was young if it had been in any way feasible. I had no bent for the medical profession, and still less for what every one thinks the most womanly of avocations — that of the trained nurse. I could nurse my own relatives more or less well, but did not distinguished myself in that way, and I could not devote myself to strangers.

XIV SPECULATION, CHARITY, AND A BOOK

I have been strongly tempted to omit altogether the next book which I wrote; but, as this is to be a sincere narrative of my life and its work, I must pierce the veil of anonymity and own up to *An Agnostic's Progress*. I had been impressed with the very different difficulties the soul of man has to encounter nowadays from those so triumphantly overcome by Christian in the great work of John Bunyan in the first part of *The Pilgrim's Progress*. He cannot now get out of the Slough of Despond by planting his foot on the stepping stones of the Promises. He cannot, like Hopeful, pluck from his bosom the Key of Promise which opens every lock in Doubting Castle when the two pilgrims are shut in it by Giant Despair, when they are caught trespassing on his grounds. Even assured Christians, we know, may occasionally trespass on these grounds of doubt; but the weapons of modern warfare are not of the seventeenth century. The Interpreter's House in the old allegory dealt only with things found in the Bible, the only channel of revelation to John Bunyan. To the modern pilgrim God reveals Himself in Nature, in art, in literature, and in history. The Interpreter's Hand had to do with all these things. Vanity Fair is not a place through which all pilgrims must pass as quickly as possible, shutting their eyes and stopping their ears so that they should neither see nor hear the wicked things that are done and said there. Vanity Fair is the world in which we all have to live and do our work well, or neglect it. Pope and Pagan are not the old giants who used to devour pilgrims, but who can now only gnash their teeth at them in impotent rage. They are live forces, quite active, and with agents and supporters alert to capture souls. Of all the influences which affected for evil my young life I perhaps resented most Mrs Sherwood's *Infant's Progress*. There were three children in it going

Speculation, Charity, and a Book

from the City of Destruction to the Celestial City by the route laid down by John Bunyan; but they were handicapped even more severely than the good Christian himself with his heavy burden — for that fell off his back at the first sight of the Cross and Him who was nailed to it, accepted by the eye of Faith as the one Sacrifice for the sins of the world — for the three little ones, Humble Mind, Playful, and Peace, were accompanied always and everywhere by an imp called Inbred Sin, who never ceased to tempt them to evil.

The doctrine of innate human depravity is one of the most paralysing dogmas that human fear invented or priestcraft encouraged. I did not think of publishing *An Agnostic's Progress* at first. I wrote it to relieve my own mind. I wanted to satisfy myself that reverent agnostics were by no means materialists; that man's nature might or might not be consciously immortal, but it was spiritual; that in the duties which lay before each of us towards ourselves and towards our fellow-creatures, there was scope for spiritual energy and spiritual emotion. I was penetrated by Browning's great idea expressed over and over again — the expansion of Paul's dictum that faith is not certainty, but a belief without sufficient proof, a belief which leads to right action and to self-sacrifice. Of the seventy years of life which one might hope to live and work in, I had no mean idea. I asked in the newspaper, "Is life so short?" and answered, "No". I expanded and spiritualized the idea in a sermon, and I again answered emphatically "No". I saw the continuation and the expansion of true ideas by succeeding generations. To the question put sometimes peevishly, "Is life worth living?" I replied with equal emphasis, "Yes". My mother told me of old times. I recalled half a century of progress, and I hoped the forward movement would continue. I read the manuscript of *An Agnostic's Progress* to Mr and Mrs Barr Smith, and they thought so well of it that they offered to take it to England on one of their many visits to the old country, where they had no doubt it would find a publisher. Trubner's reader reported most favourably of the book, and we thought there was an immediate prospect of its publication; but Mr Trubner died, and the matter was not taken up by his successor, and my friends did what I had expressly said they were not to do, and had it printed and published at their own expense. There were many printer's errors in it, but it was on the whole well reviewed, though it did not sell well. *The Spectator* joined issue with me on the point that it is only through the wicket gate of Doubt that we can come to any faith that is of value; but I am satisfied that I took the right stand there. My mother was in no way disquieted or

disturbed by my writing the book, and few of my friends read it or knew about it. I still appeared so engrossed with work on *The Register* and *The Observer* that my time was quite well enough accounted for. I tried for a prize of £100 offered by *The Sydney Mail* with a novel called *Handfasted*, but was not successful, for the judge feared that it was calculated to loosen the marriage tie — it was too socialistic, and consequently dangerous.

XV JOURNALISM AND POLITICS

My friend the late Professor Pearson had entered into active political life in Melbourne, and was a regular writer for *The Age*. Perhaps no other man underwent more obloquy from his old friends for taking the side of Graham Berry, especially as he was a Freetrader, and the popular party was Protectionist. He justified his action by saying that a mistake in the fiscal policy of a country should not prevent a real Democrat from siding with the party which opposed monopoly, especially in land. He saw in "lalifundia" — huge estates — the ruin of the Roman Empire, and its prevalence in the United Kingdom was the greatest danger ahead of it. In these young countries the tendency to build up large holdings was naturally fostered by what was the earliest of our industries. Sheepfarming is not greatly pursued in the United States or Canada, because of the rigorous winter — but Australia is the favourite home of the merino sheep. Originally there was no need to buy land, or even to pay rent to the Government for it; the land had no value till settlement gave it. The squatter leased it on easy terms, and bought it only when it had sufficient value to be desired by agriculturists or by selectors who posed as agriculturists. When he bought it he generally complained of the price these selectors compelled him to pay, but it was then secure; and, with the growth of population and the railroads and other improvements, these enforced purchasers, even in 1877, had built up vast estates in single hands in every State in Australia. In *The Melbourne Review* for April 1877, Professor Pearson sketched a plan of land taxation, which was afterwards carried out, in which the area of land held was the test for graduated taxation. Henry George had not then declared his gospel; and, although I felt that there was something very faulty in the scheme, I did not declare in my article on the subject that an acre in Collins Street might be of more value than fifty thousand acres of pastoral land five hundred miles from the seaboard, and was therefore more fitly liable to taxation for the advantage of the whole community, who had

given to that acre this exceptional value. I did not declare it because I did not believe it. But I thought that the end aimed at — the breaking up of large estates — could be better and more safely affected, though not so quickly, by a change in the incidence of succession duties.

Some time after I saw a single copy of Henry George's *Progress and Poverty* on Robertson's shelves, and bought it, and it was I who after reading this book opened in the three most important Australian colonies the question of the taxation of land values. An article I wrote went into *The Register*, and Mr Liston, of Kapunda, read it, and spoke of it at a farmers' meeting. I had then a commission from *The Sydney Morning Herald* to write on any important subject, and I wrote on this. It appeared, like a previous article on Howell's "Conflicts of Capital and Labour", as an unsigned article. A new review, *The Victorian*, had been started by Mortimer Franklyn, which paid contributors; and, now that I was a professional journalist, I thought myself entitled to ask remuneration. I sent to the new periodical, published in Melbourne, a fuller treatment of the book than had been given to the two newspapers, under the title of "A Californian Political Economist". This fell into the hands of Henry George himself, in a reading room in San Francisco, and he wrote an acknowledgement of it to me. In South Australia the first tax on unimproved land values was imposed. It was small — only a halfpenny in the pound, but without any exemption; and its imposition was encouraged by the fact that we had had bad seasons and a falling revenue. The income tax in England was originally a war tax, and they say that if there is not a war the United States will never be able to impose an income tax. The separate states have not the power to impose such a tax. Henry George said to me in his home in New York: "I wonder at you, with your zeal and enthusiasm, and your power of speaking, devoting yourself to such a small matter as proportional representation, when you see the great land question before you." I replied that to me it was not a small matter. I cannot, however, write my autobiography without giving prominence to the fact that I was the pioneer in Australia in this as in the other matter of proportional representation.

XVI SORROW AND CHANGE

My dear mother died about eight o'clock on the evening of 8 December 1887, quietly and painlessly. With her death, which was an exceedingly great loss to me, practically ended my quiet

life of literary work. Henceforth I was free to devote my efforts to the fuller public work for which I had so often longed, but which my mother's devotion to and dependence on me rendered impossible. But I missed her untiring sympathy, for with all her love for the old days and the old friends there was no movement for the advancement of her adopted land that did not claim her devoted attention.

* * *

Crowded and interesting as my life had been hitherto, the best was yet to be. My realization of Browning's beautiful line from "Rabbi Ben Ezra" — "The last of life, for which the first was made", came when I saw opening before me possibilities for public service undreamed of in my earlier years. For the advancement of effective voting I had so far confined my efforts to the newspapers. My brother John had suggested the change of name from proportional representation to effective voting as one more likely to catch the popular ear, and I had proposed a modification of Hare's original plan of having one huge electorate, and suggested instead the adoption of six-member districts. The state as one electorate returning forty-two members for the Assembly may be magnificent, and may also be the pure essence of democracy, but it is neither commonsense nor practicable. "Why not take effective voting to the people?" was suggested to me. No sooner said than done. I had ballot papers prepared and leaflets printed, and I began the public campaign which has gone on ever since. During a visit to Melbourne as a member of a charities conference it was first discovered that I had some of the gifts of a public speaker. My friend, the Rev. Charles Strong, had invited me to lecture before his working men's club at Collingwood, and I chose as my subject "Effective Voting".

When on my return Mr Barr Smith, who had long grasped the principle of justice underlying effective voting, and was eager for its adoption, offered to finance a lecturing tour through the state, I jumped at the offer. There was the opportunity for which I had been waiting for years. I got up at unearthly hours to catch trains, and sometimes succeeded only through the timely lifts of kindly drivers. Once I went in a carrier's van, because I had missed the early morning cars. I travelled thousands of miles in all weathers to carry to the people the gospel of electoral reform. Disappointments were frequent, and sometimes disheartening; but the silver lining of every cloud turned up somewhere, and I look back on that first lecturing tour as a time of the sowing of good seed, the harvest of which is now beginning to ripen. I had no advance agents to announce my arrival, and at one town in the north I

found nobody at the station to meet me. I spent the most miserable two and a half hours of my life waiting Micawber-like for something to turn up; and it turned up in the person of the village blacksmith. I spoke to him, and explained my mission to the town. He had heard nothing of any meeting. Incidentally I discovered that my correspondent was in Adelaide, and had evidently forgotten all about my coming. "Well," I said to the blacksmith, "if you can get together a dozen intelligent men I will explain effective voting to them." He looked at me with a dumbfounded air, and then burst out, "Good G— —, madam, there are not three intelligent men in the town." But the old order has changed, and in 1909 Mrs Young addressed an enthusiastic audience of 150 in the same town on the same subject. The town, moreover, is in a parliamentary district, in which every candidate at the recent general election — and there were seven of them — supported effective voting. Far down in the south I went to a little village containing seven churches, which accounted (said the local doctor) for the extreme backwardness of its inhabitants. "They have so many church affairs to attend to that there is no time to think of anything else." At the close of this lecturing tour *The Register* undertook the public count through its columns, which did so much to bring the reform before the people of South Australia. Public interest was well aroused on the matter before my long projected trip to America took shape. "Come and teach us how to vote," my American friends had been writing to me for years; but I felt that it was a big order for a little woman of sixty-eight to undertake the conversion to electoral reform of sixty millions of the most conceited people in the world. Still I went. I left Adelaide bound for America on 4 April 1893, as a Government commissioner and delegate to the Great World's Fair Congresses in Chicago.

XVII IMPRESSIONS OF AMERICA

Alfred Cridge, who reminded me so much of my brother David that I felt at home with him immediately, had prepared the way for my lectures on effective voting in San Francisco. He was an even greater enthusiast than I. "America needs the reform more than Australia," he used to say. But if America needs effective voting to check corruption, Australia needs it just as much to prevent the degradation of political life in the Commonwealth and states to the level of American politics. My lectures in San Francisco, as elsewhere in America, were well attended, and even better

received. Party politics had crushed out the best elements of political life, and to be independent of either party gave a candidate, as an agent told Judge Lindsay when he was contesting the governorship of Colorado, "as much chance as a snowball would have in hell". So that reformers everywhere were eager to hear of a system of voting that would free the electors from the tyranny of parties, and at the same time render a candidate independent of the votes of heckling minorities, and dependent only on the votes of the men who believed in him and his politics. I met men and women interested in public affairs — some of them well known, others most worthy to be known, and all willing to lend the weight of their character and intelligence to the betterment of human conditions at home and abroad. Among these were Judge Maguire, a leader of the Bar in San Francisco and a member of the State Legislature, who had fought trusts, "grafters", and "boodlers" through the whole of his public career, and Mr James Barry, proprietor of *The Star*.

"You come from Australia, the home of the secret ballot?" was the greeting I often received, and that really was my passport to the hearts of reformers all over America. From all sides I heard that it was to the energy and zeal of the Single-taxers in the various states — a well-organized and compact body — that the adoption of the secret ballot was due. To that celebrated journalist, poetess, and economic writer, Charlotte Perkins Stetson, who was a cultured Bostonian, living in San Francisco, I owed one of the best women's meetings I ever addressed. The subject was "State children and the compulsory clauses in our Education Act", and everywhere in the States people were interested in the splendid work of our State Children's Department and educational methods. Intelligence and not wealth I found to be the passport to social life among the Americans I met. At a social evening ladies as well as their escorts were expected to remove bonnets and mantles in the hall, instead of being invited into a private room as in Australia — a custom I thought curious until usage made it familiar. The homeliness and unostentatiousness of the middle class American were captivating. My interests have always been in people and in the things that make for human happiness or misery rather than in the beauties of Nature, art, or architecture. I want to know how the people live, what wages are, what the amount of comfort they can buy; how the people are fed, taught, and amused; how the burden of taxation falls; how justice is executed; how much or how little liberty the people enjoy. And these things I learned to a great extent from my social intercourse with those cultured reformers of America. Among these people I had not the

depressing feeling of immensity and hugeness which marred my enjoyment when I arrived at New York. My literary lectures on the Brownings and George Eliot were much appreciated, especially in the East, where I found paying audiences in the fall or autumn of the year. These lectures have been delivered many times in Australia; and, as the result of the Browning lecture given in the Unitarian Schoolroom in Wakefield Street, Adelaide, I received from the pen of Mr J. B. Mather a clever epigram. The room was large and sparsely filled, and to the modest back seat taken by my friend my voice scarcely penetrated. So he amused himself and me by writing:

> I have no doubt that words of sense
> Are falling from the lips of Spence.
> Alas! that Echo should be drowning
> Both words of Spence and sense of Browning.

* * *

The great war in America strengthened the Federal bond, while it loosened the attachment to the special state in which the United States citizen lives. Railroads and telegraphs have done much to make Americans homogeneous, and the school system grapples bravely with the greater task of Americanizing the children of foreigners, who arrive in such vast numbers. Canada allowed the inhabitants of lower Canada to keep their language, their laws, and their denominational schools; and the consequence is that these Canadian–British subjects are more French than the French, more conservative than the Tories, and more Catholic than Irish or Italians. Education is absolutely free in America up to the age of eighteen; but I never heard an American complain of being taxed to educate other people's children. In Auburn I met Harriet Tribman, called the "Moses of her people" — an old black woman who could neither read nor write, but who had escaped from slavery when young, and had made nineteen journeys south, and been instrumental in the escape of three hundred slaves. To listen to her was to be transferred to the pages of *Uncle Tom's Cabin*. Her language was just like that of Tom and old Jeff. A pious Christian, she was full of good works still. Her shanty was a refuge for the sick, blind, and maimed of her own people. I went all over Harvard University under the guidance of Professor Ashley, to whom our Chief Justice had given me a letter of introduction. He got up a drawing-room meeting for me, at which I met Dr Gordon Ames, pastor of the Unitarian Church of the Disciples. He invited me to preach his thanksgiving service for him on the following Thursday, which I was delighted to do. Mrs Ames

was the factory inspector of women and children in Massachusetts, and was probably the wisest woman I met in my travels. She spoke to me of the evils of stimulating the religious sentiment too young, and said that the hushed awe with which most people spoke of God and His constant presence filled a child's mind with fear.

* * *

I account it one of the great privileges of my visit to America that Mrs Garrison introduced me to Oliver Wendell Holmes, and by appointment I had an hour and a half's chat with him in the last year of his long life. He was the only survivor of a famous band of New England writers. Longfellow, Emerson, Hawthorn, Bryant, Lowell, Whittier, and Whitman were dead. His memory was failing, and he forgot some of his own characters; but Elsie Venner he remembered perfectly and he woke to full animination when I objected to the fatalism of heredity as being about as paralysing to effort as the fatalism of Calvinism. As a medical man (and we are apt to forget the physician in the author) he took strong views of heredity. As a worker among our destitute children, I considered environment the greater factor of the two, and spoke of children of the most worthless parents who had turned out well when placed early in respectable and kindly homes. Before I left, the author presented me with an autograph copy of one of his books — a much-prized gift. He was reading Cotton Mather's *Memorabilia*, not for theology, but for gossip. It was the only chronicle of the small beer of current events in the days of the witch persecutions, and the expulsion of the Quakers, Baptists, and other schismatics. I have often felt proud that of all the famous men I have mentioned in this connection there was only one not a Unitarian, and that was Whittier, the Quaker poet of abolition; and his theology was of the mildest.

XVIII BRITAIN, THE CONTINENT, AND HOME AGAIN

I went by steamer to Glasgow, as I found the fares by that route cheaper than to Liverpool. Municipal work in that city was then attracting world-wide attention, and I enquired into the methods of taxation and the management of public works, much to my advantage. The cooperative works at Shields Hall were another source of interest to me.

* * *

It was through the kind liberality of Miss Florence Davenport Hill that a pamphlet, recording the speeches and results of the voting

at River House, Chelsea, was printed and circulated. When I visited Miss Hill and her sister and found them as eager for social and political reform as they had been twenty-nine years earlier, I had another proof of the eternal youth which large and high interests keep within us in spite of advancing years. Miss Davenport Hill had been a member of the London School Board for fifteen years, and was re-elected after I left England. Years of her life had been devoted to work for the children of the state, and she was a member of the Board of Guardians for the populous union of St Pancras. Everyone acknowledged the great good that the admission of women to those boards had done. I spent a pleasant time at Toynbee Hall, a university centre, in the poorest part of London, founded by men. Canon and Mrs Barrett were intensely interested in South Australian work for state children. Similar university centres which I visited in America, like Hull House, in Chicago, were founded by women graduates. Mrs Fawcett I met several times, but Mrs Garrett Anderson only once. When the suffrage was granted to the women of South Australia I received a letter of congratulation from Dr Helen Blackburn, one of the first women to take a medical degree. Nowadays women doctors are accepted as part of our daily life, and it is owing to the brave pioneers of the women's cause, Drs Elizabeth Blackwell, Helen Blackburn, Garrett Anderson, and other like noble souls, that the social and political prestige of women has advanced so tremendously all over the English-speaking world. It only remains now for a few women, full of enthusiasm of humanity and gifted with the power of public speaking, to gain another and important step for the womanhood of the world in the direction of economic freedom. Before leaving England I was gratified at receiving a cheque from Mrs Westlake, contributed by the English proportionalists, to help me in the cause. This was the second gift of the kind I had received, for my friends in San Francisco had already helped me financially on my way to reform. Socially I liked the atmosphere of America better than that of England, but politically England was infinitely more advanced. Steadily and surely a safer democracy seems to be evolving in the old country than in the Transatlantic Republic. I left England at the end of September 1894.

* * *

I reached South Australia on 12 December 1894, after an absence of twenty months. I found the women's suffrage movement wavering in the balance. It had apparently come with a rush — as unexpected as it was welcome to those whose strenuous exertions at last seemed likely to be crowned with success. Though sympathetic

to the cause, I had always been regarded as a weak-kneed sister by the real workers. I had failed to see the advantage of having a vote that might leave me after an election a disfranchised voter, instead of an unenfranchised woman. People talk of citizens being disenfranchised for the Legislative Council when they really mean that they are unenfranchised. You can scarcely be disfranchised if you have never been enfranchised; and I have regarded the enfranchisement of the people on the roll as more important for the time being than adding new names to the rolls. This would only tend to increase the disproportion between the representative and the represented. But I rejoiced when the Women's Suffrage Bill was carried, for I believe that women have thought more and accepted the responsibilities of voting to a greater extent than was ever expected of them. During the week I was accorded a welcome home in the old Academy of Music, Rundle Street, where I listened with embarrassment to the avalanche of eulogium that overwhelmed me. "What a good thing it is, Miss Spence, that you have only one idea", a gentleman once said to me on my country tour. He wished thus to express his feeling concerning my singleness of purpose towards effective voting. But at this welcome home I felt that others realized what I had often said myself. It is really because I have so many ideas for making life better, wiser, and pleasanter — all of which effective voting will aid — that I seem so absorbed in the one reform. My opinions on other matters I give for what they are worth — for discussion, for acceptance or rejection. My opinions on equitable representation I hold absolutely, subject to criticism of methods, but impregnable as to principle.

XIX PROGRESS OF EFFECTIVE VOTING

. . . The following year was especially interesting to the women of South Australia, and, indeed, to suffragists all over the world, for at the general election of 1896 women, for the first time in Australia, had the right to vote. New Zealand had preceded us with this reform, but the first election in this state found many women voters fairly well equipped to accept their responsibilities as citizens of the state. But in the full realization by the majority of women of their whole duties of citizenship I have been distinctly disappointed. Not that they have been on the whole less patriotic and less zealous than men voters; but, like their brothers, they have allowed their interest in public affairs to stop short at the act of voting, as if the right to vote were the beginning and the end of

political life. There has been too great a tendency on the part of women to allow reform work — particularly women's branches of it — to be done by a few disinterested and public-spirited women. Not only is the home the centre of woman's sphere, as it should be, but in too many cases it is permitted to be its limitation. The larger social life has been ignored, and women have consequently failed to have the effect on public life of which their political privilege is capable.

* * *

Our disappointment over the maintenance of the block vote for the election of ten delegates to the Federal Convention led to my brother John's suggestion that I should become a candidate. Startling as the suggestion was, so many of my friends supported it that I agreed to do so. I maintained that the fundamental necessity of a democratic constitution such as we hoped would evolve from the combined efforts of the ablest men in the Australian states was a just system of representation; and it was as the advocate of effective voting that I took my stand. My personal observation in the United States and Canada had impressed me with the dangers inseparable from the election of Federal Legislatures by local majorities — sometimes by minorities — where money and influences could be employed, particularly where a line in a tariff spelt a fortune to a section of the people, in the manipulation of the floating vote. Parties may boast of their voting strength and their compactness, but their voting strength under the present system of voting is only as strong as its weakest link, discordant or discontented minorities, will permit it to be. The stronger a party is in the Legislature the more is expected from it by every little section of voters to whom it owes its victory at the polls. The impelling force of responsibility which makes all Governments "go slow" creates the greatest discontent among impatient followers of the rank and file, and where a few votes may turn the scale at any general election a Government is often compelled to choose between yielding to the demands of its more clamorous followers at the expense of the general taxpayer or submitting to a ministerial defeat.

As much as we may talk of democracy in Australia, we are far from realizing a truly democratic ideal. A state in a pure democracy draws no nice and invidious distinctions between man and man. She disclaims the right of favouring either property, education, talent, or virtue. She conceives that all alike have an interest in good government, and that all who form the community, of full age and untainted by crime, should have a right to their share in the representation. She allows education to exert its legitimate

power through the press; talent in every department of business, property in its social and material advantages; virtue and religion to influence public opinion and the public conscience. But she views all men as politically equal, and rightly so, if the equality is to be as real in operation as in theory. If the equality is actual in the representation of the citizens — truth and virtue, being stronger than error and vice, and wisdom being greater than folly, when a fair field is offered — the higher qualities subdue the lower and make themselves felt in every department of the state. But if the representation from defective machinery is not equal, the balance is overthrown, and neither education, talent, nor virtue can work through public opinion so as to have any beneficial influence on politics. We know that in despotisms and oligarchies, where the majority are unrepresented and the few extinguish the many, independence of thought is crushed down, talent is bribed to do service to tyranny, education is confined to a privileged class and denied to the people, property is sometimes pillaged and sometimes flattered, and even virtue is degraded by lowering its field and making subservience appear to be patience and loyalty, and religion is not unfrequently made the handmaid of oppression. Taxes fall heavily on the poor for the benefit of the rich, and the only check proceeds from the fear of rebellion. When, on the other hand, the majority extinguishes the minority, the evil effects are not so apparent. The body oppressed is smaller and generally wealthier, with many social advantages to draw off attention from the political injustice under which they suffer; but there is the same want of sympathy between class and class, moral courage is rare, talent is perverted, genius is overlooked, education is general, but superficial, and press and pulpit often timid in exposing or denouncing popular errors. An average standard of virtue is all that is aimed at, and when no higher mark is set up there is great fear of falling below the average. Therefore it is incumbent on all states to look well to it that their representative systems really secure the political equality they all profess to give, for until that is done democracy has had no fair trial.

In framing a new constitution the opportunity arose for laying the foundation of just representation, and, had I been elected, my first and last thought would have been given to the claims of the whole people to electoral justice. But the 7,500 votes which I received left me far enough from the lucky ten. Had Mr Kingston not asserted both publicly and privately that, if elected, I could not constitutionally take my seat, I might have done better. There were rumours even that my nomination paper would be rejected. But to obviate this, Mrs Young, who got it filled in, was careful to

Progress of Effective Voting

see that no name was on it that had no right there, and its presentation was delayed till five minutes before the hour of noon, in order that no time would be left to upset its validity. From a press cutting on the declaration of the poll I cull this item of news: "Several unexpected candidates were announced, but the only nomination which evoked any expressions of approval was that of Miss Spence." I was the first woman in Australia to seek election in a political contest. From the two main party lists I was, of course, excluded, but in the list of "ten best men" selected by a Liberal organization my name appeared. When the list was taken to the printer — who, I think, happened to be the late Federal member, Mr James Hutchison — he objected to the heading of the "ten best men", as one of them was a woman. He suggested that my name should be dropped, and a man's put in its place. "You can't say Miss Spence is one of the 'ten best men'. Take her name out." "Not say she's one of the 'ten best men'?" the Liberal organizer objected, "Why she's the best man of the lot." I had not expected to be elected, but I did expect that my candidature would help effective voting, and I am sure it did. Later, the league arranged a deputation to Mr Kingston, to beg him to use his influence for the adoption of the principle in time for the first Federal elections. We foresaw, and prophesied what has actually occurred — the monopoly of representation by one party in the Senate, and the consequent disfranchisement of hundreds of thousands of voters throughout the Commonwealth. But, as before, Mr Kingston declined to see the writing on the wall. The Hon. D.M. Charleston was successful in carrying through the Legislative Council a motion in favour of its application to Federal elections, but Mr Glynn in the Lower House had a harder row to hoe, and a division was never taken.

* * *

When Mrs Young and I began our work together the question was frequently asked why women alone were working for effective voting? The answer was simple. There were few men with leisure in South Australia, and, if there were, the leisured man was scarcely likely to take up reform work. When I first seized hold of this reform women as platform speakers were unheard of. Indeed, the prejudice was so strong against women in public life that although I wrote the letters to *The Melbourne Argus* it was my brother John who was nominally the correspondent. So for thirty years I wrong anonymously to the press on this subject. I waited for some man to come forward and do the platform work for me. We women are accused of waiting and waiting for the coming man, but often he doesn't come at all; and oftener still, when he

does come, we should be a great deal better without him. In this case he did not come at all, and I started to do the work myself; and, just because I was a woman working single-handed in the cause, Mrs Young joined me in the crusade against inequitable representation. For many years, however, the cause has counted to its credit men speakers and demonstrators of ability and talent all over the state, who are carrying the gospel of representative reform into every camp, both friendly and hostile.

It was said of Gibbon when his autobiography was published that he did not know the difference between himself and the Roman Empire. I have sometimes thought that the same charge might be levelled against me with regard to effective voting; but association with a reform for half a century sometimes makes it difficult to separate the interests of the person from the interests of the cause. Following on my return from America effective voting played a larger part than ever in my life. I had come back cheered by the earnestness and enthusiasm of American reformers, and I found the people of my adopted country more than ever prepared to listen to my teaching. Parties had become more clearly defined, and the results of our system of education were beginning to tell, I think, in the increased interest taken by individuals as well as by societies in social and economic questions. I found interesting people everywhere, in every mode of life, and in every class of society. My friends sometimes accused me of judging people's intelligence by the interest they took in effective voting; but, although this may have been true to a certain extent, it was not wholly correct. Certainly I felt more drawn to effective voters, but there are friendships I value highly into which my special reform work never enters. Just as the more recent years of my life have been coloured by the growth of the movement which means more to me than anything else in the world, so must the remaining chapters of this narrative bear the imprint of its influence.

XX WIDENING INTERESTS

During this period my work on the State Children's Council continued, and I never found time hang heavily on my hands; so that when Mr Kingston met me one day later in the year, and told me he particularly wished me to accept an appointment as a member of the Destitute Board, I hestitated. "I am too old," I objected. "No, no, Miss Spence," he replied laughingly, "it is only we who grow old — you have the gift of perpetual youth." But I was nearly seventy-two, and at any rate I thought I should first consult my

friends. I found them all eager that I should accept the position. I had agitated long and often for the appointment of women on all public boards, particularly where both sexes came under treatment, and I accepted the post. Although often I have found the work tiring, I have never regretted the step I took in joining the board. Experience has emphasized my early desire that two women at least should occupy positions on it. I hope that future Governments will rectify the mistake of past years by utilizing to a greater extent the valuable aid of capable and sympathetic women in the branch of public work for which they are peculiarly fitted.

* * *

We are apt to pride ourselves on the advance we have made in our civilization; but our self-glorification received a rude shock at the feelings of intolerance and race hatred that the [Boer] war brought forth. Freedom of speech became the monopoly of those who supported the war, and the person who dared to express an opinion which differed from that of the majority needed a great deal more than the ordinary allowance of moral courage. Unfortunately the intolerance so characteristic of that period is a feature, to a greater or lesser extent, of every parliamentary election in the Commonwealth. The clause in the Federal Electoral Act which makes disturbance of a political meeting a penal offence is a curious reflection on a so-called democratic community. But, though its justification can scarcely be denied even by the partisans of the noisier elements in a political crowd, its existence must be deplored by every right-minded and true-hearted citizen. In Miss Rose Scott I found a sympathizer on this question of the war; and one of the best speeches I ever heard her make was on peace and arbitration. "Mafeking Day" was celebrated while we were in Sydney, and I remember how we three — Miss Scott, Mrs Young, and I — remained indoors the whole day, at the charming home of our hostess, on Point Piper road. The black hand of death and desolation was too apparent for us to feel that we could face the almost ribald excesses of that day. I felt the war far less keenly than did my two friends; but it was bad even for me. No one called, and the only companions of our chosen solitude were the books we all loved so much, and

> The secret sympathy,
> The silver link, the silken tie,
> Which heart to heart and mind to mind,
> In body and in soul can bind.

I had hoped that the Women's National Council, a branch of which was formed in Adelaide a few years later, would have made

a great deal of the question of peace and arbitration, just as other branches have done all over the world; and when the Peace Society was inaugurated a short time ago I was glad to be able to express my sympathy with the movement by becoming a member. As I was returning from a lecturing tour in the south during this time, an old Scotch farm-wife came into the carriage where I had been knitting in solitude. She was a woman of strong feelings, and was bitterly opposed to the war. We chatted on the subject for a time, getting along famously, until she discovered that I was Miss Spence. "But you are a Unitarian!" she protested in a shocked tone. I admitted the fact. "Oh, Miss Spence," she went on, "how can you be so wicked as to deny the divinity of Christ?" I explained to her what Unitarianism was, but she held dubiously aloof for a time. Then we talked of other things. She told me of many family affairs, and when she left me at the station she said, "Ah, well, Miss Spence, I've learned something this morning, and that is that a Unitarian can be just as good and honest as other folk."

XXI PROPORTIONAL REPRESENTATION AND FEDERATION

In the debates of the Federal Convention I was naturally much interested. Many times I regretted my failure to win a seat when I saw how, in spite of warnings against, and years of lamentable experience of, a vicious system of voting, the members of the Convention went calmly on their way, accepting as a matter of course the crude and haphazard methods known to them, the unscientific system of voting so dear to the heart of the "middling" politician and the party intriguer. I believe Mr Glynn alone raised his voice in favour of proportional representation, in the Convention, as he has done consistently in every representative assembly of which he has been a member. Instead of seeing to it that the foundations of the Commonwealth were "broad based upon the people's will" by the adoption of effective voting, and thus maintaining the necessary connection between the representative and the represented, these thinkers for the people at the very outset of federation sowed the seeds of future discontent and Federal apathy. Faced with disfranchisement for three or six years, possibly for ever — so long as the present system of voting remains — it is unreasonable to expect from the people as a whole that interest in the national well-being which alone can lead to the safety of a progressive nation.

Proportional representation was for long talked of as a device

Proportional Representation and Federation

for representing minorities. It is only in recent years that the real scope of the reform has been recognized. By no other means than the adoption of the single transferable vote can the rule of the majority obtain. The fundamental principal of proportional representation is that majorities must rule, but that minorities shall be adequately represented. An intelligent minority of representatives has great weight and influence. Its voice can be heard. It can fully and truly express the views of the voters it represents. It can watch the majority and keep it straight. These clear rights of the minority are denied by the use of the multiple vote. It has also been asked — Can a Government be as strong as it needs to be when — besides the organized ministerial party and the recognized Opposition — there may be a larger number of independent members than at present who may vote either way? It is quite possible for a Government to be too strong, and this is especially dangerous in Australia, where there are so many of what are known as optional functions of government undertaken and administered by the Ministry of the day, resting on a majority in the Legislature. To maintain this ascendancy concessions are made to the personal interests of members or to local or class interests of their constituencies at the cost of the whole country.

* * *

The closing year of the century found the Effective Voting League in the thick of its first election campaign. There is little doubt that the best time for advancing a political reform is during an election, and it was interesting to note how many candidates came to our support. We had an interesting meeting at Parliament House for members just about that time. An opponent of the reform, who was present, complained that we were late in beginning our meeting. "We always begin punctually under the present system," he remarked. "Yes," some one replied, "but we always finish so badly." "Oh, I always finish well enough," was the pert rejoinder; "I generally come out on top." "Ah," retorted the other, "I was thinking of the electors." But the doubter did not come out on top at a subsequent election, and his defeat was probably the means of his discovering defects in the old system that no number of successes would have led him into acknowledging. From the two or three members who had supported Mr Glynn in the previous Parliament we increased our advocates in the Assembly during the campaign to fourteen. The agitation had been very persistent among the electors, and their approval of the reform was reflected in the minds of their representatives. We inaugurated during that year the series of citizens' meetings convened by the Mayors of the city and suburbs, which has been so successful a

feature of our long campaign for electoral justice, and at the present time very few of the mayoral chairs are occupied by men who are not keen supporters of effective voting.

The Hon. Theodore Bruce's connection with the reform dates from that year, when he presided at a meeting in the Adelaide Town Hall during the temporary absence of the Mayor. A consistent supporter of effective voting from that time, it was only natural that when in May 1909 the candidature of Mr Bruce (who was then and is now a vice-president of the league), for a seat in the Legislative Council, gave us an opportunity for working for his return, against a candidate who had stated that he was not satisfied with the working of the system of effective voting, we availed ourselves of it. So much has been written and said about the attitude of the league with regard to Parliamentary candidates that, as its President, I feel that I ought to take this opportunity of stating our reasons for that attitude. From its inception the league has declined to recognize parties in a contest at all. Its sole concern has been, and must be, to support effective voters, to whatever party they may belong. To secure the just representation of the whole electorate of whatever size, is the work of the Effective Voting League, and, whatever the individuals opinions of the members may be, as an official body they cannot help any candidate who opposes the reform for which they stand.

XXII A VISIT TO NEW SOUTH WALES

I was not neglectful of other reforms while on this campaign, and found time to interest myself in the state children's work with which my friend, Mrs Garran, was so intimately connected. We went to Liverpool one day to visit the benevolent institution for men. There were some hundreds of men there housed in a huge building reminiscent of the early convict days. If not the whole, parts of it had been built by the convicts, and the massive stone staircase suggested to our minds the horrors of convict settlement. I have always resented the injury done to this new country by the foundation of penal settlements, through which Botany Bay lost its natural connotation as a habitat for wonderful flora, and became known only as a place where convicts were sent for three-quarters of a century. Barrington's couplet, written as a prologue at the opening of the Playhouse, Sydney, in 1796, to a play given by convicts —

> True patriots we, for it be understood
> We left our country for our country's good —

was clever, but untrue. All experience proves that while it is a terrible injury to a new country to be settled by convicts, it is a real injury also to the people from whom they are sent, to shovel out of sight all their failures, and neither try to lessen their numbers nor to reclaim them to orderly civil life. It was not till Australia refused any longer to receive convicts, as Virginia had previously done, that serious efforts were made to amend the criminal code of England, or to use reformatory methods first with young and afterwards with older offenders. Another pleasant trip was one we took to Parramatta. The Government launch was courteously placed at our disposal to visit the Parramatta Home for Women, where also we found some comfortable homes for old couples. The separation of old people who would prefer to spend the last years of their life together is, I consider, an outrage on society. One of my chief desires has been to establish such homes for destitute couples in South Australia, and to every woman who may be appointed as a member of the Destitute Board in future I appeal to do her utmost to change our methods of treatment with regard to old couples, so that to the curse of poverty may not be added the cruelty of enforced separation. Women in New South Wales were striving for the franchise at that time, and we had the pleasure of speaking at one of their big meetings. And what fine public meetings they had in Sydney! People there seemed to take a greater interest in politics than here, and crowded attendances were frequent at political meetings, even when there was no election to stir them up.

XXIII MORE PUBLIC WORK

For the cooperative movement I had always felt the keenest sympathy. I saw in it the liberation of the small wage-earner from the toils of the middlemen. I thought moreover that the incentive to thrift so strongly encouraged by cooperative societies would be a tremendous gain to the community as well as to the individual. How many people owe a comfortable old age to the delight of seeing their first small profits in a cooperative concern, or their savings in a building society accumulating steadily and surely, if but slowly? And I have always had a disposition to encourage anything that would tend to lighten the burden of the worker. So that when in 1901 Mrs Agnes Milne placed before me a suggestion for the formation of a woman's cooperative clothing factory, I was glad to do what I could to further an extension in South Australia of the movement, which, from its inception in older countries,

had made so strong an appeal to my reason. A band of women workers were prepared to associate for the mutual benefit of the operatives in the shirtmaking and clothing trades. Under the title of the South Australian Co-operative Clothing Company, Limited, they proposed to take over and carry on a small private factory, owned by one of themselves, which had found it difficult to compete against large firms working with the latest machinery. I was sure of finding many sympathizers among my friends, and was successful in disposing of a fair number of shares. The movement had already gained support from thinking working women, and by the time we were ready to form ourselves into a company we were hopeful of success. I was appointed, and have since remained the first President of the board of directors; and, unless prevented by illness or absence from the state, I have never failed to be present at all meetings. The introduction of Wages Boards added to the keen competition between merchants, had made the task of carrying on successfully most difficult, but we hoped that as the idea gained publicity we should benefit proportionately. It was a great blow to us, when at the close of the first year we were able to declare a dividend of one shilling a share, the merchants closed down upon us and reduced their payments by sixpence or ninepence per dozen. But in spite of drawbacks we have maintained the struggle successfully, though sometimes at disheartening cost to the workers and officials of the society. I feel, however, that the reward of success due to this plucky band of women workers will come in the near future, for at no other time probably has the position looked more hopeful than during the present year.

* * *

Before I left for America I saw the growing power and strength of the Labour Party. I rejoiced that a new star had arisen in the political firmament. I looked to it as a party that would support every cause that tended towards righteousness. I expected it, as a reform party, to take up effective voting, because effective voting was a reform. I hoped that a party whose motto was "Trust the people" would have adopted a reform by means of which alone it would be possible for the people to gain control over its Legislature and its Government. Alas! for human hopes that depended on parties for their realization! As time after time I have seen defections from the ranks of proportionalists, and people have said to me: "Give it up, Miss Spence. Why trouble longer? Human nature is too bad," I have answered, "No; these politicians are but the ephemeral creations of a day or a month, or a year; this reform is for all time, and must prevail, and I will never give it up."

More Public Work

During my many visits to Melbourne and Sydney I had been much impressed with the influence and the power for good of the local branches of the world-famed National Council of Women. I had long hoped for the establishment of a branch in South Australia, and was delighted to fall in with a suggestion made by the Countess of Aberdeen (Vice-President-at-large of the International Council), through Lady Cockburn, that a council should be formed in South Australia. The inaugural meeting in September 1902 was splendidly attended, and it was on a resolution moved by me that the council came into existence. Lady Way was the first President, and I was one of the Vice-Presidents. I gave several addresses, and in 1904 contributed a paper on "Epileptics". In dealing with this subject I owed much to the splendid help I received from my dear friend Miss Alice Henry, of Victoria, now in Chicago, whose writings on epileptics and weak-minded children have contributed largely to the awakening of the public conscience to a sense of duty towards these social weaklings. In 1905 I contributed a paper to the quinquennial meeting of the International Council of Women, held at Berlin, on the laws relating to women and children in South Australia, and gave an account of the philanthropic institutions of the state, with special reference to the State Children's Council and Juvenile Courts. The work of the National Council in this state was disappointing to many earnest women, who had hoped to find in it a means for the social, political, and philanthropic education of the women of South Australia. Had the council been formed before we had obtained the vote there would probably have been more cohesion and a greater sustained effort to make it a useful body. But as it was there was so apparent a disinclination to touch "live" subjects that interest in the meetings dwindled, and in 1906 I resigned my position on the executive in order to have more time to spare for other public work.

* * *

Just as years before my interest had been kindled in the establishment of our system of state education, and later in the university and higher education, so more recently has the inauguration of the Froebel system of kindergarten training appealed most strongly to my reason and judgment. There was a time in the history of education, long after the necessity for expert teaching in primary and secondary schools had been recognized, when the training of the infant mind was left to the least skilled assistant on the staff of a school. With the late Mr J. A. Hartley, whose theory was that the earliest beginnings of education needed even greater skill in the teacher than the higher branches, I had long regarded the

policy as mistaken; but modern educationists have changed all that, and the training of tiny mites of two or three summers and upwards is regarded as of equal importance with that of children of a larger growth. South Australia owes its free kindergarten to the personal initiative and private munificence of the Rev. Bertram Hawker, youngest son of the late Hon. G. C. Hawker. I had already met, and admired the kindergarten work of, Miss Newton when in Sydney, and was delighted when she accepted Mr Hawker's invitation to inaugurate the system in Adelaide. Indeed, the time of her stay here during September 1905 might well have been regarded as a special invitation of educational experts, for, in addition to Miss Newton, the directors of education from New South Wales and Victoria (Messrs G. H. Knibbs and F. Tate) took part in the celebations. Many interesting meetings led up to the formation of the Kindergarten Union. My niece, Mrs J. P. Morice, was appointed honorary secretary, and I became one of the vice-presidents. On joining the union I was proud of the fact that I was the first member to pay a subscription. The free kindergarten has come to South Australia to stay, and is fast growing into an integral part of our system of education. I have rejoiced in the progress of the movement, and feel that the future will witness the realization of my ideal of a ladder that will reach from the kindergarten to the university, as outlined in articles I wrote for *The Register* at that time.

XXIV THE EIGHTIETH MILESTONE AND THE END

On 31 October 1905, I celebrated my eightieth birthday. Twelve months earlier, writing to a friend, I said: "I entered my eightieth year on Monday, and I enjoy life as much as I did at eighteen; indeed, in many respects I enjoy it more." The birthday gathering took place in the schoolroom of the Unitarian Church, the church to which I had owed so much happiness through the lifting of the dark shadows of my earlier religious beliefs. Surrounded by friends who had taken their share in the development of my beloved State, I realized one of the happiest times of my life. I had hoped that the celebration would have helped the cause of effective voting, which had been predominant in my mind since 1859. By my interests and work in so many other directions — in literature, journalism, education, philanthropy, and religion — which had been testified to by so many notable people on that occasion, I hoped to prove that I was not a mere faddist, who could be led

The Eightieth Milestone and the End

away by a chimerical fantasy. I wanted the world to understand that I was a clear-brained, commonsense woman of the world, whose views of effective voting and other political questions were as worthy of credence as her work in other directions had been worthy of acceptance. The greetings of my many friends from all parts of the Commonwealth on that day brought so much joy to me that there was little wonder I was able to conclude my birthday poem "Australian spring" with the lines:

> With eighty winters o'er my head,
> Within my heart there's Spring.

* * *

Among the many friends I had made in the other states there was none I admired more for her public spiritedness than Miss Vida Goldstein. I have been associated with her on many platforms and in many branches of work. Her versatility is great, but there is little doubt that her chief work lies in helping women and children. Her life is practically spent in battling for her sex. Although I was the first woman in Australia to become a parliamentary candidate, Miss Goldstein has since exceeded my achievements by a second candidature for the Senate. It was during her visit here last May–June as a delegate to the State Children's Congress that she inaugurated the Women's Non-party Political Association, which is apparently a growing force. In a general way the aims of the society bear a strong resemblance to those of the social students' society, many of its members having also belonged to the earlier association. It was a hopeful sign to me that it included among its members people of all political views working chiefly in the interests of women and children. Of this society also I became the first president, and the fact that on its platform was included proportional representation was an incentive for me to work for it. The education of women on public and social questions, so that they will be able to work side by side with the opposite sex for the public good, will, I think, help in the solution of social problems that are now obstacles in the path of progress. In addition to other literary work for the year 1909 I was asked by Miss Alice Henry to revise my book on state children in order to make it acceptable and applicable to American conditions. It was a big undertaking, but I think successful. The book as originally written had already done good work in Western Australia, where the conditions of infant mortality were extremely alarming, and in England also; and there is ample scope for such a work in America, which is still far behind even the most backward Australian state in its care for dependent children.

Autobiography

As a president of three societies, a vice-president of two others, a member of two of the most important boards in the state for the care of the destitute, the deserted, and the dependent, with a correspondence that touches on many parts of the Empire, and two continents besides, with my faculty for the appreciation of good literature still unimpaired, with my domestic interests so dear to me, and my constant knitting for the infants under the care of the State Inspector — I find my life as an octogenarian more varied in its occupations and interests than ever before. Looking back from the progressive heights of 1910 through the long vista of years, numbering upwards of four-fifths of a century, I rejoice at the progress the world has made. Side by side with the development of my state my life has slowly unfolded itself. My connection with many of the reforms to which is due this development has been intimate, and (I think I am justified in saying) oftentimes helpful. While other states of the Commonwealth and the Dominion of New Zealand have made remarkable progress, none has eclipsed the rapid growth of the state to which the steps of my family were directed in 1839. Its growth has been more remarkable, because it has been primarily due to its initiation of many social and political reforms which have since been adopted by other and older countries. "Australia, lead us further" is the cry of reformers in America. We have led in so many things, and though America may claim the honour of being the birthplace of the more modern theory of land values taxation, I rejoice that South Australia was the first country in the world with the courage and the foresight to adopt the tax on land values without exemption. That she is still lagging behind Tasmania and South Africa in the adoption of effective voting, as the only scientific system of electoral reform, is the sorrow of my old age. The fact that South Australia has been the happy hunting ground of the faddist has frequently been urged as a reproach against this state. Its more patriotic citizens will rejoice in the truth of the statement, and their prayer will probably be that no fewer but more advanced thinkers will arise to carry this glorious inheritance beneath the Southern Cross to higher and nobler heights of physical and human development than civilization has yet dreamed of or achieved. The Utopia of yesterday is the possession of today, and opens the way to the Utopia of tomorrow. The haunting horror of older civilizations — divorcing the people from their natural inheritance in the soil, and filling the towns with myriads of human souls dragged down by poverty, misery, and crime — is already casting its shadow over the future of Australia; but there is hope in the fact that a new generation has arisen untrammelled by

The Eightieth Milestone and the End

tradition, which, having the experience of older countries before it, and benefiting from the advantages of the freer life and the greater opportunities afforded by a new country, gives promise of ultimately finding the solution of the hitherto unsolved problem of making country life as attractive to the masses as that of the towns and cities. As time goes on the effect of education must tell, and the generations that are to come will be more enlightened and more altuistic, and the tendency of the world will be more and more, even as it is now, towards higher and nobler conceptions of human happiness. I have lived through a glorious age of progress. Born in "the wonderful century", I have watched the growth of the movement for the uplifting of the masses, from the Reform Bill of 1832 to the demands for adult suffrage. As a member of a church which allows women to speak in the pulpit, a citizen of a state which gives womanhood a vote for the Assembly, a citizen of a Commonwealth which fully enfranchises me for both Senate and Representatives, and a member of a community which was foremost in conferring university degrees on women, I have benefited from the advancement of the educational and political status of women for which the Victorian era will probably stand unrivalled in the annals of the world's history. I have lived through the period of repressed childhood, and witnessed the dawn of a new era which has made the dwellers in youth's "golden age" the most important factor in human development. I have watched the growth of Adelaide from the condition of a scattered hamlet to that of one of the finest cities in the southern hemisphere; I have seen the evolution of South Australia from a province to an important state in a great Commonwealth. All through my life I have tried to live up to the best that was in me, and I should like to be remembered as one who never swerved in her efforts to do her duty alike to herself and her fellow-citizens. Mistakes I have made, as all are liable to do, but I have done my best. And when life has closed for me, let those who knew me best speak and think of me as

> One who never turned her back, but marched breast forward,
>   Never doubted clouds would break,
> Never dreamed, though right were worsted, wrong would triumph,
> Held we fall to rise, are baffled to fight better,
>   Sleep to wake.

No nobler epitaph would I desire.

3
Literary Comment

EDITOR'S NOTE

This section contains two newspaper articles written twenty-two years apart, giving us some of Spence's opinions on the writing of literature in Australia. "The Literary Calling", published in *The Register*, Adelaide, 25 September 1880, was written in reaction to an essay by James Payn, "Sham Admiration in Literature", in the periodical the *Nineteenth Century*, March 1880):422-34, which suggested that the writing of literature was a relatively easy profession to enter. Bitter experience had taught Catherine Spence otherwise, and her article is written as a corrective to an unwise optimism.

The second article, "The Australian in Literature", from *The Register*, Adelaide, 22 November 1902, was written in response to an assessment of nationalism in literary terms, appropriate to the newly achieved Federation of Australian states (1 January 1901).

Both articles are typical in showing the topicality necessary to journalism. While they lack the considered detachment of the purely literary essay — Spence did write a few of these on contemporary English writers — they do give us a strong impression of the writer's emphasis on practicality and realism, her rejection of romantic expectations and romantic images. The qualities she recommends are those which characterize all her own literary efforts.

The Literary Calling

Mr James Payn, who is a successful novelist and a pleasant essayist, suggested about six months ago in the *Nineteenth Century* the "Literary Calling" as a profession to youths of education and ability, who found the so-called learned professions crowded and hard in their requirements. He pointed out that the market had extended in various directions, and even though the supply appeared to keep pace with it, there was ample room for any one who would bring power or skill or novelty into play. Since the publication of the article, Mr Payn has been overwhelmed with letters from literary aspirants, desiring hints, advice, and plots for stories, and also with packets of MSS for critical opinions, and accompanied by requests for a recommendation to a publisher. Not only the young have written, but he has received indignant letters from parents, blaming him for giving no practical directions for success in the review article, which has unsettled Tom at the lawyer's office, Dick at the merchant's desk, and Frank in the Civil Service, by making them hope for fortune and fame by an easier calling. Among so many letters there was necessarily no little absurdity. Because Mr Payn had said that a knowledge of Latin and Greek and of the higher mathematics was quite immaterial to a writer of modern fiction, the young people seem to have picked up the idea that no knowledge at all was required; when the fact is that it needs a great deal of varied knowledge, both of character and ordinary events, and that the faculty of observation, which is the most of all neglected in school and college and university, Mr Payn insisted on as to be cultivated strenuously and systematically. A large proportion of his correspondents, being able to write fair grammatical English and to work up a theme on any given subject, thought they only wanted "a story", and

asked to be furnished with a plot — a thing so valuable to a professional litterateur that a request for his watch and chain would have been much more modest. He lays down the rule that those who cannot invent a plot or seize on a workable story from the things they see, hear, and read of every day, are naturally incapacitated for the trade. But there is another class nearly as much debarred from succesful authorship; those who have imagined or adopted stories which would be telling in skilful hands, but who cannot fill them out or make lifelike people to move through them, or tell even a true narrative with any thread of sequence carried consistently out.

Mr Payn says that many of his correspondents, not feeling equal to much plot, shelter themselves under the high moral purpose of their work, and instance Mrs Gaskell's *Cranford,* which they believe their work greatly resembles, as a protest against the sensational fiction which panders to an unhealthy popular taste. In the harmlessness of purpose and the absence of plot, the MSS resembled *Cranford,* but in no other point — the delicacy, the humour, and the tenderness of those village sketches were absolutely absent also, and the unrelieved baldness of the would-be-novel was intolerable. Admirers of *Cranford* should not forget that all Mrs Gaskell's other works had abundance of plot, and even sensational plot. There is no harm in a sensational plot if it is adequately and naturally carried out. There are more wonderful things actually happen than are ever written if we only knew all about them, as the novelist alone can let us know.

We have seen a game played by clever young people, which is described, and an example given in Miss Alcott's *Little Women.* One of the circle begins a story, and carries it on so far, then when he get his characters into a dilemma, he leaves off abruptly, and the next in order carries them on to another crisis — and passes it on to the next, and so on. This is a capital exercise for ingenuity; but it is of little service in training for writing fiction, for in a properly constructed story there should be no hap hazard. Every danger and difficulty must be provided against before it is encountered, and limits set to its disastrous effects.

We have heard of two or three young ladies, who were writing a novel, who whenever they met went into solemn conclave as to what new disaster was to happen to hero and heroine in order to keep up the interest. But this was raw amateur work, and however partnerships in novels and dramas are carried on by such people as Besant and Rice, Charles Reed and Boucicault, we believe with Mr Payn that the novel should be blocked out by one mind, and fixed in its main lines in a completed whole before the pen touches

The Literary Calling

the paper. To go on wobbling from side to side with no definite end, is as mischievous in fiction as it would be in road-making. We want the nearest practial line between one point and another, and we must settle the ultimate terminus before we begin. The more interesting and fertile country we can go through the better, but we must not rush off hither and thither in search of it. And the novelist has this advantage over the road surveyor, that his scenery and surroundings are very much at his own command; he can bring the mountain to Mahomet, and does not need to take Mahomet to the mountain.

Some accessory scenes and chapters are added in the working out, the *dramatis personae* as they are developed grow upon the author and demand a wider field of action; conversations characteristic of the speakers lead back and lead out in various directions, but the general plan ought always to be undisturbed. If through some unlucky chance it is materially disturbed, and wrenched from its original setting, even an uncritical reader feels something is wrong. The generally educated public is sharp to note faults in a writer in those things which can be taught, and will not tolerate bad grammar, or mistakes in common matters of history or mythology, and any great improbability or inconsistence in the story rarely escapes censure. But when they say, as they do very often, that they could write a better book themselves, they scarcely know how much goes to the making of a readable book. If they tried, they would find out how hard it is to make the beginning sufficiently dignified, natural, and interesting — then the middle must be kept from dragging and from getting confused, which in the desire to bring in sufficient incidents is very apt to happen; and, finally, the hardest task of all — the conclusion, must carefully gather all the threads of the narrative and fasten them off in a satisfactory manner.

After all other difficulties are over, comes that of giving a book a proper title; for if you chance on one that has been used before, you infringe a copyright, and are liable to prosecution. This may perhaps partly account for the strange unmeaning names so much in vogue, and indeed we know that the publisher, who has only read the book by proxy, often prevents the author from giving it a name which is appropriate, because it sounds like that of some other novel, or because it does not appear to him to be a taking title. These two combined causes may cause the adoption of snatches of songs or well-known quotations, such as *Home, Sweet Home, Good-bye, Sweetheart, Good-bye*, and *Coming through the rye*; but one regrets to see such fine titles as Julian

Literary Comment

Hawthorne's *Idolatry,* or Mr Cunningham's *Late Laurels*, used up on tales only slight connected with them.

It is not merely that the ordinary reader would find it difficult to write a good novel, even practised litterateurs in other directions often make sad failures, in this commonly thought the easiest and lightest department of authorship.

We got hold of a novel the other day called *Harding the Money-Spinner*, and were induced to read it right through by the preface. The author was a Mr Keon, a highly educated man connected with the London Press. He was a friend of Lord Lytton's, and on one occasion when on a visit to him the editor of a weekly Conservative newspaper came to offer the great novelist *carte blanche* for a serial story, which the latter declined absolutely. But he introduced his friend as no doubt able and willing to furnish a satisfactory story, and to the arrangement which ensued *Harding the Money-Spinner* owed his existence. Though the work of a clever man, it is not a good novel. There was sufficient story, but not handled with any sense of proportion, for three-fourths of the book is occupied with the doings, the loves, and the ambitions of a precocious youth of nineteen, and the money-spinning which took place afterwards is crowded into a few chapters.

There are continued interruptions to make reflections or prognostication. A pressman who is always on the lookout for any opportunity of saying what is worth saying, gets into a habit that is fatal to the interest of a novel. Even Thackeray's genius could not always prevent us being impatient of so many interruptions in the person of the showman, for if the author continually reminds you that these are merely puppets he is playing with, how can he expect his readers to believe in their reality. What you have got to say in the way of moralizing, may be expressed by means of your characters, and even then, not because you want it said, but because it would be natural for them to say it; for whenever the thing is forced it fails of all effect. And this experienced man of the world, Mr Keon, exaggerates the perfections and accomplishments of one of his heroes, and the insufferable vulgarity of his parvenu, quite as much as might have been expected from a young inexperienced female novelist. A much more ignorant person might have written a better novel.

With regard to the construction of a plot, Mr Payn tells us that his first story, *Lost Sir Massingberd*, grew out of a reading in natural history about enormous trees apparently alive, but decayed inside, and the idea struck him that if a man fell into a fork of such tree he might die there without help. He did not want to make the story harrowing, but to have as a victim a man who was a good

riddance, and he took the character of the detested baronet from a local tradition. This necessitated the carrying back the tale to a previous century, when such tyrannical and oppressive conduct was possible. This is always a difficulty, and in modern days such removal detracts greatly from the popularity of a work of fiction. The historical novel or romance is not what it was in the days of Scott; the writer is judged by very severe codes by the critic, and the more he studies to make his work consistent with the time, the less sympathy he meets with from the general reader. But none the less at the time *Lost Sir Massingberd* was a success. It was the first serial story published in *Chambers Journal,* and the birth of the book from an imagined fact and real character is probably representative of the origin of many plots. One author may make very elaborate plots, while another will perhaps take a shred half-worked out from one of them, and make it his *pièce de résistance* for a whole novel. And no doubt he so alters and modifies it that the author from whom he steals it does not know it again. To take a whole true story and give it a fictitious setting is rarely successful, because without the circumstances in which it grew it does not appear probably; but there are other points not so apparent which militate against it. The reason why truth is said to be stranger than fiction, is because in what we receive as truth we do not really know as much of the story as a great artist can let us see in fiction. The inner springs of character are open to the great poet, dramatist, and novelist, and he can arrange all the circumstances, and all the people by whom his characters are surrounded so as to give full play to their natural and complete development. When we see a book advertised as founded on fact, we generally find it a very improbable or uninteresting story. Footnotes to some unlikely incident pitchforked in, saying that it is a fact which actually occurred, are great mistakes in art, for the whole story ought to be taken for granted as real, and such an assertion as to the truth of one isolated fact shakes our confidence in the main narrative, even more than Thackeray's stopping to talk to his reader about his own creations.

With regard to our own personal experience in life, it is precisely those passages which have been most valuable and most fertilizing to mind, heart, and soul, that no one tells. All the things that we have experienced that are worth the world's knowing are so bound up, not only with our own secret griefs, faults, and humiliations, but with those of others, that it would be sacrilege and high treason to reveal them to the public. And this is what makes biographies as a rule so meagre and unsatisfactory. You may come into contact with a character so richly endowed by nature, and

withal so generous and so tolerant, that you feel sure there has been much in the life of struggle and of victory, and yet when that life comes to be written it may tell little or none of those things. But a man or woman of genius may take that character and conceive it as it was in its youth, with all its potentialities as yet unknown, put it into circumstances which it never actually went through, and surround it with a various group of human beings, who will drawn out its strength and its weakness, and may thus make of the fictitious story a more faithful and a more helpful portrait than any commonplace relative or friend could make of what goes by the name of authentic biography.

The creative omnipotence of the poet and the novelist, who summons so many spirits to do his bidding, has no counterpart in any other walk of literature. Then the novelist can dwell long and minutely on the fruitful crises of life, and pass over rapidly the flats where there is no salient feature of interest. We confess that in spite of Mr Payn's excellent advice against wobbling, that some of his novels as well as Mr Anthony Trollope's are written too much in that way, and drag out from side to side when they should move on to the conclusion.

Every one knows how much more interest is taken in that part of a biography which relates to the youthful days, in which there is growth and progress and reverse, but not full fruition; and the successful after-career of even an eminent man is not so captivating as his early struggles. All young people, and not a few older, are generally disappointed at the very slight notice taken of love and marriage, the stock-in-trade of the fictitious writer — perhaps too much so — but which certainly ought to be a very leading article. Unless with advancing years and matured powers the hero of a biography has difficulties and reverses, the reader loses his interest in him. And this the novelist instinctively feels, and after his happy or his tragical *dénouement,* he leaves his characters to their bliss or their despair, both qualities being too negative to keep up the interest of the reader. If a story is continued after marriage it is because there are storms ahead which threaten the happiness of the married pair, and if after the acquisition of a fortune, it is generally because it has to be seriously imperilled, if not wrecked. Uncertainty and vicissitude are the life blood of novel and romance, and in them there is so much prominence given to the affections, the sentiments, and the passions, that they take hold of a mass of readers who are quite unable to express such things, but yet are capable of sympathizing with them. There is a wider public for fiction than for history, biography, travel or philosophy all put together; and therefore the

The Literary Calling

healthy direction of this universal taste is no small matter. The real movers of society may be after all not the thinkers and actors on the real stage of the world, but the comparatively insignificant members of this modern calling which goes by the name of "light literature".

The Australian in Literature

It takes more than two generations to create a distinctive national character, but we can see, even in that time, that something has been done. The patronizing judgment of a leading English journal thirty years ago that the Australian was merely the Englishman in a worse climate, and with more primitive conditions, would not be repeated now. Our climate, in spite of its drawbacks of excessive heat and dryness in summer, is a better one than that of the British Isles, and our conditions can be modified and improved by Australian enterprise and Australian commonsense. Federation must play a part in the development of patriotism, and in time it will lessen the jealousy of the states with regard to each other, though in early days it may appear to intensify it. It is, perhaps, when we travel abroad, and come upon the seed of the eucalyptus planted in California or near Rome, or have a sight of wattle bloom grown in an English hothouse, that the strong ties that bind us to our fair Southern Land are most keenly felt. But what is the figure that the Australian makes in the literature which is indigenous to its soil? Henry Kendall and Marcus Clarke and Adam Lindsay Gordon struck the keynote of pessimism; and in prose as well as in verse the deadbeat, the remittance man, the gaunt shepherd with his starving flocks and herds, the free selector on an arid patch, the drink shanty where the rouseabouts and shearers knock down their cheques, the race meeting where high and low, rich and poor, are filled with the gambler's spirit and cursed with the gambler's ill-luck, fill the foreground of the picture of Australian life. There are occasional episodes more cheerful and more tender, but the impression given to the outside world is that in the fight with Nature, which is man's task everywhere, he is oftener worsted in Australia than anywhere else. Misfortune is

The Australian in Literature

more picturesque than prosperity. Balzac said vice was better for literary purposes than virtue, and there is a modern wave of pessimism in literature which is felt all over the world. Australia, being the most distant place where the black sheep of the family can be sent, has been utilized for the relegation of the unfit — who may come back for another tug at the paternal purse-strings — and the remittance man, who is promised pecuniary help so long as he remains where he is sent; and these may be called picturesque, but they are neither useful nor ornamental.

Australia's splendid climate has tempted hundreds and thousands of delicate men who could not live and work in England to make the change to the antipodes, in many cases with the greatest success. In all the professions, especially in the church and in the press, Australia's intellectual life has been enriched by the labours of such men, whom nothing but health would have induced to leave the land of their birth. Dr Andrew Garran, who died last year at the age of seventy-five, had fifty years of good work on the press — of Adelaide first, and then on that of Sydney — and in the New South Wales Legislature, after having wintered in Madeira, where there was no work to do, and where there was a depression population of invalids. No one had a higher idea of the pleasantness of Australian life, or of the greatness of the Australian future, than this veteran journalist to the end of his life. We should not take the opinions of wealthy Australian travellers picking out the English summer, going to the most lovely spots, moving from place to place, and impressed by the completeness and the finish of all the arrangements made for their comfort, but we should see how young Australians who have to live all the year round in London, in Manchester, or in Edinburgh, long for the bright skies, the pure air, the grand vistas of their native land. The tales told "While the Billy Boils" are not all tragedies. There are deadbeats all over the world, more's the pity, but the Australian tramp is not so wretched as the tramp where the rain it raineth every day, or where frost and snow intensify the pangs of hunger and the need of shelter and fire.

No one would think in reading the poems and sketches which are said to be so characteristic of Australia that the prevalent note of Australia is good humour and commonsense. This is what Mr Percy Rowland, writing in *The Nineteenth Century* for September, after some years' residence in Australia, emphatically declares; but, curiously, he says that though there is so much good humour, there is not much original humour. Our omnibus drivers and cabbies have not the skill in repartee of the Irish jarvie or of the London bus driver. But he owns that we can appreciate a joke when we hear it, and that is a step in the right direction. We are

still sensitive to outside criticism — the Americans were so up to their great civil war — we had a financial crisis which did us much good. The Australian is a born speculator, sprung from a race of speculators; but since the crisis enterprise has been directed more towards production, and there have been continuous, varied, and patient experiments, individual and cooperative, to make the best and the most of the soil and the climate and the labour we have. Where is there a more patient, polite, or good-humoured crowd than in Australia? Visitors from England and foreign countries at the inauguration of the Commonwealth in Sydney, and at the opening of the Federal Parliament by the Duke of York in Melbourne, could not admire too much the orderly, well dressed, cheerful crowds who waited hours on the line of march. Even our race meetings command the praise that they are managed better and are more respectable than such gatherings elsewhere. Why should our poets and storytellers ignore the joyousness of Australian life, the eagerness with which outings are organized for old and young for both sexes, not only excursions by day but moonlight trips in summer, where the billy is boiled and simple fare is eaten with relish? How few think that the ubiquitous sandwich sacred to picnics, and such hospitality as is open to slender means, was introduced by Lord Sandwich, an inveterate gambler, to prevent the high play in which he delighted being interrupted by the impertinence of supper? An epigram of the time couples him with a brother peer, Lord Spencer, who also made an innovation, but his was in dress:

> Two noble lords whom, if I quote,
>   Some folks will call me sinner;
> The one invented half a coat,
>   The other half a dinner.

Ralph Nickleby may keep the memory of the Spencerian literature, but the sandwich will live as long as the Sandwich Islands, which also had their name from the worthless First Lord of the Admiralty. Australia has one great handicap — to use an appropriate phrase for the horse-loving Commonwealth — in its prolonged and excessive droughts, but these are not universal; and the enterprise and the patience and the capital of the Australians will minimize the evils where they can be dealt with, and their prudence will lead them to leave hopeless districts severely alone. We want, as Matthew Arnold says of life, "to see Australia steadily and see it whole". The one-sided pictures which our pessimistic poets and writers present are false in the impression they make on the outside world and our ourselves. They lead us to forget the beauty and the brightness of the world we live in.

4
Social and Legal Reform

Women and Children

EDITOR'S NOTE

"Marriage Rights and Wrongs" was published in *The Register*, Adelaide, 15 July 1878, and "The Boarding-Out System of South Australia" in the *Sydney Morning Herald,* 25 March 1878.

While these two articles were written in the same year, 1878, when Catherine Spence first became a full-time journalist with the Adelaide *Register*, their concerns were lifelong for Spence. She began her work with destitute children in 1865, and her interest in child welfare and education was still finding active expression in 1905, when she helped found South Australia's first free kindergartens. The reform of marriage and legitimacy laws became central issues in two of her novels, *Gathered In* (1878) and *Handfasted* (written 1879).

Some deletions have been made to "The Boarding-Out System", and are shown by asterisks.

Marriage Rights and Wrongs

In taking up an old-fashioned novel — one of Richardson's, for example — and reading it in the light of modern ideas, nothing strikes the reader more forcibly than its exaggerated view of marital and parental rights as over and against the rights of wives and children, and the very low idea which even good people then entertained of the responsibilities of the stronger and the rights of the weaker to justice and consideration. Modern opinions reverse the view, and the wider the knowledge and the greater the power the more they are held to be a trust for the benefit and protection of the ignorant and the feeble. But although this is the prevailing tone of the best literature and of the most cultivated society, such a view takes a long time to reach that stratum of society where it is most needed. It takes a long time even to give force to law, which is one of the most efficacious means of educating public opinion; and the Statute-book and the police courts still show that offences by the weaker against the stronger are considered aggravated, while those by the stronger against the weaker are taken with extenuating circumstances.

Public opinion in England as expressed in the law and enforced by the law is yet considerably behind the educated intelligence of the age with regard to marriage rights and marriage wrongs. Any offence or crime committed by a wife against her husband is still looked on as a sort of petty treason, and so late as 1760 the murder of a husband by his wife was punished by the severe sentence of burning, while any offence or violence committed by the husband against a wife is reckoned as so much less heinous than any similar crime against any other person, because she is regarded as somehow his property. A wife is liable to the heaviest punishment for transgressions which on the husband's part would

be expiated by a fine. There can be no question that adultery is a greater offence in a wife than in a husband, but taking the cases otherwise on their own merits it will be found that owing to the difference in physical strength between the sexes the woman who injures her husband does it by deceit and guile. If she takes life, it is by poison; if she is unfaithful, she tries to keep it secret. Her only open weapon is her tongue, and though it is provoking enough it makes no visible wound; whereas in the incomparably more numerous cases among the poorer classes of injury by men towards their wives the strong hand and violent blow and loud curse have a remarkable frankness about them. There is comparatively little secret made of the existence of the rival on whom the family earnings are squandered; there is little delicacy or subterfuge as to language, or gesture, or blow, or kick. Work may be done or let alone; the wages may be spent in every form of vicious indulgence; the earnings of wife or children may be all at the command of the head of the household; but there is little sense of shame on his part for doing what he likes with his own, and he has a consciousness that if his wife cannot stand this, and brings him up before the police court, the punishment awarded will cost her as dear as himself, and that he can pay her out when he returns to the bosom of his family with all his marital and parental rights in full force.

Again and again has flogging been recommended for brutal assaults on women and children as being summary, cheap, and essentially retributive, and as injuring as little as possible the family of the culprit; but although the evidence of judges, magistrates, and recorders has been overwhelming as to its being advisable nothing has been done. According to Miss Cobbe, in the *Contemporary Review* for April, six thousand women in Great Britain have during the short time of three years been brutally assaulted — that is maimed, blinded, burned, trampled on, and in many cases murdered outright — without any fresh legislation to enforce the remedy recommended. In a government which moves forward, if it moves at all, from parliamentary pressure, this question appears not to obtain sufficient backing, even from an assembly of educated gentlemen probably more chivalrous at heart than any other constituent body in the world. There can be little doubt that the swift, sharp, humbling punishment of flogging would have great influence on the effective public opinion which surrounds the culprits in the Black Country and in those large manufacturing towns in Great Britain where ignorance, good but variable wages, poor houses, and bad air lead to drink, vice, and brutality. But there is another point of view to which attention may fairly be directed. Will the flogged husband return

to his home and his duties in a better frame of mind than the fined and imprisoned one? And will wives not dread the immediate return even more than the delayed one to such an extent as to prevent them even more than at present from bringing the offenders to justice? This is one of the greatest difficulties in dealing with this class of crimes, for often lingering affection, and still oftener fear, makes the wife weaken her case, and keep back the worst wrongs she has endured. Such cruelty as is often brought before the police courts would in a higher rank of life be considered sufficient ground for judicial separation, and often for absolute divorce; but there is at present no adequate means within the reach of a woman of protecting her person or even her earnings against her husband's claims. If affection still lingers — if for the sake of the children she wishes to give him another chance — she will probably not apply for such separation; but if it is only fear, such a Bill as has been drawn out by Mr Alfred D. Hill, of Birmingham, would meet the case. This would allow the same court which sentences the husband to give the injured wife a protection-order for her earnings and the custody of her children, and also enforce an order for the husband to pay his wife such weekly sums for her own and her children's maintenance as the court sees fit. Magistrates are already empowered to give the wife protection for her earnings in the case of desertion, which is a minor offence. In many of the cases of wife-beating there is adultery as well as cruelty on the part of the husband, which should give the wife a claim for an absolute divorce. Cruelty, even of the most aggravated kind, without proved adultery is not at present held to authorize divorce, but it is well worthy of consideration whether in the interest of public morals where the offence has been great and deep, not repented of on one side, or condoned on the other, the release from marriage bonds should not be made complete after the lapse of a reasonable time from the judicial separation, the sum which the first husband is bound to pay being diminished if the wife makes a new marriage. The difficulty in enforcing the payment of a weekly amount is felt in England, and an order would be still more easily evaded here. Wife-desertion is a question which affects all the colonies, each one complaining that wives and families are deserted by their natural head and are made burdensome to the state. An intercolonial union might give increased energy to the search for the defaulters. Miss Cobbe mentions that the Recorder of Hereford last January sentenced a man to be whipped who had left his wife and family four times and thrown them on the Union.

It is being forcibly urged by some advanced thinkers that there

are two grounds for absolute divorce which are not at present recognized at all. The first is sentence to penal servitude for a long term of years. Affection may and very often indeed does survive, especially in the case of wives towards husbands, for whose temptations the most liberal allowances are made, and whose repentence is believed in. Women having a strong affection for their husbands will wait any number of years, and will be ready to take them by the hand to help them by every means in their power up the steep path which may win back a good name. But when love is dead; when the wife or husband knows better than judge or jury the depths of wickedness into which their partner has sunk, when there is no feeling of hope or trust to bridge over the long years of separation, why, it is argued, enforce the tie for life on the innocent party because vows have been made which the guilty one has made it impossible to fulfil? The second case of omission is when one party is under restraint as a lunatic with no chance of recovery. This affords perhaps stronger ground for dissolving the marriage bond and for allowing a second legal marriage. Every physician in charge of a lunatic asylum will tell of patients who have been admitted there in the prime of life, and have dragged on for ten, twenty, and thirty years, leaving their partners virtually widowed but unable to make another marriage. Such a physican will speak of many a working-man earning in the colonies from thirty to forty shillings a week with his wife in the asylum from puerperal mania, and left with two or three or more young children, obliged to go to his daily task at six in the morning and remain at it until the evening. So long as there is a chance of recovery the husband and children make a shift somehow; but as months and years roll on, and no favourable symptom presents itself, the comfortless home and the expense, and perhaps the scandal arising from employing any woman as servant, lead in many instances to the establishment of an immoral bond between him and some female disposed to act as the head of his household. The man is at the disadvantage that no respectable woman can take the position, but anything he feels is better than the anarchy which prevailed before.

In spite of the man being the breadwinner of a houshold, it is often harder for a widower to do well for a family than for a widow. His work takes him much away, and he cannot hire efficient female help at home. A widow, too, is more pitied and helped both by public and private charity than a widower. But the condition of either a poor woman or one who is widowed is far better than that of one with a partner hopelessly insane. The bulk of recoveries take place within six months, and if there is no sign

of improvement in eighteen months or two years the chance of restoration to reason is infinitesimally small. It may be insisted that people who vow to cleave to each other in sickness and in health cannot be absolved from that vow by any force of malady, but it must be remembered that permanent mental disease necessitating restraint renders cohabitation altogether out of the question. Therefore after the lapse of a reasonable time, and subject to the carefully considered judgment of an expert in mental disease that recovery is practically impossible, is it not fair to provide that the marriage bond shall be legally dissolved? If, contrary to all expectations, the patient should recover, and find that his or her rights have been superseded, he or she will have suffered a grievous misfortune, which may cloud even the great joy of restoration to the duties and pleasures of life; but against this it must be born in mind that under the present state of things the many husbands and wives who are condemned to widowhood or to an illegal and immoral substitute for marriage are all suffering misfortunes which are not slight. Marriage is a divine institution, because it is so well adapted to human necessities, because its permanency promotes repose and hope and trust, and because it builds up the family in the purest, the most loving, and the most secure manner; but in those exceptional cases where its permanency leads to violence and tyranny, and where it utterly fails to build up the family in love and trust, there is surely ground for the view that the rigid lines must be overstepped and some reasonable qualifications be allowed in the interests of true morality and social order.

The Boarding-Out System of South Australia

The Charity Commission that was appointed by Sir Henry Parkes strongly recommended the adoption in this colony of the system of boarding-out young children, in lieu of aggregating them in large masses at Randwick. There has, however, been an apparent hesitation in adopting this advice. Having understood that the system was working satisfactorily in South Australia, we applied to one of the best authorities on the subject there, for a full, true, and particular account. In response to this application we have received a communication, the first part of which we have now the pleasure of laying before our readers, and to which we bespeak the special attention of politicians, and of the charitable.
— *Ed*. SMH

Instead of charity being the easiest duty in the world, as it is, perhaps, the pleasantest, it appears, in our modern times, to be the most difficult; and there is scarcely a form or mode in which it operates, either on a large or small scale, which is not open to the charge of doing serious mischief, either directly or indirectly, to such an extent as sometimes to neutralize the benefit it bestows. The thoughtful philanthropist feels bewildered and chilled by the small real progress made by the most sincere goodwill and the best organized efforts to lighten the burden of the world. It seems so long to wait till education and the destruction of erroneous opinions have made the world so just that there is little need of charity, and he chafes at the gigantic evil he sees, which isolated efforts seem scarcely to touch, while organized societies often foster the mischief they aim at relieving. It would appear that without the wisdom of the serpent charity cannot have the harmlessness of the dove. But there is one branch of philanthropy which seems at

The Boarding-Out System

once benevolent and safe, and that is, the striking at vice and pauperism at the root by removing the children of the state from establishments which, however splendid and well-organized, are not homes, and dispersing them over the country in respectable cottage homes, where they may take root, and find that individual care and personal liking, which cannot be found where children are numbered by hundreds.

The system of placing out such children, which has been adopted in South Australia since April 1872, has been so successful as an economic reform, and still more strikingly as a moral and social reform, that I think it is worthy of the candid attention of the authorities and the general public of New South Wales to consider how far the example may be imitated with some adaptation to slightly different circumstances. It shows one feature so different from those of England and Scotland, in the enormous number of children who have been bona-fide adopted, and temporarily adopted without subsidy, that it may be supposed to be the characteristic of a young and rising colony. In Victoria, however, which has tried the system more recently, almost all the children are subsidized. New South Wales is at present decidedly more prosperous than Victoria, and although it has not the same large proportion of small farmers in its population that South Australia has, it has a great number of well-to-do people in every walk in life, to whom a child would be no burden, but a help and a comfort.

Having been intimately connected with the movement from the first, one of those who urged its adoption on the government for some time before the request found any favour, a member of the committee, and a visitor since the Auxiliary Boarding-out Society was formed to cooperate in the supervision of the children, the present writer is qualified to speak on the subject, and as in the course of this experience difficulties have occasionally been encountered and drawbacks felt, this account is not intended to be the *couleur-de-rose* picture of a partizan, but the plain and truthful statement of a practical worker.

In grappling with the evils of pauperism in all countries, anything which does not strike at the root must be necessarily superficial and temporary. As the highest authority has it, "The poor ye have always with you"; and the chance of becoming poor, like the chance of becoming rich, is one of the elements in the grand system of discipline by which humanity is trained. I would even go further and say, "The vicious ye have always with you". The liability to yield to temptation, like the power to resist it, is the necessary condition of our being; but no nation should by its institutions or by its public opinion encourage the fatal caste-like

Social and Legal Reform: Women and Children

regime of hereditary poverty, hereditary shiftlessness, and hereditary vice and crime; and the community which best protects the young from being dragged down by the civil example and training of the old, and endeavours to raise all such who fall into the hands of the state to a higher level, is the community which will make the most of all that is good, wise, and strong in its population.

The state sees that all children are educated, and will even use compulsion to effect that desirable result; but the state, as represented by educated men, is too apt to think that if the necessary reading, writing, and arithmetic are imparted, it is no matter how or where these things are learned, and that an industrial school, well organized, and carefully inspected, will turn out as good results, perhaps even better results, than poor homes, governed by average men and women, sometimes wise and patient, sometimes foolish and hasty. They forget that in the average home and in the common school there are a thousand influences playing round the children and the family which are unknown to a large establishment, where it is done by rule, and with the regularity of clockwork; that if there is a sharp word, or a box on the ear sometimes, there is a kiss or a caress, or an indulgence at another time; that, instead of the dispassionate, even-handed, but sometimes cold justice, which is all that the best of such industrial schools can exercise, there is individual care and individual love for each member of the family to the others; and that, in place of routine to deaden faculty and ingenuity, there are constant opportunities and emergencies to call out both.

Even the book-lessons, however well they may be taught, lie quite outside of the interest which ought to work on the affections, whereas the lessons learned at common schools by children coming from ordinary homes are interesting to father and mother, who plan what their boy or girl will be fit for, who ask the bright scholar to run up the butcher's, or baker's, or grocer's bill, to see if it is all right — who like to hear them read, and who look with pride on their fair writing. As what we know never influences the conduct when it is not connected with what we feel, so, in this so-called iron age, the great desideratum is to touch the heart and the conscience while we inform and discipline the mind.

* * *

In 1860, the destitute children, amounting at that date to 130, were removed from a very insufficient building to a new industrial school, pleasantly situated at Magill, about four miles from Adelaide, which was calculated to accommodate 230 inmates. Such children fell into the hands of the Destitute Board, either as orphans without relatives able or willing to provide for them, as

The Boarding-Out System

the children of parents either abandoned in character or unable from sickness or widowhood to support them; or as brought up as neglected children before the police court, and sentenced to the Industrial School for a longer or shorter term.

Under the South Australian Act such children were to be kept at the school till they reached the age of thirteen, when they were to be sent out to service; but in many instances they proved but unsatisfactory, for they were generally dull, shiftless, and without interest in their work or their employers.

Even with this outlet at thirteen, the admission of children increased till, in the year 1871, the building was completely filled, and the government resolved to comply with the request of a handful of enthusiasts — of whom Miss Emily Clark was the most earnest and indefatigable in her efforts — and try the experiment of boarding out some of the inmates. This was offered to suitable persons at the cost of each child's maintenance at the school, which was reckoned (exclusive of the cost of building) at five shillings a week for board and clothing and supervision, the cost of education and medical attendance being defrayed by the government.

The most careful inquiries were made as to the character of applicants for such children, and a system of inspection provided for, both by the chairman of the Destitute Board, and by visitors affiliated to the Adelaide Central Boarding Act Committee, who were bound to see the children at their homes once a quarter, but on no set day, and report on their health, appearance, conduct, sleeping accommodation, attendance at school, church, and Sunday-school, and above all, to see if the children appeared happy, and the foster parents kind. In this year 1872, no less than seventy children were thus placed out, but the eagerness of the community to take them either altogether, or with the contingency of parting with them at the end of a certain number of years, caused the Board to decline granting the very moderate subsidy at first offered, and for the last four years there have never been more than thirty children paid for.

In no country or colony with which I am acquainted has the system been carried out at so great a pecuniary saving to the state as in South Australia. Out of 273 children under the age of sixteen who are placed out, either on subsidy or adopted without subsidy, or at service under certain limitations, the number actually paid for is only twenty-five, and as the supervision has been done mainly by voluntary efforts, there has been no addition to the staff required, while the reduction of expenses at the Magill School has been enormous. The manner in which the community

has come forward to take their share in the good work, shows both good circumstances and good will. Only in a prosperous country can little hands be so helpful as to make the cost of food and clothing disregarded by the class of small farmers, market-gardeners, artisans, and shopkeepers, who have absorbed the bulk of the children, and the 273 at present out do not represent the whole results, for at least 300 have passed the age of sixteen (when supervision ends, somewhat too early, I think) since the adoption of the system. Only kindness of heart would lead people to bear with the waywardness, the little deceits and dishonesties born of fear and repression and destitution, the slovenly or dirty habits which recur when the child is removed from the strict order and discipline of the industrial school, and the delicate health which is inherited from sickly or vicious parents, or is the result of neglect in earlier years.

If there is serious cause of complaint on either side, if the foster parents are dissatisfied or the child seems unhappy, the child is removed, and another place is tried, often with better success. There is a small proportion who are constantly being moved about, being unattractive in appearance and stubborn in temper. Even they sometimes fall on their feet, and are borne with because they can do well, and work fairly when they please. Any case of harsh treatment is inquired into, and reported on, and the child removed at once; but in visiting at the Industrial School, and talking to such children, I have invariably found that they prefer the free life, even with the buffet, to the safety and mechanical routine of the school; that the greater variety of food made amends for its occasional irregularity; that the alternation of school work with other employments, such as gathering fruit, bringing in cows, chopping wood, or minding a baby, had charms beyond what could be found in the narrow circle of the school grounds; and that the spending of a chance penny on sweets gave more pleasure than the lavish distribution of gifts from kind friends at Christmas or Easter.

* * *

Crime

EDITOR'S NOTE

"Heredity and Environment" was delivered before (and printed at the request of) the Criminological Society of South Australia, 23 October 1897 by Catherine H. Spence.

By the time this paper was delivered, in 1897, Spence was a well-known and respected public speaker. Her writings and active involvement in social and political reform gave her the moral and intellectual authority to address social problems with the confidence that her opinions would be influential. Her repudiation of the fatalism of heredity as a socal or spiritual determinent had its origins in her youth, when she abandoned Presbyterianism chiefly because of its emphasis on the inheritance of Original Sin with the restrictions on free will that implied. Only then did Spence become free to involve herself in reform work based on the optimistic belief that people's moral character could be changed for the better if their conditions of life and work were improved.

Asterisks indicate where deletions have been made.

Heredity and Environment

The many-sided problems of this age cannot be solved by going back even to the greatest masters of thought in olden times. Even the highest authority of all, although He may indicate the spirit in which social reforms and the betterment of human conditions should be sought for and worked out, could not lay down methods of work for us, or warn against dangers which the world He lived in had no experience of. The supreme lesson taught by Christ, the brotherhood of man, makes one thing clear, that we should seek to lift the fallen, whether from poverty, from sickness, from weakness, or from sin, up to the better level in the spirit of love and sympathy, and that all punishment should be disciplinary and not revengeful. But each age should approach its own problems, not only with all the accumulated experience of the past, but with all the wisdom and inspiration of the living men and women who seek to follow Christ's example. These living men and women may, however, be one-sided and, though zealous and disinterested, give too much weight to partial truths. They are absolutely confident in their own outlook, their own inlook, and their own onlook, to use James Hinton's words, for the objective, the subjective, and the speculative. We need to compare conflicting theories so as to find a working hypothesis.

In the great question as to the extent and the limitation of heredity, and the influences of environment on character and on conditions, there are two great schools of thought. In an old classic for children, *The Evenings at Home*, I received my first lesson on the subject in the apologue of "Nature and Education". Each took a tree, and each did its best for its own, and its worst for the other. Education or environment spoiled Nature's pine, the parent of which had been the main-mast of a man-of-war. The tree

fostered by education was made unsightly by nature, but grafting made it produce tolerable fruit. In conclusion Nature says, "Ah, sister, I see it is in your power to spoil the best of my works." "Ah, sister," said Education, "it is a hard matter to contend against you. However, much may be done by taking pains." And it is only by the belief that much may be done that we are led to take pains, and direct intelligent thought towards betterment.

This utilitarian theory was good as far as it went, and it was a much higher thing than the materialism which seems in our day to have taken hold of so many of the advocates of over-mastering heredity. Zola, for instance, shows us only bodies with their coarse tastes, their selfish desires, their lower ambitions. He proposes to write as a philanthropist, and conceives that it is only by telling the truth about life that one can lead to its being made better. But "it needs a soul to move a body even to a cleaner sty", as Robert Browning says, and materialism can no more cast out materialism than Satan can cast out Satan. Moreover, when the physiologist reigns alone, the picture of human nature is false as well as painful.

We all know how paralysing to human effort was the Calvinistic doctrine of election and reprobation — the unchangeable decrees of God, who had made one vessel to honour and another to dishonour — the conviction that no efforts and no prayers could change our own destinies or the destinies of those who were dear to us. An old friend of mine, whose father was an extreme Calvinist, a Glassite, I think, told me that when he was a boy his father did not ask him to go to church. If he was elected he would be saved; if he was not, all the opportunities he had would only increase his condemnation.

But seriously, I think we may consider that no Calvinistic doctrine of election and reprobation is more cruel and hopeless than the law of heredity as laid down by Zola and Ibsen. According to these pessimists who ride heredity to death, we inherit only the vices, the weaknesses, and the diseases of our ancestors. If this is really the case the world would become worse and worse in each succeeding generation. Who of us is free from taint?

In almost all his works Ibsen hangs his story on the peg of heredity, and if we are to believe him, heredity cannot be fought against. In such a tragedy as *Ghosts* we see the son reproducing the evil acts of his father, though he had not been brought up by him, but by a mother of very different nature and temperament. Ibsen's fellow-countryman, Bjornsen, takes the contrary view of the matter. He says that if we know that our ancestors drank and gambled or were violent-tempered or immoral, we can avoid the

pitfall, because we know it is there. Ibsen's son, Sigurd, in 1892, married Bjornsen's beautiful daughter, Bergliot, and they possess a grandchild in common.

It is useless to speculate which side of the shield young Tancred Ibsen will look upon, or whether he will hold the middle course. Heredity, though an enormous factor in our constitution, need not be regarded as an over-mastering fate, for each human being has an almost limitless parentage to draw upon. Each child has both a father and a mother, and two grandparents on both sides, increasing as you go back. The law of atavism, or reverting to a past generation, comes in to save the children even of drunkards and libertines. I inherit my crooked little fingers from my father's mother, but I did not inherit the consumption of which she and most of her children died. Her children had not this crooked finger. I inherit my reddish hair from my mother's father, but not his rheumatism or gout. Not one of his eight sons and daughters had this coloured hair. In most things I hold from my mother, but from my father and the red-haired grandfather, who were both too speculative, I inherit hope, which is invaluable for a social and political reformer.

I hope you will excuse these personal notes, because they bear upon the extent and limitations of heredity. And it depends greatly on the environment which of the hereditary traits will take persistent hold on the character.

Although we are liable to inherit the diseases and the sins of our parents and ancestors, we inherit a great deal more. We inherit their health and their virtues. We inherit the recuperative power which every human being possesses, though many may not have been able to exert it. And we inherit from them possibilities which circumstances prevented them from developing. The most notable instance of this is that working bees and ants, which are all sterile, must have inherited latent possibilities for a life quite different from that of father or mother.

It is many years since I read a paper of Francis Galton's, in which he accounts for the anomaly that while generally speaking the children of men of genius show ability, in some cases when the genius was exceptionally great no child showed ability, by the supposition that the parent had used up all his potentialities and left none to bequeath. Although the paper was strong for heredity, it took such a wide grasp of the subject that it was a cheerful revelation to me.

When a young man told me he could not help drinking to excess because his father had done so, I said, "You are your mother's son as well as your father's, and she did not drink". She was the most

saintly of women. Why could he not draw from the heredity on her side? But, alas, the environment of the son was too much like that of the father. Both were brilliant, with great social gifts, and the environment of men makes these things temptations at present. Who will dare to say that it will be so in the future? Nothing has more impressed me as to this than the contrast between men and women of a century ago and even later. I can recollect when men drank freely at all times of the day and on all occasions, when gentlemen rarely returned from a dinner party without having had a great deal too much. But the women of the same class, though there was no blue or white ribbonism, though they might take beer, wine, or even spirits, were, I think, quite as temperate as now, if not more so. Sophia Western, for instance, was the daughter of a drunken, swearing, foul-mouthed squire, and her mother was dead, but she appears as the type of a sweet, virtuous, innocent girl, and no one thinks it impossible or unnatural. It was no disgrace to Squire Western to live as he lived and to talk as he talked, but an English girl would be disgraced if she imitated him.

But besides drawing on a much wider ancestry than the immediate parents, we have more than we inherit, or where could the law of progress come in? Each generation, each child who is born, comes into a slightly different world, fed by more experience, blown upon by fresh influences. And each individual comes into the world, not with a body merely, but with a soul. And this soul is susceptibe of impressions, not only from the outer material world, but from other souls also impressed by the old and the new, by the material and the ideal.

The terrible family record in which the history of several generations is worked out by Zola, where the taint seemed to be deepened by transmission, may be supposed to be supported by Richard Dugdale's *History of the Jukes.* This book is cited continually as proving heredity, whereas those who read the book through, instead of merely accepting allusions to it which are one-sided and defective, see clearly that it forms the strongest argument for change of environment that ever was brought forward. The assumed name of "Jukes" is given to the descendants of a worthless woman, who emigrated to America a hundred and fifty years ago, from whom hundreds of criminals, paupers, and prostitutes descended.

But how were the Jukes dealt with during this period? No helping hand removed the children from their vicious and criminal surroundings; neither Church nor school compelled them to come in.

The ancestral breeding spot of this family nestles along the

forest-covered margin of five lakes, so rocky as to be at some parts inaccessible. It may be called one of the crime-cradles of the state of New York, for in subsequent examinations of convicts in the different state prisons, a number of them were found to be the descendants of families equivalent to the Jukes, and emerging from this nest. Most of the ancestors were squatters upon the soil, and in some cases have become owners by tax-title or by occupancy. They lived in log or stone houses, similar to slave hovels, all ages, sexes, relations and strangers "bunking" indiscriminately. "To this day," writes Dugdale, "some of the Jukes occupy the self-same shanties, built nearly a century ago. The essential features of the habitat have remained stationary, and the social habits seem to survive in conformity to the persistency of the domiciliary environment. During the last thirty years, however, there have been better houses built, owing to the establishment of factories, and that has brought considerable improvement."

The Rev. Oscar McCulloch, in *The Tribe of Ishmael, a Study in Social Degeneration,* has carried out the history of thirty families, which, like the Jukes, were a pest and a cost to society. He says there is reason to believe that much of this came from the old convict stock which England threw into the American plantations in the seventeenth and eighteenth centuries. Any one who has read the Tennessee stories of Egbert Cradock (Miss Murfee), or who recollects the mean whites of Mrs Beecher Stowe's tales, may account for this by heredity from an old convict stock. But consider the environment! When this white convict's sentence expired, he found himself in a society where all the field labour and all the domestic service was done either by black slaves or by assigned convict servants. He had learned no trade. He became one of the strongest advocates for negro slavery, because his colour made him eternally their superior.

The expired convict was apt to take to the bush, which is not so barren in the southern states as in Australia. He learned the use of a gun and a bowie knife. He was disposed to be a nomad. There were no schools for his children to go to. He did not settle down to industrial life as the Australian expiree did. He saw that all white men must work that they might eat. The environment in New South Wales and in Tasmania might have been improved upon, but it was far better than that in Virginia, Carolina, and Georgia.

The extraordinary number of murders committed in the United States as compared with other English-speaking countries, is attributed by Mr Douglas Morrison mainly to heredity. So many Italians, Hungarians, and others who have little respect for

human life, settle in America. An American friend of mine, while acknowledging that this is a contributory cause, considers that the bad administration of the law is the main factor.

Many murders are undetected. Even where there is the clearest proof of guilt, juries will not convict or judges sentence. When the murderer is actually sentenced, the carrying of it out is delayed for months, and even years, and especially if the criminal has influential friends, it may never be carried out at all.

I read in a San Francisco paper that if there was the same swiftness and certainty of punishment as overtook Butler, the homicides in the United States would be reduced to one-half or one-third of the present number — ten thousand yearly. Lynch law, detestable as it is in a civilized country, could only have been resorted to by a people who distrusted the ordinary course of law.

Oscar McCulloch says distinctly that in the tribe of Ishmael there was much sexual immorality, but little intemperance. The crime was chiefly thieving and larceny, but there had been a good many murders. There was some wandering Indian blood in the tribe. The licentiousness which characterized all the men and women, and Dugdale says the same of the Jukes, resulted in mental weakness, general incapacity, and unfitness for hard work. Outdoor relief administered without judgment, and indiscriminate charity encouraged this idle wandering life. He himself had known three generations of Ishmaelite beggars.

McCulloch's remedies are first to stop outdoor relief; second, to check indiscriminate charity, falsely so-called; and third, to get hold of the children.

Dugdale's utterances as to intemperance among the Jukes is guarded. He hesitates to accept the current opinion as to the part which ardent spirits play in the carnival of crime. Certain diseases and mental disorders precede the appetite for stimulants, so that the true cause of their use is the antecedent hereditary or induced physical exhaustion. The remedy is healthy, well-balanced constitutions. The intemperance question in Dugdale's opinion is one for the physician and educator rather than for the legislator.

Both our observers object to institutional life, which breaks down the self-reliance of inmates, especially for children. But in New York, Dugdale's state, and in Indiana, McCulloch's state, there is no boarding out, and all the children of the state are in institutions.

When we see what can be done, and what has been done, with our Australian Jukes and Ishmaelites when young by putting them into decent homes, and giving them as companions at school and church, at work and at play, the children of industrious and

law-abiding citizens, we are bound to protest against the paralysing doctrine of hereditary crime.

Dr Dugdale has in other writings less quoted than *The Jukes* in a series of articles in the *Atlantic Monthly* entitled "The Progress of Crime in Society", proved that crime tends to lessen as detection and punishment become more certain, and as the attractions of industrial life become greater. By the progress of society a criminal career ought to become more and more difficult, and may be narrowed down till it will become possible only for the most clever and the most dexterous, who are just those who could do as well, and indeed even better, in honest callings. I wish the criminology societies of the world would republish these articles. They are the work of a man who has made a lifelong study of the subject, and a man whose earnestness and enthusiasm made him fearless. He drove his sleigh into the midst of the Juke habitat alone. The stout young countryman whom he had hired to accompany him left him when he learned his destination, saying, "I think too much of my life to risk it among highwaymen and murderers. Why, sir, they'll cut your throat for the buffalo robe you have, to say nothing of your span of horses." But always severely earnest in whatever he thought it worth his while to undertake, he proceeded alone, and after talking some time, and making some observations he wished, he partook of a meal with those outcasts, and departed unmolested. Not only this, but he had so won their hearts by the magnetism of his strong humanity that two stalwart young highwaymen volunteered to escort him through the rough places, and when outside the "Cradles" they wished him good day, and a safe journey back to his hotel.

One very important generalization laid down by Dugdale (page 50) is especially valuable for this society, as showing the hopefulness of dealing with criminals, especially with the young. It is this:

> Hereditary pauperism seems to be more fixed than hereditary crime, for very much crime is the misdirection of faculty, and is amenable to discipline, while very much of pauperism is due to the absence of vital power, being in many cases identical with such lines of organic disease of mind or body as insanity, consumption, syphilis, which cause from generation to generation the successive extinction of capacity, till death supervenes.

Here, too, we have the authority of Mr Douglas Morrison much quoted as to juvenile crime, that it is fortunate for society that the cares of parenthood are largely incompatible with a life of crime. In consequence of this, criminals who have children are often anxious to get rid of them. Such children fall upon the poor

law, or are disposed of in one way or another, so that the parental calling may not be unduly hampered. At other times criminals who have children send them out to beg, and in this way a large number of them are committed to industrial schools. It is chiefly for these reasons that in English-speaking countries the criminal calling does not descend in the majority of cases from father to son. It descends by apprenticeship, and not as a rule by parenthood. Now the pauper spirit and condition is eminently hereditary, and the poor fare, the narrow limitations, the low associations of the English workhouse and the American poorhouse are not likely to give the vitality that these poor children need to set them free from the hereditary taint. Again let me quote from the *Jukes* (p. 49):

> Criminal careers are more easily modified by environment, because crime, more especially contrived crime, is an index of capacity, and whenever capacity is found, there environment is most effective in producing modifications of career.

And again —

> We must distinctly accept as an accepted educational axiom, that the moral nature, which really means the holding of the emotions and the passions under the dominion of the judgment by the exercise of will, is the last developed of the elements of character. Dr Maudsley, that great authority, says it is not mature till from the thirtieth to the thirty-third year. For this reason this all important will is most modified by the nature of the environment.

It used to be a maxim that the first thing to be done in education was to *break a child's will,* so as to produce instant and unreasoning obedience. Even good Susannah Wesley, mother of John and Charles Wesley, in her dealings with her very numerous family, held it her duty to break the will, forgetting that if the *ipse dixit* of the parent is made the only law of life, the child has no guiding rule for his conduct in the world. The will should be trained and strengthened, for it is indeed the real "*ego*". It is one of the most fatal influences of institutional life that the child, accustomed to absolute rule and authority, to minute regulations for every hour of the day and every contingency that arises, has developed no will power, no faculty of choice between the evil and the good — between the good and the better. The strict mother, who boasted that she had brought up a family who never disobeyed or questioned her, was amazed to see that as her sons approached manhood they ran away from home, and went, many of them, into evil ways, against which she had equipped them with no defence. I do not say that parents should accompany every command with

the reasons for it. Far from that; but it should be made manifest that nothing unreasonable or arbitrary should be demanded, and that things are to be done because they are right and proper; not merely because the parents order them. If, when a parent has made a mistake, he or she acknowledges it and regrets it, the children will be far more ready to confess their offences, which are, in more cases than not, only their mistakes.

"We are too apt," says Guyan, "to judge children's actions objectively, to measure them by our own rules, our own precepts, our own ideals. The child's ideal cannot be, and ought not to be, thus developed; we must, therefore, pay special attention to the force of will displayed by the child, to its self-control, to its power of internal resistance. This or that mark of will which thwarts us, puts us out, and wounds us, may in reality be the mark of internal and subjective progress. The moral will is the power of acting along the lines of the greatest resistance, and it is a thing of very slow growth. It is as dangerous to stimulate a child to moral precocity as to intellectual precocity." All children naturally romance, but that is not lying. The foundation of the real lie is fear, for a lie is the child's only weapon. Perhaps in the case of children who have harsh or unreasonable parents truth is developed in intercourse with schoolfellows in a society of equals, long before it is exercised to superiors and masters. I believe that games give children their first introduction in justice. Fair play and equal opportunity for all — this is my idea of democratic education. All games have rules which should be obeyed. The umpire needed to settle dispute as to the game is the earliest example of a court of law, and the subordination of disputes to judges to whom the people delegate power.

* * *

No severity of punishment will deter from a lucrative profession which may last a long while without detection, particularly if the state of public feeling, or the uncertainty of the law, often lets the detected criminal escape. When we see how high wages will induce men to go into such unhealthy trades as needle-grinding, where the average life is only forty years, one can scarcely wonder that the professional thief, who spends two-thirds of his life in criminal licence and vicious self-indulgence, and one-third in prison, where he is fed and clothed, and generally recruits his health during these sequestrations, is not led to repentance and reform by our present regime. Criminal satistics in England prove that with the abolition of the death penalty for minor offences, the greater certainty of the sentence made a change for the better, but the most marked improvement there has been since the aboli-

tion of transportation, which was, according to Archbishop Whately, a system begun in defiance of all reason, and persevered in in defiance of all experience! From 1828 to 1838 the average convict population of Great Britain was fifty thousand, while from four to five thousand were transported every year to her penal settlements, of whom most of the number stayed in the colonies or died there. From the day transportation was checked in 1853, and finally abolished in 1867 in West Australia, where it took hold after the eastern Australian colonies had indignantly repudiated it, the crime rate in England has been steadily reduced. In 1881, when Dugdale wrote, he said there were only ten thousand convict prisoners and two thousand ticket-of-leave men in England. In old times there were 199 prisons in England. Even twenty years ago there were 113 prisons in England; now there are only 58. Absolute uniformity prevails in them all with regard to diet, discipline, and regulations. This is a great pity. In America experiments can be made in various states, and the results are published for the benefit of the world. Uniformity is a refuge for stupidity.

It would appear to be an anomaly that the fewer men are in prison, the fewer thieves we have at large; but the reason is clear. Transportation, which yearly sent out of England thousands of practised thieves, while the effective temptation remained the same, other thousands, more easily caught, took their place. When a country has to punish its criminals on its own soil, with reasonable vigilance on the part of the police, and especially with sufficient industrial outlets, the criminal profession is narrowed into lines which only special dexterity, ingenuity, and perseverance can follow. I quote from Dugdale's words:

> In such visitations as the Great Plague of London, or in times of disorganization during riots, we know that people supposed to be honest and law-abiding plunder and steal, because the police are paralysed, and property is supposed to be no man's, and if not taken by Dick will be seized by Harry. Effective checks are in abeyance, and temptations to crime are increased. In bad times, when employers discharge their workmen it is, of course, their worst, the least skilful, and the most unsteady, who are thrust out. The professional thieves find their preserves poached on by new hands easily detected, and an increase in crime is, singulary enough, accompanied by a decrease in the arrests for drunkenness. The old hands do not earn so much to spend in that way. On the return of commercial prosperity, the discharged hands, or at least those of them who are not in the grip of the law, will be re-engaged; the crime ratio will fall, and the proportion of arrests for drunkenness and misdemeanors arising out of drunkenness will rise.

Social and Legal Reform: Crime

But unfortunately we cannot, in this phase of the world's history, have prosperity without an immense impulse to speculation. When the currency was in progress of inflation in America, during the Civil War, when a land boom or a mining boom is inflating values in Australia, the continuous rise in prices presents such chances to become suddenly rich, that numerous clerks, trustees, and directors in public institutions, pledge other people's securities in order to borrow money for their speculations. With the decline of price numberless embezzlements and defalcations are revealed. These are not committed by the criminal class at all. They are mainly confined to the greatly tempted among lawyers, bankers, trustees, Church members, all of whom know perfectly well the ethical wrong of these acts. Every one of these offences is punishable by penal servitude and social disgrace, and yet, with the prospects of enormous profits, they take the risk. And in order to escape detection when it is imminent, even greater risks are run, and greater crimes committed. "*More effective auditing* would be a far better check to such courses than the severest penalties of the law" is Dugdale's pregnant advice.

In the case of the young, the gaol is an undoubted school of crime. Every effort should be used to keep boys and girls out of gaol. As soon as possible, boys and girls sent to reformatory schools should be dispersed where the environment is more normal, and better than that of fellow-offenders and officials. But from my experience here in South Australia, there are very few of the homes from which young offenders come, that are better than a good disciplinary institution. Order, routine, and cleanliness, prompt obedience, regular work, accompanied by plenty of wholesome food and fresh air, and time and facilities for recreation, are the very best things for children whose homes are dirty and disorderly, and whose parents are vicious and careless. Six or twelve months of such discipline is generally needed by young offenders before they can be sent out into the world. If they respond to it earlier, the State Children's Council have it in their power to transfer them to the Industrial School and place them out at once.

I do not think it right to deprive reformatory children of their play for longer than a few days. Games, according to Mr Guyan, in his book on *Education and Heredity*, in the Contemporary Sciences series, are far more important in physical and mental development than drill and gymnastics. Happiness is the most powerful of tonics, and the extreme interest felt in games, and the riotous delight which children take in their rougher frolics are of as much importance as the accompanying exertion. And I have already showed their moral teaching.

Heredity and Environment

Heredity, as we know, comes down to us from countless ancestors, and environment means a great deal more than superficial thinkers associate with the term. The home and the family are first in order, and *it is the worst part of evil heredity that it is likely to perpetuate a bad environment.* There is constant talk of the want of parental control being answerable for the increase of juvenile delinquency, but the want of parental sympathy is at the root of the lack of control. The child needing punishment is the child lacking affection. Lavish on it enough love and blows will be unnecessary, for love begets love, the most powerful weapon in all education.

A mother may be clean and tidy, and give her children well-cooked food and suitable clothes, but if she pushes them aside because she is always too busy to spare five minutes for their troubles or their joys, when she seems happiest when they are out of her way, and off her hands; when she never speaks to them but to give a command or to administer a reproof, when she is as angry about noise and spoiling clothes as about lying and cruelty, she need not be surprised if they go elsewhere for companionship and guidance. Parents are too apt to treat their children when they are little as if they were never to grow up, and then as they are growing up they check them as if they were still little. All through our childish years habits are forming, and it is no small thing whether the habits are good or bad, whether they tend to make the impulses and emotions our masters, or enthrone the intelligent will as their master.

When fathers and mothers bring their little children before the magistrate as uncontrollable, they often speak the truth, they are uncontrollable by *them*. You may say that we need a reformatory for the parents even more than for the youngsters, but let us not be too hard on the parents. They may be ignorant of what a good home should be. They may never have seen one. They enter on marriage and parenthood under the influence of one of the strongest instincts of human nature, and in poor homes in poor streets, with uncertain employment, it is not so easy to be model fathers and mothers.

* * *

Next to the home, the immediate neighbourhood is of importance. I am always very sorry when poverty drives decent families into very small houses in streets where there are doubtful characters. In a town there is not space in the home for play, and the street has to be the gathering place. I saw the opening of a playground in one of the worst quarters of Chicago, the greatest possible boon, but Chicago needed fifty or a hundred of such open spaces.

Social and Legal Reform: Crime

I regret very much that our beautiful squares, meant to be the lungs and playgrounds of the city, are so invaded by men of indifferent character that they are not quite safe for our little ones without some escort.

Perhaps of as much importance in environment is the day school. Here many children learn their first lessons in order, cleanliness, obedience, and politeness, as well as the lessons which are especially the object of public education. Without discipline, order, and obedience, large classes could not be taught at all. M. Guyan quotes from Tolstoy his amusing account of the schools he established for the Russian peasant children on his estate, where the children themselves suggest what they want to learn, and may refuse to learn anything else, where they play and fight at their own sweet will, and then tired out may turn to their books. Some children could learn much even on this strange voluntary system, and some inveterate dunces learn little even by the best methods, but eighty-five per cent of children born will learn comparably more where there is discipline than without it. And they also learn respect for others, by authority first, but afterwards reason approves of it. There is nothing school children despise more than weakness and vacillation on the part of those in authority.

There are two points on which wise parents and teachers and friends may help their young lads and girls, and these are in the choice of companions and of books. These may be most helpful or most mischievous. If parents took note of what companions their children associated with, and encouraged them to bring their friends home, they might give a great deal of pleasure, and might check undesirable intimacies. They should make a point of reading some of the books their children prefer. The choice of a profession or trade is also a most important one for environment. If the youth's heart goes with his work, the work is the best moral antiseptic in the world.

It is well for us when we reach the age to claim citizens' rights, that we should have grown up in a law-honouring and law-abiding community. The public opinion which influences us is that which is nearest to us — that of our mates and equals. A healthy public opinion is more powerful than the law. In an educated and intelligent community it supports the administration of the law if it is intelligent and honest, and such law reacts in the moralizing of public opinion.

If the church only keeps hold of our children while they go to Sunday-school, and lets them drift as they reach manhood and womanhood, it fails in its great mission. The church environment is strong but partial. The classes from which the professional

criminal and the hereditary pauper are drawn are scarcely touched by the Churches of the presnt day. The Salvation Army reaches people whom the organized churches do not touch, and it has a knack of setting its converts to work for something more than their own salvation, which is real salvation to those who practise it. The most earnest churches are stimulated by this example, and many of them now have a social wing.

But this is a criminological society, and perhaps I have dwelt too much on the preventive work to be done in the home, in the school, in the national institutions, and in the church. The question more immediately before us is what is to be done in the reclamation of the criminal and the misdemeanant. We cannot change the heredity: how can we change the environment? I do not think we have advanced far in reformatory spirit or reformatory methods at the Adelaide Gaol or at the Yatala Labor Prison. The sentences seem punitive, rather than disciplinary or elevating. We are promised a paper on the Elmira Reform Prison for Adults in New York State before the end of the year. The founding of this was the bright spot at the end of Richard Dugdale's life, and Charles Dudley Warner told me that he had confidence in its methods and its manager. How far are our methods reformatory? How far are they capable of improvement?

* * *

Richard Dugdale considers that every gaol should turn out a man a good deal better than it found him, and for the offences against the pocket — theft, embezzlement, forgery, etc. — believes that after some disciplinary treatment a ticket-of-leave might be given, to be forfeited on relapse into crime. "Gaols will continue to be necessary for the life confinement of murderers and of criminals addicted to offences of gross violence, a class requiring absolute restraint", but he says they are not needed for thieves. It seems strange to look forward to a time when they might be all at large, but during the interval the prison is the great field for experiment.

I quote from Dugdale again:

> The prisons in America and elsewhere are costly failures, built often in violation of all hygienic requirements, with a barren discipline and a stupid system of labor, turning out convicts yearly into the world without instruction in trade, in manners, or in books. It was not till capital punishment for minor offences was abolished that the police in Great Britain were rendered efficient. It was not till transportation was discontinued that conditional liberation was adopted, and that there was any intelligent effort made for the industrial and educational training of youthful offenders. And perhaps it will not be till prisons are virtually abolished that the question of hereditary crime will be studied so

as to get to the root of the physical and moral conditions which keep up the entailable attributes of the malefactor.

In speaking of crime as necessarily decreasing with the progress of society and the development of individualism, I do not include with crime vice. The are some vices which grow with the luxury which is fed by individualism; not that I mean that the man who does the work obtains the luxuries, but national wealth, which figures in statistics, and is brought forward to show how large a share each of us has by the doctrine of averages, always goes on increasing in an industrial nation. It is wrong to say that if the working classes have high wages they will spent it on vice and debauchery. A well-paid working class in steady employment is a moralizing force. The standard of comfortable living rises, and the workers respect themselves. In the large accession of innocent pleasures which are open to a well-paid working people, there is a valuable antidote to the coarser indulgences of bygone days. Young Australia drinks less than the previous generation. I should be glad if I could say it gambled less. This vice is on the increase in all civilized countries, and is especially rampant in Australia in connection with horse-racing, and with all trials of skill and speed in games and contests.

In uncivilized countries there are many murders, and very few suicides; in civilized society there are few murders and many suicides. As civilization advances crimes of violence decrease, and crimes of fraud and contrivance increase. Crimes of violence were met by the strong hand of the law, but the more refined and subtle offences, which are most prevalent nowadays, must be encountered by all the wisdom, the insight, and the patience which the collective conscience of society can evolve and apply.

Progress

EDITOR'S NOTE

"Some Social Aspects of South Australian Life", by A Colonist of 1839 — C. H. Spence, was published in *The Register*, 26 October–9 November 1878.

This series of articles written in 1878, perhaps the most prolific single year of journalistic writing in Spence's life, represents an assessment of South Australia's achievements from one of its earliest settlers. She might well have concentrated on the actual achievements of legislation, the statistics of growth and progress, but characteristically she is concerned instead with the quality of people's lives, past, present and future. Every line of this writing expresses her conviction of South Australia's superiority, not only in a colonial, but in a world context. As a social experiment she saw the colony as a success, its future promising to be as satisfying as its past.

There has been some deletion in the final article, "Husbands and Wives".

Some Social Aspects of South Australian Life

If a colonist is observant and thoughtful he has it in his power to contribute many valuable suggestions on economical and social questions to older communities than his own. If his field of vision has been limited and affairs appear on a small scale compared to theirs he has the counterbalancing advantage of seeing things with greater clearness and distinctness than can be done in a large, complex, and highly civilized society. He can distinguish the necessary from the useful, the useful from the agreeable; he has had so often to choose between these things for himself without regard to the opinions or prejudices of other people that he has learned their real comparative value. When newly arrived English people wonder at so much being different from what it is at home while there is a good deal the same old colonists recall the time when the differences were much more marked than they are now or than they will ever be again; for they are gradually approximating to English ways of living so far as the difference of climate will allow.

The colonists who arrived in South Australia in the end of 1839 found that some little progress had been made in the building of the city of Adelaide, though in some of the back streets one could only trace them by seeing that the trees were felled, which was done before the houses were built; but as for cultivation there was nothing. A drought had caused a dearth in the older colonies of New South Wales and Tasmania, on which South Australia depended for bread, and the quartern-loaf rose from 2s. 9d till it reached the price of 4s., while meat was also dear (9d to 1s. per pound) though not in the same proportion. Sheep and cattle could be transported on their own legs, and the pluck and endurance of a small band of overlanders, as they were called, had already form-

ed the nucleus of the flocks and herds which have since produced so much wealth to the colony. But the early pioneers did not themselves reap the full benefit of their adventurous efforts. The bold and the enterprising are rarely saving men in any country, and the alternations in a young and small community are so great and so sudden that the market is easily glutted, and the very success of the efforts leading to competition lessens greatly the individual chances of reward.

It must have taken a large sum to keep a population of about twelve thousand alive at these rates, especially as the profits upon all imported goods both to wholesale and retail traders were raised by the enormous expense of living. The Wakefield system of colonization had been extolled as sure to avert the crisis which all colonies had previously gone through, for the simultaneous arrival in due proportions of capital and labour was expected to secure steady and industrial progress. But neither labour nor capital was employed to produce anything. Instead of the two male and two female immigrants being employed on the eight-acre section they were ostensibly sent to cultivate for the purchaser, they were employed in building houses for themselves and others in Adelaide, and when that failed — when capital was drained for food supplies — on costly government works paid for in bills on England, afterwards protested. It was well for South Australia that the crisis did come, that government works were stopped, and people driven to the country. Everybody took simultaneously to farming and gardening, flocks and herds increased in number — faster than the consumers of beef and mutton — and the result was a time of almost fabulous cheapness and an extraordinary scarcity of money. The necessaries of life were produced in superabundance, the comforts were slowly reached, and the luxuries had to be done without. There was very little difference in the actual circumstances of different classes — some had property and some had none; but property was unsaleable for money, and barter only exchanged one unsaleable article for another. Nobody employed hired labour who could possibly do the work himself, and every one had to turn his or her hand to a great deal of miscellaneous work, most of which would be called menial and degrading in an older comunity, where large classes have been from time immemorial set apart for drudgery, and where other classes would rather sacrifice anything than take a part of it. Thus gradually the financial position of the colony improved by means of the well-directed industry of the settlers, and they owed much to the helpfulness and good management of the wives, sisters, and daughters of each household. Even before the discovery of the Burra Mine there was

Social and Legal Reform: Progress

substantial progress made, and strangers from the other colonies were surprised at the extent of cultivation we had attained to. When the rich gold discoveries of Victoria drew away at least three-fourths of the male population there was left behind a body of capable women, whose independent character and various acquirements made them equal to keeping things surprisingly well attended to under trying conditions. The money gained at Eaglehawk or Bendigo was not needed to repair losses, but generally expended in enlarging the holdings and improving the comfort of the homes to which the great body of the adventurers returned.

In the early days of a free colony we see something of that Utopia, where man learns the usefulness, the dignity, and the blessedness of labour, where work is paid for according to its hardness and its disagreeableness, and not after the standard of overcrowded countries where bread is dear and human life and strength cheap. And in such a colonial community we can also see that intelligence improves the quality of the work done; that the educated labourer has more foresight and endurance, more enterprise and resource, than the ignorant, and thus turns his work to better account. Perhaps never in any human society did circumstances realize the ideas of the community of labour and the equality of the sexes so fully as in South Australia in its early days. The immigration was chiefly family immigration. The Wakefield system secured that the free immigrants should be equal in the two sexes, and although the voluntary settlers were not balanced by the same rule the disproportion on the whole was very slight compared to that in the other colonies. In the outside settlements men preponderated greatly; in the town and suburbs and in the agricultural districts the numbers were nearly equal. The consequence was that women were not so scarce as to be spoiled or so abundant as to be neglected. Every girl knew that if she was tolerably pleasant she could be married. Beauty and grace had of course their peculiar attraction here as elsewhere, but a certain degree of usefulness combined with good temper was recognized as the chief recommendation for a wife. In the early days of the colonies a wife was not looked on as a hindrance or an expense, but as a help and a comfort. Girls did not look for establishments; parents did not press for settlements; a trousseau might cost £15 — it was handsome if it cost £25; there were no wedding presents, no cards; the cake might be made at home or dispensed with altogether. There was only one carriage in the colony for many years, which, though belonging to a private person, was hired for such as wanted to do the thing genteelly. In a country with an unlimited extent of land only waiting for the plough or for pastoral enter-

Social Aspects of South Australian Life

prise starving was out of the question, and as for falling in social position, that depended on character and not on income; so that the good old natural fashion of young people taking a liking for each other, and after a somewhat short but happy courtship being bound together for life was followed with boldness and with success. They began life with youth and love and hope and trust, and what better beginning can there be all the world over? A newcomer in the decade we speak of, between the financial crisis and the great exodus to the Victorian diggings, remarked, on the simplicity of our arrangements, "Why! it is nothing to get married here! A few mats and cane-bottomed chairs, and the house is furnished". And there were many four-roomed cottages thus furnished, where there was as much happiness on the part of their young possessors as can be found in much more ambitious houses nowadays. If we go into society now and see the heads of families who take a prominent position it is not too much to say that a large proportion of them began the world thus, and that the simplicity of tastes and the combined economy of the young people were the chief causes of their material prosperity.

The acquirements and accomplishments of colonial girls, though they might have looked meagre at a Cambridge middle-class examination, had this advantage — that they were adapted for the daily exigencies of life. They were varied and useful, and made them admirable partners for men who had to make their way in the world, either in town or country. Domestic servants were scarce, and wages, compared with prices, very high, and the colonists were poor, so that all ranks had to dispense with hired domestics at times, and every woman was bound to know something about household work. It is far too common nowadays to despise such unintellectual employment but the work must be done by someone, and it can be done in an intelligent as well as in a stupid, mechanical manner. Perhaps in time people may come to see that driving a pen over creamlaid notepaper and writing a nice little note is no more dignified than driving a smoothing-iron over linens and laces; that cooking a dinner so as to get the best meal for a family with the least waste is as intelligent a thing as defining the chemical constituents of meat, bread, and other eatables; that keeping a house clean and tidy is as good a work of art as making an indifferent drawing of it, and that the arrangements great and small which conduce to the comfort of a family every day and all day long, may require as much thought, and call forth as much talent as is required for the composition of one-half of our popular literature. So long as these things are looked on as inferior and only fit for what we are too apt to call "the lower

orders" they will be done in an inferior manner. It is only by upholding the dignity of the work that the workers gain self-respect.

Mrs Sutherland Orr, in the July number of the *Nineteenth Century,* takes up a somewhat striking view of this subject. She says that those who uphold the necessity for the higher education of women, and the opening up to them of new fields of labour, plead that the ordinary work will be done better; but Mrs Orr asserts that even if they increase their capacity the highly cultivated women lose the time and the inclination for domestic work. This however, in our opinion, applies only to those who have talent sufficient to carry them into special pursuits. If a woman has a genius for art or for literature, or perseverance and industry to qualify herself for a profession, she must depute to others those domestic duties which she has not time to discharge, but her intelligence will make her a better organizer, and will enable her to exercise more effective control over her subordinates than if she spends her time in the frivolities of dress and visiting or the whirl of dissipation. For the rank and file, those who have no special vocation, the higher education should improve the quality of the work which ordinary middle-class women have to do. The progress of civilization and the subdivision of labour, aided by machinery, withdraw many of the best class from domestic service. Where girls have homes the good pay and the comparative independence of factory life offer most powerful attractions. This tends to raise the wages of domestic servants all over the world. Their work will acquire more dignity as it is better paid; and the costly labour-saving machines which are introduced act both ways — towards the reduction of their number, and towards enabling people with small incomes to dispense with hired help altogether.

But this steady wave of advance has ebbs and flows. Things which should move simultaneously precede or lag behind each other. The sewing-machine, born of the urgent needs of the American housewife, was invented before the middle-class woman was prepared for the leisure she might gain from it for better and wiser ends, and the accumulation of work, tasteless or otherwise, which it enables her to put on the garments of her family has led to the introduction of a style of dress elaborate, costly, and inconvenient, under which the sensible groan, and against which the moralist preaches in vain. In going through a clothing factory one cannot help observing how quickly, cheaply, and well men's garments might be made, with no waste of stuff and at fairly remunerative payment for all the workers. But when watching the yards, we may say miles, of flouncing, kilting, ruching, puffing, and piping — the cutting up of stuff into small portions in order

to stick it on again, so as to make the garments of little or no use to the poor to whom they ought to revert; the covering of costly stuff with more costly trimming — one feels for the moment really sorry that the irresponsible machine should lend itself so fatally to the vagaries of fashion; that people who ride in carriages or sweep gracefully through drawing-rooms should set the fashion for the working women of the world; and that in order to have the dignity of a train all the pedestrians should have to hold up a heavy trimmed skirt, which we should imagine doubles — at least to the middle-aged — the fatigue of walking. A protest has been made against it in a leading English periodical for the conservation of energy, as the writer is aware that any appeal about its expense and its want of beauty has no effect on the leaders of fashion or their blind followers. The main objection to us is its heavy cost both in time and money, and it is a question whether the very means by which so many young ladies of the present day fancy they are making themselves agreeable in the eyes of the other sex is not one of the greatest stumbling-blocks to marriage after the old simple fashion, with love and hope and the world for the winning.

In the old days of which we speak if the money could be found to buy a dress there was not much difficulty about the making. The style was simple, the material generally cheap and there was almost always satisfaction with the result. Did these Adelaide girls then enjoy life? What was their education? What were their amusements? The book education was perhaps superficial, but the education of circumstances was admirable. Few of them had such thorough teaching as the artisan and day-labourer's children can now obtain at a government school, but young people can pick up much from intelligent parents, and books possessed or borrowed were much more carefully and profitably read than the abundant literature which is within easy reach at present. They had a knowledge of things — not of the mere names of things — a quickness of apprehension, a readiness and fearlessness of expression that made them acquit themselves very fairly in society. They did not like to fall below the place in the social scale which their parents had held in the old country, and that kept up a certain degree of genuine refinement of manner, while their definite and recognized occupations made them independent and full of resource. They lived their own life, and did not live merely to influence others. To say that men are to do all the work of the world and women merely to influence the manner in which they do that work is to make a division of sphere both unnecessary and mischievous. Women being the weaker are far more influenced by men than

men by them. The stronger sex have also all the conventional authority which society and the laws give to them, and it is only by giving woman worthy occupation that you can prevent her from succumbing entirely to the opinions, the tastes, and the wishes of others. She is naturally only too anxious to be agreeable and fearful of the responsibility of independent thought and action.

"But," says an English reader, "do you really think that such work as you describe — cooking, washing, ironing, child-tending, and needlework — is to be compared to the literary work, the art work, the charitable work of the great sisterhood of single women in the old country? Where in the colonies at that time was there really a worthy sphere for capable and educated women such as has been opened to them in the mother-country?"

For literature and art there was no market in South Australia; for the charitable work there was comparatively no need. We only maintain that the average woman stood very fairly in comparison with her analogue in England, and that the happier community is that where there is a fair share of work and the rewards of work for everybody, and not where such a phalanx of labourers need to dedicate their lives to the redressing of the evils of the social system, and so to relieve a small proportion of the sufferings of the poor, the ignorant, and the neglected. Honour to the heroic band who have done so much, though they lay bare much that they cannot cure, but let us hope that under our happier conditions a system will be provided which will require less charity because it is characterized by more justice. Better than the acquiring of collosal fortunes by individuals is the more equal distribution of wealth in a community, and although the prospect of a rise to a higher class is a wonderful stimulus to energy and thrift, it is perhaps of more consequence that the material and moral condition of the hewers of wood and drawers of water should be tolerably comfortable.

And as for our pleasures we had few, but they were keenly relished. There was no theatre worthy of the name, parties were rare, concerts rarer. Life was too busy to be cut up by dissipation, and although there was all the hospitality of a cheap country, and our houses had a wonderful elasticity in the way of accommodating guests, the sort of entertainments given were of a simple description. The delight of driving in a summer evening for a dozen miles to a country evening party in a spring-cart, with simple white muslin dresses done up in a square parcel and brothers requested not to crush them, and dancing till daylight to such music as the guests could furnish can scarcely be appreciated nowadays. The girls of the house, with perhaps assistance from brothers or

neighbours, had taken up the carpet, cleaned the room, set out supper in the verandah, arranged a few flowers, made the creams and pastry, and either cooked or superintended the cooking of all that was on the table. The wine was of home manufacture, the fruit came from the garden, the poultry was furnished from the adjoining yard. Scarcely anything on the table had cost money, and yet to the eyes of all the party it looked very well, and was given with the most overflowing hospitality. When we see the very pretty floral decorations which are now *de rigueur* at such gatherings, and compare them with the single nosegay for a centrepiece which was usual then, we recognize the fact that the girls who had to prepare and cook food and take up carpets had not time for such pretty frivolities. And the young men who shared their hospitality knew that a wife from such a home would be no helpless Dora Copperfield or absorbed Mrs Jellaby, but that his dinners and his buttons would be attended to. The simple dresses struck no awe into his soul as to their cost; and if he stayed all night and saw the girls in their morning dresses putting things straight, as he lent a hand he felt that there was no risk run if he asked such a woman to share his fate but the greatest good-luck if she would accept his offer.

But civilization has marched on, and there is no going back. Not again can we hope to see what was only a transition state of society. It was perhaps only a half refinement; not that of highly educated people, which it appears to require at least a thousand a year to keep up, and for the preservation of which so many of our middle and upper class men and women in England, and here too in an increasing ratio, are doomed to celibacy. But what we would contend for is that it was a measure of education and refinement, not for our betters to descend to, but to which our working classes may rise. Why should it be regarded as the inexorable law of nature that useful labours should be disjoined from education and refinement, that the hardest and the most disagreeable work is to be solaced by the fewest and the coarsest of pleasures? It may seem altogether too remote to be spoken of yet, except in a whisper, but perhaps fifty years hence enlightened philanthropy, just legislation, universal education, and the sympathy of class with class may raise the standard for all, so that the labours, the habits, and the pleasures of working people may be somewhat like those of the early settlers of the better class in such a colony as this of South Australia.

SOME PRESENT SOCIAL ASPECTS OF COLONIAL LIFE

In spite of what was said in a previous article on a few very pleasant phases of early colonial life we have no reason to fold our hands in idle regret for the irrevocable past. Along with some drawbacks there is much substantial advance. It is gratifying to see that the old dwellers in tents and in four-roomed cottages have now handsome mansions and can ride in easy carriages. We derive so much advantage in every way from the progress of the colony — from good roads and gas and water supply, and postal and telegraph facilities, and railway trains and fast steamers, and fine gardens, and abundant books — that it would be a retrograde movement to go back to the collection of scattered cottages and desolate-looking park lands of 1846 or thereabouts. At no time could the wages of the labouring classes purchase more than they can now, and we need have no quarrel with the prosperous on account of the prosperity in which all have some share. But in proportion as the conditions of life become more complex they should be met by more ingenuity, more culture, and a deeper sense of duty, and the suddenness of our accumulation of wealth has scarcely prepared our little community for some necessary modifications of our social arrangements.

The widespread movement which is going on all over the world for the admission of women to new fields of labour springs from more than a single cause. The marriage difficulty is the most apparent, and has been more fully discussed than any other. In all old countries men have to leave their homes to rough it in foreign lands where women of their own class cannot follow them, and Englishmen go on working in climates where wives and children sicken and die. Consequently there is an over-plus of women, which reaches its greatest number in the British Islands, where the numerous colonies spread over all the world tempt the young and the adventurous. The pressure for the means of subsistence without sinking in the social scale make serious discrepancies in the originally equal number of the sexes who are born, and all over England, and especially in rural and provincial society, the number of marriageable women greatly exceeds that of marrying men; and this is most seen in the middle and upper classes. Some political economists, like Mr W. R. Greg, say that the superabundant women should be shipped off to the colonies where men preponderate; but "the penniless gentlewoman (as the *Quarterly Reviewer* justly remarks) would not go to the wilds even if she could, and she is right; the work she could do is not in demand there, and

marriage is an object not to be taken by assault, but to be approached indirectly". And even in the Australian colonies, where Mr Greg sees that women are in the minority, in spite of the greatest material prosperity the marriage rate is at present below that of the British Islands.

* * *

In olden times in England and elsewhere when a man had made a large business he took care to bring up one or more of his sons to help him during his life and to succeed him after death. Failing a son he saw great advantage in a son-in-law with a turn for business. Nowadays the rich merchant or manufacturer educates his son at schools and university, where a wealthy and leisured aristocracy give the tone to an aspiring plutocracy, and where the effective public opinion is in favour of out-of-doors sport and the most perfect and costly things in the way of amusement, and rather antagonistic than otherwise to study, and still more so to the steady regular work and the forethought and the organization by which great businesses are made and held together. And strange to say, not only the inexperienced girls but the shrewd fathers fancy there is more security for happiness in marriage with a man to whom £20,000 or £30,000 has been bequeathed than with one who has the capacity for acquiring twice as much with fair chances. The English *Spectator* says that it needs nearly as much ability to keep up a great business as to govern a state, and that as this talent is not hereditary such large concerns either fall to pieces in incomplete hands or have to be disposed of at a loss. In Australia there are not a few of our energetic pioneers who have not had sons or sons-in-law with the taste or capacity to keep in their grasp the great businesses left to them. And for this the misdirection of the education of those sons and sons-in-law is much to blame.

The movement for a wider range of employments for women arises in great part from another cause than the marriage difficulty. All the avocations which the middle-class woman used to pursue at home, by which she saved money if she did not earn it, are slipping one by one from her by the encroachments of machinery and the profitable subdivision of labour. In olden days women of all ranks spun and wove the thread of which the garments of the family were made. Now she scarcely even puts the material together, and if she does it is by the help of a machine which can put in from three hundred to a thousand stitches a minute instead of twenty-five. Even within the memory of the middle-aged there was brewing and baking, pickling and preserving, fine cooking and pastry-making, and some kinds of laundry and other work, that were rarely left to servants. In our early colonial days the

Social and Legal Reform: Progress

sphere of work was widened beyond even that, and girls could and did hang paper, glaze windows, chop wood, and use hammer and nails very deftly. The enormous increase of wealth and the demand for everything being of the best has tended to cause home-made things to be despised. Nothing struck the present writer so much on a visit to the old country as the change in the work of the middle-class women and the preference for the laundress's gloss, the confectioner's pastry, the manufacturer's pickles, the dressmaker's perfect cut and fit; and English society is consequently getting filled up with idle gentlewomen for whom there is no work and no room. The young generation, seeing the pitiable condition of those who cannot dig and are ashamed to beg, are knocking vigorously at the doors which have so long been kept shut, but their eagerness is as great for the employment as for the remuneration. It is not the easy life or the life of luxury that is the best or the happiest — it is the *interesting* life, and to women as to men the most interesting life is one of gratified activity. The laundress who earns her children's bread by ironing flounces or picking out laces, and takes a pride in doing these things well, has a more interesting life than the wearer of them if the latter has no definite occupation and tries to kill time over weak or sensational novels, or moves from one scene of gaiety to another in the vain hope of being amused from outside. Life all amusement is more intolerable than life all labour.

The sisterhoods and the various charitable pursuits of one class of female workers, the earnest studies of another, the various new avocations into which women are pressing are all evidence of their eagerness to serve in some way or other the community in which they live. Where means are sufficient they work for love; where a livelihood is needed they relieve their parents by working for money. In spite of the remonstrances of alarmed parents who object to the expense of the training, and perhaps think that the chances of marrige are lessened by an education which puts the girl intellectually above most of her equals in social position of the other sex; in spite of the half-jealous, half-tender opposition of most men, who regret that the winning grace of dependence should be sacrificed; in spite of the theories of economists, who insist that the competition of the women must lower the price of all work into which they enter, and increase the evil by reducing the number of marrying men, the urgency of the need keeps up a steadily increasing band of women eager for employment. Even in South Australia we see this band turning in the direction of education — for one male pupil teacher that offers there are three or four females. In early days there were a few governesses, a few

dressmakers, and no difficulty in getting servants if you could pay the wages. Now there are hundreds, we may say thousands, in factories, in shops, in photographers' rooms; there are ten times more women employed as dressmakers in proportion, and servants were never so scarce. A lady who advertised in this journal for a lady-help who could assist with children and was clever with her needle got twelve applications from most promising young women. If she had advertised for a cook, nursemaid, or needlewoman she might not have had one. A correspondent of the London *Spectator* said he advertised for a superior nurse, and got two unsuitable applicants; he advertised for a nursery governess at the same salary for the same duties, only with the addition of teaching two little children, and the number of applications was forty-three. Just as in old days people who could not afford a first-class passage to Adelaide took an intermediate and paid double what the third-class did for the same food and the same attendance only having the private cabin with the power of shutting the door, so will middle-class girls do better work for the same pay as servants if they are not severed from the family they serve.

We are at presnt in a transition state. A few years hence every man with a life-income who has more than one or two daughters will bring them up to some remunerative employment. To save them from the humiliating position of seeing in marriage their only refuge from poverty and neglect, to allow them to take a dispassionate view of an offer and only to be attracted to the solemn life-union by love, the middle-class father will make it his business to provide them with a livelihood either by his savings or their own efforts. In spite of all sentimental objections our colonial experience proves that the useful woman was quite as affectionate a wife and mother as the useless ones. All the mischiefs past, present, and likely to be done by strong-minded women can scarcely compare with what have been inflicted on the other sex from time immemorial by weak-minded ones. If the French mother has an imperiousness and even *férocité* about the marriage of her daughters, at least she does not, like the English mother, throw them out dowerless and helpless into the world. The first care of the French middle-class people is to secure a *dot* for their daughter before she reaches the age for marriage, and then to look out for someone of similar means and otherwise suitable to marry her before she has had any opportunity of falling in love elsewhere. This very often results in failure, for middle-aged people who have outlived their illusions do not always know what best suits the young; but in the great majority of cases, especially among the bourgeois class, the marriages turn out happily. No

wife is so useful as that of the Parisian shopkeeper — there is a community of interests between the partners for life, and she retains the absolute disposal of her portion of the joint capital. All over the world it is the idle classes who show the greatest failures, and whether it is the idleness of great wealth severed from the duties and responsibilities which ought to accompany it or the idleness of lazy drunkenness in the lowest strata of society the results in married unhappiness are equally disastrous. In the history of the idle classes, written for the amusement of their imitators and admirers, which forms the staple of modern fiction, we see the worship of money, the love of luxury, and the revolt against marriage all brought prominently forward. There may be some truth in the pictures, but the necessity for saying something new and startling in narratives where love, virtuous or the reverse, forms the leading interest naturally leads to much exaggeration. In the barriers between people who love each other the money question is made supreme, whereas Sir Walter Scott took birth, or political differences, or family arrangements more frequently as the hindrance than mere disparity of worldly means. And the rosewater descriptions of life, the furniture and decorations, the swift silent service which are *comme il faut* (one cannot get on without a French phrase in dealing with these books), the sordid descriptions of middle-class poverty with its necessary makeshifts, make that really more forbidding to the young and the impressionable than elegant vice or startling crime. We may be in a bad decade of the century in politics and in art — the loosening of the bonds of religious obligation has affected many classes injuriously — but we are not half so bad as the fashionable literature represents us, and we need some powerful satirist to make ridiculous what is so demoralizing.

In reading a novel of Ouida or of Balzac one feels both irritated and depressed — the slapdash broad colours of the one, the microscopic and terrible analysis of the other, show the seamy side of the character of both men and women, while those who are not wicked are mostly fools. When clever and experienced men say that their descriptions are true to human nature, and extol Balzac's subtlety and insight, we do not wonder at those who have been sheltered by their sex from actual knowledge of the evil that is in the world feeling heartsick and heartsore. But a greater genius than Balzac would see beauties as well as deformities; and as more intimate knowledge of any human soul makes us generally love it the better in spite of faults, so we believe that the cynic is the most short-sighted of observers. If the microscope is looked through with eyes of love and not of scorn how different its revelations!

Men and women live together in society, but they do not know each other until some great passion of love lays bare to each the inner and the better secrets of the heart. This and this alone explains the wonderful way in which lovers whom the world thinks commonplace are transfigured to each other when they really love. The girl who appears to other young men ignorant or frivolous or haughty shows tenderness, receptiveness, and submission; the lover who seems to other girls conceited or cynical or self-centred opens to the woman who is to share his life all the better and higher side of his character. What he would not wear on his sleeve for daws to peck at he reveals to her. The man thought niggardly is generous to her. The man believed to be flippant, to her shows himself earnest; and if the same kind of confidence and the same kind of sympathy are kept up throughout married life the characters grow from within outward, so that all eyes can see somewhat of their real beauty.

Robert Browning in his last address to his living wife — "One Word More", which concludes his "Men and Women" — regrets that he cannot, like Dante or Raphael, go out of his own line to give his special tribute to the object of his love; that he cannot like the poet paint a picture, or like the painter write a century of sonnets for her only; that he had only this one gift of verse to give her, only that she would see more in his fifty men and women than the world could do; and goes on to say that though the moon only shows one side to the earth, if the moon, according to the old myths, ever loved a mortal, she would turn that side which had never been seen by Galileo or Newton to the object of her passion.

> And, God be thanked, the meanest of His creatures
> Boasts two soul-sides — one to face the world with
> And one to show a woman when he loves her.

THE SOCIAL OUTLOOK FOR THE FUTURE

There is an ever-recurring scare that every new improvement or reform which is pressed upon society — though it meets an acknowledged want and can scarcely be prevented — will be carried too far and may work greater evils than it cures. We have already mentioned the objection from the economic side to the competition of women in the fields of better-paid work that they will reduce the wages of the men whose privilege it has hitherto been to work for them, and thus make marriage more difficult than before. Labour-saving machinery has been thus feared as

Social and Legal Reform: Progress

leading to over-production, and the sewing machine itself was expected to throw nine-tenths of the sempstresses out of employment and to reduce their miserable wages, and yet there is no doubt that it has been distinctly friendly to the whole class. When Thomas Hood wrote his powerful and pathetic "Song of the Shirt" in the Christmas number of *Punch* for 1843 it was no fancy picture that he drew. A woman brought up for some petty theft told the magistrate she made men's striped cotton shirts at 1½d each, and he asked how many she could make in a day, and she replied — "If I make a long day, working from 6 in the morning till 12 at night, I can make four". A middlewoman known to the writer, who had taken the work to and from the needlewomen for the wholesale houses, about 1841, said the pay used to be 2½d in her time, but the competition of women who could sew and could do nothing else reduced it after she left London for Australia. Now, going through an Adelaide factory, we see such working men's shirts made by one machinest and two quick or three slower tackers and finishers. The shirts are cut; the machine and the thread furnished by the wholesale house. The machinist gets 2s. 2d a dozen, the tackers and finishers divide between them 4s. 4d, which makes the price for making each shirt 6½d. If they are clever hands they can each make 20s. or more a week in the working day of eight hours, and as there is only ten per cent of duty on ready-made clothing the payment in England cannot be much less than here. In every step of the process of making the cotton into garments there has been a great improvement in the condition of the labourer. The free workman has taken the place of the slave on the plantations. Factory and workshop legislation has reduced the hours of labour for all, and especially protected women and children from overwork, and provided for ventilation and healthier conditions for the spinners and weavers; and the sewing machine has improved the position of the needlewomen, and yet the working man can buy for the same, or perhaps even less money, a shirt as good in material and very much better than when it seemed to cost so many "human creatures' lives".

What competition of an additional phalanx of women as workers could be as disturbing as this development of mechanical contrivance, which was so dreaded, but which turned out so beneficial? And to tie the hands of half of the human race in order that there should be more work for the other half to do can scarcely be wise economy. Already a very large number of single women are earning their own livelihood in other ways than in the time-honoured ones of domestic service and of teaching, to the raising of the payment for these branches of industry. And so far even

Social Aspects of South Australian Life

Mrs Sutherland Orr acknowledges that the movement has done nothing but good, although she dreads its being carried to extremes. She dreads the loss of the peculiarly feminine characteristics and the decomposition of society if all women leave their retired domestic sphere and rush into professions, and the ablest and the best forswear matrimony and maternity. But society has been threatened with subversion, as Mrs Fawcett puts it, from every innovation, political and social, which an earnest minority has advocated, and yet it continues to stand firm. Society is too tough to be undermined and disintegrated by a fresh application of the principles of free trade. They are already free to discharge if they please many kinds of important unpaid work. Some women, no doubt, will blunder and rush into careers for which they are not fitted; but there is no need for legislating against that any more than for making laws to prevent deaf men from serving on juries or cripples from enlisting in the army. Things will find their level if they are only left alone. Mrs Orr suggests that, in preference to leaving the domestic duties for rougher outside work, the women should reconquer their own sphere by the better performance of household work; but that is really being done simultaneously with the opening of other fields, if we may judge by the enthusiasm about sick nursing and cookery and art needlework, and here in the colonies servants will always be so scarce and so dear as to make domestic duties honourable. There is no desire shown by the ladies of the movement to push men out of their employments or to step into professions by any easy path — all they ask is a fair field and no favour, and they are likely to get it, for the opening of the profession of medicine after so long a struggle is a decisive triumph. The question arises how far will existing social arrangements be altered or modified by this change, the which will not be confined to England and America, but which is spreading and will spread further on the Continent and is even now felt in the colonies. We are not so far removed in Australia from the heart of civilization as not to respond spontaneously to so large a movement, and it has been already shown in the preceding articles that colonial society is quite changed from the primitive type when middle-class women had sufficient domestic employments to occupy their hands and to satisfy their hearts.

And first with regard to *education*, when an appreciable and increasing number of girls want their teaching for service and not for show the middle-class schools must present something better than the pretentious programme of the young ladies' seminary. The felt want in England has been met by the establishment of the

Social and Legal Reform: Progress

Girls' Public Day Schools Company, Limited. The first of this Company's schools was opened in Chelsea in 1873, and now there are fifteen in operation with two thousand scholars in attendance and capital subscribed for six more; the fees are from three to five guineas per term according to the age of the pupils, and there are only three terms in the year. There are no extras except books and new music. The instruction is thorough and up to the highest modern standards. There is a training college for teachers in connection with the school, and the Company pays a dividend of five per cent on the subscribed capital. Each school is built to accommodate 250 pupils. The head teacher receives a salary of £250, with a capitation fee of twenty shillings on each pupil over the number of 100 in attendance. The great City Companies have been liberal with scholarships, and the schools appear to be altogether successful. Such a Company has an element of strength which private schoolmistresses have not; it can lay down a course of instruction and discipline to be carried out regardless of the whims of wealthy and influential parents. In girls' schools as at present constituted accomplishments take a very disproportionate place. The Commission recently appointed to enquire into them reported that music alone occupied as much of a girl's time as was given to history, drawing, arithmetic, German, geography, writing, French, grammar, and the use of the globes all put together; that arithmetic at expensive schools occupied one-thirteenth part of the school hours, at the cheaper ones one-tenth, and in almost all cases was miserably ill-taught; and that after ten years spent in learning French the girls could not converse for five minutes in the language, the jargon talked at school being utterly barbarous and ungrammatical. The teachers complained that all their attempts after wiser proportion in study were thwarted by the parents, especially by the mothers. "What is the use of arithmetic for Julia? Her husband will keep her accounts for her after she is married." The great aim was to arm Julia with the showy accomplishments and the fashionable air which would catch the husband.

If the advanced schools for girls are opened here under the Education Department they are likely to absorb those who mean to turn their talents to account. If the government does not undertake this task we may probably see some such expedient as a Joint-Stock Company resorted to. And one of the first fields of enterprise for our coming women will be teaching in an improved manner. The middle-class governess for country families, whose salary rarely exceeds £30 a year if she professes to teach music, and is considerably less if she has not that accomplishment, will

have her position improved by the knowledge that in a state school she might rise to £200 and £250, and in an advanced school to still higher payment and a better social position. Certified teachers will command good salaries from private employers, and there will be a recognized test of efficiency which will benefit the whole body of teachers. The Commission already quoted says that if governesses were better instructed there would be little need to employ masters for teaching even advanced classes of girls. It is because they do not know thoroughly the subjects in the curriculum that the master is resorted to. There need be little fear of any general entrance on the part of women into professions; the education is too long and too costly for any large number of parents to afford it to girls who may marry; but young women with exceptional ability and energy and patience will no doubt enter if the doors are open, and will probably succeed. These qualities are not so abundant in the world that we should war against the admission of such women. Much mechanical and light clerical work will be competed for successfully by young women. When arithmetic is properly taught to them they may be employed, as in France, largely in bookkeeping. The Civil Service may be invaded in other directions than the Telegraph Department, where in the central London office eight hundred girls are now employed with satisfactory results. It is just possible that the Civil Service might benefit from the admission of a class whose ranks may be thinned by marriage, especially as the prettiest and the most attractive are often not the best workers. A stupid or idle boy is a fixture in a government office, and he has no temptation to leave it. It was considered to be a piece of vanity and also of ignorance on Miss Martineau's part when she said that she in common with all literary women had many offers of marriage, for the male horror of blues is proverbial. But it was true so far. Miss Martineau was believed to be earning £1,000 a year by her pen, which she could do as well after marriage as before, and there is little doubt that under these circumstances she would have had many suitors even if she had been twice as deaf and dogmatic. Mrs Garrett-Anderson carries on her large and lucrative medical practice, and Mrs Allingham works at her exquisite water-colour painting as diligently as ever, and according to all accounts both ladies are most affectionate wives and mothers. There can be no doubt that women with such a career would only marry for love. The class of domestic servants who have gone amongst strangers to earn their own living are still full of family affections and amenable to words of love, so that in their case we see no narrowing and hardening of the nature. Those who think that all women

need the sanctity of home and parental influence to keep them good and womanly should see their principles fully carried out in Spain, where it is not considered proper for a girl to go to service without either her mother, or her aunt, or other watchful relative going with her for her protection. As in the case of our domestic servants, as a general rule when the middle-class woman of the future consents to marry she must choose not between destitution and marriage but between the modest competence she can earn and the modest competence her lover offers. If love is cast in the balance the joint home will have wonderful attractions; if love is absent the independent life will be felt to be the best. And the savings she has or ought to have been making for sickness or old age will be thrown into the common stock or be secured for future needs. It is not the large income that makes marriage prudent — it is the habitual living within it on both sides; and when women become in any large measure independent workers they will learn the management of money and the value of small economies. An artisan earning fifty shillings a week and a domestic servant earning with her board and lodging twelve shillings who spend every penny as they earn it would run a great risk in marrying. On both sides there should be savings, and both should do their part towards providing the necessary furnishing of a household.

The influence of a large class of intelligent and educated women being engaged in independent work will be felt upon *Dress and Fashion*. Hitherto it has been absolutely powerless, for there is sufficient hostile criticism directed against women's advance in other directions without then running counter to society and making themselves conspicious by dressing for convenience and beauty. The movement about twenty years ago was premature; the Bloomer costume, which a glance at an old number of the *Art Journal* shows as convenient, inexpensive, and modest, was put down not only by ridicule, which is legitimate enough, but by so-called gentlemen inducing women of bad character to wear it. We have little hope that the suggestion made in the August *Cornhill* of a recourse to the Greek costume will be followed; but in time the working women will be strong enough to please themselves and dress without slavish compliance with the dicta of fashion.

Society too will be modified. Working women cannot spare time for morning calls or strength for dissipation carried on to late hours. Mrs Garrett-Anderson and Mrs Allingham have adopted the French system of evening receptions; and although they cannot set any fashion for the upper ten thousand, middle-class people whose daughters have a career to follow out will adopt this inexpensive and eminently social manner of meeting

their friends of both sexes. Men and women will have more common ground; if there will be less outward deference on one side and less softness on the other there will be more mutual respect and more thorough understanding. The standard of morals will be equalized in a large degree. Girls will not be surrounded with dulness which is called innocence. They will not be supposed to know nothing of evil that is in the world, but will make it their business to discover through fathers and brothers whether a man's moral character is good or not, and consider it their duty to treat him accordingly. And fashionable society itself will stand in awe of this bar of judgment, which will be strong in literature, strong in art, and strong in morals, and the wealthy roué will no longer find entrance into decent circles even there.

As to *politics*, the woman's suffrage movement proceeds slowly — at the present rate of progress it will not be carried in ten years — but if Lord Beaconsfield appreciates the reactionary effect of admitting a large class of the most Conservative electors to be found in Britain he may at the next critical juncture when he wants to out-manoeuvre the Liberals throw in his powerful aid to a radical reform which would be of immediate service to him. The first admission of women to political privileges we confess to looking on with some alarm; but it will doubless be carried, and women will in time be educated to exercise the franchise wisely. At present the mass of women do not wish for them, partly because they dread the responsibility, partly because they care little about politics either abstract or practical, but mainly because the other sex, by which they are so largely influenced, discourage and ridicule the strong-minded women who are eager for political rights, and in all movements there are always some people who come to the front to throw discredit upon the cause. The political power, when it is attained, although reactionary at first in general politics, will however be at once directed towards the reform of some injustices which press hard on women. The *Quarterly Review* for July contains this striking passage: "Among the anomalies of a country like England, the stronghold of old customs, and the leader of modern progress, where liberty and prejudice are alike strong, there are few stronger than the over-protection of one and the over-neglect of another part of the female population; which gives the prosperous and pampered woman every indulgence, and the poor and forlorn woman no rights." That anomaly there is little doubt that any Parliament where women's votes have been felt will rectify. And when women have been generally trained to independent work some of the objections to divorce in certain cases will be removed, for she will

not be so helpless for the maintenance of her children as she is now. Very probably one of the first laws which will be modified will be that which makes breach of promise actionable. As Mrs Fawcett says: "No one, man or woman, ought to be forced into marriage by fear of social or legal penalties".

And this leads us to the last branch of the subject on which we mean to treat, the marriage question and public morals. It is a fact which is not sufficently recognized that there are some men and a great many women who have a vocation for celibacy. Who has not often seen as old-maidish a woman as can be found in the ranks of spinsterhood who seems to have married because it was the thing to be married and because she gained in social position and in material ease, but who was a cold wife and an indifferent mother? Who on the other hand has not seen a motherly old maid who was the tenderest of aunts, the most sympathizing of friends, the most faithful of confidants. Fortunately for the old maid, if she has not children of her own she can fill up gaps made by death or parental incompetence, but we are always sorry for the husband and children of the woman who was married by mistake.

There are other women like Harriet Martineau, who rightly or wrongly feel their characters too distinctive and their objects in life too important to allow them to sink to a secondary place and merge their individuality in that of another. The removal of all artificial restrictions on woman's work will make it more honourable to be single, and therefore will remove the strongest temptation to a loveless marriage. In France, where the parents accumulate the *dot* and arrange the marriages of both sons and daughters, celibacy is rare. In the United States, except in the older ones where women are in a great preponderance, where the girls and the young men have the greatest freedom of intercourse and have the entire management of their own love affairs, marriage is all but universal. The half-and-half method of England results in an increasing ratio of celibacy in the middle and higher classes. The tendency of things in England and the colonies is in favour of the young folks managing for themselves, and marriage is a thing so momentous and so personal that it must be the better way. And this will tend to what is delicately called the "initiative" being occasionally taken by the weaker sex. When the girl has the advantage in wealth or rank, or even sometimes in intellect, the man she loves may not have the courage or the presumption to ask her, but she may legitimately go more than half-way if her heart is really implicated — of course running the risk of a rejection both painful and humiliating, and binding the man she has

honoured to the secrecy which ought to be kept in all rejections of a man's love by the woman he has failed to win.

The eager partizans of women's rights assert that the opening of honest and remunerative employment to women must infallibly improve public morals greatly; that all mercenary love, whether temporary or for life, will be discouraged thereby; that the career open to talent will make it more pleasant and more honourable to be single than it has ever been; and that men will find it cheaper and better to marry a helper than a hindrance. On the other hand the equally sincere and benevolent advocate of the old ways argues that when the competition is successful it will press hard on the earnings of the professional and other middle-class men who now wish to marry, and that a movement which at its best tends to delay marriage cannot be expected to extinguish or even to diminish the greatest social evil under which we groan.

So long as human nature is what it is people cannot be made virtuous by Act of Parliament, or by the most favourable social arrangements, and a movement broadly beneficial may have some bad effects; but we may reasonably expect that women will not be dragged into hopeless vice by destitution, or by that cruel treatment of lesser sins which drives them to despair; that only those who love vice will follow it for a livelihood, and that all who can be saved will be redeemed. And with regard to the other sex, we can believe they will be induced to marry with more courage if they are confronted by women bright, capable, and self-reliant, who know the value of money by having to earn and administer it, who have some trained intelligence, and capacity for business, which will make them helpful always and in times of sickness or misfortune capable of adding to the family exchequer — who can take an intelligent interest in public matters without neglecting their household or their children, and whose ideas are not concentrated on dress, servants, and the keeping up appearances, but are turned towards rational objects in which the married pair may work hand in hand. These things may be called utopian or premature, but no one can thoughtfully watch the stream of tendency all over the world without being convinced that they are at our gates, and the sooner our community is prepared for them the more wisely they will be met, and the less mischief will accompany the benefits they may be expected to bring.

HUSBANDS AND WIVES

A very bright little woman said to us the other day, "Well, I may

provoke my husband sometimes, but I am thankful to say I never bore him — and that would be infinitely worse." No doubt the rigid censor of morals might take exception to our friend's standard of conjugal offences, as he would do to Julia Mannering's reply to her father when he said she must be either a fool outright or more disposed to make mischief than he had thought. "Put the best construction on what I say and do, papa; I would not be thought a fool for the world." Still we would maintain that in the present phase of society in all ranks of life to be bored is the greatest evil under the sun, and a successful crusade against dulness would have as great moral effect as an equally successful battle with vice. It is the "weariness of this unintelligible world", it is "the dreary intercourse of daily life" that presses upon both the thinking and the unthinking men and women of our day. Our forefathers would stand any amount of monotony, and could find pleasures in what we and our children would consider intolerably slow. In the delightful life of Lord Macaulay we see the quiet homelife of the Puritan family of Zachary Macaulay, where public amusements were forbidden, where the gatherings were of grave people associated for great public objects and the young people only crossed the forbidden line which excluded novels, and the evenings were passed in reading aloud to each other. What wonderful familiarity with literature this family-reading gives — what scope for little jokes, quotations and allusions — one can see by the letters which passed between the brother and his much-loved sisters. But such things have had their day, and the young man of our time would elevate his eyebrows at the suggestion that this would be a "good-enough line" for one evening in a month. He wants change, variety, amusement from outside, and when led by circumstances and by passions which still exercise a powerful spell over the human race he falls in love and marries, the difficulty is how to make his fireside attractive enough for him to prefer his home to any other place and his wife to any other woman.

Thackeray says there can be nothing more maddeningly irritating than to have to sit opposite to a handsome stupid woman (he does not say whether it would be better if she were ugly) at meals and at the hearth day after day who has nothing but "Yes, my dear", and "Exactly so, my love", to reply to any remarks of yours, while her own are so far removed from the objects, the amusements, or the perplexities of your life that you can only return the same unmeaning acquiescence. Better an occasional spar that shows that there are weapons common to both; better a pronounced difference of opinion with regard to people and

Social Aspects of South Australian Life

things and ideas than that severance of interests which too often exists not only between husband and wife but also between the men and women of households in general. We do not think it is found to so great an extent in America, but in England and in the colonies it begins to show itself strongly when the boys and girls are sent to different schools and take to quite different games and amusements. It receives a severe but temporary check at the time of life when both sets of young people are liable to the first stirrings of passion; when they seek each other's society in preference, and their intercourse is full of wonderful possibilities for the future; but it is too apt to recur when after the morning glory of even a love marriage is over, and the husband gets absorbed in his business cares, and the wife in her domestic duties, her social engagements, and the exigencies of keeping up appearances as to dress, furniture, and appointments satisfactory to that public opinion by which she is mainly influenced. As a rule our marriages are made from pure affection, and there is a romantic halo round them which is very good to begin life with; but it has to pull the young people through a good deal of tear and wear, and even the most conscientious do not foresee the direction from which their greatest dangers are likely to come.

* * *

While sympathizing to a considerable extent with what we have called the half-jealous, half-tender protest on the part of most men against the higher education of women, and the opening to middle-class girls of independent careers which social pressure renders necessary and which must be conceded if society is to hold together at all, we cannot help confessing that both sexes have suffered a great deal from the want of an education and training which would make the marriage bond more coherent. It is not that the love of a marriage founded originally on affection is dead. In times of sickness, of adversity, and of bereavement it starts up fresh and strong and enduring; but what we want is to make the intercourse of daily life more pleasant and sympathetic. A man does not want to talk "shop" — indeed if his work is hard or exhausting he likes to shut it off from his home-life altogether as a general rule; but there are many occasions in which he would be glad to consult on business matters the only human being whose interests are identical with his own, but who living apart from the turmoil and the competition of life could take a dispassionate and a purely equitable view of any important question, and who if she only was capable of understanding its bearing could help a man through a difficulty or nerve him to a sacrifice for which he alone would be unequal. A course of retrenchment

for which she sees good reason can be entered into and carried out without the innumerable difficulties which beset a one-sided conviction, and what is more it is done with positive satisfaction and pleasure on both sides. How many men there are who would be saved from political dishonour, from commercial disgrace, and from paltering with conscience in religious matters if their wives had the intelligence to comprehend fully the importance of honesty in all these great concerns and habitually made themselves acquainted with their husbands' feelings as well as their actions and could throw their influence into the right scale.

Mr J. S. Mill has said that if a wife does not push her husband forward morally and mentally she always holds him back, and he pleads for the emancipation of women on the ground that in modern society all strong attachments are those formed between the sexes, because the old male friendships are dead or dying out. We are not so sure that he is right on the latter point, for club-life opposes a strong rivalry to the influence of women; but we know that there can be no more fatal mistake for a rising and ambitious young man to make than either for the sake of beauty, or money, or a temporary advance in position, to marry a woman who socially and intellectually cannot rise with him. We see this mistake sometimes committed through overmastering passion, and we excuse it though we lament it, but when we see it committed open-eyed can scarcely be so charitable.

The higher education of women, which will act as a powerful stimulant and corrective on that of men, is coming, and also the opening of independent careers to middle-class girls. In a brilliant little American comedy which we saw recently admirably acted by amateurs — supposed to be a satire on the woman's rights movement, but in reality meant to show the exaggerated fears of "Noodledom" of a reversal of the order of nature if any concessions are made to the weaker sex — "The coming woman" says that the life of "waiting for the coming man, who perhaps never comes or if he does had perhaps better have stayed away", is a wearisome and a humiliating one. We cannot in Australia escape the influence of the great wave which is surging from Russia in the old world to the furthest western settlements of the Anglo-Saxon in the new. Many thoughtful people however look upon the movement with fear, lest education pursued for a direct object may fail in many important points in conducing to the beauty and the happiness of life. We want not only to increase the working power of the world by untying many fettered hands and cultivating many dormant capacities; we want to increase the pleasantness of the world for its whole body of inhabitants by

retaining the woman's special gifts of observation, tact, and sympathy — the result, says Herbert Spencer, of the accumulated experience of uncounted generations of woman in rude ages, in which these qualities were her only armour and her only weapons against the tyranny and caprice of her absolute master. The book-knowledge may be pursued at the expense of the observing faculties, the eagerness for independence may injure the tact, and the sympathy may suffer, not from the increased knowledge (which *coeteris paribus* makes it larger and more delicate), but from its being turned mainly to self-regarding objects. None of these losses however are necessarily consequent upon the new movement, and as after all the old order of things is founded on the immutable laws of human nature, and far the greater number of our girls will look forward to be wives and mothers, we feel convinced that in spite of slight and temporary reaction and a few blunders of individuals the complete development of all that is best in the feminine nature will be really fostered, and that wider knowledge, and larger experience will make women not less but more pleasant in their domestic relations, as well as call forth fuller confidence and more faithful love from their husbands, their brothers, and their sons. The wisest statesmen, economists, and philanthropists see in the cultivation of the taste for innocent amusement the greatest if not the only defence against the worst evils which beset our English and colonial communities. The pulpit and the press are comparatively powerless with the class of people who most need reform, but by substituting something which will contrast as pleasantly with the monotony of toil as vicious excess, and if possible something in which respectable women of their own class can participate, the demons of drink and vice and crime may be combated. And of this we are sure, that when we exorcise the fiend of dulness from the home he will carry with him to some distant limbo seven other spirits more wicked than himself.

5
Politics

EDITOR'S NOTE

Spence had mock ballot papers printed to help demonstrate, at public meetings, just how proportional representation worked. This pamphlet on "Effective Voting" as she called it, *What is Effective Voting and How is it to be Secured?*, is a particularly significant one for, as its appeal to women indicates, it was produced for that historic 1896 election in South Australia, when Australian women voted for the first time in a state election, preceding their English counterparts by many years. The pamphlet combines a succinct account of how proportional representation works, and the reasons for its superiority as an electoral method, with a particular appeal for support for the system from the new female voters. This pamphlet is held in the Catherine Spence collection in the Archives of the South Australian Library.

"The Dangerous Classes", from *The Register*, 4 December 1878, is typical of Spence's political writing in its avoidance of a partisan position and for the commonsense basis for its analysis.

What is Effective Voting and How is it to be Secured?

Effective voting, or proportional representation, means that instead of elections being decided by majorities in small districts, by which nearly half of the votes are wasted, all the votes are to be used in large districts, and the representatives are returned in proportion to the number of voters who hold certain opinions all over the enlarged constituencies. There will not be more members of Parliament elected, probably there will be fewer, under the improved system.

The reasons why we should seek to change our present system are as follows:

1. Effective voting is fair and just
Under our present system a very few votes, even one single vote more, given to two candidates than to the others makes these men represent the district. Those who did not vote for them are unrepresented — indeed, they are misrepresented by men of different convictions and aims. Under the Hare-Spence system every vote counts for someone the elector approves of.

2. Effective voting is peaceful
As no vote counts *against* anyone — as no two or three votes can make thousands of votes useless, the bitterness of party strife will be lessened. Under our present method the business of party politicians and election committees is to make all votes ineffective but those given to their particular favourites. Under a system of absolute fairness each party will get the representation its numbers entitle it to — no less and no more.

3. Effective voting is honest
Bribery and undue influence is often successful in securing as many votes as change a minority into a majority. No one would be foolish enough to bribe under the Hare-Spence system,

because each bought vote would only count one in a quota of thousands.

4. Effective voting is educative to the electors

Instead of having to choose from four or five candidates, generally representing two parties only, the electors would have a choice of a dozen or more, and of these there is sure to be some worth voting for. There would always be independent candidates, so that that large body of opinion in every constituency, which cannot endorse extreme party views, would be represented. When independent candidates have a fair chance of election, independent thought will be strengthened all over the country.

5. Effective voting would moralize the candidates

Instead of keeping back his real opinions, lest he should risk losing votes, the candidate would be encouraged to speak out the best that is in him to attract those who think with him, or who may be persuaded to think with him. If these are the sixth part of a six-member district or a tenth part of a ten-member district, he would be returned as their representative though all the rest differed from him. No one who has not watched the dodges and evasions of candidates and their committees can estimate the elevation of the character of public men if this cut-throat competition for votes were put an end to.

6. Effective voting will be cheaper for the country

The enlargement of the districts will greatly lessen the demand for the expenditure of public money for localities. It lowers the character of our ministries to sanction unwise expenditure of public money in order to keep or to win the votes of the members for the district to be benefited.

The only argument against the reform is that it is new and untried, except in Switzerland. The real opposition comes from the rival parties, which fear that a system of perfect righteousness would diminish their strength. They know the present system and can pull the ropes, and they do not want independent representatives who cannot be relied on in the day of battle. But representation was not meant to be "War by Election". Its true meaning, that the elected body — the Parliament — should be the mirror of the convictions and aspirations of the whole people, has been clouded by this majority fight. Inside Parliament the majority vote must decide — but for the composition of Parliament itself, we must have equitable representation of all opinions and of all classes.

I appeal to the new voters — the women — to change neck-to-neck competition for all or nothing in our present districts, into a peaceful cooperation. Thus, too, the women will not only have

Effective Voting

the vote, but an effective vote, neither wasted in a useless majority nor extinguished in a defeated minority.

HOW IS THIS REFORM TO BE CARRIED OUT?

1. By enlargement of districts. The present electorates must be redistributed soon. It is absurd that eleven thousand electors in East Torrens, and nearly ten thousand in Sturt, should send no more men to Parliament than seven hundred in the Northern Territory and a little over two thousand in Encounter Bay.

At the next election we shall see as many votes thrown away on unsuccessful candidates in these two large districts as will return eight or ten elsewhere. For convenience, I have taken a six-member district as my illustration, because Adelaide returns six members, and it might well be taken as a whole, but I should prefer districts to return nine or ten.

The ballot paper I use for a six-member district contains twelve names of well-known men belonging to the Conservative, the Labor, the Ministerial Party, and several candidates of outside parties.

BALLOT PAPER
Your vote will be used for one candidate, according to your preference.

The quota is found by dividing the number of votes given by the number of representatives required.

You may vote for six names or fewer by the numbers 1, 2, 3, 4, 5, 6.

If your first choice has already secured his quota, or if he cannot obtain it, your vote will be transferred to your next choice, and USED, NOT WASTED.

    CHARLESTON   [   ]
    DOWNER   [   ]
    DUNCAN   [   ]
    GLYNN   [   ]
    GUTHRIE   [   ]
    HARROLD   [   ]
    HOLDER   [   ]
    KINGSTON   [   ]
    MAGAREY   [   ]
    McPHERSON   [   ]
    SYMON   [   ]
    TAYLOR   [   ]

Some such list of candidates would appear on the ballot paper of every enlarged district.

2. All the change in the duty of the elector is that instead of marking two names with a cross, he marks the candidates he

prefers with the figures, 1, 2, 3, 4, 5, 6. *This is all the elector has to do*. He makes as sure that his first choice will get his vote as if he had plumped for him, but without the risk of losing it in case he has not the required number, for in that case it is transferred to his next choice.

3. The rest of the business is for the returning officer and the scrutineers. The quota required for the return of a representative is found by dividing all the votes given in the district by the number of representatives required.

If 12,000 votes are cast in a six-member district the quota is 2,000.

A favourite candidate may received more than 2,000 first choices, and after the quota is credited to him the surplus votes can be allotted according to second choice in a perfectly scientific way.

After the surplus is disposed of the returning officer declares the candidate who has fewest votes *not elected*, and proceeds to distribute his votes according to second choice, or if second choice is already elected by full quota, he passes the vote to third. Then he takes the votes of the man next lowest, and distributes them in the same way. He then proceeds, always distributing the votes of the man who has fewest votes till all are thrown out but the number who are needed for the district, who are then declared elected.

Out of 3,824 votes which I collected for the same twelve candidates at various meetings in 1892–93 all over the province there were only two voters unrepresented. One had given a single choice for a candidate who was second lowest on the poll, and the other had picked out the six candidates of various parties who were unsuccessful.

The process is as easy for the voter as the present way, and much more interesting.

It will probably take twice as long for the scrutineers and the returning officers as the present method, but it will secure that the real majority out of doors is the majority in Parliament, and it will give adequate and independent representation to minorities.

Nothing is needed to carry out this reform except that the people of South Australia should demand it. If it is made a test question at all polling places at this coming election I believe it would secure a majority in its favour.

Nothing can be said against it. It is absolutely just. It treads on no one's corns. It hurts no one's honest interests. If candidates say they do not understand it, tell them that it is time they did. It is the urgent need of all countries in the world, for it would purify

political life, and allow peaceful progress to be made by evolution, rather than by dangerous and disastrous revolution.

Let South Australia and South Australian women lead the way!

C. H. Spence
Eildon, St Peters
March 1896

The Dangerous Classes

It is not an uncommon thing for educated people to give the title of the dangerous class to the discontented poor — to the proletariat who has no stake in the country, who has nothing to lose, and may reasonably imagine that he has everything to gain by a social or political revolution. So far from education acting as a universal safeguard against the possibility of physical force and against the danger of large numbers clutching at the wealth and attacking the privileges of the minority it sometimes brings a profounder discontent than ignorance, and it enables masses to combine for more effective action than was possible in the time when life was harder and its prizes much less attainable by those who seemed born to do the rough work of life. But it is a mere conventionalism to restrict the term dangerous classes to the poor and the numerous. Every class is dangerous which has unchecked power, which exacts all its legal rights and forgets its national and social duties. The self-indulgent rich are the dangerous class until they have been brought under the will of the indignant and envious poor, and it is quite possible for the very hope and strength of our English nation and colonies — the intelligent middle class — to be dangerous to the safety of the state if it holds in its hands the supreme power and uses it for selfish or for class interests.

Looking back on the history of France, who were the dangerous classes during the century that preceded the Revolution? The despotic sovereign, the idle and luxurious nobles, who parted with their political power as a check on the monarch on condition of retaining all their social privileges and their insolent authority over all beneath them, and the church, which banded itself with the strong, and never as a political or social power

helped the weak and the oppressed — these were responsible for the long-gathered vengeance which they provoked. Had these dangerous classes either from within or from without awakened to a sense of public duty towards those whom they believed Providence had set under them would not the French Revolution have been a progressive movement instead of a frightful catastrophe? After the turning-point which led to the subversion of the monarchy, of the aristocracy, and the church the dangerous classes were the unchecked ignorant but not more selfish — probably much less selfish — Democrats. They were violent, they were cruel, their hands were stained with much innocent blood, but there was a wonderful cleanness with regard to money, and, with all their excesses, a love of the republic strong and inspiring. But this one class was a dangerous class, because it had no restraining power within the commonwealth. Its sole danger was from foreign foes, only to be withstood by enormous armies hastily levied and poorly equipped, but fired by real national enthusiasm and recruited from the new peasant proprietors of the soil, who felt they had so much to fight for that life could be thrown away gloriously for the sake of France.

The army and the general of the army next took the position of the dangerous classes, and a military despotism dependent for its continuance on foreign conquest, drained France of blood and money and at last left her at the mercy of a European coalition which made her take back her Bourbons and stay the march of freedom for herself and for Europe. After this the dangerous classes were the despotic and superstitious abettors of the retrograde movement and all the middle class who for the sake of peace or place or emolument strengthened the hands of the unwise government. The dangerous classes under Louis Philippe were the bourgeois and the bureaucrats, who derived all the advantages of peace and security, and were careless about the miseries of the poor or the freedom of the press. And again we see that in the time of Louis Napoleon the dangerous classes were not so much the discontented poor as the self-indulgent rich, and still more the apathetic peasant and bourgeois, who could carry any measure, but who thought of their own private interests and not of their public duties. In the discussion which has been lately carried on in the *Nineteenth Century* as to whether the popular judgment on political matters is more correct than that of the higher orders the weight of argument was in favour of the popular judgment being more quickly responsive to generous sympathy and to broad principles of justice, but too easily led by mistakes in public policy from one-sided ideas of the right and the wrong of a

national quarrel. If the blood of England is up England will go to war for an idea, though it is a wrong one.

It has been because England has had so long the right of public meeting, the right of petition, and a free anonymous press, that what in other countries would produce revolution in her leads to reform, sometimes slow, sometimes rapid. A measure apparently lost this session is merely delayed to the next; all means of agitation and of discussion are still open, and the greatest victories of freedom have been won by patience. Even without universal suffrage the power of the non-voter is felt in the country, and the curiously anomalous nature of the constitution, which cannot be imitated by foreign nations or even by English colonies tempers the actual absolute supremacy of the House of Commons, while the unrecognized powers — the press and the non-voters, comprising a very large proportion of the adult population — exert through public opinion a constant influence which cannot be defied. The recognized checks on the Commons — the Queen and the Lords — only maintain power by never straining it. The unrecognized powers have a reserve force, which it is to the interest of the Queen, Lords, and Commons to respect, and not to permit them to strain. In our attempts to make a brand new House of Lords or an Upper House respectable enough to delay or to modify democratic legislation, all the English colonies find it extremely difficult to adjust the balance of power so as to make the check beneficial and not hurtful. The rough-and-ready criterion of wealth is often the only one taken into consideration in choosing a representative for the Council, and it is fancied that a man who has managed his own affairs well will be the best man to manage the affairs of the colony. But our rich men often have been so engrossed with the adding of pound to pound and flock to flock and acre to acre that broad political principles, either of honour or of large expediency, are lost in the hand-to-mouth kind of legislation which suits personal interests and personal convenience. A selfish plutocracy in a rising colony is as dangerous a class as a selfish democracy; indeed we think that the transparently fallacious arguments of a rich man against property taxation have less excuse than equally one-sided arguments from the working man's point of view. Whilst condemning utterly Mr Berry's extreme measures one cannot help seeing that the proceedings of the Upper House in Victoria made them a dangerous class, and if the war goes on *à l'outrance* and the persistence of the Council leads to their being shorn of their legitimate powers then the unchecked democracy, now a source of infinite peril to the state, will be emphatically *the* dangerous class until some other constitutional

mode of representing the opinions which contain the complementary or the modifying portions of political truth can be devised and carried out.

With regard to the attitude of the press towards both bodies of the legislature the public takes the opinions of journalists for what they are worth, and anonymity neither strengthens nor weakens their effect. And the correspondence columns of every respectable journal are open to bona fide opponents; those who consider themselves aggrieved can either anonymously or with the full privilege of their name and character combat the arguments of the leading article by counter-arguments. The compulsory signature of articles in France and other countries was not devised for the protection of the people from being overawed by the imposing "we", but for the convenience of the despotic government in order that an obnoxious writer − obnoxious probably in proportion to his truthfulness − might be silenced, fined, or imprisoned. In spite of the sensitive view of some non-members to press criticism from impecunious anonymous writers, they are only prevented from becoming the dangerous classes by the freedom of criticism − by its being possible to blame, to ridicule, or to denounce them. If the German press could freely condemn or laugh at Prince Bismarck he and his supporters would not be the dangerous class there, with the probability that suppressed public opinion may ere long turn the tables and give birth to a strong and very dangerous class in the Fatherland of the future. Free criticism, free public meetings, and a free press are the only safeguards for any nation from the mischievous sway of any one preponderating power.

6
Religion

EDITOR'S NOTE

Catherine Spence wrote more than a hundred sermons, delivered over the years between 1878 and 1908. Many of these still exist in manuscript form (most of them held in the South Australian Library Archives in Adelaide). They are often only drafts, never intended for publication. The sentences, therefore, are sometimes clumsy and overlong, the punctuation is rather casual.

This is an excerpt from the first sermon preached by Catherine Spence in the Wakefield Street Unitarian Christian Church on 24 November 1878.

Excerpt from Spence's First Sermon

In the book of Genesis at the 5th chapter and the 22nd verse you will find there four words "Enoch walked with God", and in the Gospel according to Luke, chapter 17, verse 5, you find also four words "Lord, increase our faith".

When we consider the various needs which the various Christian churches have upheld as essential to salvation, the contrast with them this brief chronicle of the life and death of a patriarchal saint of the earliest times, who had no Bible, no knowledge of a personal Christ and Saviour — no Church — no Sabbath — and no Sacraments — and who so far as we can gather from contemporary and succeeding records, had no belief or expectation of the glorious immortality which awaited him, for so far as we can understand the brief record, it was by escaping from death and not by passing through it that he was taken into the higher life — we are led to pause and enquire what was the quality of the faith that saved him; what was the walk with God which could be thus beautiful and exalting when according to our modern ideas there were no means of grace by which Enoch might have risen from earth to heaven.

In this church — at this time — there are avowedly assembled men and women of the most different shades of religious belief. In other churches there *may* by dissentients — this there *must*. The [illegible] deed, as it is called, of the fatherhood of God (the mission of Christ), the brotherhood of man and the hope of immortality and conscious re-union with those we have lost; and those whom when our time comes, we must leave — would appear to Christians of other denominations sufficiently wide to embrace the few worshippers here. No complicated scheme of salvation to be held in its entirety — no nicely balanced offices of a mysterious

Trinity to be accurately distinguished by the intellect — no absolute surrender of our human will to prevenient or compelling grace — no Church or Book or Sacrament to rely upon, it would seem that when people had got down to a need so short, so simple, and so cheerful, that they would hold it in perfect unity.

But it is not so; the sense of the Infinite, which is the basis of all religion, is felt in various ways by the worshippers here. Part of our number may be called properly *Unitarian Christians*, for it is through the words and works of Jesus Christ, through obedience to his precepts and the inspiration of his example that they draw near to God — a smaller body may be denominated *Theists*, for it is from the All-Father Himself that they look for ever-present grace and help. And a smaller body still, who may be found here, may be called *Secularists* and in them the conception of the Infinite fills the soul with the sense of inexorable law, shutting out prayer and scarcely admitting of worship. But in all there is the consciousness of a Power out of ourselves which guides the Universe — which transcends our faculties — which we submit to, either in exalting faith or in dumb endurance but which we cannot in any way move by our prayers or by our sacrifice however large.

Everywhere in the life of Christ we see that it is the *quality* and not the quantity of faith that saves the soul. Those who are bid to come in to inherit the kingdom prepared for them from the foundation of the world have no idea that the works of charity and mercy they had done in life were in any way meritorious as religious duties, or done for Christ. Those who prophesied in the name of Christ, and who had heard him teach in their streets, had no doubt of their favourable reception — but the sort of faith that consisted with working iniquity, was not saving faith. And those who wash the outside of the cup and the platter, and rest in formal observance of Sabbath and ordinances and traditions of the elders, and leave out the weightier matters of the law of justice and mercy and the faith which works by love, receive the hardest condemnation which the otherwise gentle Messiah ever pronounced. And yet Christian Churches to this day build upon the foundations of the Pharisees in the very name of Christ.

The great wave of unbelief that is now passing over the world is less appalling to our brotherhood than to more dogmatic churches. Our faith is not at the mercy of a disputed text, or a critical examination of the historical evidence as to the authenticity of a book. We can undismayed regard science as having put back indefinitely the date of the creation of the world and of man. We can part with the myth of Eden, and of the universal flood, and the ark, typical of the chosen people to whom alone for many cen-

turies God vouchsafed to reveal himself. Our faith is not in ancient records, but in the relations of the human soul to the Infinite God — and these are closer and stronger now than they ever were. In those who, like Kepler, devoutly think God's thoughts after Him as they trace the mechanism of the Heavens; to those who patiently observe the laws of Nature so as to make obedience to them beneficient to all mankind, to them who labour among the poor, the sick, the sorrowful, and the sinful, to help and to heal, God is as near as — yea far nearer than when he was supposed to go before the Israelites in a pillar of cloud by day and a pillar of fire by night.

But there are those among us who work, as it were, blindly; who have little or no faith in the personal God and the conscious immortality which are our ostensible creed for whom argument avails not — prayer is unmeaning — and the testimony of the great body of God's people in all ages past cannot overcome the sense that the fact of future existence is by no means *proved*. Those who never doubted it when it was a great *fear*; when they thought it was a curse to the great majority, now feel, like poor Burns, that it is too good news to be true when it is transformed to a great *hope*. And the two beliefs are not inseparable — for some who doubt the conscious immortality, cling to the faith in the personal God, who cares for them here and now. And they, like Enoch, may walk with God in a faith the more sublime because it is so absolutely disinterested. Belief is an operation of the intellect dependent on proof. It is quite independent of the will — it does not come because it would be compatible and pleasant and respectable, and satisfactory to our friends. The careless or the forgetful may start into faith at the touch of sorrow and the fear of loss — and

> Lips say "God be merciful"
> Who ne'er said "God be praised"

but there are many earnest souls who grope in darkness and to whom no light is shown. Still there remains one article of our faith that is universally applicable and universally helpful — and that is the brotherhood of man — the sense of our duty towards each other in all relations of life. The justice the wisdom the charity we should show to those of like nature with ourselves — the common duties of every day, and the special duties of every opportunity. In this the sceptic can work with the believer, not so cheerfully, perhaps not so effectively, but yet to the utmost of the powers which God has given him — and his consciousness that this may be the only field of activity granted is to a nature in any way

Religion

noble, a spur to exertion. And when Hope does not point the way to other worlds, sometimes an intensity of energy is bestowed on this; sometimes memory of the lost ones is cherished more tenderly more faithfully because there seems to be no second act in the drama — and those who can only stretch "lame hands of faith" towards God, may confidently and lovingly stretch them out for the service of His children.

And yet nothing in death is more mysterious than birth. It would seem *a priori* more likely that an intelligent soul with all its individual powers and capacities should be indestructible than that some of its qualities should be modified and transmitted from one generation to another. But one fact we *know* and the other we dimly guess at. Only the better thoughts of human nature which are *inculcated* here, in the church, should give us better hopes for human destiny; for as we grieve to lose the lovely and the good and the noble, so may we conceive that the Father of our spirits, in whose hands we are for time and for eternity will keep those whom he too must love for higher and longer service.

The faith in human nature was seized upon by Auguste Comte as some sort of lever when he abandoned his faith in God, and he built up a fantastic sort of Panthcism of heroes and saints for the worship of Humanity with a ritual and officiating priesthood and Saint's days for the Sunday rest. But it is only the Infinite we can worship, let us see that we do not fail in the service.

> Abou Ben Adhem (may his tribe increase)
> Awoke one night from a deep dream of peace,
> And saw within the moonlight in his room,
> Making it rich, and like a lily in bloom
> An angel writing in a book of gold —
> Exceeding peace had made Ben Adhem bold,
> And to the presence in the room he said,
> "What writest thou?" The vision raised his head,
> And with a look made of all sweet accord,
> Answered "The names of those who love the Lord."
> "And is mine one?" said Abou. "Nay, not so,"
> Replied the angel. Abou spoke more low
> But cheerly still; and said, "I pray thee, then
> Write me as one that loved his fellow men."
>
> The Angel wrote and vanished. The next night
> It came again with a great waking light,
> And showed the names whom love of God had blessed
> And lo! Ben Adhem's name led all the rest.

There are times when we can see nothing clear before us but duty, sometimes tolerably easy, sometimes exceedingly difficult

Sermon

— but the *quality* of our faith the *savingness* of our faith is to be proved by the obedience we pay to this demand of the conscience — this sublime imperative which speaks to the secularist as to the spiritualist — which admits of no parley — which is not even satisfied with what is high, if a higher is attainable — which raises its demands as they are acceded to, till we reach step by step that land of Beulah, where duty is not only the command of the conscience, but the delight of the heart; that Heaven on earth which is the foretaste and earnest of a Heaven hereafter. The cowardly soul which avoids duty, bids farewell to happiness. One may get material prosperity — one may satisfy ambitious desires — one may even preserve health without being good — but happiness is inseparable from holiness. And in the pitch of duty we may not find just what we expect or do what we intended, but we do what we can and leave the rest to God, who sees the end from the beginning and the whole from a part.

* * *

Select Bibliography

PUBLISHED WORKS OF CATHERINE HELEN SPENCE

Bibliography of Catherine Helen Spence. Adelaide: Libraries Board of South Australia, 1967.
   A really comprehensive bibliography of the works of Catherine Spence will probably never be possible as many of her newspaper contributions were printed anonymously.

Fiction

Clara Morison: a Tale of South Australia during the gold fever. London: J.W Parker, 1854, 2 vols. London: Ward Lock, 1862, 1 vol. Adelaide: Rigby, 1971, with Introduction by Susan Eade (Magarey).

Tender and True: a colonial tale. London: Smith Elder, 1856.

Mr Hogarth's Will. London: Bentley, 1865. First serialized as "Uphill Work" in the *Weekly Mail*, 1864.

The Author's Daughter. London: Bentley, 1868. First serialized as "Hugh Lindsay's Guest" in *The Adelaide Observer*, 1867.

An Agnostic's Progress from the Known to the Unknown. London: Williams and Norgate, 1884.

A Week in the Future. Sydney, 1889. Serialized in the *Centennial Magazine*, 1888-89.

Gathered In. Ed. B.L. Waters and G.A. Wilkes. Sydney: Sydney University Press, 1977. Serialized in *The Adelaide Observer*, 1881-82.

Handfasted: a romance. Melbourne: Penguin Books, 1984.

Select Bibliography

Non-Fiction

Catherine Helen Spence: An Autobiography. Edited and introduced by Jeanne F. Young. Adelaide: W.K. Thomas and Co., 1910. Adelaide: Libraries Board of South Australia, 1975, reprinted from *The Register*, April–December, 1910.

Pamphlets

A Plea for Pure Democracy. Mr Hare's reform bill applied to South Australia. Adelaide: W.C. Rigby, 1861.
The Laws We Live Under. Adelaide: Government Printing Office, 1880.
Each in His Own Tongue: two sermons. Adelaide: Vardon and Pritchard, Printers, 1904.

Periodical Articles

"An Australian's Impression of England" (unsigned). *Cornhill Magazine* (1866): 110-20.
"George Eliot". *Melbourne Review* (1876): 146-63.
"Two Theories for the working of bi-cameral legislatures". *Melbourne Review* 4 (1879): 177-87.
"Honoré de Balzac: a psychological study". *Melbourne Review* 4 (1879): 348-57.
"George Eliot's life and works". *Melbourne Review* 10 (1885): 217-44.
"An Australian's Impressions of America". *Harper's Monthly* (July 1894): 244-51.

BIOGRAPHICAL AND CRITICAL STUDIES

Cooper, Janet. *Catherine Spence*. Great Australians Series. Melbourne: Oxford University Press, 1972.
Eade (Magarey), Susan. Introduction to *Clara Morison*. Adelaide: Rigby, 1971.
Magarey, Susan. "Radical Woman: Catherine Spence". In *Rebels and Radicals*, ed. Eric Fry. Sydney: Allen and Unwin, 1983.
———. *Unbridling the Tongues of Women: a biography of Catherine Spence 1825-1910*. Sydney: Hale and Iremonger, 1985.
Sinnett, Frederick. "The Fiction Fields of Australia". *Journal of Australasia* 1 (July–December 1856).

Select Bibliography

Thomson, Helen. "Catherine Helen Spence: Pragmatic Utopian". In *Who Is She: Images of Woman in Australian Fiction*, ed. Shirley Walker. St Lucia: University of Queensland Press, 1983.

Walker, R.B. "Catherine Helen Spence, Unitarian Utopian". *Australian Literary Studies* 5, no. 1 (May 1971).

Wightman, Jennifer. "A Practical Dreamer: Catherine Helen Spence". *Meanjin* 33, no. 1 (March 1974).

Young, J.F. *Catherine Helen Spence: a study and an appreciation*. Melbourne: Lothian, 1937.